D1567342

From Innovation to Cash Flows

Value Creation by Structuring High Technology Alliances

CONSTANCE LÜTOLF-CARROLL

with the collaboration of

ANTTI PIRNES *and* WITHERS LLP

WILEY

John Wiley & Sons, Inc.

Published by John Wiley & Sons, Inc., Hoboken, New Jersey.
Published simultaneously in Canada.

For general information on our other products and services or for technical support, please contact our Customer Care Department within the United States at (800) 762-2974, outside the United States at (317) 572-3993 or fax (317) 572-4002.

Wiley also publishes its books in a variety of electronic formats. Some content that appears in print may not be available in electronic books. For more information about Wiley products, visit our web site at www.wiley.com.

Library of Congress Cataloging-in-Publication Data

Lütolf-Carroll, Constance, 1955–
   From innovation to cash flows: value creation by structuring high technology alliances / Constance Lütolf-Carroll, Antti Pirnes.
         p.   cm. –   (Wiley finance series)
   Includes bibliographical references and index.
   ISBN 978-0-470-11809-2 (cloth)
 1. New business enterprises.   2. Entrepreneurship.   3. Cash flow.
 4. Intellectual property.   I. Pirnes, Antti, 1973–   II. Title.
   HD62.5.L89 2009
   658′.046–dc22

                                          2008047047

Printed in the United States of America

10   9   8   7   6   5   4   3   2   1

To Marc and Daniel
and
To Mia, Santeri, and Arttu

Contents

Foreword

This is a book written for persons who have an idea with commercial potential, such as inventors, engineers, scientists, or managers, or anyone else with the initiative to develop the idea. If you are such a person and have a serious desire to do something with your idea, you will find this book to be invaluable. Readers will benefit from the substantial complementary careers of the authors, who have drawn on years of professional experience ranging over engagements as entrepreneurs and equity investors as well as patent and business intelligence. Lütolf-Carroll and Pirnes have included in one volume all of the building blocks you will need to assemble in your first months as a new entrepreneur. In the process, they will help you identify key pitfalls that you must avoid, and arm you with the tools to avoid them.

The book is aimed directly at first-time entrepreneurs. While there is a large number of books on innovation and entrepreneurship, this book is unique. Those other books will tell you what to do as an innovator, such as pursuing disruptive technologies, opening up your innovation process to external sources of ideas and technologies, constructing more open business models to create and capture value from your ideas, or co-creating value with your customers.[1] This book is distinctive, because it tells you how to turn your idea into a profitable business. As the title suggests, the book will take you from your initial innovation, all the way through to your generation of positive cash flows.

This combination of savvy business advice and extensive legal documents is original, and the authors deserve our thanks for pulling them together. The book contains, among other items, valuable investment documents, such as alternative valuation mechanisms for a new venture, a typical term sheet for a venture capital investment (which is drafted before the money is received by the entrepreneur), an investment agreement (where the money actually is received by the entrepreneur), and even a discussion of a venture capital investment that went wrong.

The authors also understand the importance to entrepreneurs of protecting one's intellectual property. So in this book we find sample nondisclosure agreements, licensing agreements, discussions of effective and ineffective patent applications, patent maps that show areas of opportunity or vulnerability, comparisons of trademark, copyright, and trade secrecy documents, and advice on when to use which means of protection.

Successful entrepreneurship increasingly requires a global perspective, even from the inception of the business. This volume helps here as well, showing the many legal differences between U.S. and English law with regard to intellectual property protections and also between English and Continental European law. As you seek to create your business in one region, it is vital to understand these legal distinctions as you later expand your business into other regions, where different rules apply.

Finally, the book offers very helpful, very detailed examples of how to organize, negotiate, establish, and then manage strategic alliances. Again, the book provides excellent documentation of how alliances can be constructed, from start to finish. Transaction terms, termination provisions, intellectual property, risk management, and ongoing mediation of alliance disputes are all discussed.

This is a book to be read and then revisited. You will want to come back to this book time and again for references, for sample documents, and for sage advice on how to take the next step. It is no exaggeration to say that you may save thousands of dollars in legal costs alone from using the material in this book. And your chances of being a successful entrepreneur will likely increase as well.

HENRY CHESBROUGH
Adjunct Professor and Executive Director
Center for Open Innovation Haas School of Business
UC Berkeley

KARL S. PISTER
Dean and Roy W. Carlson Professor of Engineering Emeritus
UC Berkeley

Preface

Our book is for all who wish to start up a high technology business or who have an interest in developing and managing strategic alliances with high-tech companies.

From Innovation to Cash Flows is written by a global team of experts from law, science, engineering, and business, having years of experience working closely with high-tech entrepreneurs and scientists from around the world. We collaborated and pooled our know-how and especially our cross-cultural expertise to write this book for you. Inside the book's pages and on our web site (www.innovationtocashflows.com) you will find real-life cases, sample legal contracts, useful valuation tools, and practical strategy frameworks to help you start up your high technology business and improve your venture's chances for success in these turbulent times.

Divided into six parts, the book explores the process of entrepreneurship from the creative inception of an idea, to turning that idea into a protectable invention, and then into an innovation—which is the commercialization of an invention into a new process, product, or service that benefits a customer who buys it. In different chapters, we examine how to develop a venture's business strategy and create a viable business model. We discuss in depth the design, structure, negotiation, and management of strategic alliances. We show our readers how to value a high-tech start-up in order to obtain investor financing. Readers learn how to model the financial terms of a licensing agreement and employ exit strategies that make it possible for investors in the business to harvest their holdings, if they so desire.

Investors expect today's high-tech entrepreneurs to possess both breadth and depth of knowledge. Readers will see, step by step, how to protect their scientific inventions and license a variety of intellectual property (IP) rights. They will learn about state of the art tools to draw patent maps of the competitive landscape and find out what rivals are doing to advance their research. They will learn about effective and ineffective intellectual property strategies. The book explains in clear and simple language the latest on trade secrets, know-how, patent, trademark, copyright, and design registration laws. We discuss the legal terms and contract clauses that frequently are included in technology transfer, strategic alliances, joint ventures, and shareholder investment agreements.

Our aim is to create a practical how-to-get-started manual that appeals to the first-time entrepreneur as well as to write a readable reference book that benefits an experienced entrepreneur who desires to do better the next time around. Our readers need not be experts in business, law, high technology, or intellectual property rights. However, if you do have expertise in any of these areas, we hope you will be interested in reading our interpretation of the issues specific to high-tech venture start-ups.

In short, what is the rationale for the book? Here's our answer. High-tech entrepreneurs need to:

- Understand intellectual property rights but are often baffled by the legal terminology that surrounds it.
- Value their start-up businesses but might not know how to do so.
- Select good advisory teams and know what questions to ask of these specialists in commercial contracts, intellectual property, or finance.
- Understand best practices in carrying out due diligence.
- Structure and negotiate strategic alliances that create economic value.
- Understand how to turn innovation into sustainable cash flows that will attract investor financing.

We hope that a single comprehensive volume like ours—which is integrative and interdisciplinary and that weaves the challenges of starting up a high-tech venture with the management of IP rights, valuation of emerging technologies, and structuring of collaborative alliances for long-term value creation—provides you with useful insights and long-lasting value for your money.

Depending on the background and knowledge of the reader, the variety of strategic alliances we discuss might be surprising. We explain how different high-tech industries tend to use particular combinations of strategic alliances to achieve their aims. We explore outsourcing and offshoring alliances, technology transfer and pharmaceutical licensing arrangements, codevelopment and comarketing agreements, early-stage research consortia, equity and nonequity joint ventures.

When it comes to describing how to structure strategic alliances, we are very pragmatic and include sample contracts and useful checklists to guide you through the process. We have tried to cover concepts, methods, principles, and attitudes (both managerial and investor) toward sharing risks and rewards. We emphasize the governance issues of strategic alliances and of shareholder arrangements from various perspectives: that of the entrepreneur, the outside member of the board of directors, and the lead investor.

We have striven to keep perspective—to balance the needs of the novice with the expectations of the expert. For instance, we wanted you to see how patent searching is actually done in real life, not just refer you to incomprehensible databases and let you fend for yourselves. We wanted you to see a real investor term sheet or memorandum of understanding so you could read it ahead of time and prepare your own questions to bring up with your legal counsel before you negotiate for the first time with an angel investor or venture capitalist. The same chapters will help you when you negotiate with the personnel in your university's technology transfer office about protecting your invention. We also hope our book provides you with lasting insights that make the time you spend with your IP lawyers and financial advisors more strategic, more productive, and more rewarding—long after your venture is up and running.

Where we saw a special need for a book like ours was where entrepreneurs needed to manage IP rights in turbulent and fast-moving market conditions. Strategic alliances are often the best way to leverage two companies' complementary resources and capabilities where conditions are especially risky and ambiguous. Here we discuss real options and how to construct contracts that provide you with more flexibility and protection against downside losses while enabling you to share in upside rewards.

Part and parcel of designing, structuring, and negotiating either financing or strategic alliances for your new venture is being able to value the cash flows related to the agreements. We have written about venture valuation issues with an eye to lawyers and scientists; we also have written about entrepreneurial finance keeping in mind the needs of MBAs, executive MBAs, and graduate students enrolled in advanced degree programs.

From Innovation to Cash Flows will be an invaluable guide for executives taking courses on mergers and acquisitions, strategic alliances, intellectual property rights, or managing high technology entrepreneurial firms. To satisfy the learning needs of these various audiences, we introduce and explain basic concepts and vocabulary, and then apply the theory, valuation tools, or strategy frameworks to practical cases, illustrated with short stories, and numerical examples. To use the financial models, readers need to have only a very basic understanding of electronic spreadsheets. For the numerical examples, a simple financial calculator is all that is required.

We and our contributing author team have examined issues related to high-technology strategic alliances from many diverse perspectives and through many different cross-cultural lenses. But we all had one comprehensive aim in mind: to help equip you as an entrepreneur for your journey in launching, scaling up, managing, and, when the time is ripe, harvesting your venture successfully.

A NOTE TO TEACHERS WHO WISH TO ADOPT THIS BOOK

Universities today are in a race to compress ever-growing amounts of new theories and knowledge into their curriculums, even as the time frame for these programs is shortened. Student capacity to absorb information is taxed. Depending on the core curriculum and how the electives are chosen, many science or engineering students will graduate with bachelors, masters, or even doctoral degrees and have only a superficial understanding of finance and accounting, hardly any exposure to law (it depends on the school and the type of major), and little exposure, if at all, to advanced strategy or marketing. Similarly, graduates in the law will have gaps in their knowledge about subjects which are mandatory in business or science curriculums. This book is our response to further interdisciplinary learning in executive education.

When developing curricula for executives in MBA or Executive MBA programs, it is challenging for the teacher to find a versatile textbook that can meet the diverse learning needs of demanding students from different backgrounds, professions, interests, work experiences, and cultures. Usually the teacher can only recommend one book for an elective, when three may be needed for an interdisciplinary course.

From Innovation to Cash Flows should appeal to those teachers looking for a comprehensive and flexible textbook. This book is suitable for MBA and Executive MBA students enrolled in advanced strategy, venture finance, or entrepreneurship courses. This book will give executives a better understanding of strategic alliance issues and deepen their knowledge about intellectual property rights and contractual agreements. Lütolf-Carroll developed and classroom tested the cases she wrote for this book on the MBA and EMBA students taking her courses at ESADE, SDA

Bocconi, RSM-Erasmus University, and Helsinki School of Economics (soon to become part of Aalto University).

Many of the book's chapters have important supplementary materials that are available free to all readers. These files are located on our web site at www.innovationtocashflows.com. Instructions on the web site explain how to log onto the password-protected parts of the web site and download the supplements. The materials include useful chapter appendixes and mini-case studies; an extensive business, legal and scientific glossary compiled by our book's contributors; a sample confidentiality agreement; inventor disclosure guidelines; plus fully functional electronic spreadsheets to the book's valuation cases. In addition, downloadable from the web site are four complementary capstone cases from leading business schools Stanford, Darden and Ivey. These capstone cases allow students to practice and integrate concepts introduced in the text.

The team of contributing authors welcomes your feedback, suggestions for further improvements, and enhancements. Please advise us of any errors or omissions. We look forward to hearing from you. Visit our book's web site and send us your comments at www.innovationtocashflows.com.

Acknowledgments

Writing a book is a labor of love, fraught with challenges and hurdles all along the way. We have found this to be all the more true when the book is written by a group of authors and contributors hailing from diverse cultures, professions, and time zones, who are working together as a team for the first time and attempting to address a topic as broad and complex as high-technology entrepreneurship and alliances. It is no surprise, therefore, and a special source of satisfaction to us, that we can acknowledge the contributions of so many talented people from so many walks of life. The book is richer for their diversity.

This book would not have been possible without the support and backing of Anthony Indaimo, chairman of Withers LLP. Anthony marshaled his firm's collective international legal expertise to write the legal chapters for our readers. Without Withers' support, our book, frankly, would have withered on a limb (no pun intended). We are deeply indebted to each and every contributing author from Withers LLP and W.P. Thompson & Co. for the time and effort each devoted to our cause.

Conan Chitham deserves special mention as he became the anointed "project coordinator" for Withers on "the book." Conan contributed Chapter 14 on technology transfer agreements, reviewed the IP portions of the manuscript, and coordinated the various teams in London, Milan, and New York, who supplied material for the book. Anthony Indaimo, Nadia Ignatius, Gabriel Monzon-Cortarelli of Withers LLP contributed Chapter 9 on contract law and incorporation issues. Anthony and Nadia also authored Chapter 10 on investment agreements. They would like to thank these colleagues for their able assistance: Noelle Brown, Andrea Conzatti, Julie Junghanns, and Concetta Lipani, in Milan; Mirin Diver, in London; and Dan Crosby, and Justin Zamparelli who provided U.S. advice for the contract law chapter.

Richard Lord contributed Chapter 16 on due diligence and reviewed commercial aspects of the other legal chapters. John Maycock, Caroline Hughes, and Nicole Hirst contributed Chapter 11 on the IP landscape: copyright, industrial designs, know-how, trade secrets, and trademarks. They also read and commented on the other IP chapters in the book. Sanford J. Davis of Withers Bergman LLP in New York made timely reviews of the online Appendixes 17.3 and 18.1. We thank Tim Bamford of Withers LLP for reviewing those portions of the manuscript pertaining to patent infringement issues; we are especially grateful for Tim's invitation to Tom Brand of W.P. Thompson & Co. to join our team.

Tom Brand of W.P. Thompson & Co. contributed Chapters 12 and 13 on patent basics and patent strategies and the Formula One car example in Chapter 2. We thank W.P. Thompson & Co. for contributing these resource materials: Appendixes 2.2 and 2.3 guidelines for Setting Up an Invention Disclosure System for Your Company, and the Sample Invention Disclosure Form (accessible by logging onto www.innovationtocashflows.com). Tom would like to acknowledge the research assistance and drafting support provided by these members of his firm: David Read, Robert Gregory, Alistair McKinnon, Simon Bradbury, Lyle Ellis, Tom Hutchinson, Andrew Crawford, and Chevaun Tarrach.

Behind the scenes, Withers LLP provided considerable production, copyediting, and proofreading services for drafts of the manuscript. We are grateful to Felicity Ballentyne, Manager, Central Word Processing Department, in Withers' London office, for being cheerful, willing, professional, and efficient. She provided us with staff support around the clock. We especially acknowledge the able production advice and contributions of Carl Davies. We appreciate the services provided on our behalf by these copyeditors and proofreaders: Jane Browning, Alethea Reid, Alicia Jeffers, Claude Doherty, Jumoke Adejimola, William Maycock, Lauren Mayot, and Claire Harris in London.

Dr. Margaret Mullally contributed Chapter 8 on how alliances complete the value chain in biotechnology and pharmaceutical business models. Margaret would like to thank Luigi Jonk for his constant support and encouragement of her writing for the book. We are deeply grateful to Margaret for reading multiple drafts of various portions of the manuscript. She painstakingly wrote us countless queries and suggestions on the strategy and alliances chapters and commented on the earliest versions of the valuation chapters. Our book is better structured because of her editing. Margaret was a wonderful sparring partner with whom we could test out our ideas and theories. She stimulated our creativity and gave us a huge shot of energy halfway through the process of writing the book. We appreciate all of her contributions and the care and passion she showed toward the project.

Marc Perret of Gilde Healthcare and his wife, Maria Nadal, have both been staunch supporters of Connie's research and teaching for many years, at ESADE Business School and at Rotterdam School of Management. Marc's wisdom and experiences, first as a senior executive in Novartis and then as a general partner at Gilde Healthcare, have influenced her thinking about venture capital, entrepreneurial finance, and alliance strategies. Marc unselfishly shared his valuable time on numerous occasions over the years. He offered many ideas for the book and has also contributed to the development of Connie's investment management courses. The chapters on managing alliances and the role of venture capitalists on boards of directors of start-ups, in particular, benefited from her conversations with Marc Perret.

We would not have been able to complete the task without the effort and support of many friends and family members who helped us behind the scenes. About two years ago, when the manuscript was still in its very earliest stages of creation, we received hearty encouragement from Dr. Martti Kulvik and Dr. Raine Hermans, who read and provided guidance and ideas for the first drafts. Martti also commented on the final version of the biotechnology chapter. P.K. Rantalainen and Kristina Rantalainen offered early words of encouragement. Juhana Rauramo shared with us his insights on how venture capitalists in Finland think about valuing the alliances of medical technology start-ups. His comments got us thinking harder about the venture capitalists' role in influencing the choice of exit strategies—thoughts that were eventually incorporated into the examples of Chapter 19 on venture capital methods of valuation.

Antti is especially grateful to Teemu Järvinen, who reviewed many of the book's chapters and gave encouraging comments throughout the long process; to Kimmo Hautala, who read and commented on the competitive intelligence and patent search chapter; and to Jari Rantala, for reading early drafts of the manuscript and for his comments about open source innovation. Connie is grateful to Eugene Santoro for his expert copyediting on the strategy and introduction to strategic alliance chapters. Connie and Antti both thank Connie's husband, Marc Lütolf, for commenting and offering suggestions on multiple book chapters, for copyediting and proofreading the valuation sections and conclusion, and for building the book's web site.

Connie wishes to express her appreciation to these colleagues and friends, all of whom have also offered her steady support and encouragement for the book these past two years: to Sara B. Fox, for the interview which appears in the opening chapter; to Marcelo Galmarini, for his comments on Chapters 6 and 7, and especially for his insights on valuing privately held high technology companies. His feedback was invaluable in completing the financial spreadsheet model for the case in Chapter 20. Connie thanks both Marcelo Galmarini and Alessandra Genco, for their detailed comments on online Appendixes 17.3 and 18.1. Alessandra Genco also reviewed Chapters 17 and 18. Sincere thanks to Dr. Jonathan MacQuitty, for conversations about managing and investing in early-stage biotechnology ventures; to Pablo Riveroll, who provided useful ideas on structuring strategic alliances and valuing initial public offerings; to Cheryl Fragiadakis, for her insights on academic research collaborations, which enriched several chapters in the book; to Erna M. Boogaard, for her suggestions about the structure of private equity funds and how they are managed; to Laura M. Cha, for her comments on doing cross-border due diligence and on the disclosure requirements for initial public offerings; to Leanne Tilbrook, for her suggestions on formal insolvency procedures and corporate restructurings in the United Kingdom compared to U.S. practices, and for her helpful comments and proofreading of Chapter 20, the Glossary, several online appendixes, and for her meticulous review of the galley proofs for Chapters 1 to 7, 9 and 10.

Connie would like to thank all these academic colleagues for their support and stimulating ideas: to Professor Robert F. Bruner, dean of Darden Business School, for his mentoring over the years and for generously allowing us to reprint two of his cases as capstone cases; to Professor George Foster of Stanford Graduate School of Business, for sharing his insights on financial analysis and managing high-growth technology companies, and for allowing us to use his GenPharm case as one of our capstone cases; to Professor George Athanassakos, for helping us obtain permission to use the Proto 5 Case in our book; to Tracy Keys, IMD Program Manager, for her breakthrough session on reordering the sequence of topics in the book; to Professor Renzo Cenciarini of SDA Bocconi, for the chance to coteach corporate restructuring and mergers and acquisitions; and to Oriana Ghinato, for her support and encouragement. My sincere thanks to these RSM colleagues: Professor Michael J. Page, former Dean of Post-Experience Programs of RSM Erasmus University and Executive Director of the Rotterdam School of Management B.V. and now Dean of Business and the McCallum Graduate School at Bentley College; Dianne Bevelander, Luis Umaña, Lesley-Ann Calvert, and to all my friends and program managers at RSM for their caring, sense of humor, and continuous encouragement; Dr. Anne Herbert of Helsinki School of Economics (soon to become Aalto University), for inspiration on our walks; Professor Jyrki Wallenius and Asta Malinen for the multi-year opportunity to collaborate in various MBA programs at Helsinki School of Economics; and to these friends and colleagues at ESADE for help on balancing teaching duties with time to write the book: Jordi Brunat, Olaya Garcia, Gloria Battlori, Montse Olle, and

Dr. Carmen Ansotegui. For behind-the-scenes support, thanks to M. Àngles Augé, Nuria Monteagudo, Mercè Gratacós, Teresa Rioboo, and Dr. Michele Quintano. To Dr. Carlos Losada, ESADE Director General, and Dr. Xavier Mendoza, Deputy Director General, thanks to both of you for providing decades of support for innovative "active learning" teaching in ESADE, and especially to Xavier Mendoza, for our coteaching, for first tutoring me about cross-border strategic alliances, and for your guidance on the strategic alliance literature.

Antti and Connie thank Mr. Olli Haveri from Poickeus Oy, Helsinki, Finland, for creating all the illustrations and figures for this book, including the Remmey patent and patent landscape and the Tarzan yell drawings. Without Olli's artistic help and that of his team, we could never have met the publisher's requirements.

Finally, we are honored that both Dr. Henry Chesbrough and Dr. Karl S. Pister of UC Berkeley collaborated on the foreword for our book. Connie is grateful to Karl for a friendship that began 33 years ago when she was his civil engineering student at Cal. Hank Chesbrough's three books on open innovation were a source of inspiration to Connie and Antti for writing this one. We are admirers of yours, first as a manager in the hard-disk drive industry, then as an assistant professor at Harvard, and now Executive Director of the Open Innovation Center, Haas School of Business, University of California, Berkeley, and widely read author. Hank and Karl's joint effort on the foreword is the kind of interdisciplinary collaboration among business, engineering, and scientific inquiry that we hope will inspire the readers of our book.

Antti and Connie acknowledge their deep gratitude to Bill Falloon, our acquisitions editor, and Senior Editor of Wiley Finance. Bill believed in us and championed "the book" from beginning to end, even as it morphed and changed along the way. We couldn't ask for a kinder, gentler, more patient, or more understanding editor. Bill also gave Connie the biography on Joe Wilson by Charles E. Ellis, which inspired her. We extend our heartfelt thanks to all of the Wiley team for their professional, steadfast, and instrumental advice, in particular, Laura Walsh, Associate Editor; Skyler Balbus, Editorial Assistant; Emilie Herman, Editorial Manager; Meg Freeborn, Development Editor; and Michael Lisk, Senior Production Editor. We acknowledge the quality and professional work of Missy Garnett and her staff at Cape Cod Compositors. We also thank Joan O'Neil, Executive Publisher, for giving us the opportunity to publish this book with John Wiley & Sons.

Finally, to all our former students and current students, friends, colleagues, and family members, we thank you for the stimulating ideas we have received from you through your e-mails, phone calls, and visits from the far corners of the world. We are grateful to all of you. Now the whole team of authors and contributors can proudly say, "Break out the champagne, the book is finally done!"

CONSTANCE LÜTOLF-CARROLL
Milan, Italy and Lugano, Switzerland

ANTTI PIRNES
Helsinki, Finland

Creativity and the Roles of the Inventor, Innovator, and Entrepreneur

Creativity and the Entrepreneurial Process

We begin with the premise that inspiration, motivation, hard work, and persistence are all necessary aspects of the creative entrepreneurial process. We think that the distinction between *invention* and *innovation* needs to be recognized; the nuance is subtle but important. In this chapter, we explore the roles, temperaments, and talents of the *inventor, innovator,* and *entrepreneur.* Each role needs to interact with the other roles—at various points in time—in order to get great ideas out of the laboratory and to transform these ideas into viable businesses.

To more easily explain how you might go from generating your own valuable idea to forming a business, we have created a simple wheel of progress (shown in Figure 1.1). This wheel illustrates how you might proceed, step by step, from the initial brainstorming of a valuable idea, to protecting your invention, to devising a business model, to forming collaborative high-technology alliances, to valuing the cash flows, to seizing the moment when the time is ripe to harvest parts of the business, and, thereafter, to start the cycle over again.

We recognize, however, that no start-up follows such a simple linear route from innovation to cash flows. At each step, there are forks and twists and turns in the path. For instance, it could be that instead of harvesting or selling parts of the business as originally planned, you and your investors might need to contribute more capital to the venture to keep it alive. Or, alternatively, you may need to grow the venture faster to keep rivals at bay. Some older alliances might need to be dissolved and new ones formed in order to launch a pipeline of innovative new products. Hence we like the image of our readers starting and stopping their wheels, maybe even spinning them forward and backward, allowing for frequent adjustments depending on serendipity, setbacks, good fortune, and their own learning along the way.

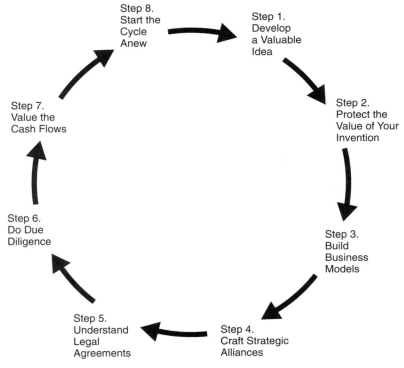

FIGURE 1.1   Going from Idea to Collaborative Alliance

GETTING THAT BRIGHT IDEA

Great scientific ideas abound. Few make it to market. Even fewer turn into splendid businesses. Why? Part of the mystery may be intrinsic to the persona and temperament of the scientist. Inquisitive, hardworking, focused on doing great research, scientists may be so absorbed in the science that they are ignorant of the commercial and legal aspects of doing business that are critical to creating value from their discoveries.

For our readers who are scientists and inventors, recognizing when you might actually have a valuable idea, no matter how small it may seem to you initially, is the first step to eventually obtaining a patent and getting official recognition for an invention. As Robert Browning says in his verse, the low man "sees it and does it."

How can you get started? How do you train your instincts to "see it"—in other words, to recognize when you might be seeing a valuable opportunity? More important, how do you crank up the internal motivation to actually "do it"? And have the courage and stamina to persevere one step at a time, until you realize your dream? This process sounds daunting, even overwhelming, to many people. How do you even know where to begin?

That low man seeks a little thing to do,
Sees it and does it:
This high man, with a great thing to pursue,
Dies ere he knows it.
That low man goes on adding one to one,
His hundred's soon hit:
This high man, aiming at a million,
Misses by a unit.

                                        —Robert Browning[1]

We suggest that you begin by being observant. Renaissance genius Leonardo da Vinci is credited with having extraordinary powers of observation. He was capable of seeing it where others could only look at it and stare. Leonardo was able to connect the dots and draw links in his mind that others, frankly, did not see.[2] In so doing, he made new meaning out of his research and experiments. Certainly part of the creative genius of Leonardo da Vinci was his persistence, patience, and determination. He also lived a very long and healthy life, unlike many others of his day, which helped him to be productive, more so than most mortals. Assuming you are not Leonardo, how can *you* get started on figuring out the next creative idea?

Inspiration and Fresh Innovative Ideas

It is within you to create. It is part of our human makeup. We invent tools to survive in the wilderness and in the urban jungle. We invent stories to make us laugh and to pass on our family history. We send each other drawings and pictures to console our friends and keep up our spirits. We all have many talents. Indeed, we have an innate sense of design that helps us to put together familiar pieces into new patterns and compositions. We create by allowing our inner selves some peace of mind. We need that peace. It frees our hearts to take on a bit of risk and think out of the box. To be creative, most of us need to overcome our fear of being judged and to overturn our anxious feelings that we might fail. To be creative is to take risks and to reach out in new ways. We need to turn off the e-mail. Quiet the chattering mind. Learn to be still and to reflect.

All of us will have our own way to reach down into that part of ourselves that is our creative "essence."[3] Some will do it by being alone—taking a walk along the beach on a foggy morning. Others will retreat to the mountaintop. A few will go to a tropical jungle and seek adventure or danger. Some will stimulate their creative selves by enjoying painting, playing music, or taking a hot sauna.

Sometimes the best ideas are the ones that solve everyday problems—such as how to manufacture a candy box that can be opened without making a loud noise in the movie theater, or how to explain to a worker on a construction site (whose mother tongue is not the same as yours) that he needs to bring to you a certain tool. This is a typical problem anywhere in the world where you have nonnative speakers working on building sites. The solution to the first problem, we do not know (yet). For the latter one, maybe you could come up with a search engine or photo dictionary integrated into your mobile phone that shows photographs of construction tools when queried. We leave it to our readers to pursue this idea.

We do not pretend to be experts in creativity, but we do suggest that it is worthwhile to read about what others have learned and what helps them pursue personal and professional development. Over the years, we have accumulated a small treasure trove of books on creativity. In particular, we highlight two books. We especially recommend the classic by Richard Nelson Bolles, *What Color Is Your Parachute?*, which is supposedly the world's best-selling job-hunting book.[4] We have found Bolles's advice and exercises fun, rewarding, and stimulating, especially if you are in a transition or "inflection" point in your job and need to repot and find fresh soil, maybe even a different career path. Our other recommendation is *How to Think like Leonardo da Vinci—Seven Steps to Genius Every Day* by Michael J. Gelb.[5] We like it because the exercises in the book help you learn and practice Leonardo's renaissance principles: curiosity, experiential observation, refinement of the senses, embracement of ambiguity and paradox, balance of art and science, awareness of the body, and appreciation for the interconnectedness of all things (systems thinking). Gelb teaches his readers about drawing, shading, and perspective. He helps you listen to music, do breathing exercises, and create your own notebooks like Leonardo's. The advice is not limited to reading words, but engages all your senses and stimulates all parts of your brain, left side and right side.

For some of us, becoming a more creative scientist, engineer, designer, lawyer, doctor, investor, or manager may mean learning the art and practice of pathfinding. *Pathfinding* means being a problem seeker—in other words, being the scout who finds the trail and indicates the path for others to follow. It means figuring out which problems to solve and which questions to ask. Problem seekers ask the right questions. They intentionally look and see around the corners. They are determined to solve life's mysteries.

Dr. Harold Leavitt, a much-beloved organizational behavior professor to generations of business students, taught the popular elective course called Implementation at Stanford University Graduate School of Business. Leavitt authored many books, including a short one titled *Corporate Pathfinders: How Visionary Managers Use Imaginative Strategies to Shape the Future of Their Companies*.[6] In the book, he creates a simple three-part model about management. In the model, he draws three mental boxes: box #1 he labels "pathfinding," box #2 is "problem solving," and box #3 is "implementing." As Leavitt puts it:

> [T]he central issue of pathfinding is not influence or persuasion, nor is it reasoning or systematic analysis. The key word here is mission. The pathfinding part of managing is the homeland of the visionary, the dreamer, the innovator, the creator, the entrepreneur, and the charismatic leader: how do I decide what I want to be when I grow up? What should this organization try to become if it could become anything imaginable? What do we really want to do with this company? The #1 pathfinding world is highly personal and subjective, with answers, where there are any, emerging more from within the self than from a diagnosis of what's out there. Pathfinding is the ephemeral part of managing that deals with values, aesthetics, and beliefs. Putting faith before evidence, pathfinders often violate #2 problem solving precepts. But they also build new worlds.[7]

According to Leavitt, #2 problem solving is the analytical part of management, where economic forecasts, strategic plans, and financial controls dominate. Reading, writing, and arithmetic are all analytical skills. Many of the core courses in a typical business school curriculum involve problem solving and analysis, starting with critical thinking and ending with decision science, advanced statistics, and consumer behavior models.

For Leavitt, #3 implementing means getting things done through others. Managers need to persuade and induce change in other people's attitudes and behavior through social interaction. It inevitably involves emotions. "[G]etting people to do what you want them to do is much more a gutsy than an intellectual process."[8] Top-performing salespeople, staff sergeants, lobbyists, and product managers have all learned implementation skills on their jobs. They know how to influence people. They do this effectively by tapping into human emotions and consequently getting change to happen.

Leavitt believes that visionary managers should spend more of their time on #1 pathfinding and less time focused on #2 problem-solving or #3 implementing. Not that he discounts the importance of #2 or #3 activities, but in the early and mid-1980s, Leavitt was writing in reaction to the overemphasis in business schools on analysis and the underemphasis on the "softer" people-related problems and how-to-get-things-done problems that managers regularly face. Back then, teaching the creative, softer side of management was much rarer than today.

For a flavor of Leavitt's pioneering thinking and writing, read his delightful research paper titled "On Teaching What We Haven't Taught."[9] In this paper, Leavitt writes: "Among the right things we don't usually teach, but should, is the soft end of the managing process; which I believe is what most of us mean when we now talk about 'leadership,' 'vision,' 'sense of responsibility,' 'imagination' and 'entrepreneurship.'"[10]

Twenty-five years from the time of Leavitt's *Pathfinders'* book, we see growing evidence that top-tier business schools are radically overhauling their curriculums in response to globalization, competition, and the need to pay more attention to developing global leadership skills, particularly interdisciplinary thinking, cross-cultural people skills, and creative pathfinding.[11] Leading faculties are developing more active-learning-type experiences to help executives develop their emotional intelligence[12] and other soft skills[13] and use them to envision and to implement strategic change within their organizations.[14]

FROM IDEA TO INVENTION

To invent something is either to think up something new or to make something new. Novelty is what separates an ordinary idea from a true invention. New scientific discoveries, technologies, products, services, and organizational methods qualify as inventions.

What exactly are inventions? Inventions may be tangible or intangible. Examples of *tangible* inventions—something you can touch or see—would be a new surgical device or a novel mechanical robot. An example of an *intangible* invention—something not perceptible by the senses—would be a brand-new process for combining software and graphics. The intangible part of the invention process would be the invisible, creative insight for a new game-user interface, most likely arising from a game programmer's inspiration, experience, and effort.

Nintendo's introduction of the Wii interface, with movement consoles, is a good example. The innovative Wii console allows millions of youngsters—and their parents—to have an active and visual experience of sports play. Nintendo redefined its old Game Boy paradigm from a passive finger-exercise game into a stand-up motion experience. Kids and parents can play electronic bowling, baseball, tennis, and golf simply by swinging their wands (which becomes their sports equipment) and timing their swing with the electronic ball (bowling ball, baseball, tennis ball, or golf ball). Neither the Sony PS3 nor Microsoft Xbox 360 consoles have the same motion capabilities as the Wii.

Difference between an Innovation and an Invention

The word *innovation* comes from the Latin root *innovatus,* which is the past participle of the verb *innovare,* meaning "to renew." *Innovation,* according to Webster's dictionary, "is the act or process of innovating," where *innovating* means "to change customary methods or to change the way things are done." Our point is that many inventions utilize the work and knowledge of others who went before. Rarely is something invented spontaneously from scratch. Most often the breakthrough or the insight comes from a novel combination of existing elements. We define *innovation* as the commercialization of an invention. "To commercialize" something means "to sell a product or a service to a customer who is willing to pay for it." The link between invention and innovation is the customer. Linking your invention to a paying customer is what changes your invention into an innovation. The customer is crucial.

The typical customer decides what to buy by comparing similar products and services. For each offering, the customer weighs the sales price versus the expected benefits or results to be attained from using the product or service. In marketing parlance, managers use the term *value proposition* to refer to the company's statement of why a customer should buy its products or use its services (over rivals' offerings). It must clearly and succinctly explain how the customer will benefit. The benefits must be perceptible and valuable in the eyes of the customer. The results may be economic (e.g., savings on raw material, labor, or delivery time) or they may be based on intangible benefits (e.g., higher perceived image, quality, comfort, or luxury experience).

A product or service with a stronger value proposition offers more benefits to the customer than a rival product or service with a weaker value proposition. The stronger the value proposition, the higher the price that the seller may charge. For instance, opera fans are willing to pay more for opening-night tickets to La Scala, in Milan, Italy, one of the most famous opera houses in the world, than they would be willing to pay for tickets at a lesser-known theater on a night that is not the opening gala. La Scala has more appeal—a much stronger value proposition—than that of "other" opera houses.

Inventions and innovations abound in many fields of endeavor. Consider for a moment the innovative shape and form of Swiss Re's London headquarters building located on St. Mary Axe in the City of London, affectionately referred to as the Gherkin. This landmark building redefined the meaning of urban space in London. Architects Foster & Partners designed the building in close collaboration with the client Swiss Re and London City planners.

The design process was interactive and iterative. It started by combining the client's need for functional commercial space that met investment-quality criteria with architectural inspiration, experience, and playfulness. The architects developed many designs and built many three-dimensional models of the spatial elements. They matched their ideas to the challenges of the historic site, located in the heart of London. After presenting their preliminary ideas, more client discussions followed, as well as consultation with statutory bodies such as English Heritage, whose approval would also be required. The team then revised the designs. More dialogue with city planners suggested that the architects raise the height of the building, making an even bolder statement on the city skyline than initially envisioned. Only when construction was under way, and the building was being built, could people on the streets see that the interplay of shape, space, materials, and color were rightly balanced into an innovative and startling new skyscraper.

Is the Gherkin an invention or an innovation? Our answer is both. Technically, it contained numerous *inventions*: The architects, engineers, and contractors developed new types of fittings and couplings for the steel structure. We also answer that the shape is *innovative*—since the tower sold in 2007 for a higher price than for other commercial buildings of a less novel profile. The "green building" design also incorporated innovative heating, cooling, and ventilation systems, which save energy costs and reduce the building's carbon footprint. Thus, the design of the building in many ways created value for the owner (Swiss Re at the time), the tenants, and the city.

We base our answers on firsthand interviews conducted with Sara B. Fox, project director, who was responsible for representing Swiss Re's interests during the construction phase of the building project as well as on information contained in Mirjam von Arx's documentary film *Building the Gherkin*.[15]

DISTINCT ROLES OF INVENTOR, INNOVATOR, AND ENTREPRENEUR

The people who are good at inventing things (such as scientists) are not necessarily the same people who are good at innovating (who sometimes are new product developers, marketers, and business development types). The entrepreneur is the one who brings vision, drive, people, and capital together, to back the inventors who discover things, the innovators who dream about their customers, the manufacturers who know how to produce products, and the salespeople who can sell them. The entrepreneur leads and molds these elements into a thriving business.

The word *entrepreneur* is derived from the French verb *entreprendre*, which means "to undertake." In the old days, *entrepreneur* referred to any particularly bold, difficult, dangerous, or important project or business venture. Entrepreneurs take on the challenge of growing business ventures. The roles of inventor, innovators, and entrepreneurs are different, but viable technology businesses need all three types.

How the Roles Are Intertwined

We said earlier, in our definition of innovation, that *innovation is what links invention to a customer's needs*. What does this mean? It means that the innovator has the ability, or personal experience, to see how an invention or a new technology might satisfy a customer's needs. Therefore, in order to combine the roles of being an "inventor" and an "innovator," you need to put yourself into the shoes of customers and experience the invention as they would. Ask yourself: What are the customers' needs? How might my invention satisfy those needs? What can be changed to make it work better and enable customers to be more productive? (If they are drilling a tunnel, for example, how can they drill that tunnel cheaper, faster, and better?) What benefits will customers receive from using this new tool or product or service? Are customers willing to pay for those benefits? If yes, how strong is the value proposition to them? How important and how urgent is the need? If you have trouble visualizing your target customer, then we advise you to find someone else who can help you think about customers and their needs. Most likely it should be someone experienced in business development or who is seasoned in sales or high-technology marketing.

Hard Work of the Inventor-Turned-Innovator

To illustrate how an inventor recognized customers' needs and used these insights to turn his invention into an innovation, let us look at the example of Chester F. Carlson, the inventor of xerography. To see how an entrepreneur took Carlson's innovation and turned it into a great company, let us examine the story of Joe Wilson, the mover and shaker behind the transformation of the old Haloid Company, his family's ailing business, into the great Xerox Corporation.

According to Charles D. Ellis, the author of Joe Wilson's biography,[16] Carlson graduated from the prestigious California Institute of Technology in 1930, during the Great Depression, with a physics degree and about $1,400 in debt.[17] Ellis writes about Carlson's struggles to find a job: "Carlson sent out 82 letters asking about work, but got only two replies, one interview, and no offers until he finally was hired by Bell Labs to test materials in New York City."[18] About a year later, Carlson transferred to Bell Labs' patent department but was laid off in 1933 due to the worsening depression. Eventually he found other work at the patent law firm of Austin & Dix, but only a year later, in 1934, "he was about to be laid off again when he got a job in the patent department at [the law firm of] P.R. Mallory and Company."[19] Over the next seven years, while working during the day, "he studied nights at New York Law School, earned his law degree, and rose to become head of Mallory's patent department."[20] Carlson spent many hours in the New York Public Library because he could not afford to buy his own books. At the library, he was frustrated "by the cost and mindless time taken to make copies of important drawings and charts."[21] He became convinced there had to be a better way than the expensive and "slow photostat process then available at 25¢ a page."[22]

In 1934, while still employed at Mallory, Carlson witnessed time and again the need for "a dozen or more copies of *patent specifications*."[23] In those days, copying meant using an old-fashioned typewriter with multiple pieces of carbon paper stuck into the machine. The copying was tedious and often plagued by typing errors and mistakes. "Seeing this situation, Carlson began thinking about low-cost copying . . . not duplicating, which required a stencil or master."[24] Once, while working with a colleague late at night, the two (according to Ellis) had this conversation:

> Carlson: *"There must be a better way of making these copies!"*
> Colleague: "Sure," came the reply, but *"nobody has ever found it."*
> Carlson: *"Maybe nobody has ever tried."*[25]

Ellis writes that "[f]or the next six months, Carlson spent evenings and weekends in the New York Library, reading all the books and literature available on printing and duplicating, and especially on photoconductivity."[26]

Ellis, quotes Carlson, describes much later his own thinking at the time [around 1934]: "I recognized a very great need then for a machine that would be right in an office where you could bring a document to it, push it in a slot, press a button, and get a copy out. I set for myself a spare-time project of trying to fill that need. I wanted a copying process, not a duplicating process."[27]

Years later, Carlson reflected:

Of course, I don't think inventions of this kind come just overnight as a sudden flash. I think there's got to be a long incubation period. First one has to recognize the problem, saturate himself with the problem and the technology or the field of science where a solution might be found. He must let his subconscious mind work on it for a long period, perhaps years, until the right elements eventually fit together in his thinking.[28]

Entrepreneurs See Value Not Only in *What* Was Invented but Also *Who* Invented It

In 1940, Carlson learned he had "received the first of his four basic patents on the process called electrophotography."[29] These strong basic patents, years later, would catch the attention of Haloid's then chief executive, Joe Wilson:

Finally arriving in Columbus, Ohio, [Haloid's attorney at the time Sol Linowitz and CEO Joe Wilson] went to Battelle for a demonstration of Carlson's invention. It was not the greatest show on earth. The Battelle team took from a shoebox a piece of cat fur, a transparent ruler, a metal plate, and a bright light. After rubbing the plate with the fur and shining the light through the ruler and onto the plate, some off-white lines showed upon the dark surface. Then the plate was dusted with dark powder and, after brushing it clean, was pressed against some paper—and there, somewhat blurred, were the lines of the ruler. As Joe Wilson looked closely at the plate through his bifocals, one of the Battelle demonstrators said proudly, "That's it!"
Wilson said one word: "Magnificent!"
Linowitz said two words, asking incredulously: "That's it?"
"Yes," came [Wilson's] reply. "That's it."[30]

Reading Carlson's and Wilson's story, we are again reminded of a line from the poem by Robert Browning we quoted earlier:
"That low man seeks a little thing to do,
Sees it and does it."

In this case, it seems to us that Carlson's brilliance was in recognizing a big customer need for convenient copying. He then dedicated years of his life "doing it." He was persistent and determined, and had the technical skills and knowledge to see the merit in what he was thinking. Moreover, he was able to combine his physics and broad science background from his years at Cal Tech with his own self-taught knowledge—gleaned through extensive reading and years of experiments.

Furthermore, he also protected his invention thoroughly and carefully (the subject of our next chapter). Carlson filed for his first patent on October 18, 1937. However, filing for a patent would not be enough; he would have to build a working model to demonstrate that the concept could be put to practical use—which months later Carlson did, but only with the help of a skilled immigrant craftsman looking for some part-time work, Otto Kornei. The first working model was so complex and cumbersome that nobody cared. In fact, nobody was impressed that Chester Carlson, at age 32, had produced the first novel technology "in 150 years" for "putting words and pictures on paper."[31]

Besides knowing the science and having the stubbornness, stamina, and persistence for years of hard work, Carlson was an *expert in patent law*, something that furthered his cause. He had learned a lot about writing patent definitions and claims from working at Bell Lab's patent office and at P.R. Mallory and Company. Interestingly enough, "the definitions in Carlson's patents are all in words—with no numbers—and are so broad they dominate all other patents in the field." Frank Steinhilper, Haloid's head of patents, later describes Carlson's xerography patent as "maybe the best patent ever written in the U.S."[32]

We believe that Joe Wilson's entrepreneurial instincts and his own years of careful preparation running the Haloid Company—and perhaps also the desperate state of the family business[33]—led him to recognize the value in Carlson's copying process, when others, such as attorney Sol Linowitz, failed to do so. Of course, Wilson failed in his own way, too; he severely underestimated the time and money it would take to turn the invention into a copying machine that worked. It ended up taking 12 more years of long and hard work.

> *While Carlson's creative genius and Battelle's remarkable development skills were crucial, Joe Wilson's vision, disciplined persistence, and organizational leadership were essential. If the development of Carlson's technology had been left in the hands of Battelle, it would probably have languished and died there. . . . What was needed was an entrepreneur with vision who could appreciate the commercial possibilities and recognize the profit potential that would justify the large financial commitments required.[34]*

In these two stories of Chester Carlson and Joe Wilson, we see clearly illustrated how innovation is the act or process of taking an invention and linking it to a specific customer's needs by discovering applications that are of practical benefit to that customer. Carlson was good at the science and was a pathfinder in recognizing when he had a great idea. However, he did not have the business acumen or the financial resources to take his idea out of the lab and turn it into a business. For that step, he needed Joe Wilson, the entrepreneur.

> *Entrepreneurs differ greatly from promoters who swing for the fences: the entrepreneur's persistent priority is a disciplined, managed minimization of risk. While casual observers may celebrate [Joe] Wilson's ultimately astounding financial success, his real achievement as a leader and manager were in his rigorous financial discipline, his focus on developing a new technology, and his remarkable capacity to keep his organization committed to his vision for many long, lean years while going through the uncertainties of deliberate transformational change.[35]*

An inventor turned innovator (the case of Chester Carlson) often lacks the financing and production resources required to launch a product or service into the market in the time frame and with the scale required for success. If the innovator runs out of money, time, or product, the customer will be reached by someone else who is right behind with his or her variation of the idea. Furthermore, one product is usually insufficient to build a viable and sustainable business.

Avoid the One-Product Business

The one-product business is known as a one-hit wonder because it is named after the pop singers who have one hit song, rising to the top of the music charts, but then who fade from sight, after never managing to record another hit.[36] These single-product operations are very often mom-and-pop businesses; that is, they are microbusinesses typically started up by one or two family members—usually Mom and Dad—who mind the shop.

One-hit wonders are also characteristic of many young high-technology start-ups, who are given one round of financing by venture capitalists, then must demonstrate the viability of their emerging new technology. Many of these single-product high-tech start-ups will go out of business within a few years, unless they are exceptionally successful early on. Why? They run out of money or they are destroyed by a rival firm launching a better product extension or they are beaten by a new entrant that has been successful in innovating and developing an even better technology. For more examples of high-technology one-hit wonders and the problems associated with them, see Chesbrough 2006.[37]

For instance, Atari was an early sensation in the video games hardware industry, but it stumbled and was superseded by Nintendo's third-generation NES game console, which sold 60 million units. Nintendo, in turn, barely held onto its lead in the fourth generation, with its Super NES against a new rival, Sega, which introduced the Genesis console. In the fifth round, Nintendo launched its Nintendo 64 machine, and survived, whereas Sega's Saturn console was beaten by Sony's launch of its first PlayStation, which went on to sell over 100 million consoles. In the sixth round, Nintendo launched Game Cube (21.2 million units sold); Sega came out with Dreamcast (10.6 million units); and Sony launched PlayStation 2 (140 million units), which handsomely beat Microsoft's Xbox new entrant. By year-end 2006, in the seventh round, Nintendo had unexpectedly good success with its innovative Wii (3.2 million units) targeted to casual users; whereas Microsoft's Xbox 360 (at 10.4 million units) was beating Sony's PS3 (2.2 million units), which had a troubled launch.[38]

Yes, we recognize it is true that many businesses must begin with one product, not only in mom-and-pop retail settings but also in high-technology ventures. Initially, many high-technology enterprises focus on one particular technology platform and one or two key customer applications. Even so, if the aim is to build a sustainable high-growth business, relying on a single product is too risky. If that one product fails, the company will go bankrupt.

In general, continuous innovation for high-technology businesses is essential to growing and sustaining a thriving pipeline of products. Continuous innovation is like bringing water to fertile desert soil. With water, the desert blooms. Same with innovation; it is the sustenance for a fledgling business. But even a canal full of water is not enough if the people running the business do not stay committed to the vision—which brings us back, full circle, to the story of the drive and determination of Joe Wilson and Chester Carlson in bringing to fruition their dream about solving the world's need for copying documents in a better way.

CLOSING THOUGHTS

Wilson and Carlson and the others involved in saving the Haloid Company and turning it into the great Xerox Corporation are an inspiring example of a great entrepreneurial team. In general, founding leaders of sustainable companies typically will have the tenacity and vision to launch not only a series of innovations to market but also to draw together a team of diverse people, energize them to be enthusiastic about the company's mission, and get them to work together. It takes determination, patience, salesmanship, and sometimes the skills of a peacemaker to pull it off. Entrepreneurs are a special set of company founders. Entrepreneurs are business builders. They tend to surround themselves with the right team to take on their ambitious projects, and together they scale up these projects and product pipelines into viable enterprises.

So, a *solid* business requires three essential ingredients: an innovation, a product or service, and a paying customer. A *thriving* business requires depth of leadership, vision, entrepreneurship, continuous innovation, new product development processes, manufacturing or service skills, capital, and salesmanship. All the basic business functions combined: research and development, production, sales and marketing, finance, and human resources. We can imagine hearing Professor Leavitt say that a thriving business needs leadership capable of pathfinding—the Joe Wilsons of this world—who have a gift for envisioning a better and brighter future and the drive and energy to bring this view to fruition.

The entrepreneur is the one who with her creativity and her team puts together the business models and figures out what parts of the value-added chain to participate in and what parts to outsource. Then typically it is the entrepreneur who raises money from friends and family, then works with financial advisors to value the business. She and her chief financial officer will give the three-minute elevator pitch to venture capitalists or to local bankers in order to raise more funds to launch and start the enterprise. Once the business is under way, the entrepreneur will lead the team that negotiates the strategic partnerships and alliances that are crucial for the fledging firm to survive. Each of these steps is depicted in our wheel of progress. We invite you to read on in this book to learn how to spin the wheel and get your ideas out of the lab and into the marketplace. It never hurts to also have a bit of luck on your side. As the old saying goes, "When all else fails, read the manual and hope to get lucky!"

CHAPTER 2

Protecting Your Invention

At first we were going to call this chapter "Protecting Your Idea," but the more we learned about how intellectual property laws work, we decided the better title was "Protecting Your Invention." Tom Brand, of W.P. Thompson & Co. and one of our book's contributors, likes to illustrate the difference between an idea and an invention by telling a story—the one about the "toaster that never burns the toast—nice idea, but it's not an invention until you can actually make the thing, or at least show how it can be made." The same is true for the notion of a perpetual motion machine—nice idea, but how do you make it work in real life?

The main purpose of this chapter is to introduce our readers to the basics about intellectual property. We explain what it is and how the law gives inventors certain rights to protect their inventions in return for encouraging the growth of human knowledge. We then illustrate with a true story the struggles of one inventor who, even after being granted his first patent, still went through many a frustration trying to commercialize his invention. In the end, he failed, where somebody else succeeded. We try to figure out what went wrong and why.

We then take our readers on a quick spin through the world of Formula One motor racing. We illustrate how the manufacturers of Formula One racecars use all five types of intellectual property to protect their state-of-the-art innovations and enhance the strength of their brands. We hope these stories and examples help you reap good harvests from your inventions. A more in-depth examination of the legal and strategic aspects of intellectual property rights may be found in Part Four: Understanding Legal Agreements.

WHAT IS INTELLECTUAL PROPERTY?

Intellectual property is what the human mind creates that has the potential to be commercially valuable. The term *intellectual property* covers a wide range of creative outputs: songs, movies, paintings, graphic arts of all types, advertisements, architectural drawings, sketches, cartoons, chemical formulas, electronic components, machine tools, mechanical gadgets, modified biomolecules, robots, and software.

Legalized concepts of intellectual property exist to promote the flow of human endeavor, not to staunch it. The point of intellectual property, generally speaking, is to reward the progenitor for sharing the fruits of his intellect with others, and thereby to encourage growth in the sum of human knowledge. However, intellectual property law is not able to protect ideas, discoveries, personal thoughts, philosophical ruminations, or views about religion or any other intangible mental activity. To be protected under intellectual property, these ideas must be made tangible and explicit. No work of *copyright* ever stopped two friends putting the world to rights over a long lunch, and no patent on a gene ever stopped a human being from expressing the product of that gene naturally or passing on the ability to do so to his or her children.

The commercial value of intellectual property comes from the legal power of the owner to control the rights for using the property and to charge for its use. If the owner of the property receives some kind of payment (a royalty, a fee, or a *license* payment) in exchange for the use of the created property, the ownership of the intellectual property has commercial value. That is why every scientist, business manager, and senior executive must learn about intellectual property laws and how intellectual property rights work. As an inventor, you also need to know the best way to protect your invention if you ever wish to reap the rewards of your labor. We illustrate how with two examples:

- Lesley-Ann writes a story about a Sherpa romance in the Himalayas and publishes it in a book. As the author, she has the legal right to prevent others from reprinting and distributing her book, turning it into a movie, a DVD, or a television soap opera based on the novel. This right is what can produce a stream of revenues for Lesley-Ann to supplement her meager salary at a university. She can sell the publishing rights to her book to a publisher, the movie rights to a Hollywood producer, and the television rights to a broadcaster in exchange for royalties, based on the number of books sold, movies viewed, and TV shows syndicated.
- John invents a novel process for inserting modified genetic material into the cells of a laboratory mouse, specially bred and used as a model for human colon cancer. His process was discovered during experiments done while searching for a colon cancer treatment. He applies for and receives a patent. In exchange for publishing the details of his procedure (in his patent) he obtains a *monopoly right* granted by the government. This monopoly right is like a toll bridge—anybody wishing to cross the bridge has to pay John a toll or fee. In this instance, John decides to charge a license fee to anyone who wishes to use his patented process. If no one wants to use his patent (analogous to no one crossing the toll bridge), John will not make any money from owning his patent. Indeed, quite the opposite, since John will have had to invest significant sums of money in getting the patent in the first place and will have to continue to pay regular maintenance fees to the government to keep the patent in force.

HOW INTELLECTUAL PROPERTY LAW WORKS

Intellectual property law is a broad term for the statutes (laws), government regulations, and court decisions that together determine who owns what intellectual property and the rights that go along with that ownership. Intellectual property laws spell out:

- The conditions under which intellectual property rights may be sold or licensed (a license works like a rental plan) to other parties and for what specific purposes.

- How to resolve and settle disputes arising from contracts marketing intellectual property (like publishing books or showing advertisements).
- How to take advantage of the government programs and processes that establish or enhance the protection of intellectual property rights (such as registration processes).

Intellectual property law works by offering protection to the owner of intellectual property. How? By giving the owner the right to file a lawsuit asking a court to decide if rights have been violated and to enforce the proper punishment if there has been a transgression. Note that intellectual property laws offer affirmative rather than defensive protection. What do we mean? Intellectual property laws serve not as a defensive shield for the property owner so much as a quiver of arrows that can be brought forth and used when needed to halt unauthorized access. In other words, intellectual property rights will not stop a trespasser from crossing your land. But the laws do give the property owner the right to point an arrow and take the trespasser to court. For example, if the copyright owner requests it, a court will halt unauthorized copying of material under copyright protection. But if the copyright owner chooses not to exercise those rights and not enforce the copyright (in other words, decides not to sue the *infringer*), no action will be taken and the copier will get away with the infringement.

BASIC FORMS OF INTELLECTUAL PROPERTY

Establishing property rights for an innovation is what allows the owner of those rights to appropriate profits from the innovation. Intellectual property is a form of property right. In general, intellectual property law consists of five basic legal categories aimed at a particular type of intellectual creation. Each category has its own nomenclature and characteristics, although sometimes the boundaries of these categories can overlap with respect to a particular type of intellectual property (especially for newer domains, such as computer software or biotechnology).

1. *Copyrights* are exclusive production, publication, or sales rights to artistic creations, literary, dramatic, or musical works, such as plays, articles, books, (technical) drawings, photographs, maps, or songs. In exchange for the copyright, the work must be published and released to the public. In some jurisdictions copyright subsists automatically, whereas in others it must be registered. (See Chapter 11 for more on copyrights.)
2. *Trademarks* are distinctive words, symbols, logos, slogans, shapes, or other marks used to identify the goods or services provided by an enterprise. Trademarks identify brands and protect distinctive packaging and containers and any other devices that are used by businesses to identify the source of their goods and services and distinguish them from rivals. For example, an important source of revenue for the fashion industry is licensing brands to licensees and collecting royalties in exchange for the use of the trademark. Trademarks have force as unregistered rights in many jurisdictions, but even so, it is generally preferable for trademark owners to seek registration wherever possible. (See Chapter 11 for more on trademarks.)

3. *Designs* protect generally aesthetic creations, the shapes of products or their configurations, or the pattern or ornament placed on them. Designs must generally be new, and, in this sense, they are similar to patents (they are called design patents in the United States)—although there is no requirement for inventiveness. They are also akin to certain types of trademark in that they relate to the appearance of a product rather than its technical function. Designs can be both unregistered and registered, with registered designs generally affording certain advantages in terms of the scope and longevity of the monopoly right and the ease of its enforcement. (See Chapter 11 for more on design rights.)

4. *Patents* establish monopoly rights to a new and useful product, process, substance, or design for a limited time. The invention should not be obvious. In exchange for the exclusive right to use the invention, the patent holder must divulge the information in the patent application (which contains the claims of the invention) to the public. The idea is that patents protect the owner for a period of time, but then the invention needs to become available to society. The length of exclusivity depends on the type of patent. Most commonly, a patent will last for a maximum of 20 years from its filing date, but there are exceptions for pharmaceutical products, which can last up to five years longer. Not all countries operate the 20-year term, although most do. Patents must be registered; there is no such thing as an unregistered patent right. (See Chapters 12, 13, and 15 for more on patent law, patent strategies, and patent searching.)

5. *Trade secrets* are chemical formulas, processes, designs, patterns, or ways of compiling information used by a business to gain competitive advantage over its rivals. The Coca-Cola Company protects the recipe for Coca-Cola as a trade secret. Trade secrets involve confidential information that would cause irreparable damage to the business if revealed and made public. (See Chapter 11 for more on trade secrets and know-how.)

In the United States, the courts may be asked to intervene when one business uses unfair tactics to compete against another business. Unfair competition is not usually considered part of intellectual property law, as it targets business practices rather than property laws. However, because the abuse of trademarks or brand names can lure customers unfairly, trademark law can overlap with unfair competition laws. Under the U.S. body of law called *unfair competition law*, a business can obtain a court order restraining a competitor from engaging in unfair business practices. A complete discussion of unfair competition laws is beyond the scope of this book (nor is it our primary focus), but we mention the topic again in Chapter 14 during the discussion on technology transfer agreements.

INTERNATIONAL TREATMENT OF INTELLECTUAL PROPERTY LAW

Each nation chooses how to define property rights for its citizens. The English Parliament passed the Statute of Monopolies in 1623 to establish the basis of English patent law. The United States Congress defined copyright and patent rights in the U.S. Constitution signed by the country's founders in 1776. The U.S. Constitution places copyright and patent rights under the jurisdiction of the federal government, so these laws are implemented exclusively through federal statutes. U.S. trade secret law is based on state legislation and state court case precedents. U.S. trademark and U.S. unfair competition laws are a mixture of both federal and state statutes, and also court case precedents. In Chapter 11 we discuss intellectual property laws and explain how some countries follow either common law principles (primarily those countries of Anglo-Saxon origin and former British colonies), or civil law principles (countries whose laws derive from German-Romanic laws) or a mixture of the two. Chapter 11 is written mainly from the English law perspective, whereas Chapter 12 describes the history of patents in several contexts and presents primarily a continental European view on patents. We think discussing various perspectives will be more interesting to our readers than confining our comments to one nation's laws. It also reflects the different nationalities of our writing team: Swiss, American, Finnish, Australian, English, Irish, and Italian.

INNOVATION PROCESS: DIFFUSION AND ADOPTION

Ideas leak. In today's interconnected and global world, they leak far and wide, and very fast. How do inventions and innovations spread? Robert M. Grant depicts the development of technology as a process of moving from basic knowledge creation to invention, to innovation. He then indicates that innovation diffuses through society via one of two mechanisms: imitation on the supply side (competitors do the imitating), and adoption on the demand side (customers do the adopting).[1]

We, however, do not see the diffusion in such linear terms. In today's outsourced world, customers and suppliers can do the imitating just as easily as competitors can do the adopting. The diffusion process of innovation is truly a picture of Brownian motion, with plenty of random movements, twists, and turns, in the cloud chamber of high technology. High technology is characterized by turbulence. Disturb the surface with a disruptive technology, and the waves can propagate far and wide, sometimes reaching nooks and crannies that the original inventor could scarcely have imagined.

These days numerous high-technology businesses are burdened with inventions that have never been turned into viable commercial products or applications. Clearly not all ideas turn into patentable inventions. Nor do all patents turn into innovations. Why don't they? Sometimes the invention may not be novel or nonobvious enough to merit a patent. Perhaps the innovative idea is overlooked because the inventor does not think it worth the bother or expense to apply for a patent. In other cases, the inventor neglects a potentially patentable invention because the person considers it only a small tweak in an idea or process, involving very little new technology but a lot of marketing, and therefore not scientifically "worthy of patenting." However, even if not a major breakthrough, the tiny modification may be patentable and could conceivably turn into a practical and valuable innovation.

If you are working in a university setting, we encourage you to consult your university technology transfer office early in the discovery process for patent advice. If you are working in a larger company, you should seek the advice of your firm's technology licensing group. If you are involved in a start-up company, seek the advice of patent experts early in your research work. Do not let the opportunity to patent or otherwise protect your invention leak away. On our password-protected web site at www.innovationtocashflows.com we offer you advice on how to implement an invention disclosure system for your venture. Refer to these links on the web site for the downloadable files:

- Appendix 2.2: Guidelines for Setting Up an Invention Disclosure System for Your Company.
- Appendix 2.3: Sample Invention Disclosure Form.

TRUE STORY: REUSABLE BOOK TAB INVENTION

Sometimes the inventor does have a patent, but a patent alone is not enough to form a commercially viable venture. The example that comes to mind is the patent that Robert H. Remmey III had on his invention of using rectangular slips of paper as tabs or as bookmarkers. In 1975 Remmey filed U.S. Patent application U.S.19750560322. Patent Title: Notation related book markers. We reproduce Remmey's granted patent so our readers can see what it looks like. (See Appendix 2.1 at the end of this chapter.)

The novelty about Remmey's book tabs was that they could be lifted on and off and reused many times. Mr. Remmey filed for a patent *before* 3M launched its innovative and now-ubiquitous yellow Post-it Notes and *before* the introduction of the colored Post-it "tabs" often used by students to index books or mark key places in notes. Having a patent on what turned out to be such a remarkable idea was not enough to commercialize it. In the case of Remmey's invention, three problems loomed: finding (1) the right glue, (2) a willing manufacturer, and (3) access to good distributors to commercialize the product. At the time of the initial patent application, Remmey did not know of any readily available sticky adhesive that could keep the bit of paper in place while still allowing it to be removed and repositioned easily—without leaving a mark on the original surface of the paper. The real problem was not the idea; it was the glue. To be successful, Remmey knew he would have to identify the right adhesive, plus convince a major manufacturer to produce and especially to sell his idea to the consumer. He thought his best shot was with a label manufacturer.

So he began contacting all the office supply and label companies of the day (this was back in the mid-1970s). As happens with many inventors, Remmey's proposal was turned down time and again by all the big manufacturers, although Avery-Dennison, a major label manufacturer, did express a keen interest in the idea. Even so, in the end, the idea of collaborating on the new form of "sticker" was rejected. Remmey gave up the quest in frustration. In perfect hindsight, we can now say that nobody in Avery-Dennison had the foresight to foresee the full market potential. According to Remmey's recollections, neither he nor Avery-Dennison was aware of what was going on in 3M at around the same time.

In 1968, Spencer Silver, a retired corporate scientist, in the Office Supplies Division of the 3M Corporation, developed an adhesive that, according to Silver, "kind of sparkled in the light."* Silver spent a few years trying to interest others in taking on his adhesive and using it in a product. There were no takers, but Silver kept looking. Then Art Fry, a colleague of Silver's, took up the idea when the paper bookmark in his choir hymnal kept falling out and drifting to the floor, disrupting his singing. He thought perhaps he could use Silver's adhesive to coat a portion of the bookmark but keep the protruding part uncoated so it would not be sticky.

Fry's idea was quite similar to Remmey's. The differences were that 3M had a special adhesive, Fry knew about it, and he had the insight to realize he had created not just a bookmark but a *way to leave notes and communicate messages to his boss,* Bob Melinda. The rest is history. Fry and Melinda took things one step at a time. They solved numerous adhesive and manufacturing problems. They championed the yellow pads internally and relied on 3M's secretaries and employees to convince higher-ups that the sticky little papers would be useful and popular. In 1980, 12 years after Silver's adhesive discovery, 3M launched Post-it Notes across the United States. A quarter of a century later, Post-its have become one of 3M's most popular lines of products, with over 400 product variations sold in more than 100 countries around the world. Developing the Post-it Notes took 3M a long time, a lot of false starts, and the persistence of an insider who refused to give up.

Sadly, Remmey did not make any money from his patent on reusable book tabs. The invention never went into production, and no licensing rights were ever sold. The original Remmey patent is now a family heirloom. Remmey's commercial successes came in real estate development. During the late 1960s through the mid-1970s, Remmey collaborated with his father, Robert H. Remmey Jr., and together they developed and built the first condominium and the first planned residential community in La Jolla, California. Although not patentable inventions, they were commercially viable innovations.

*3M Corporation 2007.

APPROPRIATING THE PROFITS OF INNOVATION

If there is a lesson to be learned from the dot-com boom (and bust) of 2000–2001, we would say it should be this: "Don't let all the value created go to the customer, make sure that some of the profits stick to the firm." Many dot-coms raised millions, burned through their cash, and crashed. Why? They generated revenues but no profits.

To understand the term *appropriation of profit,* think about the movie business. There is a healthy tug-of-war between what star actors get paid, producers make, distribution channels require, and shareholders get to keep. The take from a blockbuster movie will be divided up and allocated according to who owns the intellectual property rights to the screenplay, who has the most bargaining power, and who "owns" the human capital and know-how. How embedded is the talent? If the star actors walk off the set because they are unhappy with their share of the film's proceeds, will the film still be worth seeing? Some of the same dilemmas facing movie studios and film producers challenge the Italian fashion industry. When Valentino goes, who will replace him? Or Dolce & Gabbana? Or Giorgio Armani? The key to the future sustainability of businesses that are highly dependent on creative talent is to somehow embed that genius into the genetic fabric and know-how of the firm.

The term *economic value added* is the spread between what a firm is able to charge for its goods and services and the expenses required to stay in business. The business terms *economic rent* or *economic returns* have the same meaning as economic value-added. "Keeping a fair share of the profits" is what strategists call "appropriating the economic returns to competitive advantage."[2] In the dictionary, the verb *appropriate* means "to take for one's own use." It also means "to set aside," as in to set aside funds to build a new school (to appropriate funds for the building project). Going back to our dot-com example, we already noted that many dot-coms went bust in the dot-com boom because despite being able to scale up rapidly and generate high-revenue growth rates, they never turned a profit. That is why we emphasize the importance of generating value not only for stakeholders but also for shareholders. The success of eBay, Amazon, and Google lies in their ability to create economic value not only for their customers (or communities of users) but also for their shareholders. Our cardinal rule of business is that a company needs to create value and retain an equitable portion of that economic value added in order to be able eventually to reward its shareholders with dividends.

Appropriation of value within an industry divides up the economic returns among the suppliers, customers, innovators, and competitors involved. Grant puts it this way: "The profitability of an innovation to the innovator depends on the value created by the innovation and the share of that value that the innovator is able to appropriate."[3]

Sometimes, but not always, the innovator is able to sustain the *first-mover advantages,* which are the economic and strategic advantages that accrue to the first few entrants into an emerging industry or market territory, and keep ahead of the competition. Early entrants may gain economies of scale or scope or learning curve advantages that enable them to dominate their value chains. Sometimes, however, it pays to be the second-mover or "follow-the-leader" entrant. The successful second mover will be able to learn from the mistakes of the first mover and either executes the strategy better or leverages capabilities and resources to greater advantage to overcome the lead of the first mover.[4] Profits for Intel in microprocessors, Quantum in disk drives, Sharp in flat-panel displays, and Microsoft in operating software came in being later entrants and supplying key components to their respective industries. In the California gold rush, legend says it was the entrepreneurs who set up the hardware and grocery stores who garnered the biggest fortunes (selling the pots, pans, and key foodstuffs to the gold diggers). As we all know, most of the gold diggers went bust hunting for golden nuggets.

The ability to envision how to earn profits from an idea or invention is critical to converting that invention into an innovation. The successful innovator needs to see the connection between the idea and the marketplace. Just like an interior designer can envision how a particular piece of furniture or a carpet sample will look in a client's new bedroom, the visionary innovator can picture how the invention will fit into the lifestyle of the customer or enhance the productivity of the component manufacturer. The savvy architecture firm employing that interior designer will embed this designer's know-how into the systems, processes, and routines of the firm so that it will be able to retain clients if the star designer picks up her computer and leaves.

HOW TO DECIDE WHICH INTELLECTUAL PROPERTY TOOLS TO APPLY

Choosing which type of intellectual property protection to pursue depends on the kind of invention being protected. Although each category of intellectual property law is aimed at a particular type of intellectual property, occasionally trade secret, copyright, patent, and trademark laws overlap and intersect with each other. We describe some common instances when this situation arises next.

- *Trade secrets and copyrights.* It might make sense to place a work of expression (such as computer software source code) under trade secret protection and copyright up until the time that it is distributed to the public on an unrestricted basis. The trade secret law will allow the programmer to get a jump on competitors, while the copyright law automatically applies for any work of expression the minute it becomes fixed in a tangible form. In other words, the programmer does not have to do anything to get the copyright protection under U.S. law. (In Chapter 11, we discuss how computer code is protected differently under English compared to U.S. law.)
- *Copyright and trademark.* These laws may apply to the same item. For instance, the creative graphic artwork in a package design may be protected by copyright. At the same time, the "look" and "feel" of the container may be protected as *trade dress* (a form of trademark). The difference between these two is that copyright protects the literal expression while trademark protects whatever is used to designate the source of a product or service being used in the market.
- *Patent, copyright, and trademark.* Patent law may cross over with copyright and trademark law in the way a product is configured and designed. For instance, the team of industrial artists creating a distinctive piece of costume jewelry or inventing a new ergonometric design of a surgical tool could conceivably use all three approaches to protect their intellectual property. The same would be true for protecting patentable processes, such as the copying process invented by Chester Carlson of Xerox Corporation and known as xerography. Product and process patents, trade secrets, confidential information, trademarks—all these types of intellectual property protection would be applicable.

HOW TO IDENTIFY INTELLECTUAL PROPERTY IN YOUR ORGANIZATION

The famous Italian car designer, engineering firm, and car manufacturer Pininfarina,[5] based in Turin, Italy, could seek a design patent for a new, unobvious, nonfunctional design of a new set of "spoiler" fins on a sleek prototype Ferrari sports car. Trade-mark laws could be used to protect the appearance of the spoilers if they were used to distinguish the car from other Pininfarina models in the market, such as the Alfa Spider, the Mitsubishi Colt CZC, and the Volvo C70. Copyright law may also be used to protect certain expressive aspects of the design. (For details on the creative design collaborations Pininfarina has had over the years with Ferrari, Maserati, Alfa-Romeo, Fiat, Lancia, Peugeot, and GM, see www.pininfarina.com/index/storiaModelli/collaborazioni.html).

To pursue the example of the motoring industry for a moment, let us consider the very top end of that market—the racing industry—as a template to help us identify the various different categories of intellectual property and provide some suggestions on how to identify those categories within your own organization.

All categories of intellectual property (patents, designs, trademarks, copyrights and confidential information, trade secrets) are recognizable in many commercial products of any complexity. A Formula One car contains more intellectual property than could be covered in one chapter but, by way of example:

- *Patents*: on engine components, exhaust and transmission systems, tire compo-sition, and engine oil ingredients.
- *Designs*: on tire tread pattern, chassis shape and individual chassis components, driver's helmet, clothing, boots, and gloves.
- *Trademarks*: on whatever brand names appear on the car.
- *Copyrights*: in connection with the original chassis design drawings.
- *Confidential information*: no doubt a vast quantity unseen in the vehicle.

Other types of rights akin to intellectual property (e.g., image rights) surround celebrities. Eddie Irvine, a famous Formula One driver, for example, was able to enforce such rights against a radio station, Talksport, who used his image without permission.[6]

Patents are intended to protect technical developments that have the necessary qualities of novelty, inventive step, and industrial applicability, about which we shall hear more in Chapter 12. Patent claims may be directed toward novel compositions (e.g., a new engine oil formulation), novel articles of manufacture (e.g., a new car-buretor), and novel methods and processes for manufacturing or for achieving a desired result (e.g., a novel process for measuring the pressure within a car tire or for rapid filling of a fuel tank). Although patentable inventions are necessarily tech-nical in character, they are not necessarily complex themselves. Thus, while a novel carburetor design may be complex in character, relatively simple concepts (such as the positioning of gripping elements on a driving glove to achieve a better grip) can equally well form the basis for a patentable invention, provided the development in question achieves some technical superiority over the *prior art,* which is not obvious at the date of the invention. It is worth remembering that what seems obvious to your technical team as a result of development work proceeding over, say, a six-month period may not be obvious to anyone else, or at least to the mythical person "skilled in the art" looking in from the outside. It is commonplace for a patent attorney to identify as a patentable invention a development that has not been recognized as such by the inventors. Most patents are obtained for inventions that represent small advancements in the art, not great leaps into new technological areas, although of course some of the most important inventions are.

Registered designs (and also unregistered design rights) also protect novel articles of manufacture, but these go to the appearance of the article rather than its technical characteristics. Thus, a new racing helmet may have any number of technical innovations (e.g., relating to the material used to manufacture the helmet, or to a mechanism for releasing the helmet quickly in an emergency), but it is the appearance of the helmet, often its aesthetic appeal, that will be the subject of a registered design or design right. If the helmet looks appealing, that in itself is a selling point and a competitive advantage that can be protected by means of a design.

Trademarks represent a separate category of intellectual property intended to protect any element that identifies the commercial source of the article, material, or process in question. This "indicator of origin" function of a trademark is most commonly applied to trade names, such as Ferrari, BMW, Harley-Davidson, and the like. However, slogans can also act as indicators of commercial origin, and can therefore be protected as trademarks; "the ultimate driving machine" and "*vorsprung durch technik*"[7] being famous examples from the motoring industry. Using those slogans fulfills the function required of trademark, namely to identify the commercial origin of the goods. Similarly, logos that also serve the same function can be made the subjects of trademark protection. Also protectable these days in some cases are the shapes of particular articles of manufacture. The shape of a particular sports car, for example, is in some cases instantly recognizable and therefore has a trade origin function. To a lesser and less important extent, other origin indicators, such as smells and sounds, have also been protected.

Copyrights protect artistic endeavor in various types of work, including text documents, data sheets, drawings, product configurations, and packaging designs.

Confidential information and trade secret laws vary considerably from country to country but generally are designed to protect information that is secret from disclosure by, for example, suppliers, distributors, and members of staff who leave the organization in question.

The factors that determine how to identify potentially exploitable intellectual property are somewhat different for these various categories of intellectual property. However, they all have something in common: Successful identification of intellectual property can come about only through *increased awareness* on the part of the people who deal day to day with the subject matter in question.

DEVELOPING AN EFFECTIVE INVENTION DISCLOSURE PROCESS

As far as patentable inventions are concerned, it is useful to have in place a system for invention disclosure. In a technical department, staff members should in any event keep carefully dated and corroborated records of experiments and development work in which they are involved. If, during a particular development program, a member of staff believes that a patentable invention has been made, an invention disclosure record should be completed and passed to a designated manager for further assessment. A typical invention disclosure record should identify in key details the closest prior art, whether it is in documentary form (e.g., relevant patents or papers), and should explain the key novel features of the invention with respect to this prior art and, importantly, what technical advantage is thereby achieved. This record should be supported by data summarized from the inventor's contemporaneous notes. (Go to our password-protected web site at www.innovationtocashflows.com and refer to the links labeled Appendices 2.2 and 2.3 for suggestions on how to put in place an invention disclosure system in your company and to download a free sample invention disclosure form.)

To summarize, we have identified five separate categories of intellectual property: patents, designs, trademarks, copyright, and confidential information or trade secrets. Each type of intellectual property ought to be the subject of separate consideration within a company, as each is important in different ways. They also should be considered in combination.

One of the most important ways in which a company can better develop its intellectual property position is to educate employees as to what can be protected and what might conceivably provide the company with competitive advantage. Key messages in this respect should be reinforced by an ongoing program to raise awareness. Employee participation should be acknowledged, recognized, and rewarded. Above all, a management structure should exist to consider intellectual property issues on a regular basis and to react, quickly if necessary, to a situation developing on the ground.

CHAPTER TAKEAWAYS

- We hope to have made clear the distinction between having a creative idea and protecting your invention. We encourage you to review the lesson every time you smell burned toast or see a Post-it Note.
- Inventors may choose from five categories of intellectual property to protect their inventions: patents, designs, trademarks, copyrights, and confidential information or trade secrets.
- Often it is best to use a *combination* of intellectual property rights and competitive strategies (such as secrecy, faster learning, quicker new product introductions, and more nimble strategy execution). (Strategy is the topic of the next two chapters.)
- Companies should be keenly interested in protecting their trademarks, brands, trade secrets, and confidential information. The key to success is employee education, continuing awareness, and cooperation.
- We recommend setting up an invention disclosure system and offer employees rewards and incentives to use it. Go to www.innovationtocashflows.com where you will find:
  - Appendix 2.2: Guidelines for Setting Up an Invention Disclosure System for Your Company
  - Appendix 2.3: Sample Invention Disclosure Form

APPENDIX 2.1   REMMEY'S GRANTED PATENT

United States Patent [19]   [11]   3,958,816
Remmey, III   [45]   May 25, 1976

[54] **NOTATION RELATED BOOK MARKERS**

[76] Inventor: **Robert H. Remmey, III**, 7752 Fay
             Ave., La Jolla, Calif. 92037

[22] Filed: **Mar. 21, 1975**

[21] Appl. No.: **560,322**

[52] **U.S. Cl.** .... 283/38; 35/35 R;
                                               281/31; 283/42
[51] **Int. Cl.^{2}** B42F 21/00
[58] **Field of Search** 283/36-43;
                                         281/31; 35/35 R; 40/2, 23 A

[56]   References Cited
                       UNITED STATES PATENTS
1,862,530   6/1932   Dickman .... 281/31 X
3,372,858   3/1968   Brody .... 281/31 X
3,473,827 10/1969   Leadbetter 283/36
3,583,358   6/1971   Hanson .... 40/23 A X

Primary Examiner—Lawrence Charles
Attorney, Agent, or Firm—James C. Wray

[57]   ABSTRACT

In a marking apparatus and method for books, double sided tabs have adhesive so that the tabs may be adhered to pages of books, with a number-bearing portion of the tab extending from the page. Adhesive occupies one-half of one side of the tab, and numbers are written in opposite directions on opposite sides of the tab so that the tab may be affixed to a left or right page of a book to clearly mark the page and the point on the page to which it refers. Learning key cards have numbers corresponding to the tabs. Brief notes are written on the lines, and the cards are attached to the front leaf of a book. The tabs are attached directly to the learning key, or they are attached on the inside of a cover or opposite leaf of the book. An envelope or jacket-type holder is adhesive-backed for fastening to an inside of the book, and the tabs are mounted on a release coating on the outside of the envelope-pocket. Learning key cards, each with individual numbers corresponding to the tabs, are inserted in the pocket so that an entire card is available for notes in reference to the corresponding tab.

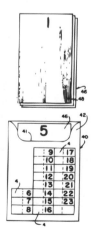

10 Claims, 10 Drawing Figures

NOTATION RELATED BOOK MARKERS

Background of the Invention

All learning comes from organized knowledge. Psychological research has proved that learning most readily occurs when one links new ideas, information or knowledge with some experience or knowledge that he already has. Research has also shown that if one reviews what he has read within 1 hour, he will recall later up to 90%. If he reviews within 2 hours, the recall rate drops to 70%. Reviewing 4 to 8 hours later drops the recall rate still further. For best learning results, one uses the markers to identify material he wishes to learn, writes brief descriptions of that in the key in the front of the book and then 1 hour later reviews his material.

Professors and students, scientists and general readers insert many slips of paper as markers in the various books they use. Most students and other frequent users of books also identify study passages in some way, by turning down corners, by underlining with markers, or by some systematic or irregular method.

Before preparing a patent application a search was conducted in the U.S. Patent Office in Class 116, Indicators, subclass 119, Book Marks. Examples of the most pertinent which were found are:

3,583,358
3,680,229
3,324,823
2,984,205

In U.S. Pat. No. 3,583,358, colored and numbered tabs having a portion of one surface coated with an adhesive are mounted in a matchbook-like holder for separately removing the tabs and marking pages of a book. That patent does not teach the mounting of the tabs on a plate or pocket which is in turn mounted inside a cover or on a fly-leaf of a book. That disclosure does not teach the use of a learning key card or cards physically and informationally related to the tabs.

U.S. Pat. No. 3,680,229 was selected as an example of symbols related to a book appearing on a card. Those symbols are used to identify whole books and not pages, and apparently those symbols are permanent in nature. The symbols and cards of U.S. Pat. No. 3,680,229 do not suggest the present invention.

U.S. Pat. No. 3,324,823 was selected for its showing of a marker attached to a related card. The entire marker and card are integral and are inserted together within pages of a book.

U.S. Pat. No. 2,984,205 was selected for its showing of notes combined with a mark. The marker and notes are combined in use and are not the same as the present invention.

No prior art disclosure suggests the present invention.

Summary of the Invention

Briefly, the invention consists of a marking apparatus and method for books. Basic to the invention are double sided tabs which have adhesive so that the tabs may be adhered to pages of books, with a number-bearing portion of the tab extending from the page. Adhesive occupies one-half of one side of the tab. Numbers are written in opposite directions on opposite sides of the tab, so that the tab may be affixed to a left or right page of a book to clearly mark the page and the point on the page to which it refers.

Included in the invention is a learning key. In one form of the invention, the learning key card is a lined card with numbers corresponding to the tabs. Brief notes are written on the lines. The card is adhesive-backed for attaching to the front leaf of a book. In that form of the invention, before use the tabs are attached directly to the learning key. In a modification, the tabs are provided on another card, which is adhesive-backed for attachment on the inside of a cover or opposite leaf of the book.

In another form of the invention, an envelope or jacket-type holder is adhesive-backed for fastening to an inside of the book, and the tabs are mounted on a release coating on the outside of the envelope-pocket. Learning key cards, each with individual numbers corresponding to the tabs, are inserted in the pocket so that an entire card is available for notes in reference to the corresponding tab.

The more refined model combines a pocket, note cards and the detachable "tips" all into one packet to be attached via adhesive on its back to an inside of the book for immediate use.

This allows for more copious note-taking. Each "tip" is easily removable and has pressure-sensitive adhesive on half of one side for marking the page and/or paragraph. The note cards are sub-classified with either numbers or letters. The purpose of the present invention is to help organize knowledge in useful ways. The present invention uses markers to identify significant passages or sections, to classify or link categories, and to identify passages for frequent and ready referral. One writes in the marker in the front of the book some detail of each identified passage or section. For best learning results one uses the markers to identify material he wishes to learn, writes brief descriptions of that in the key in the front of a book and then one hour later reviews his material.

The combined markers and note recording cards of the present invention make learning easier with less effort and increase one's ability to recall and use what has been read. The system of the present invention personalizes books with self-made notes and comments contained together for rapid review. The markers are removable and will not deface books. They may be used on library or borrowed books. One can expect higher resale value for used texts by removing the markers and adhesive-backed note packages. The notes become a permanent part of one's own library for easy filing and recording of information and for ready availability for review.

A selection of markers is offered in various packages for different uses and purposes, and they are available in a variety of colors. A small kit offers 1 to 30 tips, middle size 1 to 60 and a large package 1 to 100 tips. Special kits are offered with a hollow plastic tip in a larger size so the user can write in his own headings.

The product of the invention consists of two related parts: the marker tip, which is a tab that is coated on approximately one-half of one side with a pressure sensitive adhesive. That is used by inserting it along the edge of a page in a book, magazine or other printed material. It is inserted in such a way that about half the tab is visible when the book is closed.

The specified adhesive is one that readily may be removed from the surface of the page without leaving any residue or discoloration and has minimal deleterious effects on the paper. The adhesive quality is such that it will adhere to the page over an extended period of time if left permanently inserted in the book. The markers vary in size, shape and color. The marker tips may be made of paper or plastic or a plastic coated paper. The markers may come numbered, or alphabetized, or plain (so that they may be written upon) or as hollow plastic tabs, so that labels may be inserted. The numbers or letters may appear on one or both sides of the tabs. The markers may come packaged in different quantities and/or singly or in combinations of colors, shapes and sizes.

The markers may be packaged with a convenient protective strip over the adhesive area for protection until used (as on a "Band-Aid"). This protective cover is readily removable so that the tab is instantly ready for insertion on the page.

The marker is inserted in the book to identify a certain page, paragraph or sentence. The markers are attached along the edges of the pages of the book in an orderly index fashion to identify certain pages, or the markers are attached in such a way as to identify specific paragraphs or sentences.

The second related part of the invention is a coded index of one or more pages with lined blank spaces which may be written upon, or an envelope containing coded file cards with lined blank spaces which may be written upon. The index or envelope has a backing of strips of pressure sensitive adhesive of the same specifications as used on the "tip."

The coded index or envelope containing the coded cards may be inserted in the front, back or on a "flyleaf" of a book. The envelope is of such a size to accommodate one of the following size coded cards:

3 × 5 inches

4 × 6 inches

5 × 8 inches

The purpose for the coding of the markers and the index is so that a convenient cross-reference is made available to the user in organizing the information to which he wants ready access.

In one embodiment of the invention a plurality of page markers are provided. Each page markers is generally rectangular in shape and has identification means readable in opposite directions on opposite sides of one-half of the marker. An attaching means, which is preferably a pressure-sensitive adhesive, is secured to one-half of one face of each marker in a position remote from the identification means. The adhesive means may be any well-known adhesive which permanently attaches to paper and which is readily releasable from a shiny release coating such as a coating on a peelable release sheet. The identification means in a preferred embodiment occupies one-half of the marker, an area that is substantially square, and the adhesive attaching means occupies approximately one-half of the marker in an area that is substantially square.

A key card means is configured for attaching to a book, preferably within a book, and usually on the inside of the front or rear cover or on a flyleaf. In a preferred embodiment, the key card means has a pressure-sensitive adhesive on a rear face. The front face of the key card means may be lined, or otherwise sectioned, with identification means corresponding to marker identifications associated with each section.

In a preferred embodiment, a marker mounting means is connected to the key card means for holding the markers before the markers are attached to edge of pages. A person, before reading a book, mounts a key card means within the book. Then, as a person reads a book and notices parts which he wishes to mark, he removes a marker from the marker-holding means connected to the key card means and places the marker adjacent the passage in the book which he wishes to mark. Then he writes notes on the key card means at a position associated with the identification number of the marker. As an example, the key card means may be a single card with lines and identification numbers on its face. A coating may be placed on a portion of the card to hold adhesive markers until the markers are pulled from the coating for positioning on a page. One part of the card is free of coating so that notes may be written on that part.

In a preferred embodiment of the invention, the key card means is an envelope having a rear face covered by a pressure-sensitive adhesive mounting means with a peelable release sheet for guarding the adhesive mounting means until ready for use. The front face of the key card means envelope has a release coating for temporarily securing the markers until they are used on the pages. Included in the key card means envelope are plurality of cards, each marked with an identification corresponding to an identification on a marker. When a marker is attached to a page by a passage, the card corresponding to that marker is removed from the envelope, notes are placed on that card, and the card is returned to the envelope.

The markers are constructed so that the markers may be attached to book pages to mark the entire page, in which case the markers are arranged in a neat, progressive order on the book. The markers are also capable of being used to identify particular passages on a page, in which case the markers are attached to the pages according to the position of the passage to be marked.

One object of the invention is the provision of book notation system apparatus comprising a plurality of page markers having identification means for identifying individual markers, the markers having attaching means for attaching the markers to pages of a book, and key card means for receiving information related to individual markers, the key card means having identification means related to the marker identification means, and the key card means having mounting means for mounting the key card means in a book remote from marker marker means are attached to edges of pages.

Another object of the invention is the provision of the book notation system apparatus with double-sided markers, having marker identification means mounted in different directions on opposite sides of the markers, and having adhesive attaching means applied to one-half of one face of each marker remote from the identification means.

A further object of the invention is the provision of a book notation system apparatus wherein markers are rectangular, wherein the identification means occupies one-half of each marker, and wherein the adhesive attaching means occupies one-half of one face of the marker.

The invention has as another object the provision of book notation system markers wherein the identification area is substantially square and wherein the attaching means occupies a substantially square area on one face of the marker.

Another object of the invention is the provision of a book notation system apparatus comprising a mounting card means for holding markers before the markers are placed on edges of pages, the mounting card means having an adhesive means on one face of the card and having a release coating on an opposite face of the card for releasably holding the attaching means of the markers.

Another object of the invention is the provision of a book notation marking apparatus wherein the note-receiving key card means and a marker mounting card means are connected.

The invention has as another object the provision of a book notation apparatus wherein a marker mounting means is on a frontal surface of a note-receiving key card means opposite the mounting means on a rear surface of the key card means.

A further object of the invention is the provision of a book notation system apparatus with a key card means comprising an envelope having a rear face on which a key card mounting adhesive is arranged for attaching the key card means to the book, and having a front face on which a marker mounting means is arranged for mounting a plurality of markers before use on pages of the book, and having a plurality of cards in a pocket in the envelope, each of the cards being identified with an identification corresponding to each of the markers.

This invention has as a further object the provision of a book notation system apparatus wherein a note-receiving key card means comprises a card having an adhesive back and a plurality of lines individually identified by identification means associated with the lines for individually relating to a plurality of markers.

These and further and other objects of the invention are apparent in the dis-closure which includes the above and following specification and claims and the drawings.

Brief Description of the Drawings

FIG. 1 is a perspective view of a book on which markers have been mounted, showing the key card means and the marker mounting means inside the cover of the book.

FIG. 2 is a front elevational view of a single marker.

FIG. 3 is an edge elevation of the marker of FIG. 2.

FIG. 4 is a rear elevation of the marker of FIGS. 2 and 3.

FIG. 5 is an example of a card constructed according to the invention, in which the key card means has associated therewith a marker mounting means for holding the markers until they are affixed to edges of pages of a book.

FIG. 6 shows a preferred embodiment of the invention in which the key card means is an adhesive-backed envelope with a face for mounting markers until they are used in the book and with a pocket which receives cards on which notes are written.

FIGS. 7 and 8 show front and side views of markers arranged in order in a book.

FIGS. 9 and 10 show front and side views of markers arranged in a book to mark selected passages on pages.

Detailed Description of the Drawings

Referring to FIG. 1, a book notation system apparatus is generally indicated by the numeral 1. The apparatus is mounted on a book 2. A plurality of markers 4 are mounted on the apparatus for removal and use by removal from the marker mounting means and by attachment to edges of pages as indicated at 4′.

U.S. Patent   **May 25,1976**   **3,958,816**

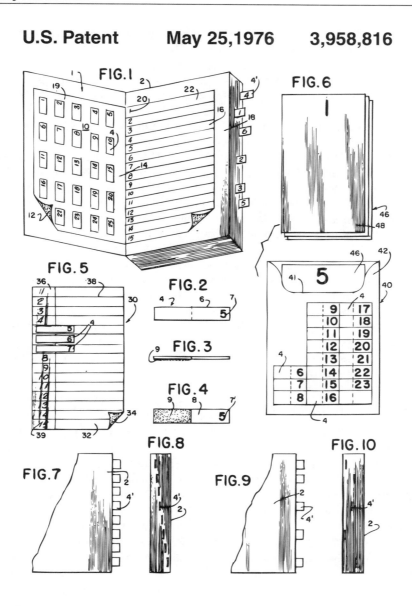

As shown in FIGS. 2, 3, and 4, the markers 4 have a front face portion 6 on which identification numbers 7 appear. As shown in FIGS. 3 and 4, adhesive 9 is applied to half of the rear face. The other portion 8 of the rear face has a numerical identification 7′ which is oppositely directed to the identification 7 on the front face. That permits the markers to be positioned directly adjacent the passage to be marked in a book.

Referring to FIG. 1, in one embodiment, the markers 4 are mounted on a marker mounting card 10 before the markers are detached for attaching to edges of the pages. The marker mounting means 10 has an adhesive back 12 and has a front face 14 which holds the markers in numerical order. In FIG. 1 all of the markers are shown mounted on the card for clarity, notwithstanding that markers **1-6** have been removed for attaching to the edges of pages. The marker holding means is attached to the key card means **16**. An adhesive backing on key card **16** is secured to a flyleaf **18** of the book. In a preferred embodiment of the invention, a release coating **19** on the face of marker holding card **14** releasably holds the adhesive **9** of the markers until the markers are ready to be removed for attaching to pages of the book.

On the key card **16** numbers **20** identify note-taking spaces **22** which are associated with like numbered markers **4′** on edges of the pages.

An alternate key card means **30** is shown in FIG. **5**. The key card **32** has an adhesive backing **34** and has a coated side area **36** for releasably receiving the adhesive **9** of the markers. Note-taking areas **38** are left uncoated, and the numbers **39** associated with those areas are visible through the transparent release coating.

In the preferred form of the invention shown in FIG. **6**, the key card means comprises an envelope **40** having a pocket **41**. A front face **42** of the envelope is coated with a slippery surface for holding markers **4** until they are ready to be used on the book. A rear face of the envelope is covered with an adhesive coating for mounting the envelope on the inside of a cover or on a flyleaf of a book.

A plurality of cards **46** are included in the key card means. The cards are slipped out of the pocket **41** and notes are written on the faces **48** of the individual cards, and the cards are returned to the envelope, permanently mounting the notes in the book.

FIGS. **7** and **8** show the mounting of markers **4′** on pages of a book to identify whole pages. In that embodiment, the markers are arranged in numerical order for ease of locating the particular markers.

FIGS. **9** and **10** show the markers **4′** attached to edges of pages of a book **2**. In the **9** and **10** figures, the markers have been randomly arranged on the pages, to indicate that the markers are positioned directly by passages on the pages which are being marked.

While the invention has been described with reference to specific embodiments, it will be obvious to those skilled in the art that variations and modifications of the invention may be made without departing from the scope of the invention. The scope of the invention is defined in the following claims.

I claim:

1. A book notation system apparatus comprising a plurality of page markers having identification marks for identifying individual markers, the markers having adhesive attaching means for attaching the markers to pages of a book, separate key card means for receiving information related to individual markers, the key card means having a front face and a rear face and release coating marker-holding means on the front face of the key card means, for holding the markers by the adhesive attaching means, the key card means having identification means related to the marker identification marks and having areas for writing notations along the identification means, and the key card means having mounting means on the rear face for mounting the key card means in a book remote from marker means which are attached to edges of pages.

2. The book notation system apparatus of claim **1** wherein the markers comprise double-sided markers, wherein the marker identification marks are mounted in different directions on opposite sides of the marker and wherein the attaching means

comprises an adhesive applied to one-half of one face of the marker remote from the identification marks.

3. The apparatus of claim 2 wherein the marker is rectangular, wherein the identification marks occupies an area one-half of the marker, and wherein the attaching means occupies one-half of one face of the marker.

4. The apparatus of claim 3 wherein the identification area is substantially square and wherein the attaching mean occupies a substantially square area on one face of the marker.

5. The apparatus of claim 1 the marker holding means further comprising a mounting card means for holding markers before the markers are placed on edges of pages, the mounting card means having an adhesive means on one face of the card and having a release coating on an opposite face of the card for releasably holding the attaching means of the markers.

6. The apparatus of claim 5 wherein the key card means and marker mounting card means are connected.

7. The apparatus of claim 6 wherein the marker mounting means is on a frontal surface of the key card means opposite the mounting means on a rear surface of the key card means.

8. The apparatus of claim 7 wherein the key card means comprises an envelope having a rear face on which the key card mounting means is arranged for attaching the key card means to the book and having a front face on which the marker mounting means is arranged for mounting a plurality of markers before use on pages of the book and the identification means comprising a plurality of cards in a pocket in the envelope, each of the cards being identified with an identification corresponding to each of the markers.

9. The apparatus of claim 4 wherein the key card means comprises a card having an adhesive back and a plurality of lines individually identified by identification means associated with the lines for individually relating to the markers.

10. The book notation system apparatus of claim 1 wherein the key card mounting means comprises adhesive on one page of the key card means, and further comprising a marker release coating on a face of the key card means spaced from the first face for releasably holding the markers.

Building Business Models

Understanding Strategy Basics

In this introductory chapter on *strategy*, we invite you to think about how to define a strategic direction for your new venture. Strategy is important because it will help guide decision making during the start-up phase of your venture and beyond. We describe the challenge of creating a strategy under conditions of high uncertainty and rapid technological change. We encourage you—in your role as an entrepreneur—to formulate a sound strategy for your company or organization, daunting as it may be. We go through the basic building blocks that a business strategy should have. We also try to answer likely questions on how to create a strategy.

FROM STRATEGY AS PLAN TO STRATEGY AS DIRECTION

The emphasis in devising strategy today has shifted from strategy as planning to strategy as setting a *strategic direction*. We like to think of two distinctly different images to make this point. Imagine for a moment what would happen if a new venture's strategic plan were to be written down in a Word document or set of presentation slides and suddenly (and most likely surreptitiously) released on the Internet. Instantly, any competitors on the web would know exactly what the organization was planning to do. Any strategic surprises that the company had in store for rivals would be revealed, and the competitors would be able to counterattack. Obviously, we do not advise this approach at all. If the only competitive advantage a start-up has is its strategic plan, it is not a very enduring advantage.

In contrast, think of being a management team out on the Sahara desert. Your company gave you some simple coordinates and taught you the strategic thinking skills needed to navigate your way across the desert. If the team gets separated, you could still find each other because you all know the common goal and destination. With a simple change of coordinates, your team's strategic direction could be changed flexibly and reliably.

Which approach would you rather have to navigate over unfamiliar terrain? We prefer the second and believe that it is much better to have managers develop their sense of *strategic thinking* than relying on written strategic plans and documents to tell them what to do. This is especially true for fast-paced high-tech start-ups operating in turbulent markets. In his widely-used MBA textbook *Contemporary*

Strategy Analysis, Georgetown University professor Robert M. Grant expresses his opinion about strategy:

> *When the firm is buffeted by unforeseen threats and where new opportunities are constantly appearing, then strategy becomes a vital tool to navigate the firm through stormy seas.*[1]

INTRODUCTION TO THE STRATEGIC MANAGEMENT PROCESS

A *strategy* typically refers to a set of activities or actions that need to be carried out in order to achieve an organization's long-term aims. We introduce and define the firm's *value chain* of activities as a means to meet customer needs. The value chain for a manufacturing business would include research and development (R&D), new product design, purchase of raw materials or components, manufacture or assembly, distribution, sales, and after-sales service support. A similar value chain could be envisioned for a service organization. The value chain also includes the overhead support activities, such as planning, marketing, logistics, human resources, finance, accounting, legal, public and regulatory affairs, investor relations, information technology (IT), and the like. The organization of the enterprise is the means by which these various activities are to be implemented and the strategy's aims accomplished.

Naturally, over time, each firm develops and evolves differently. Firm history matters when thinking about how to instigate organizational changes. So, too, does the rate of change and industry turbulence experienced by the start-up. Sometimes luck plays an important role in whether a firm survives. At other times, the critical factor may be how well the entrepreneurial team leads the organization or is able to execute its strategy compared to rivals. In fact, the external environment surrounding the firm is often described as an *ecosystem,* with many factors in the system interacting with each other and with chance variables.

To take into account the firm's ecosystem, we develop within this chapter an overall framework for gathering the inputs and generating the insights needed to understand the firm's competitive environment. We explore some of the basic tools and conceptual frameworks most commonly used in doing strategic analysis. These tools help managers do what is known as a *situational analysis,* which consists of both external analysis and *internal analysis.*

External analysis is essentially a comprehensive scan of the venture's external environment. It generally includes the political, economic, social, technological, legal, and environmental forces that may impinge on the business. A thorough analysis should consider the implications of any long-term and emerging scenarios, trends, or market conditions of significance to the firm. The analysis should aim to uncover the *key success factors*[2] required to compete and thrive in the targeted industry. Managers will want a detailed assessment of the strategies and intentions of competitors, including each one's value chain and business system. Finally, the external analysis may compare the ecosystems of high-tech clusters, including university and industry support networks, in order to help managers decide where to locate different parts of their organization's value chain. We describe how to use seven frameworks for external analysis.

Internal analysis is an *organizational audit* and assessment of the firm's internal resources (both tangible and intangible assets) and capabilities (the organization's skills). We cover three basic approaches:

1. The resource-based view of strategy identifies and appraises the organization's resources and capabilities as a prelude to strategy formulation.
2. The 7-S Framework (strategy, structure, system, style, staff, skills, and shared values) offers a simple, easy-to-remember "integrated systems approach" to auditing an organization's resources and capabilities.
3. The PARC approach refers to the *p*eople and the *ARC*s of the firm: its *a*rchitecture, *r*outines, and *c*ulture. The PARC conceptual framework is particularly useful when considering how to resolve problems of organizational design.

We talk more extensively about internal analysis and its various applications toward the end of this chapter.

Once the situational analysis is complete, the firm's managers need to reflect and come up with various strategy alternatives. Most managers stop at devising just one strategy option. We suggest developing at least three possible choices, each of which should be viable and feasible. Being successful at dreaming up creative and distinctly different strategies often requires thinking out of the box and finding new ways of perceiving the competitive landscape compared to the ways entrenched players frame decisions and think about the industry.

When formulating the strategies, keep in mind this principle: Build on the firm's key strengths and mitigate the key weaknesses to the greatest degree possible. Managers should identify any *strategic gaps* between what resources and capabilities the firm has and what it needs. Managers should think about how to bridge these gaps for each strategic option. Gaps may be closed through further research and development (R&D) or new product development, by carrying out business combinations (mergers and acquisitions) or by transacting strategic collaborations (joint ventures or strategic alliances), which we discuss further in Part Three, "Crafting Strategic Alliances."

Choosing the best strategy among the three or more strategy options will be a process of selecting decision criteria, weighing the pros and cons, and using your team's judgment on what is best for your firm. The important point is to chart a course and figure out the best way to journey along it.

WHY IS STRATEGY IMPORTANT FOR ANY ENTERPRISE?

Organizations ought to have a set of processes for making important decisions and plans. They need routines and procedures for carrying them out. In our own start-up experiences, we have found that it is a good idea to take the necessary time early on to get the buy-in and commitment of the senior management team and investors on the strategic direction of the venture. Any start-up team will need some time to formulate, evaluate, and decide on a strategic direction. Ideally it ought to be a direction the entire team will commit to and help to implement, especially since the team will be deeply involved in communicating the vision, mission, and strategy of the new venture firm to various stakeholders.

Clarity on strategic direction is essential in order to get others involved in implementing the plan. A lack of strategic direction or miscommunication of the strategy creates uncertainty for everyone involved. From listening to other executives talk about their start-ups, we know that little agreement among the leadership team on a strategic direction inevitably leads to arguments and lost opportunities.

Developing a strategy statement will help any start-up team be better prepared to face the challenges ahead. At its simplest, a strategy statement may be a one- or two-page summary of where you see the firm heading for the next three to five years. If properly used and applied correctly, the strategic tools and conceptual frameworks we present in this chapter will enable you to do an even better job in formulating your venture's strategy and honing its sustainable competitive edge.

STRATEGY IN A RAPIDLY CHANGING HIGH-TECHNOLOGY ENVIRONMENT

High-tech start-ups face the daunting challenge of navigating a rapidly changing and highly uncertain external environment. Entrepreneurial founders will have an idea of what business opportunity they intend to pursue. Typically the team will have some sort of a *business plan* (even if it is inside their heads) that sketches out the strategy; contains the sales, profits, and cash flow forecasts; estimates the capital investment requirements; and includes a series of action steps to implement it.

Guides on how to write a business plan are discussed in Note 3 of this chapter.[3] For additional recommended articles, books, and blogs on finance, entrepreneurship, venture capital, and other related topics, log onto our web site at www.innovationtocashflows.com and browse or download the file "Resources."

Besides a business plan, with its financial forecasts, you will need a *business model* for your venture. We introduce the concept of a business model here and devote Chapter 5 to defining, explaining, and discussing business models in greater detail as they are very important, not only in and of themselves but also because they are essential to securing outside investor backing and venture capital funding.

Briefly, business models show potential investors how the firm intends to reach a target market by satisfying certain customer needs. Like the business plan, the business model outlines the revenue and cost model and states the targeted operating margins. The business model explains how management intends to scale up and grow the business to achieve certain expected financial milestones and market penetration targets. It shows what parts of the value chain of the business will be done inside the firm and what parts will be done outside. Included in the business model is an explanation of how the organization will manage its network of alliances and strategic partnerships. Defining a clear strategy that creates a sustainable competitive advantage is a fundamental part of any business model. Indeed, we show you how to do this in this chapter. Finally, the business model ought to have an *exit strategy* for the venture's investors. Venture capital investors will want to harvest in a timely manner all or a portion of their equity stake in the venture, in order to reap a satisfactory expected *return on investment*. Note that we say "expected" return on investment. Funding new ventures, especially early-stage, high-tech start-ups, is risky. There is no such thing as a guaranteed high return on the investor's money.

Strategy making, especially in an entrepreneurial setting, is very much a dynamic and iterative process. Expect that your venture's strategy will change as setbacks occur, learning happens, and results turn out differently than expected.

HOW OFTEN SHOULD YOU CHANGE YOUR VENTURE'S STRATEGY?

The frequency with which your team needs to revise the organization's long-term goals and strategy will depend on the rate of change in your industry and market and the *time horizon*. Managers competing in fast-moving markets need to make more frequent adjustments to their strategic plans than those managers facing more tranquil, mature industry environments. For instance, the time horizon will be much shorter for medical technologies and other consumer electronics sectors, where new products are launched every 18 to 24 months, than for the petroleum business and pharmaceutical industries, where longer time frames are the norm. Sometimes developing a new oil field in a remote location takes over a decade. Similarly, identifying and developing a new therapeutic drug compound takes anywhere from 10 to 15 years. (See "Risks and Uncertainty Associated with Drug Development" in Chapter 8 and refer to Figure 8.8.)

The frequency with which your team needs to update the firm's goals and strategy also depends on the size of the company and how frequently and how formally the strategic planning process is carried out. Larger companies with hundreds or thousands of employees must have more elaborate and formal strategic planning processes, often done on an annual planning cycle, than smaller companies. In contrast, small start-up companies rely on a handful of managers and employees to make important strategic decisions, often in informal consultation with each other. Usually the business strategy is formulated in the minds of the founder or founding team through a process of informal conversations, interspersed with reading, market research, reflection, some quantitative and qualitative analysis, plus solicitation of firsthand information and ideas from potential customers, suppliers, contacts made in trade fairs, formal or informal web searches, and the like.

The strategy will inevitably be changed, refined, and honed in later discussions with potential investors. It is a very fluid process. Indeed, small firms require a flexible planning process that can adapt quickly to change. Furthermore, companies that are growing very fast, and are rapidly scaling up and hiring many new employees, need to think very carefully about how they are going to bring new managers up to speed on the strategic direction of the company.

Consequently there is no one right way to formulate strategy and create a strategic management process. Each firm must find its own unique way, depending on individual circumstances and industry context.

HOW DO MANAGERS FORMULATE A STRATEGY?

We suggest managers begin by understanding the definition of the term *strategy*. Michael E. Porter, in a *Harvard Business Review* article called "What Is Strategy?" says that "competitive strategy is about being different. It means deliberately choosing a different set of activities to deliver a unique mix of value."[4] He adds that the "essence of strategy is about *making choices* [our emphasis]." The definition we like to use also emphasizes the decision-making aspects of strategic thinking and the importance of focusing on specific managerial actions. (See next box.)

A GOOD STRATEGY FOCUSES ON SPECIFIC MANAGERIAL DECISIONS AND ACTIONS

Strategy is

a specific pattern

of managerial decisions and actions

taken to achieve superior long-term goals

and performance targets.[5]

What Should Be Included in the Strategy?

Entrepreneurs who need to formulate a business strategy for the very first time often wonder what to include. (Please keep in mind that the term *business strategy* is synonymous with the term *competitive strategy*. We use both interchangeably in this book, and you will see both words in textbooks on strategy.) Professors Garth Saloner and Andrea Shephard, both on the faculty of Stanford Graduate School of Business, and Joel Podolny, former dean of Yale School of Management and current dean of Apple University, are co-authors of the textbook *Strategic Management* (2001). In their book, they write that a competitive business strategy ought to contain four key elements that we list and explain in the following paragraphs.[6]

FOUR KEY ELEMENTS OF A COMPETITIVE STRATEGY

1. Goals
2. Scope
3. Sustainable competitive advantage
4. Strategic rationale

Goals: The *Where* of the Strategy Long-term goals provide enduring guidance on the direction toward which the strategy is aimed. To reach a long-term goal, managers ought to ask their team to create objectives. Objectives should not be confused with long-term goals. Objectives should be measurable, attainable, and achievable by a predetermined date (in other words, a target that is a reasonable stretch, not so demanding that the person responsible for doing it gives up hope of achieving it in time). Objectives also need to be significant (not superficial or superfluous) and aid in making progress toward the goal.

Scope: The *What* of the Strategy   The scope gives a clear definition of the products, markets, geographies, technologies, and processes in which the firm will engage. Defining the scope of the strategy is very much a process of saying no to many ideas and suggestions. It is setting clear boundaries for what the firm will do and what it will not do.

Sustainable Competitive Advantage: The *How* of the Strategy   The competitive advantage defines how the firm intends to achieve its long-term goals within its chosen scope. The competitive advantage should state the compelling reasons to expect that the organization will be able to compete effectively over the long term (in other words, in a sustainable way). What will keep actual and potential rivals from chipping away at operating margins and stealing customers? What will be done to ensure that suppliers, partners, or the government do not take all the economic value that is created for themselves? When it turns out that the competitive advantage is not feasible, or attractive, or enduring enough, the team should revise the organization's goals and scope, devising other strategies with a stronger competitive edge. Another possibility would be for the team to try to fill any critical gaps in resources or capabilities through steps like negotiating collaborative outsourcing contracts with vendors, subcontractors, or alliance partners. We discuss measures like these in later chapters.

Strategic Rationale: The *Why* of the Strategy   The rationale is the team's coherent and convincing explanation of why the strategy will work. It is the logic supporting the competitive advantage and explains the core arguments for why the firm will be able to succeed. If the reasons are not compelling, the team should start anew and revise the competitive strategy.

Finally, we close this section with this advice from Saloner, Shepard, and Podolny (2001):

> *Until one is able to articulate how the goals, scope, and competitive advantage come together to provide a coherent and convincing case for firm success, you have only a list of elements, not a strategy.*[7]

THREE LEVELS OF STRATEGY AND HOW THEY INTERRELATE

Before delving into further details on the strategy process, we want to set the context for the types of strategies commonly found in firms and, quite importantly, *how they interrelate*. Typically there are three levels of strategy:

1. *Corporate strategy* normally is the responsibility of senior managers at headquarters for the larger company. For start-up firms, the entrepreneur and other founders establish the corporate strategy working closely with other members of the venture team.
2. *Business strategy* usually is the responsibility of the senior management team leading a business unit. For start-up ventures, the entrepreneur is responsible for developing the business strategy. The line separating corporate-level strategy from business-level strategy is quite blurry for single-business companies and

FIGURE 3.1 Three Levels of Strategy: Corporate, Business, and Functional

smaller start-ups. One team most likely will devise *both* the corporate and the business strategy. In the case of the high-tech start-up, these strategies are often made with the advice and input of the lead investors and the expertise of the firm's scientific advisory board.

3. *Functional strategies* are developed respectively by the heads of research, new product development, finance, manufacturing, logistics, purchasing, marketing, or sales. We depict these levels schematically and also show a checklist of key questions pertaining to each in Figure 3.1.

Corporate Strategy Focuses on the Scope of the Firm

The role of corporate strategy is to define the *scope* of the firm. At this high level, the company's senior management and board of directors are wrestling with two big issues: how to grow and where to compete.

How to Grow?   The definition of scope should include in which industries and in which markets the firm will grow. The key questions to ask are:

- Which businesses should we enter?
- What specific markets and competitors should we target?
- With what products and technologies should we reach our target customers?

By default, defining the corporate scope will also tell the firm's managers which industries and markets it will *not* enter.

As we said, normally the senior most general managers in headquarters, especially if it is a large enterprise, shepherd the corporate strategy process and decide the general guidelines for what will and will not be included in the corporate strategy discussions. These discussions will also include the input of the board of directors, particularly if they involve corporate combinations (mergers and acquisitions) or major divestitures. For start-up firms, the entrepreneur and other founders will establish the corporate strategy, which must be vetted by the board of directors if the venture requires their approval of certain corporate actions.

Some of the hardest issues managers tasked with designing a corporate strategy face are forecasting industry growth trends and envisioning the future of their industry. These managers need to be mindful of new entrants, changing customer needs, new technology trends, and a variety of other variables. We show you how to do this in the section "Basic Tools for External Analysis" later in this chapter. After identifying the trends, the senior management team members need to reflect and imagine the implications of these long-term trends for their business. Once they think they understand what the implications are, they need to connect their conclusions with concrete strategies and actions. In other words, they need to follow up and take steps to deploy resources or capabilities to take advantage of the identified long-term trends. In Chapter 15, we share more ideas on how to identify and evaluate competitive trends. In particular, we discuss state-of-the-art tools and techniques to carry out patent searches and turn the data into patent maps, which can yield useful insights on what high-tech competitors are doing in their research and development activities.

Where to Compete?   Determining where to compete is a function of two main factors, market attractiveness and intensity of competition. To understand market attractiveness, it is useful to think about potential industry earnings (PIE). Potential industry earnings are the total value created by the industry (the value to the final buyers of the goods or services produced) less the value of the resources required to produce those goods or services. In other words, they are the value added or the economic rents of the industry. We illustrate the concept of value creation or *economic value added* in Figure 3.2.

Determining the value-added potential of an industry (or the overall size of the PIE) is one way of measuring industry attractiveness. The bigger the PIE, the more attractive is the market. What is the size of the existing PIE for a particular target industry? What factors can make the potential industry earnings grow bigger and faster, or, put differently, how can the industry as a whole create more value added? Will the industry players be increasing advertising spend? Launching new products? These types of actions tend to stimulate sales and increase industry growth rates. Alternatively, new cost-savings technology might be introduced that improves a firm's efficiency and enhances operating margins. Such an industry-wide innovation would make the spread between revenues and operating costs larger and also would increase the PIE.

Besides the size, it is also important to determine the market shares of current players in an industry and how the percentages are likely to change in the future. Competitor analysis considers those incumbents already in the market plus any new entrants threatening to enter from outside the industry. The intensity of competition

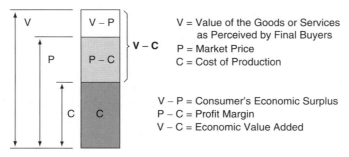

FIGURE 3.2   Value Creation or Economic Value Added

(or industry rivalry) shows up in changing market share allocations. It is often helpful to simulate how the market share allocations might change depending on different underlying assumptions of market supply and demand. Managers ought to use scenario analysis to do various types of contingency planning.

Like bears attracted to honey, new entrants are attracted to industries with lucrative potential industry earnings. Managers need to understand not only the dynamics of competitive rivalry but also the influence of industry life cycle (how an industry emerges, matures, and declines) on operating margins. In general, company operating margins erode and become more commodity-like as an industry matures.

Corporate Strategy in a Nutshell   In summary, the purpose of corporate strategy is to define the scope of the firm. It means deciding what the basic business of the firm is. How do we grow? Where do we compete? It describes which markets will be entered, with what products or services, and against which expected rivals. It also makes the fundamental choices on technologies used to serve the chosen customer base. Basically, it delineates the boundaries of the business.

Realistically, the answer to the corporate strategy questions of how to grow and where to compete tend to boil down to eight main options, each of which we explain in the paragraphs to follow.

1. Stick to the firm's core competency.
2. Develop new markets for the same products.
3. Develop new products for the same customers.
4. Expand by forward integration along the value chain.
5. Expand by backward integration along the value chain.
6. Expand by horizontal diversification into a new but related value chain.
7. Launch a completely new business venture.
8. Exit the market.

Stick to the Firm's Core Competency   Sticking to the firm's core competency means focusing on what you do best. As used in strategy, the term *core competency* refers to the *critical capabilities* of the organization. In order to determine what a "core" competency is for a company versus an ordinary competency, the manager needs to ask: What is the organization capable of doing better than its rivals?

A firm's critical capabilities are defined as the combination of internal routines, processes, and proprietary know-how that, when put to use in combination with the firm's other resources, enable the organization to do things better and faster than rivals. In other words, a core competency results in *superior firm performance* relative to competitors.

Professors C.K. Prahalad and Gary Hamel coined the term *core competence* in their classic *Harvard Business Review* article "The Core Competence of the Corporation."[8] Professor John Kay, of the London Business School, introduced the term *critical capabilities* in his book *Foundations of Corporate Success: How Business Strategies Add Value*.[9] We use the terms *core competence, core competencies,* and *critical capabilities* interchangeably.[10]

Prahalad and Hamel[11] write that "core competencies are the collective learning in the organization, especially how to coordinate diverse production skills and integrate multiple streams of technologies." They suggest that managers use three tests to identify core competencies in a company:

1. Core competencies should allow the firm to enter new markets.
2. Core competencies "should make a significant contribution to the perceived customer benefits of the end product."[12]
3. Core competencies should be difficult for rivals to imitate.

According to Professor Jay Barney, an organization's capabilities combined with its resources create sustainable competitive advantage for the firm only if the capabilities and resources pass certain tests. He clarifies and specifies that resources and capabilities are *valuable,* only if they exploit a market opportunity; *rare,* only if there are not enough for all rivals to have them; *hard to imitate,* only if they are difficult to copy, unique to the firm, and therefore cannot be easily duplicated; and *nonsubstitutable,* only if they cannot be replaced by other common resources or capabilities.[13] When resources and capabilities pass these tests and have these characteristics, then they are likely to provide the firm with a durable competitive advantage. As implied above, the collective learning of the firm—its core skills, organizational routines, and processes—often comes bundled and intertwined with specific resources of the firm. We give three examples from different sectors to illustrate the concepts of core competencies and resources and how they work in combination to become a platform for corporate growth.

1. The Japanese automotive giant Honda Motor Company, Ltd. (NYSE: HMC) is known for its core competencies in designing, developing, and building engines. Honda used this core competency to enter many new and different markets, ranging from motorcycles to automobiles. See Richard T. Pascale for more about Honda's emergent "bottom-up" strategy-making processes, which contradicts the stereotype of the "top-down" approach to strategy believed to be the norm for most Japanese conglomerates at that time.[14]
2. A fictional manufacturer has built a new state-of-the-art facility that incorporates a sophisticated computer-aided control system to monitor product quality around the clock. The core capability or key company skill would be quality performance. The delivery of this performance would be dependent on an interrelated system of operator know-how, statistical sampling techniques, modern machinery, and software.
3. In the financial services industry, an imaginary hedge fund has core skills in risk management. These firm capabilities are intimately linked to custom software and a proprietary database belonging to its trading platforms. These platforms are constantly being used by skilled trading teams doing global risk arbitrage on a continuous basis. The fund intends to use its risk management skills to enter new niches of the financial markets.

Remember that for a skill to be considered a *core* competency or *distinctive* capability (as opposed to a mere competency or an ordinary capability), it must enable the organization to achieve superior organizational performance when *compared to rivals.* Since a core competency is a skill or capability, it will not diminish with use; instead, it will be enhanced through use. This last thought is helpful when trying to decide whether something is a resource or a capability. A resource may be either a tangible or intangible asset; a capability is a skill or competency. Keep in mind that the skill or competency may be inseparably linked to a specific resource or asset, much as a musician's performance is enhanced if the artist is playing on a fine-quality instrument.

Develop New Markets for the Same Products   Developing new markets for the same products means taking the same products to new customers, often by international expansion. For instance, a promoter launches a rock-concert tour in New York City and then rolls out the show to other major venues in Europe, Asia, and Latin America. Or a start-up beverage company launches a new iced herbal drink in California. The company then takes it to Hawaii, then across the Pacific Ocean to new customers living in New Zealand and Australia.

Develop New Products for the Same Customers   Developing new products for the same customers means providing existing customers with an expanded range of product choices or services. For example, leading resort hotels around the world are expanding their menu of spa services to include sophisticated wellness programs. These include multiple methods of massage, aromatherapies, mud baths, controlled-temperature Jacuzzis plus dry Finnish saunas and wet Turkish steam baths. These may be followed by various skin-care treatments using exotic ingredients and peeling creams. In addition, the facilities include indoor and outdoor pools, relaxation and meditation areas, and so on.

Expand by Forward Integration   In this option, companies intend to move further down their existing value chain and enter businesses that are deemed closer to the final customer. For instance, in the petroleum business value chain, *upstream activities* are defined as exploring for crude oil, drilling wells, and shipping the crude oil either by tankers or pipeline to the refineries for further processing. The *downstream activities* begin at the refinery. They include refining the crude oil into finished products, such as jet fuels, gasoline, diesel, and heavier bunker oil products. Further downstream, the finished gasoline product is piped to storage tanks and eventually trucked to retail gasoline stations. If an oil company was specialized in the upstream activities of exploration and production, it could decide to forward- integrate into the refining part of the value chain. Similarly a firm dedicated only to refining would forward-integrate into the retail part of the chain if it acquired or built its own system of gasoline stations combined with convenience stores (see Figure 3.3).

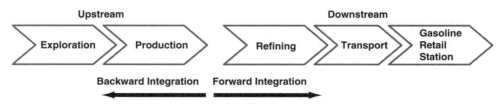

FIGURE 3.3   Petroleum Industry's Value Chain

Expand by Backward Integration   To expand by backward integration means the company's managers decide to grow by going "up" the industry's value chain, away from the end user and toward the raw materials part of the value chain. For instance, a pulp and paper mill owner would expand by backward integration if it purchased large tracks of timberlands and harvested the forests to supply its pulp mills. Similarly a steel plant expands by backward integration when it buys smelting capacity for refining the ore or if it were to purchase a mine and start digging for iron ore. A retail store backward-integrates when it moves into the wholesale part of its distribution chain.

Expand by Horizontal Integration   At times, a firm may decide to take over a rival in the same stage of the value chain in order to gain greater economies of scale or more market share. This may occur when industries consolidate. An example is when Mittal Steel, the world's largest steel producer, announced a $33 billion takeover of the world's second largest steel producer, Arcelor, in January 2006. Mittal Steel is the huge conglomerate built and controlled by Lakshmi Mittal and his family. After six months of takeover discussions, Arcelor's board voted to merge with Mittal, and the new group became Arcelor Mittal (NYSE:MT) in June 2006. The company is domiciled and headquartered in Luxembourg.

Another example of horizontal integration is when a petroleum refining company decides to expand into petrochemicals by building a new plant to process hydrocarbons. For instance, ethylene is a hydrocarbon feedstock that is widely used in the petrochemical industry. Instead of the petroleum refinery producing refined end-products like jet, gasoline, or diesel fuels, now the new plant produces different end-products based on ethylene, such as ethylene glycol (antifreeze for cars) or styrene (used in plastics).

Expand by Unrelated Diversification   At times, it may be necessary for a company to diversify away from a maturing core business. An unrelated diversification means leaving old customers and familiar products and markets behind. The organization is trying something completely new, often by means of acquisition, joint venture, or internal R&D. Completely unrelated diversifications tend to be riskier than related diversifications. Many such diversifications struggle.

Launch a New Venture   Launching a new business is the case of any new start-up technology firm. The new venture, if it starts from scratch, is called a greenfield operation. Starting up from scratch typically is the most difficult and riskiest approach. The reason is that the venture does not yet have the scale of operation or cash flow from an existing business to support it during the launch stage.

Alternatively, a new venture may be created and nurtured, or "incubated," within a larger corporation. When it is ready to stand on its own, the parent company sets it loose. It then is left to grow without further help or support from the parent company. This process is known as corporate venturing, and it is often done by new ventures groups within major corporations. Intel Corporation, in Silicon Valley, has run a very successful new ventures group, as has Nokia, in Espoo (Helsinki), Finland. We talk more about the role of corporations spawning new ventures later in this chapter. (Refer to Figure 3.10, "The Genealogy of Hybritech—A Prolific Anchor Company," found in the section, "Porter's Cluster Theory".) See also Chapter 4 for details on various types of corporate restructuring strategies (e.g., refer to the sections "Spin-Off," "Carve-Out," and "Split-Off").

Exit the Market   Exiting the market usually is a tough decision for senior executives to make and one that they go to great pains to avoid. It typically means divesting business assets, selling plant and equipment, and laying off employees. Any contracted services need to be stopped and long-term commitments to customers and other stakeholders renegotiated. We have more to say about harvest or exit strategies in Chapter 4.

Business Strategy Focuses on Creating a Sustainable Competitive Advantage

Business strategy is the second level of strategy. The fundamental problem addressed in business strategy is how the enterprise is able to compete. It is at the level of business strategy where competitive advantage needs to be achieved in order to allow the firm to survive and prosper over the long term. When devising a competitive strategy, you *always* need to consider the behavior, strategic commitment, and financial strength of your rivals and take into account their likely reactions to any strategic moves you make.

Our advice for fledgling start-ups is not to try to do too many things at once. Having a razor-sharp strategic focus is critical to a small firm. This means you and your fellow founders may end up making more decisions for your venture about what you will *not* do than what you will do. Be selective and do not overcommit your scarce resources of time, treasure, or talent.

How Do We Compete?   The two fundamentals for creating a sustainable competitive advantage are rather simple to say and very hard to do. The first key is to create an innovative product or service that generates value for your customers and keeps them coming back time after time for more. The second key is to do things that make money. In other words, generate economic value for the firm by offering products and services so compelling that customers are willing to pay more for these goods and services than it costs to provide them. Recall the old saying: "Until you have a paying customer, you don't have a business."

When developing a business strategy, you need to be *as specific* as possible about the target market and the target customer. Define the product or service or the bundle of products and services you intend to deliver to that customer. Identify not only who is the customer but also who influences the purchase decision and who are the final end users. For example, consider a high-tech manufacturing start-up firm. The founding team of this business may need to satisfy the needs of end users who will be served at the retail level. However, the final end user may not be the *real customer* of the firm. The true customer might be a component manufacturer further up the value chain. (We have more to say about identifying your target customer in Chapter 5.)

Deciding where to locate and carry out key activities of the value chain is also very important when contemplating how to establish a competitive advantage. Geographically, the target customer and target market may be tied to a specific territory; then again, the target market may be location independent. This is especially true for a virtual company whose activities are outsourced (done outside the firm but still within the firm's home market) or offshored (activities of the firm's value chain done in overseas locations by contracted third parties unrelated to the firm). With the Internet and modern means of communications, many start-ups need to be thinking globally from the very first day they set up their domain name and put out their "open for business" sign on their virtual storefront. As another example, virtual IT software companies are contracting skilled programmers located practically anywhere in the world. (We explore the role of outsourcing and offshoring and how these and various other collaboration modes affect a firm's value chain and business model in much more detail in Part Three, "Understanding Strategic Alliances.") As part of the on-going strategy process, the team will likely seek out and evaluate various technology options, choose which fundamental technology platforms are going to be adopted, and decide how they will be incorporated into manufacturing processes, IT systems, after-sales customer support services, and the like. Furthermore, the business team will need to gather competitive data, develop target pricing schemes, and estimate product demand curves, in order to forecast future revenues, expenses, cash flows, and necessary capital expenditures over the specified time horizon. (For more on financial matters, see Part Six, "Valuing Company Cash Flows.")

Functional Strategy Focuses on the Fit with Corporate and Business Strategies

Functional strategy is the third level of strategy. Functional managers should be concerned with the strategic fit between their particular function (marketing, finance, production, and so forth) and the overall business strategy. How consistently do the functional strategies fit together? How well do they support the business strategy and contribute to creating competitive advantage? For instance, if the firm's strategy is to compete on price, is it doing everything it can to be a low-cost producer? If the strategy is one of being a niche player, competing on perceived benefits, is the product offering truly differentiated compared to competitor's products? To be effective, the firm's functional managers need to mesh their strategies with each other and with the overall strategy of the business and ensure that it is in harmony with the firm's external environment. If strategic alignment is not present, then execution of the strategy becomes problematic and the reasons why the strategy is out of kilter with the external environment need to be explored, analyzed, and addressed. We offer further guidance on how to do this toward the end of this chapter.

BASIC TOOLS FOR EXTERNAL ANALYSIS

We have described the overall strategy process and explained how it might work in both a new venture setting and in a more mature corporation. In this section, we examine the most common tools that executives use to scan, analyze, and make sense of the firm's external environment. In Chapter 15, we cover more advanced techniques to do competitive analysis for high-tech firms. For now, we concentrate on these basic conceptual frameworks:

- Political, economic, social, technological, legal, and environmental (PESTLE) analysis
- Key success factors of an industry

- Five Forces framework for analyzing industry competition
- McKinsey business system
- Porter's value chain
- Value net—extending the Five Forces framework
- Porter's cluster theory or national diamond

Normally, most executives are aware of the macroeconomic forces that affect their firms. What they do not have a lot of time to do is stop and contemplate these trends. Professor Thomas A. Malnight, director of the Advanced Strategic Management program of the International Institute for Management Development (IMD),[15] and Tracey Keys, program manager, at the IMD, surveyed a diverse group of 289 senior executives as one part of the IMD's flagship executive education program "Orchestrating Winning Performance." They set up a series of group exercises in which nine global trends were presented and discussed. They then asked the managers to reflect about the trends and answer a detailed questionnaire. The point of the exercise was to get managers to think critically about four questions for their organizations:

1. What is really happening in the world today?
2. What does this mean for us over the longer term?
3. What should we do about the most significant trends?
4. What decisions can we make to take action?

The survey results are published on the IMD web site.[16] What Malnight and Keys discovered is that many senior executives are not taking time out to adequately reflect. They fail to connect the dots in the big picture and to realize the implications of long-term fundamental changes on their businesses. The IMD survey conclusions are further supported by a detailed survey conducted by McKinsey & Company in March 2008. The survey shows that "most business executives agree that global social, environmental and business trends are generally more important to corporate strategy than they were five years ago. But relatively few companies act on these trends, and many of those that do, appear to be acting tentatively, and have yet to see positive results."[17]

Analyzing the External Environment Using the PESTLE Framework

One approach to help executives analyze and think more deeply about the external environment is to conduct what is referred to as a political, economic, social, technological, legal, and environmental (PESTLE) analysis. Each element is explained next. Managers may hire outside experts to facilitate and assist in their identification of significant trends and their interpretation. However, it is very important that senior managers learn how to reflect on the significance of these trends for their own company and to make the time and effort to do so. To encourage this type of integrative thinking and behavior, many leading business schools are fundamentally changing their curriculums to be more interdisciplinary and global. They are teaching senior executives how to become better gatherers of fresh sources of information; to be better spotters and interpreters of emerging trends; and to become more expert at exercising managerial judgment on what to do and how to take advantage of important trends for their organizations.

Political Analysis   For instance, democratic elections might change the leadership of the ruling parties in various regions around the world. Newly elected parties might change the rules of the game and allow sensitive sectors of their country's economy, such as financial institutions, energy resources, or telecommunications companies, to be taken over by the government. In other countries, government action liberalizes the economy by imposing new regulations or rules to deregulate various industries. These are just a few examples of the rules and legislative changes that should be weighed in a political assessment. Other examples may be found in the Economist Intelligence Unit's Country Briefing reports (see www.EIU.com).

Economic Analysis   All organizations are affected to some degree or another by global, national, regional, and local economic conditions. Inflation, interest rates, exchange rate shifts, business cycles (booms or recessions), and the availability of loans and credit can have either a favorable or a negative impact on expected industry profitability.

Social Analysis   Demographic trends, birth rates, longevity, disposable income levels, social values, religious beliefs, racial conflicts, the growing disparity between rich and poor, and the rising importance of social networking are examples of social influences and trends.

Technological Analysis   As an example, changes in the computer industry have also affected and changed the information technology (IT) services sector. Competition for IT outsourcing services has gone global. As systems integration and data management have become more important to users, IT outsourcing service providers have had to adapt their businesses if they wish to keep customers loyal. (Advanced tools to search for emerging technological trends are covered in Chapter 15.)

Legal Analysis   The reliability, credibility, and speed at which the courts and legal justice systems of a country may work can influence how firms compete. Examples of legal issues are the recognition of intellectual property rights, enforceability of contracts, strength of antitrust laws, protection of basic human rights, and so forth.

Environmental Analysis   The scientific evidence on global warming has led many policy makers and government bodies to conclude that citizens, corporations, and nation-states need to reduce carbon emissions. Solutions most likely will involve implementing stricter energy conservation measures, stimulating the development of alternative noncarbon-based energy sources, and inducing changes in consumer behavior. Sustainable development may be defined as "development meeting the needs of the present without compromising the ability of future generations to meet their own needs."[18] Sustainable development and emerging environmental trends will create many opportunities for entrepreneurs desiring to start-up new enterprises. Trends to keep in mind will be: the design and construction of more environmentally friendly buildings; new products and transportation services that save energy; innovative ways to reclaim, recycle, and purify water; ways to reduce waste; and new technologies to eliminate dangerous particulates in the air.

When doing the PESTLE analysis, keep in mind these questions:

- What external forces are impinging on our organization?
- How many factors influence the environment surrounding our enterprise?
- Are these factors interrelated?
- Which of these factors do we think are the most important at the present time?
- Which of these factors do we imagine will be the most significant in a few years time? In a decade or more?
- How rapidly do we expect these factors to cause changes in society and the world?

When pondering the challenges that lie ahead, it is often advisable to do a PESTLE analysis on a particular portion or region of the world and then examine the specific country or geographical area which is of primary interest. Remember that in turbulent environments, simple extrapolation of trends does not work. PESTLE analysis will stimulate strategic thinking about multiple factors and their relationships over time. It is an excellent tool for systematically scanning the environment and aiding managerial reflection on the implications of global trends.

Discovering the Key Success Factors of an Industry

In performing an industry analysis, key success factors (KSFs) help to capture the customer's perspective. They are a cross-check for managers who go out too far on the core competency limb of their technology platform and leave the customer in limbo. (See the story box "The Tale of Sandvik Tools.") To develop KSFs, executives should ask three questions about the industry in which they are competing or thinking about entering. (Refer to Figure 3.4.)

In the KSF framework, the first two questions refer to the revenue-generation part of the industry. These questions deal with what to sell and how high a price to charge. The third question is asking what the firm needs to do to survive competition in its industry. Put another way, it asks what minimum requirements must a company satisfy in order to enter a market and compete successfully. These are the sine qua non or essential conditions that a company must fulfill in terms of position, resources, or capabilities in order to survive in the industry.

An example will demonstrate how to apply the KSF concepts. In the super-premium ice-cream market, Ben & Jerry's Homemade (now owned by Unilever) has long battled against the mighty Häagen-Daz brand (now owned by Nestlé). In super-premium ice cream (with real butterfat, all-natural ingredients, and big chunks of texture), the customer needs quality and freshness, innovative and tasty

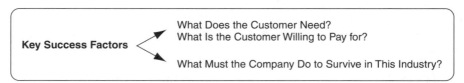

FIGURE 3.4   Key Success Factors of an Industry
Source: Adapted from Robert M. Grant, *Contemporary Strategy Analysis*, 6th ed. (Oxford, England: Wiley-Blackwell, 2008), p. 88. Used by permission.

flavor sensations, and eye-catching packaging. The Ben & Jerry's and Häagen-Daz customer is willing to pay for self-indulgence and brand recognition. The Ben & Jerry's customer is also willing to pay for the firm's policies of social consciousness and sustainable development. The sine qua non of the industry is distribution, distribution, distribution. If the cartons of premium ice cream cannot be found in the freezers of convenience stores or supermarkets, then any ice cream maker will fail.

Indeed, the end of Ben & Jerry's independence came on its acceptance of the takeover tender offer by Unilever. One of the main reasons that Ben & Jerry's board of directors agreed to accept Unilever's offer was that it gave Ben & Jerry's access to Unilever's global ice cream distribution channels. Access to distribution was a KSF for survival in the premium ice-cream market. Without better distribution, Ben & Jerry's could not grow overseas. The decision by the board, however, was difficult and controversial, as it cost Ben & Jerry's Homemade its independence. Today, Unilever and Nestlé are still engaged in fierce competition to woo super-premium ice-cream lovers to their respective brands all around the world.

THE TALE OF SANDVIK TOOLS

Taking core competencies to the limit means that some firms—especially high-tech firms led by engineers in love with their technology—will launch wonderfully complex new products, all state of the art, but then fail miserably in the market and wonder why. The overengineered features may be underappreciated by the customer who must perceive the benefits of the product before buying it and then be willing to pay for these benefits. This reminds us of the old saying that experienced sales managers inevitably tell new hires: "Sell the benefits, not the features."

Customers buy goods and services to satisfy real and perceived needs. They also buy things for emotional fulfillment. An example brings this point home. European-based tool company Sandvik AB of Sweden made a strategic mistake when it launched ergonometric hand tools into the U.S. market. Although ergonometric design was appreciated by European craftsmen, it was not a benefit that U.S. retail customers, purchasing hand tools at Home Depot stores, were willing to pay for, especially since they would rather switch to a power tool than use a hand tool repetitively. In the end, Sandvik sold the business to Snap-On Tools. The latter company had a special niche serving automobile mechanics, who did do repetitive work with cold-forged hand tools and who were willing to pay for safety and ergonometric design. Whereas Sandvik had the brand recognition, distribution channels, and correct product to be successful in Europe, it lacked all three industry key success factors when it tried to enter the United States. Consequently, there was no strategic fit between the company's ergonometric hand tool product and the needs of the U.S. market; the customers were not satisfied, and Sandvik ended up exiting the market.

Lesson to be learned: In order to work, a core competency approach to strategy needs to be matched to the value proposition being offered to customers. Finding the fit between customer expectations and what must be done to survive in an industry involves examining the industry's key success factors.

Assessing Industry Competition with Porter's Five Forces

The book *Competitive Strategy* introduced Michael Porter's Five Forces framework.[19] This conceptual tool provides a convenient shorthand way of describing the intensity of competitive forces in an industry. It also associates that rivalry with an expected level of industry profitability. Therefore, MBA students often use Porter's framework as the starting point for conducting an industry analysis when doing a business case study. The framework assesses five sources of competitive pressure arrayed as a diamond. As shown in Figure 3.5, competition from buyers and suppliers is shown along the vertical axis. Competition from new entrants coming into the market and offering new products or services and competition from companies offering substitute products or services is shown along the horizontal axis. Industry rivalry (intensity of competition) is placed in the center. Competitive rivals are organizations or companies with similar products or services targeting the same customer group. Industry rivalry results when these competitors are at odds with each other—for instance, when they engage in price wars and similar such competitive retaliations.

Rivalry is more likely to occur in industries with high fixed costs and high capital intensity (e.g., steel or commodity chemicals). Keeping capacity utilization rates high would be a priority in these industries. (The utilization rate of a plant is its actual output divided by potential output expressed as a percentage.) Therefore, price wars in such industries are common. Where there are high "exit barriers" to an industry, high rivalry is also likely. An example of a high exit barrier is the cost to reduce personnel because of labor laws. Under these circumstances, shutting

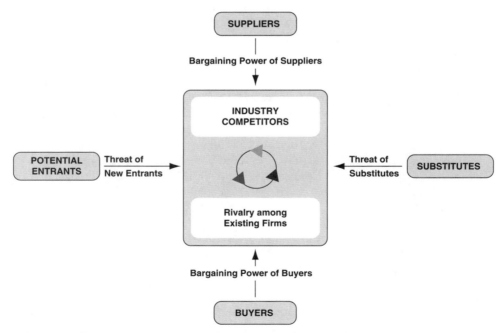

FIGURE 3.5 Porter's Five Forces Framework of Industry Competition
Source: Reprinted with the permission of The Free Press, A Division of Simon & Schuster, Inc., from *Competitive Strategy: Techniques for Analyzing Industries and Competitors* by Michael E. Porter. Copyright © 1980, 1998 by The Free Press. All rights reserved.

down excess capacity and laying off workers (making workers redundant) is very expensive. Incumbent players are likely to avoid shutting down factories for as long as possible, so they keep lowering prices to keep local plants operating. This example of an exit barrier related to labor laws also demonstrates how an external condition may lead to industry rivalry.

McKinsey's Business System

In 1980, the strategy consultants McKinsey & Company were the first to conceptualize a business system as a tool for analyzing the value chain and cost structure of an industry.[20] One purpose of the business system analysis was to help consultants determine the stages within the value chain where the most value was added as raw materials were transformed into finished products. The tool also helped pinpoint where the most value was being lost and hence where there were possibilities for restructuring the value chain. Restructuring the value chain is when a firm decides to outsource parts of its value chain to third parties or to offshore parts of its value chain to third parties overseas. Industry value chains are decoupled or deconstructed when the companies competing in an industry choose no longer to be fully integrated in all the stages of the value chain but to specialize in one or the other step. The business system tool may be applied not only to manufacturing businesses but also to service industries, such as insurance, hotels, and airlines. Refer to Figure 3.6.

Firm Processes and Porter's Value Chain

In his book *Competitive Advantage,* Michael Porter built on the McKinsey business system concept. Porter's value chain focuses on the process capabilities of the firm.[21] It may be used to compare one firm and benchmark the efficiency of its processes versus rivals. As shown in Figure 3.7, Porter expanded the notion of a value chain to include support activities (firm infrastructure, human resource management, technology development, financial management and control) and primary activities

Business system for a technology-based manufacturing company

Technology	Product design	Manufacturing	Marketing	Distribution	Service
• Source • Sophistication • Patents • Product, process choices	• Function • Physical characteristics • Aesthetics • Quality	• Integration • Raw materials • Capacity • Location • Procurement • Parts production • Assembly	• Prices • Advertising, promotion • Sales force • Package • Brand	• Channels • Integration • Inventory • Warehousing • Transport	• Warranty • Speed • Captive vs. independent service providers • Prices

FIGURE 3.6 McKinsey Business System
Source: Exhibit from "The microeconomics of industry supply" June 2000, *The McKinsey Quarterly,* www.mckinseyquarterly.com. McKinsey & Company. All rights reserved. Reprinted by permission.

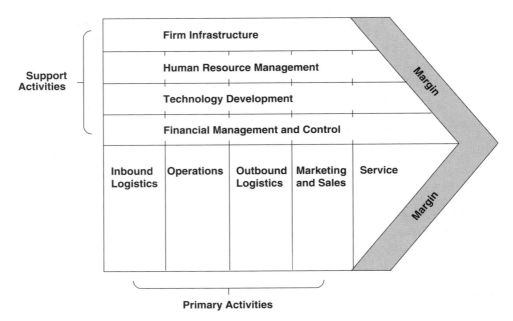

FIGURE 3.7 Porter's Generic Value Chain
Source: Reprinted with the permission of The Free Press, A Division of Simon & Schuster, Inc., from *Competitive Advantage: Creating and Sustaining Superior Performance* by Michael E. Porter. Copyright © 1985, 1998 by Michael E. Porter. All rights reserved.

(logistics for incoming supplies, operations, logistics for outbound products, marketing and sales, and service).

Strategists find Porter's value chain especially useful to identify and categorize a firm's capabilities in a systematic, well-accepted fashion that goes beyond the traditional functional analysis of activities into finance, marketing, manufacturing, human resources, and the like. Porter's framework was one of the earliest to look at the process flows within the firm. His value chain helps diagnose coordination links between various administrative support activities, the purchasing and logistics functions, and downstream customer support interfaces. The notion of looking at the firm from a process flow perspective is now taken for granted in most supply chain management systems. Administrative process flows are also a feature in most customer resource management (CRM) systems and enterprise resource planning (ERP) systems.

Value Net Extends the Five Forces Framework

Professors Adam Brandenburger of Harvard Business School and Barry Nalebuff of Yale University are experts in game theory and the study of strategic interactions. They coauthored the book *Co-opetition* and popularized a strategy framework they called the "Value Net."[22] The value net introduces the idea of collaborative forces into industry analysis. (See Figure 3.8.)

Business relationships often have dual natures. At times, the relationship is cooperative while at other times it is competitive. The value net recognizes the

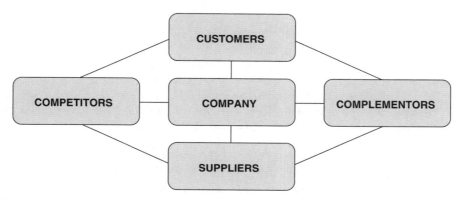

FIGURE 3.8 Value Net Includes Cooperative Forces
Source: Illustration adapted from *Co-opetition* by Adam M. Brandenburger and Barry J. Nalebuff. Copyright © 1996 by Adam M. Brandenburger and Barry J. Nalebuff. Used by permission of Doubleday, a division of Random House, Inc., and the authors.

cooperative-competitive duality of these relationships in many industries. To illustrate the duality, we cite a financial services example. Co-opetition is commonplace in investment banking circles. For instance, for one capital market transaction, investment banks may be fiercely competing against each other, whereas in the very next deal, the same banks would be collaborating together as part of an underwriting syndicate for, say, a client's initial public offering of shares. As another example, major pharmaceutical companies might be competitors and collaborators at the same time. Two drug companies might fiercely compete for the best scientists and researchers in the upstream part of the value chain (early drug discovery stage); at the same time, these two companies might be strategic partners in the downstream part of the chain where they have formed a joint venture to codevelop a leading therapeutic compound and a comarketing alliance to sell drug products in various parts of the world.

Complements Enhance the Customer's Perception of Value Added   We think the value net framework extends and enhances Porter's Five Forces framework. Two criticisms of the Five Forces framework are that it is static and that it ignores collaborative forces as a driver of industry dynamics. In other words, it does not include the notion of "economic complements." *Complements* are goods that, when bundled together with a product or service, tend to *enhance* the value added perceived by the customer. Substitutes do the opposite; they tend to *reduce* the value added perceived by the customer. For example, two different energy drinks are substitutes for each other if after drinking a large amount of one of them the runner's immediate desire for another is reduced. Either energy drink will do; the runner is no longer thirsty. The drinks are substitutes for each other.

A Caesar salad can be used to illustrate the idea of complements. Including one packet of premade Caesar salad dressing and one packet of toasted croutons would be two "complements" found inside the bag of prewashed, precut, and ready-to-eat prepared romaine lettuce displayed in the salad section of the supermarket. The croutons and Caesar salad dressing are complementors to the basic commodity, the lettuce. Taken as a whole, the consumer is willing to pay more for three ingredients than for separate batches of each. Why? In the eyes of some customers, it may save them from wasting time and ingredients.

Another classic case that illustrates the strategic importance of complementors is Nintendo's story.[23] In the early 1990s, Nintendo earned enormous profits on its combination of video games software and game machine; at that time it was the Nintendo Entertainment System (NES). The consumers valued the video games that were created by Nintendo's ace designer, Sigeru Miyamoto (Donkey Kong, Super Mario Brothers, and the Legend of Zelda) plus those produced by independent software houses. Nintendo cleverly captured a large part of the value potential of the entire system and retained it for itself. In other words, Nintendo "appropriated the economic rents of its value network," in the jargon of economists. It accomplished this feat by controlling the value network through hardware and software measures. Nintendo built a security chip inside its hardware to ensure that only Nintendo-approved game cartridges could run on the NES system. Moreover, software houses had to receive permission from Nintendo to only write games for the NES. Thus, Nintendo controlled the value network. Furthermore, Nintendo established a dominant relationship with game developers by issuing developer licenses to the many producers of games software that wanted to take advantage of the popularity of the NES. Nintendo avoided the earlier mistake of Atari, which was destroyed when the game market flooded with poor-quality games. Unlike Atari, Nintendo maintained tight quality control over the specification of game content and manufactured all of the games of which it approved. Nintendo made money "by charging its licensees a large markup on every game cartridge."[24] Nintendo went on to achieve a 90-plus percent share of the Japanese and U.S. 8-bit video games markets—a remarkable achievement for a century-old Japanese company with historical roots in making playing cards, then toys, then arcade games.

Why emphasize the notion of industry complementors so much? The reason is because industry complements are critical in many high-tech industries. Many computer manufacturers and other consumer electronics makers depend on bundling hardware with software for their launch and ultimate market acceptance. As Professor David Teece describes, "the base innovation ('hardware') requires an investment in producing complementary goods ('software') specialized for that innovation, in order to make the entire system useful."[25] As described in Gallagher and Park, many video game console makers will intentionally lose money or break even on the hardware game consoles so that they can make money from the software royalties on the games.[26] Complements add up; they matter.

Porter's Cluster Theory

In his book *The Competitive Advantage of Nations*, Michael Porter presents his theory of cluster competitiveness referred to as his "cluster theory" or known as the "Diamond of National Competitiveness" (because of the diamondlike shape of the drawing).[27] (Refer to Figure 3.9.) He suggests that competitive advantage in the global economy is intimately tied to where firms decide to locate various activities of their value chain. Organizations located in the world's leading centers for doing that particular activity are at an advantage compared to firms located elsewhere. This theory has gained widespread acceptance and been put to practical use

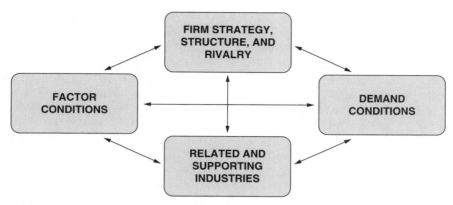

FIGURE 3.9 Porter's Cluster Theory: The Diamond of National Competitive Advantage
Source: Reprinted with the permission of *Harvard Business Review*. Exhibit from "The Competitive Advantage of Nations" by Michael E. Porter, March–April, 1990. Copyright © 1990 by the Harvard Business School Publishing Corporation. All rights reserved.

by national and regional economic planners and policy makers. Numerous public and private organizations have sponsored economic development measures to stimulate the growth of clusters in nearly every nation. With the cluster theory, Porter considers innovation as a means for upgrading and renewing the resources and capabilities, not only of companies but also of nations. The cluster theory takes a more dynamic view of competition than Porter's previous Five Forces framework, which portrays a static view of industry boundaries and rivalry. Cluster theory considers global strategy issues. It is particularly useful for managers who need to decide where to locate value chain activities around the world.

A criticism of this model is that it is silent about the role of headquarters. It does not address the issue of how the firm as a whole should be organized to take advantage of the individual units, each of which is situated in an area where it can supposedly gain location-based advantage. Nor does it specify the "learning" mechanism by which the global firm is able to tap into the knowledge and skills created in various clusters and transmit this know-how to other parts of the firm. Nevertheless, cluster theory provides a systematic approach for appraising the economic competitiveness of one cluster compared to another. It also helps to identify in which specific aspects or factors one hub is stronger or weaker than another. We illustrate how to use Porter's cluster theory by applying it to the San Diego Biotechnology hub. Log onto our web site at www.innovationtocashflows.com and download Appendix 3.1, "Porter's Cluster Theory Applied to San Diego's Biotechnology Cluster."

What Is a *Cluster*? A *cluster* is a geographically concentrated "critical mass" of companies, universities, and related organizations that interact with each other and have some sort of relationship to each other. By "critical mass," we mean that there is a sufficient number of companies or research institutes or universities to attract specialized providers of services or supplies or resources. The relationships may be of various types. For instance, the companies might be complementors of each other's products or services. Or they could jointly share resources. Or they could be rivals, competing in the same market niches using similar processes or technologies. Some clusters may be knowledge centers, consisting of a group of world-renowned universities or research institutes. Napa Valley, California, is known as a famous wine cluster. Warsaw, Indiana, a town of 12,000 people, is famous for the manufacture of orthopedics products—it is the world's leading cluster for making artificial hips. For generations, South Carolina has been a center for fine wood furniture making. Carlsbad, California, is a more recent cluster for developing high-tech golf clubs and other golfing sports equipment.

High-tech clusters in electronics, information, and communications technology (ICT) and in biotechnology rely on highly educated workforces. These clusters evolve in close proximity to major research universities and research institutes. For instance, Silicon Valley, California, is a high-tech cluster supported by the research and talent coming from world-renowned universities such as Stanford, UC Berkeley, and UC San Francisco. Route 128 in Massachusetts is supported by Boston's leading research universities, including the Massachusetts Institute of Technology and Harvard.

Around the world, there are numerous biotechnology and life science clusters. In the United States, leading biotech clusters include San Francisco, San Diego, and Los Angeles, in California; Boston, Massachusetts; Minneapolis-St. Paul, Minnesota; and the "Research Triangle" in North Carolina. In Canada, Toronto is the largest biotech cluster. In England, noted bioscience clusters are located at Oxford and Cambridge. In Continental Europe, important hubs include Paris, France; "BioValley," a trinational bio-cluster on the borders of Switzerland, Germany, and France; and "BioTech," a cluster in Münich, Germany. In Scandinavia, important biomedical hubs are "Medicon Valley" in Denmark and southern Sweden; "Bio-Uppsala" closer to Stockholm, Sweden; and the biotechnology clusters in Helsinki, and Turku, Finland.

The web site prepared by William Hoffman, MBBNet, of the University of Minnesota (www.mbbnet.umn.edu/hoff/hoff_w.html) shows a global map with the locations of leading biotechnology clusters.

What Are the Origins of Clusters?   Many of the world's successful clusters have evolved through a series of unplanned, serendipitous events often going back generation to generation of skilled craftsman plying their trade. For instance, outside of Barcelona, Spain, in a city called Sabadell, is a textile cluster that has specialized in weaving ultrafine wools for centuries. The area around Como, near Lake Como, is known as the silk cluster of northern Italy. The Sassuolo ceramic cluster, northwest of Bologna, in the Emilia-Romagna region of Italy, dates back to the 1600s and is famous for making fine-quality Italian ceramic tiles based on local clays. More recently, Sassuolo has been experiencing intense global competition, first from less expensive Spanish tiles and more recently from Chinese tile manufacturers.

National and regional governments, sometimes working alone and sometimes working with nonprofit organizations or private sponsors, have used various economic policy measures and have spent large sums of money to try to stimulate the growth of new clusters—especially in desired high-tech sectors, such as biotechnology, nanotech, electronics, and telecommunications. These efforts have met with mixed results; the intended clusters do not always take hold and thrive. What does seem to work, and sometimes spontaneously, is that a cluster starts forming around a strong anchor company. An *anchor company* is one that spawns or incubates ventures. In other words, it ends up spinning off a number of smaller companies in response to employee initiative, entrepreneurship, and market opportunities.

A good example of one such anchor company is PARC (Palo Alto Research Company), founded in 1970, in Palo Alto, California, as part of Xerox Research and now an independent research company. PARC has contributed to the formation of over 30 companies. It was intimately involved in the creation of laser printing, distributed computing and Ethernet, the graphical user interface (GUI), object-oriented programming, and ubiquitous computing (www.parc.com).

There are many other examples of anchor companies that have stimulated the formation of clusters. For instance, the mobile phone hub that has built up around Nokia's headquarters is located in Espoo, near Helsinki, Finland. The same is true for the wireless hub supporting the growth of Qualcomm, in San Diego, California, a leading ICT company.

A particularly prolific biotech anchor company was Hybritech, founded in San Diego, which eventually was acquired by Eli Lilly & Company. The companies related to Hybritech became part of the nucleus for San Diego's biotechnology cluster. See Figure 3.10 for Hybritech's "genealogical tree."

External Analysis: Summary and Conclusions

In this section, we have examined the most commonly used tools and conceptual frameworks for conducting an external analysis of the firm's environment. The Five Forces framework helps managers to determine industry rivalry and attractiveness. The PESTLE tool is a way to examine global trends and assess their implications for an organization. The key success factors of an industry is a tool to help the manager keep the customer perspective in mind when formulating strategy based on the core competencies or distinctive capabilities of the firm. The McKinsey business system is fundamental to analyzing the value chain. Porter's value chain approach extends the business system by focusing attention on the organization's support activities and process capabilities. The value net introduces the notion of complements and collaborative forces to industry analysis. Cluster theory or the national diamond theory helps to identify those factors of competitiveness that are location specific and innovation dependent. Cluster theory helps managers decide where to locate various portions of the value chain. It also has been used as a policy tool to guide national and regional economic development of clusters around the world, with particular interest by most countries on stimulating the growth of high-tech clusters.

INTERNAL ANALYSIS AND ORGANIZATIONAL DESIGN

We now turn to the problem of how to conduct an internal analysis of the organization. We will use the results to formulate better strategies and to design better organizations. In this section, we cover three different approaches:

1. Resource-based view of strategy
2. Seven-S framework
3. People, architecture, routines, and culture (PARCs) of the firm

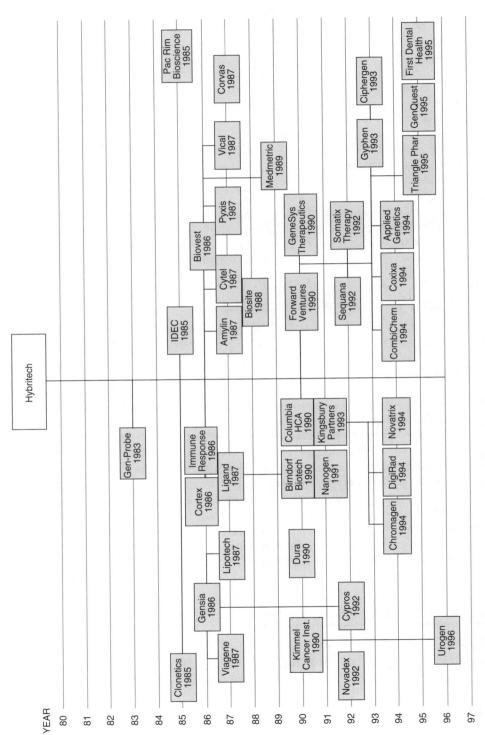

FIGURE 3.10 The Genealogy of Hybritech—A Prolific Anchor Company
Source: Data supplied by UCSD Connect, University of California, San Diego.

Resource-Based View of Strategy

The resource-based view of strategy was first developed in 1959 by Edith Penrose, in her seminal book *The Theory of the Growth of the Firm.*[28] Later authors amplified and enhanced upon her research. Refer to Wernerfelt, to Barney, and to Grant.[29] For a list of recommended strategy books, log onto our web site at www.innovationtocashflows.com and go to "Resources."

When managers are scanning the internal environment of a firm, they are searching for answers to the fundamental question: What can this firm do better than its competitors? The resource-based view of strategy helps a team of managers identify the underlying sources of a company's competitive advantage.

In the next section, we introduce a simple five-step procedure that can be used by managers to systematically appraise any company's resources and organizational capabilities. (The procedure modifies and refines a three-step method suggested by Grant.[30]) Either Grant's or our step-by-step evaluation system will enable a management team to practice and to apply the resource-based view of strategy to competitor analysis.

Conducting An Appraisal of a Firm's Resources and Capabilities

Step 1. *Identify the resources and organizational capabilities of the firm.* In the next section, we explain how to distinguish a resource from an organizational capability.

Step 2. *Examine the relationships and links among the resources and capabilities.* Capabilities are often inseparable from the resources on which they depend. It is important to understand the interrelationships among the various pieces and how they work together. (Particularly important is to see how the link between various industry key success factors ties into the company's capabilities. Refer to Figure 3.11).

Step 3. *Appraise each resource and capability for strategic importance and relative strength.* The *strategic importance* of a resource or capability is determined by the degree to which it helps the firm establish a competitive advantage over its rivals. Next comes the rating of each pertinent resource and capability in terms of relative strength. *Relative strength* is determined by measuring how each of the firm's resources and capabilities compares to equivalent resources and capabilities of competitors. Where does the firm have superior, equal, or deficient strength in each resource or capability compared to its main rivals? We suggest giving a numerical rating for each factor and then plotting the results on a diagram showing relative strength on one axis and strategic importance on the other (refer to Figure 3.12).

Step 4. *Develop the strategy implications. Understand the company's strategically important strengths and weaknesses.* Do this by scrutinizing and discussing the chart prepared in Step 3. Determine where there are strategic gaps (deficiencies) in critically important and relevant capabilities and resources. Strategic gap analysis is vital and should come before strategy formulation. Once all four steps are completed, then the manager is finished with the internal analysis of the organization. What comes next is to

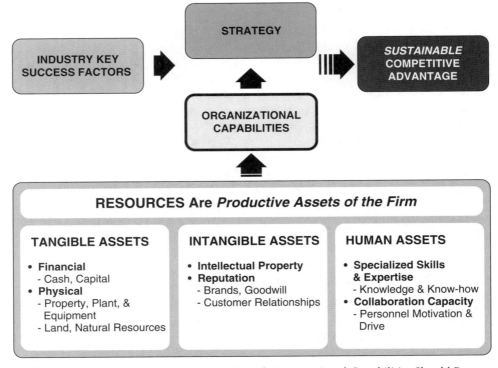

FIGURE 3.11   Industry Key Success Factors and Organizational Capabilities Should Be Brought Together to Create Competitive Advantage
Source: Adapted from Robert M. Grant. *Contemporary Strategy Analysis,* 6th ed. (Oxford, England: Wiley-Blackwell, 2008), p. 131. Used with permission.

formulate the business strategies so as to achieve a sustainable competitive advantage.

Step 5. *Formulate strategic options.* We discuss this in more detail in the section titled "Leveraging Strategically Important Strengths, Mitigating Strategically Important Weaknesses." We recommend devising at least three distinct business strategies. Managers should ensure that the team considers a variety of different but robust (meaning not trivial) strategic options to avoid tunnel vision. Only after all feasible and practical alternatives have been explored should the team reach a final decision. The decision-criteria should be agreed upon in advance. The end result should be the team's recommended business strategy.

Identifying Resources and Capabilities

Resources are the productive assets owned by the firm. They may be *tangible assets,* such as financial assets (cash, securities, or debt capacity) or *physical assets* (plant and equipment, land, natural resources, etc.). They may also be *intangible assets,* such as intellectual property assets (consisting of patents, copyrights, trademarks, designs,

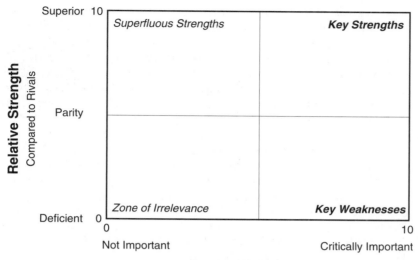

FIGURE 3.12 Doing the Strategic Appraisal: Focus on the Critical and Relevant Resources and Capabilities
Source: Reprinted from Robert M. Grant. *Contemporary Strategy Analysis,* 6th ed. (Oxford, England: Wiley-Blackwell, 2008). Used by permission.

confidential information, or trade secrets), or goodwill assets related to the firm's reputation (brands, customer loyalty), or the company's knowledge assets (useful information systematically stored in databases). *Human resources* are the people in the firm, their motivation, their willingness to collaborate, and their skills or know-how. Some strategy textbook authors include human resources in "resources of the firm"; others prefer to deal with human resources as a separate element. Definitions may vary slightly.

Organizational capabilities (or capabilities) are the collective skills of the firm. These are its core competencies plus other noncore capabilities. These skills need to have been institutionalized into the organization's systems, processes, or knowledge bases. The firm's resources—its tangible and intangible assets and its human resources—are often intimately linked to the firm's organizational capabilities. In other words, the capabilities and the resources cannot be separated. Be mindful once more that core competencies must be properly linked with the industry key success factors. If a technological capability is not linked to the industry's KSFs, then the firm could enter new markets based on its core competencies and leave the customer behind. (Recall "The Tale of Sandvik Tools.")

Resources and Capabilities Appraisal Process

Sometimes managers attempt to do strategic gap analysis (step 4, discussed before) with a widely used technique known as strengths, weaknesses, opportunities, and threats (SWOT) analysis. In the SWOT approach, *strengths and weaknesses* refer to the firm's internal environment; *opportunities and threats* are what the company perceives as happening in the external environment. We advise against using SWOT. For scanning opportunities and threats, we prefer the processes described earlier in this chapter for doing a comprehensive scan of the environment rather than a simple list of opportunities and threats. Moreover, we find the five step appraisal process to be a better approach to doing internal analysis than simply listing a firm's strengths and weaknesses. Although easy to remember, the SWOT technique has serious flaws as a strategy tool. In practice, it is often misused.

For instance, SWOT does not distinguish between what is strategically important from what is strategically unimportant. In other words, it does not distinguish when a resource or capability might be strong but is superfluous or not needed, because it is strategically irrelevant. The example to bring this point home is to put yourself in the imaginary role of being the world's greatest piccolo player but unable to get a job. Why? Because all the orchestras that are hiring musicians are in need of trumpet players, not piccolo players. Your expertise as a piccolo player is superfluous. It is not in demand. The other flaw of SWOT is that it does not distinguish the weaknesses that may be ignored from the ones that ought to be corrected or mitigated. For instance, if a weakness is of no strategic significance, then it may be best for the company to sell the resource or outsource the activity to a third party. The firm has better uses for its capital and time than investing in a weakness that is not strategically important—especially since the payoff from the investment is not going to enhance competitive advantage.

Leveraging Strategically Important Strengths, Mitigating Strategically Important Weaknesses

As we described earlier, with the first four steps of internal analysis completed, the fifth step is to formulate strategic options. We recommended that three distinct business strategies be devised, each of which should achieve sustainable competitive advantage but in a different way. Creating a number of strategic options helps the team to think more creatively about strategic possibilities and viable alternatives. Each strategy should clearly state the chosen long-term goals, scope, competitive advantage, and strategic rationale. Each one should be a robust and feasible alternative.

The principle to keep in mind is to devise strategies that exploit the firm's strategically important strengths while mitigating its strategically important weaknesses. A good strategy ought to deploy the assets of the firm (its resources and people) in such a way that it exploits the firm's unique strengths and capabilities to the greatest extent possible. This is called leveraging the resources and capabilities of the firm to strategic advantage.

Normally there are many feasible ways to accomplish the chosen goals, scope, competitive advantage, and strategic rationale of any given strategy. For instance, the mechanisms for carrying out the strategy might be to invest more in internal development, sign additional external research collaborations, conclude strategic partnership deals, and do joint ventures and strategic alliances, as well as perform mergers and acquisitions. We cover these topics and especially how to structure collaborative alliances in Part Three, "Crafting Strategic Alliances"; Part Four,

"Understanding Legal Arrangements"; and in Chapter 20, "Valuing and Structuring High Technology Strategic Alliances."

Deciding what to do about strategically important (key) weaknesses is more problematic; converting key weaknesses into key strengths usually takes a long time. It also costs money. The bad news is that despite management's best efforts, the conversion may not work out as planned. A very small start-up usually lacks both time and money and has little room for errors and mistakes. Hence it is advisable for a start-up firm to concentrate on exploiting its strengths whenever possible, especially at the beginning. For a larger firm with more time and money, and hence more margin for error, various possibilities are open to management for correcting key weaknesses or at least mitigating them to some degree. Typical steps to be considered would be to:

- Increase internal new product development especially through the use of cross-functional, multidisciplinary teams.
- Invest in more R&D to build up the intellectual property assets or organizational capabilities that are important but weaker than those of rivals and where management believes there is a good chance to succeed.
- Create carefully crafted strategic alliances or joint ventures by selectively picking partners that may also provide learning opportunities and allow the company's weaker capabilities to be developed along with its other strengths.
- Acquire the missing capabilities or resources through a focused program of mergers and acquisitions (M&A). Again, if the firm is very weak in a certain critical capability, it may not have the in-house expertise to identify good M&A prospects and qualify them properly in the due diligence process. (See Chapter 16.) This could lead to problems with postmerger integration.

Again, we cover these aspects in later chapters and especially how to mitigate the risks of structuring collaborative alliances in Part Five, "Competitive Intelligence and Due Diligence."

Fictional Case Study to Illustrate How to Do a Strategy Appraisal

To illustrate step by step how to do an appraisal of a start-up company's resources and capabilities, we wrote a case study about an imaginary company that we called WineOnline.com. In the story, the venture's founders wish to launch an online wine market for trading bottles of wine. The company's vision is to become the world's biggest online wine market and wine trading platform on the Internet. We do a complete inventory of its resources and capabilities and apply the tools and process just described for steps 1 through 4. We do not do step 5 (strategy formulation) as the start-up already had a strategy in place. What we do instead is a detailed critique of what went wrong with the venture's launch and why the strategy that the team chose may have failed. For the case study example, log onto our web site at www.innovationtocashflows.com and refer to Appendix 3.2, "Fictional Case Study of WineOnline.com."

Creating Competitive Advantage

In Figure 3.11, we depicted the relationships among resources (tangible, intangible, and human), organizational capabilities, industry key success factors, and competitive advantage. Next, we discuss how capabilities and firm position combine with resources to create superior competitive advantage.

An important aspect to keep in mind is that merely owning resources does not give a firm a superior sustainable advantage. For instance, just because a retailer happens to own valuable real estate assets, such as downtown store locations, does not necessarily mean that the retailer has outstanding capabilities and merchandizing skills. A rival retailer coming into town that is able to acquire equally good locations and that benefits from outstanding operating skills would have a stronger competitive advantage than the retailer with only the good real estate assets. The same holds true for a company owning a mine; ownership does not necessarily create an advantage. What if the mine is no longer operating?

Similarly a high-tech start-up might own one or two strong patents, but these patents alone do not give it a competitive advantage. The patents give competitive advantage to the firm only when they are put to productive use in the business, say by protecting a particular process or product. Otherwise, the start-up would be better off selling the patents or licensing the rights to someone else who could use them. What would help to create competitive advantage for the start-up are the organizational skills of managing the overall patent portfolio and being expert at negotiating technology transfer agreements involving licensing rights for a valuable royalty rate and up-front milestone payments. (See Chapters 8, 14, and 20 for more information on royalty rates and up-front milestone payments.)

In summary, organizational capabilities combine with the firm's position in the market to create competitive advantage; resources alone do not confer competitive advantage until they are put to productive use. As a final example, consider how a firm's position in an industry can help it create competitive advantage, especially if that position is combined with superior organizational capabilities. Picture a large energy company that is a low-cost leader in its industry. It enjoys economies of scale due to its dominant market share position compared to smaller rivals. Furthermore, it builds on this competitive positioning by a relentless focus on cost efficiencies in all its operations and processes. A dominant position combined with organizational efficiency is what creates superior competitive advantage for this company.

Strategy from the Inside or the Outside

Sometimes the dilemma facing novices is knowing how and where to begin the process of strategy formulation: Some strategy textbooks begin the process by starting from the outside, beginning with external analysis, while others start from the inside and begin with internal analysis. Either way works so long as *both* perspectives are captured.

- The outside-looking inward approach means creating a strategy based on doing the external analyses and industry studies. This leads to identifying the key success factors of the industry, then asking: What resources and capabilities are needed to deliver these industry KSFs?

- The inside-looking outward approach is to formulate strategy by asking what can the firm do better than its rivals. This methodology is known as the core competency approach to strategy formulation. The important point is not to stop at the core competencies but to link the organizational capabilities to the KSFs of the industry and to the customer perspective.

When done properly, either way of formulating strategy is acceptable. The point is to take the firm's position into account with the external analysis of the industry and link it to the firm's organizational capabilities through the process of internal analysis. This way the strategist is taking into account all the pertinent factors necessary to create competitive advantage: strategic positioning combined with organizational capabilities and their underlying resources.

Practical Challenges When Using the Core Competencies Approach to Strategy

In the real world (away from textbooks), when the strategy team begins to identify the firm's core competencies or distinctive capabilities, the internal audit often yields ambiguous results. This is particularly true if the organization's core competencies are complex. Complexity arises because the expertise and know-how are combined with intangibles, such as the firm's reputation, customer loyalty, and various organizational processes, including sophisticated computer systems and operating routines. It may not be easy to tell what it is that makes one firm outstanding and another in the same industry only mediocre. Since it is difficult to identify and reach a consensus about an organization's "core" competencies, the ambiguity may lead to a case of wishful thinking on the part of management. We are reminded of the Dilbert cartoon where the pointy-haired boss says, "We need to find a way to close the gap between our strategy and our capabilities." Then Wally, the lazy engineer, pipes back, "Why don't we just pretend we're good at something and call it our strategy."[31]

UNDERSTANDING ORGANIZATIONS AND THEIR CULTURES

There are many ways to describe and understand the internal context of an organization and come to appreciate its unique culture. We introduce two more methodologies. A classic method that has withstood the test of time is the Seven-S Framework, developed jointly by Anthony Athos, Thomas J. Peters, Richard T. Pascale, Julien R. Philips, and Robert H Waterman Jr. while they were working at McKinsey & Company.[32] The second method is called PARC, for the People, Architecture, Routines, and Culture of the firm. (Note that this PARC approach has nothing to do with the Palo Alto Research Center [PARC] that was founded by Xerox Research.) The People, Architecture, Routines, and Culture approach leads us into a discussion on the problems of organizational design. There we contemplate the problem of the new venture starting up and how the entrepreneur might consider designing the new organization to fit the environment and the strategy of the start-up.

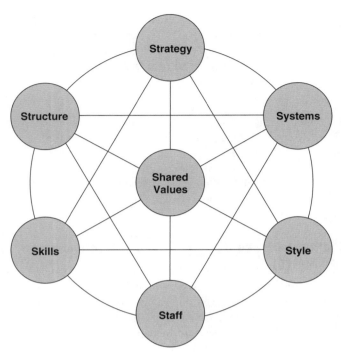

Seven-S Framework

The Seven-S framework is a simple tool used to audit organizations. By using it, a manager is able to compare systematically the internal features and processes of two or more firms. The original Seven S's were strategy, structure, system, style, staff, skills, and superordinate goals, although now most strategy textbooks substitute "shared values" for "superordinate goals." Each element is interrelated to the other, thus creating a system view of an organization's culture and organizational design. (Refer to Figure 3.13.)

Strategy　*Strategy* consists of analysis of environment, competition, customer needs, and the firm's own strengths and weaknesses, leading to a plan or course of action that determines the allocation of a firm's scarce resources, over time, to reach identified goals.

Structure　*Structure* is the organizational architecture of the firm as depicted in its organizational chart. Is the firm organized by divisions? By functions? Is management responsibility centralized or decentralized? Looking beyond the formal organization, the analyst should also describe how the separate entities of the organization are tied together. Do they share solid or dotted-line reporting relationships? Where are the centers of decision-making status, power, and control?

Systems   *Systems* refers to the formal planning and budget, financial reporting, and information processing systems of the firm. It also includes the recruiting and compensation policies applied to the employees by the firm's human resources systems. It also (and importantly) includes the firm's informal routines, usually referred to as this-is-how-things-are-done-around-here routine. How are individual and team performance measured and rewarded? How do the resource allocation and budget systems work in practice? What are the formats (face-to-face? e-mail? phone? dinners?) for informal meetings? How are conflicts resolved?

Staff   *Staff* refers to the demographic, educational, and professional background of the employees who work within the firm. What are the most important personnel selection criteria and promotion factors? For instance, who are the role models? How diverse are the personnel and senior management? Is the company run by engineers or brand managers? Does senior management have MBAs or PhDs? What kinds of work experiences are considered key for promotion—for instance, a typical career path might mean time spent in the finance function or handling key accounts, or managing new product development or being responsible for a region overseas. What sorts of language skills are found in the firm?

Style   *Style* provides a description of the culture of the firm. How do managers behave toward each other? Is teamwork recognized and rewarded? What are common communication patterns: trusting or fearful? Does the organization appear to make consensual decisions, or is it led by one or two strong leaders or key groups? Is the organization timid or bold when it comes to adopting change? Does the culture appear to be more open or closed? How is time allocated, and where do people spend their time? Are managers out in the field with customers? Who are the role models?

Shared Values   The term *shared values* refers to the significant meanings or central beliefs that organizational members share. These overarching values may serve as tiebreakers when making decisions. What are the espoused values compared to what really takes place? What are the transcendent values? How is the organization serving society? What are the internal shared values binding one employee to the next? How does the company behave toward its stakeholders and the environment?

Skills   *Skills* consist of the one or two core competencies or distinctive capabilities of the organization that truly differentiate it from the competition.

CHALLENGES OF ORGANIZATIONAL DESIGN

To frame the problems of organizational design, we turn to the People, Architecture, Routines and Culture or PARC framework. Organizational design and strategy should depend on each other, especially when considering the start-up situation of a new high-technology firm. The organizational design should be developed in accordance with the firm's strategy. Consequently, there is no such thing as one best design for a start-up. Although it is true that each organization faces the same big issues, namely the *coordination problem* and the *cooperation problem,*[33] the organizational solution to these issues will vary widely.

- The essence of the *coordination* problem is coordinating the efforts of the individuals, teams, and groups within the firm. The other aspect is coordinating the deployment of the firm's resources or assets in an effective and efficient way.
- The *cooperation* (or incentive) problem refers to the need to get people to cooperate to work together. Management needs to "elicit the right amount and type of effort in the presence of hidden information and hidden action."[34] For that, organizations offer various forms of incentives and use different monitoring and control schemes. Not everyone working in a firm shares the same goals or motivations. Overcoming goal conflicts or so-called agency problems (when employees pursue self-serving goals instead of the firm's goals) is what we mean when we talk about the cooperation problem. Resolving the agency problem requires an organization design effective ways to reward, monitor, and supervise people within the hierarchy of the firm.

PARC Framework

To work on coordination and cooperation issues, management has at its disposal at least three design parameters or elements. The three levers are the Architecture, Routines and Culture of the firm.[35] To these three, some authors add the People in the organization. These four components collectively make up the PARCs of the firm and what we refer to as the PARC framework.[36] (See Figure 3.14.)

Briefly, the elements of organizational design are summarized next using our synthesis of the schema developed by various authors:[37]

- *Architecture* is designing the "boundaries of the firm" (what activities are done inside the firm and what activities are done outside by third parties). It includes

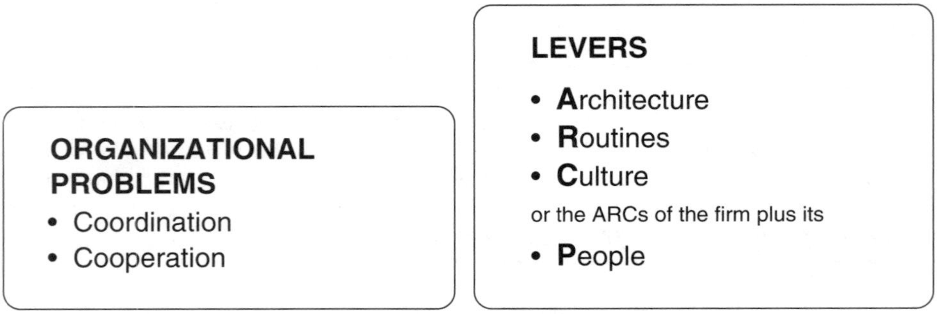

ORGANIZATIONAL PROBLEMS
- Coordination
- Cooperation

LEVERS
- **A**rchitecture
- **R**outines
- **C**ulture
or the ARCs of the firm plus its
- **P**eople

FIGURE 3.14   Basic Organizational Problems and Levers to Work on Them
Source: Adapted from Garth Saloner, Andrea Shepard, and Joel M. Podolny, *Strategic Management* (Hoboken, NJ: John Wiley & Sons, 2004), 65–92.

such parameters as the financing, ownership, and governance structure of the firm. Besides the reporting relationships and formal organizational chart, the Architecture of different firms varies in terms of their use of personal networks that link people across the firm and to others outside the firm's boundaries. The linking mechanism might refer to management's informal and formal decisions such as putting key personnel on ad hoc internal task forces, or assigning them to special functional teams, or formally nominating them to serve on outside committees that set industry standards. Architecture roughly corresponds to the structure portion of the Seven-S framework, but it includes other aspects as well.

- *Routines* include all the managerial processes, policies, and procedures that shape managerial decision making. They cover both formal and informal processes for how decisions are made, resources are deployed, performance is monitored, and results are rewarded. They include how information is solicited, gathered, filtered, transformed, and transmitted to management. Routines also include how decision authority is distributed within the firm, and roughly correspond to the strategy and systems portion of the Seven-S framework.
- *Culture* includes the softer aspects of the fundamental shared values of the people in the firm. It encompasses the shared values and beliefs of the people working within the organization and how their mental models work; how their mind-sets frame their interpretation of events taking place inside and outside the organization. It is more or less a combination of the shared values, staff, and style portions of the Seven-S framework.

Using Organizational Design to Strategic Advantage

The entrepreneurial team leading a start-up company is faced with a complicated organizational design problem. A firm's performance depends on interactions taking place among three main variables: the strategy, the organization, and the environment or ecosystem of the firm. Ideally the strategy and the organizational design needs are aligned and have a suitable fit with the firm's environment; yet consideration also needs to be given to the future, so that as the environment shifts, the firm's strategy and organization can cope with the inevitable but unpredictable changes.

We can frame the economic optimization problem facing the entrepreneur as one of trying to maximize firm performance given these constraints: the strategy, the organization, and the environment.[38] The choice variables for a business strategy are its goals, scope, competitive advantage, and strategic rationale. The organizational design variables for the firm are its people, architecture, routines, and culture. With so many variables and combinations, it should be clearly seen that there is no single "magic formula" to create economic value and enable the firm to keep ahead of its competitive rivals. In the language of mathematics, it is a complex system, and there are many possible solutions. We draw two important conclusions. First, firm performance depends on three variables: strategy, organization, and environment; therefore, companies can choose to create economic value in multiple ways. Second, the strategy and the organizational design must be developed simultaneously, as both are intimately linked to the firm's activities and ultimately its performance. What we have just explained is a dynamic, contingent way of viewing strategy and organizational design.

Pulling It All Together: Combining the Environment, the Organization, and the Strategy

We have described the complete processes of external and internal analysis. We have summarized how the strategic management process works. We also have discussed the challenges of organizational design and strategic fit in an environment that constantly changes. What lies ahead is tying together the strategic context environmental analysis and the organizational design to create a compelling and sustainable strategy that can be implemented and carried out.

Author John Roberts, leading economist, scholar, educator, and expert on business strategy and organization, elaborates more on the concept of strategic fit and organizational change in his book *The Modern Firm*, which won *The Economist*'s Best Business Book prize for 2004:

> *There is a logic underlying the idea of "fit." Certain strategies and organizational designs do fit one another and the environment, and thus produce good performance, and others do not. ... These relations arise for both technological and behavioral reasons. Recognizing these relations and understanding their implications can guide the [strategy] design problem.*[39]

Organizational Design: Tightly Coupled or Loosely Coupled?

Roberts goes on to discuss how some firms have organizational designs that are "tightly coupled" and others that are "loosely coupled." *Tightly coupled* means "the extent to which the organization is finely tuned to maximize performance against a particular strategy and environment." *Loosely coupled* means the organization is "designed to work reasonably well in the face of change."[40]

What are the implications of coupling? It implies that a tightly coupled organization will have functional strategies and policies that fit well with one another. They also will mesh well with the overall company strategy and with external environment—that is, until such a time as the firm's environment undergoes drastic change. When the environment turns turbulent, the necessary information about markets and technologies may not reach top executives in time to allow for top-down strategy formulation.

With rapidly changing environments, a loosely coupled organizational design comes to the fore. These designs are sometimes called a flexible or modular architecture for the firm. Contractual strategic alliances are an ideal organizational design solution for forming a loosely coupled organization, especially for a small start-up trying to keep its options open while coping with turbulence in the high-technology environment.

An example of a high-technology start-up company that grew very rapidly and was able to scale up its operations successfully because of its modular architecture and flexible organizational design is Cisco Systems, Inc. (www.cisco.com) of San Jose, California, which develops Internet Protocol–based networking hardware and software solutions. Cisco exploits internal R&D efforts with strategic alliances, minority investments, and acquisitions. It has an exceptional track record in integrating high-technology acquisitions. Part of the reason for its outstanding success is the loosely coupled and modular design of its organizational architecture, which makes swapping out maturing businesses and swapping in newer acquired businesses much easier than for rivals that are more tightly coupled.

HOW ORGANIZATIONS SURVIVE TURBULENCE AND CHANGE

If you are successful in creating a business, particularly if it is a family-owned business, you eventually might ask: How can we help our firm keep on creating a sustainable advantage for generation after generation? Strategy scholars will answer that there is no one simple recipe to achieve this. Current academic theories of strategy cannot predict accurately which firms will thrive and which will perish in the ecosystems out there in the messy real world. The truth is that based on current scholarly research and best practice, today's managers ought to accept that, so far, there are only incomplete and partial answers to this simple yet fundamental question: How do we keep a firm viable for generations?

What we do know is that managing the management succession process is extremely important in *any* business, not just a family business, wishing to pass the firm down from one generation to the next. Corporate governance is also important. We deal with this topic in Chapter 10.

Strategy scholars suggest that part of the secret for enduring success, especially in high-technology environments, is to create a culture and organizational design that is more nimble, more flexible, more responsive, and allows for faster learning than other rivals. Professor David J. Teece of the University of California, Berkeley, and his colleagues refer to these *dynamic capabilities* as the "firm's ability to integrate, build, and reconfigure internal and external competences to address rapidly changing environments."[41] We agree that part of the key to enduring success is becoming a more agile and forward-looking organization.

The joint research of Professors Michael Tushman of Harvard University and Charles O'Reilly III of Stanford University (both noted scholars in management and innovation) helps to illuminate how a firm may become more agile and forward looking. Based on their field research, Tushman and O'Reilly believe that organizations have to "simultaneously manage two forces, stability and change."[42] They call this juggling act instilling "ambidexterity as a dynamic capability" within the organization—which means sustaining incremental change while simultaneously leading revolutionary change in different parts of the organization.[43] In Chapter 4, we show you how to diagnose the strategic change context of your firm's industry so you can tell whether it is experiencing incremental or evolutionary change or if your industry is undergoing disruptive or revolutionary change.

Motivating People to Use the Strategy

We also think that part of the key to enduring success is motivating the people working for the organization and convincing them that they are capable of doing more than they thought they could. Corporate culture and the behavior of senior management are influential in this process.

Being better at executing strategy is another key factor for enduring success. Rene McPherson, chief executive officer of Dana Corporation and former dean of the Stanford Graduate School of Business, used to say to his colleagues at the business school: "Developing a strategy is the easy part; the hard part is getting people to do it."[44] From his years of managerial experience, McPherson knew that if the strategy planners are separated from the doers (the people carrying out the plans), then the managerial buy-in and acceptance of the strategy will be missing. Implementation will inevitably be problematic. Briefly, we think some practical solutions to the knowing–doing gap would be for organizations to:

- Integrate the doers and the planners.
- Have line managers doing their own planning and analysis.
- Focus on strategic thinking for *everybody*, not just for corporate staff or outside strategy consultants.
- Become a learning organization capable of transferring and assimilating knowledge from one part of the organization to another.

REFLECTIONS ON STRATEGY IN THE ENTREPRENEURIAL CONTEXT

Better strategic thinking is a benefit of carrying out a strategy process with your team of managers. No written plan will ever be a substitute for strategic thinking. Strategic thinking, however, should *not* be a once-a-year exercise. It should be incorporated into the team's everyday thinking and approach to business. It is a mind-set, not a set of documents or slides.

High-technology firms, in particular, must navigate rapidly changing external environments. They must have a process that allows them to make strategic decisions more rapidly and to change their strategy more frequently than the annual planning process used by many firms in other industries. They need to be agile, flexible, and responsive to market needs. Expect a high-technology firm's strategy to change and evolve quickly as events unfold.

For your own high-technology start-up, do not allow the excuses that "our industry is changing too fast" or "we have no time to do strategy" to avoid deciding on a strategic direction and formulating strategies with your team. With its judgment and managerial experience, the team determines when to adjust the navigation coordinates for the strategic direction and how frequently to make any adjustments. Widely varying firm circumstances and industry contexts make generalizations unwise. There are no strict rules on how to make these decisions.

We do recommend that you and your management team articulate the long-term goals, scope, sustainable competitive advantage, and strategic rationale of your organization's business strategy. Each member of the senior management team should agree on these elements. Be cognizant that setting a clear sense of direction for the firm enables *any* manager, not just the most senior ones, to make better decisions. Communication of the strategy is vital. So, too, is soliciting feedback on the strategy and the progress made toward its implementation from all levels of the organization and from across the functions. If one of the purposes of strategy is to help coordinate and bring a sense of direction to the firm, all managers must be able to understand the strategy, know their role in carrying it out, and be able to communicate it clearly to their employees.

As an entrepreneur, we hope you cultivate a habit of constantly scanning the external environment to recognize strategic opportunities early. Top managers need to take the time to identify significant long-term global trends. More important, they also must stop and make time to reflect about the implications of these trends for their organization. Contemplating the trends is not enough. They need to follow through and do something about the conclusions, either by deploying assets or by building up new capabilities. This way the company will be ready to take advantage of the trends. As we said in Chapter 1, strategic insight and spotting opportunity is where creative ideas incubate and innovation begins.

We have barely scratched the surface of strategy in this chapter. Even so, we hope we have lifted the veil somewhat on the most commonly used analytical tools and frameworks. Our aim was to help you get started on thinking more strategically and dynamically. In our next chapter, we journey on to more advanced strategy topics in which we discuss ways managers gain scale, restructure, and harvest businesses as the need or opportunity arises.

CHAPTER TAKEAWAYS

- Conceptually there are three levels of strategy: corporate, business, and functional. We recommend starting at the business level when formulating a competitive strategy for your high-tech venture.
- The basic elements of a business strategy are long-term goals, scope, sustainable competitive advantage, and strategic rationale.
- Formulate strategies that build competitive advantage around your organization's strengths, provided they are of strategic importance to your industry and will create value for your target customers.
- Appraising an organization's resources and capabilities is a way to determine whether you can deliver your product or service to the customer alone or if you need to access resources or capabilities through a contractual relationship (alliance or joint venture) or by means of a corporate combination (merger or acquisition). We discuss this more in later chapters.
- Creativity aids in strategy formulation and organizational design. There is no one template on how to do use creativity to enhance a firm's competitive strategy or organizational culture. Each organization will need to discover its own way and come up with its own unique solutions.
- Hiring talented, committed, and dedicated people who share the venture's vision and values is vital. So, too, is communication. If these talented people do not understand the strategy, how can they help implement it?
- It is ever so much easier to create strategies than to get them done. Seek out the early involvement and commitment of the managers tasked with carrying out the strategy. Doing so will aid in achieving the strategy.
- Go to www.innovationtocashflows.com, where you will find:
    - Appendix 3.1: Porter's Cluster Theory Applied to San Diego's Biotechnology Cluster.
    - Appendix 3.2: Fictional Case Study of WineOnline.com.

CHAPTER 4

Strategies to Grow, Restructure, or Harvest Your Business

In this chapter, we examine some of the ways managers may grow, restructure, or harvest businesses, depending on their firm's strategic aims and stage of development. It is important for entrepreneurs to understand not only avenues toward growth but also how corporate restructurings may yield interesting opportunities for start-ups that are able to take advantage of them. Furthermore, boards of directors, investors, company founders, and senior managers will each play a role in deciding how best to harvest their equity stakes in the venture. Sometimes the exit strategy may mean passing the company on to the next generation of owners; at other times, it may mean taking a private firm public or selling out to a larger rival. These are all weighty decisions. They require expert information and financial, tax, and legal advice, and should be made only after careful analysis and reflection. In the end, a consensus will need to emerge on the best ways the firm should implement a desired strategy or series of contingent strategies, depending on how events unfold in the future.

Here we explain and explore the use of mergers and acquisitions (M&A), minority investments, cross-shareholding agreements, and joint ventures as important means by which firms may enter new markets, gain scale quickly, and thereby grow faster. We discuss the mechanisms commonly used to reduce the size or to change the focus of an existing company via sales of minority interests, spin-offs, carve-outs, split-offs, and tracking stock. (We explain the meaning of these terms in this chapter.) Although there are many ways to divest, exit, or harvest businesses, we describe only the most common ones: management buyouts, leveraged buyouts, trade sales, initial public offerings (IPOs), liquidations, and financial reorganizations.

We know from our own experiences as entrepreneurs that corporate restructurings offer many opportunities, especially for small start-ups. For instance, many high-technology ventures will be headed up by senior managers who have left the corporate scene, either voluntarily or involuntarily, as a result of a restructuring.[1] Often the first customer of such a start-up will be the chief executive's former firm, which may wish to downsize and outsource certain activities or functions to colleagues they trust. All might be fine for a while. Yet if that former firm were to undergo yet another merger or takeover, the new venture's most important customer relationships might be ruptured or even disappear because of the subsequent restructuring. Consequently, it is important to understand the ways that corporations carry out their strategies, as these corporate actions may impact, either positively or negatively, your own entrepreneurial venture—if not immediately, then maybe in a few years' time.

For instance, in a positive set of scenarios, your first venture may be one of the fortunate few that flourishes. Perhaps you or your investors want to exit by selling a stake in the company to a larger multinational or to a private equity group, perhaps leading eventually to a listing on a public stock exchange.

It could also be that your company or your family business might go through a crisis and need to sell parts (or all) of itself to a multinational corporation or to a private equity investor syndicate experienced in distressed company turnarounds. In an even worse scenario, your venture or family firm might be forced into liquidation and face bankruptcy if it has burned through its cash or is incapable of meeting loan covenants or returning to profitability. It is wise to think through these end-game scenarios and reflect ahead of time about the appropriate response. Are you and your team prepared if the worst-case scenario materializes?

Before immediately taking action, however, we emphasize that all managers should accurately diagnose the situational context facing their firm and its industry. Executives must understand the external and internal context of the firm. They need to figure out how long a time frame they have in which to carry out any planned strategic changes. Crisis management, whether in a large firm or a small one, will require drastic and quick action on the part of senior management to stem the flow of losses and conserve cash. While it is true that existing processes can be fine-tuned relatively quickly, much more time is needed to extend a firm's core capabilities or to make a radical transformational overhaul. Managers should not only consider what strategic options they have but also reflect carefully on how long they have to do them. It may help narrow the choices from what is possible to what is feasible.

We hope that this chapter helps you think through all these varied options more strategically. In so doing, you should be better prepared to ask the right questions of your board members, senior management team, and financial and legal advisors. We also hope it enables you to think more broadly about the kinds of strategic actions you can take to enhance your firm's performance, depending on your particular context.

GROWING

The board of directors expects senior management to answer the basic corporate strategy question: "How to grow?" Sometimes senior management will seek to grow the firm by investing in research and developing new products. If the work is carried out within the boundaries of the firm, then financial and legal advisers will often say that management has chosen the route of *organic growth*. At other times, the firm needs to go outside the boundaries of the firm. If the firm taps other companies' or other organizations' capabilities or resources, then financial and legal advisers will say that management has chosen the route of *inorganic growth*. As shown in Figure 4.1, a large firm has a wide variety of options for inorganic growth: It can do mergers and acquisitions, make minority investments in external companies (either publicly trading or privately held), create joint ventures, or build strategic alliance partnerships with innovative ventures or research organizations in order to extend the firm's global reach, competencies, and access to missing resources.

In reality, the processes of innovation and stimulating firm growth are very fluid and dynamic, unlike the static boxes of our drawing. As firms carry out their strategies by linking up to external partners, their own organizations are likely to

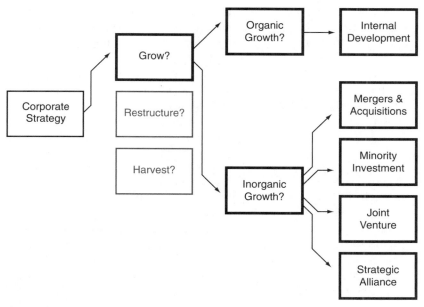

FIGURE 4.1 Ways to Grow

change as they grow and learn in the process. Hence we think the terms *organic* and *inorganic* growth are somewhat misleading—especially if you agree with us that all growth is a learning process and should be viewed as natural and organic. We think all firms depend, in a myriad of ways, on their various stakeholders to help them grow and innovate.[2]

Even so, the nomenclature lingers on of organic growth versus inorganic growth—sometimes referred to as the make-or-buy decision (i.e., make it inside the company or buy the resources and capabilities from the outside). These terms are commonly used on Wall Street or the City of London and especially in the financial press, so we define these words so that our readers are clear about their meaning. Keep in mind, however, that we prefer a much more porous and dynamic view of innovation. As you look at Figure 4.1, visualize the participants in transactions learning and changing whenever they are involved in strategic alliances, joint ventures, or mergers and acquisitions. Know, too, that exposure to outside influences typically stimulates a firm's internal research and development processes.

Merger

In a *merger*, the firms involved in the transaction are joined and absorbed, one into the other. They will lose their separate identities and, according to law, will become a consolidated new entity. For instance, the Swiss merger of Ciba-Geigy and Sandoz took place in 1996. Out of the restructured life sciences portions of the two companies emerged a new global healthcare company known as Novartis AG (NYSE: NVS). The corporate name Novartis means "New Arts." It was purposely chosen to signal the intent to create a new corporate culture right from the beginning of the fusion. This was especially important, yet difficult to do, as the origins of Geigy dated back to 1758, whereas Ciba was founded in 1859. When these two proud rivals merged in 1970, they chose the name Ciba-Geigy and kept the brand names in the corporate name. Sandoz, although younger than Geigy, also had a proud history, dating back 110 years. Sandoz, located in Basel, Switzerland, near the Rhine River, had started operations in 1886 as a chemical company. Hence the creation of Novartis involved the postmerger integration of three distinct cultures: that of Geigy, Ciba, and Sandoz.

Acquisition

In an *acquisition*, one firm purchases and takes over the other—either by buying out its assets or by buying up a controlling equity stake and assuming the target's liabilities. For instance, ING, the Dutch banking behemoth, acquired Barings, the venerated merchant bank whose customers included the Queen of England, for a symbolic one pound sterling for its equity, while at the same time ING assumed Barings' debts, obligations, and open trading positions. The rogue trader Nick Leeson, in Singapore, had put the venerable merchant bank's capital position in jeopardy with his unauthorized trades, which led to the takeover and rescue by ING.

Minority Investments and Cross-Shareholding Arrangements

In a *minority investment*, the buyer makes a small equity investment in the target firm (or the seller). To be considered a minority shareholding, the amount must be less than a controlling stake (in other words, less than 50 percent). For accounting purposes, a minority stake is usually not consolidated on the balance sheet if it is less than 25 percent.

A *cross-shareholding arrangement* is a form of minority investment and occurs when two or more firms take *mutual* equity stakes in each other. This is quite common in Italy and France and many other countries. In Japan, the term *keiretsu* refers to a network of businesses that own stakes in one another as a sign of collaboration, commitment, and mutual support. Often keiretsu involve cross-holdings between large manufacturers and suppliers of components or raw materials. *Zaibutsu* refers to collaboration only between the four largest companies in Japan. In South Korea, the major family-controlled business conglomerates that arose in the country after World War II are called *cheabols*. Like the keiretsu in Japan, the *cheabols* often have numerous cross-shareholdings among their satellite companies. Famous South Korean *cheabols* include LG and Samsung Group.

Joint Ventures

In a *joint venture*, typically a *separate* legal entity is set up (called the joint venture company). Joint ventures may be either equity joint ventures or nonequity joint ventures. (Types of joint ventures are discussed further in Chapter 6.) Equity commitments help to align each party's goals and economic interests while sharing the risks of the new venture. By creating a separate legal entity, the risks of lawsuits arising from the activities of the joint venture are "ring-fenced" (kept away from the parent companies). Isolating legal risks may be important, for instance, in the pharmaceutical industry, where a separate joint venture may be set up to do late-stage clinical trials of a risky new treatment, where the risk of subsequent litigation may be higher than normal. The joint venture shareholder agreement should specify investment rights, operational responsibilities, voting control, exit alternatives, and generally the allocation of risks and rewards. Each party to the joint venture may choose to contribute capital, intellectual property rights, or experience and know-how to the new entity. Know-how is often transferred by assigning key personnel to work for the joint venture as employees. The proportions and rights of ownership are negotiable among the various parties and will depend on relative bargaining power and skill at negotiating and crafting agreements. (For more on shareholder agreements and points to consider when drafting legal documents of investment terms, refer to Chapters 9 and 10.)

Sometimes joint ventures are set up between two firms on an even 50 percent–50 percent basis as a sign of mutual trust and collaborative spirit. Conventional wisdom suggests that this even split of power can lead to conflicts when choosing strategies or making decisions, although this is not always the case. To reduce the potential for deadlock, one party may be given the right to exercise the tie-breaking vote. As mentioned, it is important to define the roles of the parties to a joint venture and also decide on how to dissolve a joint venture, as this type of organizational structure tends to be unstable. For example, in the oil business, it is common to set up joint ventures to explore and drill for crude oil and gas. One joint venture partner is named the managing partner and is responsible for operating the joint venture company. The other parties, the investing partners, do not have responsibility for operating decisions or control of the venture. The joint venture would be dissolved if the operators find insufficient crude oil or gas reserves to exploit profitably. (For more on energy joint ventures, see Chapter 6.)

RESTRUCTURING

If the executive team decides it is best to restructure the firm, there are a number of different methods to carry out this decision, as shown in Figure 4.2. The basic idea of restructuring under crisis conditions is to stop losses, also known as the bleeding of red ink, and conserve precious cash. Managers should then concentrate on stabilizing the condition of the core business and seek ways to future revenue and profit growth. If the firm is not in critical condition—in other words, not in the midst of a crisis—the executive team has more time to do a more fundamental transformation of the firm. We discuss these trade-offs in more detail toward the end of the chapter.

Sale of Minority Interests

Here the firm that wishes to restructure sells an equity stake to another firm. In doing so, the seller gains an infusion of fresh capital and a new shareholder that might be willing to contribute specialized know-how, technology, or resources. An alternative to selling a minority stake to an interested third party is to offer the shares in a public offering. At times, family businesses sell off a minority interest in the firm to a larger

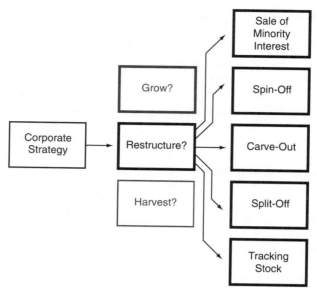

FIGURE 4.2 Ways to Restructure

company with the idea of eventually having the larger firm take over the business (if it all works out). This is what happened to a leading ice-cream manufacturer and distributor Dreyer's Grand Ice Cream of Oakland, California. Initially it sold a 23 percent equity stake in itself to Swiss multinational Nestlé (SWS: NESN), of Vevey, Switzerland. In June 2002, Nestlé consolidated its holdings in Dreyer's to a 67 percent controlling stake, then in January 2006, Nestlé SA acquired 100 percent of Dreyer's Grand Ice Cream Holdings, Inc. Dreyer's became a wholly-owned subsidiary of Nestlé.[3]

Spin-Off

In a spin-off, a publicly listed parent company typically distributes shares of a subsidiary or business entity to the parent's shareholders in the form of a stock dividend. That means no cash is exchanged. Where there was one listed company before the transaction, afterward there will be two. Examples of spin-offs include: Lucent Technologies that was spun off from AT&T in 1996; Agilent Technologies was formed in 1999 by a spin-off of Hewlett-Packard's former test-and-measurement equipment division. A famous example of a spin-off was the 1995 breakup of the ITT conglomerate[4] into these separate businesses: diversified industrial, insurance, and hotels and gaming.

Two spin-offs were part of the Ciba-Geigy and Sandoz restructuring and merger that created Novartis, the pharmaceutical example we described earlier in the "Merger" section. The spin-off operations took place in two phases. In 1995, Sandoz moved first and spun off its specialty chemicals division into a new entity called the Clariant Corporation (CLN traded on Virt-X), based in Muttenz (near Basel), Switzerland.[5] In 1997, Novartis spun off its specialty chemicals businesses into a separate listed company called Ciba Specialty Chemicals Inc., which was the largest spin-off in Europe at that time. Ten years later, in 2007, Ciba Specialty Chemicals Inc. rebranded itself to Ciba, Inc. (SWX: CIBN). Sandoz and then Novartis both had the same intent in doing the spin-offs: to focus on the core pharmaceutical businesses and exit from specialty chemicals.

Carve-Out

In a *carve-out,* the parent company reorganizes a subsidiary, which is to be broken off and placed in a separate entity. Then the parent company sells a minority stake in the subsidiary (usually 20 percent or less) to the public by doing an initial public offering (IPO). The parent company gets cash in exchange for the shares, reduces its holding in the subsidiary, and creates more transparency for outside shareholders and analysts to value the parent's remaining businesses. The listed subsidiary benefits from more analyst scrutiny and coverage. After the IPO, the parent company may decide to spin-off the remaining interests to its shareholders, or it may choose to reacquire the subsidiary once its value has been recognized by the market, or it may do an exchange of shares, explained next. Consequently, an equity carve-out gives management the flexibility to decide later on what it wants to do with the subsidiary. Thus an equity carve-out is like a *real option,* which, in this case, means that it gives management the option to delay a decision. It is a way of signaling to the capital markets that corporate management desires to refocus its core business without losing control over the carved-out subsidiary.

Example of a Combined Carve-Out and Exchange of Shares   During 2006, McDonald's Corporation (NYSE: MCD) of Oak Brook, Illinois, carried out a disposal of its equity investment in Chipotle's Mexican Grill founded in Denver, Colorado. McDonald's chose to make this disposal in various stages, by combining an equity carve-out and IPO followed by a subsequent tax-free exchange of shares. This is how McDonald's did it, according to its filings with the Securities Exchange Commission (SEC). In January 2006 Chipotle (NYSE: CMG) completed an initial primary public offering of 6.1 Class A common shares resulting in net proceeds to Chipotle of $121 million and a tax-free gain to McDonald's of $32 million (reflecting an increase in the carrying value of the company's investment as a result of the public offering). Concurrently with the Chipotle IPO, McDonald's sold an additional stake of 3 million Chipotle shares. In May 2006 McDonald's sold another portion of its equity investment in Chipotle's to the public. Then, in October 2006, McDonald's and Chipotle completely separated through a tax-free exchange of 16.5 million shares of Chipotle's Class B common stock for 18.6 million shares of McDonald's common stock. McDonald's received $329 million in cash proceeds and reacquired 18.6 million shares of its own stock via the tax-free exchange.[6]

Split-Off

A *split-off* (or exchange of shares) is a type of corporate reorganization where the stock of a subsidiary is exchanged for shares in the parent company. This creates a freestanding firm, no longer a subsidiary of the parent company. The owners of the split-off company are a subset of the former parent's shareholders (namely those shareholders who agreed to the split-off terms). For example, Viacom announced a split-off of its interest in Blockbuster in 2004. Viacom offered its shareholders the chance to receive stock in Blockbuster in exchange for an appropriate amount of Viacom stock.

Tracking Stock

The parent company issues a specially designed type of common stock (also known as designer stock) to track the performance of a particular division or subsidiary. When the parent company issues the tracking stock, all revenues and expenses of the applicable division are separated from the parent company's financial statements and bound to the tracking stock. There is no transfer of ownership, either in the form of equity interests or claims on the assets of the business. This means that the parent company still controls the subsidiary. The purpose of creating a tracking stock is to separate a subsidiary's higher growth from the parent's slower growth (or to provide more visibility to the division's profits as opposed to the parent company's losses.) Another reason to issue tracking stock is to highlight a subsidiary's high-growth prospects from a larger parent company's slower growth pattern. A famous tracking stock was the one issued by AT&T during the days of the Internet frenzy. On October 25, 2000, AT&T announced plans to offer AT&T common shareholders the chance to exchange shares of AT&T common (stock symbol "T") for shares of AT&T Wireless Group tracking stock (stock symbol "AWE") (AT&T).[7] The stock market subsequently crashed. Between November 2000 and January 2001, disgruntled purchasers of the AT&T Wireless Group tracking stock shares filed various class action lawsuits alleging violations of the U.S. federal securities laws—including the failure to disclose ongoing business problems at AT&T Wireless (Stanford Law School Class Action Clearinghouse).[8]

HARVESTING

Harvesting a business may signal many things. True, a "for sale" sign may mean a company is in distress and needs to being taken over and revitalized. It may also mean the opposite—that an organization has achieved all its milestones and its venture capital investors wish to take some of their invested money off the table at a handsome premium. Sometimes, in a family firm, the family members controlling the company are not unanimous about their wish to sell. A trade sale to another industrial buyer could signal that a family business has grown beyond the managerial capabilities of the early founders and that a faction of the family, with a majority of votes, wishes to bring in more professional management and a wider investor base to get the company to the next level of growth. The real reasons for a sale always merit close scrutiny. Try to understand the motivations of the buyer and seller in any transaction.

Some experienced managers cringe when thinking about how to completely exit a market or harvest a business. Emotionally, divestiture may be one of the most difficult decisions for senior managers to justify and carry out, especially if they have been working all their careers for the business unit or company to be sold. Exiting a business is not simple, especially as many nonmarket factors (political, social,

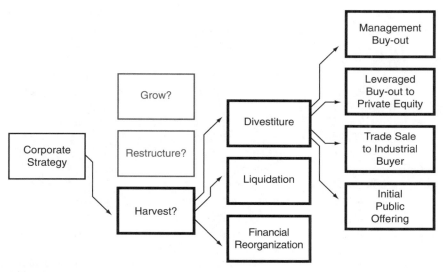

FIGURE 4.3 Ways to Harvest

regulatory, environmental, etc.) must be taken into account. For instance, in order to shutter a unionized plant, labor union support would be needed. Management would need to present the rationale for the closing with employees and local community and political leaders, and simultaneously inform the media any time job cuts are at stake. These issues and many more are involved in divestitures.

Divestiture means selling the entire business subsidiary (or business unit) or pieces of the businesses assets (e.g., a manufacturing plant, equipment, or real estate), typically to an unrelated party. In Figure 4.3, we highlight four types of sales: (1) management buy-out (MBO); (2) leveraged buy-out (LBO); (3) trade sale, which is typically to someone who is "in the same trade," that is, an industrial buyer often in the same sector, as opposed to a pure financial buyer such as a private equity firm or merchant bank; and (4) initial public offering.

Management Buy-Out

In a *management buy-out*, existing management (or select members of management) makes an offer to the existing shareholders to buy them out. Sometimes management acts alone; sometimes it acts in concert with other private equity players. To pay for the shares, management is: independently wealthy; has the reputation and capacity to borrow money from a bank; or can use the company's spare debt capacity to tap the capital markets for additional borrowings. In other words, the management typically puts itself, or the company, or both into debt to buy out the firm's existing shareholders.

The hope of the new owners-managers is that they can turn around the operations and make the company leaner (or meaner). They believe they have the expertise, focus, drive, and determination to operate the business faster and more insightfully than before. By making operational changes, they typically intend to increase revenues, lower costs, and thereby improve operating margins and increase operating cash flows. They will then use the additional cash flow to pay back the debt they assumed in doing the management buy-out. When making operational changes, they must be careful to remain in compliance with any bank debt covenants or other loan restrictions. Management buy-outs increase the financial risk of the company since it will be more highly leveraged (have more debt) than before the transaction. An example of an MBO would be the now private company SynCo Bio Partners BV, based in Amsterdam, the Netherlands. SynCo Bio Partners is a small contract manufacturing organization that specializes in biopharmaceuticals production. SynCo Bio Partners was formed as the result of a management buy-out by Dr. William J. Rutter, founder of Chiron Corporation, a pioneering biotechnology company based in Emeryville, California. Currently, Rutter serves as Chairman of the SynCo Bio Partner's Board of Directors, and is still active in the company, providing scientific and business advice.[9]

Leveraged Buy-Out

A *leveraged buy-out* is similar to a management buy-out, only unrelated parties are involved in the transaction. In other words, existing management is not part of the investor team wishing to gain control of the target. Suitable candidates for an LBO are a cash-generating business with unrealized debt capacity. Traditionally LBOs were done on more mature manufacturing businesses, which did not require large capital investments, rather than riskier, fast-growing high-technology businesses. Firms famous for doing LBOs are Kohlberg Kravis Roberts & Co., The Blackstone Group, The Carlyle Group, and Bain Capital.[10] Numerous business case studies have been written about LBOs. Business cases can be ordered from the major case clearinghouses of Harvard, Darden, Ivey, or the European Case Clearing House.

Trade Sale

In a *trade sale,* the business is sold either to a company competing in the same market (a direct rival) or to a firm that would like to enter the market (a new entrant). For example, the typical exit path for a life science investor begins early in the investment decision-making process. Biotechnology venture capitalists often consult with trade buyers (e.g., large pharmaceutical firms or major medical device manufacturers) to determine their potential interest in buying out the venture at a later stage in the development cycle. The alternative to a trade sale is either an IPO of equity shares or a sale to a financial party (either another private equity firm or a pure financial investor). The web sites of venture capital groups list which companies in their portfolios they have sold or taken public.

Initial Public Offering

An *initial public offering* is when a company's shareholders take a private firm and turn it into a publicly traded company by listing a portion of the shares on a stock exchange where the public may buy and sell them through qualified market makers and dealers. The normal process is for the company to hire a lead manager or organize a syndicate of investment banks that agree to underwrite the offering and place the shares in the market. If the shares are being issued by the company, and the proceeds from the sale go to it, the offering is called a *primary offering*. If the shares are being sold by existing shareholders (e.g., by the venture capital investors or the founders), the sale is known as a *secondary offering*. In a secondary offering, the proceeds go to the selling shareholders, not to the company. Strict regulations govern IPOs. For more information on them, read about them on the Investopedia web site (www.investopedia.com).

Liquidation

Liquidation is when a company is placed into bankruptcy (in the United States such a filing is done according to Chapter 7, Title 11 of the U.S. Bankruptcy Code). Liquidation is a terminal procedure for a company, meaning that the company ceases to exist at the end of the process.

In a voluntary liquidation, the shareholders agree to terminate the corporation's activities. In a compulsory liquidation, the insolvent company is placed in liquidation by order of the court that is acting according to the jurisdiction's bankruptcy code. Insolvency means that a party is unable to pay its creditors. Insolvency may be of two types: It may be related to a shortage of cash flow (cash flow insolvency) or to a balance sheet problem (balance sheet insolvency).

Sometimes a company or an individual is unable to pay liabilities as they become due because of insufficient cash flow. (For instance, an individual cannot meet his monthly mortgage payments due to insufficient liquid funds. Consequently, this person winds up defaulting on his home loan and the mortgage bank takes over ownership of the house.) Conversely, if liabilities exceed assets, the result is negative net assets on the balance sheet—a condition called balance sheet insolvency. However, the indebted party might still avoid default, if cash flow is sufficient to meet current debt obligations. (For instance, an individual is heavily indebted but has sufficient income to keep making monthly mortgage payments and thereby avoid defaulting on his home mortgage.)

A company with balance sheet insolvency may be able to avoid defaulting on its debt, if it can restructure its loans and strengthen its balance sheet in time, whereas a company with cash flow insolvency is at immediate risk of defaulting on its debt, unless the creditors promptly restructure the terms and conditions of the loan. Consequently the term insolvency is *not* a synonym for bankruptcy; the condition of bankruptcy is a determination that must be made by a court of law.

The differences between "liquidation," "bankruptcy," or "insolvency proceedings" vary according to each country's laws and the legal jurisdiction of the case. To illustrate the cross-border differences, in the United Kingdom, bankruptcy (in a strictly legal sense) refers only to individuals. Companies and other corporations enter into differently named legal insolvency procedures called "liquidation" and "administration," which we describe in the section "Financial Reorganization or Restructuring." In the United States, individuals as well as companies may go bankrupt. Depending on the situation, bankruptcy filings may be done according to one of several chapters of the U.S. Bankruptcy Code, such as Title 11, Chapter 7 (liquidation of assets); Chapter 11 (company or individual "reorganizations"); or Chapter 13 (debt restructuring and repayment with lowered debt covenant or payment plans).

In general, during a liquidation process, whether in the United States or the United Kingdom, the liquidator will attempt a distressed asset sale ("fire sale") of the company's business and assets. In other words, the liquidator may auction off to the highest bidder the company's assets and business or sell them at a substantial discount to a third party. As a result, the liquidation price may be far less than the fair market price if the company were still operating. After any sale (or failing any sale), the company is then wound up and dissolved (ceases to exist legally). As liquidation procedures are complex, it is advisable to consult with experienced legal and financial specialists when insolvency concerns arise.

Financial Reorganization or Restructuring

Financial reorganizations or *restructurings* are called recapitalizations if the debt-equity capital structure of a firm is changed. Sometimes financial reorganizations occur in the bankruptcy process (known in the United States as *reorganization in bankruptcy*). Chapter 11, Title 11 of the U.S. Bankruptcy Code covers, in general, reorganizations. In the United Kingdom, these types of recapitalizations are called "restructuring" (possibly through administration). The term *administration* is a specific type of formal insolvency procedure in the United Kingdom. It gives companies a breathing space to restructure, as it provides a moratorium period in which creditors cannot enforce against the company.

At other times—meaning outside of bankruptcy or insolvency proceedings—firms voluntarily take on more debt or repurchase their own equity shares, in order to fend off hostile raiders. The repurchase of shares as part of a voluntary financial reorganization is called a *leveraged restructuring*.

Log onto our web site at www.innovationtocashflows.com and browse "Resources" for a list of recommended finance textbooks on M&A, corporate reorganizations, and financial restructurings.

DIAGNOSING THE SITUATIONAL CONTEXT OF THE INDUSTRY

When deciding which corporate strategy is appropriate, executives need to carefully diagnose the situational context. A critical component to enact strategy is for senior leaders to exercise judgment and experience when picking the right rhythm and pace for carrying out a change effort. It is it helpful for executives to keep in mind not only the *nature of change* confronting their firm but also the available *time horizon* they have in which to implement strategic change.

Incremental or Evolutionary Change versus Disruptive or Revolutionary Change

Firms are always challenged by turbulence and change in their external environments. However, the magnitude of change varies. Is it an earthquake or a small tremor that is rocking your industry? Evolutionary or incremental changes can be distinguished from revolutionary or disruptive changes mainly by intensity—a series of small tremors characterizes an incremental change in contrast to a violent earthquake, which is more like a dramatic, revolutionary change.

Incremental or evolutionary change is the result of gradual industry adaptation to more or less foreseeable environmental developments. The competitive response by the industry players to incremental change is often subtle. Your firm may see the launch of newer product line extensions by rivals or experience a series of cumulative process improvements by suppliers of critical components. Evolutionary change does not usually challenge existing organizational routines, systems, structures, thought processes, or mental paradigms. It is a slow, gradual change. Most of the time, existing routines are able to cope with the scale of change.

Discontinuous or revolutionary change is a radical change process that is often disruptive to industry boundaries. It typically stems from unpredictable external forces, resulting in paradigm shifts in the way players compete in an industry. To illustrate disruptive or revolutionary change, imagine when a critical mass of key customers switches from one technology platform to another, such as when music lovers began changing from their vinyl records and old-fashioned record players and trying out new cassette tape players. Then came the switch from cassettes to more advanced optical compact disc players. Now music lovers are adapting to iPods. Another illustration is the changeover under way in the television broadcasting as the industry upgrades from analog to digital systems.

Disruptive change can pose a life-or-death threat for companies of any size. These sorts of major technology switchovers can be as threatening for the small, one-product start-up as for the large dinosaur corporation that is lagging behind rivals and is incapable of changing gears in time to compete in the new technology domain.[11] Small firms have the advantage of being more agile than larger firms; if they make a big mistake, however, it may be their last, since they typically have scarcer resources, especially money and human capital.

Larger firms may have more money and people to cushion mistakes, but they are susceptible to other factors: inertia, arrogance, old routines, and being locked into their former ways of viewing the world and framing strategic decisions. The theme of the paradox of success, sometimes called the success syndrome, is found in the writings of various authors on strategy, innovation, and the management of technology. For instance, Dorothy A. Leonard-Barton coined the phrase "how core competences may turn into core rigidities."[12] She points out that as a firm becomes more specialized and more successful at what it does best, it may be sowing the seeds of future problems and creating the conditions for stalemating innovation. Her message is that the flip side of a firm's core competence is that it may become the firm's future core rigidity.

Actually, recognizing when radical change is on the horizon is not always easy. Firms of any size may be blinded by the "tyranny of success" and by habitual ways of doing business. They may be incapable of changing their old ways in time. Based on extensive field research, Professors Michael A. Tushman of Harvard Business School and Charles O'Reilly III of Stanford University Graduate School of Business describe the need for the "ambidextrous organization which juggles incremental changes while simultaneously leading revolutionary change." They go on to say: "Great leaders need to be architects, network builders, and jugglers, fostering a culture that celebrates stability and change—in order to increase the firm's chances for success tomorrow."[13] We return to this bit of advice at the end of the next section.

Time Horizon: Short or Long Term

As we said, the definition of what is short term or long term depends very much on industry context and the firm's situation. For instance, what industry executives consider to be short term is orders of magnitude quicker for makers of wireless mobile telephone handsets than for manufacturers of heavy construction equipment. Managers need to diagnose carefully the time horizon they have in order to set the pace and rhythm for carrying out their strategic change agenda. The time horizon will also vary depending on the specifics of the situation confronting the firm's managers.

As shown in Figure 4.4, if the industry is experiencing incremental or evolutionary change, the appropriate management responses are likely to be either fine-tuning over the short time horizon or gaining new competencies over a longer time horizon. *Fine-tuning* means gaining efficiencies from incremental process improvements or more sales through the launch of product enhancements to existing product lines.

Gaining new competencies will take more time. They may be accomplished by launching multidisciplinary new product innovations. They may also be achieved by sending key employees and managers through advanced training and education programs as part of an ongoing talent renewal process. Furthermore, new competencies may be learned by participating in alliance collaborations or joint ventures and by making and properly integrating mergers and acquisitions.

However, if the industry is experiencing discontinuous change, the firm may already be in a crisis state where it is rapidly losing market share, bleeding cash, and staring down hostile stakeholders. Then the time horizon for taking action to save the company may be quite short. In a crisis, stemming the flow of bleeding red ink must be a top priority. Conserving cash is critical. Managerial indecision and delay is not an option. Action steps, and of the right sort, must be decided quickly.

If the industry is in the midst of an earthquake—a revolutionary, discontinuous, or disruptive change—and your firm is *not* in a precarious crisis situation, then

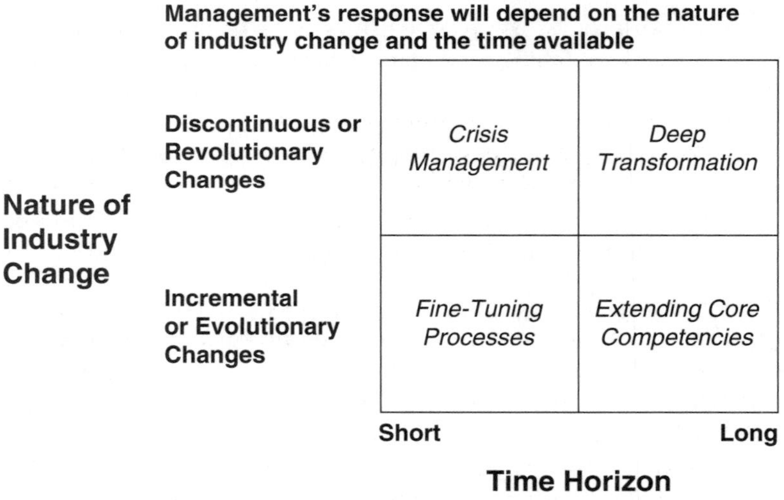

Management's response will depend on the nature of industry change and the time available

Nature of Industry Change		Short	Long
Discontinuous or Revolutionary Changes		*Crisis Management*	*Deep Transformation*
Incremental or Evolutionary Changes		*Fine-Tuning Processes*	*Extending Core Competencies*

Time Horizon

FIGURE 4.4   Which Strategic Change Process Is Appropriate?

management should consider carrying out a *transformational change* program. Merely extending existing competencies is not sufficient under these conditions. Managers need to play a whole new game and enact a paradigm shift within their organizations.

Tushman and O'Reilly put it this way:

> *The real test of leadership, then, is to be able to compete successfully in both the short-term through increasing the alignment or fit among strategy, structure, individual competencies, culture, and processes while simultaneously preparing for the inevitable organization revolutions required by shifting innovation streams. Managing an organization that can succeed at both incremental and radical innovation is like juggling.... For organizations, success for both today and tomorrow requires managers who can simultaneously juggle several inconsistent organizational architectures and cultures and who can build and manage ambidextrous organizations.*[14]

We agree. For the long-term survival of the firm, particularly under conditions of disruptive industry changes, the leaders of high-technology companies need to become ambidextrous jugglers.

CLOSING THOUGHTS

Earlier in this chapter, we explored the three main choices you and your team are likely to face in crafting the future strategy of a company: to grow, to restructure, or to harvest. We underline that all three of these choices (not just growth) may be faced by entrepreneurs in dynamic start-up situations. Sometimes in order to survive, a plant needs to be pruned or repotted. The same is true in start-ups. Setbacks are likely to occur that will require management to redeploy assets and resources. Sometimes drastic pruning is needed to save the firm, and the pruning may or may not work out as hoped. As we all know, one year the harvest may be bountiful; the next year the harvest yields next to nothing. It all depends on many factors, some of which (like the weather) are not under the farmer's control. The same truth applies when restructuring or harvesting a business. Timing the restructuring or the exit is extremely important, but it is not always within management's control. Moreover, the restructuring or the harvest can take many pathways: minority equity sales, spin-offs, carve-outs, split-offs, tracking stocks, or doing MBOs, LBOs, IPOs, or trade sales. Sometimes the best approach may be to go into liquidation or financial reorganization. All these techniques (and many more) are ways managers can expertly prune and harvest companies. Entrepreneurs should be informed about these approaches. The aim of this chapter is to show the range of strategic options available and how to implement each one effectively.

We also underlined the context for carrying out a change program. Think through whether your industry is undergoing revolutionary or evolutionary change. Combine the industry conditions with the specific situation facing your firm (crisis? or no crisis?) in order to determine the time horizon you have in which to maneuver.

As we said, given a short time horizon, managers have limited maneuvering room and basically two options: either crisis management—where stopping losses and conserving cash are the top priorities—or fine-tuning the existing processes, if industry conditions are more benign.

With a longer time horizon, more degrees of freedom are possible. If the industry is undergoing disruptive change (like the switch from analog to digital in the television broadcasting industry), then managers need to think about enacting deep transformational change of a fundamental nature. If the industry is experiencing only incremental changes, then keeping up might merely be a matter of extending competencies on an ongoing basis. Corporate managers or entrepreneurs always need to be mindful of the pace, rhythm, and intensity of the strategic change required depending on industry circumstances and the needs of their particular organization.

In the next chapter, we put into perspective all the tools and strategies discussed so far, as we describe the key elements of a business model. In the business model, all things should come together. The very last element of the business model is the organization's competitive strategy and the strategic rationale supporting it. Even if two firms propose the same business model, they could still experience different results. On one hand, the difference in results may depend on how committed each organization is to implementing the strategy and capable of executing on the action plans. On the other hand, the two firms could also experience variance in performance depending on the turbulence in their external environments.

With dynamic, fast-moving industries, the speed and agility with which firms, large or small, are able to adapt and modify their strategies can be a key source of competitive advantage. Managers need to be adept at managing both in the short term while simultaneously preparing for the inevitable industry disruption coming from shifting innovation streams. So even if you might think the feasible choices are limited in the beginning for the start-up firm, it is good to be aware of the breadth of possibilities. Especially since market turbulence, the pressures of globalization, and the dynamics of industry restructuring may yield interesting opportunities for the alert start-up team who is prepared to spot them.

CHAPTER TAKEAWAYS

- The processes of innovation and stimulating firm growth are fluid and dynamic. As firms carry out their strategies by linking up to external partners, their own organizations are likely to change as they grow and learn in the process. All growth is a learning process and should be viewed as natural and organic.
- Managers have many means at their disposal to accelerate growth, enter markets, and gain scale, including open innovation processes, mergers and acquisitions, minority investments, cross-shareholding arrangements, and joint ventures.
- At some point in time, nearly all start-ups will run into trouble. Learning how to manage failure is just as important as learning how to manage success. It may become critical for you to know how to shrink, refocus, divest, or restructure unsuccessful operations when times get tough.
- Liquidation is when a company is placed into bankruptcy and wound up. During some bankruptcies, a financial reorganization may be appropriate. Leveraged restructuring is when a company changes its capital structure by repurchasing its

own shares as part of a voluntary financial reorganization. Leveraged restructurings are one way to fend off hostile raiders.

- Harvesting and exiting a business can signal many things, either positive or negative. Always seek to understand the motivations of the buyer and seller in any corporate transaction and search for the real reasons behind any sale.
- As divestitures, insolvency procedures, and corporate restructurings are complex, it is wise to seek expert legal and financial advice early in the process.

Key Elements of a Business Model

Venture capitalists (VCs) coined the term *business model* and the media then popularized the notion during the e-commerce boom of the late 1990s. Even though many people banter around the term, the intended meaning varies widely, depending on the personal experience and professional background of the person who is uttering the phrase. To avoid misunderstandings, we explain what we think is meant by a business model. We then explain *why* a business model matters, how it is *not* the same thing as a business plan (which many people think it is), and illustrate how a business model also incorporates competitive strategy—but is not a substitute for it.

This chapter discusses business models primarily from the point of view of the venture capitalist rather than the venture's founders. The reason is that many high-technology start-ups require venture funding to finance their early-stage development. For the founders who need financing, we think it is a good idea to reverse roles. Put yourself in the shoes of the potential investor who must scrutinize and evaluate your business model before deciding whether to place funds into the new company.

In the end, the ability of your team to implement your venture's business model may very well depend on the firm having the right resources and capabilities at the right time and place. Some of these resources will be furnished by the VCs and others will be supplied by *complementors*. Complementors enhance the value of a product or service. They are third parties that are outside the company's immediate value chain. (See Chapter 3 for more on these strategy terms or log on to our web site at www.innovationtocashflows.com and use our extensive Glossary.)

WHAT IS YOUR BUSINESS MODEL?

When a venture capitalist asks, "What is your business model?" what he or she really means is:

- What is the revenue model?
- What is the cost model?
- How is the business going to make money?
- How capital intensive is the business?
- Is the business scalable? Is it global?

- Can the business grow rapidly? Can it get big, quick?
- How does the business achieve short-term and long-term competitive advantage vis-à-vis rivals?
- What is the exit strategy for the venture capital?
- What is the time to exit?[1]

In the early days of venture capital in Silicon Valley, investors used to ask company founders to prepare and present their business plans (documents laying out the founders' ideas on how they were going to make things or sell services that would make money and could be sold to customers).

However, in today's more turbulent and complicated world, when VCs ask founders to pitch their business model, they are asking for much more than a business plan and its financial spreadsheets containing revenue, expense, and cash flow forecasts. They want to know the answers to all the questions just posed and then maybe even some more.

Professor Henry Chesbrough, executive director of the Center for Open Innovation at the Haas School of Business, University of California at Berkeley, and an expert on managing technology and innovation, writes that a business model has two important purposes. "It must create value within the value chain; and it must capture a piece of value for the focal firm in that chain."[2] Chesbrough and his Harvard University colleague Richard Rosenbloom describe the reasons why founders need a business model in six steps. (See the next box.)

SIX FUNCTIONS OF A BUSINESS MODEL

1. To articulate the *value proposition*, that is, the value created for users by the offering based on technology.
2. To identify a *market segment*, that is, the users to whom the technology is useful and the purpose for which it will be used.
3. To define the structure of the firm's *value chain*, which is required to create and distribute the offering, and to determine the *complementary assets* needed to support the firm's position in this chain.
4. To specify the *revenue generation mechanism(s)* for the firm, and estimate the *cost structure* and *target margins* of producing the offering, given the value proposition and value chain structure chosen.
5. To describe the position of the firm within the *value network* linking suppliers and customers, including identification of potential complementary firms and competitors.
6. To formulate the *competitive strategy* by which the innovating firm will gain and hold advantage over rivals.

Source: Henry W. Chesbrough. *Open Innovation: The New Imperative for Creating and Profiting from Technology* (Boston: Harvard Business School Press, 2003, 64–65).

CREATING THE BUSINESS MODEL STEP BY STEP

As the entrepreneur, creating a complete business model will help you structure the business design problem into a logical sequence of decisions:

1. *Try to picture customers and their needs and sketch out the entire purchase decision process.* Imagine how customers are going to use the technology, product, or service and for what purposes. What benefits will they gain from its use? These benefits are the value that is being created for customers—in other words, the value proposition.

    Distinct customer groups may very well perceive benefits or experience them differently. Consequently, the value propositions vary, depending on the target customer group. This is the reason for clearly identifying the target customer. Also, try to identify who might be the purchase decision maker, who else might influence the buying decision process, and who will be the final end user. Each role may be assigned to different persons or groups within the value chain.

    Let us elaborate a bit more on the difference between the customer and the final end user. The customer for your technology, product, or service may not necessarily be the same person or entity as the end user. It could be that your customer is an *original equipment manufacturer*. For instance, your start-up might be designing and manufacturing a critical component for an artificial hip. So your customer would be the medical device manufacturer. The end user would be the hip-transplant patient. It will be vital for your sales team to identify the key purchase decision makers who will decide and authorize your component versus competitors' offerings. They are the gatekeepers to the sales process. The customer, however, would most likely be the product manager responsible for delivering the new artificial hip product line to the market, on time and within budget. The end user is the patient receiving a new artificial hip.

2. *Segment the market.* Once you have identified possible customers, then group them according to how they will respond to your product or service. (This process is called segmenting the market.) How price and quality sensitive are the customers in the different market niches? How would you reach them? What distribution channels would serve them?

3. *Visualize the business system or value chain.* Sketch the sequence of steps from design, prototype production, field testing, laboratory scale-up, manufacture, wholesale distribution, to retail sales of the business. Take a preliminary decision on how much of the work is going to be done inside the firm and how much will be outsourced or accessed via strategic partnerships.

4. *Charge for your product or service and get paid for it.* This is called the revenue generation mechanism. Figure out how you are going to have the customer pay for your product or services in order to make a revenue forecast and when you expect to be paid. Will it be based on a price per unit? A lump-sum fee? An agent commission? A broker fee? A subscription rate? A percentage of gross sales? An hourly billing rate? Do you expect payments to be made in cash, by credit card, or through some sort of negotiated exchange of services?

5. *Estimate the fixed and variable expenses of your business.* This is part of determining the cost structure of the business. Knowing your costs and overheads

is an important part of any entrepreneur's job. If you do not know how to do the financials, you will need to hire help. Experienced salespeople and managers involved in business development will be good sources of information to help you develop pricing models and set realistic target operating margins. Will you extend credit terms to your customers? Will your suppliers extend credit to you? How much working capital will be needed? It is critical to understand the sources of cash flowing into the firm and the sources of cash flowing out. The *burn rate* is how fast a start-up uses up cash.

6. *Decide about the capital intensity of the business.* This is another aspect to the cost structure of the business. Will it be asset heavy (in other words, requiring a lot of fixed investment), or will it be asset light (more like a *virtual company,* where most production aspects of the business are outsourced)? To save on fixed labor costs and high employee benefits, the workforce might consist instead of subcontractors, who are selected and contracted according to project needs. Asset-light organizations are typical for many high-technology service businesses, software development, or application service providers.

7. *View the business as part of an ecosystem that includes the alliance network and the value network.*[3] The *alliance network* is the overall ecosystem of social networks, both formal and informal, that surround your firm. A *value network* is a subset of players within the alliance network. The value network consists of the third parties (suppliers or distributors) that are outside the immediate value chain but that complement your technology, product, or service with value-added technology, services, or products of their own. In the jargon of economics, a *complementor* is a supplier whose product or service when bundled with yours enhances the overall value of the combined offering. (Refer again to Chapter 3, where we introduced the notion of complements).

   We can review the concept of a complement with a few examples: If a razor is the basic product, then the razor blades are the complements. If the product is a camera, then the roll of film would be the complement. Without the film, an old-fashioned camera is pretty useless for taking pictures. For an ink-jet printer, the ink cartridges would be complements. Likewise for a personal computer: The hardware manufacturers bundle the PC components with other operating system software and applications, which are the complements. In essence, complements may be either *critical* components (such as the PC operating system, without it the PC will not work) or *nonessential* but highly valued (such as an enhanced equation editor within the Excel spreadsheet or Word document, particularly useful for scientists, engineers, and economists who need to work with formulas).

   Other aspects of creating and managing an alliance network that are particularly important to a biotechnology firm are the role, influence, and advice provided by a distinguished scientific advisory board and highly qualified board of directors. These external advisors usually are scientific experts, experienced entrepreneurs, or seasoned venture capitalists. They may provide a wealth of knowledge and management depth that every biotechnology or biopharmaceutical start-up needs. Chapter 8 specifically discusses the many ways alliance networks complete the value chain in the pharmaceutical and biopharmaceutical industries, what we refer to as the (bio)pharmaceutical industry. Chapter 10 covers investment term sheets (heads of terms) as well as the governance issues of shareholder agreements. Chapter 10 also mentions the tensions between founders and investors when deciding on the board of directors for early stage start-up companies.

8. *Articulate the competitive strategy.* This means the entrepreneur needs to define the goals, scope, sustainable competitive advantage, and strategic logic of the business.[4] Make sure the strategic logic or rationale supporting the strategy is compelling and persuasive. If not, the venture capitalist will not fund the proposal. (We explained how to formulate competitive strategies in Chapter 3.)

9. *Decide on an "exit strategy" and "exit time horizon" for the early-stage investors.* These early investors could be friends and family, *angel investors,* or early *seed money* venture capitalists. (See "Glossary" at www.innovation tocashflows.com for key term definitions and Chapters 19 for descriptions of each investor type.) An exit strategy means figuring out how the venture capitalists can cash out of their investment. The exit time horizon is the period of time the VCs intend to invest in the venture, at the end of which they will sell their shares and collect any capital gains. Time horizons vary. They are three to five years in most high-tech sectors, although in biotechnology the exit time is usually longer, and may be up to 10 years. Typical exit routes are: (1) sell the investors' shares in the company to a larger company in the same industry (known as a trade sale); (2) take the privately held company and turn it into a public company by selling shares in an initial public offering (IPO) and listing the company's shares on a stock exchange; or (3) sell the company to another private equity firm (the venture capitalists will sell out to other equity investors who provide later rounds of financing). The normal venture financing route is seed capital, venture capital (first round, second round, to third round of financing), then either an IPO or a trade sale. The quicker that VCs can complete their exit strategy for each round of financing, the higher their return on invested capital—measured as the *internal rate of return*—and the happier will be the limited partners who, in turn, have invested their money in the VCs' venture fund (which is usually structured as a limited partnership fund). Refer to Chapter 4 for more on harvest or exit strategies. See Chapter 9 and 10 for more on investor contracts. Refer to Chapter 19 for more on venture capital funds and how VCs value high-tech start-ups.

These nine steps, in a nutshell, are the basic elements of what is taught in the entrepreneurship or new ventures courses of most business schools. We have covered a lot of ground very quickly.

CHAPTER TAKEAWAYS

- The business model is much more than the venture's business plan or profit and loss forecasts. It is much more than the strategy for your venture. The business model describes the complete system for how you will: connect to your target customers; charge for your products or services; and grow and leverage your firm's resources and capabilities with those of your alliance networks.
- "What is your business model?" is likely to be the first question the venture capitalists will ask you when you go to them seeking capital to fund your venture.

- "What is the exit strategy?" is really asking how venture capitalists will be able to sell their investment shares and cash out of the deal. Typical exits are to sell their shares to a trade buyer (usually a bigger company in the same industry); take the company public by listing the company on a stock exchange and selling shares to the market in an initial public offering; or sell shares to another financial group (either another private equity firm or a merchant bank syndicate).
- Venture capitalists must keep their money working for their investors; that means they will seek to exit at a target multiple of value (usually a multiple of sales or a multiple of earnings) and within an agreed time period. We discuss the investor's perspective in greater depth and explain how to value a company, using discounted cash flows and various kinds of multiples, in Part Six: Valuing Company Cash Flows.

Crafting Strategic Alliances

Introduction to Strategic Alliances

The purpose of Part Three, "Crafting Strategic Alliances," is to explore and better understand alliances. For the next three chapters, we examine how high-technology strategic alliances may be used as vehicles for achieving the growth, capability development, and learning aims of your venture's business model. As an entrepreneur starting up a company, you and your team will need to define the boundaries of your firm—what activities and parts of the value chain will you do inside? What things will be done by third parties? Then you will need to select where these activities will be located—on domestic shores or foreign soil?

There are many alliance choices awaiting scrutiny. You will need to mentally sift and sort through a wide range of alliance modes to determine the ones most suited to leverage your venture's unique resources and capabilities. For those chief executive officers (CEOs) of high-technology start-ups seeking venture funding, it is imperative that you and your team select a growth vehicle that has the potential to expand your firm's market reach and scale. Forming that first successful alliance is important to build momentum and enhance your venture's reputation as a credible partner. With that first early win, it will be easier to entice other potential partners to join later alliances. Step by step you will eventually grow and develop an effective alliance network. Be mindful, however, that in all cases, you and your start-up team will need to judge carefully whether pursuing growth through an alliance structure is the right path to take or if your company would be better off if it pursued some other vehicle in order to accomplish its aims—such as doing mergers and acquisitions or raising money for more internal development. Alliances are not always the best choice to advance your strategic goals; each situation must be decided on its own merits, after careful analysis of facts, circumstances, and current market conditions.

In Chapter 6, we explore the nature of alliances, define industry deconstruction, and examine how it stimulates alliance formation, and determine the various types of strategic collaborations commonly encountered in high-technology industries (defined as those industries with intense research and development (R&D), combined with state-of-the-art technology). In Chapter 7, we describe the reasons why companies choose to make alliances, then we spend the latter part of that chapter showing you how to do an alliance step by step. In Chapter 8, we focus on alliances in the biotechnology, pharmaceutical, and medical device industries.

WHAT IS AN ALLIANCE?

The term *alliance* covers a wide multitude of different kinds and modes of collaboration, from simple and informal handshake agreements, to complex outsourcing subcontract agreements, technology transfer contracts, or joint venture investment agreements. We summarize the types of alliance agreements into three main categories: informal, formal, and equity. We depict each type of alliance in Figure 6.1 and then explain them.

Informal Agreements

At its simplest, an alliance may be a verbal agreement to collaborate between two parties. We classify these as "loose" or informal relationships. These informal agreements may be based on the centuries-old idea that "My word is my bond." They are grounded on perceived trust, often friendship, and may be based on family, social, university, or other business ties. If the trust is betrayed or problems arise in the relationship, such loose verbal agreements may give cause for personal consternation or even worse consequences, especially if the alliance turns out to be related to a more mission-critical or significant activity than originally envisioned. Consequently, in many societies, many business collaborations are not loose agreements but are written down in formal contracts that explicitly state the promises and commitments made by the negotiating parties.

The key message we wish to convey, however, is that regardless of whether it is an oral agreement or a written contract, the fundamental foundation on which

Type of Alliance Relationships	
Loose or Informal Relationship	Family Ties
	Social Networks
	Opportunistic Alliances (short term and fluid in nature)
Formal Contractual Relationship	Subcontracting agreements
	Nonequity Joint Ventures (a contractual joint venture)
	Technology Transfer Agreements (licensing of IP or know-how)
	Franchising (a type of licensing agreement)
Equity Ownership in a Company Structure	Equity Joint Venture
	Minority Investment

FIGURE 6.1   Common Types of Alliances

any collaboration is built is trust. Gaining the respect and trust of the other party is essential for the collaboration to succeed and flourish.

Family Ties   All over the world, family clans form alliances for mutual defense or support. For instance, in South Korea, family members keep track of each other in "family books" dating back multiple generations. Korean society expects the eldest son to provide family leadership and support; he is the one who is responsible for taking care of others in the family, especially the infirm or elderly. (Refer to the first item in Figure 6.1.)

Social Networks   May be very powerful and long lasting. They provide solidarity and support to the respective members of the network or business association who have banded together for mutual advantage in a trust-based relationship. Entrepreneurs employ various networks to obtain information, resources, and knowledge to help them get started in their businesses. Networks help to build up an entrepreneur's social capital (reputation and credibility). In Chinese society, for example, the concept of *guānxi* (one's personal network) is a central cultural precept for the giving and receiving of favors and influence.

Of course, there is also a dark side to networks and networking. In Italy, infamous criminal networks are the Cosa Nostra of Sicily, the Camorra near Naples, and the 'Ndrangheta near Calabria. Mafias and their powerful equivalents exist all over the world; they are not limited to Italy.

Numerous social networks exist—alumni associations, religious organizations, charity, philanthropic, and other types of nongovernmental organizations (NGOs), such as those working toward social causes like bettering the environment, furthering world peace, and defending human rights. Networks might also be loose federations of experts who volunteer their time and energies to create products or services, such as the open source community (www.opensource.org), which is a dedicated group of volunteer computer software programmers who use open source development methods for creating code and programs that rely on peer review and free redistribution of software.[1]

Opportunistic Alliances   Might spring up around particular business or social ventures. They are quite common in academic research circles, where two or three doctoral students might band together to do a field study, or company researchers decide to pursue a particular development project. The alliances may be informal, spontaneous, and fluid. They may quickly dissipate or evolve into something more structured and permanent depending on the personal chemistry of the teams involved and the importance of the project or venture.

Consortia are temporary partnerships or associations. Although we classify them under opportunistic alliances, they fit into a number of the other categories as well, as their form and nature vary widely. Some consortia operate like loose umbrella organizations and have ad hoc membership rules. Other consortia are more formal and may require members to join a foundation.[2] (Refer to the Symbian Foundation discussed later in this chapter under "Equity Joint Ventures.")

Basic research consortia consist of groups formed to carry out complex, large, and multidisciplinary research efforts, sometimes over long periods of time. Networks of academic institutions, NGOs, privately funded research centers, government-sponsored research laboratories, or corporate members may decide to partner and to collectively accomplish what no one member could do alone. In the next few paragraphs, we explain how such research consortia may be set up and structured as contractual collaboration agreements. (For further information on how to access innovation through academic collaboration, refer to Chapter 8.)

Research consortia are structured in many different ways, and the details vary from country to country. Typically, however, they consist of a series of contractual agreements among the various parties. For example, the global energy company BP Plc (www.bp.com), acting through its U.S. subsidiary BP Technology Ventures Inc. signed a master partnership agreement with the Regents of the University of California that created the Energy Biosciences Institute (EBI). EBI is a major research consortium among BP, the University of California, Berkeley, the Lawrence Berkeley National Laboratory,[3] and the University of Illinois at Urbana-Champaign (UIUC). BP will initially fund the Energy Biosciences Institute with a 10-year grant amounting to $500 million. EBI's mandate is to research innovative clean and renewable fuels (including solar and biofuels) and apply biotechnology to the energy sector, with the aim of reducing the level of carbon emissions from motor vehicles, and thus address the societal challenge of finding, enhancing, and then gaining widespread adoption of alternatives to petroleum-based fuels (www.energybiosciencesinstitute.org).

Research consortia usually depend on industry support or government funded research grants to finance their operations. The way it works is that interested parties form alliances, make proposals, and bid for the grant. To enhance their chances of winning the BP grant money, UC Berkeley and UIUC teamed up with Lawrence Berkeley Laboratory. The three collaborators drafted and submitted a joint proposal to BP. Together they proposed to combine social policy, scientific, and engineering expertise to research the selection, breeding, development, and processing of nonfood plant species (biomass) that could be used for making clean biofuels.[4]

Afterward, representatives from BP screened the bids. In the final selection process, they chose UC Berkeley-UIUC over competing proposals from the Massachusetts Institute of Technology, Cambridge University, and others. Very often one partner in a large research consortium is designated the lead coordinator and made responsible for administering the research project. In the case of the Energy Bioscience Institute, the lead coordinator is UC Berkeley. (See note 5 for further information on EBI's governance and management structure.)[5]

Normally, research consortia are bound by contractual agreements, such as a memorandum of understanding (or letter of intent) and basic confidentiality agreements. (Refer to Chapters 9 and 10 for definitions and details about these kinds of agreements.) The allocation of intellectual property (IP) rights must be decided ahead of time by the consortia partners, to reduce the potential for later conflicts on who keeps what IP rights. (Refer to the discussion in Chapter 8 for further advice to entrepreneurs when negotiating patent and other IP rights.) The decisions and agreements on IP rights for a research consortium may be incorporated into the master memorandum of understanding or documented in a series of separate agreements. For instance, the BP-UC Regents Master Agreement is a matter of public record.[6]

Research performance for many consortia is overseen by a board of governance, and progress is monitored through annual or semiannual reviews of research milestones and project deliverables. Sometimes research consortia evolve and their structures are modified into other legal vehicles (equity joint ventures or incorporated companies), especially if valuable intellectual property is developed and the partners agree a different structure will be better for exploiting the IP at a later stage. (Refer to Chapter 8, "Access to Innovation through Collaboration with Academic Groups," for a discussion of how academic research collaborations advance early-stage drug discovery.)

Formal Contractual Agreements

When considering formal contractual agreements, it helps to group them into short-term contracts (perhaps a single transaction) or long-term contracts that may involve a series of multiple and repeated transactions over a defined period of time.

An example of a short-term contract is a market contract for buying or selling foreign exchange or some other commodity. Such "spot contracts" reflect the current market price of an underlying financial instrument, commodity, good, or service. For example, when a commodities trader located in Zug, Switzerland, buys a large crude oil contract in the global petroleum market, the contract is honored through a spot transaction where money is exchanged for the delivered good, in this case, a tanker of crude oil sent to the port of Rotterdam.

Similarly, when a major engineering construction company puts out a single tender request to procure a quantity of high-pressure valves for a utility project, it is an order that may be satisfied by a number of qualified vendors or suppliers. The engineering company will award the contract to the vendor offering the lowest bid that still meets the specified product quality and delivery conditions. The terms are easily specified, and the competitive bids comparable. Both of these sample contracts would be relatively straightforward procurement contracts, and neither would be particularly strategic in nature. These contracts involve no long-term exchange of core competencies or proprietary know-how, therefore they are considered to be ordinary collaborations, not strategic alliances.

Long-term contracts are often used when closer supplier and customer relationships are needed. A long-term contract helps reduce opportunistic behavior (where one party takes advantage of the other) and provides more security and lower risk, particularly if the parties must make transaction-specific or project-specific investments that are not reusable elsewhere. However, the downside of these binding long-term contracts is they may lock the parties into untenable positions. These long-term contracts may prove to be too inflexible since it is nearly impossible to foresee all the circumstances that may arise during the course of a project, particularly in turbulent and changing industries. Smart negotiators will figure out ways to insert various types of "trigger clauses" that allow for the renegotiation of certain contract clauses if key assumptions turn out to be incorrect or conditions shift unexpectedly. It is common, too, to allow for change orders, if the client changes the original scope of the work specified in the contract.

Subcontracting Agreements   With subcontracting, a company or organization chooses to award parts of a particular service or process to a third party. Often these awards are made on the basis of competitive bids, but they may also be made through negotiated contract agreements. For instance, in the building trades, a general contractor would have overall responsibility for preparing the bids on various construction jobs. Once the bid is won, the general contractor is liable for completing the terms of the contract and delivering the project to the client. In order to construct a building, the general contractor parcels out pieces of the project to subcontractors who are experts in their particular crafts, such as carpenters, plumbers, electricians, plasterers, mechanical (heating and air conditioning), and telecommunications specialists. The general contractor, as a principal, is fully liable for the work of any subcontractors acting as an agent while they are carrying out the obligations of the contract. Consequently, most general contractors (at least in the United States) are required to carry various liability insurances. (For more on liability protections, refer to Chapter 9's discussion on company incorporation issues and limited partnership vehicles.)

Another very common type of subcontract agreement would be for occasional work, as, for example, when a firm hires temporary staff to help do the inventory audit at the end of the fiscal year or to do some seasonal assembly work. These workers are hired to do specific tasks and then let go. These occasional service contracts are not strategic.

A typical subcontractor situation arises when software development companies hire computer programmers on a temporary basis from a firm that does "body shopping" (supplying low-cost computer programmers—bodies—to other firms in exchange for a markup on the hourly fee that will be paid to the programmer).

Not all subcontracting is strategic in nature; it depends on how critical it is to the firm's competitive advantage and strategic capabilities development. In some outsourcing contracts, the processed work is returned to the firm that subcontracted it. In other cases it may also be passed on to another partner in the supply chain for further processing. Then typically only a small percentage of the value added is appropriated by the subcontractor.

The use of subcontracting to complete major projects is common in many industries. We discuss outsourcing decisions and turnkey projects (both are forms of contracting) in greater detail later in this chapter; see "Vertical Integration Decisions" and "Strategic Alliances," respectively.

Nonequity Joint Venture   As mentioned in Chapter 4, there are two types of joint ventures: equity and nonequity joint ventures (or contractual joint ventures). In an equity joint venture, two parties remain independent but jointly set up a newly created company. (See later discussion under "Equity Joint Ventures.")

In a nonequity joint venture, no equity investment is involved; instead, the two parties sign a long-term contractual agreement to collaborate. This is the simplest form of association for joint ventures under which the parties to the joint venture agree to associate as independent contractors rather than shareholders in a company or partners in a legal partnership.[7] Such a vehicle is purely a contractual cooperation agreement. This mode of collaboration is suitable where the parties want to signal commitment without the formality and permanence of a corporate vehicle. The basic objectives will be substantially similar to that of a shareholders' agreement; the essential differences are the absence of a separate legal vehicle and the possibility that the nonequity joint venture may pertain to a project of a finite life. In many ways, it is quite similar to the consortium discussed earlier. (See Chapter 9 for more on company formation.)

For instance (and this is a low-tech example even though nonequity joint ventures are also used in high tech), IKEA, the giant Swedish-based furniture retailer, operates a series of nonequity buyer-supplier alliances around the world that are structured as nonequity joint ventures. According to Professor Paul Beamish, an authority on international joint ventures, IKEA "provides component suppliers with product design, technical assistance, leased equipment and even loans. IKEA's suppliers get new skills, direct access to a large and growing retailer, and steadier sales."[8] The benefit for both sides is a sense of partnership and loyalty from IKEA to its suppliers and from the suppliers toward IKEA. The customers ultimately benefit from the volume procurement of lower-cost but higher-quality furniture, designed to IKEA's specifications.

Technology Transfer Agreements *Technology transfer agreements* are licensing agreements. As briefly introduced in Chapter 2, licensing agreements can be considered as similar to a lease (or rental) contract for an apartment. The *licensor* is the firm (or person) that owns the license. The *licensee* is the firm (or person) that wishes to use the license and, in turn, will pay a royalty or fee for using it to the owner. Similarly, the *lessor* is the owner, the landlord, the firm, or person that owns the apartment building. The *lessee* is the user, the tenant, the person that gains the use of the apartment, for a fixed period of time, in exchange for a monthly lease payment.

Technology transfer agreements are the instruments of choice when trying to transfer protectable intellectual property rights from, for example, a start-up high-tech venture to a third party, such as another strategic partner involved in a different part of the value chain or an investor group placing funds into the venture. The license agreement allows the licensor to transfer the rights to use its various kinds of intellectual property either separately or bundled together. The IP would be its patents, trademarks, designs, copyrights, trade secrets, or proprietary technological know-how. Once the IP is identified and the rights specified, then the agreement also defines the time frame and geographical territory where these rights may be exercised. The firm that buys the rights gives in exchange a combination usually of lump-sum advances, royalties, and milestone payments. (See Chapter 14, where we discuss technology transfer agreements and the legal clauses found in these agreements in greater detail, and Chapter 20, where we illustrate how to value and negotiate such a patent licensing and technology transfer agreement.)

Technology transfer agreements are a very common form of strategic alliance in technology-intensive and science-driven industries like biotechnology, nanotechnology, medical devices, semiconductors, and telecommunications, and many other industries where brands and registered designs are valuable (e.g., fashionable clothes, luxury accessories, and consumer electronics).

Franchising *Franchising* is a business system used by companies to execute their growth strategy, penetrate markets, and extend their geographical reach by using other people's money, labor, and energy. Franchising has become one of the most prevalent and successful forms of new business start-up in the United States.[9] Franchising is a booming trend in both developed and emerging markets, particularly in fast food, retailing, auto parts, quick copy shops, and various service businesses—especially professional services, such as accounting, tax, and real estate brokerage.

The *franchisor* is the seller of the franchise; the *franchisee* is the buyer of the franchise. The franchisor is the owner of a trademarked product, brand, business format, or service that grants the exclusive right to market, sell, or distribute a product or provide a service in a designated territory to the franchisee. In return for the use of these rights, brand, and business concept, the owner receives payment of a franchise fee, royalties (typically on net sales), and the franchisee's promise to conform to the quality standards of the franchise and comply with any other specifications in the contract. McDonald's Corporation, based in Oakbrook, Illinois, and Yum! Brands, Inc., based in Louisville, Kentucky, (owner of KFC, Long John Silver's, Pizza Hut, and Taco Bell) are rapidly and successfully expanding their franchises in China, South Korea, other parts of Asia, and the rest of the world. A recent PricewaterhouseCoopers study found that the franchising sector generates 21 million jobs in the United States alone and yielded $2.3 trillion in economic output.[10]

For instance, MySQL created the world's most popular open source relational database software, with over 100 million copies of its software downloaded or distributed as of June 2008. The company MySQL AB was founded in 1995 by two Swedes and a Finn; it was acquired by Sun Microsystems[11] for $1 billion ($800 million in cash and $200 million in stock options). MySQL employed a software franchising strategy to offer training for its database. In addition to its own training, MySQL partnered with many other companies around the world to extend its training reach into a global network. In its software franchise business model, MySQL would authorize other developers to use its brand names and trademarks and helped them create associated organizations to do open source support and custom software development in particular geographic areas or vertical markets.

With all franchising and licensing arrangements, the owner must consider the capabilities, reliability, and trustworthiness of the counterparties. This is particularly crucial when licensing high-profile luxury brand names; the owner of the brand trademark must carefully protect the brand's reputation and use by the licensees so as not to dilute the value of the brand.

Equity Ownership Agreements

In Figure 6.1 we mention two important types of equity ownership agreements that arise in alliances: equity joint ventures and minority investments. Equity ownership changes the nature of the alliance collaboration in important ways by lengthening the possible time of collaboration and changing the risk and reward profile of the joint endeavor. Chapters 9 and 10 explain the key legal, liability, and corporate governance issues to take into consideration when forming a new company, partnership, or equity joint venture vehicle.

Equity Joint Ventures   In the eyes of the law, a joint stock company (or incorporated company) is assumed to have an indefinite life span. Therefore, in principle, equity joint ventures have an unlimited duration as compared to a contractual agreement, which has a specified time horizon, after which the contract must be renewed or it expires. Consequently, equity joint ventures usually are set up as a sign of both parties commitment to a long-term collaboration. As said in Chapter 4, when a joint venture is formed, generally one party contributes a combination of cash, resources, and capabilities to fund the joint venture; the other party, usually the start-up company, contributes its "sweat equity" into the new joint venture, meaning its intellectual property assets (patent portfolio and associated rights), technological know-how, and so forth. Both firms will choose key people from their respective firms to join the new joint venture, which then has its own independent identity.

Some joint ventures are fully vertically integrated and do many activities in a business's value chain. Other joint ventures are focused on only one small part of the overall value chain. A focused joint venture may be set up specifically to do research, or development, or manufacture, or sales, or customer relationship management support. Joint ventures are widely used in all high-technology and engineering-driven industries, such as wireless mobile devices, media, cable, consumer electronics, pharmaceutical, biotechnology, automotive, specialty chemicals, energy, and so on.

For instance, Sony Corporation and Ericsson teamed up in 2001 to form a 50/50 equity joint venture with the goal of becoming a global leading provider of mobile multimedia devices.[12] The joint venture, Sony Ericsson, does product research, design, and development as well as manufacturing, marketing, sales, distribution, and customer services. The global management is based in London, whereas R&D is done in Sweden, the United Kingdom, France, the Netherlands, India, Japan, China, and the United States.

On June 24, 2008, Nokia, Sony Ericsson, Motorola, and Japan's NTT DOCOMO announced their intent to unite the Symbian operating system (Symbian OS) with three other operating systems, to create one unified open mobile software platform for advanced smart phones and other mobile devices. Nokia said it planned to acquire for $411 million the remaining shares of Symbian Ltd. that it did not already own (52 percent), and then contribute the Symbian OS and Nokia S60 software to a new Symbian Foundation[13] Symbian, Ltd., based in London, is a software licensing company that develops and licenses Symbian OS, the market-leading open operating system for mobile phones. Symbian's operating system had about a two-thirds global market share, as of end 2007, according to Canalys, a market research firm based in Reading, England.[14]

The new Symbian Foundation would make the operating system platform available to its members as a royalty-free open source Eclipse Public License.[15] The foundation will be guided by an alliance of the world's leading mobile device manufacturers and chip makers, including Nokia, Samsung, Sony Ericsson, LG Electronics, and Motorola. The same terms would be offered to the network operators AT&T Wireless, NTT DOCOMO of Japan, and Vodafone of Britain.

This move by Nokia sets the stage for a new standards war against Google and Microsoft for the next generation of mobile devices. "In smart phone operating systems, Symbian had a 65 percent share at the end of 2007, compared to a 12 percent share for Microsoft Windows Mobile, 11 percent for Research in Motion (maker of the popular BlackBerry), 7 percent for Apple, and 5 percent for the Linux open source system, according to Canalys."[16] Psion Ltd. was the company that originally created the early joint venture consortium with Ericsson, Nokia, and Motorola to develop the Symbian mobile phone OS. In 2004 Nokia doubled its share in Symbian by acquiring Psion's stake.[17]

Minority Investments   Companies try to discourage opportunistic behavior in their alliances partners by carefully considering the allocation of risks and rewards when negotiating joint ventures and minority investments. By becoming equity partners, economic interests and risks of the venture are better aligned, as both upside rewards and downside losses are shared according to the ownership percentage each partner has in the company.

The difficulty in specifying complete contracts for long-term supplier agreements enhances the attractiveness of long-term partnership arrangements that often involve minority investments. This trend is particularly noticeable in the automotive industry, where there has been a major shift away from arm's-length supplier contracts to long-term collaborations with a handful of key global suppliers. In many instances, competitive tenders and the requirement for multiple bidders are being replaced by single-supplier arrangements. All the automotive majors have a host of international alliances and joint ventures, ranging from minority stakes to equity joint ventures with a variety of suppliers and other automotive rivals.

STRATEGIC ALLIANCES

A *strategic alliance* is a negotiated collaboration agreement of strategic importance between two or more parties, firms, or organizations that keep their own identities. The parties decide to pool, share, exchange, or integrate specific resources or capabilities in order to carry out vital tasks. They mutually strive to achieve agreed on strategic goals. A joint venture that involves a significant pooling of assets and technological know-how is considered a strategic alliance rather than a merger or acquisition, because the parties that create the joint venture (the parent companies) remain separate entities. In a merger or acquisition, either the target company or its assets are completely absorbed into the buyer and become a new entity.

The terms *resources* or *capabilities* in the preceding definition have the same meanings as in Chapter 3. *Resources* include a firm's productive tangible or intangible assets, including the firm's human resources; *capabilities* refers to what a firm can do.

The following statements are true about strategic alliances:

- A strategic alliance is a negotiated collaboration agreement of long-term significance between two or more firms or organizations.
- The partners decide to pool, share, exchange, or integrate specific resources and capabilities to carry out vital tasks.
- The firms remain separate businesses, which distinguishes alliances from mergers and acquisitions.
- A joint venture is classified as a strategic alliance if it is of strategic importance to both parties.

When Is an Alliance a *Strategic* Alliance?

Asking this question is very important because sometimes ordinary alliances turn out to be much more strategic than managers had initially expected. What seemed like a simple outsourcing decision may turn out to have far-reaching strategic consequences later on, especially if control over proprietary technological know-how is lost or the firm loses out on an opportunity to develop new knowledge or capabilities vital to its future survival.

A strategic alliance is of greater strategic importance to your firm than an ordinary collaboration or everyday type of short-term contract. Your organization must recognize that a strategic alliance implies a *serious commitment* among two or more parties to collaborate to achieve mutual aims. The parties to the strategic alliance agreement may be actual competitors, potential competitors, or noncompetitors. There is always the possibility of a rival gaining advantage over an unwary partner in any strategic alliance. Typically, although to varying degrees, a strategic alliance implies the sharing of proprietary know-how, confidential trade secrets, organizational information about routines and processes, market intelligence, or important intellectual property rights. Strategic alliances may range from formal joint ventures, in which two or more firms have equity stakes (such as the Sony Ericsson joint venture mentioned earlier) to shorter-term contractual arrangements, in which two firms agree, for example, to cooperate by developing and launching a new film project or drug product or comarket an important new web-based online service.

A minority equity investment may or may not be a strategic investment; it depends on how the deal was structured. If it is a purely passive investment, then the minority stake would *not* be the basis for a strategic alliance. However, if the minority interest were made to facilitate strategic collaboration and align the interests and commitment of both parties toward future development goals, then it could be a strategic alliance.

For instance, strategic alliances are very common in the airline industries where multiple airlines join forces to jointly share airplane seating capacity (a practice called code sharing). They also cooperate in order to offer their customers global service, better-quality service, more ticketing choices, smoother baggage transfers, better access to airport lounges, and more appealing frequent flyer reward programs. Airlines participating in the network enhance their economies of scale and gain market power. Strategic alliances in the airlines industry tend to create more profits than full mergers because of network externalities: The more partners in the alliance, the greater the perceived value of the alliance to the airline's customers. Alliance networks have become a crucial key success factor to remain competitive in the airline industry; these days being a member of a powerful alliance network is essential.

Another common situation involves IT outsourcing. If the scope of the work for the IT project is very large and if it is of vital importance to the company, the IT outsourcing project would be considered strategic in nature, and we would classify the project as a strategic alliance. (We discuss global trends in information, communications, and technology [ICT] industry outsourcing later in this chapter.)

Strategic alliances normally require senior management commitment and some measure of trust among the parties in order to work. Companies can form strategic alliances with a vast array of players: universities, industry R&D consortia, technology suppliers, NGOs, competitors, customers, distributors, or governmental bodies and agencies. Entrepreneurs have dreamed up many possible permutations and combinations when it comes to creating strategic alliances. We show in the next section that the dynamics of an industry, especially the structure of its value chain, can determine the opportunity for alliance formation.

FORCES OF DECONSTRUCTION OF THE VALUE CHAIN

An industry's value chain is likely to evolve as the industry matures. How the value chain will evolve and to what extent change occurs depends on the initial starting conditions in the industry. *Deconstruction of the value chain* refers to the process whereby integrated portions of a value chain decouple into separate fragments. In some high-technology industries, the forces of deconstruction will split apart the industry's value chain as the industry matures. In other cases, for instance, the opposite takes place, and an industry that begins as an assembly-line operation of standardized components may evolve toward more vertical integration as the stronger players seek advantages from economies of scale and better coordination by producing the components in-house.

How does deconstruction happen? Specialist companies enter into the space being occupied by fully integrated companies. These specialists are focused providers. They operate as independent third parties and compete by offering better and cheaper alternatives to activities and services that are being done in-house. They are more efficient, for example, because they produce only one component compared to a vertically integrated corporation that produces multiple components. They are more responsive and quicker, less bureaucratic than a more complacent in-house group. Eventually the forces of competition prevail.

Why does deconstruction occur? A partial answer is that if a series of horizontally organized specialists are able to perform better than a vertical system, the industry will deconstruct. It may also be a reaction to an antitrust settlement where a dominant, vertically integrated player is split up and forced to compete in a deregulated industry. How fast it happens and to what extent often depends on the trade-off in each industry between coordination, which is the main advantage of vertical integration, and greater competition and efficiency, which are the main advantages of specialization.

As industries mature, many value chains are decoupling and experiencing competition across different stages of the value chain (refer to Figure 6.2). Some of the many forces causing deconstruction today include globalization, faster communications, enhanced real-time Internet-based information systems, improved logistics systems, modern container port facilities, better transport systems across all modes (truck, rail, air, and ship), and industry deregulation. Deconstruction means that even small companies can participate in selective parts of the value chain or can actually coordinate a number of sections through alliance formation. Many successful microcompanies have become global niche players as a result.

As an example, take the deconstruction of the "old" mainframe computer industry where IBM used to be the dominant player against these other vertically integrated competitors: Digital Equipment Corporation (DEC), Sperry Univac, and Wang. Andy Grove, CEO of Intel, in his book *Only the Paranoid Survive* was the first to use the phrase *moving from "vertical" to "horizontal"* to describe the shift in industry's value chain from mainframe computers to the personal computing era of desktop computers.[18]

In mainframes, IBM was completely vertically integrated. It owned its own basic R&D laboratories, designed and developed its own computer processing units, produced its own mainframe hardware, and developed and wrote its own operating systems and applications software. It also controlled its own sales force, service organization, and distribution channels. Similar patterns applied to DEC, Sperry Univac, and Wang. (Refer to Figure 6.3.)

In contrast, the personal computer (PC) industry, at least in the early days, was "horizontally" organized. (Refer to Figure 6.4 on page 122.) In the PC industry, each layer consisted of firms competing to produce a different component used in the overall system. This meant that the firms competing in one segment—say,

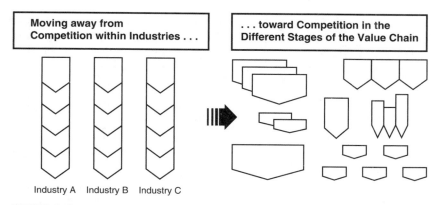

FIGURE 6.2 Industry Deconstruction
Source: Prepared by Constance Lütolf-Carroll in collaboration with Professor Renzo A. Cenciarini, SDA Bocconi. Used with permission.

microprocessors—were not the same ones competing in the other segments—for instance, computer assembly, operating systems, or applications software.

Each industry structure has its pros and cons. The advantage of the vertical arrangement is that the design, manufacture, and integration of components can be coordinated by the dominant player into a unified system. However, when the industry is organized horizontally, the interfaces can be quite problematic (e.g., getting the printer peripherals to be compatible with the computer and the applications software working with the operating system). A standardized interface among the industry players must be developed, agreed upon, and maintained, which adds to costs.

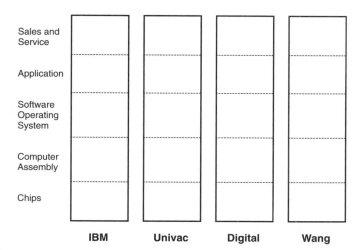

FIGURE 6.3 Vertically Integrated Mainframe Computer Industry in the mid-1990s
Source: Data based on author's recollections and data from Saloner, Shepard, and Podolny (2001, 288–289).

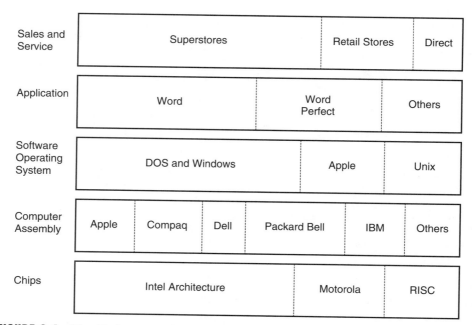

Sales and Service	Superstores		Retail Stores	Direct
Application	Word		Word Perfect	Others
Software Operating System	DOS and Windows		Apple	Unix
Computer Assembly	Apple | Compaq | Dell	Packard Bell	IBM	Others
Chips	Intel Architecture		Motorola	RISC

FIGURE 6.4   Very Early Years of the Personal Computer Industry
Source: Data based on the author's recollections and data from Saloner, Shepard, and Podolny (2001, 288–289).

Counterbalancing the cost of developing standards, however, is the superior ability of the horizontal structure to provide differentiated product components, from which the assemblers can mix and match to suit customized needs. Overall, there is a trade-off between the benefits of coordination and the benefits of specialization and market competition. Although it is hard to generalize, most industries tend toward the vertical organization when the benefits from coordination are higher. When specialization benefits are higher, then industries tend toward disintermediation and deconstruction of the value chain. At any time, most industries are in between the two extremes.

Today, we are witnessing an important trend favoring deconstruction in the pharmaceutical and biopharmaceutical industries. We discuss this trend in more depth in Chapter 8, when we describe the emerging business models in biotechnology and the transition from fully integrated pharmaceutical players to virtually integrated networks of pharmaceutical or biopharmaceutical firms.

The main implication of deconstruction is the growing importance of networks of firms collaborating together, either through partnerships and alliances or by means of electronic marketplaces. The key point to notice is that most global corporations are collaborating with suppliers and alliance partners in much different ways from just a few years ago. What began as a trend—simply to get costs down, primarily by shifting labor-intensive manufacturing jobs to emerging countries with lower hourly wages—has rapidly evolved toward companies seeking higher forms of global collaboration. The competitive pressures are relentless for more seamless supply chains, quicker response times, greater product choice, and 24/7 coverage. As more strategic parts of the value chain are being outsourced, more knowledge-intensive activities and jobs, including R&D, engineering design, and higher levels of value-added manufacturing and business processing, are going offshore.

Since deconstruction of the value chain and moving parts of it around the globe is so important to so many firms in the global economy, we focus next on these types of contractual relationships within the vast array of alliances from which we have to choose.

VERTICAL INTEGRATION DECISIONS

The entrepreneur and her team need to make important decisions about the boundaries of the firm—in other words, on its corporate scope. (Refer to Chapter 3 under "Corporate and Business Strategies.") The team must decide on the degree of vertical integration of the company: what activities are going to be done inside the company and what things are going to be done by other organizations or companies outside the firm. Some executives refer to this as the make-or-buy decision. Be mindful that it is just more than a simple "Who can do it cheaper?" calculation. Choosing the degree of vertical integration is a strategic decision. When making the decision, consider the implications carefully. Capabilities are enhanced through use. If your employees are going to learn to do something well, they need to practice doing it and exercise their skills at accomplishing the activity. Furthermore, they need to continually refresh and renew that learning going forward. This is the principle of dynamic capabilities that we discussed in Chapter 3 (the ability to learn faster and better than your competitors). Going to a third party and having it do an activity at arm's length will likely prevent your company's personnel from having the chance to learn how to do it. If the outsourced activity is a noncrucial part of the value chain, so be it. However, if it deals with the firm's core competency, and it is critically interconnected to other parts of the firm's resources and capabilities, this should give rise for some deep reflection on the part of management. The team will need to think through the advantages and disadvantages of keeping the activity inside (and not outsourcing the assets, skills, and critical know-how embedded in that activity). It could be that the team would be better off setting up an *equity-based* vehicle where the upside and downside risks and rewards are more evenly shared, more control can be maintained, and learning can take place side by side with the other party. For instance, it might make more sense to set up an equity joint venture (with a well-balanced governance structure) than pursuing an outsourcing contract.

Gaining know-how of the type that can be learned only by working in close proximity to others (e.g., a master craftsman and an apprentice) is why the governments in many countries favor setting up international equity joint ventures with foreign companies. Then the employees from both sides get to rub elbows and work together. The smart ones observe and learn and continuously report back to the parent company what they have been learning. It is well-known that over the last few decades, employees at Asian companies have been better at observing and transferring the learning and knowledge back to their parent group than employees in many western companies. As knowledge-based management systems have become more popular, and as more companies try to develop global linkages across their companies, we expect a lot more emphasis on capturing and retaining knowledge from outside and bringing it into the firm more effectively and productively.

On the positive side of going outside the firm, the entrepreneur may encounter different kinds of markets, called *product markets* by economists, in which to procure certain important raw materials or components. Or the start-up firm may be able to rely on the local labor markets, called *factor markets*, to hire the human resources needed to carry out certain activities. In Chapter 3 we discussed the importance of locating within the appropriate cluster to gain proximity to skilled and knowledgeable people. These days, many product and factor markets are migrating to electronic trading platforms, thanks to the Internet and modern telecommunications. Since these electronic markets often are very competitive, they tend to keep the players that participate in them on their toes. A risk that any firm faces as it grows larger, and especially if it becomes too vertically integrated, is that it might lose its competitive edge and become too inflexible. Sometimes creating internal competition between in-house operations and external market sourcing is a good way to keep the organization nimble.

The high-technology entrepreneur is faced with a two-pronged decision. Should your firm do a particular activity or produce a particular component inside the firm (in-house) or go outside (to third parties vendors or suppliers)? Once the firm decides the make-or-buy decision, it needs to decide where to find the vendors: Does the firm look for local vendors (in the same domestic market) or search offshore for foreign vendors (go abroad)? If we map these decision choices, we get a two-by-two decision box, as shown in Figure 6.5.

Decision to Stay Local

It could very well be that for personal or family reasons, the entrepreneur decides to stay local. Staying on home soil simplifies things a lot: It avoids foreign languages, problems of cross-cultural misunderstandings, easier networking to make contacts

Value Chain Activities	Local?	Offshore?
Make? Do it in-house	**Locally Integrated** Do it locally and in-house	**Captive Offshoring** Do it overseas but in-house
Buy? Go outside, contract with third parties	**Local Outsourcing** Use external suppliers but do it locally	**Offshore Outsourcing**[*] Use external suppliers but do it overseas

FIGURE 6.5 Decision Choices: Make or Buy, Local or Offshore?
[*]"Near-shoring" is when the third party is located in a nearby country but still on the same continent.

and find solutions to problems, and so forth. If the choice is to stay local, then the decision breaks down into two pieces:

1. *Locally integrated* is when a company completes the activity in-house by its own employees in its own local facilities. It is referred to as in-house manufacturing or an in-house service capability.
2. *Local outsourcing* is when a company uses domestic vendors (third-party contractors) to carry out business activities in the same country.

For example, imagine a small Swiss start-up software company that specializes in developing Internet applications software and also does some web site development. Most of its customers are located in Switzerland, although some are multinationals and have global operations. An urgent project has come up and the small firm needs to find some skilled programmers quickly. If local software programmers are subcontracted to write computer code, and they carry out the work in Switzerland for the Swiss firm that hires them, this would be an example of a locally outsourced job. As another example, if an Italian manufacturing firm located in Bologna, Italy, decides not to manufacture in-house a key component of a machine tool but instead chooses to subcontract the work to a local supplier, this is a local outsourcing decision.

Decision to Go Abroad

Our Swiss computer software company eventually learns about a better way to staff its application software projects overseas. Through a friend of a friend in London, it has learned about some excellent programmers who work from India, thereby presenting them with an offshore opportunity. *Offshoring* is a form of outsourcing; it is when the activity to be accomplished is relocated away from domestic shores and onto foreign shores. As shown in Figure 6.5, there are two types of offshoring.

1. *Captive offshoring* is when a company keeps and maintains a function or business process under its complete control (in other words, it keeps it completely in-house) but moves the operations to a company facility in a different country. It is basically the relocating of a part of the company's operation to another foreign country.
2. *Offshore outsourcing* is when a company outsources a function or process to another foreign country through an independent third party. The company no longer has its personnel doing that activity. It could very well be that the third party will have sophisticated systems and secure facilities so that the work being done for one company is kept confidential and isolated.

"Near-shoring" refers to an outsourcing agreement where the third party is located in a nearby country but still on the same continent, according to Darrell Rigby of management consultancy Bain & Company.[19] In Latin America, the North American Free Trade Agreement treaty has increased cross-border near-shoring between Canada and the United States and between the United States and Mexico. Similar cross-border near-shoring activity has increased because of Mercosur (Mercado

Común del Sur), which is the regional trade agreement in South America, and the enlargement of the European Union in Europe.

If the outsourcing or offshoring contract is of minor importance to the firm, involving only noncore activities, then it is simply a subcontract agreement and an ordinary alliance. However, if the nature of the work is of critical importance, touches the firm's core competencies, and its failure would have major disruptive consequences for the firm, then the relationship should be classified as a strategic alliance and ought to be viewed as an integral part of the firm's overall strategy and business model.

Trends in ICT Offshoring

Global outsourcing has changed the nature of competition in services. Business processes consist of back-office services (e.g., payroll, order processing) and front-office services (e.g., customer care). Both types of functions, front and back office, are being moved from developed countries, such as the United States and Europe, to offshore centers, in particular, to India and to other developing nations (where language proficiency and service levels are adequate). This lift-and-shift trend has major ramifications for the world's engineering profession and for the ITC industry in particular. Certainly it is the most important trend transforming the Indian software industry, and it is affecting the business models of many other software service providers located in Eastern Europe, South America, and Asia, particularly the Philippines. We are paraphrasing the title of a working paper by two Stanford scholars, both of whom are experts on offshoring issues, when we say that many firms "went for cost reasons and stayed for quality."[20]

Indeed, numerous companies of all sizes (from the largest multinationals to tiny family businesses) competing in many different industries (banking, financial services, consumer credit, insurance, industrial, retail, etc.) have shifted a fraction, a majority, or all of their ICT infrastructure systems, networks, code and applications programming, call centers, or front- and back-office infrastructure to high-tech clusters specializing in certain activities and located in foreign countries.[21] Bain & Company suggest that some of the key strategic drivers for doing more offshoring is to gain proximity to emerging market customers and to access growing pools of highly skilled talent.[22]

Globalization, the search for lower costs, higher productivity, less time zone disruptions, and more qualified technical personnel have made cities like Bangalore, Hyderabad, Mumbai, Delhi, Budapest, Prague, and Moscow hubs for major IT and business processing centers.

To illustrate, in India, the leading Indian software companies that are heavily involved in providing both offshoring and outsourcing services and advisory are Tata Consulting Services (TCS), Infosys, and Wipro Technologies. The National Association of Software and Services Companies (NASSCOM®) is the most important trade association for the software, IT, and business processing industry in India. NASSCOM's web site (www.nasscom.in) provides a wide array of publications on the very latest Indian software industry trends and the growth statistics.

Professors Joseph W. Rottman and Mary C. Lacity, both of the University of Missouri-St. Louis, conducted field interviews during 2006 to identify the best, worst, and emerging practices for offshore outsourcing of IT work. They identify the 15 "best" practices to help clients and suppliers actually realize the benefits expected from offshoring IT work.[23]

Harvard Business School professor Alan MacCormack conducted a yearlong study in collaboration with colleagues from Wipro Technologies, the third largest Indian software company. Together they examined 45 global collaboration projects, interviewed over 150 managers, and identified the "best practices that companies use to move from the initial cost-lowering goals of [offshore] outsourcing to the revenue generating goals of global collaboration."[24]

STRATEGIC ALLIANCES WITH A HIGH COMPONENT OF TECHNOLOGY

Having described the main types of strategic alliances, we next examine the situations in which managers tend to use strategic alliances in a wide variety of high-technology industries. These strategic alliances range from large-scale engineering projects in the utilities, defense, or energy sectors, to industrial collaborations in the automotive, specialty chemicals, pharmaceuticals, medical device, or biotechnology industries, to fast-moving consumer electronics, advanced mobile telephone devices, consumer games, and software markets.

Turnkey Projects

Sometimes an owner contemplating a major construction project wants to deal with only one party for all services—design, engineering, procurement, and construction—in connection with the work; this is a so-called *turnkey project* or stand-alone project. When finished, the new plant is supposed to be ready to operate for the owner at the "turn of a key." In the software industry, the term *turnkey* often describes the design, development, and installation of a large-scale IT system or major software applications project.

In a design, engineer, procure, and construct turnkey project, the engineering contractor does not assume operating responsibilities after project delivery. In a design, engineer, procure, construct, *and operate* turnkey project, the engineering contractor operates the plant for the owner and is paid under a service and maintenance contract.

The semiconductor, chemical, petrochemical, petroleum refining, pharmaceutical, steel, military defense, and utility industries all use turnkey projects that involve the design and installation of sophisticated state-of-the-art equipment, electronic instruments, highly automated processes, and proprietary technologies. Selling turnkey projects is a way for some owners to export their process technologies to other countries. For instance, a major energy company will sell as a turnkey project a multibillion-dollar state-of-the-art petrochemical complex destined for the Middle East.

Key to the development of these projects is the integration of multiple engineering and scientific disciplines, coupled with skilled project management and financing know-how. The owners of the new plant and the staff of the engineering and construction firms must work closely together to develop the scope of work, schedule, financing, and implementation details.

Turnkey agreements are negotiated contracts characterized by the transfer of patented equipment, processes, and products (formulas, chemical catalysts, or active ingredients), transfer of engineering know-how and designs (blueprints, operating manuals, etc.), and technical assistance, services, and training. The major firms that design and build these plants tend to specialize in particular industries where they have decades of experience and know-how on how best to bid, finance, and deliver these projects.

To be a *strategic alliance*, the turnkey project agreement would have to be critically important for the contracting parties, such as in the capital-intensive industries mentioned above, but this criterion could also apply to major software development projects, which are less capital intensive but highly knowledge intensive. If a major, multiyear, multi-user software development project fails, it can have critical consequences for all the parties involved.

Project management skills are of vital importance to oversee the successful completion of these large turnkey projects. For engineering construction firms, the management of complex, technology-driven projects—if done properly and well—can be a source of tremendous competitive advantage for clients.

According to June 2008 predictions published in the *McKinsey Quarterly*, global capital spending is expected to exceed $71 trillion during the years 2008 to 2013—a one-third increase from the levels of 2002 to 2007.[25] According to a Dow-Jones Financial News report, Citibank analysts are projecting that infrastructure spending alone—in emerging markets—will average $2 trillion per annum between 2008 and 2015. Over a slightly longer time horizon, Merrill Lynch, in the same Dow-Jones report, projected that infrastructure spending rates in emerging markets would be 10 percent higher than Citibank's forecast or $2.2 trillion per annum over the next 10 years, starting in 2008.[26]

With the worsening of the global financial crisis in August, 2008, the above-mentioned infrastructure and capital goods forecasts now appear to be too optimistic. Even so, after much political wrangling in Congress, President Barack Obama signed into law in February, 2009, a major $787 billion economic recovery package to immediately fund $150 billion in infrastructure and energy projects. Governments in Europe, Asia, and South America have also devised domestic stimulus plans to counter the growing global recession as consumers, banks, and institutional investors deleverage their balance sheets. If all these promised public works projects are realized, they still will represent huge investments in capital goods and infrastructure. The immediate implications are heavy demand for already scarce engineering talent and a global search to find qualified and experienced project managers.

Technical Assistance and Training Agreements of a Long-Term Strategic Nature

These are agreements in which operating personnel are given specialized and ongoing assistance and training on how to safely maintain and operate highly sophisticated plant and equipment or software systems. Technical assistance agreements may be an important component of infrastructure projects. For instance, operator training programs frequently accompany major civil engineering projects, such as large-scale dams, airports, or advanced water treatment facilities (including salt water desalinization plants, wastewater treatment facilities, or ultra-clean water purification systems). Local operators need to be trained on how to operate the computerized process control systems or other sophisticated electronics. Other examples where safety is a particular concern would be training and transferring technical know-how to operators in state-of-the-art nuclear power plants, semiconductor plants, submarines, aircraft carriers, stealth fighter planes, and hazardous waste treatment facilities for dangerous chemical, biological, or radioactive substances.

Professional Service Contracts

In these agreements, qualified professionals and experts offer their consulting services on a contract basis in exchange for payment. To be a strategic alliance, these services would have to form part of a long-term contractual relationship or partnership. Such professional services are provided by consulting engineers, architects, product designers, software programmers, commercial lawyers, patent attorneys, patent litigation experts, accountants, small business advisors and small business brokers, investment bankers, market researchers, and contract research firms.

Joint Purchasing or Procurement Agreements

These types of procurement contracts (buyer-supplier agreements) arise when two or more companies agree to combine purchase orders for raw materials or other component supplies in order to exploit economies of scale and reduce transaction costs. These types of joint purchasing alliances are common in many sectors where procurement of raw materials, components, or equipment is crucially important, including, for instance, commodity and specialty chemicals, automotive, military, government, and education. They may be based on competitive bids or be collaborative agreements with preferred vendors.

For instance, universities rely on educational discounts for purchasing all sorts of laboratory and office equipment, computer hardware and software, and supplies. The same is true for campus science parks and "incubators" housing start-up companies. A science park will negotiate attractive discounts with vendors of laboratory equipment, consumables, and the like. In the case of life science research laboratories, expensive reagents and chemicals are used to make defined media for the growth of bacteria or animal cells. Restriction enzymes may be used daily in molecular biology for DNA cloning experiments or routine checks. These very expensive consumables typically are bought in long-term joint purchasing agreements.

Production-Sharing Agreements

Production-sharing agreements (PSAs) are contractual arrangements frequently used to explore and develop energy resources. Typically a state with petroleum minerals will contract the services of a foreign international energy company or a consortium of major energy companies (which we will refer to as the energy contractor) to explore, drill, and produce crude oil or gas. In these negotiations, the state will be represented either by the ruling government or by the national oil company. The energy contractor bears all the risk of finding the petroleum minerals and pays for all the exploration, drilling, and production costs. If no crude oil or gas is found, the energy contractor receives no compensation. If the energy contractor is successful and finds sufficient oil or gas, the contractor recovers its investment costs and capital expenditures by claiming a portion of the oil or gas that is eventually produced and sold. The negotiated terms of these production-sharing agreements vary, depending on the current price of crude oil, the remoteness of the place where the oil and gas reserves are located, the country risk incurred, and the negotiating strength of the government.[27]

Codevelopment Agreements

When two or more companies agree to share the costs and ownership of intellectual property derived from basic research or new product development, this is called a *codevelopment agreement*. These long-term collaboration contracts may be for jointly creating intricate prototypes, testing laboratory-scale models or mock-ups, or technical assistance in debugging novel manufacturing processes. These types of agreements are common in a wide variety of industries; we cite two examples, one from the automobile industry and the other from the life sciences.

Codevelopment in the Automotive Sector   In June 2007, General Motors awarded a codevelopment contract to design and build a prototype energy storage system for the GM Chevrolet "E-Flex" electric vehicle propulsion system. The codevelopment partner is Continental Automotive Systems, a division of global giant Continental AG, based in Hamburg, Germany, with 2006 sales of €14.8 billion. The two parties are also jointly researching and exploring various aspects of using state-of-the-art lithium ion battery technology.[28]

Codevelopment in the Biotechnology Sector   Genzyme, based in San Francisco, California, is one of the world's leading global biotechnology firms with 2007 sales exceeding $3 billion and more than 9,000 employees (www.Genzyme.com). Genzyme has grown by its highly successful strategies of "in-licensing" (licensing technology from outside the firm and bringing it inside) as opposed to "out-licensing" (taking technology from inside the firm and licensing it out to other firms). In biopharmaceuticals, both in-licensing and out-licensing strategies are common between smaller biotechnology research-driven firms and larger pharmaceuticals manufacturers. These life science collaborations are characterized by complex strategic contractual relationships, typically involving multiple patent licensing agreements, extensive scientific advisory networks, special issues of corporate governance, all combined under an umbrella of very high technological risk and final market uncertainty. Developing patent strategies and contingent contracts that capture the real options issues involved in the life sciences is critical for success in launching a business venture in biotechnology or related fields. (Refer to Chapter 8 for more about the evolving business models being devised by biotechnology start-up ventures and their alliance partners.)

Copacking or Coproduction Agreements

In *copacking*, a client firm hires another manufacturer that has spare capacity to process ingredients or package products in special containers or bottles. Such *copacking agreements* might also be termed "copackaging agreements," "private-label manufacturing," or "comanufacturing" agreements. Copacking outsourcing contracts are very common, for instance, in fast-moving consumer goods, over-the-counter (OTC) self-medication industries, and many others. Typically a manufacturing firm has spare capacity in one or more of its specialized container filling lines or packing and labeling equipment systems (e.g., putting a medicated gel into a new type of soft-squeeze tube). Production managers working for this brand-name company may decide they can make better use of the spare capacity by producing private-label goods (unbranded goods) for other customers, such as major supermarket or drugstore chains, which then apply their house brand to the finished product. For example, supermarket chains might order the same ingredients, use the same "recipes," and even use the same manufacturers to make up large-volume orders of various items (e.g., breakfast cereals, tomato sauces, canned corn, cookies, or toiletry products). Instead of having the branded company's label on the container, the supermarket chain will substitute its own "house" brand label. Normally these private-label goods are sold to customers at a discount to comparable branded goods.

Copacking arrangements may also arise between intermediate product good manufacturers and specialist packaging firms, for instance, that have special blister-pack equipment, plastic-foil-wrapping machines, labeling equipment, and so forth, which might be expensive, difficult to operate, and outside the core competence of the intermediate product good producer. The specialist copacker will produce finished goods, packaged, wrapped, and labeled, all according to the manufacturer's specifications and final retail customers' requirements. Copacking is a way for manufacturing businesses to utilize spare capacity. The disadvantages are that a manufacturer may be overwhelmed by the volume, complexity, or demands of the customers for whom it is copacking. The trade-offs of extra marginal profits must be counterbalanced by the costs of commitment, loss of schedule flexibility, and service requirements of adding outside customers to the normal backlog of work.

The term *coproduction* has a wide range of meanings. In a general sense, co-production refers to any jointly produced service or any cooperative manufacturing agreement. Coproduction may refer to the way services are jointly performed by both provider and user collaborating together. This is common in education, for instance, where teacher and student must work together for learning to occur. In Hollywood, a film is coproduced when two or more production companies collaborate and shoot scenes for the movie in each other's production facilities (e.g., a French film company may shoot scenes in a German studio, while post-production work is done in Italy). In scientific research, coproduction has a different meaning. It often refers to two or more scientists (or scientific organizations) collaborating together to carry out joint research or produce new technologies or make new prototypes.

In a cooperative manufacturing arrangement (e.g., technology transfer between one multinational company with a foreign government or company), then the copro-duction agreement will provide for the transfer of sufficient production information to enable the commercial producer to manufacture the component, either in whole or in part. For instance, the arrangement would include engineering, quality assurance, and assistance with material specification or procurement.

Comarketing Agreements

In *comarketing agreements*, one company typically owns a patented or branded product and allows another company to sell the branded product in a specific geographical territory. For instance, two pharmaceutical companies, one strong in marketing for the United States and the other strong in the Japanese market, might have a comarketing agreement whereby one firm's patented drug is sold and marketed in the United States in exchange for the other firm's patented drug being sold in Japan. These arrangements take advantage of the differential strengths of the two companies' sales forces; one might have a strong product but weaker sales force coverage for a particular therapeutic treatment area (e.g., cardiovascular medicines), and one might have global sales and distribution channels in Asia that are beyond the reach of the other partner.

In Appendix 6.1, at the end of this chapter, we summarize the main types of alliances and investment modes and compare their contractual features. We touch on the duration of the agreements and the kinds of resources and rights that may be transferred, and provide a quick overview of the typical compensation methods found in these contractual agreements, minority investments, or equity joint venture relationships. These topics are discussed more thoroughly in later chapters of the book.

Reflections on Alliances

As you can see from reading this chapter, alliances come in many diverse shapes and forms. Alliances may be used for any number of purposes and appear in every sort of industry context. The nature of the alliances ranges from loose and informal networks to complicated, formal consortia with interlocking interests. Some alliances have simple reasons for being; others, such as some technology consortia, are aiming to set new technology standards and win the next round in an ongoing competitive race for global market share leadership of their advanced devices and latest innovations. The types of alliances adopted will vary, but knowing when and where to make an alliance can mean success or failure of your commercialization strategy.

Strategic alliance formation is a way for many small companies to survive in turbulent high-technology industries. Ventures may need strategic alliances to carry out R&D, to develop their products, to manufacture and test these products, to go more quickly to market, and to penetrate new niches. A start-up company generally does not have the financial wherewithal to go it alone. It cannot be specialized in all aspects of the value chain and still maintain its state-of-the-art edge in its own technological domain. It needs to combine resources with others to gain economies of scale and increase the breadth of its own product or service offerings.

As industries go through their life cycle, from birth to decline, very often the value chain of the industry will morph, at times leaning toward convergence, at other times deconstructing and splintering into discrete sections. Turbulence and deconstruction lead to increased alliance formation and create new opportunities for the entrepreneurial firm.

In the next chapter, we explore further why parties decide to collaborate and then discuss how to craft, structure, negotiate, and monitor the progress of a strategic alliance.

CHAPTER TAKEAWAYS

- Alliances take many shapes and forms. They may be informal or loose networks, more formal contractual relationships, or equity-based investments in limited liability companies (joint stock companies).

- Each situation is unique. Entrepreneurs may use any or all of the three types of alliances or none of them, depending on the aims and initial conditions of the start-up.
- Choose carefully. A careful strategic internal and external analysis and strategic gap assessment (similar to what we did in Chapter 3) should soon reveal if alliances are necessary for the short or long term.
- Alliance formation is not always necessary. If the entrepreneurial enterprise already possesses the in-house resources and capabilities and financing to develop and market a new product or service, it may be able to advance the commercialization on its own. Most start-ups are not born so well endowed, nor do they have sufficient financial strength to do it on their own; most need partners.
- Spot industry turbulence and the drivers of change. Deconstruction of an industry's value chain often leads to increased alliance formation. For a small company, this creates many opportunities to seek out and find new partners.
- Trust is the key ingredient. For a collaboration to succeed, the partners must respect and trust each other and be willing to share important information and keep each other informed of any changes in the execution of the strategy or problems in the relationship.

APPENDIX 6.1 COMPARISON OF MAIN ALLIANCE MODES AND THEIR CONTRACTUAL FEATURES

TABLE 6.1   Contractual Features of Different Alliance Modes

Type of Alliance	Transfer of Resources and Rights	Typical Compensation Arrangements
Subcontracts (especially those sent out for competitive bids)	Limited to what is specified in the contract. Limited duration.	Cost plus markup, sometimes with unlimited ceiling, other times with a not-to-exceed clause. If scope of work is well defined, then fixed cost, subject to change orders.
Contractual joint venture	Limited to resources and rights specified in the contract, e.g., might be limited to a sales and marketing joint venture. Limited duration.	Function of the change in costs and revenues of the venture, firm, or dominant partner.
Technology transfer licensing agreement	See Chapter 14 for details on how these licensing agreements work. In general, they specify the rights to be licensed, the nature of the grant, and termination conditions. Rights are limited to defined uses, geographical territory. Contract has a limited duration.	See Chapter 14 for details on the financial structure and payment mechanisms. In general, contracts typically include royalties, up-front cash payments, and eventual milestones payments.

(Continued)

TABLE 6.1   (*Continued*)

Type of Alliance	Transfer of Resources and Rights	Typical Compensation Arrangements
Franchising	Contract specifies which IP rights may be licensed, for what field of use, and where (which geographical territory). Limited duration subject to renewal.	Royalty as a percent of sales plus markups on components or ingredients supplied.
Equity joint venture	Full range of resources, capabilities, and IP rights. Unlimited duration unless defined in the agreement.	Dividends plus any capital gains on shares sold to another investor.
Minority investment	Extent of collaboration depends on the actual agreement and the investor's role, passive or active, and level of commitment.	Dividends plus any capital gains on shares sold to another investor.
Turnkey project	Usually stand-alone projects that may be worth in the billions of dollars. Complex technology transfer, specialized equipment designs, and sophisticated technical assistance and training often combined in these projects.	Fixed price, staged payments depending on degree of project completion. May have severe penalty clauses for late completion.
Technical assistance and training	May be small in scale and scope but could be larger, especially for software and complex industrial projects when operators need to be trained.	Often a lump-sum amount. May also be based as a percentage of sales if related to software implementation projects.
Professional services contracts	May refer to a variety of professional, managerial, consulting, engineering, or software services. Usually involves transfer of managerial know-how and expertise. Duration limited by contract.	Remuneration may be structured many ways. Common conditions are monthly or annual retainer fees, fixed lump sums, a percentage paid on completion of various phases of a project, an hourly billing rate (time plus expenses), an exchange of services, or even stock options in lieu of cash.
Joint purchasing agreements or procurement contracts (buyer-supplier agreements)	Usually limited to specific resources (materials, equipment, components). Often done on a competitive bid basis but may also be structured as a collaborative agreement with preferred vendors, such as in the automotive industry.	Depends. Sometimes involve scaled volume discounts, or cost-plus markups or incentives, where rewards are shared based on either decreased costs or increased revenues. Often done on competitive bid basis but may be structured as a collaborative agreement.

TABLE 6.1 *(Continued)*

Type of Alliance	Transfer of Resources and Rights	Typical Compensation Arrangements
Codevelopment agreements	Depends on the industry context, purpose of the development, and the agreement structure. Research agreements are particularly complex, due to the range of IP issues involved. Life is limited to contract duration.	Depends on the negotiated agreement. See Chapter 8 (for biotechnology and biopharmaceutical specifics) and Chapters 10 and 14 (for structuring contingent payments and other financial terms) for these types of deals.
Coproduction (or copacking) agreements	Depends on the industry context, purpose of the alliance, and the agreement specifics. Life limited to contract duration.	Depends on agreement. See Chapters 8 and 14 for details.
Comarketing agreements	Depends on the industry context and specific contract terms. Life limited to contract duration.	Depends on agreement. See Chapters 8 and 14 for details.

CHAPTER 7

Managing Alliances

In the last chapter, we explored how specialist firms deconstruct an industry's value chain. By virtue of their actions, they end up rearranging and transforming pieces of that value chain into new business models. We saw how the upstarts in personal computers dismantled the vertically integrated mainframe industry and created a radically new horizontal structure. Right now, in high-technology consumer electronics, particularly in video game platforms, wireless mobile phones, and personal computers, all kinds of formerly separate technologies are converging into novel products. Designers and manufacturers borrow bits and pieces from parallel industries (e.g., digital cameras, music downloading and networking software, and ultra-thin screens) to dream up new product combinations, such as video chatting on a PC while laughing at a funny YouTube video clip. In so doing, leading firms and their innovative small business partners are fully engaged in innovating, blurring, transforming, and merging the boundaries of industries, business models, value chains, and alliance networks. Firms are managing innovation and using collaboration to gain competitive advantage over their rivals. Deconstruction and convergence are turbulent and unpredictable change processes. We argue that global collaboration is a way forward for firms being slammed in the waves of global competition.

In this chapter, we provide advice for planning and carrying out your venture's first strategic alliance. Perhaps even more important, we make suggestions on how to *manage* it over its life cycle. Our focus is on strategic alliances, as these critical collaborations frequently arise during the start-up phase of a small high-technology business, just when the entrepreneurial team is overloaded with work and has way too many tasks to accomplish. For the chief executive officer (CEO) to take time away from day-to-day crisis management to do some serious reflection on things such as alliance goals and partner search criteria might seem like a pipedream. But we insist the CEO needs to do the things we discuss in this chapter *before* rather than *after* the strategic alliance agreement is signed.

FILLING THE STRATEGIC GAPS

Sooner or later the entrepreneurial team discovers strategic gaps that must be filled as quickly as possible or else the venture's momentum will stall or falter. We refer to this as the "uh-oh" moment. These gaps may appear as strategic weaknesses in resources, organizational capabilities, or market positioning. They could also be gaps in technological or managerial know-how or experience. The holes are usually closed by buying in expertise, collaborating, and learning from others. It is impossible for the start-up team to be master of all trades. Therefore, strategic collaboration is a necessity for many small firms. Under certain conditions it can make a lot of sense for a start-up business to join forces with other more mature businesses.

However, rather than follow a systematic approach to filling their strategic gaps, some small firms have a tendency to bump into their collaboration partners on a haphazard basis. They have a need, they realize they might be in trouble, they look around quickly, they find a nearby partner, and off they run. It either works out, in which case they continue, or it fails, and the partnership is terminated, often with the help of expensive legal and financial advisors. We call it strategic collaboration on the fly.

DOING IT BETTER

We recommend a better approach. You and your entrepreneurial team ought to have a very clear view of *why* you are trying to create value through collaboration and *how* you are going to strengthen your core business by leveraging the complementary resources of a partner firm. Here are some examples. Sharing a sale force, distribution channel, or logistics network with another larger firm can benefit your start-up company by giving it immediate access to one or more market segments. The venture can take advantage of the heavy investments made by others and speed up the delivery of its own new products or services to new customers. At the same time, your venture is benefiting from more efficient economies of scale in distribution, allowing it to cut costs and improve service quality at the same time. Through collaboration it gains from economies of learning. If your organization can learn new skills and apply those capabilities to larger volumes of business, your team will be able to go down the learning curve faster and achieve greater efficiencies in organizational processes and costs than a rival firm that tries to do it all by itself. That is, *if* the alliance is a success story. If it fails, your venture might be worse off than the rival that chose a different path.

Attaining the promised benefits from a collaborative effort is never easy. Managing an alliance is fraught with difficulties. At the beginning it will be much harder and more time-consuming to do something through an alliance than attempting to do it alone. It will take a lot more planning, coordinating, discussing, and negotiating than you may expect, but it will be worth the effort if it works out.

In this chapter, we hope to save you time. We hope to equip you with a road map, a set of checklists and activities that will help you guide your team through the process of formulating and managing strategic alliances. At the end of the process, you and your team will know about the importance of defining the purpose of the alliance and will learn how to select the right partner and what activities are needed to plan, structure, and prepare to negotiate your first alliance deal. You will see the wisdom of planning carefully for the alliance launch even while negotiating with the other side. We also discuss some of the options for managing the nuts and bolts of the alliance, checking its performance, and measuring the results. Here is our road map, step by step, to help you:

1. Decide on the strategic logic for the collaboration.
2. Select the right partnering candidates.

3. Design, structure, and negotiate the alliance.
4. Manage the alliance.
5. Measure and assess performance.
6. Check on the merits of continuing the alliance. Either adjust or exit.
7. Start the cycle anew. Strive to create a connected network of alliances.

STEP 1: DECIDE ON THE STRATEGIC LOGIC FOR THE COLLABORATION

A strategic alliance is a strategic commitment. You need to decide up front and with deep reflection exactly *why* you and your team want to collaborate over the long term with a strategic partner.

- What is the real purpose or strategic intent of the alliance?
- What are the long-term strategic aims and goals of the collaboration?
- What realistically can be expected by collaborating?
- What is the strategic logic driving the economics of the deal for both sides?
- What value is going to be created for customers and ultimately shareholders through this alliance?

Try to keep an open mind, especially at the beginning, as you do this strategic reflection. After all, it might make more sense *not* to negotiate a strategic collaboration but rather have your venture:

1. Do it alone (e.g., pursue in-house research and development [R&D]).
2. Rely on separate vendor contracts to purchase off-the-shelf components rather than manufacture them in a complicated joint venture.
3. Hire the talent directly instead of sharing key people in an academic research collaboration.
4. Accept a merger in order to consolidate the global earnings stream from a technology platform that your venture developed, but that only the partner is capable of distributing and selling around the world.
5. Pay a control premium to carry out an acquisition and block a rival from doing the same—rather than hope the target company will do an alliance and things will work out. (Acquisitions tend to be more costly for buyers than doing alliances because of the need to pay the target company shareholders a control premium, but sometimes they are the best way for the buyer to consolidate control over interconnected technology platforms or to wring cost savings out of the completed transaction.)

Collaborations, like mergers and acquisitions, are messy. They always require a lot of hard work to carry out. Getting people to join forces and share know-how is never easy. Cultures clash, people can be obstinate. Delays and project cost overruns are inevitable. Some people feel very threatened about collaborating. They may fear they will lose power if they share too much, or they may not like the intrusion, or they may worry about losing their jobs.

As the CEO of a start-up venture, it may pay to play the role of devil's advocate. Be skeptical. Ask probing questions. Seek specific facts and evidence to corroborate the benefits to be achieved by any proposed collaboration or joint venture. Do not underestimate the costs, especially the managerial time you and your senior team will need to commit to make the strategic alliance work.

Nearly Half of Alliances Fail to Earn Their Cost of Capital

Explore the risks and downsides if the strategic alliance or joint venture were to fail. Have a contingency plan. Be aware that alliances are fragile structures. As quickly as they can be formed, they can also fall apart. To cite one example of many such research studies, McKinsey and Company assessed the outcomes of over 2,000 alliance announcements in a large field study conducted during 2001. The success rate for the alliances in their sample set was only 53 percent, where "success" was defined as each partner having achieved returns greater than the cost of capital.[1]

Over the years, the 50 percent average success rate has not changed much; furthermore, the success rate for mergers and acquisitions (M&As) is not altogether different; about half fail. Be aware of the risks of both alliances and business combinations.

For evidence and stories about M&A fiascos, we recommend the carefully researched book *Deals from Hell: M&A Lessons that Rise above the Ashes* by Robert F. Bruner.[2] Bruner writes:

> *anticipating M&A failure can enhance success. . . . [S]uccess depends on vitally adopting the right attitude about M&A as a path of corporate growth. It is no formula for surefire success; rewards are extremely difficult to sustain over time; risks are legion; it is to be undertaken only with very serious planning and preparation; and the effort should be motivated by the right values and respect for investors.[3]*

We wish to convey exactly the same message when it comes to managing and maintaining strategic alliance relationships: Management choices and processes *do* matter. The devil is in the details. We cannot emphasize enough the importance of careful preparation and planning. You need to make the commitment to the strategic alliance, to make timely decisions, and to carefully execute on the details of any joint venture or alliance collaboration.

We also recommend that you consider a wide range of strategic options. Explore the costs and benefits of each before narrowing down to a specific alliance decision too quickly. We encourage you to listen carefully to your board of directors, especially to those with strategic alliance, joint venture, or M&A experiences. They will help you think through various strategic options as you ultimately decide on the best path to take.

If your venture is financed with venture capital, then pay close attention to the exit strategy requirements of the venture capitalists on your board of directors. The venture capitalists will have certain goals and time schedules for harvesting the funds they have invested in your company. A timely exit is what they expect to achieve, and the alliance strategy will be interwoven into that decision. (Refer to Chapter 19, where we discuss venture capitalists' views on exit strategies in greater detail.)

Balance the Trade-Offs between Yielding Control and Gaining Benefits

When considering collaboration with another organization, be mindful that there is always a trade-off between "yielding control" and "gaining benefits." Yielding control can mean many things. For example, your venture may lose the ability to make strategic decisions about the direction of its new product launch. Or your marketing manager may be unable to make the critical decisions on brand image and channel positioning for an improved service-product bundle being offered to a potentially large and important consumer market. (See the story about Raisio, a small Finnish company with a big innovation, later in this chapter. Raisio carefully negotiated a strategic alliance collaboration that seemed like a perfect match at the beginning and then turned into a worst-case scenario.)

Losing control might also mean yielding on the future direction of important R&D projects in a joint venture, or losing out on picking key managers for important positions in competition with the other partner. Many high-technology ventures are concerned about losing control over the use of shared technology and proprietary trade secrets, and rightly so. We address these concerns at length in Chapter 9 and raise them again in Chapters 11 and 14. Worrisome, too, is losing direct contact with the final customers or end users and their needs because a so-called partner in a comarketing alliance may refuse to cooperate and share important customer data. Then, too, plenty of outsourcing deals, licensing agreements, and joint ventures have led to the creation of future competitors in soon-to-be important markets. These worries can become nightmares. All are valid managerial concerns that need to be taken into account *before* entering into collaboration with another party. Taking the time to identify and select the right partner at the very beginning is the best way to prevent many of these problems. (See Step 2.)

Benefits to Be Gained   Having discussed the downsides about yielding control, what are the benefits to be gained by giving up control? There are numerous benefits attainable for small ventures that do go ahead and pursue alliances. As we show in Chapter 8, strategic alliances and joint ventures can stimulate innovation and organizational learning, especially in science-driven ventures. In fact, alliances and alliance networks are deeply woven into the value chains of biotechnology and medical technology companies. We were hard-pressed to find examples of start-ups going it alone in those sectors. Each one we studied was symbiotically dependent on other alliance partners. Alliance management is a critical skill for entrepreneurs contemplating entry into these life science industries.

As we already observed in Chapter 4, joint ventures make sense when value creation is facilitated by physically integrating assets and capabilities and placing them side by side in a separate joint venture company, a company with its own culture and independent financing. As we pointed out in Chapter 6, an equity joint venture might be the *only* viable alternative to capture the know-how and specialized assets inside another company, especially if the other party is unwilling to be bought or do a merger, or if the party is not allowed to be merged or bought due to government regulations or foreign ownership restrictions.

When to Favor Strategic Alliances over M&As   Various studies have shown that joint ventures and strategic alliances are preferable to mergers and acquisitions under certain conditions—conditions that we suggest usually prevail in the realm of high-technology ventures. For instance, research conducted by McKinsey and Company for more than a decade (field studies conducted in 1991, 2001, and 2004) has shown that strategic alliances and joint ventures have a slightly higher success rate than M&As when the aims are to (1) enter a new territory, (2) develop a product area, (3) grow in new customer segments, or (4) develop entirely new capabilities. James Bamford, David Ernst, and David G. Fubini write "Alliances have *lower* success rates [than mergers and acquisitions] when control is important—for instance, when the goal is consolidation of operations or improved performance."[4]

Thus, if the strategic intent is to consolidate market positions and achieve synergies through cost consolidation or restructuring, then pursuing a M&A is a slightly better risk. If the strategic intent is more open-ended and learning oriented, pursuing strategic alliances might yield slightly better results. We emphasize, however, that these "success rate" differences are small. Each situation needs to be assessed individually and strategically on a case-by-case basis, especially if the transaction being contemplated is one involving international partners. Cross-border strategic alliances and joint ventures tend to be more problematic, even for larger companies with years of experience doing alliances.

Cross-Border Joint Ventures and Alliances In another well-known study on cross-border joint ventures and alliances, conducted in 1991, McKinsey consultants Joel Bleeke and David Ernst examined the partnerships of 150 companies ranked by market capitalization. (They used the top 50 joint ventures in size from the United States, Europe and Japan).[5] They learned that:

- Both cross-border acquisitions and cross-border alliances have about a 50 percent success rate.
- Alliances are more effective for penetrating related businesses or new geographical territories. Acquisitions work better for core businesses and existing geographical markets.
- "Alliances between strong and weak partners rarely work. They do not provide the missing skills needed for growth, and they lead to mediocre performance."[6]
- Of the joint ventures that are terminated, more than 75 percent end up by one of the parties buying out the other. (In other words, one parent usually purchases the position of the other parent company, in order to end the joint venture relationship.)
- Successful alliances need autonomy and flexibility to evolve and to adapt their initial objectives to suit new circumstances and partner aims.

There is no magic wand to guarantee that strategic alliances or business combinations will work out for your venture. The world is too risky for that. Despite decades of research and numerous studies, alliance success rates still hover around 50 percent, and we predict that it will continue to be so. Here is why:

- Alliances are most suitable for the riskiest business conditions.
- Alliances are good where ambitious, ambiguous, novel, and pioneering exploration is desired.
- Under conditions like these, we think a high breakup rate is normal.

While some alliances may be like fragile boats, there also are some that behave like extremely flexible and adaptable rubber lifeboats—again a feature that may work out about half the time:

- Alliance flexibility becomes attractive when managers seek to keep their options open.
- Alliance flexibility can be frustrating when it enables "the other side" to dance around commitments and deliverables.

In the end, each strategic alliance and joint venture deal varies. The people initiating, negotiating, and managing any alliance will face novel circumstances and unknown market conditions whenever they do a deal. That is what makes the study of strategic alliances an exciting and somewhat treacherous territory for authors of books like ours. It is hard to generalize. But consider for a moment, the alternative for a small start-up. You either collaborate and it works, or you do not collaborate and your high-technology start-up venture might fail anyway. To help improve the odds of your start-up venture's survival, we think it helps to be prepared. As the old saying goes, "Forewarned is forearmed." In that spirit, we offer you our first checklist and set of activities.

Step 1 Checklist: Deciding on the Strategic Logic

The following activities and questions are designed to help you and your team decide on the strategic rationale for doing a strategic alliance.

Activity A

Each group member should prepare these questions individually and then when the group meets, constructively discuss as a team each person's view and proposals. The group should then try to reach a consensus on the main purpose and overall aims of the proposed collaboration. Typically there is more than one aim for collaboration. Avoid making a laundry list of too many aims. Set realistic expectations for the alliance.

Why are we seeking to collaborate? Is it to

- ☐ Obtain more financing?
- ☐ Help test and evaluate new products in development?
- ☐ Share research and development costs?
- ☐ Tap new market applications?
- ☐ Gain specialized knowledge?
- ☐ Enhance our venture's reputation and credibility in the scientific and business communities?
- ☐ Leapfrog to a new technology platform?
- ☐ Prevent a rival from setting an industry standard?
- ☐ Improve contacts with governmental agencies or legislative committees?
- ☐ Enhance the venture's ability to bear risks?

- ☐ Stimulate growth, development, learning of personnel? If so, in what specific ways?
- ☐ Co-opt a rival?
- ☐ Gain access to and knowledge about potential customers?
- ☐ Gain clout in distribution?
- ☐ Gain scale in manufacturing capacity?
- ☐ Grow internationally?

Activity B

Brainstorm these next questions as a team. Have one person record the group's comments and serve as process moderator.

1. How does the proposed alliance fit in with our venture's overall vision and mission?
2. What are our specific long-term goals for this strategic alliance?
3. What are our priorities?
4. What are our specific short-term objectives and milestones for carrying out the strategic alliance?
5. For how long do we envision this strategic alliance should endure?

Activity C

Summarize the group's decisions. Write down the strategic intent for the alliance. Develop the strategy statement for the alliance. (Recall that a good business strategy should have a well-defined set of goals, scope, sustainable competitive advantage, and a compelling strategic logic. Review Chapter 3 if you are unsure how to create a strategy.) Make a list of these key points:

- ☐ Immediate short-term goals of the alliance relationship
- ☐ Long-term goals (specify time horizon) of the alliance relationship
- ☐ Capabilities, resources, and positioning essential to achieving these goals, both now *and in the future*
- ☐ Capabilities, resources, and positioning you look for in a partner, both now *and in the future*
- ☐ Capabilities, resources, and positioning that can be shared with that partner, both now *and in the future*

STEP 2: SELECT THE RIGHT PARTNERING CANDIDATES

After doing Step 1, you and your team should have a clearer idea of the strategy for the strategic alliance. Later on you may need to revisit this strategy and revise it. But at least for now, you have made some initial choices.

In Step 2, our aim is to translate the strategy into a set of decision criteria that will be helpful when you begin the partner search and selection process. These decision criteria will help you narrow down the field of potential partners systematically and effectively.

1. *Decide* who *is going to be on the decision criteria task force.* Being responsible for setting the partner criteria is a key role. Assign a small group of senior people to do the job—maybe yourself, your chief financial officer (if those are separate roles), chief scientific officer, and head of business development. Ensure they dedicate a reasonable amount of time to carry out the process adequately and achieve a good result. Starting a search process to pick an alliance partner without adequate criteria is a waste of time. Focus on managing the process.

2. *Develop partner search criteria.* Making a good analysis of your potential partner depends on developing objective measures a priori, then assessing the competencies and resources of potential candidates. Your team needs to develop a simple system for making comparisons and to discuss the merits or demerits of the potential list of candidates.

3. *Assign roles.* Once you have drafted the partner selection criteria, assign members various roles and responsibilities for facilitating the search. Give each person deadlines to meet. Make sure one person is assigned responsibility and authority to systematically keep track of the search results in a database. By keeping track of your search results for this first alliance, you are building up a competitive knowledge base that you can use for doing future alliances. Be organized.

4. *Seek diverse sources of information.* The best advice for picking the right partner is to search widely using a variety of different networks and information search techniques. There is no substitute for doing an intensive amount of competitive intelligence searching and carefully conducting due diligence on any potential partners. (Refer to Chapter 15 for more on how to do competitive searches and patent investigations. Refer to Chapter 16 for advice on how to do due diligence.)

5. *Get out of your usual comfort zone and widen your search patterns.* You and your colleagues should think out of the box. Do not fall back on old habits and rely too heavily on the most convenient advisors (the people who you rub elbows with each day, in the cafeteria of your business incubator) or with whom you are most familiar (former PhD research advisors or other faculty mentors). Instead, try to conscientiously widen your search patterns. The more time and effort that you and your team place on this step of widening your search, the more *diverse* knowledge you will glean on the competitive situation you face in the field.

6. *Personal networks and direct private contacts are indispensable.* Try to develop as much reliable private information and private sources of insights as you can. Business development managers, hedge fund managers, and investment bankers will tell you the same thing: The closer you can get to the primary source information, and the earlier you discover it before competitors, the likelier it is that you will find more advantageous pricing opportunities. Perhaps, too, by being early, you will find more flexibility on negotiating terms. There is no substitute for face-to-face meetings. Try to get to know the potential partner as well as possible before committing to an important strategic alliance or JV arrangement. However, before you make the contacts, think through how you

are going to handle the initial approach. (We discuss two possible strategies in the next section, "Making the Initial Contact with the Potential Alliance Partner.")

7. *Do seek information from informed and reliable third parties.* Naturally your firm should collect and make sense of as much publicly available information on potential partners as possible. But also regularly collect and screen data from informed third parties. For example, seek out contacts in firms that have had previous alliance agreements with the potential partners. Learn what their experience was with that partner. Listen to former employees. Contact the investment bankers and scientific advisors of the potential partner, who may have had dealings with them, and learn their views about the reputation and reliability of the other party. (See the section in Chapter 16 called "Strategic Alliances" for more on conducting alliance partner due diligence).

8. *"You don't always get what you pay for but you always pay for what you get"* is an anonymous quip from the investment business but also rings true when it comes time to buy competitor intelligence.[7] Proprietary databases of information are going to be more expensive than free ones, but that is because there is a cost to information acquisition, filtering, and making meaning out of all the noise and data. If your partner search generates bewilderment rather than clear, useful information, perhaps you should invest in some proprietary information about recent partnering experiences.

9. *Visit industry "partnering" forums.* The companies that are attending such forums are of the same mind-set as you are, so it is easier to get to know each other. (See Chapter 15 for more on partnering forums or else log onto our web site at www.innovationtocashflows.com and browse the file called "Resources" for the URLs of specific partnering forums).

10. *Intermediary "matchmakers" may be needed in some countries.* In China, Japan, and South Korea, for instance (but in many other countries too), it may be advisable to use a "matchmaker" (a type of broker) to make the initial contact between your firm and a potential partner. This means that you first need to conduct a search to find the right matchmaker who will then enable you to connect with the right person (maybe in the government) who then will connect you to the potential partner company. In the United States and Europe, things might be different. U.S. and European firms use intermediaries less frequently to broker strategic alliances. These firms will be inclined to make the approach directly through their own network of contacts. Again, there are no hard-and-fast rules.

11. *All the time, deals get brokered and deals get discovered.* Sometimes discovery is through luck and serendipity, but most of the time it is through hard work and dedicated search effort. Stay alert, be dynamic, and position yourself strategically where you can gain access to good quality and fresh information about talented people and promising deals. That's our main advice.

Making the Initial Contact with the Potential Alliance Partner

You need to clarify with your team how you are going to approach the top three or so potential alliance candidates, particularly if these potential partners are firms with which your company has never worked. The two main options are (1) to do the approach sequentially or (2) to broadcast your venture's alliance intentions more openly. For more insights, see Lucius Cary.[8]

- *In the sequential approach, potential partners are approached one by one.* Start with number one; move to number two if one says no; move to number three if two says no; and so forth. This approach works best if time is not a critical factor in setting up the alliance. The reason is that each candidate might take several weeks or even months studying the proposal, doing their own market research, due diligence fact checking, and analysis. The risk your venture runs is that the other party decides not to make the commitment, possibly for reasons unrelated to your proposal (it has other strategic priorities, is overloaded and has no spare manpower—there are numerous reasons to say no). Then your team will need to start over again with the next candidate. Meanwhile precious time to market is being lost. The process can be quite time-consuming and very stressful, particularly after three or four iterations of the cycle.
- *In the open approach, the idea is to send out feelers to test the interest of the leading potential candidates more or less at the same time.* This has the advantage of stimulating a beauty-contest atmosphere and may lead to interest on the part of suitors vying to get in on the deal. It can also backfire. You do not want to appear to be "shopping the deal," as then people get suspicious and might just as quickly lose interest.

We believe that it is unwise to give armchair advice without knowing the facts of each situation. The choice of approach very much depends on whether you have already taken measures to protect your intellectual property by means of copyrights, trademarks, or design registration. (See Chapter 11 for advice on copyrights, trademarks, or design registration processes.) If you are seeking an alliance because you need money and expertise to proceed with a patent registration, then it would be a real blunder to tell people openly about your ideas and plans. It might also prevent you from getting a patent in the first place. (See Chapters 12 and 13 for more on patent basics and patent strategies.)

We also think the approach very much depends on the country in which you are doing business and its local customs. In continental Europe, a more nuanced, discreet, and cautious approach would likely work better. In the end, the choice between using an open approach or a sequential approach will depend on your own reading of local business practices, cross-cultural experiences, and the advice you receive from local contacts. Our point is simply to raise the issues and make you aware of other cross-cultural ways of approaching suitable partners that might be different than in your home country. In all cases, it will be beneficial for your venture if you, and your start-up team, do the following:

- Contemplate your approach for initiating alliance discussions. Decide who should make the initial approach and in what sequence the potential candidates will be contacted.
- Carefully consider what exchange of information you are willing to enter into about your own proprietary know-how and strategies.

For further tips on legal protections for your intellectual property, we recommend that you log onto our web site, www.innovationtocashflows.com, and either download or browse these useful supplements:

- Appendix 2.2, "Guidelines for Setting Up an Invention Disclosure System for Your Company"
- Appendix 2.3, "Sample Invention Disclosure Form"
- Appendix 9.1, "Sample Confidentiality Agreement"

Step 2 Checklist: Selecting the Right Partnering Candidates

The next series of activities will help you and your team think about the partner search and selection process.

Activity A

Sketch the value chain of your business model and try to see how putting your venture's value chain together with that of each potential partner could create synergies for both parties. Determine at what stages in the value chain there are likely possibilities for collaboration. The team should make a list of potential partnering possibilities. Assign one person to keep track of all the names of potential candidates that surface during the brainstorming session.

- ☐ Research the leads of potential partners that arise during the brainstorming sessions and competitive intelligence searches.
- ☐ Using the search criteria, narrow down the list of possible candidates to a smaller sample.
- ☐ Screen the shorter list of potential candidates by preparing briefing materials about each one in preparation for the next round of teamwork.
- ☐ Develop a list of the resources, capabilities, and strategic market positioning for each potential candidate that would be useful to access in the collaborative alliance (from the point of view of your venture).
- ☐ Really think ahead. Are the desired capabilities and resources those that are needed now and *in the future*?

Activity B

The team should discuss each strategic alliance partner on the short list of candidates. We suggest screening, filtering, and qualifying them using a set of qualitative questions. (See the next checklist and refer to the particular section in Chapter 16 called "Conducting Due Diligence: Strategic Alliances" for more questions on partner selection.) Record the results for each candidate and develop a rating system for ranking them on their suitable fit.

- ☐ Does this potential partner have the necessary financial, market, or development resources to carry the project to completion?
- ☐ Is the potential partner's organization seriously interested in pursuing the opportunity?

☐ Will the senior management of the counterparty be involved? (If so, how many other commitments will these persons have to juggle at the same time?)

☐ What is the reputation of the people with whom you will be directly working? Is it one of honesty and integrity? Are they reliable? Do they deliver what they promise? Could you work together?

☐ Is there a fit between their values and ethics and those of your own firm?

☐ Does the company have a previous track record of successful partnering?

☐ Is the potential partner technically qualified and considered a leader in the field?

☐ What proof of expertise is available (pending patent applications, granted patents, leading journal publications, research grants, and technical standards committee memberships)?

☐ Are there any other concerns about this candidate that should be investigated further?

Activity C

The team should now summarize their discussions about each strategic alliance partner on the shorter list of candidates. The team needs to decide on a process by which the final short list of candidates is narrowed down to the first, second, and third choices.

STEP 3: DESIGN, STRUCTURE, AND NEGOTIATE THE ALLIANCE

Step 3 is presented as a logical sequence of activities and discusses each phase (design, structure, negotiate) as if these processes take place in distinct phases, one right after the other. In fact, what happens in real life is that these three phases are interrelated and interconnected. As the strategic alliance design progresses, various possible legal, financial, and tax structures for the deal will emerge. The possible legal structures will need to be discussed and fleshed out in consultation with the venture's legal counsel who are specialists in forming joint venture companies or limited partnership vehicles. If it looks like a technology agreement will be a key part of the negotiations, then the entrepreneur is well advised to seek legal counsel from intellectual property specialists to help structure the deal from their respective points of view: patents, trademarks, registered designs, trade secrets, or copyrights.

Meanwhile, the chief financial officer and head of business development ought to be engaged in making financial models and valuing different variations of the possible deal structures. They should be trying to quantify the economic benefits of various deal options and the financial implications of the deal alternatives on the strategy of the venture. At some point in this process, experts in accounting and tax issues will weigh into the discussion, and so the process evolves, changes, and completes a few loops, possibly even before the negotiation phase begins with the first potential strategic alliance candidate.

The timing of when these various experts are called into the picture depends very much on the size of the deal and the budget of the venture. For a very small transaction or a start-up strapped for cash, often these expensive advisors are brought into the process at a very late stage—sometimes too late. Experienced advisors can be very helpful early in the process when the entrepreneurial team is still formulating its ideas about deal structure. For any large transaction then, legal, intellectual property, tax, and accounting advice are indispensable throughout the alliance structuring and negotiation phases.

Once the negotiations begin with the alliance candidate (the "other party"), more issues and questions may arise that will affect the venture team's initial thoughts about their own intent and purposes for doing the strategic alliance.

The negotiations will inevitably cause them to rethink some elements of the overall strategy for the alliance. These "upstream changes" in strategy have a cascade effect and will influence "downstream" contract choices, such as the type of legal structure or clauses required. The terms and conditions written into the various agreements will need to be adjusted and modified by the lawyers.

Meanwhile, on the process side of the negotiations, other activities are happening in parallel to the work being done by the teams. As soon as the negotiations start, the managers and advisory teams on both sides are getting acquainted. They capture their first impressions and size each other up. Later on, as the negotiations intensify, they start testing assumptions about each other's commitment, seriousness, suitability, and qualifications for getting the alliance to work.

Surprise

The next statement will come as a surprise to many start-up entrepreneurs doing their first strategic alliance: The reality is that in most large corporations, the people *doing* the negotiations for the alliance will *not* be the people eventually tasked with managing and carrying it out. This rightly causes a lot of concern for the venture team managers. After all, in a small company, the ones negotiating the deal will be doing the deal. Normally, there are not that many people in a start-up for the situation to be otherwise. But do *not assume* that is true for the other side, especially if it is a larger corporation.

Passing the Baton

The best analogy we can think of is to describe the alliance process as a relay race. One runner starts off with the baton. The first runner must pass the baton to the next runner or the team loses the race. Consequently, we need to think very carefully how to keep our side and the other side from dropping the baton between the time when the negotiations are under way and verbal promises are made, and the actual launch of the strategic alliance, when a new team is likely to come onboard from the larger corporation. Plan and assume that the new team coming onboard will have had virtually no preparation from the negotiation team on any aspect of the strategic alliance. This is a realistic portrayal of what often happens. The baton gets dropped by the other party, and often the small venture ends up suffering the consequences.

This sad story is why we include in our checklist a series of questions that you can ask to try to pin down the other side on exactly what its processes are going to be for the handover—our term for what happens to the alliance process when the negotiation phase is over and the alliance launch begins. With this long prelude, we now begin the three phases of Step 3 on our road map.

Designing the Alliance

A useful way to begin designing the alliance is to take the hypothetical role of the party sitting on the other side of the bargaining table. Discuss the questions with your team. View the deal from the perspective of the alliance candidate with whom the venture team will be negotiating. Then flip sides and view the questions from your venture's point of view. Seek a balance of interests. Think along multiple issues and meshing multiple objectives and interests.

Step 3 Checklist: Designing the Alliance

The first set of questions covers the subject matter or specific contents of the alliance. The second set refers to the process of managing the alliance. The third set addresses alliance risks, controls, and governance mechanisms.

Content Questions

These queries ask about the subject matter of the alliance agreement. In answering these questions, the alliance team collects the needed facts and evidence which the negotiating team will be able to use to develop supporting arguments and stories for the upcoming alliance negotiations.

- ☐ How can both sides benefit?
- ☐ What can we bring to the bargaining table? What is the main reason why the other party would be interested in doing an alliance with us?
- ☐ Are the short-term goals, objectives, and priorities of the other party aligned with our goals, objectives, and priorities? If not, what are the differences? What about the long-term goals, objectives, and priorities? Is there alignment or divergence with our goals, objectives, and priorities for the alliance?
- ☐ Especially for a joint venture, is there congruence between what the sponsors of the joint venture see as the aims and what the subgroups participating in the joint venture see as the aims? If these views are not aligned, is there a way to bring them back into alignment?
- ☐ What is the value we are bringing to the customer with the strategic alliance? Will the customer be willing to pay for the perceived benefits?
- ☐ What are the specific economic benefits for the other party if it does the alliance? Enumerate these benefits and quantify using the financial modeling tools and techniques we describe in Chapters 17 to 20. (In Chapter 17, we show you how to do discounted cash flow valuations. In Chapter 20, we show how to develop economic trade-off tables to quantify various deal options during the heat of negotiations. See the Advanced Dermal Delivery Inc. case in Chapter 20.)

☐ The bottom line: Does the partnership create economic benefits and make commercial sense for both sides? If not, dig deeper and ask why are we doing the deal? Are there other strategic reasons for doing it?

☐ Do not focus solely on the numbers. Specify and enumerate the *nontangible* benefits. Write them down.

☐ Why is the other party willing to pay to get access to our patents, trade secrets, or other intellectual property?

☐ In what specific ways would our innovative technological know-how and processes help the other side win competitive advantage?

☐ What role would this relationship play in our industry?

☐ Which partner is responsible for what component of the value equation?

☐ What strategic gaps are being filled by the partner?

☐ Where does the competitive advantage lie in the future? What skills are needed? Will the rewards be shared fairly?

Process Questions

The following questions ask about process, or how the venture team proposes to engage the hearts and minds of the other parties to the alliance.

☐ Are we allowing adequate face-to-face meeting time with the other party so we are able to get to know each other better, both formally and informally?

☐ How can we build cross-disciplinary and cross-functional task force teams and get people to participate on these teams?

☐ Do we really trust our partners? Is their expertise and experience adequate?

☐ Which partner is the most receptive learner? Do both partners have a willingness and capacity to learn from the other? (The technical term is *absorptive learning capacity*.)

☐ How can we keep the people committed to the alliance goals and keep them fully engaged?

☐ What happens if there are delays? What triggers do we have to set off the alarm bells that the alliance is getting derailed? Do we have contingency plans in case things are late?

☐ How can we ensure that critical issues do not get buried or brushed aside during the negotiations and launch phases?

☐ How can we ensure that any verbal promises or understandings made in the negotiations are put into writing and included in formal processes during the launch phase? In other words, what can we do to get the concrete details specified that are critical to managing the alliance, and have these handed over and passed along to the team who will be actually managing the alliance, not just negotiating it.

Risk, Control, and Governance Questions

The last set of questions asks for team reflection about the alliance governance structure. The questions seek information from the team on the potential risks. The final questions ask for the team's input on ways to mitigate these risks. Bring up the salient points and concerns with legal counsel when you discuss possible deal structures (Step 4).

- ☐ What are the risks of doing this particular alliance?
- ☐ How likely are these risks? Can we quantify the chances of their happening?
- ☐ What is the proper legal mechanism for establishing the partner relationship?
- ☐ Who is governing this alliance? (In a joint venture, the board of directors typically governs the alliance. In a strategic alliance, the governance structure needs to be clearly understood.)
- ☐ For equity joint ventures: Are the voting rights aligned with the economic contributions of the parties to the JV?
- ☐ What control rights do the lenders and preferred shareholders have over common shareholders? (These terms are explained in Chapters 9 and 10.)
- ☐ How are the decision-making roles allocated?
- ☐ Do we have a specific plan to decide on who is allocated what roles during the alliance launch process?
- ☐ Do we fear opportunistic behavior from this partner? Why? What mechanisms can be put in place to prevent one party from dominating to the detriment of the other?
- ☐ Are we sharing the benefits fairly?
- ☐ What are the implications of sharing proprietary know-how and licensing intellectual property? If it were to leak into the wrong hands, what are the consequences for our venture? What steps can we put in place to try to prevent this from happening?
- ☐ Are we vulnerable to changes in strategy by the other party? What is the appropriate response if such a circumstance arises?
- ☐ Do we risk damage to our products, brands, or company reputation by misbehavior from our outsourcing partner?
- ☐ Are we exposed to financial risk if the other party faces financial difficulties? Can we protect ourselves from any such liabilities through proper legal structures?
- ☐ Have we conducted thorough due diligence to find out if the other party has exposure to legal risks (environmental liabilities, product quality problems, or pending civil or criminal lawsuits) that we should protect ourselves against?
- ☐ What are the triggers we would like to have to terminate the agreement and extricate ourselves from the relationship, if things take a turn for the worse and there is no other remedy but exit?

Structuring the Alliance

In this phase, we convey a few simple principles about deal structuring in anticipation of much deeper coverage of shareholder agreements and technology transfer agreements in the legal portions of the book. (Refer to Chapters 9 to 14 and

Chapter 16.) Strategic alliances, if well designed, properly crafted, and carefully implemented, have the potential to offer you and your entrepreneurial team of managers multiple opportunities for value creation. As we said earlier, despite managers' best intentions, strategic alliances and joint ventures experience high failure rates. Therefore, a key principle to keep in mind in structuring any strategic alliance deal is to try to keep your management options open. You are going to be dealing with situations of high uncertainty and ambiguity and therefore high expected risks. We introduce two powerful concepts of dealing with uncertainty, conflict, and ambiguity: *real options* and *contingent rights*.

What Is a Real Option?   An investor holds a real option "when he or she buys the right—but not the obligation to invest or disinvest in a real (nonfinancial asset) at a future time called the expiration date."[9] The presence of real options enhances the worth of a capital investment project. For instance, managers will proactively make decisions to accelerate capital investments when good fortune reigns; or they will reverse course and postpone investments or even abandon them to mitigate losses when recessionary times prevail or disaster looms.

The notion of managerial flexibility having some sort of investment value was recognized after World War II by experts on capital budgeting.[10] Experienced corporate managers were going ahead and approving major capital investments even though traditional finance valuation methods (using discounted cash flows to determine a net present value) were showing negative numbers. (We explain the meaning of *discounted cash flow* and *net present value* and how to apply them in Chapter 17.)

The discrepancy between theory and management's actual investment decisions can be explained by incorporating the value of real options, or management's flexibility to change or alter investment decisions, into the project's valuation equation. In other words, the value of an investment project is worth its net present value plus the value of any real options.

Academic scholars and specialists in the field are continuing to search for better methods to quantify the value of real options.[11] At the beginning, theorists attempted to value real options by drawing (imperfect) analogies to simple financial options. In practice, most real options are highly complex. They involve interdependencies that violate the assumptions of independency and stochastic processes that are used to model financial options. Real options, except in very simple situations, are normally quite difficult to model even using today's most advanced numerical methods. Even though we may not be able to value them precisely, there is a great deal of value in conceptualizing strategic decisions and investment proposals using real options thinking. For readers interested in learning how real options compare to financial options, log onto our web site at www.innovation-tocashflows.com and go to the file: Appendix 7.1, "Real Options versus Financial Options."

These are the four basic types of real options:

1. *Expansion or growth options.* Management can exercise the right to unbottleneck existing plant capacity, add new production capacity, or accelerate the next round of financing if conditions are favorable. Venture capitalists use these types of expansion options all the time when they make staged investments: They put

in a small amount of money in the first financing round of a start-up and wait to see what happens. If the results look promising, then they deploy more money in the second financing round. The money is released only on completion of certain goals and targets (milestones), such as reaching a certain sales volume of units sold or successfully completing prototype tests. (For examples, refer to Chapters 8, 14, 19, and 20.)

2. *Deferment options.* These are investment timing options that allow management to postpone making an investment until a future time. For example, a venture buys some patents. The venture pays annual upkeep fees to keep the patents current, and in so doing, it "Pays to play." (Refer to Chapter 13.) Basically management is taking an option on future exploitation of the patents. Perhaps someone will license the rights to the patents; or management will decide to invest and commercialize the patents by incorporating them into a new product and selling it. More examples are buying undeveloped land zoned for commercial development, or mineral extraction rights (a mine or an oilfield).

3. *Abandonment options.* If the investment project or venture does not work out, then management can stop investing before the conclusion date to avoid further losses. (This is like a put option.) These types of real options are very important in structuring strategic alliance, joint venture, or new company investment agreements. (Refer to Chapter 10 under "Termination Clauses.")

4. *Liquidation options.* If the company fails, then common shareholders are the last to be paid if there is any money left after all the assets have been sold. (Refer to Chapters 4, 17, and 18 on what happens in a liquidation sale.) Equity shareholders are said to have a residual claim on the company. When professionals are valuing companies under financial distress, with high levels of debt and losses, the equity may still be worth something if the company is restructured and certain assets used elsewhere. For a high-technology company, sometimes the rights to the intellectual property inside the bankrupt company are quite valuable. When signing any type of shareholder or alliance agreement, be sure to understand what is going to happen to the intellectual property rights in case of failure. You do not want to inadvertently lose control over your venture's most valuable assets due to a misunderstood contract clause on liquidation rights. (See Chapters 9, 10, and 14 for more details.)

Contingent Rights Are a Form of Real Option   Contingent rights are a subset of real options that depend on some future event happening or some promise taking place (e.g., they are contingent on securing a broadcasting license or obtaining a government grant). Contingent rights are also useful in dealing with conflict stemming from different parties' views of future outcomes, outcomes that are unknowable and unpredictable at the time of drafting the contract or negotiating the alliance agreement. For instance, one side might have an extremely optimistic view of the market success of a new nanotechnology; the other side is not so sure it will work out without heavy investment. No one knows a priori who is right and who is wrong, or if something else will happen unexpectedly in between. Contingent rights are useful for settling such differences of opinion and reaching a consensus in a fair way, depending on what evolves in the future. (Such mechanisms include things like "royalty ratchets" or "grant-backs." (See Chapter 14 for definitions and examples.)

Consequently, it is very important for today's alliance managers to become skillful at identifying real options and creating contingent rights. You can use these skills when designing, structuring, and negotiating strategic alliance and joint venture agreements. Contingent rights give managers the flexibility to exercise their judgment and discretion, especially when taking decisions under conditions of high uncertainty and ambiguity.

The principle to remember is that *managers can increase the strategic value of their business by actively seeking to create real options and negotiating for contingent rights*. Said another way, it is worthwhile to negotiate hard for the right to exercise managerial flexibility over investment decisions. Strive to build flexibility into the agreement to deal with circumstances that may (or may not) happen in the future. It is also worthwhile to bargain for the right to mitigate losses, reserving the right to postpone commitments if anticipated conditions should deteriorate unexpectedly. Deferment options, for instance, often take the form of contingent payments, which include not only staged investment rounds (described earlier) but escrow funds (money set aside in an escrow account until certain things are done), stock options or convertible securities, or holdback allowances (e.g., holding back that last 15 percent payment until the alliance partner finishes up all details of the job).[12]

When it comes to actually drafting the legal documents, tell your lawyers your views on the real options you envision in the deal and the risks you have enumerated in your advanced preparations. It will be their task to translate these real options and contingent rights into the appropriate legal contracts.

Choosing the Proper Legal Vehicle for the Deal   Discuss with your legal advisors what legal structure makes the most sense for the deal you are envisioning: Should it be a contractual relationship agreement? Partnership? Limited liability company? Some sort of equity joint venture? These company incorporation or partnership choices have very different trade-offs in terms of money required, tax and dividend payment implications, control of resources, degree of complexity, corporate governance, degree of commitment, and time, effort, and learning transfer. (See Chapter 9 for details.) The legal documents used will vary, depending on the type of vehicle chosen to implement the goals and aims of the alliance. For joint ventures, the key will be navigating the shareholder agreements (see Chapters 9 and 10). For deals involving intellectual property rights (say licensing a group of patents, codeveloping a novel drug compound, or obtaining a trademark license), then the key document will be the technology transfer agreement (see Chapter 14).

We list some possible ways of thinking about the various trade-offs in Table 7.1, where we compare the general advantages and disadvantages of alternative structures that may be used to exploit your innovation through strategic alliance partnering.

In broad strokes, we can say that there is a continuum of transaction types. It is also true that one size does not fit all. It pays to recognize the *uniqueness* of each alliance, particularly in terms of sharing control, risks, or rewards. At the risk of oversimplifying, we summarize the trade-offs in terms of sorting out two key parameters: the degree of partner commitment and the degree of asset integration. Think about these parameters as you work with your legal and business development teams to come up with the right balance for your particular deal.

TABLE 7.1 Decision Trade-Offs in Risks, Rewards, and Control When Structuring High-Technology Alliances to Exploit Innovation

Decision Trade-Offs	Do-It-Yourself	Form a Joint Company to Spread Risks and Lower Up-Front Investment	Signal Intent to Create a Strategically Significant Relationship	Create a Non-Strategic (Simple) Buyer-Vendor Collaboration	Exploit Own Intellectual Property (IP) Rights By Licensing It to Others
Typical business approach or legal structure	Conduct internal research, product development, and commercialization.	Create an equity joint venture.	Conclude an important strategic alliance agreement.	Structure an outsourcing contract for specific products and services.	Conclude technology transfer agreements.
Expected duration of the relationship	Unlimited life.	Unlimited life due to equity nature of the commitment.	Duration specified in the contractual agreement.	Duration specified in the contractual agreement.	Duration specified in the contractual agreement.
Concerns over governance and control	No risk sharing. Substantial investment committed, usually for a long period of time. Venture could run out of cash. Management might not have requisite skills or experience to do all that is required.	Joint venture relationship sours. Culture clashes between joint venture partners or between the joint venture company and parent companies of the partners. Because of equity nature of commitment, duration may be unlimited.	Informal structure may be unstable. Easy to form, also easy to have the alliance come apart. Limited life.	Outsourcing may have been initiated to lower costs of noncore functions; however, relationship could evolve to become more strategic if dependency develops between supplier and partner. Owner could experience problems monitoring and controlling the outsourced function.	Difficult to control. Partner acquiring the license (the licensee) may not complete contract obligations. Vice versa, the licensee is also dependent on the licensor.

(Continued)

TABLE 7.1 (Continued)

Decision Trade-Offs	Do-It-Yourself	Form a Joint Company to Spread Risks and Lower Up-Front Investment	Signal Intent to Create a Strategically Significant Relationship	Create a Non-Strategic (Simple) Buyer-Vendor Collaboration	Exploit Own Intellectual Property (IP) Rights By Licensing It to Others
Required resources	Substantial investments and resource commitments, often for a long period of time.	Allows pooling of resources and capabilities of two or more firms into separate entity. Due to equity nature of commitment, duration may be unlimited.	Strategic alliances are similar to joint ventures in that resources and capabilities are normally shared.	Limited internal resources.	In general, licensing requires least amount of financial resources compared to alternatives. Do need to pay money to keep patents current. Can be expensive to enforce IP rights through litigation. Some countries have lax enforcement of IP rights.
Examples	Larry Page and Sergey Brin set up and launch to develop and market their Internet search technology.	The Xerox-Fuji joint venture is considered the gold standard on how to manage a joint venture.	Ballard formed a strategic alliance with DaimlerChrysler to develop hydrogen fuel cells for automotive applications.	Many financial services firms have outsourced IT processing functions to trusted suppliers; others see IT as a core competency.	Qualcomm of San Diego, CA, has built up core competency in licensing intellectual property and managing IP rights.

Increasing degree of partner commitment
- Higher risk sharing
- More complexity

Increasing degree of asset integration
- Assets are joined, intertwined, and codeveloped
- More difficult to separate the asset ownership in case of failure
- Higher need to protect against *inadvertent* intellectual property rights transfer upon takeover, liquidation, or termination
- More complex governance and control issues
- Takes longer to set up
- Greater costs

We close this stage with a reflection by Robert F. Bruner, who has taught many MBAs and executives the art of deal design. Bruner counsels:

> *Deal design in part is an engineering problem, optimizing across objectives and constraints. . . . [D]eal design in part is a bargaining problem, seeking the structure that satisfies both sides. . . . [In part] it is economic problem solving. . . . Think of a deal as a whole system where each component interacts with the others. . . . Effective deal design is a learning process. Learning is incorporated through feedback loops in the deal design effort. . . . The chief lesson is that one should manage complexity and strive for simplicity.*[13]

Negotiating the Alliance

Negotiation is a skill that one learns through practice and experience. We highly recommend that you (or the people negotiating on your behalf) be adequately trained on how to negotiate. If you have not done so already, or if you need a refresher course, take a seminar where you can test out and try new negotiation techniques with coaching, peer and observer feedback, taping sessions, and role-play exercises. *The key to success in negotiations is careful preparation.*

We have listed a small selection of excellent books about negotiation in Resources under the Strategy section. The authors of these books are acknowledged experts in the field and have decades of experience teaching executives the art of negotiation. Reading about negotiations helps broaden the mind and will make you more aware of the numerous issues involved in complex negotiations. Reading can help you prepare, but it is no substitute for skill development through practice.

Rehearsing, however, is an excellent way to flex your mental muscles and exercise the way you intend to articulate your ideas during an upcoming negotiation session. We strongly urge you to practice. Test your choice of words, body language, and mental attitude before walking into a negotiation session. *Never go into a negotiation unprepared.* (Log onto our web site at www.innovationtocash flows.com and download the file called Appendix 7.2, "Overview of the Negotiation Process" for practical tips and expert advice on how to prepare and negotiate better.) Before entering into negotiations, you should combine your team's qualitative reasons for doing the deal with the financial forecast models and trade-off tables of the various proposals you wish to negotiate. See Chapters 17 to 20 to learn more about valuation methods that are used for building a spreadsheet financial model of an alliance. It pays to do the financial forecasts beforehand and quantify the deal options. You will be much better prepared for the negotiations and more likely to get what you ask for if you know what you want.

Rudyard Kipling supposedly said, "If you don't get what you want, it's a sign either that you did not seriously want it or that you tried to bargain over the price."[14] We might add that if you don't get what you want, it might also be a sign you need to prepare better next time and to think more creatively of how to seek out win-win options. Do not get stalemated on to haggling over price. Focus on terms and conditions and processes.

For example, carefully consider when and how to take advantage of your firm's resources and those of your alliance partners. This advice applies to setting milestones and goals for the alliance. At this point it is important to take a contingent view: If this event or milestone is accomplished (or not), then what is our next move? Do we have a backup plan in case the other party is not willing to negotiate a certain set of terms or conditions? Think about how to keep the flow of the negotiation moving and not backing up or stalling.

Naturally, the results of any negotiation will depend on the experience, skills, respective commitments, market conditions, financial needs, and bargaining strength of the parties involved. It also will depend on the deal structuring process and your commitment to invest the time and effort to prepare for any negotiations. There are many variables and trade-offs to be made. Developing a mental attitude toward contingent thinking and strategic trade-offs over time is very important.

STEP 4: MANAGING THE ALLIANCE

In this step, the team's task is to role-play and to rehearse the upcoming strategic alliance negotiations. Just as the success in the first days of a start-up encourages entrepreneurs to work harder, take more risks, and gain momentum launching the venture, the early phases of the alliance are the most critical.

Managing the JV or Alliance Launch

Bamford, Ernst, and Fubini's McKinsey & Company study of 2004 was designed to answer the dilemma of why joint venture and corporate alliance success remains out of reach despite so much research on the topic. These senior management consultants were perplexed by the fact that the average success rate for alliances had not improved much over the last decade or so despite so many scholarly books and publications documenting well-known reasons for JV and alliance failures—the most common being changes in strategy by one party or the other, clashes among incompatible partners (or corporate cultures), inequitable or unrealistic deals, and poor management process or assignment of weak managers to the JV or alliance.

Here is their summary of their findings:

> *Joint venture and strategic alliance success remains elusive for most companies because they don't pay enough attention to launch planning and execution. The launch phase begins with the parent companies' signing of a memorandum of understanding and continues through the first 100 days of*

the JV or alliance's operation. During this period, it's critical for the parents to convene a team dedicated to exposing inherent tensions early. Specifically, the launch team must tackle four basic challenges. First, build and maintain strategic alignment across the separate corporate entities, each of which has its own goals, market pressures, and shareholders. Second, create a shared governance system for the two parent companies. Third, manage the economic interdependencies between the corporate parents and the JV. And fourth, build a cohesive, high-performing organization for the JV or alliance. Many venture CEOs lament that alliances are treated as dumping grounds for underperforming executives, rather than as magnets for high-potential managers. . . . If organizations under-invest in launch project management, they can jeopardize the long-term health of their ventures.[15]

Clearly the choice of partner will have a direct effect on how the launch phase is managed. No venture wants to work with a bigger partner that is using the strategic alliance or joint venture as "dumping grounds for underperforming executives." If that is happening, raise the red flag of alarm early (and see Step 6 on dealing with conflicts).

Obviously it is easier to build trust with a company (and people) that you already know than to build new relationships from scratch. If the partner is new, both sides need to spend considerably more resources (time and money) in getting to know each other and establishing a solid working relationship. A trial period for collaboration (a honeymoon) is often a wise solution—provided that the confidentiality issues are handled with care. Some alliances propose conducting feasibility studies or pilot development projects to test out the relationship in a low-profile manner.

Managing the Alliance and Helping It Gain Traction

How you and your partners choose to frame the strategic intent of the alliance ends up strongly influencing the way it is ultimately managed. We discuss this theme again regarding measuring and assessing alliance performance. The way the alliance should be managed depends on the alliance aims, its economic drivers, the way it is structured, and also the importance and commitment the two sides attach to the relationship. According to research conducted by MacCormack, Forbath, Brooks, and Kalaher[16] there are three critical errors that managers commit time and time again when it comes to managing alliances:

1. They focus *solely on lowering costs*, failing to consider the broader strategic role of collaboration. Even though managers know that there are more ways to increase operating margins than simply lowering costs, sometimes a focus on costs is driven by poor accounting systems or inappropriate managerial incentive and compensation schemes.
2. They *do not organize effectively for collaboration*, believing that innovation can be managed much like production and partners treated like "suppliers." There exists too much of an outsourcing mentality, where the aim is to bargain for efficiencies rather than to search for savings while also seeking improved effectiveness and new opportunities.

3. They *underinvest in time and money in building collaborative capabilities*, as-suming that their existing people and processes are already equipped for the challenge.

In contrast, MacCormack and his coauthors discovered that successful firms in their survey sample developed an explicit strategy for *collaboration* and *make organizational changes to aid performance in these efforts*. Ultimately, these actions allowed them to identify and exploit new business opportunities more successfully.

The last sentence begs the question: What organizational changes are required for collaboration to occur? Part of the answer comes from what is learned during the prelaunch negotiation phase of the relationship and also from the initial jockeying for informal positions of power and influence during the launch. It is vitally important to make sure the roles of the parties are clarified and that the balance of interests is fair, or else trouble will emerge later on. Be sure to ask the basic *management* questions and try to obtain behaviorally specific commitments on the details. We share the flavor of such a conversation next:

- Who decides on the strategy and the processes around here?
- Who carries out the strategy and processes?
- How do we agree on the strategy and the processes?
- Is the strategy enough, or do we have in place mechanisms to incorporate minority views and listen to constructive criticisms?
- Or do we need more than one strategy? If so, how do we authorize such rebel causes and exploratory thinking?
- How do we change the strategy?
- How quickly can we change if we need to? Can we design the alliance around modular units to enhance our future flexibility? What other processes can we put in place to gain strategic flexibility?

Once you launch the alliance, keep in mind that most likely your potential partners will not share the same strategic intent or goals for the alliance as your team envisions. Your potential partners might have opposite goals, or they might try to pursue a different combination of goals. They may attach importance to certain priorities that are different from those of your venture. In this phase, you must listen attentively and decipher your partner's true goals and motivations for doing the strategic alliance. Failing to see eye to eye on the importance and resources required to make the alliance work is a key cause of alliance conflicts. Managing an alliance requires an ongoing attentiveness to the other party's needs and priorities. Listening is not a one-time thing, to be done at the negotiations and then forgotten; listening needs to happen throughout the life of the relationship.

Successful Joint Venture Evolves over Time

It is quite normal for the alliance goals and strategic needs to change and evolve as the partnership or joint venture matures, strategies change, and people directly involved in the alliance come and go.

Consider Xerox and Fuji Photo Film in Japan. Harvard Professor Benjamin Gomes-Casseres, an expert on managing international alliances, describes how the goals of the Fuji Xerox joint venture evolved and how the two partners were able to adapt and accommodate to the changing needs.

Rank Xerox and Fuji Photo Film, the two partners in Fuji Xerox, had different goals for the 50-50 joint venture formed in 1962. Rank Xerox, which was responsible for Xerox's international sales, wanted to sell in Japan, where government regulations required a local partner. Fuji Photo Film wanted to learn xerography, which it saw as a means for diversifying away from silver-based photography. . . . Over time, the joint ventures and the partners developed additional goals—Fuji Xerox began supplying Xerox and Rank Xerox with products, Fuji Xerox took over the task of learning xerography, and, by the 1980s, Xerox Corporation itself began learning product design and quality management skills from Fuji Xerox.[17]

Step 4 Checklist: Managing the Alliance

The next set of questions will help you and your team focus on the management of the alliance.

- ☐ Have we positioned our best people in this alliance?
- ☐ Are we providing them with adequate resources to get the job done?
- ☐ Are we all communicating regularly and effectively?
- ☐ Do we and the other party have the buy-in required to keep this alliance going?
- ☐ Are we giving relationships sufficient time and attention to develop?
- ☐ Are we regularly reviewing our progress?
- ☐ Are we willing to make hard choices? Are we communicating those choices to our partners? Do they know and understand the choices we are facing?
- ☐ Can we live with the choices we must make? Can our partners? How can we manage their reactions to our decisions? And are we managing our reactions to their decisions?
- ☐ Are we willing to compromise for the sake of this alliance?
- ☐ Are we contributing as much as we are getting back?
- ☐ How fast will we expand? Are we poised to build on the alliance capabilities?
- ☐ Why does this alliance still fit in with our company's business? Are we maintaining it for cash? For technology? For market access?
- ☐ Are we making the most of the trust and interdependence we have built with our partners?
- ☐ Are we dealing with tough issues as they arise?
- ☐ Should this alliance evolve into a self-supporting business? Should we spin it off into a separate company?

STEP 5: MEASURE AND ASSESS PERFORMANCE

Do you have in place a system to measure the success of your most critical external relationships? It is surprising to find out how many ventures and their alliance partners overlook the importance of measuring and assessing performance on a regular and ongoing basis. Part of the reason is that strategic alliances are sometimes placed outside of the normal financial systems of two companies. It is difficult to measure the success of these critical relationships because of a lack of proper financial systems integration. There also is the problem of a dominance of financial measures to the exclusion of strategic considerations (such real options as gaining managerial flexibility, strategic agility, new innovative learning capacity, etc.).

If financial considerations rule the performance assessment system, then the strategic alliance may suffer these consequences:

- Results tend to be short-term
- Little incentive to invest in the business
- Lack of clarity on whether pure financial metrics track with longer-term value creation (particularly true for early-stage R&D collaborations)

If performance metrics are to be linked to strategy, a different approach is needed than focusing purely on financial measures, one that helps to:

- Tie vision and strategy and link them to operations
- Bring clarity to measurement
- Help communicate the strategic plans to the people on the front lines doing the work
- Aid consensus building and manager buy-in

Clearly there are multiple metrics by which to value the success of an alliance, beyond the cost of capital criteria cited earlier. Often the key is to negotiate milestones tied to financing rounds. These milestones need to be realistic and contingent on deadlines or events that are objective, and the results must be measurable. Vague descriptions of milestones as aspirations rather than realistic targets will only lead to trouble and disputes down the road.

Defining Performance Metrics

As we have said all along, strategic alliances warrant the time, attention, and commitment of senior leaders in the organization, not only in the early negotiation phases but also as part of an ongoing performance review and benchmarking process. Since these types of contractual relationships are a key part of implementing your venture's alliance strategy, it is wise to reflect on how you are framing the decision about whether an alliance can be judged a success or failure.

How managers perceive the partnership will depend on which lens they are using to view it. The goals and points of view about alliances vary widely, depending on conventional wisdom and a particular industry's beliefs about how partners ought to behave and how business should be done.

A popular approach to thinking about performance metrics is to use the balanced scorecard jointly developed by Robert S. Kaplan of Harvard Business School and

David P. Norton.[18] The balanced scorecard translates the vision and strategy of a business into a set of performance measures. In this approach, there are four "lenses" or "perspectives" commonly used to frame business decisions: the internal process perspective, the customer perspective, the financial markets perspective, and the learning and growth perspective.

Internal Process Perspective For instance, purchasing managers or executives designing a major outsourcing project may frame the alliance partner decision as a means to achieve these ends:

- Reduce waste
- Lower production costs
- Enhance business unit productivity

Such a view is focused primarily on reducing costs. It may be driven by a need to strip away overheads, improve integration across business units, and enhance new product coordination efforts by outsourcing less critical components using make-or-buy criteria ranked purely on cost metrics. In this paradigm, the firm scours the world seeking the cheapest sources of supply (of raw materials or labor inputs). Executives will decide to make the product internally or outsource manufacturing to a third party depending on which alternative is cheaper. If offshoring is even cheaper, this option will be favored over outsourcing at home. This paradigm frames alliance issues in a framework of lower transaction costs and lower production costs. Firms whose internal management accounting systems look only at the bottom line of operating costs might find themselves falling into this viewpoint and ignoring other perspectives.

Customer Perspective The customer perspective frames the partnering discussion in terms of delivering value to a target customer in the most effective way possible. There is more emphasis on quality and less concern for costs compared to purely considering transaction costs or product exchanges. Flexibility is rewarded even if it costs a bit more up front. The customer wants deliverables and is willing to pay for them but only if they are received on time; it will not pay for broken promises. The customer perspective also considers other alliance goals, such as helping a firm extend its product reach into new international markets, spreading the adoption of new technology to new users, and perhaps even helping create a dominant standard for the industry.

Financial Markets Perspective This perspective could be the stock market's or the venture capitalist's viewpoint, depending on whether the alliance is made up of public trading companies or privately held firms. It takes into account the vantage point of the supplier of capital. Equity markets generally will react favorably to a company's announcement of a new value-creating strategic alliance or the formation of an important joint venture with a well-connected or well-endowed partner. Alliance measurement metrics frequently discussed in this mind-set are better operating margins, increased free cash flow, and higher earnings per share. Quicker time to market often means a quicker time to exit for the venture capitalist funding a private venture. For a publicly traded high-technology firm, well-performing strategic alliances and joint ventures translate into higher earnings growth expectations, higher price-earnings multiples, and greater market capitalization. (See Part Six, "Valuing Company Cash Flows" for explanations of these financial terms and concepts.)

Learning and Growth Perspective This perspective emphasizes the importance of enhancing the firm's capacity to absorb new skills and become a better partner. The goal here is to learn how to learn faster and more effectively than rivals when striving to gain dynamic new capabilities. Learning partnerships strive to develop new know-how and skills by participating in cutting-edge research and development consortia.

Depending on the chosen perspective, and depending if both sides agree to frame the alliance relationship in the same way, you should be able to come up with jointly agreed on performance metrics by which to measure the progress of the alliance.

Step 5 Checklist: Measure and Assess Performance

These questions will help you and your team evaluate and measure the progress of the alliance.

- ☐ Have we explicitly defined what we mean by the "success" of this alliance or joint venture?
- ☐ Have we aligned our performance metrics to the strategic intent, goals, and objectives we hope to achieve?
- ☐ Are we measuring what we need to know to make timely management decisions?
- ☐ Do we have a regular review system set up for assessing and monitoring and measuring performance?
- ☐ Are our management incentive and compensation schemes linked to the performance assessment system?
- ☐ Do we have both short-term and long-term incentives in the compensation schemes? Do the incentives reward the right kind of behaviors we want to encourage in the alliance or JV?
- ☐ Is there a feedback loop to senior management of the parent companies (in the case of a JV) to alert them to any problems or deficiencies?
- ☐ When performance problems arise, is there a management process in place for dealing with them *before* they escalate into a major crisis? (See Step 6.)

STEP 6: CHECK THE MERITS OF CONTINUING THE ALLIANCE, EITHER ADJUST OR EXIT

According to Robert M. Grant, the strategy gurus Gary Hamel and C.K. Prahalad have said this about alliances: "[What matters] is not the size of a firm's resource base, but the firm's ability to extend its reach through leveraging."[19] Like using a long pole to lever your own strength and lift up a big rock, collaboration is a way of gaining strength through others. Even so, poles lifting big rocks have been known to break. At times, the biggest barrier to success you face as a smaller venture is trying "to lift the big rock" on the other end of your pole, especially if that big rock is a giant corporate partner. The larger partner might lose interest in your small alliance, especially if it hits a few bumps during the critical early stages of the alliance or joint venture. Seen from the point of view of the larger company, small ventures tend to promise way too much and deliver too little, too late. Conflicts are going to arise.

Alliance management is challenging because alliances, in general, are more open-ended and ambiguous than acquisitions, where there is generally a clear winner and loser. Alliances by nature are more fluid: The management structure is more flexible and easier to change than in a merger or acquisition. When new people come into the alliance, as often happens, it may be unclear who is supposed to decide certain issues, who will participate in meetings, what issues will be negotiated, and which interests will be in conflict. To manage alliances well, you need to do good reconnaissance and constantly be diagnosing the changing landscape. James March puts it well in the next quote—all we would do is substitute the words *strategic alliance management* for *strategic management* in the first line:

> *Strategic Management is the art of dealing intelligently with three grand problems of decision making:*
>
> 1. *The problem of* ignorance
> 2. *The problem of* conflict
> 3. *The problem of* ambiguity[20]

Sometimes events spin out of control, for reasons beyond the control of either party; because one side or the other committed a strategic blunder; or because the government made a regulatory decision that did not turn out as the parties had anticipated. Many strands of the alliance unraveling together may eventually end up in a major fiasco.

It is very important to pay attention to the termination clauses in your alliance contract agreement (or shareholder agreement). Just like divorces, alliance terminations can be contentious, and potentially costly. Care and attention need to be paid on how you plan to terminate the strategic alliance and extricate the assets from the partnership. Again, as we did earlier, we advise you to seek legal counsel to protect against inadvertent transfer of intellectual property rights upon termination. (See Chapter 10 for a brief discussion of liquidation rights and change of control clauses in shareholder agreements.)

The next story about the Raisio Group, located in Raisio, Finland, highlights the difficulties of choosing the right alliance partner and, even if that goes well, the challenges of modifying the alliance strategy in time, if things start going wrong.

THE RAISIO STORY

I remember hearing the story about the Raisio Group, a Finnish company that invented and launched Benecol, a novel cholesterol-reducing margarine compound from one of my Finnish investment students. At that time, in early 1997, he was thinking about buying shares in the company. Institutional and retail investors were intrigued by the possibilities. During 1996, Raisio's shares rose so high as to make it the second most valuable public company on the Helsinki

(Continued)

THE RAISIO STORY (*Continued*)

Stock Exchange (after Nokia). The active ingredient in the Benecol margarine was stanol ester, which was attracting the interest of food processors all over the world. Raisio's company history was in grain milling in the town of Raisio located in southwestern Finland. During 1997, negotiations were under way between the Raisio Group and Johnson & Johnson's U.S. subsidiary, American McNeil Consumer Products Company. According to Raisio's filings in its 1997 annual report, "a cooperation agreement was signed which gives McNeil the sole right to use the Benecol trademark and patents on the US, Canadian, and Mexico markets. The Raisio Group retains the right to supply the stanol ester required for the products. McNeil aimed to introduce the first products during 1998. Raisio received a lump sum payment for assignment [sale] of these license rights and would have received remunerations related to operative development and royalties for the sales of Benecol products and for deliveries of stanol ester. In November 1997 a further letter of intent was signed between the two parties leading to a final cooperation agreement signed on March 2, 1998. [The revised terms added most of Europe and Japan to the original North American markets, while Raisio kept the Finnish market for itself.]"[*]

At the time the first strategic collaboration agreement was signed, Johnson & Johnson was already a global behemoth in health-related products. Its sales revenue (turnover) was $21.6 billion in 1996, and it had operations in over 50 countries (Raisio Annual Report 1997, 39). The terms of the agreement meant close cooperation between Raisio and Johnson & Johnson (J&J). Raisio would supply J&J with stanol ester, and the two companies would collaborate together to coordinate medical and clinical research and marketing, and cooperate in product development on a project-by-project basis.[†]

The alliance hit a major crisis in the year 2000. Losses mounted in the Benecol Division and reached €44 million by June 2000.[‡] According to Raisio, the problem appeared to be in the structure of the worldwide license agreement with J&J. As reported in Grant: "J&J's worldwide license meant that Raisio was completely dependent on J&J's commitment to Benecol and the success of J&J's marketing strategy."[§] J&J made a key assumption when it submitted Benecol Margarine to the Food and Drug Administration (FDA) as a "dietary supplement" rather than as a "food product without any explicit health claims." The assumption turned out to be wrong. The FDA rejected the dietary supplement claim unless J&J could provide it with clinical evidence of stanol ester's safety and efficacy, clinical trials that would have been time consuming and costly. Therefore, J&J halted the planned U.S. launch and repositioned the product as a food product without any health-related claims, but the delay meant precious time had been lost in the U.S. market.

[*]Raisio Annual Report 1997, 39.
[†]"Raisio Group and the Benecol Launch," 174.
[‡]Raisio Group Annual Report 2000, 5.
[§]Grant "Raisio Group and the Benecol Launch," 179.

Meanwhile in Europe, the Benecol strategy was vulnerable to rival Unilever, which had launched its own new product response based on a different active ingredient called sterol ester. Unilever's new margarine, Pro-activ, cost 20 percent less than Benecol's product on supermarket shelves. Consumers were price sensitive, and Unilever soon had twice the market share of Benecol.*

Questions

1. What lessons do you think Raisio learned from this strategic alliance with J&J?
2. Could either Raisio or J&J have done anything differently to have prevented the problems?
3. What would you have done instead if you were in Raisio's position?

*Ibid., 176, quoting www.nutraingredients.com.

Source: This story draws on the annual reports of the Raisio Group and the cases written by Robert M. Grant, "Raisio Group and the Benecol Launch (A) and (B)," in *Cases to Accompany Contemporary Strategy Analysis*, 6th ed. (Malden, MA: Blackwell Publishing, 2008), 163–184, and the case by Michael H. Moffett and Stacey Wolff Howard, "Benecol: Raisio's Global Nutriceutical," Thunderbird School of Global Management, Case No. A06-99-0004, 1999.

Step 6 Checklist: Check on the Merits of Continuing the Alliance

Use this meeting checklist to review the progress of the alliance and to help resolve conflicts. Such reviews will help you and your team choose whether to continue with the alliance or prepare to exit from it.

Progress Review Meeting

Meeting Agenda: Review the progress of the alliance.[21]

Who Should Attend: Key alliance managers only (no staff, no outsiders).

When: Anytime a significant change occurs, unanticipated problems arise, or an important milestone is attained.

Where: Neutral location. (Plan adequate time for both social and business interaction.)

Preparations before the Meeting

☐ What were the strategic intentions of both parties in forming the strategic alliance? What were the agreed-on goals and strategies for the alliance?

☐ What have been the accomplishments since the last review (deadlines met, milestones, projects completed)? Review the missed goals, failures, or near misses.

☐ What have been the disappointments or failures?

☐ Have there been any major happenings to the parent companies (in the case of a joint venture); or to the investors in your venture or the other parties to the alliance (new CEOs, takeovers, bankruptcies, mergers)?

☐ Think about significant trends or shifts in the industry, competition, political, economic, social, technological, legal, or environmental arenas that might affect the alliance or its external relationships since the last review session. What have been the unexpected opportunities? Was the alliance able to pursue them? Why or why not?

☐ What obstacles have arisen?

☐ What changes have taken place in key personnel? Which ones are pending?

☐ What other issues or concerns do you have about the alliance?

☐ What specific changes do you propose be made?

Process Rules: Keep the Meeting Confidential

☐ "Listening" should prevail over "blaming."

☐ Acknowledge and praise successes.

☐ Seek to identify open-ended, unresolved, or hard-to-resolve issues.

☐ Search for root causes of delays or problems.

☐ Aim for a calm, objective tone throughout the meeting.

☐ Strive to bring to the surface the doubts, worries, and concerns of the other party.

☐ Seek to identify potential problems, unrecognized risks, or emerging zones of conflict.

☐ Bring out into the open the unresolved or hard-to-resolve issues.

Various Decisions and Process Outcomes Likely

Possible Decisions

☐ *Green light*: Continue current strategy.

☐ *Yellow warning light*: Need to adjust alliance strategy.

☐ *Red light*: Alliance is in jeopardy: Decide on exit alternatives.

Possible Process Outcomes

☐ Renewed agreement on how the relationship should work.

☐ Reconfirmation of JV or strategic alliance business goals and objectives.

☐ Renewed commitment to the importance of the relationship.

☐ Clarity achieved on next steps to reach key targets or milestones.

STEP 7: START THE CYCLE ANEW: STRIVE TO CREATE A CONNECTED NETWORK OF ALLIANCES

Professor Michael Watkins teaches negotiations at Harvard Business School and has written articles about analyzing complex negotiations. In his note on negotiating strategic alliances, he points out:

> *Beyond the prescription, "build alliances," practically nothing is said on where to begin, and how to proceed in doing deals. But alliance networks get built one negotiation at a time. . . . It is crucially important to start with the right early deals and to do them in the right order. Success in building momentum through a sequence of deals makes the company an increasingly attractive alliance partner, improving its bargaining position for future deals. But it requires careful attention to the dynamics of strategic deal-making.[22]*

Our recommendation is to take a dynamic view of strategic alliances and manage them over their life cycle, from the time they are conceived, to when they are given birth, to when they reach midlife crisis, to when it is time to say good-bye and move on. In an alliance network, a broader systems approach is required to manage them. An alliance network is a complex, adaptive system where changes in one part of the ecosystem will affect other parts as well.

Step 7 Checklist: Start the Cycle Anew

This checklist presents our framework for dynamically viewing strategic alliances. In this final checklist, we summarize the essential steps for crafting strategic alliances.

Understand the Strategic Intent of the Collaboration

- ☐ What is the purpose and strategic rationale of the proposed alliance?
- ☐ Why do we need to do this collaboration?
- ☐ For how long?
- ☐ What benefits are expected?
- ☐ How likely is "success," and how do we measure it?

Partner Selection

- ☐ With whom can we work?
- ☐ Does the partner share compatible objectives?
- ☐ Does it have the needed skills and capabilities?
- ☐ Can a "dating" period be arranged to get to know each other?

Structure, Design, and Negotiate

- ☐ What is in it for both of us?
- ☐ Plan for the launch even during the negotiations.

Manage the Alliance

☐ Execute the launch phase well.

☐ Build trust and commitment.

☐ Carefully manage the evolution of the relationship.

☐ Deal with cultural conflicts and surprises; do not let them fester.

Measure and Assess Performance

☐ How are we doing?

☐ Are there other benefits still to be achieved?

Recheck the Merits of Continuing

☐ Is there still trust and commitment to keep going?

☐ What are the consequences of exiting?

☐ Should we continue or quit?

CLOSING THOUGHTS

This chapter has focused on guiding you through the process of planning, designing, structuring, and negotiating your first strategic alliance. It opens the door to later chapters where you will be able to see the details more clearly and find examples to help you put what we have been saying into practice.

Alliances, particularly contractual relationship alliances, have the advantages of being quicker to set up and quicker to dissolve than a merger, acquisition, or equity joint venture. As the CEO of a high-technology venture, you need to develop a sixth sense about when to do alliances and when to avoid them; how to negotiate them; the right moment to change the aims; and when and how to terminate them. All this has to be accomplished in the usual frenzy of the day-to-day management of any start-up venture. We hope this chapter helps you go further along the road to value creation, not only through structuring high-technology alliances but also managing them well.

CHAPTER TAKEAWAYS

- Do not rush into doing a strategic alliance without first exploring if there is a better option.
- Strategic alliances are messy and hard to manage. Remember that about 50 percent of them will fail.
- Know why you are doing the alliance, and clearly define your aims and goals. Know what you want to achieve in the collaboration.
- Search carefully and thoroughly for the best strategic partner with whom to build a relationship. Early deals are crucial for gaining momentum.

- Spend time choosing the right partners. Join the best alliance networks you can find.
- Remember that in order to form your own alliance network, you need to achieve that first successful collaboration.
- Build a reputation as a reliable, trustworthy partner.
- Although there is no substitute for negotiating experience, anyone can improve negotiating skills with proper training and practice. Preparation and rehearsal and are fundamental to success in negotiations. Never walk into a negotiation unprepared.
- Build real options thinking into your strategies and contingent rights into your contracts.
- Designing and structuring alliance deals requires finding mutually satisfactory solutions across multiple parameters so that the interests of multiple parties are served.
- Alliances between strong and weak partners rarely work.
- Plan on the purpose of the strategic alliance or joint venture to evolve as it matures. The key is to stay tuned to the dynamics and adapt and evolve the managerial systems and processes accordingly.
- Log onto our book's web site at www.innovationtocashflows.com where you will find these useful supplements:
  - Appendix 7.1, "Real Options versus Financial Options"
  - Appendix 7.2, "Overview of the Negotiation Process"

How Alliances Complete the Value Chain in Biotechnology and Pharmaceutical Business Models

Margaret Mullally

This chapter illustrates to the entrepreneur how alliances form a vital component of *biotechnology*[1] and pharmaceutical business models. We focus on the healthcare industry, particularly the pharmaceutical, *biopharmaceutical,* and *medical device* sectors: pharmaceuticals,[2] biopharmaceuticals,[3] and medical devices are used in the diagnosis, alleviation, treatment, cure, or prevention of human disease. We use the term (bio)pharmaceutical to refer to a combination of pharmaceutical and biopharmaceutical research and development (R&D) within a single firm. The manufacture, testing, and use of all healthcare products are regulated to varying extents depending on the therapeutic application and type of device or drug. We describe a characteristic *drug discovery* and development pipeline and the associated value chain. We illustrate some of the risks and uncertainties associated with *drug development.* We emphasize how alliances are increasingly used in healthcare business models to mitigate those risks. Firms in this domain are becoming more reliant on strategic partnerships at many stages of their value chains. Indeed, for these industries, managing multiple, long-term strategic alliances is critical to their innovation processes and to their value creation strategies. We also elucidate some of the better-known business models and explain how these have evolved and how they exist in hybrid forms.

We suggest how recent trends in healthcare and alliance formation will influence the future business model dynamics for both small and large companies in the biotechnology and pharmaceutical industries. This chapter introduces important factors that should help entrepreneurs in this domain focus on the strategic decisions they need to make in order to participate successfully in value creation.

RISKS AND UNCERTAINTY ASSOCIATED WITH DRUG DEVELOPMENT

In the healthcare domain, the business model that any start-up company chooses should mitigate an array of risks associated with innovating, researching, developing, and commercializing a drug product, medical device, or *platform technology.* Of the many risks associated with early-stage pharmaceutical and biopharmaceutical or (bio)pharmaceutical businesses, we mention just a few risks related primarily to those business models concentrating on drug development, since these models currently are associated with the highest risk but usually are coupled with the highest expected returns for investors.

Drug Discovery and Development Cycle

The typical (bio)pharmaceutical drug has two distinct life cycles: the development life cycle before market launch and the product life cycle after it has been released for commercial sale and launched into the market. The development life cycle of a drug takes from 10 to 15 years and can be divided into distinct stages[4] through which any drug would have to proceed before being allowed to reach the marketplace.

The very earliest stages of the drug discovery and development process involve research scientists working in the laboratory to identify promising lead compounds and their molecular targets. The early stages of drug discovery are target identification, target validation, lead identification, and lead optimization as depicted in Figure 8.1.

- *Target identification.* Drugs usually act on cellular molecules in the body, which are known as targets. Target identification is the procedure of finding drug compound targets. These targets can be cellular molecules, such as proteins or peptides, nucleic acids, or polysaccharides that bind to a small molecule or peptide. Specific targets may be associated with a particular disease process.
- *Target validation.* Target validation is the procedure of verifying that cellular targets molecules identified are actually involved in the disease process of interest. Researchers validate each drug target for its suitability as a therapeutic candidate, based on the target's regulation of the biological and chemical processes in the body associated with the disease of interest.
- *Lead identification.* A lead compound is one that is believed to have the potential to treat the disease. Leads usually are developed or acquired via high-throughput screening of libraries of individual chemical or biological structures. Selected leads that specifically interact with targets are regarded as "hits." Many hundreds of hits are experimentally analyzed further for their influence on the targets related to the disease of interest.
- *Lead optimization.* This is where scientists compare the properties of various lead compounds. They provide their experience and information to help select the compound with the greatest potential to be developed further. The optimized leads are further tested in preclinical evaluation.

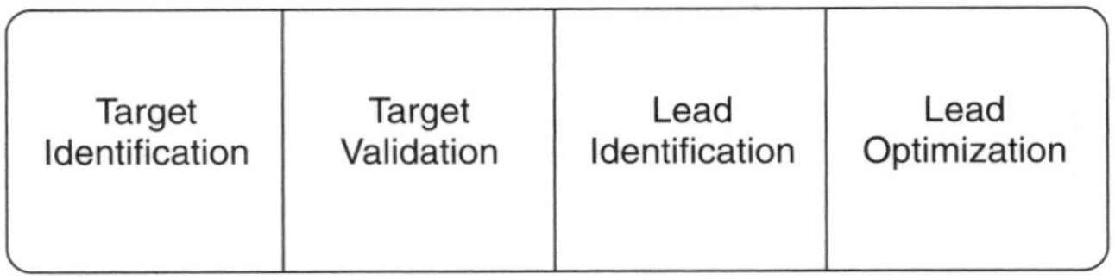

Target Identification	Target Validation	Lead Identification	Lead Optimization

FIGURE 8.1 Early Stages of Drug Discovery

Preclinical Evaluations   After promising target candidates are identified and validated and drug compound leads are qualified and optimized, the next phase of the drug development cycle begins. After a drug compound is discovered using various biological or chemical techniques, and before that drug can be sold, it must satisfy strict government safety and toxicity criteria. Consequently, the drug compound will be put through a number of stringent tests, called preclinical evaluations followed by *clinical trials*. Only successful drug compounds will proceed to final registration and regulatory review by the authorities.

Preclinical evaluations are carried out first in vitro[5] in a laboratory environment, for example, using specific assays in cell lines and then in animals, where combinations of genetic, biochemical, pathological, and environmental factors are present together in vivo (in the living organism). These tests are done in order to reveal any unexpected secondary effects and to assess the safety, toxicity, and efficacy of that drug. Preclinical tests are also used to predict the clinical dose range as determined using pharmacokinetics studies (such as absorption, distribution, metabolism, and excretion [ADME] of that drug in an animal). If a drug passes these initial tests in animals, subsequent clinical trials determine whether a drug is safe and effective in humans. Furthermore, these trials are also used to ascertain what side effects may result. Usually after preclinical testing, an Investigational New Drug (IND)[6] application is filed with the U.S. Food and Drug Administration (FDA), with the European Medicines Agency (EMEA), or with an equivalent agency in other countries. The filing of an IND is mandatory. If the FDA or EMEA or equivalent does not object to the IND filing within the specified time period, clinical testing may begin.

Clinical Trials   There are four phases in clinical trial development. Phase I is also known as the Phase I/II study and is used to determine if a drug is safe; only a small number of volunteers are treated. In the Phase I study, the drug is administered to healthy volunteers, whereas in Phase I/II, patients who have the disease to which the drug is targeted are treated. Proof of concept[7] (POC) is an exploratory study and can be shown during Phase I, but it is usually established in Phase II. POC is the first credible evidence in a target population that a drug actually functions as expected. The earlier the proof of concept, the better it is. If POC is shown not to be acceptable, then poor candidates can be eliminated early, thus potentially reducing total development costs. Only promising candidates are carried into further clinical trials. Of the drugs that make it to POC, most will still fail in subsequent phases due to lack of product efficacy, stability, or safety, or insufficient cash for further clinical trials or operations. Phase II measures efficacy in addition to safety and begins only if there is success during the first phase. If results are positive for Phase II, then a Phase III study is used to further establish efficacy and long-term safety in a large patient population.

If positive results are obtained for all three phases, then an application for approval to market the drug, known as a New Drug Application (NDA), is filed at the FDA, with the EMEA, or with an equivalent agency. If it passes FDA or EMEA approval, then it may be released for commercial sale. If launched, then the drug product is manufactured[8] on a larger scale. The company can then either commercialize the drug or comarket it if the necessary approval to do so is granted.

Following market approval and product launch, Phase IV studies are often carried out to determine long-term effects and optimal use of the drug. The time taken for each phase can vary. The time period for drug discovery through to preclinical testing may be four to six years for target identification and validation, including lead compound identification and optimization, together with subsequent preclinical testing. Typical times for clinical trials are one to two years for Phase I; approximately two years for Phase II; three to four years for Phase III; and one to two years for FDA approval. In total, it takes many years to take a drug candidate from the discovery phase to the market. For example, for antibody therapeutics the process may take up to 10 years; for other more complex drugs, up to 15 years. (See Figure 8.2.)

Risks Associated with Drug Development

Drug development involves an array of risks. *Attrition rates* are associated with the failure of clinical studies if drug efficacy, safety, toxicity, or other regulatory requirements are not met. Attrition rates of candidate drugs are high. For example, the probability of investigational compounds (at Phase I)[9] entering Phase II and Phase III is 71% and 31%, respectively, and this is depicted schematically in Figure 8.2 by the narrowing of the "funnel," or pipeline contour. Technical risks, associated with drug research and clinical development, may include, for example, those related to poor expression or production of proteins by cell lines; or problems during scale-up from laboratory or pilot scale quantities of the drug to large-scale

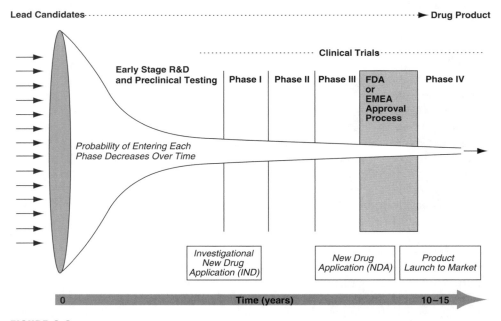

FIGURE 8.2   Schematic Representation of a Typical Drug Development Pipeline

manufacture. Compliance risks are associated with meeting regulatory procedures. These include differences between, for example, FDA and EMEA approval processes and decision criteria. Operational risks include project execution and associated personnel risks of finding, selecting, and hiring qualified people with the necessary experience. Intellectual property (IP) risks are associated with protecting IP assets, transferring associated IP rights, and discovering the freedom to operate. (See Chapter 2 and Chapters 11 to 13 for more details on IP protection and patent strategies. See Chapter 15 for more on freedom to operate searches.)

The main financial risk for a biotechnology venture is running out of cash. During the long research and development time frames, sufficient cash flow must be available to support business operations and to finance future growth options as they arise. Estimates by the Tufts Center for the Study of Drug Development, associated with Tufts University in the United States, show that capitalizing out-of-pocket costs to the point of market approval yields total drug development costs that are nearly the same for biopharmaceuticals as for pharmaceuticals (i.e., $1,241 million and $1,318 million, respectively).[10]

Market risk is defined as customer acceptance of the drug relative to competitive alternatives. In the end, financial success in producing and developing a drug requires careful consideration of market risk. It may become apparent at Phase III that a competing drug serves the patient's unmet need in a more effective way, in which case the drug candidate may be withdrawn from further clinical trials development.

VALUE CHAINS IN PHARMACEUTICALS AND (BIO)PHARMACEUTICALS

Before describing the various business models found in the healthcare sector, we first discuss a characteristic (bio)pharmaceutical value chain. The value chain in the (bio)pharmaceutical industry, depicted in Figure 8.3, is associated with the early stages of the drug discovery process shown in Figure 8.1 and the drug development pipeline depicted in Figure 8.2. This value chain may be shared either by a few or by many different players.

The transfer of IP rights at each stage of the value chain is complex, as the economic value added is often shared by several parties. Strategic alliances between and among the various players are possible. The transaction agreements may include *technology transfer* or product in-sourcing (accomplished through *in-licensing agreements*); technology or product outsourcing (often done by means of *out-licensing agreements*); and strategic alliance agreements (carried out as *codevelopment agreements*, joint ventures, or sales and marketing agreements). All the players involved, as depicted in Figure 8.3, form an extensive network. This network needs to be managed and exploited in order to create value.

For example, multidisciplinary academic research groups or consortia may carry out several steps at the earliest phases of the drug development process, such as target identification, target validation, lead identification, or optimization. These investigations may be funded by the government or by an industrial partner. IP rights created may then be transferred to that industrial partner or to a small biotechnology

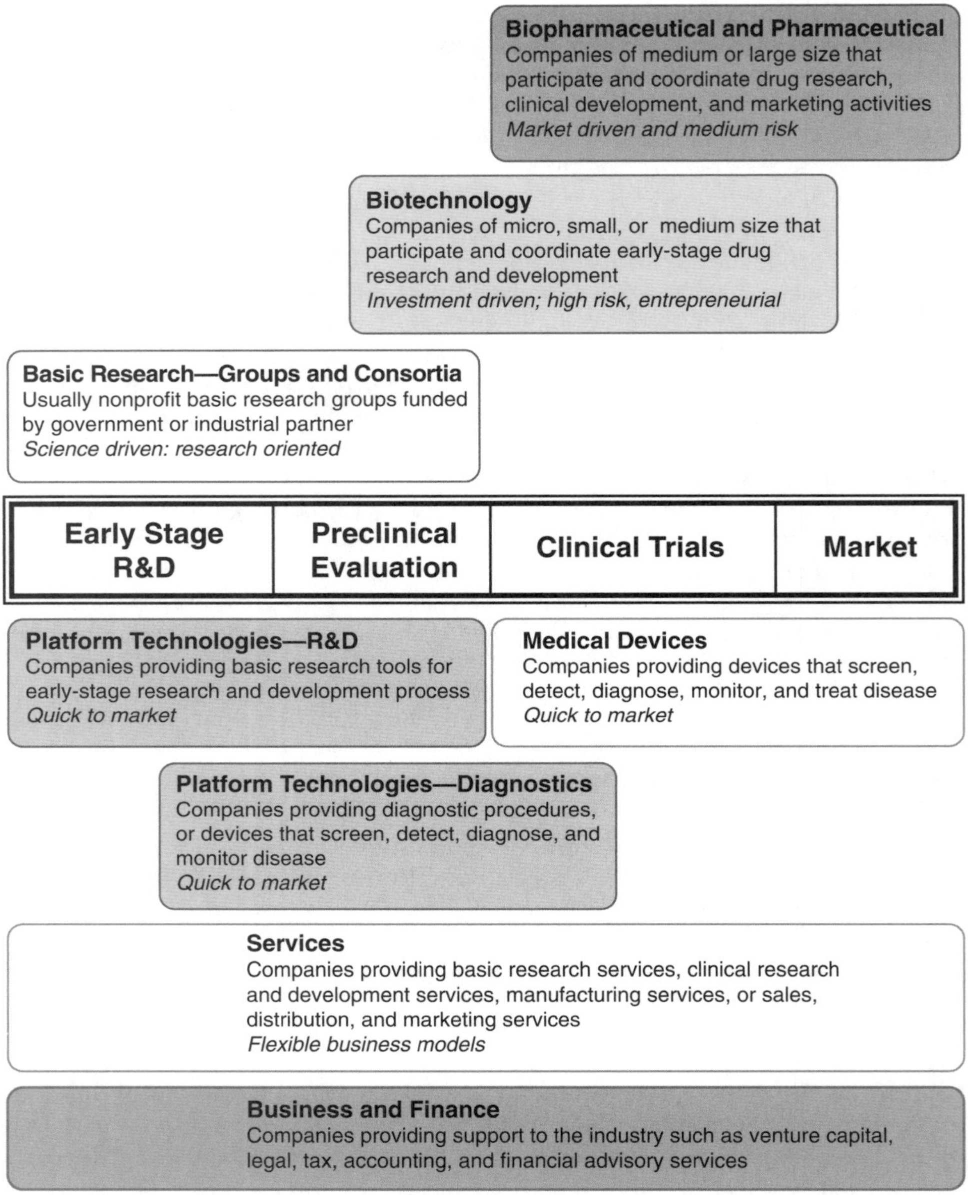

Biopharmaceutical and Pharmaceutical
Companies of medium or large size that participate and coordinate drug research, clinical development, and marketing activities
Market driven and medium risk

Biotechnology
Companies of micro, small, or medium size that participate and coordinate early-stage drug research and development
Investment driven; high risk, entrepreneurial

Basic Research—Groups and Consortia
Usually nonprofit basic research groups funded by government or industrial partner
Science driven: research oriented

Early Stage R&D	Preclinical Evaluation	Clinical Trials	Market

Platform Technologies—R&D
Companies providing basic research tools for early-stage research and development process
Quick to market

Medical Devices
Companies providing devices that screen, detect, diagnose, monitor, and treat disease
Quick to market

Platform Technologies—Diagnostics
Companies providing diagnostic procedures, or devices that screen, detect, diagnose, and monitor disease
Quick to market

Services
Companies providing basic research services, clinical research and development services, manufacturing services, or sales, distribution, and marketing services
Flexible business models

Business and Finance
Companies providing support to the industry such as venture capital, legal, tax, accounting, and financial advisory services

FIGURE 8.3 Various Players in the (Bio)Pharmaceutical Value Chain

company that will take the lead compounds into further development stages. Alternatively, a small biotechnology company may already hold IP rights to a lead compound, but due to a lack of appropriate resources it may license technology from, or use the novel services of, platform technology companies to, for example, further validate the target or optimize the half-life of the lead candidate. Platform technology companies provide a collection of "enabling" methodologies or technologies that, when bundled together, provide support for a range of scientific investigations or activities. During the early phases of drug development, biotechnology companies might also employ service companies that provide, for example, DNA sequencing or *bioinformatics* services. These service companies are often referred to as contract research companies or *contract research organizations*; they provide standard research resources. Their role is usually at the early stages of drug development and is distinct from service organizations that specialize in carrying out clinical research studies later in the value chain.

After the preclinical evaluation phase is completed, the drug will enter clinical trials, which may be carried out internally by large (bio)pharmaceutical companies or may be contracted out as a service to clinical research companies or organizations such as Quintiles Transnational Corporation (NASDAQ: QTRN) of Research Triangle Park, North Carolina. Sufficient quantities of drug product need to be manufactured according to *Good Manufacturing Practice* (GMP) and *Good Clinical Practice* (GCP) standards. This is usually handled by specialist *contract manufacturing organizations* (CMOs), such as Lonza Group Ltd. (SPI: LONN) of Basel, Switzerland. If the drug is approved by regulatory authorities, it could be distributed, marketed, and sold by a large (bio)pharmaceutical company or by *contract sales and marketing organizations* (CSOs). Innovex is the world's largest supplier of contract sales and marketing services to the (bio)pharmaceutical industry, with service capabilities in 21 countries on five continents. Innovex is part of Quintiles, a broadly diversified contract research company. Its subsidiaries do a variety of services, such as contract research, clinical trials, and contract sales and marketing.

We highlight the increasing complexity of both the (bio)pharmaceutical and pharmaceutical industries due to rising drug discovery expenses, costly clinical trials, rigorous government regulatory (including health and safety) procedures, and the huge investments in manufacturing, marketing, and distributing (bio)pharmaceutical drug products to patients. No player can survive alone in this complex industry, and the value chain cannot be managed without structuring both informal and formal alliances. As a result, (bio)pharmaceutical business models need to be constantly updated and adapted to rapidly changing industry dynamics and external nonmarket forces, such as changing government regulations, globalization, and the impact of emerging markets, which in many cases is reducing manufacturing costs while increasing demand for certain drug products.

COMPLETION OF THE BIOTECHNOLOGY AND PHARMACEUTICAL VALUE CHAIN THROUGH ALLIANCE FORMATION

Start-up companies in biotechnology need formal or informal alliances to complete their value chains and to access complementary resources and capabilities, and thereby gain new ideas, knowledge, and learning during different growth phases. These biotechnology start-ups often have less than 10 employees. Therefore they are defined to be "micro-companies" according to the small and medium-size enterprises (SMEs) classification system adopted by the European Commission.[11] Alliance formation helps these fledgling companies share risks (and rewards) with partners at different points of the value chain, thereby reducing the total risk faced by any one company in the chain. We believe that the interrelated aspects of value creation and appropriation of value are extremely important when considering biotechnology or (bio)pharmaceutical business models. Value creation is determined in this industry by many factors, including the innovative capacity of a firm, measured as the number, type, and phase of development of proprietary products in the pipeline. Another aspect of value creation includes the management of internally and externally derived IP rights and know-how. It also encompasses the development of firm capabilities such as negotiation and business development. We acknowledge all these factors; however, in the paragraphs to follow, we emphasize the role played by alliances in value creation. We also discuss the distribution of the risks and rewards among the various players in the alliance network. (Refer to Chapter 5 where we define an alliance network.)

We define a strategic alliance in the biotechnology and pharmaceutical context as any long-term and cooperative relationship that is designed to achieve mutually beneficial goals for as long as this is economically viable. Alliances may be of many types and can be formed at any link of the value chain. Alliance networks are necessary for all companies in the healthcare domain to compete in a dynamic environment. In fact, alliances are regarded as an essential part of the business model by many stakeholders. For example, early-stage biotechnology drug developers are often financed by venture capitalists, but these investors would not consider investing in a start-up company that does not have a good network of contacts, collaborators, and potential partners who could assist with commercialization strategies. Start-up biotechnology companies, in turn, need a strategy to attract investors and partners in order to bring their drugs to a development stage where value is created. The entrepreneur and the investors usually negotiate and jointly revise the business model as events unfold. This also includes the strategic partnering and exit strategies.

Increasingly, biotechnology and (bio)pharmaceutical companies use what is referred to as an open innovation business model. *Open innovation* is defined by Chesbrough as "the use of purposive inflows and outflows of knowledge to accelerate internal innovation, and expand the markets for external use of innovation, respectively. [This paradigm] assumes that firms can and should use external ideas as well as internal ideas, and internal and external paths to market, as they look to advance their technology."[12] In contrast, closed innovation is in-house, without external interactions. External collaboration in biotechnology is combined with internal IP and know-how, and we agree that this open model is necessary to capture the "cascade of knowledge flowing from biotechnology."[13] In fact, Chesbrough stresses the significance of alliances with the biotechnology domain, stating that the "open innovation explicitly incorporates the business model as a source of both value creation and value capture."[14]

The number of alliances that a small biotechnology company makes with big pharmaceutical is an indicator of the firm's stage of growth. According to the hypothesis developed by Deeds et al., "the total number of strategic alliances of a firm will have a positive relationship with the number of new products developed by the firm."[15] We could argue, however, that the structure of deals made with strategic partners, their quality, and the coordinated management of the firm's overall alliance network is of greater strategic significance than the sheer number of alliances made.

As with all types of collaboration, it is most beneficial to develop selection criteria for potential partners. Often there are no defined criteria for the formation of a strategic alliance for early-stage biotechnology companies, and each one may be formed in an opportunistic manner, tailor-made to a single product. However, critical factors for alliance formation have been identified by a Deloitte Research Life Sciences Study.[16] For example, the four most important characteristics that biotechnology companies look for in a partner have been shown to be: (1) commitment from senior management, (2) favorable deal terms, (3) market depth in a particular therapeutic area, and (4) the partner's alignment with the biotechnology firm's core strategy. Over time, a company usually learns how to structure alliances; management also learns about the criteria that are important in selecting potential partners. Partner selection is discussed further in Chapter 7.

Of the many different types of collaboration possible, we next discuss two types that should be considered by entrepreneurs within the biotechnology domain and especially among early-stage drug developers. These are collaboration with academic groups and strategic alliances with large pharmaceutical companies. Developers of platform technologies or medical devices also use alliances to complement their business model. Both kinds of collaboration, described next, allow access to external resources and capabilities. Therefore, the management of these collaborations is an integral part of their value creation strategy.

Access to Innovation through Collaboration with Academic Groups

Most start-up companies in biotechnology form both formal and informal collaborations with academic groups. These collaborations may take the form of academic research collaborations, strategic partnerships, equity or non-equity joint ventures, or minority equity participations as depicted in Figure 6.1. Early-stage academic research collaborations are usually tailor-made for each drug compound or biotech product in the pipeline. In fact, many start-up companies in biotechnology have their roots in academia or their innovations are sourced from academia. Academic collaborations provide access to new ideas and technologies, in the form of scientific advice and expertise that help to strengthen the venture's business model. For example, an early developer of drugs could use academic collaborations to identify and validate drug targets, to carry out functional assays during the pre-clinical phase of drug development, or to help substantiate claims for a patent application.

At this early stage of discussions, a start-up company needs to exercise care with respect to how proprietary rights are divided and how agreements are made with universities or other stakeholders, such as research funding organizations. Nondisclosure agreements (NDAs) or patent agreements are the most common agreements made with academic collaborators. NDAs and their uses are discussed in Chapters 9, 11, and 16. To see a sample NDA, log onto our web site located at www.innovationtocashflows.com and go to Appendix 9.1, "Sample Confidentiality Agreement."

The management of academic collaborations is also important to ensure that collaborators are cooperating with respect to commercially related deadlines and that the agreed balance between the start-up company projects and their other own research projects is maintained. Often mutual agreements are reached concerning milestones and deliverables, and these are part of the written collaborative contract between the company and the university.

If the entrepreneur who starts in a university setting would like to exploit an innovation and start his or her own company, numerous agreements, including an investor agreement will be needed. See Chapter 10 for a discussion of company incorporation issues and to see a sample investment term sheet. Usually if a scientist applies for patent protection for his invention, he will need the agreement and the financial support of the university as his employer. Technology transfer offices usually mediate these agreements for the university. If IP rights already exist, for instance, due to the earlier success of university employees being granted patents, then the entrepreneur could license these IP rights from the university; if he has the financing, he could buy them outright from the university. The situation with respect to exploitation of IP rights created in a university or academic setting differs widely between countries. Technology transfer was advanced in the United States by the Bayh-Dole Act of 1980,[17] which obliges universities to transfer technology to industry if partially or totally funded through U.S. government funds. In other countries, including those in the European Union, no one act governs the transfer of technology between universities and industry. Consequently such technology transfer agreements differ from country to country and even within countries. In some cases, technology transfer offices favor complex and often expensive license agreements, some involving up-front payments, others involving milestones payments linked to further development of the drug or technology or royalties as a percentage of sales. For a better understanding of the IP landscape, patents, patenting strategies, and technology transfer license agreements, refer to Chapters 11 through 14.

As an inventor or entrepreneur, you will need to use your negotiation skills and judgment to weigh the costs and benefits of entering into complicated agreements. One factor you should keep in mind is how investors perceive these agreements. Often venture capitalists (VCs), for example, will not be interested in financing development of your innovation if your former employer, the university, does not coinvest yet wants to keep IP rights. The value of the IP at this point is often a contentious chicken-and-the-egg point of discussion. On one hand, the university will argue that the IP would not exist without its research, which is in fact true. On the other hand, you as entrepreneur, and your potential VCs, will argue that IP has no value unless it is exploited, which is also true. In the end, IP at this stage is often assigned the value of the costs that were incurred during its lifetime. These costs are called *replication costs* if they are the costs of replicating the IP or proprietary know-how. These costs should include the costs of any failures (e.g., failed experiments or inconclusive results) related to the IP, not just the sum of the costs of successful outcomes. We discuss valuation issues in Part Six, "Valuing Company Cash Flows."

Despite some complications, SMEs and universities are nevertheless stimulated to collaborate via government subsidies or grants. This type of collaboration is one of the most important for industry access to innovations. In Europe, the EU stimulates the collaboration between SMEs and universities, for instance, through programs that support an SME to "develop its capacity for innovation." These programs include the cooperation programme, the European Technology Platforms (ETPs), and Research for the Benefit of SMEs. Information concerning such programs is available from the European Community Research and Development Information Service, referred to as CORDIS (http://cordis.europa.eu). In the United States, grants are provided by the National Institutes of Health (NIH) (www.nih.gov) and the National Science Foundation (NSF) (www.nsf.gov). For example, Small Business Innovation Research (SBIR) grants are provided by the NSF. Log onto our web site at www.innovationtocashflows.com and go to "Resources" and search for the section, "Government Agencies, Science and Research Organizations, and Disease Associations" for a list of useful Web sites.

Mutualism between Biotechnology and Pharmaceutical Companies

The business models of large pharmaceutical companies such as GlaxoSmithKline Plc (LSE: GSK; NYSE: GSK) of Middlesex, the United Kingdom, or AstraZeneca (NYSE: AZN) of London, the United Kingdom, are generally different from start-up biotechnology ventures, and the nature of their drugs have until recently been chemical based. In our characterization, these large companies have traditionally adopted the fully integrated pharmaceutical company (FIPCO) business model. However, over the past decade, larger pharmaceutical companies have experienced difficulties in expanding their drug portfolios. There is a general decline in productivity as measured by the average research and development (R&D) cost per new approved drug, which includes the amount spent on failed drugs. Over the past decade, the number of New Molecular Entities (NMEs) and Biologic License Applications (BLAs) granted by the FDA, for example, has dropped significantly. Yet the amount of R&D spending continues to rise. In addition, generics are now entering the market more rapidly after the expiration of patent protection. For example, these days, when a patent expires, 90 percent of blockbuster revenues may be lost in a few weeks.[18] (A blockbuster is defined as a drug with over $1 billion in sales.)This means that pharmaceutical companies are experiencing what is referred to as an innovation gap, as shown in Figure 8.4.

To fill the innovation gap, pharmaceutical companies are taking a series of measures to replenish their pipelines based on trade-offs among strengthening in-house R&D, buying up know-how or innovative IP rights from smaller companies, and in-licensing IP rights through strategic partnering or joint ventures.

Biotechnology companies, in turn, are exploiting the innovation gap in the pharmaceutical industry pipeline. They are seeking ever more attractive deal terms and collaboration conditions from larger pharmaceutical companies for the biopharmaceutical candidates in early stages of development. In order to complete their value chains, biotechnology companies do need to attract large pharmaceutical companies as technology investors or strategic alliance partners. These partners, in turn, supply the resources and capabilities that the fledgling biotechnology firms might lack. Strategic partnering is common, as demonstrated by the partnering meetings among investors, pharmaceutical companies, and biotechnology that usually take place at global clusters for biotechnology. Details on partnering meetings are available from biotechnology and licensing trade association web sites. We also discuss partnering and social networks in Chapters 7 and 15. For more on San Diego, California's leading biotechnology cluster, log onto our web site at www.innovationtocashflows.com and search for Appendix 3.1, "Porter's Cluster Theory Applied to San Diego's Biotechnology Cluster." Access to external innovation, as described in theory by

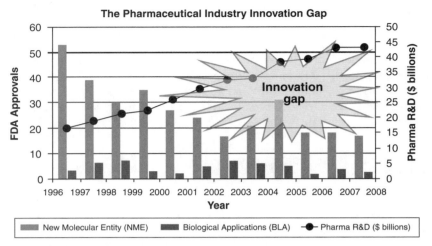

FIGURE 8.4   Pharmaceutical Industry Innovation Gap
Source: Based on data from a presentation given by G. Steven Burrill, "Biotech 2008:
A Global Transformation"—A presentation for the Wisconsin Life Sciences
Transformation Conference (2008); and from the report by Frost & Sullivan,
"Widening Innovation—Productivity Gap in the Pharmaceutical Industry—New
Challenges and Future Directions" (2008).

the open innovation model referred to earlier, is now being translated into practice.
Biotechnology and pharmaceutical companies are emerging as dependent relations
of each other in sharing a common value chain; in so doing, they are bringing novel
drug products or medical devices to the market faster than either could do alone. Like
the biological interaction between two different species, referred to as mutualism,
both species derive a fitness benefit, and often this is survival. Small biotechnology
companies provide innovation to large pharmaceutical companies, much like the
mycorrhizal fungi provide inorganic compounds such as nitrogen to larger trees and
plants, while these plants provide a source of energy in the form of carbohydrates to
the fungi.

Importance of Deal Structure for Cash Generation   Through in- or out-licensing,
pharmaceutical and biotechnology companies access new technologies, novel products and proprietary know-how. Deal structuring and bargaining skill come together
to determine how cash payments will be transferred among the parties in such licensing or technology transfer agreements. Individual licensing agreements will differ
from each other in terms of contents and scope. In creating a strategic alliance through
the licensing of IP rights, a series of complex and interrelated factors are involved.
The cost versus benefit of each option needs to be weighed. Important factors to be
considered when navigating a patent licensing contract or negotiating a technology
transfer agreement are described further in Chapter 14.

For pharmaceutical and biotechnology companies, the structuring of deals with
respect to commercialization rights needs to be creative in order to have both parties benefit from access to resources, capabilities, and knowledge. However, small
biotechnology companies have the priority need to generate cash flow, as well as

other needs, such as learning. The agreed percentage royalty is typically higher if it is a *front-loaded licensing deal*, meaning an up-front cash payment is given to the biotechnology firm by the pharmaceutical company with later payments coming in the form of royalties once product is sold in the market. The problem for the biotechnology firm with this type of agreement is that royalty payments may not be seen for 10 to 15 years, the time it takes for a (bio)pharmaceutical to make its way through the product development pipeline.

In contrast to a front-loaded deal, a *back-loaded licensing deal* typically involves a smaller, initial up-front cash payment but offers the attraction of further cash payments contingent on accomplishing specified milestones. Therefore, a back-loaded deal may be more favorable for the start-up biotechnology company that needs more frequent infusions of cash in order to continue operations. The back-loaded, or "staged," investment deal means that the biotechnology company can push its product into later stages of the development cycle before having to pass it on to the next player in the value chain. Such deals may be difficult for small biotechnology companies to negotiate with a large pharmaceutical company, due perhaps to the degree of dependency on such a partner and the greater perceived bargaining power of the larger company. However, by optimal structuring of these deals, smaller companies can secure both near-term and future cash flows to sustain operations and to advance a value creation strategy. In some cases, small companies can access the investor's expertise and know-how in making such deals. Royalty agreements are part of the *royalty income pharmaceutical company (RIPCO) business model* to be described. Further information about royalty rates and deals can be obtained from proprietary deal databases such as PharmaDeals, a division of PharmaVentures Ltd., Oxford, England (www.pharmaventures.com), and Recombinant Capital (Recap), Walnut Creek, California (www.recap.com). Typical royalty rates for each phase of drug development are shown in Figure 8.5. The royalty rates are generally lower for products at the preclinical evaluation phase compared to products in later phases of clinical trials.

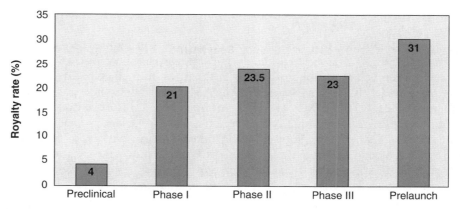

FIGURE 8.5   Average Royalty Rates in Single-Product Global Deals, 1997 to Mid-2007
Source: Adapted from Everild Haynes, "Royalty Rates in Pharmaceutical Licensing Deals," *Pharmadeals Review* (November 2007): 12

Until recently, the structure of deals meant that biotechnology companies took most of the initial risks during the R&D phases. Now sharing of these risks is becoming more common as the (bio)pharmaceutical industry attempts to close the innovation gap. Small biotechnology companies are retaining more control over copromotion, codevelopment, and commercialization,[19] and thus more transfer of knowledge and learning occurs at later phases of the value chain. The average value of early-stage deals between the biotechnology and pharmaceutical industries has risen from $65.3 million in 2001 to $125.1 million in 2005. Additionally, midstage deals (preclinical development–Phase I) increased in this same time span from $29 million to $172 million—an almost 600 percent increase. We believe that the current innovation gap in the pharmaceutical pipeline favors the kinds of deal structure where risk is shared by multiple partners.

BUSINESS MODELS IN PHARMACEUTICALS AND (BIO)PHARMACEUTICALS

We have described a typical value chain within the biopharmaceutical domain and have identified some of the risks involved with drug development, in particular. We have portrayed how alliances are structured to complete the value chain. Here we explore the business models that are common for drug developers, medical device developers, and those companies that enable drug or medical device development. We emphasize that many hybrid forms of these business models do exist.

Fully Integrated Pharmaceutical Company Model

The FIPCO model is based on the view that a start-up (bio)pharmaceutical company can gather enough financing and expertise to carry out all drug discovery and development steps independently. These include basic research and development, filing of INDs through clinical trials Phases I, II, III, and IV. If the drug candidate is successful and makes it through clinical trials, it must be launched, marketed, and sold through various distribution channels, ranging from pharmacies, to health maintenance organizations and government medical systems. All activities in the value chain are completed under one corporate roof, without access to external resources and capabilities.

Investors consider this model as both high risk and high expected return on investment. FIPCO is associated mainly with the development of own proprietary products. Prominent examples of companies that traditionally employed FIPCO as their basic model are Amgen Inc. (NASDAQ: AMGN) of Thousand Oaks, California; Genentech Inc. (NYSE: DNA) of South San Francisco, California; and Biogen Inc. (NASDAQ: BIIB) of Cambridge, Massachusetts. These large biopharmaceutical companies are considered the champions of the biotechnology industry. In 1976, Robert A. Swanson, a venture capitalist, and Herbert Boyer, a biochemistry and biophysics professor at the University of California at San Francisco, founded Genentech with $100,000 financed from a venture capital firm, Kleiner Perkins Inc. The value of this investment increased 783 times before an IPO value of $78 million in 1980. The FIPCO model was made popular in the United States and the United Kingdom during the 1980s and up to the early 1990s in Europe. Nowadays, due to the high capital costs involved, it is impossible that start-ups would use this model, since they would not raise the required finance or have the other resources or capabilities to push product(s) derived from their own in-house technology and know-how through all phases of the value chain.

The FIPCO model is outdated because even established players use alliances at the earliest stages of the pipeline. For example, Genentech has considerable cash resources which the company is using to build future growth prospects through focused partnership activities. Some of Genentech's activities include the partnering of Rituxan® (rituximab), a treatment for non-Hodgkin's lymphoma (NHL) and rheumatoid arthritis with Idec Pharmaceuticals Corporation (now Biogen Idec Inc.). Genentech is also comarketing Tarceva® (erlotinib), a treatment for non–small cell lung cancer and pancreatic cancer, with OSI Pharmaceuticals Inc. (NASDAQ: OSIP) of Long Island, New York. Biogen Idec Inc. has a pipeline of drug candidates that address diseases such as multiple sclerosis, lymphoma, and rheumatoid arthritis. OSI Pharmaceuticals is a biotechnology company focused on treatments for oncology, diabetes, and obesity.

An exception to the move away from the FIPCO model is the research, development and sale of *orphan drugs*. Orphan drugs are used to treat very rare diseases. Approximately 30 million people living in the EU and 25 million Americans suffer from more than 6,000 rare diseases. *Rare diseases* are defined as those affecting fewer than 5 in 10,000 people in the EU and fewer than 200,000 people in the United States.[20] Due to the small number of patients, the companies developing drugs for rare diseases may expect relatively low profit from sales and, in some cases, a financial loss, when the costs of R&D for these drugs are taken into account. Changes in drug regulations concerning orphan drugs in 1983 by the FDA and in 1999 by EMEA means that now even orphan drugs can become blockbusters. Orphan drugs are successfully pursued within the FIPCO business model. The new legal frameworks aim to provide regulatory and financial incentives, such as protocol assistance and marketing exclusivity, to encourage (bio)pharmaceutical companies to develop and market orphan drug products.

An example of an orphan drug with blockbuster status is the drug Cerezyme from biotechnology company Genzyme Corporation (NASDAQ: GENZ) based in Cambridge, Massachusetts, used as a treatment for Gaucher's disease. This drug exceeded $1 billion in product revenues for 2007 and is available in more than 90 countries.[21] Gaucher's disease, affecting 1 in 100,000 persons, causes a harmful buildup of fatty substances in the spleen, liver, lungs, bone marrow, and brain.

Another medium-size orphan drug company is Amsterdam Molecular Therapeutics, (Euronext: AMT) headquartered in Amsterdam, the Netherlands, which is engaged in human gene therapy and went public on the Amsterdam Stock Exchange in 2006. It aspires to follow the FIPCO business model, focused on developing research and clinical development of orphan diseases in *metabolic* disorders, ocular diseases, and disorders of the central and peripheral nervous systems. For example, AMT is currently preparing to file the Marketing Authorization Dossier with the EMEA for Glybera®, a drug for hyperlipoproteinemia type I. Hyperlipoproteinemia causes recurrent episodes of pancreatitis that destroy major parts of the pancreas and cause a form of difficult-to-treat diabetes.

We now examine other business models that have evolved in the life science industry. The models described all depend on alliance formation with partners that specialize in defined parts of the value chain.

Royalty Income Pharmaceutical Company Model

The RIPCO model depends on alliance formation; it is certainly more common for a (bio)pharmaceutical or biotechnology start-up than the FIPCO model. For example, an early-stage drug developer may raise capital that allows it to finance research and to develop its own innovative product up to a particular phase of the value chain (usually Phase I or II). For a small biotechnology firm, it could mean raising equity capital in the form of seed money from angel investors, for example, or venture capital from venture capitalists. Subsequently, the product value (usually IP rights) is transferred through an out-licensing agreement to a larger firm (often a listed pharmaceutical company), which will further develop and take the product to market. The mutualism involved between small biotechnology and large pharmaceutical companies is described earlier in this chapter. In-licensing is used by pharmaceutical companies to plug the innovation gap in their pipeline. For a large pharmaceutical company, the likelihood of partnering with a smaller biotechnology company is usually higher if the drug compound under consideration has passed an earlier phase of testing (in other words, safety, tolerability and efficacy in clinical trials Phase I and Phase II) or achieved an orphan drug status. Moreover, it is essential that the drug compound be legally well protected. Partnering has a very positive impact on the share price of publicly traded pharmaceutical companies, since future cash flows are more likely for products that have already passed earlier phases of development.

Royalties are commonly a percentage of product net sales. Agreements can be made, for example, on a tiered royalty structure. Generally speaking, the product that has the higher market potential will get the better royalty rates. Often a back-loaded licensing deal (described earlier) is employed, since it can provide cash flow to support the operations of a small biotechnology company by means of an initial up-front cash payment with further payments contingent on reaching development milestones. Frequently these types of agreements also are codevelopment agreements. An example is the exclusive global collaboration agreement between POZEN (NAS-DAQ: POZN) Inc., of Chapel Hill, North Carolina, and AstraZeneca (NYSE: AZN) of London, England, that was announced in early August 2006 for the codevelopment and commercialization of proprietary fixed-dose combinations of the proton pump inhibitor esomeprazole magnesium, with the nonsteroidal anti-inflammatory drug (NSAID) naproxen, in a single tablet. The product will be indicated for use in the management of pain and inflammation associated with conditions such as osteoarthritis and rheumatoid arthritis in patients who are at risk for developing NSAID-associated gastric ulcers. Under the terms of the most recently amended agreement, AstraZeneca will pay POZEN up to $345 million, in the aggregate, for the achievement of development, regulatory, and sales milestones. POZEN will receive an immediate $30 million payment, which includes recognition of successful proof of concept, $55 million will be paid on achievement of certain development and regulatory milestones, and $260 million will be paid as sales performance milestones if certain aggregate sales thresholds are achieved. The U.S. royalty structure is a low double-digit rate for the life of the agreement. The royalty structure outside the United States is a multitier structure ranging from mid-single digits to high teens.

For the RIPCO business model to be successful, the product's market potential should be well characterized. A small biotechnology company needs to pay attention to the size of the patient population for the product concerned; the price the customer is willing to pay; and the speed with which the product can actually reach the market via the alliance under consideration. (Refer to Chapter 14.)

In the RIPCO business model, the investor's role is both financial and strategic. In addition to providing early stage financing for the venture, often the venture capitalists (VCs) will help the small biotechnology company identify suitable alliance partners, particularly in the early phases of research and product development. Furthermore, the VCs may facilitate the application for additional financing for the biotechnology venture from a larger pharmaceutical company. If the application is approved, the pharmaceutical company's investment could be made through a strategic alliance agreement for one or more research programs within the biotechnology company. Alternatively, the larger pharmaceutical company might acquire the smaller biotechnology company in a trade sale. All forms of financing are usually contingent upon reaching agreed upon R&D milestones.

No-Research, Development-Only Model

The *No-Research, Development-Only (NRDO) business model* guides existing but as-yet unapproved drugs through clinical trials and eventually toward regulatory approval. This model describes companies that license in products that have been researched and developed and have passed initial clinical investigations at, for example, pre-IND (investigational new drug) or Phase I. Alternatively, companies license in products that have received approval in other countries, develop older drug products into new indications, or take existing products and make *me-better* variants. Through in-licensing, therefore, some pharmaceutical companies concentrate on being late-stage developers of drugs (Phase III) and may also distribute and market these drugs once they are approved. The NRDO business model is therefore reliant on alliance formation. This business model is also generally dependent on outsourcing drug development to *clinical research organizations* and contract manufacturing organizations to support in-house operations.

The advantage of this business model is that, in theory, drug compounds should have already passed phases of the testing such as Phase I and so time to market should be faster. This model also helps to ensure that a company uses its resources to develop products, without maintaining a large number of personnel. However, disadvantages are that in-licensing of products for this model may involve large fees, milestone payments, and royalties, since the innovation and investment up to that point should be rewarded. Furthermore, sufficient capital needs to be available to develop a portfolio of drug compounds, increasing the likelihood that one will succeed to market launch.

An example of a small company employing this model is PanGenetics B.V. headquartered in Utrecht, the Netherlands, and near Cambridge in the United Kingdom. The company focuses on clinical application of monoclonal antibodies for treatment of immune-mediated diseases, cancer, and pain. The company's management and advisors have several decades of combined antibody development and commercial experience. They have been responsible for bringing a large number of biological products into clinical development; of them, five have been successfully marketed. The company uses this expertise to select antibody products for in-licensing based on a clear therapeutic rationale and freedom to operate. PanGenetics also owns or has exclusive rights to a substantial IP portfolio. Another example of a company that uses the NRDO model is Curalogic A/S (CO:CUR), quoted on the OMX Nordic Exchange, Copenhagen, Denmark. The in-house core competencies of Curalogic are drug development, project management, clinical development, quality assurance, (bio)pharmaceuticals development, and manufacture. Curalogic exploits its own proprietary formulation technology to develop oral immunotherapy products for the most commercially attractive allergies.

Virtually Integrated Pharmaceutical Company Model

The *virtually integrated pharmaceutical company (VIPCO) business model* is evidence of an emerging trend: deconstruction or decoupling of industry value chains. Formerly fully integrated value chains within the (bio)pharmaceuticals and biotechnology domains are deconstructing and fragmenting. The traditional FIPCO model is evolving toward the VIPCO model. In VIPCO business models, the industry players specialize in portions of the value chain. The VIPCO model may describe companies that range from small, 5- to 10-person microcompanies to large companies that keep in-house activities to a minimum and outsource (or offshore) almost all stages of their value chain. Outsourcing keeps fixed costs to a minimum; in theory, it gives greater control over variable costs. This business model accesses external sources of know-how and expertise quickly. VIPCO is flexible and is readily adaptable to changes in the external environment.

A start-up company could participate and specialize in one part of the alliance network, or alternatively it could own a drug compound and coordinate a part of the network of alliances in the VIPCO model. Some activities in the value chain are outsourced as contract services, involving little or no technology transfer. In other cases, technology transfer is extensive and IP rights are transferred as part of licensing agreements with several other players. For example, an own proprietary drug product, medical device, or technology (i.e., developed solely by the start-up without help) could be further researched or developed through an academic collaboration with a scientific institution. Subsequently, alliance partners that operate service business models could be employed to complete the value chain. For example, a drug product could enter pre-clinical evaluation through an alliance with a pre-clinical research service organization or platform technology company, before being passed to a clinical research organization (CRO), which carries out the clinical trials such as animal testing, pharmacokinetics and dynamics, efficacy, and toxicity. An alliance with a contract manufacturing organization (CMO) would ensure sufficient quantities of clinical-grade product for these trials and also for the market. The finished product could then be marketed, distributed, and sold via an alliance with a clinical sales organization (CSO) or large pharmaceutical organization.

Management of alliances, negotiation, and expertise of in- and out-licensing are critical skills for the success of this business model. IP rights and know-how issues need careful attention when alliance agreements are drafted, since some joint process development may be involved in addition to technology transfer. Strategic alliances with partners can involve sharing of risk but also of rewards in much the same way as codevelopment agreements mentioned for the RIPCO model. We predict that the virtually integrated business model will become the more dominant of the business models discussed so far.

There are many examples of smaller companies that employ the VIPCO model. Here we give two examples. One example is Speedel (www.speedel.com) based in Basel, Switzerland. In July 2008, Speedel was taken over by Novartis (www.novartis.com). Consequently, by early 2009 Speedel will be delisted from the Swiss stock exchange. Speedel is a biopharmaceutical company that specializes in the fast development of therapeutics for cardiovascular and metabolic disease, focusing on the stages from lead development to the end of Phase II. Speedel takes on the financial risk associated with research and early-stage clinical trials development in return for the exclusive rights to in-license drug product candidates from major pharmaceutical companies. Speedel's business model is to develop a drug candidate through Phase II clinical trials, then license the compound back to the pharmaceutical company for further trials and eventual commercialization if the compound is approved. For instance, Speedel's lead product candidate SPP100 (aliskiren, Tekturna®) was the first-in-class renin inhibitor (for treating cardiovascular diseases). SPP100 was in-licensed from Novartis in 1999 and licensed back to Novartis Pharma in 2002 for further development and commercialization. The FDA in the United States approved SPP100 in March 2007 and the EMEA in the EU in August 2007. Speedel's business model continues to evolve. The company founded Speedel Experimenta in April 2002 to do late-stage research. Currently Speedel seeks to conduct internally Phase III clinical trials development for selected product candidates in specialist indications. Speedel's aim is to capture and retain for itself more of the economic value being created in the research and drug development process.

Another example of a biopharmaceutical company employing the VIPCO model is AM-Pharma based in Bunnik, the Netherlands (www.am-pharma.com). This privately held company focuses on the preclinical and clinical development of therapeutics to treat inflammatory and infectious disease. The company operates the VIPCO model, employing just 20 staff, but manages alliances with academic groups, CMOs, and CROs to advance the R&D of its products. Developed products are being prepared for subsequent out-licensing via partnering agreements with large pharmaceutical companies.

Platform Technology Business Model

The *platform technology business model* describes a collection of enabling technologies or methodologies that are bundled together to provide a unique solution or service that can be accessed by clients as an entirety via a license or via service fees. Platforms technologies can be research tools or diagnostic tools (or diagnostic kits). They have diverse applications. They usually exploit a combination of scientific methodologies or technologies that can facilitate different steps in drug discovery, development, diagnosis, or monitoring of disease processes. Companies employing this model could integrate technologies derived from disciplines such as combinatorial chemistry, genomics,[22] proteomics, or systems biology to allow high-throughput screening activities engaged to discover genomic-based drugs, or to diagnose disease conditions using biochips. Technology platforms could also be used to allow gene expression profiling or to make mouse gene knock-outs.[23] Proprietary platform technologies may therefore add value by reducing the time and cost to identify and develop drug candidates.

Very often the platform technology is composed of various patented subcomponents, some of which may have to be in-licensed from external parties before being "layered" with the firm's own proprietary technology. Companies that rely on this business model might produce instruments or devices for the diagnostics or high-throughput screening markets, such as some biochips. In the case of biochips or lab-on-a-chip manufacture, there is value in the combination of know-how, trade secrets, and patent ownership or licensing rights. For example, a protein biochip technology platform is the result of combined know-how, proprietary process technologies, trade secrets, and strong intellectual patent portfolios in several areas and may include a combination of expertise in peptide chemistry, supramolecular chemistry, and other related biology and technologies. When the IP property rights needed to build the chip are sought from external sources, freedom to operate (FTO) challenges may be faced. *Freedom to operate* and *freedom to use* refer to the patentee's commercial freedom to use the technology identified in the patent, where the "patentee" is the inventor to whom the patent was issued. The concept of a patentee's freedom to use is explained more fully in Chapter 12 in the section "Patent Facts." In Chapter 15 we give a simplified case example of how to do a patent search in order to discover patent documents that affect a company's FTO. (In reality, FTO searches are complex to carry out.)

To continue the biochip story, not having FTO may mean that you will not be able to do what you initially thought you could do if the rights to a single patent are too costly or simply not available. Alternatively, a single array may require several licenses for specific probes, or ligands. Licensing each probe or ligand would result in costly royalty stacking, where you end up paying royalties on top of royalties. Often, therefore, biochip companies frequently make a basic version of the chip and allow their clients to couple their own specific probes or ligands to it. (See Chapters 12 through 14 for more on patent strategies and technology transfer licensing agreements.) If the company has a strong patent position, broad freedom to operate, an already installed customer base on which to build and scale up future products, or its technology platform offers compelling benefits with which to attract customers to switch platforms, then investors will be easier to attract.

Usually companies employing this business model require less capital than that needed to fund fully integrated (bio)pharmaceutical business models. Furthermore, revenues are visible sooner. Technologies most likely will require less total investment. In theory, platform technologies ought to be able to reach the market quicker and with less time-consuming compliance and product approval requirements than for (bio)pharmaceuticals. Companies in this sector, however, need to be skilled at managing multiple alliances in order to validate technology, promote industry standards, and gain faster product adoption by customers in the market. Also required to implement this business model is experience in new product development, regulatory expertise, manufacturing capabilities, and distribution channels to be able to deliver products and services to customers. In the case of technology platforms, usually only modest royalties or other rights are retained. Initial introduction may be to academia to allow faster adoption by researchers and clinicians and may involve incentives for the customers, such as reduced rates for basic equipment, but as part of extended service or development contracts. Hybrid business models also exist in this category, as there is an overlap with medical devices and service models.

A very well-known example of a platform technology is the research and diagnostic tool polymerase chain reaction (PCR), which enables researchers or clinicians to quickly produce millions of copies of a specific DNA sequence from a DNA or mRNA sample. PCR can be used in multiple applications, such as molecular cloning, DNA sequencing, and also for rapid detection of organism-specific DNA.

Leading global players in diagnostics are Abbott Laboratories (NYSE:ABT) of Abbott Park, Illinois, the Diagnostics Division of Roche (SWX:RO) of Basel, Switzerland, and GE Healthcare (NYSE:GE) of Fairfield, Connecticut. These players are investing heavily in platform technologies. Examples of leaders in pure-play platform technologies include Affymetrix (NASDAQ: AFFX), headquartered in Santa Clara, California; it had 2007 revenues of $371 million and net income of $12.6 million. It specializes in DNA probe arrays, reagents, scanners, and software to process and analyze complex genetic information. It competes with firms such as Agilent Technologies, Inc., Invitrogen (NASDAQ: IVGN), Beckman Coulter (NYSE: BEC), and Applied Biosystems group (NYSE: ABI). Another interesting example of a platform technology provider is Biacore Life Sciences, founded in Uppsala, Sweden, and acquired in August 2006 by GE Healthcare. Biacore is the recognized platform leader in surface plasmon resonance, which is used in areas such as pharmaceutical drug discovery, antibody characterization, proteomics, biotherapeutic development and manufacture, and many life science research applications. Biacore systems generate unique data on the interactions between proteins and other molecules. During research, development, and manufacture, these data give insights into protein functionality and disease mechanisms and play a key role in the critical decisions needed for efficient development and production of therapeutics.

The main threat to the platform technology business model is rapid technological change, the emergence of new standards, and the lack of customer adoption to new product introductions. Switching costs[24] are very important, especially when a new technology platform is being considered for adoption by a customer. This business model, unlike the (bio)pharmaceutical product model, is generally not driven by patient populations but depends instead on platform adoption by multiple decision makers at academic research institutes or hospitals or within large pharmaceutical companies. Should the technology be adopted, the switching costs should include the time and expense to adapt the GMP environment, to validate equipment and methodologies, and to train personnel. All incurred expenditures may represent a sizeable investment.

The 1990s showed huge success for the technology platform business model in terms of raising finance. However, this trend would not last with investors. According to biotechnology investors, such as Stelios Papadopoulos, former vice chairman of Cowen & Company (NASDAQ: COWN) of New York, New York, and cofounder of Exelixis (NASDAQ:EXEL) of South San Francisco, California, a company engaged in the development of treatments for cancer and other serious diseases, since the platform technology model "addressed only a tiny part of the drug discovery process, (it) risked becoming optional or redundant."[25] Papadopoulos, who sketched his vision in an industry trends supplement of *Nature Biotechnology* in 2000, advocated slowly turning the technology platform model into a proprietary R&D discovery model. There is a lower barrier to entry to this business model as compared to drug development models. However, such a hybrid model may be employed only by more mature or fully integrated companies. Millennium Pharmaceuticals, Inc. (NASDAQ: MLNM), of Cambridge, Massachusetts, is an example of a company that succeeded in this transformation, mainly through acquisition and partnering. For example, when Millennium bought Leukocyte and Cor Therapeutics, it acquired two

FDA-approved drug candidates. Takeda Pharmaceutical Company Limited (TSE: 4502), based in Osaka, Japan, announced on May 9, 2008, the successful completion of its all-cash $8.8 billion tender offer to acquire all the outstanding shares of Millennium common stock for $25 per share. Takeda is Japan's largest pharmaceutical company.

We expect, and contrary to general opinion, that there may be a second wave of technology platform business models that correspond to the imminent advance in personalized medicine. We also predict that platform technology models, although addressing a small part of the value chain, will be crucial alliance players in the VIPCO model and will serve niche markets in healthcare. Innovation will play a huge part in determining which players employing platform technology models will survive over time.

Service Business Models

Service business models are multifaceted and describe the provision of many individual or combined services, including contract discovery, research or analysis, clinical trials investigations, contract manufacturing, instrumentation maintenance and after-sales service contracts, distribution, sales, and various information, education, or bioinformatics services. In practice, even so-called fully integrated companies outsource specialized, identifiable portions of their value chain through service contracts. (See Figure 8.3.) These business models therefore complement the NDRO and VIPCO models and overlap with the platform technologies and medical device models.

So many variations exist of the service business model that a detailed description of all the possibilities is beyond the scope of this book. We suggest consulting industry directories to locate the service providers for a particular need. As an example, to identify the contract manufacturing organizations for the pharmaceuticals industry, see the Web site of Contract Pharma (www.contractpharma.com). Other contract pharmaceutical companies are listed in the "Resources" file on our web site, www.innovationtocashflows.com.

Many CMOs are privately owned. Two leading examples for contract manufacture of chemical pharmaceuticals would be Metrics, Inc. (www.metricsinc.com) of Greenville, North Carolina, and Penn Pharmaceutical Services (www.pennpharm.co.uk) of Penn, Buckinghamshire, England. Offering an even broader range of services than these two privately held manufacturers is publicly listed Patheon (TSK: PTI) of Ontario, Canada. It is focused on meeting the contract manufacturing needs of chemical pharmaceutical, biopharmaceutical, and specialty chemicals customers served by its 10 best-in-class manufacturing facilities located in the United States, Canada, and Europe.

While there are abundant examples of CMOs that are capable of making chemically based pharmaceuticals, there are relatively fewer well-established CMOs that are able to handle biological processes and manufacture biopharmaceuticals, such as vaccines *or* recombinant proteins. To meet the unmet market demand for biological processing, several major CMOs are expanding their capacity. According to the market research consultancy HighTech Business Decisions of Moraga, California, the top biopharmaceutical CMOs, based on revenues, include: Avecia Biologics (Billingham, United Kingdom), Boehringer Ingelheim (Ingelheim, Germany), Diosynth Biotechnology (Morrisville, North Carolina), Lonza (Basel, Switzerland), and Sandoz (Holzkirchen, Germany).[26]

As part of the global trend toward offshoring manufacturing, we mention the services of two firms that are benefiting. Malladi Drugs & Pharmaceuticals of Chennai Tamilnadu, India, is now the largest drug manufacturer in India and is conducting global contract manufacturing for a growing roster of clients. SynCo Bio Partners (privately owned), of Amsterdam, the Netherlands, is another example of a European manufacturer offering an attractive value proposition to biopharmaceutical customers. This contract manufacturer has the capability to flexibly produce biopharmaceuticals in just the right quantities for various phases of clinical trials. It then can scale up production and produce larger volumes for licensed compounds launched in the market. Other biopharmaceutical CMOs are modifying their service model to include some drug development services in addition to focused manufacturing for both clinical trials and full-scale market production, thus evolving toward a one-stop-shop model.

R&D outsourcing continues to increase, with contract research and clinical research organization revenues forecast to grow by 11.5% through 2011 after reaching $16 billion in 2006.[27] Examples of firms specializing in conducting Phase I to IV clinical research trials are Kendle (NASDAQ: KNDL) of Cincinnati, Ohio, and ICON plc (NASDAQ: ICLR-ADRs) of Dublin, Ireland. Offering a broader palate of contract research services is Pharmaceutical Product Development (NASDAQ: PPDI) of Wilmington, North Carolina, which not only does global clinical trials research for drug and medical device companies but also offers a range of laboratory services for the life science industry.

Moving from contract research and clinical research organizations, we turn to platform technology service models. Such models may be used anywhere in the biopharmaceutical value chain but often are found in very-early-stage research activities. We provide one example to clarify the business model concept. We focus especially on a platform technology company located in India that has acquired credibility through acquisitions of smaller companies in Europe. We expect to see many more emerging market companies pursue this strategy of acquiring local companies to obtain brands and access to customer relationships and then using both to grow in developed markets. Ocimum Biosolutions of Hyderabad, India, operates in the research information services market. It is a specialist in bioinformatics.[28] Ocimum Biosolutions provides customers with access to its biological reference databases; furthermore, it offers custom software solutions and data analysis using proprietary analytical software. In addition, it has diversified into producing microarrays and oligonucleotides besides gene expression data generation services.

In nearly all cases, companies that use a services model operate in well-defined technology or therapeutic domains that target specific areas of the (bio)pharmaceutical or biotechnology value chain. Many leading service companies have used their success in one part of the chain to either forward integrate or backward integrate into other parts of the value chain. For example, Quintiles Transnational Corporation provides not only a wide range of contract clinical research services for customer in the (bio)pharmaceutical and medical device industries but also provides contract sales services via Innovex and an investment and partnering service for emerging biotechnology companies via NovaQuest.

We believe, therefore, that although competition is fierce when using a service-based business model, and some investors (such as venture capitalists) may express little interest in this model, due to slower growth expectations and less expected return on investment over short time horizons (five years or less), this model has distinct long-term advantages. Enterprising entrepreneurs are able to exploit the service-based business model over the long term. A major advantage is that it provides the start-up with a steadier stream of cash flow earlier than some of the other business models we have discussed. It also allows the firm to grow from an established customer base, allowing access to other parts of the value chain. Furthermore, there are a multitude of ways these innovative firms can form alliances and introduce novel combinations of services and products. It is a very flexible business model.

Medical Device Business Models

Medical device companies research, develop, and produce devices for diagnosis, monitoring, alleviation, or compensation for injury, or for therapeutic purposes. Medical device companies include those that provide surgical instruments, biosensors such as those to monitor glucose levels, cardiovascular devices such as heart pacemakers or stents, transdermal patches for administration of low dosages of drugs such as those to help patients with cessation of smoking, infusion pumps for diabetes sufferers, silicone-gel-filled implants, artificial organs and orthopedic devices, and inhalers such as used by asthma sufferers. Leading medical device firms compete by using a multidisciplinary scientific and technological approach when creating and making their products.

For instance, medical device manufacturers may combine elements of electronics, software, biotechnology, nanotechnology, and so forth to create new sensors or diagnostic imaging equipment, such as specialist imaging equipment provided by Siemens (NYSE: SI) of Munich, Germany, Philips (NYSE: PHG) of Amsterdam, the Netherlands, or GE Healthcare (NYSE: GE) of Fairfield, Connecticut.

Medical devices normally are divided into different classes, which correspond to different regulatory requirements as set down by the FDA or similar government agency bodies in Europe. The product development times vary widely (from 18 months up to 5 years). They are much shorter than for drug development, which often takes a decade or longer. An important consideration is customer switching costs (in much the same way as previously described for products of the platform technology models). Alliances are used during the initial phases of development in order to validate the medical device and gain faster product adoption by professional medical users in the market. As soon as a customer base is established, customer lock-in can be achieved through customer service and education and information services. We give examples of leading medical device companies in the next paragraphs.

Varian Medical Systems (NYSE: VAR) of Palo Alto, California, is a global manufacturer of medical devices and software for treating cancer and other medical conditions with radiotherapy, radiosurgery, proton therapy, and brachytherapy. The company supplies informatics software for managing comprehensive cancer clinics, radiotherapy centers, and medical oncology practices. Varian is a premier supplier of tubes and digital detectors for X-ray imaging in medical, scientific, and various industrial applications.

Boston Scientific (NYSE: BSX) of Natick, Massachusetts, is a worldwide developer, manufacturer, and marketer of less-invasive medical devices and surgical procedures for a wide variety of medical areas, including cardiovascular, endosurgery, and neuromodulation. In 2006, Boston Scientific acquired Guidant, a world leader in the treatment of cardiac disease, for about $27.2 billion in cash and stock, in a bidding contest with Johnson & Johnson (NYSE: JNJ) of New Brunswick, New Jersey. Boston Scientific now competes directly against Johnson & Johnson (especially its Cordis Corporation subsidiary) and Medtronic Inc. (NYSE: MDT) of Minneapolis, Minnesota. Since Boston Scientific acquired Guidant, Abbott Laboratories (NYSE: ABT) of Chicago, Illinois, has become a primary competitor in the interventional cardiology market, and St. Jude Medical (NYSE: STJ) of St. Paul, Minnesota, is a rival in the cardiac rhythm management and neuromodulation markets.

Finally, Baxter International (NYSE: BAX) of Deerfield, Illinois, is a global medical device, pharmaceuticals, and biotechnology company that is focused on assisting people with chronic and complex conditions—for example, hemophilia, cancer, immune disorders, and kidney disease. Baxter specializes in bioscience, medication delivery, and renal care. In bioscience, Baxter is a leader in the manufacture of recombinant and plasma-based proteins to treat hemophilia, immune disorders, burns, and shock. Medication delivery specializes in the delivery of food and drugs to patients through intravenous systems. Renal care includes treatments for end-stage kidney disease or irreversible kidney failure, through various types of dialysis therapies, both home based and hospital or clinic based.

In general, venture capitalists investing in early-stage development of medical devices seek earlier returns but with lower expected investment returns as compared to business models in pharmaceutical or biopharmaceuticals. SMEs usually adopt different business models in medical devices from larger companies. SMEs usually depend on alliance-based models, such as the RIPCO model. SMEs often out-license and codevelop their products in strategic alliance collaborations with larger companies. Alternatively, SMEs use platform technology models, which may include the use of royalty stacking, and subsequently they out-license or provide a service to healthcare providers. In general, investors such as VCs seek to exit from their investments in medical device companies by means of a trade sale to a larger company in the same sector.

RECENT TRENDS AND EMERGING BUSINESS MODELS IN HEALTHCARE

The basic elements of a business model are described in Chapter 5. Here we reiterate and summarize some of the more important aspects of managing the biotechnology business model. We then discuss how we envisage biotechnology and (bio)pharmaceutical business models may evolve to accommodate emerging trends and changes in healthcare.

Basics of the Biotechnology Business Model: Cash, Talent, and IP Rights

Biotechnology, in general, is capital intensive. Usually it requires raising equity funds from outside investors to support research and product development over long periods of time. If a start-up biotechnology company is fortunate and is able to raise cash when equity markets are strong or booming, then it will be in a better bargaining position than those start-ups that are struggling to raise capital when market conditions are weak or flat. Any business needs working capital to fund daily operations.

In particular, a start-up biopharmaceutical company's business model is atypical: Sales revenues may not be visible for a decade or more. Operating losses are normal for many years. Hence raising sufficient capital is critical to the start-up's survival. With a high burn rate of cash, the cash reserves must be sufficient to enable the venture to achieve targeted milestones and to progress through the various phases of product development. Ideally, the company's financial structure should provide adequate flexibility for management to take advantage of future opportunities as they may arise. It should also provide a cushion to protect against unforeseeable contingencies. Our advice is to try to raise as much cash as you can for your venture, given the venture capital market conditions you encounter. In Chapter 10, we cover investment agreements. In Part Six, "Valuing Company Cash Flows," we explain how to value your venture's cash flows and discuss other financial matters pertinent to start-ups such as building financial models for modeling alliance terms and conditions.

Implementing a biotechnology company's business model requires hiring very talented personnel with multidisciplinary scientific skills, business acumen, and business development skills in negotiating IP and investor agreements. Furthermore, this high-performance team needs to work closely together and over long periods of time. Normally the founding team consists of the chief executive officer (CEO), the chief scientific officer, and the head of the business development team. During the start-up phase, the senior management team could be supported by external experts in research, clinical development, and IP rights. As the company grows, it will hire more in-house expertise and will assign executives to other senior management roles, such as chief financial officer (CFO) or chief operations officer (COO). Depending on the part of the value chain in which the biotechnology company operates, certain capabilities and resources will be more important than others. An early-stage drug development company needs strong product and patent portfolio development expertise, and sound strategies for the acquisition, exploitation, and protection of IP rights. For early drug developers, it is critical to have good working relationships with the appropriate regulatory bodies, such as the FDA and EMEA or their equivalents in other countries. For late-stage developers of drugs, it is more important to have a focused marketing structure or a strong customer service capability.

How Biotechnology and (Bio)Pharmaceutical Business Models Might Change

In addition to these basic business model requirements, a number of major current trends could have an impact on the evolution of many biotechnology and (bio)pharmaceutical business models within the healthcare domain in the coming two decades. Changes in global demographics will influence the disease areas that receive more research funding and media attention, expanding market opportunities in particular therapeutic areas. For example, the world's elderly population is currently 650 million. By 2050, the "graying" population is forecast to reach 2 billion.[29] As a result, age-related diseases, such as Alzheimer's, will become more dominant. Experts predict that by 2010, there will be almost a half million new cases of Alzheimer's disease each year in the United States; and by 2050, there will be almost 1 million new cases each year in the United States alone.[30] In addition, other diseases, such as those related to obesity, are predicted to increase. The World

Health Organization (WHO) further projects that by 2015, approximately 2.3 billion adults will be overweight and more than 700 million will be obese.[31] Aside from a response to these kinds of disease trends, we also predict that business models that contribute to disease prevention will be equally as important as those that contribute to therapies or cures in the coming two decades.

Other changes will occur through harmonization of regulations, with a reduction in regulatory costs expected as a result. Harmonization should also speed up the time to market for many drug products and medical devices. Currently discussions are conducted by the International Committee for Harmonisation, which represents the European Commission; the European Federation of Pharmaceutical Industries and Associations; the FDA; the Pharmaceutical Research and Manufacturers of America; Japan's Ministry of Health, Labor, and Welfare; and the Japan Pharmaceutical Manufacturers Association. Increased transparency as a whole will also contribute to efficient global pricing models.

In a recent podcast and presentation, G. Steven Burrill, CEO of Burrill & Company, a venture capital private equity and merchant bank specializing in life sciences, gave his vision for the year 2020.[32] He foresees the convergence of genomics, informatics, and nanotechnologies and expects they will radically change healthcare systems, from the way in which companies develop and market drugs to the way individuals pay for and receive medical services. He predicts that medical treatment will be accessible at the supermarket centers of the world. He expects that a personal organizer (such as a BlackBerry) will monitor your health, and, if problems arise, alert your doctor automatically. He believes that individuals will carry their own genome and health records on a smartcard and that nanodevices will diagnose and repair problems in the bloodstream. Although we do not envision such speedy progress within the next 12 years, we do expect a greater emphasis on personalized medicine.

But how will these trends impact the development of the business models in healthcare? If healthcare becomes more consumer driven, we envisage a revolution in business models. We anticipate that emerging disciplines such as nanotechnology and systems biology will drive healthcare innovation. We expect these disciplines to play a role in the emergence of new business models for diagnostics, drug research and development, and delivery tailored to individual needs. Already numerous high-technology companies, including biotechnology companies, are exploring new avenues to stimulate or complement their internal innovation practices, often through open innovation models. These strategies should leverage partner business models, through alliance formation, thus reducing in-house risk. Overlapping with the open innovation model proposed by Chesbrough[33] is a specific integrated innovation framework proposed by Khilji et al.[34] Their framework incorporates market-oriented mechanisms and the building of appropriate organizational capabilities—through developing effective alliances—in order to improve the efficiency and probability of success of biotechnology business models.

Opportunities in the East

Both India and China and other Asian countries will provide increasing opportunities for biotechnology companies to support their value creation and commercialization strategies, and this too will have an impact on the dynamics of the biotechnology business model. Opportunities exist to outsource and offshore many activities in the value chain, to save on R&D and manufacturing costs, to hire talented staff, and to increase access to growing emerging markets. In the foreseeable future, an increasing number of patients in Asia are likely to have more disposable income, be better able to pay even for expensive treatments, and be more able to pay for preventive medicines.

An article written by Boston Consultancy Group (BCG) outlined the opportunities for biotechnology companies wanting to collaborate more in India and China "to optimize product development and accelerate time to market."[35] BCG's findings are based on client work with executives, government research agencies, and an extensive survey of over 90 vendors and 10 major biopharmaceutical corporations operating in China and India. A huge and inexpensive talent pool is available in China and in India. Both countries have high-quality graduates from many science disciplines. The governments of China and India provide strong support and incentives for biotechnology. At the same time, the BCG study (conducted in 2006) warns of a number of downside risks: "complexities and inefficiencies" in government approvals, infrastructure, and so forth that are typical of emerging markets. In addition, the biotechnology industry faces specific legal, scientific, privacy, and ethical risks, especially related to (bio)pharmaceutical R&D. We agree that all such risks need to be well managed, especially those related to enforcement of IP rights. Nevertheless, as the BCG study illustrates, a "modular" business model like the VIPCO model has several points along the value chain where potential partnering could take place between a western start-up biotechnology company and an Indian or Chinese counterpart. Since the BCG survey, numerous companies in both India and China[36] are emerging at all points of the value chain, not only as service providers but also as virtually or partially integrated players.

For example, R&D companies from India are increasingly seeking partnering or acquisition opportunities with European and American counterparts. Biocon Ltd. of Bangalore, India, develops both novel and generic biopharmaceuticals. It acquired a 70 percent stake in a German company, AxiCorp GmbH of Friedrichsdorf, for €30 million in 2008. AxiCorp is a marketing and distribution company that will provide a channel for Biocon's generics, biosimilars, biologics, and innovative pharmaceutical products in Germany and elsewhere in Europe.[37] Avesthagen of Bangalore, India, is a leading integrated systems biology platform company that "focuses on the convergence of food, pharmaceuticals and population genetics leading towards predictive, preventive, personalized healthcare" (www.avesthagen.com). It has a number of European investors and partners.

Opportunities originating from the East will support the development of the VIPCO business models, involving alliances with several partners.

Finding New Ways to Sustain Innovation

In order to remain competitive, we envisage that innovation capacity will continue to be a dominant determinant of success for the biotechnology and (bio)pharmaceutical business model, and we predict that only a broad alliance network will continue to support this innovation. Through alliances, new ideas and opportunities can be identified faster. If a company business model allows a speedy incorporation of such ideas or opportunities, it has the greatest chance of capturing the related value. Even though start-up companies have to contend with survival in a high-risk and dynamic environment, they also need to pay close attention to stimulation of in-house creativity and innovation.

Crowd sourcing is the outsourcing of parts of a firm's value chain to the crowd, or to use the crowd to generate novel ideas to bring inside the firm. Crowd sourcing has the potential to become a more important part of some business models[38] and describes how, recently, both public and private organizations are inviting experts from outside their companies to assist them in their innovation processes. Some of the first crowd sourcing was done by offering large prizes for innovative ideas. For example, the Virgin Earth challenge is a prize offering $25 million for a commercially viable idea to remove 1 billion tons of carbon dioxide from the earth's atmosphere for 10 years, without harmful side effects. In the biotechnology domain, the Archon X PRIZE for Genomics offered by the X PRIZE Foundation (http://genomics.xprize.org/) offers a prize of $10 million to develop radically new technology that will dramatically reduce the time and cost of sequencing genomes and accelerate a new era of predictive and personalized medicine. The prize will be awarded to the first team that can build a device and use it to sequence 100 human genomes in 10 days or less, with an accuracy of no more than one error in every 100,000 bases sequenced, with sequences accurately covering at least 98 percent of the genome, and at a recurring cost of no more than $10,000 per genome. This prize links innovation to the promise of personalized medicine. Similar prizes for space, lunar, automotive, and genomics are mentioned on the X PRIZE Foundation Web site (www.xprize.org). Multinational corporations such as Kraft Foods (NYSE: KFT) of Northfield, Illinois and Procter & Gamble (NYSE: PG) of Cincinnati, Ohio, also have Internet sites specifically dedicated to crowd sourcing.

In a separate development, innovation brokerage companies are exploiting the Internet to provide easy transfer of know-how, acting as trading places for knowledge by offering sophisticated Web-based matching services. These brokerages are particularly useful for start-up companies. A user company can, for example, send a request for information or expertise via the brokerage. Experts can then respond to this request via the site. Leading innovation broker companies include Innocentive,[39] NineSigma, and YourEnCore. These companies aim to stimulate innovation. Besides public companies, some governmental agencies and NGOs are providing similar kinds of forums. Innocentive works, for example, in a partnership with the Rockefeller Foundation on the Accelerating Innovation for Development Initiative. In addition, the EU stimulates innovation by rewarding innovative research proposals and well-constructed collaborative networks with grants and subsidies. Furthermore, the EU has set up a marketplace for technology at its Community Research and Development Information Service (CORDIS) (http://cordis.europa.eu). The marketplace is intended for information exchange and training; it is often used by groups that have existing copyright or IP protection for their invention but that wish to access collaborators to develop their products further.

Crowd sourcing as a type of collaboration makes perfect economic sense for companies that want to reach outside their firms to get fresh ideas for making new products. However, this type of open innovation business model depends on a motivated group of contributing experts, the payments they receive, and their interest in the topics involved. From the IP point of the view, the questions raised are: Who is going to patent these ideas? Who will create the pricing policy for them? There are different versions of the crowd-sourcing model. In some cases, all IP rights are transferred to the brokerage upon exchange of a nominal sum of money; alternatively, the rights may be negotiated directly among the parties involved. Companies that utilize crowd sourcing or otherwise outsource their IP rights activities have to pay attention to IP rights issues. Regardless of this caution, we think it probable that crowd sourcing may be incorporated into parts of the VIPCO and platform technology business models and may also allow faster innovation.

Promise of Personalized Medicine

Following sequencing of the human genome, experts and nonexperts alike were surprised by how little human beings differ in genetic makeup from other animals. The difference amounts to as little as 5 percent in some cases—for instance, when the human genome was compared to a mouse genome. The key to unlock the complexity of human health and disease is more elusive than most of us first thought. The Human Genome Project has provided an explosion of genetic data, allowing scientists and medical researchers to identify the genetic origins of both common and rare diseases. Genomics is becoming standard practice, but knowing the sequence of a genome is merely a beginning.

There is an increased requirement for synergy between scientific disciplines and related technologies within the biotechnology domain, primarily genomics (and pharmacogenetics), proteomics, and metabolomics, in order to advance the diagnosis and study of diseases by correlating genotypic information with expressed phenotypic information. Technologies used in these disciplines can speed up target identification and build up knowledge on gene variants to help eliminate poor drug candidates, retaining those that work for a specific population of patients. *Systems biology* and *bioinformatics* are collective terms used to describe the beginning of a revolution within medical research, the biopharmaceutical industry, and public health sectors. These emerging fields offer exciting and promising advances toward predictive, preventive, and personalized medicine. Many biotechnology business models in the near future will be based either on a platform technology approach or will depend on devising innovative ways to integrate know-how from the different scientific and technology domains mentioned here.

The genetic backgrounds of common diseases, such as different types of cancer, heart disease, and diabetes, are being unraveled. Imagine the day when your doctor can review a series of your genes or your whole genome. Those who support personalized medicine envision its advantages. These include an advanced knowledge of susceptibility, which will allow for careful monitoring and early intervention. They also foresee safer and more effective medicines, since a patient's molecular profile will also show how well his or her body will metabolize a certain drug. This will allow doctors to determine the safest and most effective dosage, which is expected to increase patient compliance, since the prescribed drugs will have little or no side effects. The costs of healthcare are also predicted to decrease since preventive and tailor-made medicine will reduce the amount of medicines that patients need to take. Initiatives such as the X-prize may increase the likelihood that personalized medicine will be accessible to all.

Personalized medicine is still in its infancy, but some advances have already been made. For example, in 2005, the FDA approved AmpliChip CYP450, now produced by Roche (SWX: RO) of Basel, Switzerland. This is a DNA-based chip test that measures variations in two genes that play a role in the metabolism of some frequently prescribed drugs. This chip test has the potential to reduce the chances of unwanted drug reactions if doctors use it to guide the prescriptions of drugs known to be metabolized through one of the two measured genes. These kinds of test results have the potential to allow dosages to be adjusted for individuals whose genes lead them to metabolize drugs unusually rapidly or unusually slowly. This would result in doctors prescribing more effective dosages, with less side effects to the patients. The AmpliChip test and similar diagnostic tests are leading us closer to an era of personalized medicine. According to Felix W. Frueh, of the Office of Clinical Pharmacology and Biopharmaceutics at the FDA's Center for Drug Evaluation and Research, personalized medicine may be characterized as giving "the right dose of the right drug for the right indication for the right patient at the right time."[40] We expect personalized medicine to offer several as-yet unfulfilled promises, such as the identification of people at risk for disease.

An earlier diagnosis of disease will allow tailored treatment but will also have great implications for preventive medicine. For example, it is known that Herceptin, a treatment for breast cancer produced by Genentech, is effective in only a small population, those individuals with an overactive HER-2 gene. It is known that 25 percent of all breast cancer patients have tumors that possess this abnormal gene activity. Therefore, Herceptin can be "targeted" to the tumor as an effective treatment in a genetically defined patient group. Previously, such a drug may have been tested in patient populations only to find that it was ineffective in many cases. As a result, it may have been dropped as a treatment. In the past, drugs were prescribed in a trial-and-error manner with doctors waiting to see if a patient improved. From now on, personalized medicine will make it more likely that patients respond to a treatment.

Companies such as Genomic Health Inc. (NASDAQ: GHDX) of Redwood City, California, focus on the development and commercialization of genomic-based clinical diagnostic tests for cancer. Similar technologies can supply individualized information on the likelihood of disease occurrence or recurrence and allow response to certain types of therapy to be predicted. These tests provide information that support healthcare providers and patients in making better treatment decisions. Such information can also speed up clinical trials, since trials will be conducted only with those patients selected for likely response and safety.

ALLIANCE FORMATION CRUCIAL TO BIOTECHNOLOGY AND PHARMACEUTICAL BUSINESS MODELS

Potential investors and other key stakeholders carefully scrutinize business models in the biotechnology and (bio)pharmaceutical industries. A successful business model can take many different forms in this domain but should include strategies for cash generation, an innovation capacity, and allow the exploitation of know-how and IP from both internal and external sources. A successful business model also has an expert team implementing the model. These elements are an extension of the basic aspects of any business model (described in Chapter 5) and are incorporated into the business models of small firms and large corporations alike.

As soon as knowledge, in the form of know-how or IP, is created internally or acquired from external sources, its management becomes important and exploiting its intrinsic value is crucial for sustained growth and value creation. Where know-how or IP is not available internally, the ability to form collaborations and strategic partnerships in order to acquire or access knowledge contributes to competitive advantage. This is an important addition aspect of the biotechnology and (bio)pharmaceutical business model. In fact, the structuring and management of collaborative relationships has become a vital capability; it allows access to complementary resources and capabilities; sustains innovation; mitigates the risks associated with drug, diagnostic, or medical device development; and makes the completion of the value chain possible.

We predict a paradigm shift within healthcare within the next two decades, from a more linear process where diagnosis and treatment are based on symptoms of a disease, to an integrated and heuristic process, with diagnosis based on molecular profiles of the individual patient. Preventive medicine may even dominate over provision of treatments or cures. This paradigm shift will have a huge impact on the biotechnology and (bio)pharmaceutical business models. We predict that biotechnology or (bio)pharmaceutical companies that lead in the creation or adoption of this integrative approach to diagnosis, drug discovery, and disease prevention will be able to create and to capture significant market share. Drug development most likely will be more rapid and tailored to customer needs. In our view, the newest business models in the healthcare domain will not only integrate alliances to enhance and implement their value creation strategies but will become more specialized in focused therapeutic or technology areas. We expect that variants of the VIPCO model will become more dominant as networks of companies interact and come together, like pieces of a jigsaw puzzle, to complete an increasing number of value chains, steered by customer demands.

If done well, alliance formation in the healthcare industry increases opportunities and can allow a higher degree of flexibility to implement value creation and commercialization strategies over time, in addition to stimulating innovation and learning. We expect alliance creation and the management of alliance networks to become increasingly important to high-technology business models in the biotechnology and (bio)pharmaceutical domains.

CHAPTER TAKEAWAYS

- Choose your business model to mitigate risk. Be aware of the risks involved in developing products within biopharmaceutical, pharmaceutical, medical device, and platform technologies domains. Assess your own business model in the light of these risks by examining all its key components carefully and comparing it to the business models employed by your competitors. (Refer to Chapter 5.)
- Know your part of the value chain. For early drug developers and developers of medical devices, or platform technologies, established know-how and a strong IP portfolio together with a defined business development strategy is crucial. This is coupled to management capabilities in the technology transfer and alliance formation, in addition to developed relationships with regulatory bodies, such as the FDA and EMEA. For late-stage developers of drugs, a focused marketing structure or customer service could be more important.

- Business models may be of many types, and hybrid forms exist. Ideally the initial choice of business model could include service model components in order to generate near-future cash flows. However, hybrid models are less attractive to potential investors, such as venture capitalists.

- Hire the right people at the right time. To implement all aspects of your business model, a start-up biotechnology company needs talented people with diverse expertise and people who will work well in a team. The basic formation should include a strong business development team, skilled in cross-cultural negotiation and deal making for technology transfer agreements or for alliance partnering. The chief executive officer will play a leading role in business development and raising funding but should have the support of a chief scientific officer and internal or external experts in research, clinical or technology development, and intellectual property rights. As the company grows, it will hire more in-house expertise, in addition to assigning executives to more senior management roles, such as chief financial officer or chief operations officer.

- The VIPCO business model suits start-up companies. The model you choose should allow flexibility and the option to grow from a small start-up to a larger organization; at the very least it should allow you considerable options and independence to implement your value creation strategy over time. For example, the VIPCO model offers the most flexibility in terms of alliances formed to complete the value chain. This model also allows you to implement the decisions you make faster, as a response to changes in the dynamic environment of this industry. Customized healthcare will encourage more companies to turn to the VIPCO business model in the future.

- Identify numerous alliances that have the potential to complete your value chain. Assess these potential partners, including partners in emerging economies, using well-defined criteria, and enter alliances only when value creation can be maximized. Employ strategic alliances to reduce risks associated with product development, to access innovation, for generation of cash for operations, to provide potential customers, and to allow you to fulfill your value creation and commercialization strategies. Choosing the right alliance partner and the management of alliances is further described in Chapter 7.

- Sustain innovation. Preserve and develop your company's innovation capacity through alliances not only with academic groups but also through the use of crowd sourcing and other open innovation mechanisms. Be aware of the importance of IP rights, trade secrets, know-how, and freedom to operate; use expert advice when negotiating the transfer of these rights. For optimal value creation, you must arrange well-structured alliance agreements that also give you control over developmental decisions concerning your product or technology.

- Log onto www.innovationtocashflows.com to find these materials that supplement this chapter:
  - *Resources* (including the URLs of all referenced companies, government agencies, or scientific research organizations).
  - *Glossary* (including definitions of key biotechnology and scientific terms).
  - *Appendix 9.1*, "Sample Confidentiality Agreement."

Four

Understanding
Legal Agreements

CHAPTER 9

Contract Law, Key Legal Agreements for Business, and Incorporation Issues

Anthony Indaimo, Nadia Ignatius, and Gabriel Monzon-Cortarelli
Withers LLP

Whatever the nature or structure of the strategic alliance that you may be considering, invariably commercialization of the technology will involve the negotiation of a variety of legal documents with, for example, (1) the scientific team within a university, (2) outside research consortiums, (3) early-stage investors such as family and friends, (4) other investors such as government funding agencies or venture capitalists, or (5) strategic alliance partners such as major pharmaceutical companies.

As an entrepreneur and founder of a start-up venture, you will also have to choose, with advice from your lawyer and accountant, the most appropriate legal structure for your business. Such a choice will depend on various matters, including but not limited to: the legal structures available in the business's relevant country or countries; the type of start-up venture being undertaken; the risks associated therewith; the need to manage that risk; and the tax considerations for all parties involved in the business.

The first document you are likely to need in your discussions with the individuals or entities just mentioned will be a *confidentiality agreement*, also sometimes referred to as a *nondisclosure agreement*. This agreement is designed to give you added protection in relation to any valuable information that you may wish to, or may be asked to, disclose to third parties.

When negotiating for financing with investors for your start-up venture, you typically will begin with what is called a *term sheet* in the United States or *heads of terms* in England, also commonly referred to as a *letter of intent* (LoI) or a *memorandum of understanding* (MoU). This document (referred to here as "MoU" for simplicity) will record the main commercial terms that have been agreed with the investor, which will then form the basis of the other more formal legal documentation that you will require. Negotiating and documenting the MoU, among other things, provides a useful record or outline of the *nonbinding* terms that have been agreed on and allows the parties to see how close they are to concluding a deal.

Sometimes parties are tempted to leave the MoU less detailed (and often vague) in order to reach a preliminary agreement as quickly as possible. This strategy frequently results in more extensive (and often costly and contentious) negotiations at the time when more formal legal documentation is being prepared and there is increased pressure on entrepreneurs and the new business to close the financing transaction. Therefore, it is preferable to agree on a detailed MoU so as to avoid the loss of significant time and resources if the deal falls apart at a later stage, when the parties finally realize how divergent their positions actually are.

You might think that because the MoU usually sets out only commercial terms, which have been discussed, there is no need for a lawyer to be involved at this stage. A word of warning: You should involve your lawyer[1] as early as possible to ensure that you do not inadvertently commit yourself to something you did not intend to and certainly before you sign any documentation. For instance, you do not want to be inadvertently bound by a provision obligating the new business to deal exclusively with a particular financing source for a fixed period of time. Although a term sheet in the United States is less likely to be treated as a *legally binding* commitment than a heads of terms in England, it is strongly recommended that you engage your lawyer to assist in negotiation and preparation of the MoU whether in England or in the United States.

Once you have obtained support for your new business start-up and have potential financial backers, the next stage involves the negotiation of terms and conditions for the definitive legal agreements, such as a shareholder agreement or a technology transfer agreement. While the commercial and legal terms of each of these contracts vary, the structure is based on general principles of contract law, which is the subject matter of this chapter. In most cases, a period of negotiation precedes the conclusion of a binding contract during which time many things will be said or written. Often it is difficult, in the heat of the negotiations, to determine at precisely what point a binding contract is reached.

Clearly, you *need* to know when a binding contract is reached so that you are aware of your contractual rights and obligations. In England, and generally in the United States,[2] in order for a legally binding and valid contract to exist, four essential elements must be present. There must be:

1. Offer
2. Acceptance
3. Consideration
4. Intention to be bound

ELEMENTS CONSTITUTING A CONTRACT

When negotiating, it is important to bear in mind these contract elements to ensure that you do not inadvertently bind yourself to a contract when you only intended to reach an agreement in principle. What do these legal terms mean in practice?

Offer

An *offer* is a statement by a party of his or her readiness to contract on certain terms. The offer must be capable of acceptance and must be made by the *offeror* with the intention of being bound if accepted by the *offeree*. A party cannot be pressured or misled into making an enforceable contract. An offer can be made to an adult individual (or a group of such persons) or to a legal entity, and it can be made orally, in writing, or even by conduct.

An offer may be withdrawn or revoked by the offeror, provided that the offeree has not accepted it. This is the case even where the offer is stated to be open for a particular period, unless the offeree has given some form of consideration (see below) in order to keep that period open. This is why it is sometimes a good idea to pay a deposit to ensure that an offer cannot be revoked.

It is also worth bearing in mind that if conditions have been attached to the offer (e.g., an approval or consent being required from a third party) that then fail to be satisfied, the offer will terminate.

Acceptance

In order for a contract to be formed, the offeree must accept the offer and communicate that acceptance to the party who made the offer. An acceptance can be made in writing or by conduct. It is, however, always advisable to accept an offer in writing to avoid uncertainties. However, if the offeror has specified the form of acceptance (e.g., "accept by registered post before Friday"), this must be adhered to in order for the acceptance to be valid.

Also, to be valid, the acceptance must be unconditional. If the offeree rejects the offer and puts forward amended terms or perhaps purports to accept the offer, but changes the conditions of the acceptance, this will amount to a *counteroffer*. A counteroffer is a rejection of the offer, with a new offer being put in its place.

There is one important exception that is often overlooked: *acceptance by conduct*. For example, if a party offers to buy goods from XYZ Limited and XYZ Limited delivers the goods without signing a contract, the purchaser, in certain circumstances, may be deemed to have entered into the contract by conduct if it accepts the goods from XYZ Limited without raising the issue.

In conclusion, it is vital that communication of acceptance be clear, whatever the rule being adhered to.

Consideration

The third element necessary in some jurisdictions, such as England and the United States, to constitute a legally binding contract is that there must be consideration. *Consideration* is an English legal concept based on the idea that contracts are made for the mutual benefit of both parties, and therefore some kind of reciprocal burden must be placed on both sides. In simple terms, a promisee cannot enforce a promise unless he has given or promised something in exchange for it. For example, if Party A offers to sell goods to Party B, Party B is expected to pay for those goods. If Party A merely delivers the goods without the expectation of payment, no contract would be formed and if a disagreement arose, Party B could not legally oblige Party A to deliver the goods.

In order to enforce a promise, the promisee must be able to show that he gave some form of consideration to the promisor. For example, A promises B that if B washes A's car, A will pay £10 to C. If B washes A's car and A never pays C, is C in a position to sue A? The answer is no. It was B who gave the consideration (by washing the car), not C, and therefore C is merely a third party and has no rights under this contract. B, however, can sue A to compel A to pay the £10 to C.

This example shows that consideration, under English law, does not have to be monetary; it must simply be something that is valuable in the eyes of the law. The law requires that there be sufficient consideration although the consideration need not necessarily be adequate. The law is not concerned with the value of the consideration; it is for the parties to decide, commercially, what consideration they want. In situations where it is difficult to determine whether there is sufficient consideration or where there is no consideration, it is common under English law to include a nominal monetary payment of say £1 to avoid the risk of the contract being held unenforceable. In the United States where consideration does not have to be monetary, either, it is common to include a nominal consideration of $1 to establish valuable consideration, or for the parties expressly to acknowledge that their agreement is supported by "valuable consideration, the receipt and sufficiency of which are hereby acknowledged."

In some civil law jurisdictions, such as Italy, for example, the requirement for consideration does not exist.

Intention to Be Bound

The fourth element is that there must be an intention to be bound. In commercial circumstances, the law presumes that it was the intention of the parties to enter into a legally binding contract. This means that evidence will be required in order to prove the contrary. In practice, parties tend to deny that there is a legal intention to be bound in documents such as heads of terms or letters of intent by the use of the words *subject to contract*.

Although there is usually not an intention for the MoU to be contractually binding, such a document does create a strong moral or good-faith obligation to reach a contract on the agreed terms, which can make it difficult for parties to change their minds. If you do not intend the MoU to be binding, the document should clearly say so or should include the words *subject to contract*. Merely calling it "heads of terms" will not be sufficient to ensure that it is not legally binding. In the United States, it is customary for the term sheet or letter of intent expressly to state that it is nonbinding and subject to the execution of a *definitive agreement*, except for certain specifically identified binding terms, such as confidentiality and exclusive dealing between the parties for a limited time period.

FORM OF THE CONTRACT

It is a common misconception that a contract has to be in writing in order to be legally binding. A contract may be written or oral, or mixed (partly oral and partly written), or created by conduct or the behavior of the parties. To avoid uncertainty, it is advisable to write down any contractual agreements.

While it is important that you record the terms of the agreement in writing, it is equally important to ensure that the terms of the agreement are clear and unequivocal and that your intentions and the intentions of the other parties have not been expressed in vague or incomplete terms. If an agreement is vague or ambiguous, it may not be legally binding. The willingness of the courts to fill in any gaps will depend on the particular circumstances and also on the jurisdiction in which the matter is being litigated. In England and in the United States, for example, the courts will take the view that where the contract is written, any statements found within the body of the contract are taken to be its terms. An English or U.S. court will not usually fill in the gaps left by the parties and will not allow evidence to be added to vary or contradict its terms, although U.S. courts will look to evidence outside the four corners of the contract (e.g., correspondence between the parties during negotiations) if its terms are ambiguous or uncertain. Most U.S. and English contracts contain an *integration clause* (also known as an *entire agreements clause* in England) expressly stating that the written contract constitutes the entire integrated agreement between the parties and supersedes all prior agreements and negotiations.

CROSS-CULTURAL DIFFERENCES IN CONTRACTUAL AGREEMENTS

When dealing with contracts on an international level, it is vital to recognize that different countries have different legal traditions as well as cultural beliefs and habits that affect the way in which contracts are agreed and interpreted by the courts. A list of some of the legal differences between common law countries, such as England and the United States, and civil law countries, notably in Europe, follows.

- As mentioned earlier, English and U.S. judges have tended to take a literal approach to the interpretation of contracts. For them, the written contract is key. In contrast, European judges will tend to look behind the written terms to determine the intention of the parties and are more willing to provide relief in situations where a literal interpretation of the words would cause undue hardship.
- It is often surprising to European lawyers to see the length of English and U.S. contracts. English and U.S. courts are largely reliant on case law, which gives legal weight to previous decisions of the courts. This means that English and U.S. lawyers rely heavily on detailed drafting of contracts to address legal issues set forth in prior cases that might affect the parties' agreement. In contrast, European law is codified, which helps to simplify the drafting process as legal principles are already statutorily fixed.
- There are also fundamental differences in legal principles on which contracts are based, for example:
  - In European jurisdictions, the law generally requires parties to negotiate in good faith. Not so under English or U.S. law, where there is no such obligation. In English law contracts, good faith clauses should therefore not be relied on. U.S. courts will (very rarely) nullify a contract on the ground that it is "unconscionable" (e.g., due to the unequal bargaining power of the parties) or contrary to a strong public policy, although they will enforce virtually any agreement reached by commercially sophisticated parties.
  - In English law contracts, clauses that agree for fixed *damages* to be paid if a breach of contract occurs cannot be enforced unless the amount expressed to be payable is a genuine pre-estimate of the loss the other party will suffer as a

result of the breach. A similar rule applies in the United States, where fixed (or "liquidated") damages clauses often explicitly provide that the stated amount is a "reasonable estimate" of anticipated losses and that an actual calculation of damages would be impracticable or impossible. In contrast, civil law courts will uphold "penalties" that have been negotiated even if they may appear excessive to English eyes.

- As we have seen, consideration forms a fundamental part of the formation of a contract under English and U.S. law. In contrast, civil law codes do not always recognize it as a concept. While some civil law countries require an underlying purpose for creating the contract in the first place, there need not be consideration in the English sense.

NONDISCLOSURE AGREEMENTS

There will come the time when you will have to share some or all of your valuable information with a third party, such as a financial backer or a potential partner. Sharing the information with a third party can be risky, and ensuring that it will be used in good faith requires a great deal of trust. It is therefore extremely important to consider confidentiality issues before approaching anyone to whom you may have to divulge confidential information.

Although there are numerous duties placed on a third party by the general law not to mistreat or misuse information that has been divulged to it in confidence, you should require any party to whom you are disclosing confidential information to enter into a confidentiality agreement (also known as a nondisclosure agreement [NDA]). Such agreements are legally binding and will enable you to set out the terms under which your confidential information is exchanged. Entering into such an agreement does not mean that you give up any rights that protect you under the general law—they will be in addition to your existing rights. A formal written agreement is not only easier to enforce, but it will also help to support any claim under the general law that the information is proprietary, confidential, and valuable. What constitutes information that is capable of protection under the general law is explained in Chapter 11, "Know-How or Trade Secrets." The confidentiality agreement simply gives you added certainty and protection.

As well as the obvious benefit of a confidentiality agreement, these are some added advantages:

- *Promoting your invention.* If you are concerned about divulging your secrets and fail to provide a potential investor or partner with sufficient information, your proposal may not appear as attractive because the third party will be unable to see its full potential or merit. She may consequently decide not to invest or enter into partnership with you, and you may have lost your opportunity for all the wrong reasons. Having a confidentiality agreement in force means you may feel more comfortable in divulging more without the worry that the information you disclose will be mistreated.
- *Boundaries.* The confidentiality agreement will set out the boundaries between you and the third party. Without an agreement, it is open to either party to claim

that instructions or information could be interpreted differently. Furthermore, the agreement will provide for specific remedies if things go wrong.

- *Focus.* A legally binding agreement may help the party to whom the information is divulged to focus on the importance of keeping the information confidential. He may be encouraged to mark relevant documents as confidential and take protective measures to reduce the risks of information being leaked, steps he may not have thought to take otherwise.

- *Evidential.* The agreement could assist you in the event of litigation in order to demonstrate that it was entered into, that confidential information was actually disclosed, and may serve to support any *injunctive relief* in the event of a breach by the other party.

A word of warning: These agreements, as with all agreements, have their limits. Although the agreement will be legally binding, it cannot prevent a third party from breaching the terms. Although the main remedy for breach is an injunction (to stop disclosure of the information), it relies on your knowing that a breach is about to occur or has recently occurred. Once the information gets into the public domain, no amount of law can make the information secret again. An injunction may, by then, be of little or no use. In such circumstances, damages for breach of contract to compensate you for your loss may be the only remedy available. If the information has greater potential future value and little value now, damages will not be a satisfactory or adequate remedy. There is the added difficulty of proving that the agreement was breached. This might be difficult even with a contract but probably near impossible without one.

Despite any shortcomings, however, it is the general consensus that the benefits of having such an agreement in force outweigh the risks of not having one.

What to Disclose and When

Ideally, you should seek to enter into a confidentiality agreement at the earliest opportunity. This can often be difficult, not least because it would be perfectly reasonable for an investor, for example, to want to see the basic concept of your invention or business secret before getting involved in such formalities. It is also not unusual for larger institutions, and, in particular, multinationals and venture capitalists to refuse to enter into such an agreement until they have seen the full particulars of the invention and before they have decided whether they are interested in investing. These institutions often have a great deal of power and influence. Being in a weaker position, you may have no choice but to take the risk. What you can do is prepare yourself for this inevitability by grading your information in terms of importance and sensitivity. You should determine what must be disclosed at the earlier stages of the negotiations and keep the remaining information back if or until it becomes absolutely necessary to disclose it.

What Will the Confidentiality Agreement Say?

The confidentiality agreement ideally should be drawn up by the person disclosing the information. Some commonly used clauses that should be included in most agreements follow, although you should remember that no one type fits all. When entering into one of these agreements, you should also bear in mind that any terms that are unreasonable or impractical will be ignored by the English courts and rendered unenforceable.

- *Parties.* Be sure that all parties to whom the information will be passed are either party to the agreement, or, where this is not practical, there is a provision whereby those to whom the third party passes on information are informed of its confidentiality and are required to undertake to respect its confidential nature.
- *Property to be protected.* An important clause of the agreement will be the definition of the type and content of the information to be protected. You may want this to be as wide a definition as possible, whereas an investor or partner may seek to make it more restrictive. A balance should be found whereby you do not feel restricted by an overcomplicated and burdensome contract and the third party does not feel exposed. For example, you should consider whether the definition should include oral as well as written information, or whether it should include notes of discussions and meetings, which may be unreasonable in certain circumstances. When defining the property to be protected, you should always remember that the term must be reasonable to have any effect at all. It may therefore be helpful to also include a definition of what is not confidential, for example, information that is already in the public domain or of which the recipient is already aware or in possession.
- *Permitted purposes.* The third party to whom the information is disclosed should undertake to use the confidential information only for limited and defined permitted purposes. "Permitted purposes" should include in what limited circumstances the third party can disclose the information to others, (e.g., to other employees or banks funding the research), bearing in mind that the more people who know, the more difficult it will be to keep the information confidential. You should also try to bind such additional parties by asking the third party to place obligations on any other recipients.
- *Copies.* Provision should be made with regard to how many copies of each document can be made and in what form. This will enable you, and indeed the third party, to keep control of the confidential information and minimize the risk of it getting into the wrong hands.
- *Return of confidential information.* You will want to ensure that, after presentations and negotiations, if the project does not proceed, there is a provision for all documents or information to be destroyed or returned back to you. This is obviously difficult to police in practice, but at the very least you should keep a record of the information you have disclosed.
- *Sample confidentiality agreement.* To see a sample nondisclosure agreement, log onto our web site at www.innovationtocashflows.com and go to Appendix 9.1, "Sample Confidentiality Agreement."

SHAREHOLDERS' AGREEMENTS

If your negotiations with a potential investor or partner are successful, the next step is for you to think about the best legal vehicle to use to commercialize your idea.

Whether you decide to develop and commercialize your project through the use of a company that is already in existence (by way of sale of existing shares to the investors or a capital increase followed by a subscription of shares by the investor) or by way of establishment of, for example, a new company, the parties involved (yourself, the investors, or other partners, or cofounders) are each likely to take a stake (become a shareholder) in the equity of the company at varying costs.

A company will be governed by its constitutional documents: the *Memorandum of Association* (English term), or *Corporate Charter* or *Articles of Incorporation* or Certificate of Incorporation (U.S. terms) that set forth the company's business purpose and share capital; and the Articles of Association (English term) or Company Bylaws or simply Bylaws (U.S. terms) addressing issues of corporate governance.

Regulating the relationship between the parties as shareholders and establishing the framework for the management of the company will normally be set out in the *shareholders' agreement* or *investment agreement*. (Refer to Chapter 10 for more on incorporation issues and shareholders' agreements.)

The contents of the definitive shareholders' agreement will depend heavily on the terms of the investment and the identities of the investing parties. (Larger institutional investors typically require more detailed and complex investment agreements than "friends and family" would require.) In general, as well as defining the scope and nature of the business, a shareholders' agreement will cover:

- What each shareholder will bring to the company and what they will get out of it
- The shareholders' respective roles and responsibilities
- The division of power among the shareholders and the extent of their influence on the management of the company
- The transferability of shares, including in circumstances such as the death, disability, divorce, bankruptcy, or retirement of a shareholder
- How to deal with disputes
- In what circumstances the relationship can be terminated and the mechanics and implications if terminated

Chapter 10 discusses Shareholders' Agreements in detail. An example of a preliminary investor term sheet may be found at the conclusion of Chapter 10. (Refer to Appendix 10.1, "Investment Term Sheet," in the next chapter.)

INCORPORATION ISSUES: CHOOSING THE APPROPRIATE LEGAL STRUCTURE

As noted earlier, you will need to determine what the best legal vehicle will be to commercialize your idea. Entrepreneurs around the world can choose from a variety of legal structures for incorporating their start-up ventures, most of which provide for limited liability and have varying characteristics in terms of governance and tax treatment.

As it would be outside the scope of this book to examine all the options available in each jurisdiction, we have focused on providing an overview of legal structures available in the United States and England; however, the entrepreneur will find comfort in knowing that most western countries have legal structures with characteristics generally similar to the structures to be discussed.

Entrepreneurs customarily have three options available to them when contemplating how best to structure their business. They can:

1. Carry on business as a sole trader in the entrepreneur's own name.
2. Incorporate as a corporation, which is a separate and distinct legal entity from the individual entrepreneur having limited liability.
3. Create a partnership, ideally with limited liability.

In choosing any of these structures, entrepreneurs will need to consider the legal, tax, and commercial issues of each option before they will be able to decide which structure is the most suitable, bearing in mind:

- The anticipated capitalization and financing needs of the business
- The proposed governance structure
- Future plans for the business, such as obtaining financing through the issue of debt or listing the business on a stock exchange through an initial public offering (IPO)
- The number of parties in the business and how the relationship between them will be governed

In addition, the entrepreneurs will also need to decide who should own the intellectual property (e.g., a patent, trademark, design right, or other registerable intellectual property of the business). The two main choices are (1) the inventor personally (or the entrepreneur if the same person is the inventor); or (2) the company through which the entrepreneur is looking to commercialize the idea. These choices are discussed further in the section "Intellectual Property Issues Pertaining to Incorporation."

SOLE TRADER (SOLE PROPRIETORSHIP)

English and U.S. law, and for this matter, laws in most western jurisdictions, recognize a sole proprietorship. One of its distinguishing characteristics is that the business and the entrepreneur are considered the same, with the individual entrepreneur owning and controlling all the assets of the business. As a result, the sole proprietor has unlimited personal liability concerning the business and its assets. Creditors of the sole proprietor can seek to recover their receivables from the business and its assets as well as the entrepreneur's personal assets.

The sole proprietorship is the simplest form of legal structure. A sole proprietorship can hire employees to manage the business, but the entrepreneur assumes all of the responsibilities of the employees' decisions.

Sole proprietorships have the advantage of being able to avoid the issues of double taxation on profits (a characteristic of some incorporated structures, as we will see later). However, they are limited in terms of ownership as there can only be one owner or proprietor. Due to its inherent limitations and liabilities, this form of legal structure is not usually the preferred vehicle used by entrepreneurs to undertake their business.

CORPORATIONS

As noted earlier, a corporation is a separate and distinct legal entity from its owners. One of the principal characteristics of a corporation is that the owner is generally not liable for the debts of the corporation aside from the financial contributions made to it, except in very limited circumstances (e.g., the owner commits fraud), where the protection of limited liability is lifted.

Unlike partnerships (as we shall see), which can be a simple voluntary association of two or more persons as co-owners to carry on a business for profit, corporations take their legal status directly from the specific corporate laws under which they are created in their country of incorporation. In common law countries, incorporating a simple business can be a relatively quick process without certain formalities common in civil law countries, such as the need to execute formation documents before a notary public or comply with statutory minimum capital requirements.[3]

Corporations have the flexibility of raising funds either through equity (through the issue of shares to new investors or existing shareholders) or debt (through the issue of bonds, debentures, and other debt instruments).

A corporation can have multiple owners (shareholders) and has a distinct governance structure with a division between ownership and management. Day-to-day management responsibilities are left to directors and officers of the corporation (who may also be shareholders) who, under statutory law, owe various duties to the corporation and its shareholders, such as:

- To act within the directors' powers
- To promote the success of the company
- To exercise independent judgment
- To exercise reasonable care, skill, and diligence
- To avoid conflicts of interest
- Not to accept benefits from third parties
- To declare interests in proposed transactions or arrangements with the company

U.S. Corporations

In the United States, each state has its own corporate laws detailing the steps and documents required to create a corporation, with all state laws requiring that the business be clearly identified as an incorporated entity (by ending with words "Inc." or "Corp.," or other similar words).

If you are considering setting up a business in the United States, in essence, there are two different types of corporations available to you, which differ principally on their tax treatment and ownership structure: the C corporation (C corp.) and the Subchapter S corporation (S corp.). The S corp. is a form of corporation that has elected a special tax regime under U.S. tax laws (Subchapter S of the United States Internal Revenue Code).

Both the C corp. and the S corp. offer limited liability protection for their shareholders, and both are separate legal entities requiring the necessary filings and documents under state corporate laws in order to create them. Like any corporation, C corps. and S corps. need to adopt bylaws, issue stock, appoint directors and officers, hold annual shareholders' and directors' meetings, keep minutes of those meetings and records, and maintain a good standing by filing any reports and paying annual franchise taxes required in their state of incorporation. The principal differences between a C corp. and an S corp. are:

- S corps. do not pay any income tax, as they are pass-through entities. Income or losses are divided among and passed through to the S corp.'s shareholders who report any income or loss on their own individual income tax returns.
- C corps. have to file a corporate tax return reporting income and losses, and any income is taxed at the corporate level. When income is distributed to the shareholders as dividends, C corps. may face double taxation, as income is also taxed at the individual shareholder level.
- S corps. are limited in the number of shareholders they can have (no more than 100) while C corps. can have an unlimited number of shareholders.
- C corps. can have various classes of shares with various rights attached to them. S corps. can have only one class of shares (although such shares can have different voting rights).
- C corps. can have nonresident aliens as shareholders (such as foreign non-U.S. investors); S corps. cannot.
- C corps. tend to be the vehicle of choice for accessing the stock markets through an IPO, as public market investors are accustomed to holding shares in a C corp.

S corps. can be easily converted into C corps., assuming enough shareholders' consent. However, entrepreneurs should be aware that there could be adverse tax consequences to convert an S corp. to any form other than a C corp. (e.g., an LLC, as discussed next), especially if the assets of the S corp. have appreciated in value.

U.S. Limited Liability Company

As an alternative to the S corp. and C corp., entrepreneurs wishing to establish a business in the United States have the option to set up a limited liability company (LLC). All states have enacted specific LLC legislation setting up the steps and documents required to create an LLC.

An LLC is a hybrid entity with certain similarities to a standard corporation and a partnership. LLC members are the owners of the LLC contributing to its capital like shareholders in a corporation. Management may be delegated to an LLC manager(s), like directors and officers in a corporation. LLCs can have one or more members. One-member LLCs are referred to as "single-member LLCs" and have certain peculiarities, such as not requiring an operating agreement (the LLC's governance charter, in certain respects similar to the bylaws in a corporation). Members of the LLC participate in the management of the business, and members, managers, and employees are not held personally liable for the debts of the business.

Some of the principal advantages attributable to LLCs are:

- *Liability protection.* As for shareholders in a corporation, members in an LLC are not liable for the obligations of the LLC unless in very limited circumstances the veil of limited liability of the LLC is lifted.
- *Simplicity and lack of formalities.* LLCs can be simple to set up under a state LLC law; however, they can be as complex as the parties need them to be. LLCs can

have the benefit of a partnership-like tax treatment (they can be pass-through entities) and the relative simplicity of an S corp. Single-member LLCs can be set up without the need of a complex operating agreement. Alternatively, the LLC can have a complex operating agreement with detailed governance provisions and profit and loss attribution mechanisms between the members. LLCs are generally simpler to form and manage than, for example, a limited partnership with a corporate general partner.

- *Taxation.* When forming an LLC, entrepreneurs have the option to choose their tax treatment under the "check-the-box" tax regulation. Two or more member LLCs are normally classified as a partnership for tax purposes; single-member LLCs normally are classified as sole proprietors. Alternatively, the LLC can opt to be taxed as a standard corporation.

Some of the principal disadvantages attributable to LLCs are:

- *Developing law.* LLC legislation can vary from state to state, although various efforts have been made to create a uniform set of LLC laws that each state can implement. LLCs have not been in existence for as long as corporations or partnerships and, although case law on LLCs is being written, in many states, the courts are still developing a comprehensive set of legal precedents on matters relating to LLCs. However, most LLC statutes clearly define the organizational, governance, and internal affairs and liability of LLC members, and the lack of uniformity and developing law should not be taken as the sole reason not to form an LLC.

- *Public offerings.* As noted, typically a regular C corp. is used to going public. LLCs can have ownership units (such as shares), but they do not lend themselves to alienability. The LLC will therefore need to convert to a C corp., which can be done through a merger, under state merger laws, or alternatively by liquidating the LLC's assets and contributing them to a C corp. These procedures require planning and may or may not lead to tax consequences. Also, public market investors are accustomed to holding shares in a corporation and may resist holding shares in an LLC.

Corporations in England

Entrepreneurs looking to incorporate a business in England have in essence two corporate vehicles to choose from: the public limited company (Plc) and the private limited company (Ltd.).

A Plc would rarely be used for establishing a start-up business in England, unless the entrepreneur was looking to list on the London Stock Exchange as a means of raising finance, for example, in the AIM Market for growth companies of the London Stock Exchange.

The most common entity used by entrepreneurs establishing a presence in England is the private limited liability company (Ltd.). As the name suggests, the liability of shareholders is limited to the amount that each subscribes for his shares. A private limited company can be formed with one director, for which there are no nationality criteria, and one shareholder, and with a single share. Note that it is possible to issue shares for noncash consideration, such as services, real property, or intellectual property, without a formal valuation.

Incorporation of either a Plc or Ltd. in England is made by depositing at Companies House a prescribed form together with a memorandum of association and articles of association (bylaws). The object(s) of the company are set down in the memorandum; the articles govern the general management of the company, such as board and shareholder meetings, as well as setting out the rights of shareholders.

It is possible to buy off-the-shelf companies or to incorporate a company in one day through Companies House. However, you will need to check that the company name you want to use is available; otherwise registration will be rejected. Particular attention should be given to amending any off-the-shelf documentation to the specific governance needs of the business. Careful thought should also be given as to who will serve as the directors and officers of the entity, their term and powers, and their compensation, as well as the structure of the board of directors. Private companies have a single-tiered board with at least one director. Directors can be executive (e.g., with a service contract) or nonexecutive, with varying roles and duties. As mentioned, there are no restrictions on foreign directors.

PARTNERSHIPS

Partnership structures revolve around the basic principle of two or more individuals or entities voluntarily associating themselves as co-owners to carry on a business for profit. Partnership structures can be simple or complex with convoluted governance agreements (partnership agreements). Their principal difference with a standard corporation lies in their tax treatment in that a partnership is considered as an aggregate of individuals and not a separate entity and hence not a taxpayer. Each individual partner pays partnership income tax based on its share of the partnership.

Thanks to their flexibility and tax benefits, partnerships (with limited liability) have tended to be the preferred vehicle in specific industries, such as venture capital, hedge funds, private equity funds, real estate, and certain service industries like the legal and accounting professions.

Entrepreneurs looking to establish their business as a partnership should bear in mind there are two generic categories of partnership: those having unlimited liability among partners and those having limited liability, referred to as limited partnership (in the United States) and limited liability partnerships (in England).

U.S. Partnerships

In virtually all states in the United States, there are specific uniform laws governing the formation and laws on partnerships: the Uniform Partnership Act for general partnerships (GPs) and the Uniform Limited Partnership Act or the Revised Uniform Partnership Act for limited partnerships (LPs).[4]

A GP does not need formalities or filings with any state; two individuals simply agree to own the business and make management decisions for the business. The partners share in the profits and financial losses of the partnership and are also individually liable for the business debts. Partners have a duty to act in the best interests of the partnership.

However, in an LP, there are one or more general partners and one or more limited partners. The general partners make the management decisions of the business, while the limited partners do not. The general partners, however, also assume full responsibility for the risk, liabilities, and debts of the limited partnership. The limited partners risk only the financial contributions they make to the limited partnership. In order to avoid such general liability, LPs are usually structured so that the general partner is an LLC or a corporation benefiting from limited liability. Generally, all the partners in the limited partnership share the profits of the business. (See Chapter 19 and refer to Figure 19.1, "Structure of a Typical Venture Capital Fund," for an example of a limited partnership.)

Partnerships in England

In England, entrepreneurs can choose from a general partnership with partners having unlimited liability or a limited liability partnership (LLP), which combines the advantages of an English Ltd., in terms of the limited personal liability offered to its members, with the tax treatment of a traditional partnership, namely tax transparency. The LLP is a very flexible entity that may be adapted to various situations, such as professional partnerships, joint ventures, investment structures, and entrepreneurial businesses.

An LLP can be formed by two or more people, and there is no maximum number of members. Note that corporate entities can be members of an LLP and that there are no residence requirements. LLPs are governed by statute, the Limited Liability Partnership Act 2000, and by English common law. However, these provisions alone are not likely to be satisfactory to the members. It is therefore important, though not legally necessary, to have a properly drafted, valid partnership agreement for the LLP.

An LLP, rather than its members, will be primarily liable to its customers and clients. This is because legal relationships will be established between the LLP (rather than the members) and its customers and clients pursuant to its conditions of business or terms of engagement. LLPs have unlimited capacity. This means that they have the same capacity to enter into contracts, hold assets, sue and be sued as private individuals.

An LLP must be incorporated by registration at Companies House and is subject to certain filing requirements, such as, among other things, annual accounts and members' details. Registration is made by means of a prescribed form, including details of the members. The LLP agreement would normally deal with every aspect of the management and decision making of the LLP as well as capital contributions by members, division of profits and losses, accession to and retirement from the LLP. The LLP agreement, being a private document, is not filed at Companies House.

WHAT IS THE RIGHT CHOICE OF VEHICLE?

There is no one right answer to the question of what is the right vehicle. Often more than one type of vehicle may be suitable, and the selection process of which one to choose can be quite complex.

In the United States, LLCs have been very popular and have become the entity of choice for smaller nonlisted businesses, thanks to the combination of partnership-like aspects and the corporate-like ability to shield the owner from personal liability. In England, Ltds. and LLPs are the most commonly used legal entity.

The entrepreneur together with legal and tax advisers will need to consider the legal, tax, and commercial issues as they impact each possible formation vehicle and undertake comparative analysis of each vehicle based on its limited liability, governance flexibility, and tax efficiency.

INTELLECTUAL PROPERTY ISSUES PERTAINING TO INCORPORATION

Turning to the question of in whose name the inventor (or the entrepreneur if the same person is the inventor) should register the intellectual property, there is a tendency, at least in the early stages of a business, for an inventor (or entrepreneur) to register intellectual property in their own name. A patent application (see Chapter 12) is required to state the name of the inventor. If the patent is granted, then the patent and some or all of its associated rights may later be assigned (i.e., sold) either to the entrepreneur or their company (the "Company").

In the early stages of a business, there is some merit in keeping the legal ownership of the intellectual property separate and distinct from the Company's. This is because if the business fails and the Company becomes insolvent and is eventually liquidated, the intellectual property will remain with the entrepreneur, who may be able to exploit or commercialize the asset, especially if it has any value. However, this may not always be the case. Notwithstanding that the legal ownership of the intellectual property may be in the entrepreneur's name (as opposed to the Company's name), the Company may still be entitled to the beneficial ownership. This is more likely to be the case if the entrepreneur is the sole shareholder and director of the Company and has dedicated their entire time and attention to developing the Company's business.

In any event, as part of any due diligence that precedes an investment into the Company by a third-party investor, the question of who owns the intellectual property is crucial. A third-party investor will always want to ensure that the Company holds both the legal and beneficial ownership in the intellectual property so that the investment in the Company will be used to grow the business and, as a consequence, assist in developing and commercializing the Company's (and not the entrepreneur's) intellectual property.

If the intellectual property is owned by the entrepreneur and not the Company, a third-party investor will, as a condition of any investment into the Company, require the entrepreneur to transfer the intellectual property to the Company. This is often done for nominal consideration (e.g., in England, £1.00), especially where the Company is entitled to the beneficial interest in the asset. In fact, the legal documentation is relatively straightforward. It often takes the form of a short acknowledgment by the entrepreneur, who simply declares that he or she has effectively held the intellectual property, since its registration, for and on behalf of the Company. There are cases, however, where the transfer of the intellectual property by the entrepreneur to the Company can justifiably be made at market value. (See Chapter 18 for the explanation of market value.) These cases are the exception rather than the rule and, in any event, require the entrepreneur and the Company to obtain an independent valuation of the asset prior to any transfer. This does not, however, mean that the

Company will pay the entrepreneur cash for the transfer of the intellectual property, as the price is almost always satisfied by the Company issuing shares to the entrepreneur for the value of the independently valued intellectual property.

CHAPTER TAKEAWAYS

- Involve your lawyer sooner rather than later to avoid nasty surprises later on.
- Do not rely on oral promises; make sure all terms negotiated are recorded in writing in clear and unambiguous terms.
- Take local advice, as each jurisdiction has its own set of rules and procedures.
- Keep a record of any confidential information you disclose, and disclose only as much as is strictly necessary.
- When negotiating a shareholders' agreement, make sure that you retain some control over how the business is managed and over important decisions that need to be made.
- The choice of forming a sole proprietorship or a partnership or incorporating a company depends on many interrelated factors, including: the legal structures available in the country where it will be formed; the purpose of the venture; the risk exposure; and other legal, tax, control, and governance issues.
- Always be aware of the personal liability and exposure (to lawsuits, or to personal bankruptcy) that you may face when setting up a sole proprietorship, joining a partnership, or becoming a director of a corporation. If you do not understand what you are doing, seek expert legal, accounting, and tax advice.
- Think carefully about how to hold your intellectual property (either in your own name or that of your business entity), and seek advice on what is appropriate under the circumstances.
- Log onto our web site at www.innovationtocashflows.com where you will find these useful online materials:
  - Appendix 9.1, "Sample Confidentiality Agreement"
  - Resources
  - Glossary
  - Spreadsheets

Investment Agreements

Anthony Indaimo and Nadia Ignatius
Withers LLP

In Chapters 5 to 8, we looked at various ways in which business models and strategic alliances may be formed with the purpose of commercializing an idea or a project. In Chapter 9, we suggested that whatever the choice of vehicle for the commercialization or realization of the project, the relationship of the parties should be documented. In this chapter, we consider, in some detail, the legal issues surrounding an investment into a company and the inevitable competing interests between the founder and the investor. We also provide an example of what an entrepreneur should look out for when seeking external finance.

If outside investors are sufficiently interested in your project and are willing to inject cash in the venture vehicle, then the first step for the investors, or their legal counsel, is to prepare an investment term sheet setting out the basic terms upon which they are willing to invest and what they expect to get in return for the investment. The term sheet will outline the commercial rather than legal terms and should, depending on the level of experience, knowledge, and sophistication of the parties and the amount to be invested, be relatively straightforward. The legal terms will subsequently be contained in more detail in the definitive long-form agreement, which, in contrast to the term sheet, is a legally binding agreement, which investors or their legal counsel will prepare.

As the term sheet is signed in the early stages of a relationship and before any due diligence is carried out, it plays an important role in focusing the minds of both investors and the entrepreneur as to what they wish to achieve and can help to avoid misunderstandings later on. A term sheet is therefore a useful road map for finalizing the long-form agreement. A word of caution: Try to avoid focusing too much on the detail of the term sheet, which should properly be addressed in the long-form agreement. The risk is that if you spend too much time negotiating the term sheet, this will simply delay the process of preparing the investment agreement and add considerably to the cost of the negotiations.

Generally, the term sheet is not intended to be legally binding (except for a few clauses, such as the confidentiality clause and any exclusivity provisions) and will be subject to various conditions including, among other things, satisfactory due diligence. The term sheet does, however, create a strong moral obligation, which the parties can point to subsequently when negotiating the long-form agreement. In fact, heated discussions are often exchanged between an entrepreneur and an outside investor, with accusations of bad faith if the term sheet is not strictly adhered to, even though it is expressed not to be legally binding. In addition, in some European jurisdictions, where there is a duty to negotiate in good faith, the term sheet could be construed to be legally binding.

The long-form agreement, once signed, records the commercial arrangement between the parties as set out in the term sheet and defines the legal terms on which investors will invest in the company. Going forward, it will also govern the ongoing contractual relationship between investors and the entrepreneur as shareholders in the venture. These different legal areas could be covered in separate legal documents but are usually set out in one document. This type of agreement is commonly referred to as a subscription and shareholders' agreement, an investment agreement, or a joint venture agreement, depending on the circumstances. In this chapter, we refer to the long-form agreement covering all these areas as the investment agreement.

The investment agreement is likely to contain seven key provisions:

1. The amount and nature of the financing
2. The nature of the warranties given by the entrepreneur
3. Provisions relating to the ongoing operations and management of the company
4. Share transfer provisions (including permitted transfers and *preemption rights*)
5. Rights attaching to the investor's shares
6. *Drag-along* and *tag-along* provisions
7. Exit provisions

INVESTMENT AND FINANCE

Investors come in many shapes and sizes, from friends and family and business angel investors to sophisticated institutional, venture, or private equity funds. Each category of investor will have its own investment criteria or motive for investment—from wanting to back an ambitious and determined family member or friend to needing to deliver, in the case of a private equity fund, a minimum rate of return to the fund's own stakeholders—and will have minimum and maximum investment thresholds below or above which the investor is not willing or able to invest.

Depending on the goals—in other words, whether the business is (a) starting up, (b) wanting to produce its patented prototype, (c) expanding its product range or production capacity or rapidly growing, or (d) looking for new markets, these aims will normally determine the likely category of investor who may be willing to invest in the business. For example, most start-up companies in the early days, are financed by the founder or entrepreneur having to beg or borrow from family and friends. Highly specialized and sector-specific funds, however, may target biotechnology or technology companies that need seed, development, or expansion capital. Moreover, these funds may have a minimum investment of £1 million, £5 million or £15 million, depending on the amount of capital under management which the funds have to deploy.

An example term sheet is presented in Appendix 10.1 on page 240. This is not intended to be exhaustive, but gives you an idea of the terms an investor (who is likely to have greater bargaining strength) is going to want to see before investing in a business. The term sheet is usually of the type used where the investor is a private equity fund or at least a sophisticated investor.

The investment agreement sets out the details of how the proposed investment is to be made by the investor. If the investment is to be made using a newly formed company, the other parties (both the entrepreneur and the investor) will need to make a contribution to the new company of equal or similar value. In the case of the outside investor, this will be in the form of cash, but the agreement will also specify, based on an agreed valuation, whether any contribution is to be made by way of the transfer of assets rather than cash. For example, the entrepreneur may wish to contribute valuable intellectual property, such as know-how, design rights, copyright or patent rights, to the newly formed company. The term sheet usually includes the basis on which the parties have valued the existing company or the assets that are to be contributed to the newly formed company. (See Chapter 19, "Case Study: TSP Enterprises Seeks Venture Financing," for an illustration of how venture capitalists value companies; and Chapter 20, "Case Study: Advanced Dermal Delivery, Inc. and the Launch of the New Transdermal Patch," for more on the valuation of a patent licensing agreement.)

The investment agreement also specifies the number of shares that will be issued to each party in the share capital of the company and in what proportions each party will provide further funding for the company. Regarding the amount of funding required, most investors wish to see a business plan setting out the required level of financing and the use of proceeds for the business. In fact, it is now fairly common to attach a three-year business plan to the investment agreement that the parties have prepared and agreed on.

If an investor does not wish to contribute all of the investment in one single lump sum, it is possible for the investment agreement to specify that the investment will be made in a specified number of tranches. One reason why investors may not wish to invest in one lump sum is because they may wish to make any future funding conditional on the company achieving certain predetermined milestones. The milestones normally are the subject of intense negotiation between the parties, taking into account the specific circumstances. The milestones could be of a technical, financial or commercial nature. In agreeing to the milestones, you should be sure that the milestone is expressed in clear and unambiguous terms and that it is factual and capable of objective measurement.

Ideally, you should consider defining the milestones at the time that the term sheet is being negotiated, although it is also possible to state in the term sheet that further funding will be provided subject to the attainment of performance milestones, with the milestones being defined and negotiated in the Investment Agreement. For example, an investment in a biotechnology company might initially be made on signing the investment agreement. Thereafter, further investments may be subject to the company signing a license agreement with a pharmaceutical company in a key territory, such as the United States or Japan, or the successful commencement or completion by the biotechnology company of a certain phase (say Phase I, II, or III) of preclinical or clinical trials. In any event, it is important to define clearly the milestone and to be able to measure easily whether it has been achieved so that the cash is promptly injected into the business.

If the investment is made in one lump sum, the investment agreement will also specify whether the parties will be required, or be entitled, to contribute further funding and on what basis.

A MODERN DAY AESOP TALE: BEWARE THE WOLF IN SHEEP'S CLOTHING

The business world is littered with investment stories that started out with such hope and promise only to end in tears or, worse, in court. This example should serve as a warning for all entrepreneurs who are seeking financial investments.

Joe and Peter, 38 and 29 years old, respectively, met at a New Media conference in Las Vegas when they were working for different firms. Both were frustrated entrepreneurs and were unhappy with their jobs. Over the course of the next 18 months they spoke and met regularly about setting up a business that had, as its basis, the idea of providing a revolutionary way of servicing a sector of the leisure market that was in Joe and Peter's view quite staid, conservative, and serviced to date by what could loosely be called an old boys' club. Joe and Peter not only had a good idea; they had the drive and energy to become a new entrant in a market that, not surprisingly, was skeptical at best and threatened at worst by a pair of young upstarts.

In the beginning, Joe and Peter found things understandably quite tough, but they were encouraged by the reception they received from potential clients who were interested in learning more about what Joe and Peter's company, New Media Products, had to offer. Slowly orders began coming in. Within two years, the company's turnover had grown to approximately U.S. $4 million. The business grant or soft loan that New Media Products had obtained from its local business center, while helpful, was not sufficient to take the business to the next level. Joe and Peter were members of the local Technology Chamber of Commerce. Their interest was tweaked one day when they received an invitation from the chamber to attend a seminar titled "Access to Capital: How to Obtain Growth Capital."

They attended the seminar and were so impressed with one of the speakers of a technology fund that they made an appointment to see him and his colleagues in the fund's London office in two weeks' time.

In readiness for the meeting, Joe and Peter prepared a PowerPoint presentation setting out (a) the description of the business; (b) key clients and customers; (c) the growth opportunities; (d) financial information indicating New Media Products' financial achievements for the last two years as well as a pro forma forecast for the next three years; and (e) the amount of funds required and the use thereof. The meeting with the technology investment fund could not have gone better. In fact, two weeks later New Media Products received a letter that, in summary, stated that the fund was willing to invest U.S. $500,000 for 40 percent of the equity in New Media Products, to be issued to the fund in *preference shares* with a 7 percent annual cumulative dividend. The fund also stated that it wished to appoint to the board an "observer" who was experienced in new media and who would attend all of the company's board meetings. The fund's letter made no reference to how long it proposed to hold its investment in New Media Products—although there was a reference to a valuation mechanism in the event that the fund or the founding shareholders wished to sell their shares.

Joe and Peter could not believe their luck and could not wait to get their hands on the money. Here they were, two years after creating their own business, and a reputable institutional investor was validating their vision by wanting to become a shareholder. Moreover, the fund was also willing to augment the company's board by appointing a seasoned and experienced technology executive who would attend all board meetings and thereby bring valuable business and strategic advice. Following the successful completion of due diligence by the fund, Joe and Peter signed the long-form investment agreement and the fund duly injected U.S. $500,000 in return for which the fund received preference shares equal to 40 percent of the company's share capital. No sooner had Joe and Peter finished downing the last glass of champagne in celebration, the relationship with the fund and, in particular, the "observer" began to go wrong.

The "observer" failed to attend a number of important board meetings. Of those that he did attend, the "observer" simply observed proceedings and offered no useful business or strategic advice. Worse still, Joe was shocked to learn one day, through reading an article in the newspaper, that the fund had recently invested in one of New Media Products biggest competitors, Ultra New Media Products. When asked about this, the fund simply replied that the investment agreement did not prohibit the fund from making any investment in any similar or competing company or sector. The last straw came when Joe and Peter needed further funding. Following a tense meeting with the fund in this regard, Joe and Peter received a letter from the fund stating that not only did it not wish to provide further finance, but, in its view, the fund believed that New Media Products needed to restructure its business in order to deal with what the fund saw as inherent weaknesses in the company's business plan, given the increasingly competitive environment.

As a consequence, Joe and Peter promptly sought legal advice, which, unfortunately, did not give them much hope for the future. What Joe and Peter initially thought would be a mutually beneficial and long-term relationship with the fund suddenly felt like a weight around their necks. The relationship had become very strained quite quickly. They were advised by their lawyers that the only mechanism in the investment agreement for the shareholders or the fund to exit from New Media Products was for Joe and Peter to either purchase the fund's shares or, worse still, for them to sell their shares to the fund at a predetermined valuation, which did not take into account the fact that they held 60 percent in the company but rather valued the company as if it were a 50/50 joint venture.

PREFERRED SHARES

Ownership in a company is normally evidenced by the issue of *ordinary shares* (or *common stock* or *common equity shares*) to the shareholders. The rights attaching to those shares are set out in the company's articles of association (bylaws in the United States). Aside from any share rights in the articles, when the company is liquidated (see Chapter 4, "Liquidation"), the holders of ordinary shares receive, normally as a distribution of capital, what is left after all of the company's liabilities have been satisfied.

Investors, particularly sophisticated investors, usually do not wish to hold ordinary shares in the company but rather insist on subscribing for a preferred class of share (preference shares or preferred shares), which will give them certain preferred rights over the ordinary shares or common stock of the company—especially in a situation where the company has underperformed. Such preferential rights could include one or more of these features:

- Dividends
- Return on liquidation
- Redemption
- Conversion rights
- Voting rights
- Antidilution provisions

Dividends

The preference shares may include a preferred dividend right to receive a fixed share of income in priority to the ordinary or common shares. The dividend is usually expressed as a fixed percentage (or coupon) of the nominal value of the share, for example, 7 percent preference share. If the share is expressed as being a cumulative preference share, this means that if the dividend is not paid when due, the right to receive a dividend will accumulate until the company is able to pay the dividend. The payment of any dividend accrued will take precedence over the payment of any other dividend.

If the preference shares are *participating preference shares*, they have the right to a profit share as well as a preferred dividend. Institutional or sophisticated investors generally look for capital gains rather than an income stream on their investments. Consequently, sometimes they may not insist on a dividend right, but rather a combination of one or more of the rights set out next.

Return on Liquidation

In the event of a liquidation or winding up of the company or upon the distribution of assets on a sale, the holders of preference shares will have a preferred right to receive a return of capital in priority to all other shareholders.

Redemption

Preference shares might also contain a right to redeem (in other words, to repurchase) the shares on a specified date (e.g., within three or five years from the date of the investment) as a way of exiting from the company within a certain time frame.

The amount payable on redemption usually will be the subscription amount originally paid by the investor on the shares, plus a premium that will provide the investor with the required rate of return.

Conversion Rights

If the preference shares are *convertible shares*, investors have the right, at their option, to convert the shares into ordinary shares on the happening of certain events, such as the sale or listing of the company, which satisfies certain predetermined price and valuation requirements. Investors can then choose whether they want to rely on the preferred liquidation feature or to *liquidate* their investment through the ordinary shares. It is also worth bearing in mind that where there is an imminent initial public offering (IPO), underwriters may want to see a straightforward capital structure and therefore may insist that any preferred shares be converted to ordinary shares immediately prior to the IPO.

Voting Rights

Generally, each share carries one vote (or, in the case of convertible preferred shares, one vote per share on an as-converted basis). Investors may seek enhanced voting rights (or weighted voting rights) in relation to certain matters, such as the removal of a director.

Antidilution Provisions

The purpose of *antidilution provisions* (also known as ratchets) is to protect original outside investors so that they are not diluted by subsequent third-party investments at a lower valuation (often referred to as a "down" round). The effect of such rights is to protect the original investors' economic position against the dilutive effects of the down round. (Refer to Chapter 19, "Applying the Venture Capital Valuation Method," to learn how to calculate dilution effects from multiple investment rounds).

In agreeing to such provisions, it is important to bear in mind that not only will the founder's shareholding be diluted but that the provisions will apply to all subsequent investment rounds, not just the first one. The founder or entrepreneur, if able, should try to negotiate a *pay-to-play provision,* which provides that if the original investor does not participate in future funding, the investor loses the protection of the antidilution rights. This will then be an incentive for the investor to participate further.

If it is appropriate to include a ratchet mechanism, this should also be included in the term sheet and should be carefully considered at that time, as such mechanisms are often complicated. In particular, any tax issues should be identified at the outset.

There are two ways in which an original investor can be protected:

1. By the issue of further shares to the investor, for example, by way of a bonus issue. A bonus issue can, however, only be done in strict compliance with company law requirements. The company must have authority to do so under its articles of association (bylaws) and must have sufficient unissued shares to do so. The company must also have sufficient distributable profits to be used to pay up

the additional shares. The antidilution provision normally provides that if the company cannot, by law, make a bonus issue, the investor can subscribe for the shares at their nominal or face value. In agreeing to this, the investor will want to ensure that the nominal value of the shares is sufficiently low.

2. If the investor holds convertible preference shares, the investment will provide that the rate at which the shares are convertible (the conversion rate) will be adjusted by a formula that will take into account the dilutive effect.

A founder or entrepreneur usually accepts that, in order to obtain investor financing, she will have to agree to antidilution provisions in one form or another. There is, however, usually some scope for negotiation as to the level of protection that a founder or entrepreneur shall give to an investor.

In this regard, a full ratchet mechanism provides the greatest level of protection to investors. It provides that the investors be given such number of shares as if their initial investment price per share had been at the down-round price.

A weighted average ratchet provides that the round price should not be looked at in isolation but rather that the amount of equity issued should be considered in the context of the company's overall share structure by averaging the price across different rounds of funding. This method is fairer to the founder than a full ratchet.

TRANSFERABILITY OF SHARES AND EXIT

Once the parties have agreed on the type of shares to be issued and what rights attach to those shares, consideration will (and should) be given to what extent, if any, the shares should be transferable. Such provisions are commonly found in the articles of association (bylaws) of the company, but they could also be included in the investment agreement. In any event, it is important to ensure that the investment agreement and the articles of association do not conflict with each other.

Permitted Transfers

Investors will want to have the flexibility of being able to freely transfer the shares they hold in the company. Conversely, they will wish to see restrictions on share transfers by other shareholders, particularly the founder. Investors will also want to ensure that the founder remains involved and that ownership of the company is not altered.

Investors will, however, usually not object if the founder wishes to make certain permitted transfers. For example, the founders may wish to transfer shares to close family members or to a family trust for tax planning purposes; usually these transfers are not problematic. In the case of corporate shareholders, transfers to and from companies in the same group are also usually allowed.

Preemption Rights

If transfers are allowed, it is usual to include "preemption" rights in favor of the other shareholders. A *preemption right* is simply a right of first refusal which ensures that, if any further shares in the company are to be issued or if any shareholder wishes to transfer shares, then the other shareholders must be offered those shares first, pro-rata to their existing shareholding. This ensures that investors have some control over any dilution of their existing shareholding. This also ensures that existing shareholders retain some control over the identity of any future investors. Investors do, however, sometimes insist on having the right of first refusal ahead of all other shareholders.

The investment agreement might also contain provisions whereby on a transfer of shares by one shareholder, the other shareholders can elect either to purchase the shares of the transferor or to require the transferor to purchase their shares. These types of provisions are known as call and put options. *Put options* are particularly attractive to investors as they effectively operate as redemption rights where no such right attaches to the preferred shares. The right to require the purchase of the shares often arises if no exit has been achieved within a defined period.

Drag Along and Tag Along

It is common to include what are known as drag-along (also called *come-along*) and tag-along rights in the investment agreement.

Drag-along rights enable investors to ensure that, on an exit, the entire share capital of the company will be sold, including their own. In essence, the right requires minority shareholders in the company to sell their shares in the event of a takeover. Drag-along rights also ensure that a sale of the company is not blocked by minority shareholders refusing to sell their shares. The mechanism is equally attractive for a purchaser who may not wish to have a small minority shareholder remain in the company.

Where a drag-along right has been negotiated, minority shareholders (e.g., a founder) may seek a matching tag-along right. A tag-along right ensures that shareholders who hold a majority interest cannot sell their shares without the minority shareholders having the opportunity to participate in the sale. A tag-along right therefore gives the minority shareholders the right to require the third party to buy all remaining shares for the same price.

OTHER TERMS OF THE INVESTMENT AGREEMENT

Purpose

There is usually a clause in the investment agreement setting out the purpose for which the company must use the investor's funds.

Warranties

After the term sheet is finalized, investors will undertake the due diligence process. (Refer to Chapter 16.) The outcome of the due diligence investigations will reveal the extent to which investors will require warranties to be given by the company or the founders. The main areas that are usually covered are those areas listed in the "Warranties" paragraph of the term sheet set out in Appendix 10.1 at the end of this chapter.

Essentially, the purpose of the warranties is to enable investors to obtain as much information as possible about the business before they make their investment. After the investment agreement is signed, the warranties also provide investors with protections should any of the warranties later be proved to be untrue.

To protect themselves from liability under the warranties, the founders and the company will make appropriate disclosures against the warranties in the disclosure letter (see Chapter 16) and seek to limit their liability by reference to financial caps and time limits. The company should, in any event, seek to limit its liability to the amount of the investment received by investors.

Management

In addition to any warranties that investors may require, investors usually also require some form of board representation as a means of protecting their investment and to help them monitor the investment. This could be either by having a director on the board or by having an observer who will attend board meetings and report back to the investors. Institutional investors usually insist on board representation so that they can monitor the running of the company and the use to which the investment is being put. Universities, however, are not always concerned with board representation, being content to rely on their rights to obtain certain information (e.g., to receive annual accounts and management accounts, the right to approve the annual budget, and to receive periodic reports and reviews of the business) to enable it to monitor the business. It also means that investors will not have to be concerned about taking on director's duties, which can be onerous, particularly if the company is underperforming.

Rather than giving investors an absolute right to appoint a director, the company and the founder may wish to link board representation to a level of shareholding that investors have in the company. For example, if an investor holds a very small percentage of the shares, then the right to appoint a director is lost. Ultimately, the parties will have to negotiate on this point, and the outcome will depend largely on their respective bargaining strength.

If there is to be board representation (in whatever form), investors also require that regular board meetings be held and minutes written. The investment agreement also sets out what the quorum and notice requirements for meetings are, what matters are to be reserved for board decision alone and cannot be delegated, what voting arrangements will apply, frequency and location of board meetings, how the chairperson will be chosen, and what rights he or she will have.

Covenants

Board representation is usually accompanied by covenants that ensure that investors retain some degree of control over certain important aspects of the business. Both positive and negative covenants will normally be included in the investment agreement. The positive covenants place a positive obligation on the company to do certain things: for example, to maintain and protect the company's intellectual property rights, to maintain adequate insurance, and to comply with all relevant laws and regulations.

The negative covenants restrict the managers or the board from taking certain actions unless carried out with the consent of the investor or board representative or both. The areas in relation to which such "veto" exists are matters for negotiation. Typically however, they are fundamental matters that are key for the business and include, for example, decisions relating to any change in the nature of the company's business, any decision to sell the company's business, any decision to sell the company, removing key personnel, winding up the company, important contracts, and the company entering into any financing arrangements in excess of a preagreed level. (See further examples in the sample term sheet set out in Appendix 10.1.)

Where there is no representation at board level (e.g., there is only an observer), investors may insist on veto rights, which restrict certain actions (examples of which are set out earlier) by the company unless they are carried out with the consent of the investor at shareholder level.

The key in negotiating these provisions is to ensure that a balance is struck between the shareholders safeguarding their interests and allowing the company sufficient flexibility to operate and develop without unnecessary obstruction.

Exit Clauses

It is common to include in the investment agreement a general exit clause along these lines:

> *The parties acknowledge their intention to work toward a sale or listing of the company within [ ] calendar months of today's date and the parties acknowledge that, on such sale or quotation, the investor will not be required to give any kind of warranty or indemnity to any person (other than a warranty as to title to any shares to be sold by it at that time).*

This type of clause is included although it is doubtful whether it is enforceable because it is uncertain. In any event, it may carry moral force. On an exit, investors will want to make it clear that they will not be providing any warranties or that only limited warranties will be provided. (Refer to Chapter 19, "How Venture Capitalists Improve Their Chances for Success," for more on venture capitalist financing and the importance of exit planning.)

Restrictive Covenants

The continued participation of the founders, in particular during the early stages, will be crucial to the success of the venture. Investors therefore seek to secure the long-term commitment of the founders by putting in place what are known as "key individual" service agreements or consultancy agreements that have an initial fixed term.

In the investment agreement, investors seek to impose on the founders of the business, who are also shareholders, covenants that require the founders to act in the best interests of the company and not to have competing interests. Investors insist on this type of provision being in the investment agreement rather than an employment contract because this type of provision is more likely to be enforceable if it is in the investment agreement. It is often more difficult to enforce these types of clauses in the context of an employment relationship.

CHAPTER TAKEAWAYS

- Do your homework on any potential investor.
- There are always inevitable tensions between a founder and an investor. Understand and anticipate what the stress points are for both parties.
- Consider a nonbinding term sheet that records the key commercial terms.
- With the investor, prepare and agree to a business plan that shows the amount of investment required, the use thereof, and over what period.
- If the investment is to be made in tranches and subject to achievement of certain milestones, clearly define all performance milestones.
- If board representation is required by an investor, ensure that whoever the investor appoints (including himself) has the requisite skill, experience, and competence that complements that of the founder.
- Consider the various options for exiting the investment and determine whether the interests of the entrepreneur and the investor are aligned.
- Get advice early on.

APPENDIX 10.1 INVESTMENT TERM SHEET

This Term Sheet sets out the terms of a proposed investment in [NAME OF COMPANY] (the "**Company**") by [NAME OF INVESTOR] (the "**Investor**").

This Term Sheet does not constitute an agreement or commitment to invest in the Company or provide financing and, except as set out below, is nonbinding. A binding obligation to invest in or provide funding to the Company shall only exist upon execution of a detailed and legally binding subscription and shareholders' agreement (the "**Investment Agreement**").

Share Capital	The share capital of the Company shall be split into ordinary shares of £[AMOUNT] each ("**Ordinary Shares**"); and preference shares of £[AMOUNT] each ("**Preference Shares**").
Investment	The proposed investment of £[AMOUNT] (the "**Investment**") will be made on a fully diluted pre-investment valuation of £[AMOUNT] equal to [PERCENTAGE]% of the Company's fully diluted equity share capital. On a fully diluted basis this represents a [PERCENTAGE]% shareholding in the Company for the Investor.
Price and Amount of Investment	The Investment will be made in the form of [CUMULATIVE] [CONVERTIBLE] [REDEEMABLE] Preference Shares at a price of £[AMOUNT] per Preference Share (the "**Original Issue Price**").

[The Investment will be made in full on completion] OR [The Investment will be made available in [NUMBER] of stages, with [PERCENTAGE]% being invested at completion (First Tranche) and [PERCENTAGE]% being invested in [NUMBER] subsequent rounds (Further Tranches). [The Investor shall have the right, but no obligation, to subscribe for Preference Shares in the Further Tranches at the Initial Subscription Price.]

[The board of directors (Board) shall have the right to call Further Tranches within [PERIOD] provided that the performance milestones set out below have been satisfied.] [INSERT PERFORMANCE MILESTONES].

Use of Proceeds	The Investment must be used for the Company's working capital requirements including [DETAILS OF SPECIFIC PURPOSE].
Dividends	The Preference Shares shall have a preferential [cumulative] coupon of [PERCENTAGE]% per annum, starting on [DATE]. Any other dividends or distributions shall be payable to all shareholders on a pro rata basis, in which case, the holders of Preference Shares shall be entitled to participate on an as-if-converted basis.
Return on Liquidation	On a liquidation, winding up or dissolution, the holders of Preference Shares shall be entitled to receive (before any return to holders of Ordinary Shares) an amount equal to:
	[[NUMBER] times] the Original Issue Price [; and OR]
	any declared but unpaid dividends (if any) [; and OR]
	[the interest compounded quarterly from the date of payment at a rate of [PERCENTAGE]% per annum] (Liquidation Preference).
	The holders of Ordinary Shares shall also be entitled to recover an amount per Ordinary Share equal to the amount paid up on such Ordinary Shares.
	If, after the distributions referred to above, the Company still has assets remaining, the holders of Preference Shares will participate with other holders of Ordinary Shares pro rata to the number of shares held on an as-if-converted basis.
Recapitalization Events	Shall mean an increase, repayment, subdivision, consolidation, capitalization or variation of share capital or any other similar event.
Conversion Rights	The Preference Shares shall be convertible at any time at the option of the Investor into an equivalent number of Ordinary Shares (subject to any adjustment being made to the conversion rate following any Recapitalization Events [and to the operation of any antidilution provisions referred to below]).

(*Continued*)

Automatic Conversion	The Preference Shares shall automatically convert to Ordinary Shares, at the then applicable conversion rate:
	(a) Immediately prior to a [firmly underwritten] initial public offering (IPO) of the Ordinary Shares combined with the listing of such Ordinary Shares on an internationally recognized stock exchange [at a net offering price per share of at least [NUMBER] times the Original Issue Price (after adjusting for any Recapitalization Events) AND/OR resulting in net aggregate proceeds to the Company of not less than £[AMOUNT].] Immediately prior to any such IPO, all accrued but unpaid dividends on the Preference Shares shall be paid (save to the extent that the Company resolves to capitalize some or all of such amounts into Ordinary Shares).
	(b) With the consent of the holders of at least [PERCENTAGE]% of the unconverted Preference Shares;
	(c) If less than [PERCENTAGE]% of the Preference Shares issued [in this round of investment] remain outstanding.
	[The Board shall, subject to the requirements of the Companies Act 2006 (as amended), also be entitled to effect any conversion of the Preference Shares as above by redesignation, redemption and issue of new Ordinary Shares or otherwise as they deem fit.]
Conversion Rate	The Investment into Preference Shares shall initially be convertible into Ordinary Shares equaling, if fully converted [and taking into account any conversion rights of any other classes of share,] [PERCENTAGE]% of the Company's [initial] issued and paid up ordinary share capital ("**Conversion Rate**"). The Conversion Rate shall be adjusted from time to time pursuant to the Company's articles of association as is customary for transactions of this nature [and subject to customary anti-dilution adjustment as described below].
[Antidilution]	[The Preference Shares shall have a [full ratchet OR weighted average] antidilution protection in relation to any additional issue of shares [warrants, [convertible loan notes] or options for shares] at a price below the Original Issue Price (after adjusting for any Recapitalization Events) other than Shares issued to the Investor as a result of the Investor electing to convert its Preference Shares into Ordinary Shares.
	This protection shall operate [so as to adjust the rate at which the Preference Shares will convert into Ordinary Shares OR by the issue of Ordinary Shares at par through a capitalization of the share premium account].]
[Pay to play]	[If the Company makes a subsequent issue of shares in which the Investor is entitled to participate and the Investor elects not to do so for at least [PERCENTAGE]% of its allocation [the Investor shall lose its antidilution right in respect of any Preference Shares that it holds] OR [the Investor's Preference Shares shall automatically convert to Ordinary Shares].]

[Tag Along]	[In the event of a sale or transfer of any shares by any shareholder other than the Investor, or of a change of control of any of the shareholders other than the Investor, the Investor shall have tag-along rights to sell its holding of Preference Shares [and Ordinary Shares] to such purchaser or transferee or person obtaining control on a pro rata basis.]
	[In the event that such a sale or transfer would result in the proposed purchaser or transferee acquiring more than [PERCENTAGE]% of the entire issued share capital of the Company, the Investor shall be entitled, and at its option, to sell its entire shareholding in the Company to such purchaser or transferee on the same terms and at the same price.]
[Drag Along]	[If holders of [PERCENTAGE]% or more Preference Shares [and Ordinary Shares] agree to sell their shares to a third party, there shall be drag-along rights so that all remaining shareholders and option holders shall be required to sell their shares to the third party on the same terms, provided that [the Investor shall not be required to sell unless it receives cash or marketable securities for its shares, and] the Investor shall not be required to provide any representations and warranties to the third party concerning the Company.]
[Redemption]	[If a liquidation, winding up, dissolution or an IPO does not occur within [NUMBER] years from completion, the Preference Shares shall [provided that the Investor has not exercised its drag-along rights] be redeemable at the Investor's election for an amount in cash equal to the [Original Issue Price OR Liquidation Preference OR [OTHER AMOUNT]] plus all accrued but unpaid dividends.]
[Mandatory Redemption]	The Company shall redeem the Preference Shares [[PERIOD] in [AMOUNT] increments beginning on [DATE]] at a redemption price equal to the Original Issue Price plus all accrued but unpaid dividends (if any).
	[The holders of the Preference Shares shall receive advance notice of each redemption and shall have the option to convert any or all of the Preference Shares otherwise due to be redeemed into Ordinary Shares prior to the mandatory redemption. In the event that the Company shall fail to make:
	(a) a mandatory redemption payment to the holders of Preference Shares while having funds and distributable reserves necessary to do so, then the holder of Preference Shares shall have a majority of the votes on all matters submitted for the approval of the Company' shareholders until such defaults are rectified; or
	(b) two mandatory redemption payments to the holders of Preference Shares regardless of whether it has the funds or distributable reserves necessary to do so, then the holders of the Preference Shares shall have the right to appoint a majority of the board of directors of the Company until such default is rectified.]

(Continued)

Sale of Assets or Shares	In the event of either a sale of substantially all of the assets of the Company or the sale of shares involving a change of control, [the Company shall redeem the Preference Shares at a redemption price equal to the Original Issue Price plus all accrued but unpaid dividends] OR [the Preference Shares shall be treated in the same way as on a liquidation and the proceeds of such sale will be distributed in the same manner as for a liquidation, winding up or dissolution (see above).]
Preemptive Rights	[The Investor shall have a right of first refusal on any new issue of shares of any class.]
	OR
	[The Investor (together with the holders of other classes of shares in the Company) shall have the right to participate in any new issue of shares of any class pro rata to its holding of shares (determined on an as-if-converted basis)] (other than shares issued as consideration for the acquisition of other companies or assets and those issued pursuant to employee share option and incentive schemes).]
	[In addition, the Investor shall have the right (but no obligation) to subscribe for [PERCENTAGE]% of the next £[AMOUNT] raised by the Company in future rounds of financing on terms substantially the same (but no worse) than those offered to the third party.]
	Save for permitted transfers (see below):
	(a) the holders of Preference Shares shall have the right of first refusal on the transfer or sale of any Preference Shares; and
	(b) any transfers of any Ordinary Shares in the capital of the Company shall be subject to pro-rata preemption rights in favor of the other shareholders in the Company from time to time in each case before such shares may be offered to any third party (in the case of the holders of Preference Shares, on an as-if-converted basis).
Permitted Transfers	The Investor shall be permitted to transfer its shares to any company which is a member of the same group [and any other holder of Preference Shares], provided that the transferee shall, if not already a party to the Investment Agreement, agree to be bound by the terms of the Investment Agreement.
	[For [PERIOD] following completion, the Founders shall not be able to transfer any shares without the Investor's permission.] Thereafter, the Founders shall be permitted to transfer their shares to
	(a) any spouse, civil partner, child or grandchild (including step or adopted or illegitimate children and their issue); and
	(b) to the trustees of any family trust.

Compulsory Transfers	In the event that [NAMES OR any of the Founders] leave the Company within [NUMBER] years of completion [or [OTHER EVENTS], they shall be required to sell their shares in the Company to the remaining members of the Company (on a preemptive basis) at, in the case of a *good leaver*, fair market value or, in the case of a *bad leaver*, par value.
Warranties	The Company and each of the Founders shall provide the Investor with customary representations and warranties in the Investment Agreement in terms to be agreed in relation to the following matters:

(a) the status of the Company, including the accuracy of the register of members and confirmation that no other share capital is issued, under option or committed to be issued;

(b) the Company's latest available audited accounts;

(c) the Company's management accounts covering the period from the latest available audited accounts to completion of the proposed investment;

(d) the Company's position since the date of the audited accounts;

(e) the business plan;

(f) the ownership of the assets and details of any liabilities;

(g) details of the Company's intellectual property;

(h) details of employment and pension arrangements;

(i) taxation;

(j) the properties owned, leased or occupied by the Company including details of the terms, rights and obligations in relation to such properties;

(k) confirmation that the Company's insurance policies are current; and

(l) the Company's loan and guarantee arrangements.

Service Agreements	Each of the Founders shall [enter into a new Service Agreement with the Company and] provide the Investor with customary noncompetition, nonsolicitation, and confidentiality undertakings.
Board Composition	The Board will have a maximum of [NUMBER] directors.

[For so long as the Investor continues to hold [PERCENTAGE]% shares in the Company, it shall have the right to appoint a director ("**Investor Director**")] OR [The Investor shall have the right [at all times OR for so long as it continues to hold shares in the Company] to appoint an observer to attend board meetings.]

There will be at least [NUMBER] of board meetings in each [calendar OR financial] year.

(Continued)

The consent of the Investor Director shall be required to:

(a) authorize the issue of any further shares, grant rights to subscribe for or to convert any shares [(other than shares issued pursuant to the employee share option and incentive schemes which have been approved by the Investor)];

(b) create or grant of any option [(other than pursuant to the employee share option and incentive schemes which have been approved by the Investor)] or any other right to subscribe for shares or securities convertible into shares of the Company;

(c) declare or distribute any dividend;

(d) redeem, purchase or other acquisition of an interest in any issued share capital of the Company other than from a former employee or pursuant to the Articles;

(e) increase, repay, subdivide, consolidate, capitalize, or otherwise vary the Company's authorized share capital;

(f) incur any indebtedness in excess of £[AMOUNT];

(g) incur any capital expenditure in excess of £[AMOUNT];

(h) effect any acquisition or disposal of shares or assets that may be material to the business; or

(i) [OTHERS].

The Investor shall be provided with normal financial and operating information about the Company, [and such other information as the Investor may reasonably request] in a timely fashion.

Protective Provisions

The consent of the Investor shall be required to:

(a) amend the memorandum of association or the Articles or both;

(b) disapply preemption rights;

(c) acquire or establish a subsidiary;

(d) any material change to the nature of the Company's business; and

(e) [OTHERS].

Confidentiality

This clause is legally binding.

The matters contemplated in this Term Sheet are to be treated as confidential and should not be disclosed to any person (except with the prior written consent of the other party, or in order to comply with law or by the rules and regulations of any other regulatory body).

[The Investor, the Founders and the Company agree that they will enter into a confidentiality agreement before the Investor commences its due diligence investigation.]

In the event that the Investment does not take place, the Investor undertakes that it will not disclose or make use of for its own benefit [or for the benefit of any subsidiary or parent company] any of the information of a confidential nature relating to the Company [or the Founders] which has been disclosed to it during the course of its due diligence investigation and otherwise in connection with the Investment. These provisions do not apply to any information which is publicly available at the time of disclosure unless disclosed through breach of the undertakings in this paragraph, nor does it apply to any information disclosed by the parties to the extent that disclosure is required by any law or regulation.

If the Investor is in breach of the terms of the undertakings, the Investor agrees to pay the [reasonable] legal, accountancy and other third party professional costs, fees, disbursements and expenses incurred by the Company [and the Founders] in connection with the negotiation, preparation and implementation of this Term Sheet and the Investment.

Exclusivity

This clause is legally binding.

In consideration of [the Investor undertaking to pay the Company the sum of £[AMOUNT], receipt of which is hereby acknowledged,] the confidentiality obligations under the confidentiality paragraph, and the Investor incurring the costs of professional advisers and other expenses and expending further management time in connection with the due diligence investigations in relation to the Company [and its subsidiaries] and progressing the proposed Investment, the Company and the Founders grant the Investor a period of exclusivity on and from the date of acceptance of this term sheet until the earlier of [DATE], completion of the Investment and the date on which discussions regarding the Investment are terminated ("**Exclusivity Period**").

During the Exclusivity Period, the Company and the Founders agree and undertake to the Investor that they will not [, and shall procure that the Company's directors, employees, agents and advisers shall not] (directly or indirectly) enter into or continue, facilitate or encourage, any discussions or negotiations with any other party relating to the possible subscription or purchase of shares in the Company, or of any material part of the Company or its assets (including without limitation any shares in any subsidiary) or enter into or continue to seek negotiations with any party other than the Investor in connection with such matters (all or any of the foregoing being referred to as a Competing Investment.)

The Founders and the Company agree and undertake with the Investor to inform the Investor immediately of any third party who contacts the Founders or the Company with a view to the sale of any interest in the shares of the Company or any part of the business of the Company.

(*Continued*)

The Company and the Founders acknowledge that by relying on this term the Investor will incur significant costs, fees and expenses, and confirm that if:

a. they withdraw from negotiations with the Investor during the Exclusivity Period; or

b. they breach the undertakings and provisions in this term; [or]

[the Investor decides not to proceed with the Investment due to a materially adverse fact or circumstance of which the Investor becomes aware during the Exclusivity Period;]

they shall (without prejudice to any other remedies the Investor may have) indemnify and keep indemnified the Investor for an amount equal to all the [reasonable] costs, fees, disbursements and expenses (plus any applicable VAT) which have been or will be incurred by the Investor in connection with the proposed Investment, including without limitation the investigation of the Company [and its subsidiaries] and the negotiation of these heads of terms and other documents connected with the proposed Investment. [Such amount(s) shall be payable on production of appropriate invoices, receipts and vouchers.]

Fees and Expenses	This clause is legally binding.
	Save as expressly set out in this Term Sheet, each of the parties shall bear their own costs in relation to the Investment [save that the Company will contribute an aggregate of £[AMOUNT] to the Investor's expenses].
Governing Law	This clause is legally binding.
	This Term Sheet and any disputes or claims arising out of or in connection with its subject matter are governed by and construed in accordance with the law of England.
	This Term Sheet is for the benefit of the parties to it and is not intended to benefit, or be enforceable by, anyone else.

Agreed and Accepted
[Investor]
[The Founders]
[The Company]

CHAPTER 11

The Intellectual Property Landscape

Caroline Hughes, John Maycock, and Nicole Hirst
Withers LLP

This chapter introduces the intellectual property (IP) landscape and provides a brief overview of the legal principles and supranational regulatory frameworks that govern IP protections globally. As you learned in Chapter 2, there are five basic categories of IP rights. As patent rights are the cornerstone of most technology licensing agreements, we have devoted two chapters to patents (Chapters 12 and 13). Here we focus on:

- Copyright
- Industrial designs
- Know-how and trade secrets
- Trademarks

We explain the primary functions of these categories of IP rights and the advantages to be gained from using these in substitution for or in tandem with patent protection. In parts of this chapter, we do delve into some of the legal principles and regulation surrounding these IP rights—and, in so doing, we hope to give you a flavor of how particular rights can help protect your invention and aid commercialization. However, this chapter is not intended to provide an exhaustive analysis of the international aspects of IP rights. Nor should it be considered a substitute for seeking specific advice from an IP specialist, whether from a lawyer or a patent or trademark attorney. What we aim to provide is an overview of the key points that any innovator will need to consider when putting together an IP portfolio.

Before we get into the specifics, we give a brief recap of some of the points that were discussed in Chapter 2 as to the importance of IP rights for the innovator and a look at some of the current trends in IP.

IP PERSPECTIVE

The purpose of any IP system is to encourage innovation and creative endeavor and to reward the innovator and creator for that enterprise. As the world gets smaller and economic competition fiercer, it is essential that inventions be protected and capable of being commercialized. Intangible assets in the form of IP rights, rather than tangible or physical assets, are increasingly important in the global economy. It is therefore critical that innovators and IP rights owners are aware of their legal rights and how best to exploit and protect these valuable assets.

The importance of IP rights to the global economy has prompted many countries to carry out a review of their existing IP systems and practices, with a view to streamlining processes and harmonizing both the law and practices applied to the registration, exploitation, and protection of IP rights.[1] The key themes that have come out of such reviews are:

- How to meet the needs of IP rights owners in this global age of trade and commerce
- How to ensure that the legal framework for IP remains able to protect adequately new technology

We discuss each of these issues in brief, because it is important that the information given later in this chapter in relation to specific IP rights is read in the context of current thinking on the scope, value, and future development of intellectual property.

Global Challenge

Owning IP rights gives you exclusive rights to prevent third parties and competitors from utilizing your assets in the course of their business without your consent and without payment or other compensation. Although progress has been made by the global IP community to harmonize rights and procedures, more work remains to be done. The members belonging to the World Trade Organization (WTO) have agreed to adhere to the Trade-Related Aspects of Intellectual Property Rights (TRIPS agreement). The TRIPS agreement establishes the minimum levels of intellectual protection that each government has to provide. Refer to Appendix 11.1, "International Intellectual Property Treaties and Conventions" by logging onto our web site at www.innovationtocashflows.com. In Appendix 11.1, we summarize the most important international IP treaties and convention systems, in addition to the main European IP treaty and convention systems. For each treaty and convention system, we describe the relevant IP rights and who administers them.

Generally speaking, intellectual property rights are national rights that only give protection within a national territorial boundary. Some supranational registration systems allow for a single application to be made for multiple jurisdiction protection of particular IP rights, but we are still a long way off from a truly international IP registration system.

In all other cases, applications for registration of IP rights will have to be made in each jurisdiction where protection is required. Likewise, enforcement will have to be dealt with on a national basis. Paying maintenance fees to keep IP protection current in multiple territories is expensive. Managers need to use a rational, cost-effective approach in deciding where protection is truly needed in terms of geographical scope, especially at the early stages of developing an innovation.

Understandably, to the uninitiated, the idea of trying to navigate the maze of national and supranational IP systems and the cost of establishing and maintaining an IP portfolio may seem daunting. However, with advice from an IP specialist at an early stage and by keeping in mind some strategic principles as described in this chapter and elsewhere in this book, one can figure out the way.

Keeping Apace with Technological Development

One of the challenges of national governments is to identify where existing IP protection may not adequately cover new innovations. This has been brought to the fore with such developments as human genome technology and stem cell research, which do not sit easily within the existing patent framework and which can also give rise to ethical and public policy considerations. The rapid development of new technologies within very short periods is one of the reasons why differences have arisen in the way that different countries approach the grant of rights to certain types of innovation. A good example of this is computer software. The United States, which was at the forefront of the creation and growth of software and for whom the software industry is a large contributor to its economy, has reflected the value that it attaches to such contribution by extending patent protection to cover computer programs.

This is in contrast to the position in the United Kingdom and European Union where "programs for computers . . . as such"[2] are excluded from patent protection. In the European Union (including the United Kingdom), software can be patented only if it has a "technical effect" when run on a computer. This effect must be more than the "normal" physical interaction between program and computer. (In other words, the program must solve a technical problem rather than just a business problem.) The U.K. Patent Office gives the following example: If a computer program provides improved control of a car braking system, it is likely to be patentable, but if it merely provides an improved accounting system, it is probably not patentable. There has been a great deal of discussion in recent years on the patentability of software, including a failed attempt to introduce a new European Community directive on the patentability of computer-implemented inventions. The issues around software patentability are beyond the scope of this book.[3]

As we have discussed, IP rights are territorial. In most cases, they have force only within national boundaries. In certain cases, as we shall see, they may have force across supranational boundaries. However, there is currently no such thing as a global IP right in any of the categories of rights listed earlier. This means that one of the key considerations for any IP strategy is to identify key territories for the innovation. Key territories may not just be *target markets* for a product but might also include countries of manufacture and countries where there is a risk that copycat products could be produced.

In the next sections, we look at copyright, industrial designs, know-how and trade secrets, and trademarks in more detail. Because IP rights are geographically limited, this chapter does not attempt to cover all territories. Instead, we focus on the United States, the United Kingdom and the European Union. However, many of the issues that apply to these countries will also apply to other jurisdictions. Particularly, the IP regime in the former British Commonwealth countries (Canada, Australia, and New Zealand) follows broadly the same regime as in the United Kingdom.

COPYRIGHT

What is copyright? Copyright protects creative works. Often people are confused as to what will be protected by copyright. The scope of protection is often described by stating that copyright protects the expression of an idea but not the idea itself. In other words, there has to be something tangible to which the copyright can attach. This means that a work must be recorded in some material form before it will attract copyright protection.

The types of creative works that may be protected by copyright are:

- Original literary, dramatic, musical, or artistic works
- Sound recordings, films, or broadcasts
- Typographical arrangements of published editions
- Software

Obtaining Copyright Protection

Unlike patents and trademarks, you generally do not have to apply for copyright protection, and there are no fees, form filings, or renewals to worry about (although the position in the United States is different, where registration may affect your right to enforce your copyright). If you have created something that falls within any of the listed categories, then, provided that the work is original and that either the author or the work qualifies for copyright protection under the relevant legal regime, the copyright will arise automatically when the work is created.[4]

In the case of artistic and literary works, you do not need to show that the works have any artistic or literary merit, so copyright protection can extend to technical drawings, maps, circuit diagrams, plans, and the like. In the United Kingdom and in Europe, computer programs and certain databases can also be protected by copyright, which is useful, since protection will arise automatically, without any lengthy application process or need to keep the work secret during that process (as with an invention seeking patent protection).

The general rule is that the first owner of the copyright will be the person (or persons) who created the work. However, in some countries, including the United Kingdom, if a work is created by a person in the course of employment, then the employer will be the owner of the copyright in the work. The position is subtly different in the United States and is closer to the United Kingdom's "commissioned works" position.

The U.S. position in relation to works created during employment (and the U.S. and U.K. position in relation to commissioned works) is that the commissioning party will *not* own the copyright in the work unless the parties have agreed otherwise in writing. This means that it is crucial, where you subcontract part or all of a project in which copyright material will be created, or where you commission a third party to create a copyright work for you, that you have a written contract in place which states explicitly that the copyright in any work created by that third party will belong to you, the commissioning party.

Most copyright regimes, including the United Kingdom, recognize joint authorship of a copyright work, where more than one person has created the work.

However, joint authorship can cause difficulties when it comes to exploiting a copyright work (as, generally, consent of all authors is required in order to license or assign the copyright work). This is therefore something that should be thought about and dealt with between the joint authors as early on in the process for commercializing a copyright work as possible, to avoid unnecessary practical difficulties arising.

Who Is Eligible for Copyright Protection?

Different countries have different rules as to who is entitled to copyright protection.

U.S. Position In the United States, there is a distinction between published and unpublished works. Copyright protection is available for all *unpublished* works, regardless of the nationality or domicile of the author. For *published* works to be eligible for copyright protection in the United States, either the author or the work itself must fall within detailed criteria as to nationality or place of first publication. Generally speaking, if the author is a U.S. national or domiciled in the United States, or if the work is first published in the United States, then it will attract copyright protection. The *U.S. Copyright Office* provides comprehensive guidance on who and what qualifies for copyright protection, as well as good practical information on how to protect and enforce your copyright.[5]

U.K. Position Under the Copyright, Designs and Patents Act 1988 (CDPA), a work will be eligible for copyright protection in the United Kingdom, if either one of these criteria is met:

1. At the time the work was created, the author was a "qualifying person," for example:
   - A British citizen
   - Domiciled or resident in the United Kingdom or another country in the European Union
   - A body incorporated under the law of the United Kingdom or another country in the European Union
2. The work was first published (or broadcast, in the case of a broadcast or cable program) either in the United Kingdom or in a country to which the CDPA extends protection.

What Legal Protection Does Copyright Provide?

Copyright gives the owner the right to carry out certain acts with the copyright work and to prevent other people from carrying out those acts—known as restricted acts. The main restricted acts are reproducing the copyright work, issuing copies of it, or communicating it to the public.

In some countries, notably the United States, the copyright owner has to register its rights in the work in order to be able to sue an infringer for damages. In the United Kingdom and elsewhere, where registration is not a prerequisite to suing for infringement, the requirement to prove ownership of the copyright in the work is simply a question of fact. This is why it is important to document accurately the date of creation of any copyright works and the identity of the author, so that you have an audit trail, should it ever become necessary to evidence when and by whom the work was created. There are companies that offer a commercial registration and depositary service, to assist this process.

Although not a legal requirement, it makes sense to affix a copyright notice to your work. The standard form, recognized internationally, is © [name of copyright owner] [year of publication]. This puts people on notice that the work is copyright protected.

The copyright regime differs from country to country, but a number of international conventions have tried to harmonize the situation.[6] As a result, most countries in the world recognize and honor citizens' copyrights of other convention countries. However, it would be wrong to assume that every country will treat your copyright in the same way and afford you the same rights as your home country. If you are relying on copyright for sole, or part, protection of a product that you want to exploit commercially, you will need to seek legal advice as to whether you will have adequate legal protection in your target markets.

In particular, the length of copyright protection may vary between different countries, depending on the work in question. In the United States, the position is relatively straightforward—for works created after January 1, 1978, copyright lasts for the author's lifetime plus 70 years.[7] In the United Kingdom, the period of copyright protection depends on the type of copyright work, as illustrated in Table 11.1.

Most countries' legal systems treat copyright in the same way as any other property right, which means that copyright can be assigned, licensed, or used as collateral—making copyright works, in many cases, valuable assets. In some countries, including the United Kingdom, you can even assign the future copyright (in other words, copyright that will come into existence on creation of a future work), so that when the copyright comes into existence, ownership of that copyright will automatically vest in the *assignee*.[8] This can be particularly valuable at early-stage development of an innovation that will attract copyright protection, where you can

TABLE 11.1   Period of U.K. Copyright Protection

Copyright Work	Duration
Literary	70 years from the end of the calendar year in which the author or composer or artist dies
Dramatic	As above
Musical	As above
Artistic	As above
Original database	As above
Film	As above
Broadcast	50 years from the end of the calendar year in which the broadcast or cable program or recording was made
Cable program	As above
Sound recording	As above
Typographical arrangement	25 years from the end of the calendar year in which it was first published

Source: Copyright, Designs and Patents Act 1988 of the United Kingdom Parliament.

secure funding for the next stage of the process in exchange for the transfer of ownership of the copyright in the eventual work.

Different rules apply in terms of the formalities that you have to follow to create a valid license, assignment, or mortgage. Most countries, including the United Kingdom, require that a license, assignment, or charge must be in writing and signed by the person assigning the rights. Even where there is no legal requirement to have a written contract, we strongly recommend that you should properly document any dealings with your copyright, so that there is a robust audit trail in the event of any challenge to those rights.

Enforcing Copyright

To enforce your copyright in a protected work, you must be the owner and you will need to show that a person has infringed that work. Ownership is often forgotten in the relationship between an independent self-employed consultant and the person or company contracting for the work. It is essential to make sure that ownership of the copyright in the work ends up in the right place. An example of a situation where care should be taken is in the designing of web sites, which is often undertaken by independent contractors. Note that in the United Kingdom at least, copyright can only be assigned in writing and a verbal agreement to do so will not be effective. Any web design contract needs to clearly state who will own the copyright in the web design.

A person will infringe copyright if he does one of the "restricted acts" (as described earlier) in relation to the copyright work, without the authorization of the copyright owner. An example of copyright infringement would be where a person copies a work of modern art to make limited edition posters. It does not matter that the medium in which the work is copied is different from the original—the fact of reproducing the copyright work without the copyright owner's permission will amount to an infringement.

The typical remedies for copyright infringement are an injunction or damages or both.

DESIGNS

What is a design? Generally speaking, when we talk about a design in a legal sense, this refers to the functional shape or configuration of an industrial product. In some countries, the concept of a design may also extend to surface ornamentation or decoration, but the crucial element is the underlying article, which must have industrial application. This is a broad concept but does rule out protection for what may, in common understanding, be considered a "design" in the generic sense of the word, but which does not have any industrial application. Of course, copyright protection may be available to protect such "designs."

What Protection Is Available for Designs?

The law relating to designs varies from country to country. Some jurisdictions, such as the United Kingdom and the European Community (EC) provide a form of protection for both registered and unregistered designs (which creates a degree of overlap with copyright protection). Other jurisdictions rely on copyright alone for unregistered rights and have a separate regime for designs that are capable of registration. Some countries protect only the functional shape or configuration of a product, whereas others will also protect surface ornamentation or decoration. We summarize the main differences between "design right" (which refers to protections for unregistered design) and "registered design" in the United Kingdom as compared to the European Community in Appendix 11.2, "Comparison of Design Right and Registered Design," located on our web site at www.innovationtocashflows.com. (After logging onto the web site, go to the file labeled Appendix 11.2, and refer to Table 11A2.1, "Comparison of Design Right (for Unregistered Designs) in the United Kingdom and the European Community" and Table 11A2.2, "Comparison of Registered Design in the United Kingdom and the European Community.")

Until relatively recently, registered design protection was overlooked and considered by many as not worth the expense. Since the introduction of the Community Registered Design (CRD) in Europe, there has been an increased awareness of the availability of registered design protection and increased reliance on this form of protection either as stand-alone or, most commonly, in conjunction with other IP protection, such as trademarks and copyright, to provide the broadest possible protection for a product.

U.S. Design Patents

In the United States, designs can be protected under a design patent. A design patent is available to anyone who invents a new, original, and ornamental design for an article of manufacture. You can apply for a design patent for the configuration or shape of an article, the surface ornamentation applied to an article, or the combination of configuration and surface ornamentation. Note that you cannot apply to protect surface ornamentation alone (in the absence of an article to which it is applied). Also, the U.S. Patent and Trademark Office (USPTO) typically raises objections against applications for designs that it considers to be merely decorative elements and, therefore, more properly protected under copyright. In practice, this is where an IP attorney can add value in helping you steer a course between copyright and design patents, to maximize the available protection.

A design patent, once granted, lasts for 14 years, during which time the patent owner has the right to prevent others from importing, making, using, offering for sale, or selling the design.

The main advantage of a design patent is that there is no requirement to show copying, so that even if a third party independently creates a design that is the same as the patented design, this will be an infringement. The main disadvantage is the time and cost involved in obtaining a design patent. Typically, it will take up to two years to obtain a design patent, by which time the design that is the subject of the patent may have evolved or come to the end of its marketable life. However, there is a way around this by paying more money to go through an expedited process, typically six months from filing to grant.

One issue that must not be overlooked, not just in the case of design patents, but in the case of registered designs in other jurisdictions as well, is that the strength of the patent or design registration is almost wholly dependent on the depiction of the protected designs. Unlike utility patents, where technical drawings can be supplemented by detailed claims setting out the specification of the innovation, the protection afforded by a registered design or a design patent is based on the drawings of the article that incorporates the design. The effect of this in practice is twofold. First, you need to be clear on the final design for the product before filing an application since your protection will be limited to what has been filed. This also means that you should not look to cut costs in the preparation of your design drawings, since these will form the basis of your legal protection and it is critical that they accurately reflect your designs. Second, if you file to register an earlier *prototype design*, there is a risk that this will then become "prior art" (by which we mean all information publicly known before the date of filing the design or patent application). Prior art destroys the novelty of your later design, rendering it incapable of registration.

KNOW-HOW OR TRADE SECRETS

What is know-how? Know-how, in the form of confidential information, or trade secrets, generally refers to information of a technical nature which is of commercial value or application and which is not known to the public.

In the United Kingdom, *know-how* and *trade secrets* are generally considered to be one and the same thing: There is no legislation governing the protection of know-how or trade secrets in the United Kingdom and no statutory definition of either. The closest that the United Kingdom comes to having a defined concept of know-how is under the EC Technology Transfer Block Exemption (which deals with the licensing or other transfer of know-how and applies to the United Kingdom and the rest of the member states of the European Union), which has this definition:

> *Know-how = a package of non-patented practical information, resulting from experience and testing which is secret, substantial and identified.*[9]

In the United States, know-how is generally regarded as being technical information relating to the practical application of patented or unpatented inventions. Therefore, although know-how will often be a trade secret, the terms *know-how* and *trade secrets* are *not* generally interchangeable.

U.S. law has gone further than the United Kingdom or European Union in trying to create a statutory right in respect of trade secrets. The Uniform Trade Secrets Act was enacted as a means of trying to codify the law as it applies to trade secrets. To date it has been adopted by 45 states (notable exceptions being Massachusetts, New Jersey, New York, North Carolina, and Texas). It defines a trade secret as:

> *Information, including a formula, patterns, compilation, program, device, method, technique, or process that:*

> i. *derives independent economic value, actual or potential, from not being generally known to, and not being readily ascertainable by proper means by, other persons who can obtain economic value from its disclosure or use; and*
> ii. *is the subject of efforts that are reasonable under the circumstances to maintain its secrecy.*[10]

This definition of a *trade secret* from the American Law Institute's "Restatement of Torts" is also commonly used:

> *any formula, pattern, device or compilation of information which is used in one's business, and which gives him an opportunity to obtain an advantage over competitors who do not know or use it.*[11]

As can be seen from these definitions, there is no single universally shared legal concept of what constitutes know-how or trade secrets, and different countries offer differing degrees of legal protection to know-how or trade secrets. The international TRIPS agreement has gone some way to try to set a minimum standard of protection for confidential information as between its members. It states that for information to be legally protectable:

1. The information must be secret: in other words, not generally known or readily accessible to persons that normally deal with that kind of information;
2. It must have commercial value because it is secret; and
3. The owner must have taken reasonable steps to keep it secret.

However, how this is interpreted and implemented does differ as between WTO members, so local legal advice should always be sought. Next, we explore the legal issues surrounding know-how and trade secrets from a predominantly U.K. and U.S. perspective.

What Protection Is Available for Know-How and Trade Secrets?

It is important not to consider know-how and trade secrets in isolation, but to understand that there is a great deal of overlap between know-how and trade secrets and the other types of intellectual property rights discussed in this chapter and in the two patent chapters to follow. One thing to establish at the outset is whether your know-how or trade secret is also patentable, or capable of being registered as a registered design or trademark, or protected by copyright. You can then assess the best legal regime for protecting that know-how to gain maximum legal protection.

Some jurisdictions, including the United Kingdom, do not recognize know-how or trade secrets as a separate type of IP right. This means that there is no statutory basis for protecting know-how. Instead, know-how may be protected as confidential information under the common law concept of confidentiality. (Refer to Chapter 9, where we discuss confidentiality agreements, also referred to as non-disclosure agreements [NDAs]). The U.S. position is different. In most states (specifically those that have adopted the Uniform Trade Secrets Act [UTSA]), trade secrets are a property right and are protected under statute (although some states have adopted UTSA with modifications). In those states that have not yet adopted specific trade secrets legislation, common law protection still applies.

U.S. Position   For a trade secret to be protected, it must be secret. This means that it must not be generally known to the public. It should also not be readily ascertainable (which, in broad terms, means that it should not be obvious and should not have been published). It also means that the owner of a trade secret must make reasonable efforts to keep it secret—the rationale being that if the owner of a trade secret does not treat the information as a trade secret, then neither should the law. What this means for the innovator is that it is vitally important to establish a system of best practice processes and procedures for keeping information confidential. We discuss practical steps in more detail later in the chapter.

To qualify as a trade secret, the information must derive some independent economic value because it is kept secret. In other words, it must provide its owner with a competitive advantage over others who are unaware of the secret information.

U.K. Position   Under English law, to be protected by confidentiality, information must meet two criteria. It must have:

1. "The necessary quality of confidence about it"[12] (in other words, not something which is public property or public knowledge)
2. Been disclosed in "circumstances importing an obligation of confidence"[13]

Whether a piece of information has "the necessary quality of confidence about it" is a question of fact. Some types of information, such as secret formulas (e.g., the Coca-Cola recipe) are more readily identifiable as confidential information than others. One important point to note is that merely marking information as "confidential" will not make it confidential if the nature of the information means that it lacks the "necessary quality of confidence."

As long as it meets these criteria, any information can be confidential information, regardless of what form it takes (whether physical or electronic copy or even intangible). Examples include information that is also patentable subject matter; unpublished business methods or industrial processes; customer and supplier lists; scientific or industrial test results; source codes and algorithms.

The basic concept of the duty of confidence arises from the broad equitable principle that "he who has received information in confidence should not take unfair advantage of it." If your know-how is protected under a duty of confidence, then you have a right to a remedy where a recipient seeks to use your confidential information to your prejudice without obtaining your consent.

Obtaining Protection for Your Know-How or Trade Secrets

This section focuses on three critical points to consider in relation to protecting your know-how:

1. Identifying confidential information
2. Confidential information versus intellectual property rights
3. Maintaining confidentiality

Identifying Confidential Information

Unlike patents, trademarks, or designs—all of which can be registered—and copyright, which attaches automatically to certain types of created work, one of the key issues when you are talking about know-how is how to identify that which you wish to protect. Businesses that focus on the development of innovations or technology to generate income should have internal procedures for identifying and documenting know-how generated by the business. For example, researchers working on a research and development project will be required to document all of the inputs, methodology, and outputs of the various project tasks carried out, to capture the know-how involved in that project. Not all of this information may have the "necessary quality of confidence" to attract protection (e.g., trivial information, such as which individuals performed which tests), but best practice would be to retain all of the information, so that you have a robust audit trail. (For advice on how to set up such a documentation system, log onto our web site at www.innovationtocashflows.com and refer to Appendix 2.2, "Guidelines for Setting Up an Invention Disclosure System for Your Company" and Appendix 2.3, "Sample Invention Disclosure Form.")

One of the prime, and often overlooked, issues is that much of the know-how on a particular project may be held by just one or a few key individuals involved in the development process. The challenge for businesses is how to ensure that this know-how is extracted from those individuals in a meaningful way that allows it to be used even if those individuals subsequently exit from the business. While most well-drafted employment contracts contain a provision whereby all intellectual property rights created by an employee during the course of employment will belong to the employer, this presumes that the relevant IP rights can be identified. It is easy to see how such a clause, while good on paper, has little worth in reality if the IP right of value is know-how stored in an individual's head!

Investors, particularly, will be eager to ensure that the know-how on the basis of which they are investing has been "unlocked" in terms of being properly and completely documented. (Refer to Chapter 14 and especially to the section, "Know-how Transfer," for more discussion on this important topic.)

Confidential Information versus Intellectual Property Rights

Once you have identified your know-how, you must consider how best to protect it. Keeping it secret is one option but is a weaker form of protection than, for example, a patent registration. It may be that a combination of confidentiality and other IP rights are available to you, and you should seek specialist advice from a lawyer or a patent or trademark attorney as appropriate at as early a stage as possible.

By way of example, Table 11.2 shows a summary comparison of the protection conferred by confidentiality as opposed to patent registration.

Maintaining Confidentiality

Confidentiality can protect only that information that is kept confidential. If the information enters the public domain (whether through publication, unauthorized disclosure, or the putting onto the market of a product of which the know-how within it is easily determined), then protection is lost.

It is therefore vitally important that once information has been identified as potentially confidential, it must be kept secret. In practical terms, this means implementing adequate security in terms of where the information is stored (whether in hardcopy or electronically) to prevent unauthorized disclosure. It also means

TABLE 11.2 Comparison of the Protection Conferred by Confidentiality as Opposed to Patent Registration

Confidential Know-How	Patent Registration
No monopoly right—no right to prevent a third party who has independently come up with the same innovation from using and exploiting that innovation.	Monopoly right for 20 years—only the registered patent owner has the right to exploit the patented invention.
Susceptible to loss of rights due to inadvertent or unauthorized disclosure.	A registered patent is lost only through a successful challenge to its validity.
Enforceability can be difficult, as the person making the claim has to prove that the know–how has the necessary quality of confidence about it; was disclosed to the defendant in circumstances importing an obligation of confidence; and was disclosed by the defendant without authority.	Patent enforceability by way of infringement proceedings is a well-established cause of action but can give rise to a challenge for invalidity of the patent.
Not recognized as a property right under English law (but trade secrets recognized as a property right under U.S. law) so special thought needs to be given to licensing, assignment, or mortgaging.	Recognized as a property right and therefore capable of being licensed, assigned, or mortgaged.

ensuring that access to that information is limited to those individuals who have a strict need to know. This may include restricting physical access to areas where processes or testing are being carried out. Many businesses keep an access log, to enable them to track who has had access to the information and at what time (similar to what is done during due diligence as explained in Chapter 16).[14] Practical steps to bear in mind include:

- Best practice guidelines about the identification, handling, recording, and disclosure of confidential information (including document retention policies)
- Physical security and storage (including encryption of electronic documents and data storage systems and networks)
- Central control of drawings, prototypes, and similar information capable of being readily understood or reverse engineered
- Training of employees and subcontractors
- Standard confidentiality clauses in employee or subcontractor contracts

Employees and any contractors working on a particular development project should be subject to robust confidentiality obligations in their terms of employment or service contracts. These obligations should be drafted so as to apply (so far as is legally possible) even after their employment or contract has expired.

While confidentiality agreements are a useful part of your armory, avoid over-reliance on them. The safest course of action, if confidentiality is your only form of protection for your innovation, is to keep details of the innovation secret. If you must disclose details of the innovation—for example, to secure funding for further development—you should insist on the recipient of the information signing a robust confidentiality agreement. If you can disclose only generic detail, then do so. If you have to disclose the technical detail, a confidentiality agreement is vital. As we have already discussed at the beginning of this chapter and will emphasize again in the chapters relating to patents, public disclosure of an invention may be fatal to any patent application in a number of countries, including the United Kingdom. If you think that your invention might be capable of attracting patent protection, then you should not disclose any detail of it without placing the recipient under an obligation to keep that detail confidential. See Chapter 9 for more on confidentiality agreements and also log onto our web site at www.innovationtocashflows.com to find Appendix 9.1, "Sample Confidentiality Agreement."

Remember, once the information is in the public domain, your rights in that information are likely to have evaporated and cannot be resurrected. Therefore, if you become aware of a possible disclosure of your confidential information, you must take adequate steps to seek to prevent such disclosure.

Enforcing Rights in Confidential Information

If the confidential information has not yet been disclosed, but disclosure is threatened or imminent, then the usual remedy would be to obtain an *interim injunction*, pending a trial on the facts of the case (which, if the claimant is successful, will result in a *permanent injunction* to restrain the party that wishes to disclose from doing so). An application for an interim injunction must be made promptly after you become aware of the threatened disclosure; delay in applying could result in the court refusing to grant an injunction on the basis that it is no longer an appropriate remedy.

Once disclosure has occurred, the only remedy available is damages, which may not come close to compensating for the disclosure.

TRADEMARKS

What is a trademark? A trademark is a sign or indicator used by an individual, business organization, or other legal entity to:

- Identify the provenance of its products and services (or both) to the public or consumers
- Distinguish its products or services from those of third parties

The main purpose of a trademark, therefore, is to serve as a badge of origin.

This section focuses on *registered* trademark rights, since, in most countries, you must register a trademark in order to obtain protection. However, some countries, including the United Kingdom, the United States, France, and Germany, also recognize *unregistered* trademark rights. At the very end of this section, we give a brief summary of the protection given to such unregistered rights by the law of passing off (in the United Kingdom) and unfair competition laws (in the United States, France, and Germany). The basic point to take away is that registered rights offer better protection than unregistered rights.

What Can be Registered as a Trademark?

Each country has its own definition of what constitutes a trademark and what can be registered, but all are based on the idea that the mark must be able to act as an indication of the source of the products or services to which the mark is applied. The U.S. Trademarks Act[15] refers to a trademark as being a "word, name, symbol, or device, or any combination thereof," and the emphasis is very much on the mark being used (or a good faith intention that the mark will be used) in commerce as a means of distinguishing a person's goods or services from another person's goods or services.

If you want to register a trademark in the United Kingdom, or if you want to register a trademark that covers all countries of the European Union (known as a *Community Trade Mark* [CTM]), the key requirement for either jurisdiction is that the mark is a sign that is capable of being represented graphically and can distinguish the goods and services that bear the mark from goods and services of a third party. The key criteria that must be met for either a U.K. or a CTM registration are "graphical representation" and *"distinctiveness."*

In theory, this means that you can apply to register a smell, a taste, a sound, a color, or a three-dimensional shape as either a U.K. trademark or as a Community Trade Mark. However, the vast majority of registered trademarks are simple words or words in stylized or logo form. Applicants (and trademarks registries) have struggled with the graphical representation requirement when trying to register nonword marks. The example presented in the next box illustrates the difficulties.

TARZAN

Edgar Rice Burroughs, Inc. (the successor in title to the author of the *Tarzan* novels) applied to register the *Tarzan* "yell" as a Community Trade Mark (sound mark). The application comprised this spectrogram and waveform of the sound and accompanying written description:

> The mark consists of the yell of the fictional character TARZAN, the yell consisting of five distinct phases, namely sustain, followed by ululation, followed by sustain, but at a higher frequency, followed by ululation, followed by sustain at the starting frequency, and being represented by the representations set out below, the upper representation being a plot, over the time of the yell, of the normalized envelope of the air pressure waveform and the lower representation being a normalized spectrogram of the yell consisting of a three-dimensional depiction of the frequency content (colors as shown) versus the frequency (vertical axis) over the time of the yell (horizontal axis).*

*Decision of Fourth Board of Appeal of Office for Harmonization in the Internal Market of September 27, 2007 – R 708/2006–4 – Tarzan Yell (Sound Mark).

The application was refused because the graphical representation (in the form of the spectrogram and words) was not sufficiently clear, precise, self-contained, easily accessible, intelligible, durable, and objective (which is the test that was prescribed in an earlier case regarding sound marks).

(Continued)

TARZAN (*Continued*)

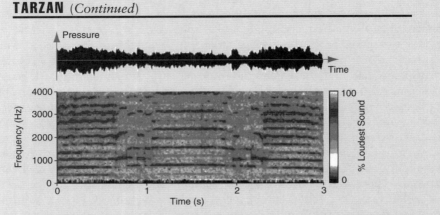

FIGURE 11.1   Tarzan "Yell" as a Community Trade Mark (Sound Mark)
Source: Decision of Fourth Board of Appeal of the Office for Harmonization
in the Internal Market of September 27, 2007 – R 708/2006-4 – Tarzan Yell
(Sound Mark).

Previously, only a musical stave (properly divided into bars and showing
a clef and musical notes) had been accepted as a graphical representation of
a sound mark. However, it is now possible to submit a sound file as part of
an electronic Community Trade Mark application, which should assist those
wishing to register sound marks.

Examples of nonword marks that have been successfully registered in the United
Kingdom include:

- A shape: the Coca-Cola bottle
- A color: like ORANGE, the key brand of France Telecom, one of the world's
  leading telecommunications operators
- A sound: the lion's roar used by MGM Corporation in the opening credits of a
  film
- A smell: the smell of fresh-cut grass, registered as a trademark for tennis balls

The "distinctiveness" element tends to come up where a person is trying to
register a mark that is either generic for the type of goods or services applied for
or that is descriptive of the goods or services applied for. For example, it is very
likely that an application to register "Deluxe Cameras," for high-end photographic
equipment or services, would be rejected, because it is wholly descriptive of the goods
that the registration would cover. You can get over the distinctiveness hurdle, but
only by showing that the mark has acquired distinctiveness through use (which means
that you would have to get your brand out into the market without the benefit of
trademark protection, in order to generate some consumer awareness in your brand
to enable you to gain trademark protection—not an ideal position to be in).

The best trademarks are those that are either invented names, such as "Kodak," or names that are common but have no connection to the relevant goods or services, for example, "Apple" for computers.

Obtaining Trademark Protection

To register a trademark, you need to apply to the trademark registry in the territory in which you are seeking registration. The formalities for registration and the costs of applying to register a trademark vary enormously from country to country, as does the time period from submitting your application to obtaining registration.

The key factors to consider, when deciding on a trademark registration strategy, are:

- *The form of the trademark.* Even putting aside the possibility of sound, smell, and taste marks, there are a number of different ways of registering a word as a trademark:
  - A plain word mark (which provides the broadest protection, since it can then be used in any number of styles, fonts, and the like)
  - A stylized word mark (meaning a word mark in a particular font and script and color, which means that the registered protection is limited to that script and font and color)
  - In logo form (in which case the registration protection is for the overall logo design rather than the word on its own)
- *Geography.* Where do you need to protect your brand? As with most other registered IP rights, trademarks are national rights, which means that you need to register your mark in each country where you need protection. There are a number of supranational systems for registration that allow you to make one application for registration covering a number of different countries, which can reduce the cost of putting together your trademark portfolio. We discuss two of these systems: (1) the Community Trade Mark, which is administered by the European Union and was mentioned earlier; and (2) the International Registration system under the Madrid Agreement and Madrid Protocol. Both of these systems are explained later in this chapter, in the section "Supranational Registration Systems." Whichever route to registration you choose, think about these points when deciding on the territorial reach of your trademark protection:
  - Where are the target markets for your branded product, in terms of both manufacturing base and sales opportunities?
  - If your product is one that is likely to attract counterfeiters, should you also apply to register your trademark in countries where counterfeiting is common?
  - Does your trademark work in different countries? In other words, get local advice as to whether the word that you have chosen as your mark does not have some unintended meaning in a different language.
  - Do you also need to register a translation or transliteration of your mark in certain markets, such as in the Far East or Middle East?
- *Specification.* What products and services do you need your trademark registration to cover? Trademarks are registered for particular classes of goods and services. (There is an international classification system, referred to as the Nice

Classification System [the agreement was concluded in Nice, France] that is used in most countries worldwide.)

- Within each class of goods or services, you can specify both a broad classification (e.g., computer programs in class 9) and a more detailed description of your particular goods or services (e.g., software for online product ordering in class 9), thereby giving you the broadest possible protection.

- Once you have obtained trademark registration, you cannot add new classes of goods or services to that registration; you have to make a new application (and pay a whole new set of application fees). Giving significant thought to the classes of goods and services at the outset can save you substantial sums in the long term, particularly since the costs of adding additional classes to your trademark application are often incremental when compared to the costs of a new application. Your trademark attorney will be able to advise you on the appropriate specification for your application.

- *Clearance searches.* Once you have established where you want to apply to register your mark and for what classes of goods or services, you may wish to carry out a clearance search of the trademark registers in the target countries. A clearance search generally searches the trademark registers for existing identical or similar marks, so that you can get a feel for whether you are likely to face any opposition to your application from third parties before you incur the costs of the applications. The costs of conducting clearance searches depend on the number of registers and classes to be searched but can be significant, so it is advisable to consult a trademark attorney or lawyer before you embark on this.

Why Register a Trademark?

Generally, registration of a trademark lasts for 10 years and is renewable for further 10-year periods on the payment of renewal fees, so, unlike patent registration, trademark protection can last indefinitely.

Registering a trademark has these advantages:

- The registered owner has the right to the exclusive use of the mark in connection with the goods or services for which it is registered.
- The registered owner has the right to sue for trademark infringement any person who uses an identical or similar mark in connection with identical or similar goods without authorization.
- In most jurisdictions, a registered trademark is an asset that can be licensed or assigned or mortgaged.
- There is no requirement to prove reputation or goodwill.
- The trademark register is open to the public; therefore, registration acts as notice to the public of a proprietor's rights in a particular mark and so has a deterrent effect.

When to Register a Trademark?

In most jurisdictions, you do not have to be using a mark in order to apply for registration—it is enough that you have a good faith intention to use it in the course of trade. Therefore, the best time to apply for registration is at the development stage of a new product and certainly prior to its launch. This ensures not only that the application is well on its way to registration by the time the product is on the market but also preempts any third party that applies for the same or similar mark, since the pending application can be cited against any such subsequent application.

Application Process

The application process is broadly the same wherever you apply to register a trademark. What will vary is the time that it takes to get through the application process. In the United Kingdom, it is possible to obtain registration of a mark in six to nine months, whereas in India, the time frame is more likely to be three years or more. The three main stages of the application process are:

1. *Examination.* The trademark registry considers whether the mark is capable of registration (depending on the registration criteria under that country's trademark laws). The trademark examiner may raise objections at this stage, in respect of which the applicant will have an opportunity to make representations. If the objections are not overcome, the application will be rejected. If no objections are raised or the objections are overcome, the mark will proceed to publication.
2. *Publication.* The trademark is advertised to allow third parties an opportunity to oppose the application (e.g., if they have an earlier conflicting registration). The opposition process varies from country to country in terms of formalities, timing, and cost. In the United Kingdom and under the CTM system, marks are advertised in the official *Trade Marks Journal* for three months for opposition purposes. In the United States, the period is 30 days from the date of publication in the *Official Gazette*.
3. *Registration.* The mark is formally registered and the registration certificate issued. In some countries, you have to pay a fee at this stage to obtain registration. In the United States, you must file an affidavit of use for a trademark registration to be valid: (1) between the 5th and 6th year following registration (extensions of time are possible if you cannot yet show evidence of use in the United States) and (2) within the year before the end of the 10-year period after registration.

Supranational Registration Systems

In this section, we describe the trademark registration systems for the European Union (administered in Alicante, Spain), followed by the International Registration system (administered in Geneva, Switzerland).

Community Trade Mark   A Community Trade Mark registration provides protection in all the member states of the European Union (currently 27). The CTM system is administered by the Office for Harmonization in the Internal Market (OHIM), based in Alicante, Spain. The application process is very straightforward—a single application (which can be submitted to a local office in one of the EU member states or directly to OHIM, and can be filed electronically, for expediency) and single point of administration. This means that a CTM application can provide significant costs savings as against making individual applications in target member states. The average time frame from application to registration is approximately 18 months to two years.

The main disadvantage of the CTM system is that a person with an existing registration in just one EU member state can block your application, which means that it would be rejected in its entirety. In this situation, your only remedy would be to convert your application into separate national applications—which would be a costly exercise.

International Registration   The International Registration (IR) system allows you to make a single application and designate the countries in which you seek protection. Your application is then sent to the national trademark registries in each of the designated countries and goes through their national application processes. If your IR applications are successful, you end up with a bundle of national rights. Member countries are signed up to either the Madrid Protocol or the Madrid Agreement (an earlier agreement that predates the Madrid Protocol). Most of the major industrial countries are members of one or the other agreement, but there are a few notable exceptions, such as India and Brazil, that do not belong to either.

The Madrid system (i.e., Madrid Protocol and Madrid Agreement) is administered by the World Intellectual Property Organization (WIPO) in Geneva, Switzerland. To be eligible to apply for an IR, you must be a person domiciled in, or a national of, or having a real and effective commercial establishment in a country that is a party to either the Madrid Protocol or to the Madrid Agreement. You must also have a "home" trademark application or registration (meaning an existing national registration in your home country) on which to base your IR.

Generally, an IR application is cheaper than applying for separate national rights in different Madrid member countries, but this depends on the number of countries designated. Because the applications go through the national systems, the overall process is no quicker than if you made individual national applications, but the administrative burden is less onerous on the applicant.

Enforcing Trademarks

It is the trademark owner's responsibility to protect its trademark rights. The exact nature of what constitutes trademark infringement will vary from country to country, so it is important to get legal advice on your rights in relation to enforcement before you take any action in a particular jurisdiction where you hold a trademark.

In most jurisdictions, including the United Kingdom and the United States, the primary remedy for trademark infringement is an injunction to prevent further infringement, together with some form of financial compensation. In the United Kingdom, the financial relief can take the form of either an award of damages to compensate the claimant for its loss or damage sustained as a result of infringing activities, or an account of profits that the infringer has made from the unlawful activities. One of the benefits of a CTM registration is that you can obtain a pan-European injunction to stop infringing acts.

Unfair Competition and Passing Off

As mentioned, if you do not have a trademark registration, then you cannot sue for trademark infringement but have to rely on the unfair competition law or *passing off* law. Not all countries provide a legal remedy for unauthorized use of unregistered trademarks.

The concept of unfair competition stems from the Paris Convention Article 10 *bis* of the 1883 Paris Convention for the Protection of Industrial Property, which provides that:

> *The countries of the union are bound to assure to nationals of such countries effective protection against unfair competition.*

A number of countries, including the United States and certain countries in Europe, such as France and Germany, have developed a general *tort* of unfair competition, designed to protect against acts of competition that are contrary to honest commercial practices. (A *tort* is a wrongful act for which someone can be sued for damages in a civil court.) What constitutes "unfair competition" varies from country to country, so local law advice should be sought before embarking on any legal proceedings. By way of example, unfair competition can cover not only use of an unregistered trademark but false advertising, bait-and-switch selling tactics, trade libel, and false representation of products or services.

The United Kingdom takes a slightly different approach and relies on various causes of action, including the torts of passing off and malicious falsehood, and certain criminal offenses, to comply with the Paris Convention requirements. To succeed in a passing off action, proprietors must show that: (a) they have *goodwill* or reputation in the trademark; (b) the defendant has used the mark without authorization in such a way as amounts to misrepresentation; and (c) they have suffered damage as a result. Passing off actions are often terribly complicated and extremely costly. Because of the requirement to establish reputation, it is very difficult to bring a successful passing off action regarding a new brand, since it is unlikely that the brand would have built up sufficient goodwill. This is why it is strongly advisable to apply to register a trademark before you begin trading under a brand.

CLOSING THOUGHTS

The global trend is toward ever greater harmonization of IP rights, some of which will be achieved under the general auspices of WIPO and TRIPS. However, other countervailing forces, such as bilateral agreements and regional treaties, will slow progress. The nature of national pride and history across so many jurisdictions makes IP harmonization a distant prospect. For now, we must content ourselves with the status quo—an imperfect system of interlocking IP rights subject to international cooperation.

The main point to remember is that for any invention more than one IP right may be able to protect it. The inventor, innovator, and high-tech entrepreneur all need to be aware of *what these rights are* and understand, in the simplest terms, *what they protect*, so that, when relevant, those rights requiring registration can be applied for on a timely basis. Cost of registration will always be a factor. A coherent IP rights strategy needs to be worked out, as early as possible, so that available funding is put to the most effective use. The IP strategy needs to cover not only what rights may be best but also territorially *where* they are needed from a commercial and strategic perspective.

CHAPTER TAKEAWAYS

- If there is a possibility that you can patent your invention or innovation, you must be very careful when it comes to disclosing or publishing details of it (even under a nondisclosure agreement). In most countries, if an invention has been published, it cannot be patented. The United States is an exception to this general rule.
- Make sure that you have your house in order, to make it easier for you and others when identifying, protecting, and exploiting your intellectual property. Keep accurate records during development stages and think about who is involved in the development of the invention and who is ultimately going to own the rights. Get written agreements in place for any type of collaborative project, setting out who owns what in terms of the IP.
- Be creative when it comes to putting together your IP portfolio. Patents are not the only means of protecting what you have created. Invest in specialist advice from various types of IP experts at the earliest possible stage. The most successful innovations in recent years are protected by a mixture of registered and unregistered rights.
- Inevitably, there will be a conflict between putting money into protecting your rights in your innovation and putting that money toward promoting or selling the innovation to generate much-needed revenue. However, you will increase your chances of attracting investment and the price you can put on that investment if you can show that the IP in your innovation is soundly protected.
- *On copyright.* If your innovation attracts copyright protection, then it will arise automatically, without you having to do anything. Check, however, if you need to register your copyright in a particular country in order to be able to enforce it (e.g., in the United States). Before you publish your copyright work in another country, check whether that country gives reciprocal copyright protection.
- *On designs.* Where possible, think about registering your designs (e.g., as a design patent in the United States or as a Community Registered Design in the European Union), so that you do not have to show copying for infringement purposes, as you would do with an unregistered design.
- *On know-how and trade secrets.* The value of know-how or trade secrets lies in it being unknown to the public. Put in place suitably robust procedures and practices for keeping your trade secrets confidential. If you must share trade secrets, make sure that you have a confidentiality or nondisclosure agreement in place (see Chapters 9, 14, and 16 for more on confidentiality agreements, know-how transfer, and due diligence processes).
- *On trademarks.* Think carefully not only about what form your trademark should take but where you want to apply to register it and what products

or services you need the trademark to cover. Take advantage, where possible, of supranational trademark systems that allow you to file one application for registration which covers a number of different countries.

- *On further supplements to this chapter.* Log onto our web site at www.innovationtocashflows.com to locate these files:
  - Appendix 11.1, "International Intellectual Property Treaties and Conventions"
  - Appendix 11.2, "Comparison of Design Right and Registered Design"

CHAPTER 12

The Basics about Patents

Tom Brand
W.P. Thompson & Co.

This chapter provides a basic grounding in the principles and mechanisms by which inventions may be protected. We begin with some brief history and an introduction to what patents are and how they are used. The principal international treaties concerning patents are introduced, and the basic mechanisms by which patents are filed, prosecuted, and granted in the major jurisdictions of Europe and the United States are explained, with some reference also to the International Patents filing system, which commonly prefaces the filing of patents in individual territories. Finally, some major trends in global patenting activity are summarized, with some statistical background concerning the world's major patent offices.

PATENT FACTS

The grant of a patent gives the proprietor a monopoly to work the invention as defined in the patent, to the exclusion of others. The *patentee* is the person or enterprise to whom the patent is issued. It is important to appreciate the difference between the exclusive right afforded by a patent and the patentee's commercial freedom to use the technology identified in the patent.

The *exclusive right* granted to the patentee is exactly that—the right to exclude others from the claimed technology. Importantly, the grant of a patent gives absolutely no right to the patentee to do anything with that technology. Rather, the patentee's commercial freedom (freedom to use) is determined by the relationship between the technology in question and third-party patents pertaining to the same technology domain. (There may, of course, be other factors affecting commercial freedom, such as contractual issues, unfair competition, or illegality.) Thus, it is perfectly possible for a patentee to own a valid patent for a new technology but to be prevented from using the technology because to do so would infringe the rights of others.

Example of Freedom to Use

Consider this example. If I invent a novel form of mechanical propulsion having two wheels and a chain, I can have a patent for my bicycle invention. My patent claims "a two-wheeled vehicle." My neighbor then sees my successful invention and, having a competitive edge, decides to improve on it by adding an engine. My neighbor obtains a perfectly valid patent on the motorbike: "a two-wheeled vehicle with an engine."

Now, I am free to make and sell bicycles, because there are no third-party patents that would prevent me from doing so. I am not, however, free to sell motorbikes, because to do so would infringe my neighbor's patent. Note that this is the case even though my patent claim—to "a two-wheeled vehicle"—includes motorbikes.

My neighbor is not entitled to make or sell bicycles, because to do so would infringe my patent. But neither can she make or sell motorbikes—because to do so would also infringe my patent.

In fact, neither of us can make or sell motorbikes. The only way for a would-be biker to get his hands on the new technology would be to persuade me and my neighbor to grant each other a cross-license on our respective patents as far as motorbikes are concerned. Licensing agreements are covered in further detail in Chapter 14.

This exclusive right of a patent is essentially granted as a contract between the state and the inventor who gains temporary protection, generally for 20 years, in reward for disclosure of the new invention. In this way, the patent system is believed to promote research and development by encouraging the inventor to disclose ideas rather than keep them secret.[1] This is the classic quid pro quo bargain between the inventor and the state. A patent is a territorial creature and (generally speaking) is enforceable only within the borders of the nation-state which granted the patent.

Although 20 years (from the filing date) is the typical life of a patent, it is important to appreciate that there are individual differences in national legal systems and the 20-year term is by no means universal, although it is by far the most common. Also, in certain areas of technology, particularly in the pharmaceutical industry, it is possible to extend a patent term by as much as five years. Such patent term extension recognizes that many years of research and clinical trials generally are needed before a patented drug can come to market and, because of the need to file a patent before any publicly available research is conducted (e.g., in clinic), the original 20-year patent term is often significantly eroded during this time.

Patents are crucial commercial tools in many different kinds of industry. Although high-tech industries clearly need to use patents to protect their innovations, the importance of patents in general and in simple mechanical fields is well exemplified by the case of Ron Hickman, the inventor of the Workmate®, a mechanically simple but ingenious work station for carpenters and other artisans. Hickman came up with the idea for the Workmate® when he accidentally sawed through the leg of a chair. He initially sold the product (the Workmate®, not the three-legged chair) to do-it-yourself enthusiasts by mail order. After he had sold over 10,000, Black & Decker offered to license his patent at £1 for each Workmate® they sold. It sold 25 million worldwide.[2]

History of Patents around the World

It is difficult to say who was awarded the first patent, and the origins of the early patent systems are uncertain. The British lay claim to the longest continuous patent system in the world, with the earliest known patent granted by King Henry VI to John of Utynam in 1449 for a method of making stained glass used in the windows of Eton College.[3] The Venetians, with a Statute of 1474,[4] issued a decree protecting new and inventive devices and methods against potential infringers, provided that they had been put into practice and communicated to the state by letters patent. However, there is also strong evidence to suggest that the ancient Greeks operated what could be considered a patent system.[5]

In England, Tudor monarchs used the patent system as a means for generating income. They granted monopolies for particular commodities, such as salt, and the system became increasingly subject to abuse. It was not uncommon for patents to be granted for inventions and trades that were not new. Often patents were granted to anyone willing to pay for the privilege, and in some instances patents were granted to allies of the royal household. In 1623 the Statute of Monopolies was passed to protect the public from such abuse by providing monopolies "for the term of 14 years or under...to be made of the sole working or making of any manner of new manufacturers within this Realm to the true and first inventor."[6] So the concept of novelty, still in use today, was enshrined in law.

Over the years, various improvements were made to the system. These include the requirement of a written specification describing how to put the invention into effect. This requirement is present today, and drafting patent specifications to disclose the invention fully is an important consideration, as a Mr. Arkwright of Bolton, Lancashire, found out in 1785. Arkwright was a barber who, fueled by the spirit of the industrial age, left his business and nagging wife to pursue his interest in inventing. His patent for a water-powered spinning machine was, however, found "invalid for want of detail."[7] The requirement that a patent specification clearly and completely disclose the invention in sufficient detail for it to be reproduced (without inventive effort) by a person skilled in the relevant art is known in modern legal terminology as sufficiency, and the stipulation that a patent specification be "sufficient" is one of the key requirements for patentability.

It was during the industrial revolution that foundations were laid for the colonial patent systems in the United States, New Zealand, and Australia, to protect the interests of industrialists who were willing to invest in the New World. Further developments included the introduction of the Paris Convention for the Protection of Industrial Property in 1883 and novelty searches (to check that the invention had not already been made) in 1902.

The Patent Commission of the United States was created in 1790, and the first U.S. patent was granted to Samuel Hopkins of Philadelphia for a method of producing potash, used for making soap, glass, and gunpowder. Today the United States stands in the vanguard of the world's most successful patent systems.

In Europe, a major development in the process of obtaining a patent was the introduction in 1973 of a multilateral system for granting patents known as the European Patent Convention (EPC) controlled by the European Patent Office (EPO). The EPC provides a single procedure that leads to the grant of a patent in each state that the applicant has chosen. (As of January 1, 2009, there are 35 member states.)

Novelty and Inventive Step

We have touched already on "sufficiency" as being a key requirement of a patent specification. This is, however, only one of three key requirements. Under the EPC (and for that matter, most other patent systems), an invention is considered patentable if it is novel and involves an inventive step.[8]

In addition to these basic requirements, there are also a number of exceptions in Europe for which patents will not generally be granted. The most important exceptions are:

- Business methods
- Methods of medical treatment and diagnosis
- Computer programs[9]

Patents in Europe are considered to be essentially technical in character—that is to say, the invention must relate to something tangible in a technical sense. A business method is considered to be essentially non-technical in character and cannot straightforwardly be patented in Europe. For example, if I devise a system for making money in the stock market by short selling the stock of companies that I predict will go down in value, that is essentially a mental act, an intangible intellectual exercise, albeit with possibly complicated rules for identifying those companies ripe for short selling. There is nothing technical about it, and even if it were a novel and inventive application of intellectual skill, it would not be patentable in Europe.

Computer programs traditionally have been treated as copyright works, and as such are considered outside the scope of the patents system in Europe.

It should, however, be stressed that in Europe, computer programs can be patented if they can be tied into some technical effect. A computer program that serves to operate a piece of machinery in an improved manner would, for example, be considered as an invention with a technical character. The same would apply to a business method, if one or more novel technical steps were required to operate the method in question.

Novelty will arise if there are differences between the invention and what is known at the *priority date* (either the date of filing the application or the date of an earlier "priority" application). An invention is not considered novel if it has been made available to the public anywhere in the world, either by use or by oral or written disclosure, prior to making an application. For example, an invention will not be novel if it was disclosed in an obscure Peruvian journal, filed deep in a public library in Lima.

Earlier disclosures are known as *prior art*, and the requirement of novelty is absolute. If the subject matter of an invention is already disclosed in the prior art, then that invention cannot be patented, and a patent application for the invention should fail. If the art in question is not known to the *examiner* at the time of the application, then, no matter, the patent is still invalid because the art is sitting there waiting to be found. Provided the art does indeed disclose the full subject matter of the invention, and provided the art was published before the priority date of the invention, anyone who finds the art can successfully challenge the patent.

The relationship between the subject matter of the invention and the closest prior art is determined by the claims of the patent. We have already discussed the fact that a patent must contain a description of the invention sufficient to disclose it to the skilled person. That is one-half of the quid pro quo bargain between the inventor and the state. The other half is that the inventor obtains (once the patent is granted) an exclusive monopoly right over the invention for a limited time period. The *scope* of that monopoly right is determined by the claims of the patent. The job of the claims is to define the invention as broadly as reasonably possible while not encompassing the prior art.

To be novel, an invention must contain at least one feature that is not unambiguously disclosed in a single prior art document (or other type of disclosure, e.g., public use or sale). Although it is quite possible for disagreements to arise as to whether an invention is novel, essentially the question is one of fact. Any disagreement about that fact arises from different interpretations of the prior art or the claimed invention, or both.

Inventive step is a more subjective topic. Inventive step arises if, when the prior art (as a whole, not just a single piece of it) is considered, the invention would not be considered obvious to a *person skilled in the art*. A person skilled in the art is a fictional unimaginative person who has implied knowledge of all the prior art that is relevant to the invention.

Excluded Inventions

Some inventions, no matter how novel or inventive, are excluded from patentability in any event in some jurisdictions. One such exclusion concerns programs for computers. While the EPO considers that inventions solely directed to such computers are not patentable, it is possible to circumvent this exclusion provided the program shows *technical character or technical effect*. A program would be considered to have technical character if, when run on a computer, it made the computer run faster or more efficiently in a novel and inventive way or controlled apparatus, equipment, or machinery associated with the computer in a manner that created some beneficial enhancement of the performance of such associated kit. If the program simply allowed the formatting of data and no more, this would not be considered to have technical character.

Methods of treatment (and diagnosis) are considered unpatentable in Europe primarily for the reason that the progenitors of European patent law considered that medics should be free to exercise their professional skills without fear of infringing patents in the process. However, it is possible to patent the use of a particular product in a method of treatment or diagnosis.

In contrast to these European exclusions, a U.S. patent will be granted to anyone who "invents or discovers any new and useful process, machine, manufacture, or composition."[10] The U.S. patent system does not place any statutory restrictions on software patents or methods of medical treatment. However, patents based on mere ideas or suggestions are excluded. In common with Europe, U.S. patents must be new and non-obvious (in other words, involve novelty and an inventive step).

FILING PATENTS—OVERVIEW OF INTERNATIONAL PATENT TREATIES

In Chapter 11 we briefly mentioned the main international patent treaties. (Refer to Appendix 11.1, especially see Table 11A1.1.) This section provides in-depth information and background on the most important patent agreements and treaties.

Paris Convention for the Protection of Industrial Property (1883)[11]

An important step in the development of worldwide patent systems was the introduction of the Paris Convention,[12] one of the first international intellectual property treaties. As a result of this treaty, patents of any contracting state are accessible to the nationals of the 173 states party to the Convention. The Paris Convention also provides that an applicant from one of the contracting states shall be able to use its first filing date as the effective filing date in another contracting state, provided that he files another application within 12 months from filing the initial application. This 12-month period can provide valuable time to assess a particular foreign market before embarking on investment. While the Paris Convention facilitates the filing of patents in multiple countries, it is essentially a procedural tool because it does not address each state's substantive laws relating to patents granted by each state. Therefore, what may be patentable in the United States will not necessarily be patentable in Europe, as applicants must comply with the various formal and substantive legal requirements in each of the states of interest. Furthermore, the United States operates a system whereby the patent will be granted to the person who first made the invention, whereas in Europe, generally the patent will be granted to the person who first files the application.

Thus, while it does not regulate any aspect of the examination procedure, the Paris Convention does establish two important rights: Foreign applicants must have the same rights as nationals, and the very important right of priority. As mentioned, an applicant who has filed a patent application in any country that is a member to the Paris Convention can, within one year after that filing, file patent applications in other countries, claiming the filing date of the first application as the effective filing date of the later applications. This way, the applicant has up to one year to decide in which countries to apply for patent protection and to make the necessary preparations (e.g., translating the application into the official languages of those countries) for doing so.

When the priority date of an earlier application is claimed, the filing date of the earlier application is regarded as the filing date of the later application when doing the novelty search. This means that only publications that exist before the filing date of the earlier application are considered. This allows an applicant to, for example, file a patent application quickly in one country, then publish the invention in a journal or show it at an exhibition, and then within 12 months of the first application file further patent applications in other countries with the benefit of the earlier priority date. The publication or presentation at the exhibition will not be damaging for the patent application, in terms of novelty, even though it completely describes the invention and was published before the filing date of those later applications.

An additional advantage of filing an application while claiming the filing date of another application is that in most countries, the patent term is determined from the actual filing date in that country. This means that this term is effectively shifted one year into the future, although patent protection lasts 20 years from the later date of filing.

You will commonly hear your professional advisor talk of the *priority date*, the very first date of filing under the Paris Convention. A patent may have more than one priority date because it is possible, during the first year after the very first filing, to file further priority applications in relation to modifications or improvements on the original disclosure. It is, however, important to bear in mind that an earlier priority date for a particular patent can be "lost" if, for example, the patent as eventually completed claims something that is not also clearly claimed or disclosed in the relevant priority application. For this reason, it is extremely important to allocate sufficient resources to the priority filing, insuring that the filing is made professionally and with as much affirming or experimental data as can be managed. It is also extremely useful to conduct a thorough search at this stage to identify the relevant art and establish the framework in which your invention can be claimed. "Do-it-yourself" priority applications, filed by individual inventors without professional help, for example, only rarely contain adequate wording in the description to support the claims that may eventually be granted once they have been examined. The best priority applications exhibit teamwork—with the inventor(s) contributing heavily toward the description and examples, but with the patent lawyer directing the claims and statements of advantage and invention, albeit with technical guidance from the inventor(s).

Patent Cooperation Treaty (1970)

In an attempt to harmonize international patent law, the Patent Cooperation Treaty (PCT) was concluded in 1970. The PCT, administered by World Intellectual Property Organization (WIPO), makes it possible to apply for patent protection simultaneously in each of the contracting states by filing a single international application rather than filing individual applications in each state. (As of October 2008, there are 139 contracting states.) However, eventually, the application will have to be divided into individual national applications for each state, and each application will have to meet the substantive laws of each state in order to obtain a granted patent.

The PCT attempts to harmonize process through the evaluation of novelty and inventive step (or patentability) made by the PCT governing body. It was thought this would lead to more uniform results in connection with the patentability of inventions in each country. Although individual countries are not bound by the determination made during the PCT process, a positive PCT decision on patentability is often persuasive evidence in a national patent office. While what is patentable in one country is not necessarily patentable in another, broadly speaking, it should be possible to obtain a similar scope of patent in multiple jurisdictions. However, there are exceptions, sometimes because of individual differences in national laws, sometimes because of subjective differences of opinion between patent examiners in different jurisdictions, and sometimes because different art can form the basis of prosecution in different countries. While broadly speaking the arguments should be the same or at least similar, often they are not.

An important concept to bear in mind here is that a good patent, almost by definition, seeks to push the boundaries of its scope right up to the edge of what is possible, so that it nudges right up against, but does not impinge on, the prior art. Any narrower and the patent is weaker than it could be. Any broader, and the patent risks encompassing the art and thereby being invalid. It is because the patent treads this very thin line at the boundary that prosecution arguments, and individual differences in prosecution arguments, are often to be had.

The major advantage of the PCT system is that it buys an applicant time and defers the costs of filing individual national applications for up to 18 months, over the 12-month priority period. This allows applicants a chance to consider the patentability of their invention, based on search results obtained in the PCT process, and provides time to assess the commercial importance of their invention.

Even with the benefit of the priority system as provided by the Paris Convention, obtaining patent protection in 25 countries still means having to start 25 separate national procedures. Although there is no system for a single unified patent covering multiple countries, the PCT makes it possible to start the process of seeking patent protection for an invention simultaneously in each of a large number of countries by filing a single "international" patent application.

There are other important advantages of filing a PCT application rather than filing one or more separate national applications. Arguably the most significant advantage is that a PCT application defers the costs associated with prosecuting applications. This gives the applicant more time to assess the value of the claimed invention and the potential markets before incurring the large costs of foreign prosecution of the application.

Of course, there are also disadvantages to a PCT application. Since with a single international application the applicant has all his eggs in one basket, therefore if the *search report* or the *International Preliminary Report on Patentability* (IPRP) (also known as the International Preliminary Examination Report [IPER]) is negative, this may result in difficulties and added cost in the national phase (meaning subsequent prosecution of the application before individual national patent offices). However, this problem can often be alleviated by filing arguments or amendments, or both, in the international phase in response to the search report and filing a demand for examination. Also, the overall cost can be higher than making separate national filings at the outset if the applicant decides to proceed in all designated counties, although these costs are deferred.

European Patent Convention (1973)

The European Patent Convention (EPC) goes even beyond what the PCT establishes. An applicant can file a single European Patent Application and designate the countries in Europe in which she wants to have patent protection. The EPO performs a novelty search and prepares a search report. Using this search report, the Examining Division (three examiners) then determines the patentability of the invention. The procedure is comparable to the national procedure, except in that it has only to be performed once regardless of how many European countries were designated.

If the Examining Division decides that the invention is patentable, the EPO grants a European patent. This is a slightly misleading name, since it does not grant any traditional patent rights. Rather, it grants the applicant, in the countries she designated, the same rights as would have been granted in the case of a national application. A European patent is therefore sometimes referred to as a bundle of rights.

Despite the name, the EPO is not an organization within the European Union. Non-EU members are also party to the EPC.

Once a European Patent has been granted, anyone has the right to oppose it within nine months after the grant. If the patent is then found to be invalid, it is revoked in all countries simultaneously. After these nine months, the patent can only be revoked separately for each country in which it was granted. This is substantially more expensive and time-consuming for the opponent.

The EPO, however, is not the final authority on patent matters in Europe. A European patent effectively grants its owner national patents in every country that is party to the EPO (or those countries the owner designated). Issues of validity and infringement must be dealt with according to the national patent law in each country.

In particular, a European patent can be declared invalid by a court in one country only for that country. This means that someone wanting to invalidate a European patent that was granted in 18 countries must start 18 separate court proceedings. Of course, once the first few proceedings are won, the rest should be relatively simple and may not even be necessary, since the patent owner will be unlikely to actually enforce the patent after that.

Europe does not have an equivalent of the U.S. Court of Appeals for the Federal Circuit, which means that, in principle, every country can rule differently on patent matters. There are some restrictions. However, Article 69 of the EPC gives a basic principle on determination of the scope of the monopoly right and the way in which it should be interpreted.

Budapest Treaty on the International Recognition of the Deposit of Microorganisms for the Purposes of Patent Procedure (1980)

In order to meet the legal requirement of sufficiency of disclosure, patent applications must disclose in their description the subject matter of the invention in a manner sufficiently clear and complete to be carried out by the person skilled in the art. When an invention involves a microorganism—for example, the Chakrabarty patent, which discloses a human-made microorganism—completely describing the invention in a written form in a way that enables third parties to carry it out is usually impossible. This is why, in the particular case of inventions involving microorganisms, including, for example, human or animal cell lines, a deposit of biological material must be made in a recognized institution. The Budapest Treaty reduces the problem of depositing multiple samples of the biological material by allowing the applicant to deposit the biological material at one recognized institution, and this deposit will be recognized in all countries party to the Budapest Treaty.

Agreement on Trade-Related Aspects of Intellectual Property Rights (1994)

The protection and enforcement of intellectual property rights traditionally has been controlled by the particular laws of each country individually. As such, these rights could vary greatly between countries. As intellectual property became more important in trade, particularly worldwide trade, these differences became a source of tension in international economic relations. New internationally agreed trade rules for intellectual property rights were seen as a way to introduce more order and predictability, and for disputes to be settled more systematically. The World Trade Organization's (WTO's) Trade-Related Aspects of Intellectual Property Rights

(TRIPS) agreement is an attempt to narrow the gaps in the way these rights are protected around the world and to bring them under common international rules.[13] It establishes minimum levels of protection that each government has to give to the intellectual property of fellow WTO members. Virtually all industrialized nations have signed up to the TRIPS agreement.

Patent Law Treaty (2000)

While the TRIPS agreement covers standards concerning the availability of patents (and other intellectual property rights), the Patent Law Treaty (PLT) aims to regulate formality requirements relating to patent applications and patents, thereby streamlining the procedures for obtaining and maintaining a patent.[14] The PLT provides maximum sets of requirements that the office of a contracting party could apply. This means that a contracting party is free to provide for requirements that are more generous from the viewpoint of applicants and owners. The provisions of the PLT apply to national and regional patent applications and patents as well as to international applications under the PCT once they have entered the "national phase."

PATENT APPLICATION PROCESSES

In this section, we describe the patent application processes under the Patent Cooperation Treaty (PCT), the European Patent Convention (EPC), and the U.S. Patent and Trademark Office (USPTO).

Patent Cooperation Treaty

Figure 12.1 is a flow diagram illustrating the PCT procedure and the approximate time scales involved.

A PCT application is always based on an earlier national application, which typically would be filed in the country in which the applicant resides. Using the right to priority, the PCT application can be filed at any time within 12 months of the filing of the first national application. It is common practice to delay the filing of the PCT application until the end of the 12-month priority period, primarily to delay costs and allow the applicant to have a better idea of the potential markets for the invention worldwide so that adequate protection can be obtained. It should also be remembered that multiple priority applications may be filed during the first 12 months and that if ongoing research is continuing after the first filing, it is likely that at some stage further priority applications will need to be considered.

The PCT application can be filed directly with the International Bureau, a division of the World Intellectual Property Organization in Geneva, Switzerland, which receives the patent application and checks that it meets the formal requirements. Alternatively the PCT application may be filed through a receiving office, generally in the applicant's state of residence or nationality. The receiving office will ensure the international application complies with the minimum and formal requirements. One of the major patent offices in the world is then appointed as the International Search

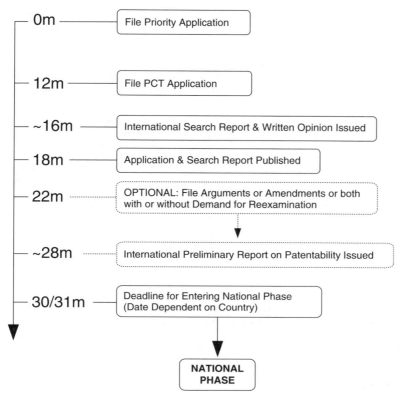

FIGURE 12.1 Patent Cooperation Treaty (PCT) Procedure
Source: WIPO Patent Report, 2007 edition, www.wipo.int/ipstats/en/statistics/patents/patent_report_2007.html#P745_41736.

Authority (ISA) and performs the literature search and draws up a written opinion on the patentability of the application. Usually this is the U.S. Patent and Trademark Office (USPTO), the European Patent Office (EPO), or the Japanese Patent Office (JPO). WIPO also publishes the patent application 18 months after filing along with the search report if issued in time, although the written opinion is never published.

Depending on the outcome of the search report and the written opinion, the applicant has several options on how to proceed. If the applicant wishes to amend the claims at this stage for any reason—for example, one or more objections were raised in the written opinion—then a request for examination (known technically as a demand) can be made along with the appropriate arguments and amendments within 22 months of the priority date (or three months from the date of transmittal of the search report, if later). If a demand is filed, then the application will be reexamined and an international preliminary examination report will be issued, normally about 28 months after the priority date.

However, if the written opinion is generally favorable, then the applicant may decide that there is no need to file arguments or amendments at this stage or both.

If this is the case, then the written opinion will be used as the international report on patentability. The applicant has the option of filing informal comments on the written opinion, which will be sent to the designated national offices the applicant elects to continue the procedure to the national phase.

The application and the international preliminary examination report are sent to the designated national offices within the prescribed time limit governed by each designated state. This is typically 30 or 31 months, although because the procedure has changed significantly in the past few years, a few member countries have yet to update their patent laws; therefore, if no demand is filed, then the national phase must be entered within 20 months of priority in these countries.

Upon receiving a national phase PCT application, the national offices immediately start with the examination, often using the search report drawn up by the International Bureau as a basis. This means that the applicant does not need to have a separate search performed at every national office, which is a substantial saving in costs (although national offices are free to do their own searches from scratch, or perform a supplementary search, which of course still costs money). However, the applicant must still convince each examiner in every country designated that the invention is patentable in light of the state of the art as described in the search report. The examiner, of course, applies his or her country's national standards for patentability, although commonly the preliminary written opinion or international report on patentability (obtained during the unified international stage of the procedure) will serve as the basis, sometimes the sole basis, for the examination. Hence, an applicant who has been able to obtain a favorable report during the international stage may reap a benefit in costs down the line by reducing the amount of prosecution in the individual national stages. If an application is to be filed in a large number of countries, the cost saving can be appreciable.

European Patent Convention

Figure 12.2 is a flow diagram illustrating the EPC procedure for an application claiming priority from a national application and the approximate timescales involved.

As with a PCT application, a European application can be filed at any time within 12 months of the first national filing for the same invention. It is not necessary to claim priority from an earlier application so the European application can be the first filing if desired. When an application is filed at the 12-month stage, it is commonly known as a *convention application*, as opposed to a *national phase application*, which results from a PCT case. In principle, there is no reason why, at the 12-month stage, an applicant cannot file both a PCT application and a number of convention applications. (It will, of course, be necessary to do this in the event that protection is sought in non-PCT contracting states, of which there are many in, for example, the Middle East, South America, and Africa.) There is also nothing to stop an applicant pursuing protection for an invention in, say, Europe and the United States by filing convention applications in those jurisdictions at the 12-month stage and then filing national phase applications 18 months later (in other words, 30 months after the priority date). Ultimately, patent offices will not allow two patents to coexist for the same invention, but if the claims of the applications are handled in different ways (e.g., amended differently), this prohibition may be avoided.

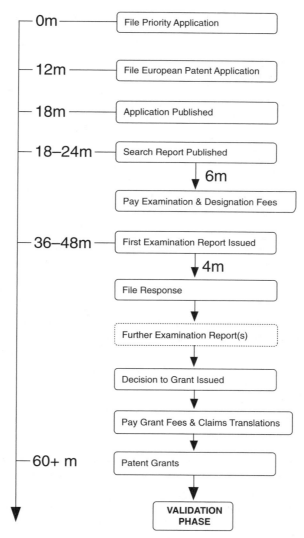

0m ——— File Priority Application

12m ——— File European Patent Application

18m ——— Application Published

18–24m ——— Search Report Published

↓ **6m**

Pay Examination & Designation Fees

36–48m ——— First Examination Report Issued

↓ **4m**

File Response

Further Examination Report(s)

Decision to Grant Issued

Pay Grant Fees & Claims Translations

60+ m ——— Patent Grants

VALIDATION PHASE

FIGURE 12.2 European Patent Convention Procedure
Source: WIPO Patent Report, 2007 edition, www.wipo.int/ipstats/en/statistics/patents/
patent_report_2007.html#P745_41736.

The European Patent Office is an example of a regional office that can be used to extend the jurisdiction of a patent into a number of individual states. There are other regional patent organizations outside of Europe, for example, in the Gulf States, in Eurasia, and in Africa.

The application is published by the EPO 18 months after the priority date, which may include the search report if completed in time. Often the search report is not completed at this stage, particularly if priority is claimed, and so the search report may be published shortly after the application.

TABLE 12.1   European Patent Convention 1973 Contracting States and Extension States as of January 2009

Code	Member State	Since	Code	Member State	Since
AT	Austria	May 1, 1979	IS	Iceland	November 1, 2004
BE	Belgium	October 7, 1977	IT	Italy	December 1, 1978
BG	Bulgaria	July 1, 2002	LI	Liechtenstein	April 1, 1980
CH	Switzerland	October 7, 1977	LT	Lithuania	December 1, 2004
CY	Cyprus	April 1, 1998	LU	Luxembourg	October 7, 1977
CZ	Czech Republic	July 1, 2002	LV	Latvia	July 1, 2005
DE	Germany	October 7, 1977	MC	Monaco	December 1, 1991
DK	Denmark	January 1, 1990	MT	Malta	March 1, 2007
EE	Estonia	July 1, 2002	NL	Netherlands	October 7, 1977
ES	Spain	October 1, 1986	NO	Norway	January 1, 2008
FI	Finland	March 1, 1996	PL	Poland	March 1, 2004
FR	France	October 7, 1977	PT	Portugal	January 1, 1992
GB	United Kingdom	October 7, 1977	RO	Romania	March 1, 2003
GR	Greece	October 1, 1986	SE	Sweden	May 1, 1978
HR	Croatia	January 1, 2008	SI	Slovenia	December 1, 2002
HU	Hungary	January 1, 2003	SK	Slovakia	July 1, 2002
IE	Ireland	August 1, 1992	TR	Turkey	November 1, 2000
			MK	the Former Yugoslav Republic of Macedonia	January 1, 2009

Extension States
AL	Albania
BA	Bosnia and Herzegovina
RS	Serbia

Source: www.epo.org/about-us/epo/member-states.html and www.wpt.co.uk/news/view.jsp?ref=74.

The publication of the search report sets a six-month deadline for paying the examination fee and the designation fees. Beginning April 2009, payment of a single designation fee is effective to designate all 35 contracting states.

There are also three "extension states" that can be designated. These countries are not members of the EPC but do recognize a European patent. (Refer to Table 12.1.)

After the examination fee is paid, an EPO examiner will, at some point, examine the application. The time scale for receiving the first examination report varies from six months after the examination fee is paid to over two years, depending on the complexity and technical field of the invention. A response is normally due to the examination report within four months of its completion. Although theoretically an examiner need only issue one examination report before refusing the application, in practice two, three, or even four written reports are issued in response to the arguments and amendments made, which means that this process can often take several years. If the examiner concludes that the invention is not patentable despite any arguments and amendments made, then he or she has the option of calling for oral proceedings. This is a face-to-face meeting with the Examining Division (consisting of three examiners) with the aim of overcoming all of the outstanding objections to the satisfaction of both the examiner and the applicant.

Once the examiner is satisfied that any objections have been overcome, he or she issues a decision to grant the application. This sets a deadline for checking any amendments made by the examiner, translating the claims into all three official languages (English, German, French) and paying the grant fees.

After the grant fees have been paid, the patent is granted. However, it must then be validated in each designated European country for which protection is sought. Typically the validation process involves translating the full patent text into each country's official language and authorizing a local agent to represent the patentee in that country. The so-called London Agreement, which came into force on May 1, 2008, reduced certain costs associated with the validation procedure, as not all countries now require a full translation of the text.

A European patent is in fact a collection of national patents with a centralized examining procedure. Therefore, once a patent is validated in each country, it essentially becomes a national patent (which means that any party who wanted to challenge the patent would have to do so in every country individually).

However, within nine months of the grant, a European patent can be opposed centrally at the EPO. If the opposition is successful, then it will have the same effect in each country in which the patent is validated. Having to challenge a patent in each European country individually is often prohibitively expensive so this opposition period can be an important stage in the life of a patent.

The procedure is slightly different if the European application derives from a PCT application since the publication and search will have already been carried out during the PCT procedure. However, the basic principles and order of the procedure remain the same.

U.S. Patent and Trademark Office

Figure 12.3 is a flow diagram illustrating the U.S. patent procedure for a typical new filing and the approximate time scales involved.

The current U.S. patent laws are somewhat different from those of most European countries. One of these differences is the distinction between a provisional patent application and a nonprovisional application. Typically for new inventions in the United States, an applicant will file a provisional patent application as soon as sufficient written documentation on the new invention has been prepared. A provisional application allows filing without any formal patent claims, oath, or declaration, or any information disclosure statement. Its purpose is to provide the means to establish an early effective filing date in a nonprovisional patent application. It also allows the term *patent pending* to be applied to articles made according to the invention.

A provisional patent application can never be granted and has a life span of only one year. Therefore, in order to obtain a patent, the applicant must file a corresponding nonprovisional patent application (officially referred to as a *utility patent*) within 12 months of filing the provisional application. The nonprovisional application must contain all the essential elements of a patent application, including at least

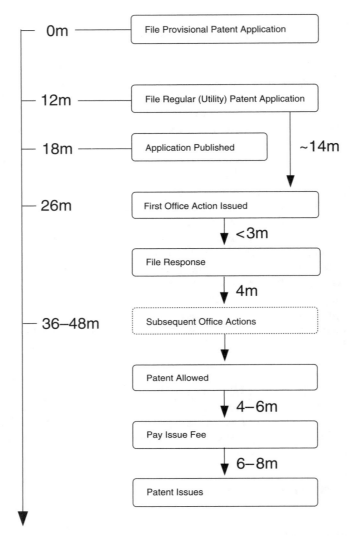

FIGURE 12.3 U.S. Patent and Trademark Office Patent Procedure
Source: WIPO Patent Report, 2007 edition, www.wipo.int/ipstats/en/statistics/patents/
patent_report_2007.html#P745_41736.

one claim. Although provisional applications are commonly used, it is important to
bear in mind that the strongest patents ultimately will result from applications filed
with these key components:

- A clear understanding of the nature and scope of the invention, in particular with
  reference to a thorough knowledge, backed up with recent specialist searching,
  of the prior art and the technical contribution (in other words, advantage or
  improvement made by the invention)

■ Rigorous experimental data or technical exemplification of the invention, preferably demonstrating variety and alternative options with respect to the key component(s) of the invention

■ Professional claim drafting performed with good understanding of the invention and access to experimental data or technical exemplification

Therefore, while a provisional application may in some cases be helpful to speed up a filing or reduce its cost a little, proper focus on these fundamentals should be maintained.

As with nearly all other countries, the patent application is published approximately 18 months after the priority date.

The application will then be examined by the USPTO, and the examiner will issue what is known as the first office action, which is very similar to the examination report issued in Europe. The office action sets out any objections raised by the examiner and sets a period of three months in which the applicant must respond (extendable by three months for a fee). This process is repeated until either all the objections are overcome or the examiner refuses the application, although even if the application is refused, it is possible to file a request for an extended examination to continue to examination procedure.

Once all of the objections are overcome to the satisfaction of the examiner, the patent is deemed allowable. At this stage the applicant must pay the issue fee, and the patent is finally granted six to eight months later.

TRENDS IN GLOBAL PATENTING ACTIVITY

The uptick in global patenting activity mirrors the changes that are under way in current worldwide industrial activity. Very high growth rates in the use of the patent system can be observed in countries in the Far East, particularly Republic of Korea and China. Such growth is not only from patent filings by resident applicants but also from foreign applicants, thus reflecting the increasing integration of these countries into worldwide industrial activity.

Historic Trends in Patent Filings

Figure 12.4 illustrates the number of patent applications filed at nine patent offices from 1883 (date of the signature of the Paris Convention for the Protection of Industrial Property) to 2005.

As can be seen, until 1960, patenting activity was concentrated in four countries—the United States, Germany, the United Kingdom, and France—and growth was very modest.

However, from 1960 onward there was a great expansion in patenting activity, partly due to the emergence of applicants from new states or regions. The chart shows that filings in Japan and Russia, for example, increased noticeably during this period.

Since 1980, the patent offices of the United States followed by the European Patent Office, the Republic of Korea, and China have all experienced significant

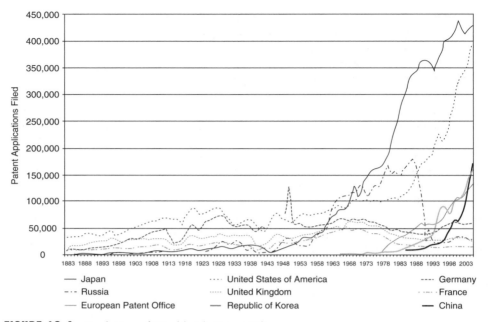

FIGURE 12.4 Evolution of Worldwide Patent Filings
Source: WIPO Patent Report, 2007 edition, www.wipo.int/ipstats/en/statistics/patents/
patent_report_2007.html#P745_41736.

growth rates in filings, while filings at European national offices (Germany, France, and the United Kingdom as shown in Figure 12.4) have declined because the European regional route (via the European Patent Office) became available.

Further, the decline in numbers of Russian applications filed in the late 1980s to early 1990s would seem to correspond with the collapse of the Soviet Union.

Top 20 Offices for Filing Patents

Figure 12.5 shows the Top 20 Offices according to the total number of patents filed in 2005 (the latest data available).

More than three-quarters (77 percent) of all patent applications in 2005 were filed at five offices—the so-called Big Five—the Japan Patent Office, the United States Patent and Trademark Office, the Korean Intellectual Property Office, the State Intellectual Property Office of China, and the European Patent Office. The figure of 77 percent represents an increase of 2 percent over 2004 (75 percent).

With an increase in patent filings of almost 33 percent over the patent filings for 2004, the patent office of China moved up one place to become the third largest recipient of patent filings in 2005.

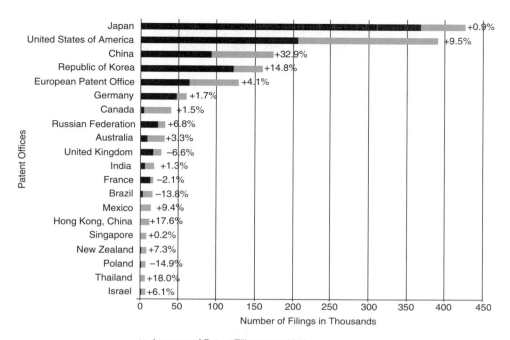

FIGURE 12.5 Top 20 Offices of Filing
Source: WIPO *Patent Report,* 2007 edition, www.wipo.int/ipstats/en/statistics/patents/
patent_report_2007.html#P745_41736.

Recent Trends

Patent filings by residents of countries in the Far East have been growing at high
rates for more than 10 years. However, these countries have remained somewhat
insular in their approach to patent activity, and filings abroad by residents of these
countries have only started to appear in significant numbers in recent years. This can
be seen in filings of PCT international applications, where filings from the Republic
of Korea and China have grown significantly since 2002, to the point where China,
Japan, and the Republic of Korea are now all among the top 10 countries of origin
of PCT applications.

Figure 12.6 illustrates the number of PCT international applications filed in 2005
and 2006 by country of origin.

Beyond the Far East

While much attention is given to the high patenting growth rates in countries in the
Far East, other industrializing countries are also showing steady increases in their
use of the patent system, particularly Brazil, India, Israel, and South Africa, where
patent applicants are all increasing their patent filings abroad.

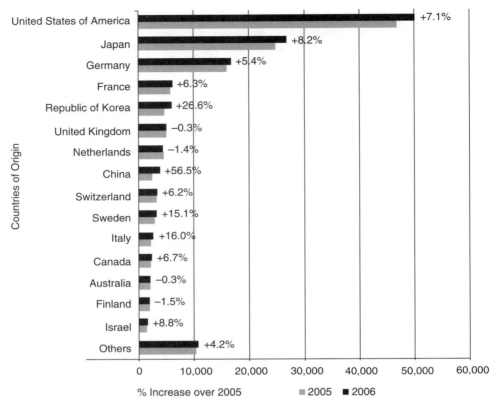

FIGURE 12.6   Resident Filings by Office
Source: WIPO Patent Report, 2007 edition, www.wipo.int/ipstats/en/statistics/patents/
patent_report_2007.html#P745_41736.

Figure 12.7 illustrates the country of residence of nonresident patent filings worldwide. In the figure, it can be seen that applicants from the United States are the largest filers of patent applications in other countries.

Balance of Power

The increase in patent filings from industrializing countries does not yet translate into international ownership of patent rights by applicants from those countries.

Figure 12.8 illustrates the number of patents in force by office in 2004 and 2005. As can be seen from the figure, there were approximately 5.6 million patents in force in 2005, of which 49 percent were owned by applicants from the two major users of the patent system: Japan and the United States. In addition, Germany, France, and the United Kingdom are also strongly represented in ownership of patent rights. Of course, the above described increases in patent filings will eventually mature into increased numbers of patents granted. It can be expected that the proportions shown in the figure will change as the ownership of patent rights worldwide become more diversified.

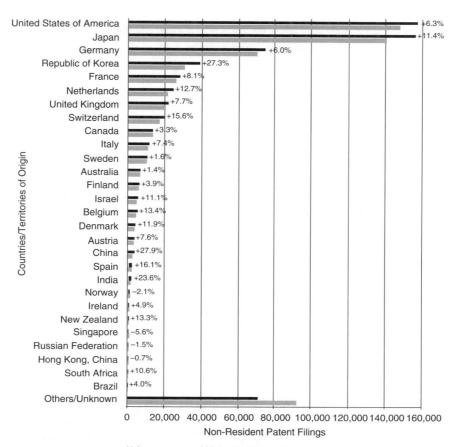

FIGURE 12.7 Nonresidential Filings by Country of Origin
Source: WIPO Patent Report, 2007 edition, www.wipo.int/ipstats/en/statistics/patents/
patent_report_2007.html#P745_41736.

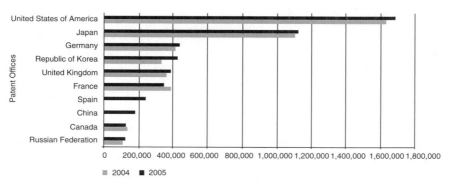

FIGURE 12.8 Patents in Force by Office
Source: WIPO Patent Report, 2007 edition, www.wipo.int/ipstats/en/statistics/patents/
patent_report_2007.html#P745_41736.

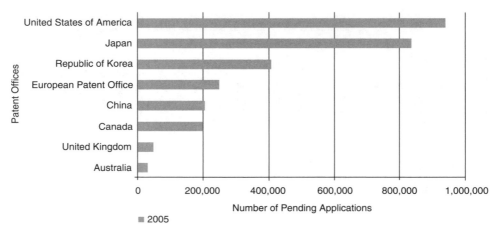

FIGURE 12.9   Pending Applications by Office
Source: WIPO Patent Report, 2007 edition, www.wipo.int/ipstats/en/statistics/patents/
patent_report_2007.html#P745_41736.

Problems Faced

As can be appreciated, these changes do not come without a cost. At certain patent offices, the workload has increased faster than the capacity to examine patent applications.

Figure 12.9 illustrates the number of applications pending in 2005 in the offices shown. As can be seen, more than 900,000 patent applications were undergoing prosecution at the USPTO in 2005. The JPO also had more than 800,000 patent applications pending in 2005, although this is largely due to changes in the time limit for request for examination, which has created a temporary increase in the examination workload in Japan.

Duration of Patent Prosecution

A downside of the increasing numbers of patent applications being filed at the patent offices of Japan and the United States is that these offices are now experiencing large backlogs of pending applications. The same is true at the European Patent Office. These offices have attempted to address this problem by recruiting more examiners, but these backlogs, which delay the grant of patent applications, remain.

A question raised by this increase in workload is the extent of duplication of effort within the system. Worldwide, 38 percent of patent applications are by non-resident applicants. Figure 12.10 illustrates the number of patent applications filed by residents and nonresidents worldwide by year of filing. These applications are usually preceded by prior applications in the applicant's country of residence and often by parallel applications in other countries. Each of these applications may be subject to a separate search and examination in each patent office.

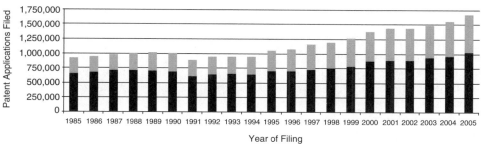

Year of Filing

▪ Patent Applications Filed by Non-Residents
▪ Patent Applications Filed by Residents

FIGURE 12.10 Patents Granted Worldwide by Year of Grants
Source: WIPO Patent Report, 2007 edition, www.wipo.int/ipstats/en/statistics/patents/
patent_report_2007.html#P745_41736.

Reducing the Backlog

In order to address this issue, a number of offices are adopting so-called Patent
Prosecution Highway (PPH) pilot procedures. The intention of these procedures is
to enable national patent offices to avoid repeating work carried out by another
patent office and to reduce the time applications are pending before grant.

So far, pilot PPH programs exist between the Korean Intellectual Property Office
and the JPO, between the USPTO and the JPO, and between the U.K. Intellectual
Property Office (UKIPO) and both the USPTO and the JPO.

In addition to these PPH programs, the EPO is testing a program to investigate
if the work carried out by a patent office when the patent is first filed can be utilized
by other patent offices in subsequent filings. The initial trial of the Utilization Pilot
Program (UPP) is to run until April 2008 for filings in Austria, Denmark, Germany,
and the United Kingdom, with the view to full-scale implementation in the future.

Further to these existing programs, the heads of the Big Five patent offices have
recently met to exchange views and enhance cooperation in the field of patents, with
work-sharing proposals; how work done by one office could be utilized by the other
offices was a main point of discussion.[15]

CLOSING THOUGHTS

The grant of a patent gives the proprietor a monopoly to work the invention as
defined in the patent, to the exclusion of others. It is important to appreciate the
difference between the exclusive right afforded by a patent and the patentee's commercial freedom to use the technology identified in the patent. In fact, it is perfectly
possible for a patentee to own a valid patent for a new technology but to be prevented
from using the technology because to do so would infringe the rights of others.

An important concept to bear in mind is that a good patent, almost by definition,
seeks to push the boundaries of its scope right up to the limit while not impinging on
the prior art. Any narrower definition, and the patent is weaker than it could be. Any
broader, and the patent risks encompassing the art, and thereby may not be granted.

It is because the patent treads this very thin line at the boundary that prosecution arguments, and individual differences in prosecution arguments, are often to be had.

While most countries have national patenting procedures, patenting in Europe is dominated by the EPC, which has 34 signatories and effectively allows a single application to progress throughout Europe. However, any granted European patent must be validated in each individual state, or those that the applicant so chooses, and this step involves some significant cost.

Patent filing trends throughout the world and in the world's major patent offices show strong and persistent growth coinciding with a world of ever-increasing commercial competitiveness, emerging new markets, and new technologies.

CHAPTER TAKEAWAYS

Key points to take away from this chapter are:

- Patents are granted for inventions that are novel and inventive with respect to the prior art.
- The prior art includes any published document or prior use or sale, or any other kind of public disclosure, provided that the disclosure predates the priority date of the patent.
- The priority date of the patent is its very first filing date, usually in the applicant's home territory.
- The Paris Convention allows a one-year period during which foreign filings may be made and still claim the earlier priority date.
- The PCT application is a common route to international patenting, as it enables the applicant provisionally to secure protection in a large number of countries at relatively low cost, at least during the early stages of the procedure.
- The PCT procedure (which itself is optional, although widely used) leads to national and in some cases regional patent applications, which themselves progress to separately granted patents, generally over a period of several years.
- Patenting in Europe is dominated by the European Patent Convention.
- The vast majority of patents are filed in one or more of these places—the United States, Europe, and Japan—although China and India are becoming increasingly important. A number of other Pacific Rim countries, such as South Korea, Singapore, and Malaysia, also witness very significant patenting activity, as do Canada and Australia.
- There are other regional patent organizations of growing importance, for example, in the Gulf States, Eurasia, and Africa.

CHAPTER 13

General Patenting Strategies in High-Technology Industries

Tom Brand
W. P. Thompson & Co.

This chapter deals with the strategic considerations necessary to develop an effective patent strategy. First, the importance of developing patent strategy at an early stage in the life of a high-tech business is emphasized and explained, and some golden rules are highlighted. Different types of patent strategy, in particular offensive and defensive, are characterized, and finally some more complex models for extracting value from patents are explored.

DEVELOPING A PATENT STRATEGY FOR EARLY-STAGE BUSINESSES

Why patent? In developing a patent strategy, businesses should always be mindful of the reasons why individuals and companies engage in patenting in the first place. The reasons fall, broadly, into two camps: (1) patents can be used to make money, and (2) patents can be used to cost your competitors money. A well-thought-out and executed patent strategy exploits both.

It is important to budget properly for patents as costs can quickly escalate. Patent filing costs tend to come in three stages: filing, examination or prosecution, and registration. The time lapse between the first and the last stage is typically about four to six years, although it can be even longer. Costs vary significantly from country to country and are highly dependent on factors such as exchange rates, translation charges, professional fees, and official fees.

While it is often difficult for a finance director to justify the cost of patents, it is important to keep in mind that patents may be making money for your business behind the scenes, or may have the potential to do so.

This story, told by a practicing patent lawyer, illustrates just one way in which a patent may subtly influence the balance sheet on which it sits as an expense: Recently a client was having difficulty justifying the cost of a patent to his board of directors, since he had been engaged, for about a year, in a costly dispute with a competitor who was alleged to have been infringing a patent. The board was doubtful that the costs were justifiable. However, the dispute was eventually settled, with the competitor paying a portion of the patent costs and becoming a customer of the client. Although the patent and the dispute had incurred significant costs, the ongoing benefit to the company was that the competitor (who would otherwise have been taking a market share from the client) became a profitable customer and actually increased the client's market share.

The lesson here is that patents have a direct cost but an indirect value. In other words, patents rarely pay for themselves directly over the short term, but, in the longer term, their value often outweighs their cost by, for example, converting competitors into customers, attracting license fees, and increasing market share. Patents should therefore be viewed as a necessary ongoing expense. As such, patents should be properly budgeted for, and that budget should be built into a business plan in much the same way as, say, marketing costs, solicitor's fees, and business expenses are included.

Budgeting for Patents

In arriving at a budget for patent costs, direct application and prosecution costs (which can be estimated fairly accurately) should be taken into consideration. Often overlooked, underestimated, or both, however, are funds to deal with minor disputes (both offensive and defensive) as and when they arise and funds to enable your patent lawyer to carry out ongoing tasks, such as searching, assessment of inventions, and providing general advice. It is also often advisable to budget for intellectual property (IP) insurance to cover you in the event of a major dispute or full-blown litigation.

A typical patent filing begins with a home application (the priority application), generally prepared with the benefit of close consultation between the inventor(s) and the patent attorney. At this stage you are paying primarily for the patent attorney's time. Although the hourly rates can be appreciable (from £250 to £500 per hour, for example), it is immensely valuable to get things right at this early stage. In the scheme of things, a typical patent filing program can cost tens or even hundreds of thousands of pounds (depending primarily on the number of countries covered by the program), and this very first stage is in many ways the most important. Correctly determining what the invention is and also determining fallback positions or safeguards (in the event of new prior art coming to light for example) in the application is essential.

The costs of a major filing program (covering, say, 30 countries) come in spikes:

Year 1. Expenditure generally up to about £15,000 to cover the cost of initial advice, searching, and priority filing.

Year 2. Expenditure generally up to about £20,000 to cover the cost of Patent Cooperation Treaty (PCT) filing, with associated advice concerning any search reports and further technological developments. This stage may be more expensive if non-PCT applications are required.

Year 3. Expenditure generally up to about £100,000 to cover the cost of converting the PCT case into separate national cases.

Years 4, 5, 6, and 7. Expenditure generally up to about £25,000 per year to cover the cost of prosecuting the separate national applications and paying registration fees once cases begin to grant.

Year 7 onward. Expenditure generally up to about £15,000 per year, covering the cost of renewal and any stragglers in prosecution terms, but then rising toward £30,000 per year as the granted patents get older and renewal fees start to rise.

If you were to commence a patent filing program and predict all of the costs arising over the subsequent six or seven years (seeing the patent through to grant in most jurisdictions), and then look at the total accumulated costs on a per county basis, a ballpark average would be:

Filing. Up to about £5,000. This includes legal fees for the preparation of supporting documents, in particular powers of attorney and priority documents, which frequently require notarization and legalization, translation charges, local attorney, and government fees.

Examination or prosecution. Up to about £3,000. This includes search and examination fee payments, legal fees in considering office actions, and where necessary filing amendments and responses.

Registration. Up to about £2,000. This includes government registration fees and local attorney costs in managing the grant procedure.

It should be stressed that there is enormous variation between countries, and costs are highly dependent on professional fees, translation charges, government fees, exchange rates, and the nature and complexity of particular proceedings.

Normally these costs would be charged as and when they occur—so filing costs would be incurred at the outset of any filing program; prosecution costs would be charged periodically over a two-, three-, or even four-year period; and registration costs would be charged at the end of the procedure. It may be possible for other charging structures to be agreed with your patent attorney.

Granted patents incur annual renewal fees to keep them in force. Generally these are of the order of £300 to £500 per patent per country, but they tend to rise as the patent gets older.

Finally, in some jurisdictions, most notably in Europe, patents are subject to oppositions filed by third parties. These proceedings can be costly, but not major in comparison with the overall cost of a large patent filing program and not major in comparison with postgrant litigation costs.

Pitfalls of Not Engaging in Patenting

The flip side is that failing to engage in patenting can cost your business money for several reasons.

First, research and development (R&D) is expensive. However, many businesses spend fortunes reinventing the wheel (i.e., developing products and services that have already been developed by someone else). Just think how much money you could save if, instead of developing a new product from scratch in-house, you could simply read and copy a "recipe" explaining exactly how to produce the same, or a similar, product. Patent specifications, in particular, contain such recipes and are freely available to read online. Moreover, if the patent application was never granted, or, if it did grant but was later abandoned, you may be able to copy and exploit the technology royalty free. Your patent lawyer or patent search specialist will be able to provide pre-R&D searching services to help you identify what, if any, similar technology already exists and whether you are free to exploit it. Moreover, the search may also help to identify any aspects of your project that you might be able to protect, and whether you may be exposed to risks of infringement down the line (in other words, whether there are existing documents of which you should be aware from a freedom-to-operate point of view).

Another way that IP can cost your business money is by you applying to protect IP that you cannot profitably exploit. Money spent patenting a commercially unviable product (a product that customers do not want, that will be too expensive for customers to buy, or that underperforms compared to competing products of a similar price) is money wasted pure and simple. It is often difficult for businesses to see this, especially when they feel committed to a particular product or service. You will need to work closely with your patent lawyer, accountants, and marketing advisors on a continuous basis to identify and abandon unwanted or ineffectual patents.

Further, IP costs businesses, by managers continuing to spend time and money on IP that the business no longer exploits. This includes continuing to pay royalties or renewal fees for IP rights that cover products or services that are approaching obsolescence or that have long since been shelved. Your patent lawyer or patent search specialist will be able to provide a periodic review service to check that you are still profitably exploiting your IP and, if not, to help you to dispose of it cost effectively. Doing this may involve abandonment of the IP rights in question, opting to make them "licenses of right" (allowing anyone a license in return for reduced renewal fees), actively seeking potential licensees, or even using online patent auction services.

By far the biggest way that IP can sap a business's resources is being sued by your competitors for infringing their IP rights. The penalties for infringing someone else's rights can be severe both financially (successful claimants can claim legal costs, damages, or an account of profits (i.e., a claim to a share of the profits made by an infringer), delivery-up (i.e., repatriation of the infringing goods), etc.) and to your reputation (a public declaration can be requested that the right in question has been infringed, not to mention the claimant's press releases, etc.). It is therefore essential that you continuously monitor your competitors' activities and commission freedom-to-use searches before rolling out any new product or service. (See Chapter 15 for more about freedom-to-use or freedom-to-operate searches.) If the searches identify any IP rights that may impede your activities, then a risk assessment will need to be carried out to assess:

- Whether your proposed product or service is likely to infringe
- The likelihood of infringement being detected and acted on
- The damage that might ensue should you be sued successfully

Your patent lawyer or other IP specialist or external technology consultants should provide search and risk assessment services to help you to decide if, and how, to proceed.

If someone has already accused you of infringing their IP rights, your patent lawyer ought to be able to advise you regarding various defensive strategies, including trying to demonstrate that the right in question is invalid, or not infringed, negotiating or mediating a settlement or license, or identifying potential cross-licenses, where applicable.

Developing a Patenting Ethos

Notwithstanding the previous text, it is rarely enough simply to throw money at patents: There should also be a strong, and ingrained, patenting ethos within the company. This requires ongoing education so that all employees are aware that their ideas may be valuable to the company. All employees should at least know about intellectual property (including patents, trademarks, copyright, and designs). The idea behind such education is not to teach your staff all about IP but to make them aware of the issues and to encourage them to discuss IP issues with senior staff as and when matters arise. (Your patent lawyer may be able to provide easy-to-understand literature or provide in-house training.) Senior staff, however, should be better informed, and you should appoint an IP coordinator to manage and oversee your patent strategy, and to be a central point of contact for your patent lawyer.[1]

Idea Farming and Employee Incentives

You should make it a policy to farm your employees' ideas on a regular basis. This can be done at monthly staff meetings, where everyone is asked if any problems have arisen, and how they tackled or overcame those problems. Alternatively, install suggestion boxes at your premises and encourage staff to deposit ideas as and when they think of them. All ideas should be properly documented, dated, and reviewed by a patent lawyer who will be able to advise you as to their potential patentability.

Encourage your staff to engage in the patenting process. Acknowledge and reward staff for their ideas by using Idea of the Month awards and cash incentives for depositing ideas.

Shore Up Ownership of Your IP

It is important to ensure that your employees' ideas are legally transferred to the company and that your employees are legally obliged to maintain confidentiality. This is usually best done by inserting IP clauses in your employees' contracts of employment. Be careful when drafting subcontractor contracts; make sure you carefully think through ownership of IP rights in these contracts as well. Again, professional legal counsel is best consulted on how to word such clauses. Of course, if you are on a very tight start-up budget, you may have to rely on do-it-yourself books, such as those published by Nolo Press in Berkeley, California (www.nolo.com), or consult online web sites, such as FindLaw (www.findlaw.com), if you cannot afford expensive attorney fees. Go to our web site at www.innovationtocashflows.com and browse the "Resources" file to find other recommended IP books and web sites).

Think Strategically

It is also important that your patent lawyer fully understands your business and knows about your competitors so that she can anticipate potential problems and identify where IP needs to be protected or enforced. Sometimes a patent lawyer will be called in to advise a client, only to discover the following state of affairs:

> *It is not unknown for companies to launch new products and then find themselves in the situation where they are unable to stop competitors from copying their ideas. In many cases, the company might have been able to stop the competitor if only it had consulted its patent lawyer pre-launch and ensured that all relevant IP rights had been secured before going to market.*

You should consider inviting your patent lawyer to sit in on high-level strategic planning meetings.

QUESTIONS TO ASK WHEN DEVISING A PATENTING STRATEGY

The first step in devising a patenting strategy is to understand how you intend to make money from the patents and see how this complements your existing business model or any proposed new business model. The subheads in this section list questions you might wish to consider.

Why Are You Patenting at All?

If you are patenting to help raise venture capital or to attract external investment, you probably will want as many patents, trademarks, and designs in your portfolio as you can afford. If, however, you plan to launch a new product, then you may better spend your available funds on product development, marketing, and production rather than patenting. Thus, in the latter case, fewer patents may be called for.

What Are You Planning to Make or Sell?

If you are a manufacturing company and intend to sell manufactured products, you will almost certainly require a patent (or patents) that cover those actual products. If you are a design and development company and wish to market designs, or concepts, for new products, you probably will require a more nebulous or blue-skies patent (or patents) that protect the underlying concepts or ideas. For example, if your company develops a novel method of encapsulating an active ingredient in a new type of particle that will harmlessly store and preserve the active ingredient for a long period of time, this new concept can and should be broadly protected with reference to all possible categories of active ingredient. Thus, the first claim of the patent may refer simply to "active ingredient" or "useful compound" or something of that sort, but then specific subclaims of the patent may be more product oriented—specifying the active ingredient as a pharmaceutical product, a flavoring, or a fire retardant, for example. If you are a manufacturing company specializing in pesticides, for example, you may come across this patent and decide that the technology could, with perhaps some adaptation, be applied in your field. In that case, you should be free to file your own patent on the encapsulated pesticide in a directed, product-specific patent.

How Far Along the Product Development Cycle Are You?

Where you are in the product development cycle will affect the form and content of the patent application(s). If you anticipate having to make changes to the design of the product before committing to production or launch, the patent specification ought to contain plenty of wiggle room so that the patent, as granted, does not exclude any possible variants of the invention. You probably will have to commit to limiting the scope of the patent to certain preferred embodiments at some stage, and if this can be done sooner rather than later, your chances of securing an early grant date are greatly increased.

What Is Your Main Market for These Goods?

If you plan to operate in only one country, it may not be worth your while to apply for overseas patents. The question to ask is: What effect would it have on your business if a competitor were to copy and exploit your idea abroad? If the answer is none, then an overseas filing strategy is probably unjustifiable. However, if you foresee potential licensing or franchising opportunities for your products, then it may be worth considering an overseas patent strategy.

What Do You Want to Be Able to Stop Your Competitors from Doing?

What you want to stop your competitors from doing will influence the type of patents you should apply for. It may also suggest not patenting at all but rather keeping ideas confidential within the company. Your patent lawyer should be able to advise you here.

DEVISING A PATENT STRATEGY: DO'S AND DON'TS

Do

- Properly budget for patents.
- Take a long-term view.
- Consult a patent lawyer and other patent experts before embarking on any new project or launching any new product.
- Continuously review your patents and your competitors' patents.
- Develop a patenting ethos within your company.
- Invest in staff training.
- Encourage and reward staff for engaging in the patenting process.
- Regularly note down any new ideas you may have and ask your patent lawyer to review them.
- Make sure your company legally owns its employees ideas.
- Engage your patent lawyer at a high level, especially in strategic planning decisions.
- Understand what you can, and want, to achieve by patenting; be realistic.

Don't

- Underestimate costs.
- Publish before you patent.
- Expect patents to pay for themselves immediately.
- Bury your head in the sand and ignore patents—you may be losing market share, hemorrhaging cash, or risk being sued.
- Allow ideas to walk out of your company by neglecting to set up and enforce confidentiality agreements.

DEFENSIVE AND OFFENSIVE PATENT STRATEGIES

In order to obtain a commercial advantage in their target market, many technology-driven businesses have adopted various patent strategies not only to protect their core products but also to prevent their competitors from encroaching on their market share. Such patent strategies can be loosely described under the terms *defensive* and *offensive*.

Broadly speaking, a *defensive patent strategy* is aimed at protecting the core products of a business by filing a small number of patent applications that cover important products and any improvements to those products that are thought to be significant. Most companies adopt this kind of defensive patent strategy.

In contrast, an *offensive patent strategy* is directed toward actively blocking the commercial activities of competitors by filing applications focusing on propriety technology that a business may have developed but has no intention to market.

While both terms can be defined individually, many larger businesses combine a mixture of defensive and offensive patent strategies. Smaller businesses automatically adopt a defensive strategy, as they effectively want to stop other parties from copying their products, for which a research and development activity will have been expended. As an offensive patent strategy requires the filing of patent applications that are not directed toward protecting core products, it is often seen as an expensive strategy to employ. Generally only the larger businesses can afford to go down this route. However, an offensive strategy can not only block competitors, it also can bring in a revenue stream if properly managed.

While patent strategies are discussed in this chapter, it should be remembered that such strategies should be included in the overall IP strategy of a business, as defensive and offensive strategies can also be employed with respect to trademarks and designs.

Defensive Patent Strategies

A defensive patent strategy is intended to protect the core products of a business. Many businesses employ a defensive patent strategy without even realizing that this is what they are doing. At the very minimum, patent applications should be filed toward the core products (or processes) in an attempt to prevent others from producing similar or identical products.

If finances permit, patent applications should also be filed to any significant improvements developed in respect of the core products. In a number of instances, these improvements relate to the things that actually allow the product to function as intended or reduce production costs. Often these improvement patent applications can prove to be essential to a business.

Last, patent applications can also be directed to prevent other parties from designing around the core patents or improvement patents.

As discussed in more detail in Chapter 12, a new application can be filed within 12 months of an earlier application claiming the benefit of the earlier filing date. For example, a first patent application can be filed for a core product. Within 12 months, a second patent application for an improvement can be filed that claims priority from the earlier application. As a patent application is usually published within 18 months of the initial filing date, if further improvements are developed between expiry of the 12-month priority period and the date of publication, applications filed during this period only have to show novelty (and not inventive step) over the earlier applications.

A defensive patent strategy should also include a focus on the location of your protection. If at all possible, patent protection should be extended to your major markets, in addition to locations where the product is likely to be manufactured. Overseas protection will of course increase costs. If finances are tight, then it might be best to spend money on protecting core products overseas than protecting improvements in a single country.

It should also be noted that if a particular product or process is hard to reverse engineer or is not "disclosed" during operation, one option may be not to file a patent application at all. While there are risks associated with maintaining a product or a process as a trade secret, the risks associated with the publishing of a patent application that details the product or process may be greater. With trade secrets, there is no problem with the expiry of a patent (usually 20 years), as the trade secret will extend in perpetuity.

Offensive Patent Strategies

An offensive patent strategy can be multifaceted but is generally intended to block the commercial activities of competitors within a propriety technology of a business. Many larger businesses operate offensive patent strategies in parallel with defensive strategies. Some defensive patent strategies of smaller businesses develop into offensive patent strategies over time. When considering the benefits of an offensive patent strategy, it should be borne in mind that a patent does not give anyone the right to do something; rather it gives the proprietor the right to prevent others from doing something that falls within the scope of the patent.

An offensive strategy generally results in a large number of patent applications being filed before any real thought has been given as to whether the innovation may be implemented within a product or service that the business provides. Indeed, applications for innovations that are seemingly unrelated to the operations of the business may also be filed. This scattergun approach may ultimately yield a number of patents that are useful in the defensive strategy as they may protect products or processes that become core to the business. The approach will also lead to a number of patents that are not useful as defensive patents to the core products or processes but are useful in preventing other parties from entering a particular technological field.

By using a scattergun approach, the cost of filing the patent applications and maintaining granted patents can be extremely expensive—especially if overseas protection ultimately is obtained. However, these costs can be reduced or recovered by licensing the patents to other parties with whom you are not in direct competition. Furthermore, there will be an intangible deterrence value associated with blocking the competition from using the relevant technology.

Two questions that are often raised, especially in very high-technology fields, is at what point during the development of an innovation should an application be filed, and should every development be protected. It would certainly be wasteful to file applications directed at every result from the R&D of a business. For example, the R&D department may have analyzed a number of different paths and chosen the best one to take forward to a product. A commonsense approach has to be taken regarding filing patent applications that will, it is hoped, block the competitors' activities in relation to the relevant technology and those that may generate a return on the R&D expenditure by way of a license. It is also worth noting that the patent has to disclose sufficiently an invention for it to be valid, so a decision has to be made regarding how early on in development the application is filed.

In addition to blocking, offensive patent strategies can also provide a valuable revenue stream that can be used to offset the cost of the patent filings, and hopefully generate added value.

To illustrate the point, imagine you manufacture vacuum cleaners and your R&D department has developed a new, platinum-coated filter to filter out the smallest of dust particles (which has not previously been possible). As platinum is an expensive metal, vacuum cleaners that incorporate the filters will be very expensive to produce. You run a quick market assessment to see whether the people who usually buy your vacuum cleaner would be prepared to pay the estimated retail cost if the vacuum provided greatly improved cleaning. It turns out that the cost would be just a little too high, and the decision is made not to push the new cleaner into production. Even so, you recognize the existence of a market need and therefore decide to pursue an offensive patent strategy. You apply for a patent on the platinum-coated filter development in the hope or expectation that you will find new revenue streams as a result. Thus, while you do not intend to go to market yourself with the product, nevertheless, you recognize that others may wish to. Your offensive patent will allow you to benefit from that circumstance.

For example, you may know that your competitor Vacuum Gold has been trying for a number of years to develop a vacuum that filters out the smallest of dust particles but has been unsuccessful to date, probably because they have been using gold instead of the essential platinum. Because of your offensive patent you are in a position to provide them with a solution to their problem, and claim a royalty, provided they are prepared to adopt your solution. On the other hand, if they use the platinum solution on their own without your permission, then provided they have not done so before the date of your invention, you can sue them for patent infringement. Even if you are not in the platinum-coated market yourself, it is likely that Vacuum Gold's incursion into that market will affect your market share. You should be able to claim damages or alternatively a share of the profits generated by the infringement.

Offensive patent strategies may also involve keeping a close watch on your competitors' pipelines. A patent watch may be put in place to establish when new applications are filed and published in the name of competitors or their inventors. If need be, you can file patent applications directed toward these new technologies to prevent further development and hamper competitors' research efforts.

Keeping track of your competitors' patent portfolio is also important, so that you have early warning of possible conflicts. For example, if a product that you are developing falls within the scope of the claims of a patent application filed by a competitor, you will want to keep a close watch on the application to see whether it proceeds to grant. If need be, you can undertake prior art searches and apply to contest the patent (i.e., apply to invalidate the patent in the United States or oppose it in Europe). Furthermore, by keeping a close eye on the competitors' patent pipeline, you can also identify any holes or gaps in its protection and file applications directed toward those holes or gaps. Patent searching can also be useful, not least because it has been estimated that up to 30 percent of European R&D is wasted on trying to develop something that already exists.

Last, the offensive strategy involves enforcing your patent rights against others. If you are successful in bringing a court action against another party for infringement of a patent, often a shock wave is sent through the industry and it takes the threat of infringing your patents more seriously.

REAL-LIFE EXAMPLES

The next examples illustrate the different approaches to patent strategy.

Consumer Electronics: Triple Vortex

Dyson developed and patented a vacuum cleaner that was marketed under Dual Cyclone; its suction was produced by means of a cyclone. A patent was granted for the invention in a number of countries some time ago.

Dyson then developed and patented a modified vacuum cleaner that was marketed under Root Cyclone. It used a number of smaller-diameter cyclones to provide a cleaner having an even greater suction.

Back in 2002, Dyson successfully sued Hoover for infringement of its patent by Hoover's Triple Vortex vacuum cleaner and was awarded record damages of over £4 million.

Dyson's patent filings were defensive as they sought to protect their core product and improvements. However, if Hoover had used an offensive patent strategy and developed and patented the "Root Cyclone" technology, then this would have caused a problem for Dyson, as when the original Dual Cyclone patent expired, not only would Hoover have been free to have produced a product similar to the Root Cyclone, but it would have been able to prevent Dyson from developing the original concept to incorporate a number of smaller cyclones to increase suction.

Pharmaceuticals: Viagra®

Pfizer originally developed sildenafil (Viagra®) for the treatment of hypertension and angina. After Phase I clinical trials, it became apparent that the drug had little effect on angina but could be useful for the treatment of erectile dysfunction.

Pfizer had filed a core patent directed toward the compound itself and a second patent directed toward the use of the compound for the treatment of erectile dysfunction.

Viagra turned into an overnight success, with annual sales at an estimated $1 billion. With that sort of success, it was only going to be a matter of time before the patents were challenged.

In 2000, the High Court in the United Kingdom ruled that the second patent directed toward the use of the compound for erectile dysfunction was invalid. Although this was a blow for Pfizer, its core patent remained in force and it is not due to expire until 2013. Therefore, no one other than Pfizer is able to produce or sell the compound for any medical condition until 2013.

Commonly in pharmaceutical inventions, a core patent application is filed that is directed toward the compound itself. Patent applications directed toward the use of the compound for particular medical conditions are also filed. Protection can also be extended further, by filing patent applications directed toward new formulations and methods of manufacturing the compound.

There is, of course, nothing stopping a competitor from adopting an offensive patent strategy and filing patent applications for new uses of the compound or new formulations and methods of manufacture before the core patent has expired.

Computing: Hyperlink

It is estimated that British Telecom Plc (BT) has some 15,000 global patents. The company has adopted an offensive patent strategy and actively licenses a large proportion of its patent portfolio. One difficulty is keeping track of the technologies that your patents cover.

After a review of its patent portfolio in 2000, BT came across a patent (filed in 1986) that it believed claimed the use of a hyperlink, used on nearly every Internet page to link users to other Internet pages. As only the U.S. patent was still in force, BT contacted a number of Internet Service Providers (ISPs) to request that they take a license under the patent. When the ISPs refused to take a license, BT then decided to try to sue Prodigy Communications as a test case. BT lost the case.

It goes to show that an offensive patent strategy can be of limited benefit if the business loses sight of what intellectual property it actually owns.

STRATEGIC PATENTING—CLAIMING FIRST TO WIN THE BATTLE

Innovation generally and protecting innovation by patenting operates on a first come, first served basis. A patenting strategy must take account of the need to identify patentable innovations within your organization quickly and efficiently and follow this ethos through in patenting.

First to file is a legal concept that defines who has the right to the grant of a patent for an invention. The first-to-file system is used in the majority of countries with the notable exception of the United States, which operates a *first-to-invent* system.

In a first-to-file system, the right to the grant of a patent for a given invention lies with the first entitled person to file a patent application for protection of that invention, regardless of the date that the actual invention was made. It is possible that there are other people elsewhere in the world making the same innovations in your technical field, and it is therefore imperative that you file before they do.

For example, imagine Frank conceives an innovative rat trap on January 1, 2007. Frank diligently works to have a patent application prepared, which is filed February 1, 2007. On January 15, 2007, Dean independently conceives the same rat trap. Conscious of the first-to-file principle, Dean immediately contacts his patent lawyer. Dean's patent lawyer files an application on January 30, 2007. In this scenario, Dean is entitled to the patent on the rat trap because he was the first entitled person to file a patent application.

Conversely, the United States uses a first-to-invent system. The act of invention in the United States is generally considered to comprise two steps: (1) conception of the invention and (2) reduction to practice of the invention.

When an inventor conceives an invention and diligently reduces the invention to practice (e.g., by filing a patent application, by practicing the invention, and so forth), the inventor's date of invention will be the date of conception. Provided that an inventor is diligent in reducing an application to practice, he or she will be the first inventor and the inventor entitled to a patent, even if another party files a patent application before the inventor.

That said, the first applicant to file has the *prima facie*[2] right to the grant of a patent. Should a second patent application be filed for the same invention, the second applicant can institute interference proceedings to determine who was the first inventor and thereby who is entitled to the grant of a patent. This can be a particularly expensive and a time-consuming process.

Returning to our example, in the United States it is likely that Frank or the U.S. Patent and Trademark Office (USPTO) would institute interference proceedings to review evidence of conception and diligence so as to determine whether Frank or Dean is entitled to the grant of a patent for the invention.

As an extension to this example, imagine Sammy conceived the same humane rat trap on January 1, 2000. Sammy kept the invention to himself and never disclosed it to anyone. Due to financial constraints, Sammy did not work on reducing the rat trap to practice for many years. Sammy finally reduced the rat trap to practice by filing a patent application on April 1, 2007. Because he did not diligently work to reduce the invention to practice, the USPTO is unlikely to consider Sammy entitled to a patent over Frank and Dean.

Interference proceedings are complicated. The patent application process can get bogged down in round after round of evidence where each party tries to assert that its research notes contain the earliest mention of a particular product or process. In turn, this delays the grant of a patent and can prevent valuable inventions from being available to the public while the dispute rages.

There are proposals to convert the United States to a first-to-file system, although this seems unlikely in the near future. That said, it is important to note that this system will not save you in the vast majority of countries. Therefore, it is best practice to ensure that patent applications are filed in a timely manner. This is one of the reasons why patent lawyers advise clients to file patent applications as quickly as is practically possible while ensuring that sufficient information is provided to support the claimed invention.

Strategic Patenting—Trolling for Patents

- **troll**[1] /trol, trol/, verb: **1** Angling. **1a** to draw (a baited line, and so forth) through the water. **1b** to fish by trolling.
- **troll**[2] /trol, trol/, noun: (in folklore) an ugly cave-dwelling being depicted as either a giant or a dwarf.[3]

Patent trolls court controversy wherever they raise their ugly heads. Typically, they are enforcers of patents who themselves have no intention to make use of a patented technology. Often they acquire patents from bankrupt companies with the intention of suing third parties for infringement. Their focus is on enforcing patent rights, and they are unlikely to have a manufacturing or research base.

The term was popularized in 2001 by Peter Detkin, formerly legal counsel at semiconductor giant Intel. At that time, Intel was fighting claims in excess of $15 billion from companies asserting patent rights that had never made a semiconductor device.[4]

T.J. Rodgers, chief executive of Cypress Semiconductor Corporation, is critical of patent trolls but makes a distinction based on a company's motivation:

> *They fall into three categories: the good, the bad and the ugly. The good companies don't go on the offensive unless the potentially infringed patent is critical to their business. The bad companies have a system to actively seek third parties who might be using their patented technology and the ugly who are basically in the business of suing people for money.*[5]

Patent trolls focus on extracting money from existing uses of technology, not from seeking new applications of a technology. They will look for signs that another company is developing a potentially infringing technology by monitoring the market and reviewing published patent applications. Once a target has been identified, whether it is an individual company or an entire industry, the trolls will develop their plan to proceed. Often they will threaten action to encourage an out-of-court settlement as the cost of defending an action can be significant, particularly in the United States. Defendants may even settle cases they consider frivolous to avoid the expense of trial.

In 1995, NTP Inc. patented the idea of sending electronic messages to a wireless device, then shelved the patent for a rainy day. In 2002, Research in Motion (RIM) developed and marketed the BlackBerry® device.

Seizing on the similarities between the technology behind the BlackBerry® device and its own patents, NTP, having failed to agree on a license with RIM, issued infringement proceedings in the United States. The U.S. court granted an injunction, and RIM was temporarily prevented from selling BlackBerry® devices in the United States. The conclusion to the proceedings came on March 3, 2006, when RIM announced that it had agreed on an out-of-court settlement to pay $612.5 million to NTP in order to resolve the lengthy dispute.

The U.S. case was followed in quick succession in the United Kingdom, where Inpro, a licensing company based in Luxembourg, issued proceedings against RIM on similar grounds. Inpro claimed that RIM's BlackBerry® service infringed its patent for a computer system that reduces the processing power used by portable computers and other devices when accessing servers over the Internet. In this case, however, the patent was found to be invalid, and RIM was able to continue to sell its product.

Key to the patent troll's way of life is that in the United Kingdom (and the United States), patents do not need to be commercialized to be valid. Some critics argue that to protect genuine commercial interests, patent trolls should be stopped. However, to achieve this, the patent system would have to be overhauled, and how is the unfinanced innovator to be protected?

There are a number of ways that you can help reduce the impact from patent trolls. These include:

- Clearance searches
- Patent watches
- Opposition to or reexamination of a granted patent
- Insurance

Clearance Searches   Before initial development or commercialization, conduct a clearance search for patent applications or patents that relate to your technology.

Patent Watches   Routinely monitor new patents and patent applications to determine if any are relevant to your technology and business activities.

Opposition to or Reexamination of a Granted Patent   In Europe, it is possible to oppose the grant of a European patent (known as *opposition*). In the United States, it is possible to request *reexamination of a granted patent*. This is what RIM did to NTP's broad patents.

Insurance   Patent infringement insurance is available to help protect you from inadvertently infringing someone's patent and to help pay the costs if someone else infringes your patent. However, such insurance is expensive—generally from about 2 to 5 percent or more of the insured amount. A copayment may also be required, ranging from 15 to 25 percent of any damage awarded.[6]

STRATEGIC PATENT CONSIDERATIONS FOR GENERICS DRUG COMPANIES

Companies working on generic agricultural or medicinal products need to be aware of specific IP issues. In this area, perhaps more than many others, activities take place that are deliberately close to the infringement boundary. This is because large amounts of money are at stake for each day that a chemical compound or composition can be sold as a therapeutically or agriculturally active material.

It is important to gather detailed and complete information on all potentially problematic IP. In any particular field that a generics company intends to enter, it is essential as a first step to determine whether there is protection, what kind it is, where it is, and when it expires. The main types of IP in this area are patents and supplementary protection certification certificates (SPCs), although data exclusivity rights may also adversely affect a party's freedom to operate.

Patent Searches

As part of the information-gathering process, a search should be carried out to determine the IP that potentially covers the products or methods with which a company is intending to work. This could be done in-house or outsourced, for example, to a firm of patent lawyers or patent search specialists. There are specific databases focused on SPCs as well as patents.

The same product or method may be covered by more than one family of patent applications, patents, or SPCs and accordingly it is important that thorough searching be carried out.

Status of Patents and Other Documents

The status of potentially problematic patents should be checked before time is spent on detailed analysis. In other words, whether patents are in force in any countries of interest should be checked. Searches for equivalents or family members of documents should also be carried out and the relationship between related documents assessed. It should be borne in mind that patent protection can be obtained via both the PCT route and via regional (say, for example, European) routes as well as via direct national routes. SPC status should also be assessed. See Chapter 12 for details on how to apply for patents.

Bearing in mind the financial implications of bringing a product to market even a day later than is necessary, the exact expiry date of patent or SPC protection should be determined.

Various databases provide information on patent and SPC status. In some cases, however, such databases are incomplete. In the event of any doubt, status should be checked with national patent offices or local attorneys or patent specialists. See Chapter 15 for an in-depth discussion of how specialists conduct these types of database searches.

Analysis of the Claims Sections of Patent Documents

Here we illustrate some of the issues involved in strategically sorting through the various patent claims in a granted patent. If in the course of an infringement search, you discover problematic IP issues, these should be brought to the attention of your patent lawyer if they pertain to patents. For other types of potential IP infringement issues, you will likely be referred to different legal experts depending on the topic (trademark, copyright, or trade secrets).

Patent claims delineate the scope of protection of a patent and are essentially of two types: products (e.g., compounds, compositions, and apparatus) and methods (e.g., methods of manufacture, processes of preparing, and uses of particular compounds or composition). A generics drug manufacturer will be mostly concerned with compounds and compositions as well as preparation processes and uses of the compounds or compositions.

Situations could be envisaged where a generics drug company is interested in working in a field to which an existing patent already relates in some broad sense, but the company still may be able to carry out some activities without infringing. For example, an existing patent may cover certain uses of compounds, but after careful assessment of the claims, a patent lawyer may conclude that a generics manufacturer may be able to work on certain other different uses without infringing.

It is therefore important to determine exactly what activities a generics company intends to carry out so that these can be compared to the patent claims.

Patenting a Generics Drug Company's Own Developments

In parallel with this process of determining a generics company's activities, it may become apparent that the company is developing material that can itself be patented.

It is possible to patent new compositions or new combinations of previously known components (particularly if these combinations bring about advantages or improvements) or developments on top of previously known technology (again, particularly if such developments result in enhancements).

The likelihood of obtaining valuable patent protection will be further enhanced if the invention is surprising in some way—for example, if it would not have been predicted that a problem could be solved in a particular way, or if prior documents had suggested a different way of tackling the problem, without recognizing the approach that the generics company found to be effective. Any material that the generics company may patent should be kept confidential until a patent application is filed.

CHAPTER TAKEAWAYS

- It is important to develop a patent strategy at the early stages of a high-tech business.
- A sound patent strategy can make money for a business and cost your competitors money.
- The cost of a patent can come as an unwelcome surprise, so it is important to budget.
- A business or individual should be aware of the potential pitfalls if choosing not to engage in patenting, especially in terms of long-term costs.
- Infringing competitors' IP rights can have a costly outcome.
- Encouraging employees to farm ideas can help develop a business's IP portfolio.
- Ideas made by employees should be legally transferred to the company, and confidentiality should be written into staff contracts.
- You should build a close working relationship with your patent lawyers to ensure they fully understand the nature of your business.
- Log onto our web site at www.innovationtocashflows to access these supplementary materials:
  - Appendix 2.2, "Guidelines for Setting Up an Invention Disclosure System for Your Company"
  - Appendix 2.3, "Sample Invention Disclosure Form"
  - "Resources," see section "Law and Intellectual Property" for recommended books; see section "Contract Law, Commercial Law and Other Intellectual Property" for online web sites related to patents and other types of intellectual property

CHAPTER 14

Navigating Technology License Agreements

Conan Chitham
Withers LLP

This chapter looks at the key tool in all technology exploitation arrangements: the technology license. It is variously referred to as a *patent license, know-how license,* or technology transfer agreement. For consistency's sake, we shall refer to it as a technology transfer agreement. It is, in essence, a license of all or part of a technology; it may include any feasible combination of intellectual property (IP) categories: copyrights, trademarks, designs, patents, confidential know-how, or trade secrets. In the United Kingdom and Europe, the term *know-how* in the context of technology licensing means secret and substantial technical information and is similar to the U.S. concept of *trade secrets* under the Uniform Trade Secrets Act.[1]

High-technology strategic alliances, joint ventures, or codevelopment deals depend on technology transfer agreements. In the case of corporate joint ventures, it is common for each participating party to place its technology into separate special-purpose legal corporations or special-purpose vehicles (SPVs); then, through the mechanism of technology transfer license agreements, the IP rights may be transferred out of the SPV and licensed for use by the joint venture.

Similarly, in a codevelopment arrangement, each party may license to the other the necessary development rights using a technology transfer agreement, including provisions for the future licensing of the resulting rights to one or both parties as appropriate. Even in mature businesses, the technology transfer agreement is a key tool. It can be used for dealing with many diverse situations, such as specialist manufacturing collaborations (perhaps producing critical components or doing specialized subassembly work in a coproduction agreement). Alternatively, the technology transfer could involve licensing the latest technology to a third party in order to extend the reach of the strategic alliance to new target customers or new distribution channels. It also could allow the market to be segmented, in other words, to make provisions for another party to undertake the sale or manufacture of a product for a different market segment—say, for example, the automotive sector instead of the aerospace market or in order to maximize the use of the technology in areas where the owner may not have core competencies or routes to the market.

So from these illustrations, we can see that technology transfer arrangements may range from limited *nonexclusive* licenses of discrete technologies for a special purpose in support of the *licensor* to a wide range of strategic alliances and codevelopment or comarketing agreements based on sharing patented technology and know-how. The right technology transfer structure at the outset can make a difference on how many options your venture may have to exploit in the future. Learning the principles of how to better structure technology transfer agreements is the purpose of this chapter.

STRUCTURE OF A BASIC TECHNOLOGY TRANSFER AGREEMENT

There are as many variations on technology transfer agreements as it is possible to imagine. However, regardless of jurisdiction,[2] all of these agreements will share a number of common features. These common features achieve a basic aim: to regulate the terms on which technical knowledge is transferred and patented technology is used by another party. Much will depend on the nature of the technology (whether it is a process, formula, product, or another sort of technology), the proposed uses by the licensee, the financial provisions, and the negotiation skills, bargaining position, and economic balance between the parties.

For the small innovation business dealing with another partner, either big or small, adopting a collaborative approach is inevitably the most rewarding. This does not mean that you should not assertively (as opposed to aggressively) negotiate your best position. But it does mean recognizing that the best value is obtained by working together to find a mutually acceptable legal position to form the foundation of a relationship going forward. In any case you should realize that technology transfer is a complex, time-consuming, and, potentially, costly process needing careful consideration not only of the deal at hand but of the future strategy for the technology and the business. You need to recognize the fundamental importance of these arrangements to the current and future prospects of the technology and the enterprises involved. It is dangerous and shortsighted not to invest the appropriate time and effort to this process. It will be key to the future success of the business.

EXAMPLE OF A LICENSE ARRANGEMENT: BASED ON A TRUE STORY

Bob, based in Europe, invented new software coding that helped to facilitate web site user participation on a massive scale in social networking sites. Early on, he licensed it via a friend of a friend to a site operator in the United States. He had been glad of the money, which helped him spend time developing further versions of the coding. He had, of course, signed a license arrangement with the site operator, but it now appears that he gave away more than he had thought at the time, when admittedly he did not focus on some of the details as much as he should have. Not only does the site operator have a long fixed-term *exclusive license*, but it has the right to call for a license of any further versions or improvement to the coding, too. This had seemed fair at the time because Bob was working with a prototype. Now it means he cannot exploit the technology in the United States except through the site operator, and this is threatening his current business.

Another factor that you will often need to take into account is the role played by universities, technology sponsors, grant bodies, government agencies, and similar early investors in the development of the technology. All of these players may have an interest in the way that the technology is being exploited. If they have funded the development of the technology, they will want to see that any licensing arrangement operates successfully for the maximum return on their investment or complies with other policies or governance rules that they may have. These organizations may have standard legal clauses or even contract terms and conditions that they will require to be included. In certain cases, they may require a right to step in and take over the licensor's responsibilities so as to secure their rights. You will need to consider whether their demands conflict with the deal you want to do and the strategic approach you have developed and, if so, how to deal with them. You may find yourself negotiating with your investors and sponsors as well as with your proposed license partner.

The degree of internationalization that your technology transfer involves will also affect the degree of complexity of the legal document. Significantly, more complex issues arise when you are transferring technology or authorizing another to use technology in different jurisdictions. As the most complex of all, multijurisdictional arrangements have to provide for a wide range of foreseeable and, most awkwardly, unforeseeable situations. For these sorts of arrangements, you will need to think carefully with your advisors about the applicable law (in other words, if it should be English law, New York law, etc.) and jurisdiction (where court proceedings can take place). You will need advice on the risks of each legal territory in which the license is taking effect or the license partner is based, the ease of enforcing your rights and any special rules of law that apply to the technology transfer in these jurisdictions.

OUTLINE OF THE AGREEMENT

The following is not intended to be a detailed drafting guide but an outline of the main commercial and technical provisions that you will need to be thinking about and dealing with when setting up a technology transfer agreement. It goes without saying that specialist legal counsel experienced in the commercialization of intellectual property should be involved in any technology transfer agreement you do. It is a very wise precaution and should add value to the process and therefore to the technology in the longer term. Technology transfer agreements are not arrangements that can be safely undertaken by amateurs or by using general precedents from third-party sources, the Internet, or textbooks alone.

Parties

The starting point must be that the parties to the agreement are clearly defined and identified. They also need to be the appropriate parties. The licensor must be the owner of the relevant rights or otherwise have the right to license them. The licensee must be the party that will exploit the rights unless specific provision is made for sublicensing. As licensor, you will need to consider sublicensing carefully to ensure your risks are properly managed. If you are the licensee, you may want to undertake due diligence to ensure that the licensor holds the rights they say they do.

A typical (and frequent) example of where a wrong licensee might be referred to improperly is where a corporate group has organized its rights to be held by one entity (perhaps a foreign holding company) rather than one of the trading companies with whom negotiations might have taken place. You need to be aware of this and make sure the internal arrangements are reflected in the agreement.

Definitions

The definitions will be critical and often do not receive the degree of attention that they deserve. However, they drive the whole of the agreement and should be the first thing to get right. Four key terms need to be defined carefully:

1. Technology
2. Territory
3. Exclusivity
4. Field of use

The main issues pertaining to each are described next.

1. *Technology.* Where it consists of granted patents alone, this may be by a relatively straightforward cross-reference to a list of relevant granted and in-force patents. Even then, care must be taken to consider future developments of the patents, the granting or refusing of any application for patents, and patents claiming priority from the listed patents in the same family. In the case of patent and know-how licenses, and in pure know-how licenses, you need to be careful about the definition of the know-how. Where the licensor is well organized and has the know-how in carefully encapsulated or recorded form, a definition process will be much easier. However, experience suggests that this is rarely the case with smaller innovation businesses; the know-how is often in the heads of the innovators and is not fully documented. In some businesses—for example, those closely associated with the academic world—more comprehensive documentation may exist, but it is not always in a state that is most useful for transfer to another. Before signing the license, each party needs to have a clear idea of what is inside and what is outside the scope of the license. If you are a licensor, you may need to undertake a careful exercise of know-how capture to describe the technology in a usable way before you can license it successfully. Inevitably in some industries there are elements of know-how that cannot be adequately described in writing or by formulas but need to be seen or demonstrated. (See "Know-How Transfer" later in this chapter.)

DEFINE IT

It is crucial to define properly the terms in any technology transfer agreement. Properly defined terms can save a great deal of confusion and help from the outset to produce a clear and well-thought-out arrangement. Some principal terms and sample definitions follow.

> **Technology** means the patents and know-how (defined next).
>
> **Patents** mean the granted patents, applications for patents listed in the schedule, and any further granted patent or patent applications made by the licensor claiming priority from them.
>
> **Know-how** means the description of the technology set out in the operating manuals in the sections labeled {KH 100.1–KH100.4} and as demonstrated in the "Know-How Transfer" sections {KH 200.1–KH200.8} of the operating manuals.
>
> **Territory** means the United States and Canada and the member states of the European Union, as constituted on January 1, 2009.

---

2. *Territory.* This term's definition needs care and precision, particularly if the territory is more than one jurisdiction. Sloppy references to North America, for example, rather than identifying legally defined territories, can cause significant problems in the licensing of the technology. You also need to be careful in referring to territory by reference to international structures such as the European Union or the North American Free Trade Agreement. You need to be clear what happens to the scope of the license when membership of these international treaty territories changes. A specific example is to define what it means for the parties signing the licensing agreement. If the European Union adds new countries, will these new territories be included or not included under the terms of the agreement?

3. *Exclusivity.* Whether the licensee is to be exclusive or not is a key issue and affects the whole nature of the agreement. Exclusivity should be defined so that there is no misunderstanding of the use or interpretation of the terms *Exclusive*, *Nonexclusive*, or *Sole* between different parties and jurisdictions. These definitions are proposed:

Exclusive means that the licensor will not authorize anybody else to nor will itself exploit the technology in the exclusive territory.

Nonexclusive means that the licensor or another third party authorized by the licensor may freely exploit the technology in the territory.

Sole means that the licensor will not license anybody else to use the technology in the territory though retains the right to do so itself.

If an exclusive license is to be granted, you need to give careful consideration to the terms and conditions of that exclusivity and their interrelationship to your own business performance and the penetration of the market with the technology. If you grant an exclusive license as a licensor without any performance obligations on the licensee, you could be made a hostage to fortune—as the licensee may effectively block the use of your own technology in that exclusive territory. Financial techniques such as inserting into the contract terms minimum guaranteed royalties are a partial answer to such issues but are not certain to achieve your aims as a licensor. In addition, therefore, you should consider inserting more direct obligations and milestones into the agreement, such as a specific launch date in the territory, targeted sales for each year (increasing annually), and best endeavors to increase the sales, frequency of product use, or market penetration. If you are dealing with a license at the outset or early on in the life of an unproved technology, then you may have some difficulty defining the criteria of success or performance milestones. This is not an excuse for avoiding the subject: From a licensor's point of view a grant of exclusivity is very valuable.

A failure to meet performance targets should be a termination event, but given the disruption that termination causes, you may want to have specific remedies that allow the license to continue, such as the removal of the exclusivity or reduction of the territorial scope of the exclusivity or the license as a whole.

EXAMPLE: A LICENSOR GRANTS AN EXCLUSIVE LICENSE FOR THE EUROPEAN UNION

The licensor of a pharmaceutical product granted an exclusive license for the European Union (at the time 22 countries). The licensee only exploited the product in one of the wealthiest countries where its return was best and it had established sales networks. These sales alone allowed it to comfortably fulfill its minimum royalty obligations, which were the only performance obligation stipulated. Demand in the other countries was not satisfied, although there were some secondary cross-border sales, so the product was known in these territories. The licensor could not itself satisfy the demands, due to the terms of the exclusivity. Not only did this lead to lost sales in the other territories, it also harmed the licensor's brand reputation due to dissatisfaction at the poor level of availability in these territories. Until the license came to an end, the licensor was powerless to take effective action.

4. *Field of use.* This refers to the specialization of use or market segmentation that a licensor can impose. For example, a license may allow use of the technology only in the consumer sector or directly to hospitals. Another example is a license that allows use of the technology in the automotive sector while reserving other uses including the aeronautical sector. This segmentation is often tied in with exclusivity and provides a useful tool to license technology for a particular purpose, market application, or other more narrowly defined undertaking to two or more exclusive licensees for a territory but with different channels to market.

All of these terms will be referred to extensively in the license and will affect the whole form and nature of the technology transfer arrangement.

Financial Considerations

Central to technology transfer licenses is what the licensor (the owner, say, of the patent) can get back in terms of financial remuneration from the licensee (the party that is "renting" the patent or paying for the right to use it). Of course, the financial costs are of equal significance to the licensee and an excessively high payment to the licensor will be detrimental to the licensee's ability to exploit the licensed rights.

The basic mechanism of remuneration for a licensor is a royalty. A royalty is a percentage calculated on either the value of sales or the incremental use of the technology, such as per item produced, or a combination of the two. Of course, a royalty can be expressed simply or involve complicated calculations of deductions, additions, rebates, or more depending on the market and the complexity of the technology. Some of the royalty may be paid as an advance that may be deducted against future royalties.

As the licensor of a patented technology and founder of a start-up business, it may be essential for you to negotiate a cash advance up front in order to keep your venture from insolvency or bankruptcy. In practical cash flow terms, it may be especially important where there has been or continues to be a considerable financial investment by you in technology development and the potential of an ongoing delay before additional financing is received.

Often, however, the opposite scenario is true. It is the licensee that has to bear the brunt of the investment in order to develop a technology, incorporate it into a product, and bring it to the customers in the designated market in the allotted territory. If this is the case, an advance may divert cash away from investing fully in the early stages of the roll-out of the licensed technology to your longer-term detriment as licensor (the owner of the patent). The rate of royalty, any advance, and the measure against which that rate is set need careful consideration, taking account of the investment that each party needs to make.

As licensor, you may well want to have some sort of minimum royalty payable under the license, especially if it is exclusive, as noted earlier. This often takes the form of an increasing year-on-year guarantee. A minimum royalty is really all about providing a minimum revenue stream for the licensor.

Be mindful that minimum royalties are not the same thing as a target goal. A target should be a more ambitious measure. Minimum royalties as well as a guarantee of income level should be used as basic measures of satisfactory performance. Failure of a licensee to meet these minimum performance measures may be used (by the licensor) to terminate a license or reduce the scope of the territory or exclusivity. While either measure—minimum royalties or guarantee of income level—obviously contains an element of incentive, it certainly is not unknown for a licensee to agree to pay minimum royalties, if only to keep the licensed technology out of the market. (Refer to earlier discussions on "Exclusivity" for more about performance obligations.) Even in less cynical cases, minimum royalties can end up being a target ceiling rather than the floor they are meant to be. To be effective performance tools, minimum royalties need to be combined with other performance obligations and measures.

For a business that is not established and with a technology that is not yet proven, the calculation of a royalty can be particularly difficult. One of the most frequently asked questions is: What is the usual rate for this sort of thing? It is a question that perplexes lawyers, accountants, and patent valuation consultants. There is no such thing as a standard or usual rate, particularly for a genuinely new technology—it is worth what someone is willing to pay. Also, the "value" of the technology may change significantly over its exploitation lifetime. It may prove to be more valuable than first thought or indeed quite the opposite. The rate of royalty and any minimum payment therefore need to be a compromise on "shared risk" versus early returns that reflects a wide range of potential outcomes to the reasonable satisfaction of both parties. This may need careful explaining to any investor who may wish to see a quicker return on its money even if this is not in the best long-term interests of the exploitation of the technology. (See Chapter 20 for details on how to quantify these potential outcomes, risks, and expected returns in a financial model.)

Contingent Payment Mechanisms   One way of dealing with the issue of initial valuation against subsequent proven valuation is providing in the contract a *contingent payment mechanism*. There are a couple of common ways of doing this. The first is known as a structured *royalty ratchet*. This is a mechanism whereby the payment is changed on a mathematical basis according to certain agreed targets. As a licensor, you may set a relatively high royalty rate of 20 percent initially. To incentivize the licensee, a ratchet may then operate to bring this royalty down to, say, 18 percent if royalties are more that $500,000 and 15 percent if royalties are more than $1 million. Alternatively, you may be keen to get the licensee to agree to a deal. You are willing to mitigate some of the licensee's risk so you initially agree to a low royalty rate, increasing as certain sales levels are reached and the technology proves its marketability. Various triggers for the ratchet can be used, such as the number of products sold incorporating the technology, the number of customers or territories dealt with, or the revenue due directly or indirectly to the technology's use.

The second mechanism is known as an *interim revaluation*. An interim revaluation is a reappraisal of the technology's worth at some agreed on point in time or upon the achievement of a particular milestone or target. An independent qualified appraiser typically does this appraisal. Using an interim revaluation may be suitable if the situation is complicated and there are no reliable guides to the technology's market value. The independent expert provides a valuation at a certain point in time, which then reboots the license royalties at an interim point, much like a rent review of a leased property. There is a risk, particularly from a licensor's point of view, that the technology will not prove as valuable as first hoped and in the end the licensor actually ends up with a lower royalty than before. The process also has its share of definitional and choice of criteria issues, but some of these can be postponed and left to the discretion and experience of the appraiser. Of course, the choice of the appraiser, and his or her selection if the parties cannot agree on the choice, is another critical issue to be documented. Usually disputes about the choice of appraiser are dealt with by appointing the president of an independent professional body to select a person. The drafting of this provision requires some care and needs to be unambiguous or the nominated person may decline to act to avoid a claim being made by one or other party.

Another financial consideration is whether a premium should be paid—in other words, an up-front lump sum for the technology license. The difference between a "premium" and an "advance" is that a premium is *not* repayable from future royalties; an advance is. When the technology has not yet proven itself, it may be difficult to ask for an up-front lump sum from the licensee.

When you (as licensee) are negotiating with a larger organization (as licensor), asking for a lump sum may be more realistic—although the larger organization is likely to want to have the funds as an advance on royalties, not as an outright advance. Essentially, the result depends on bargaining power—how much does the prospective licensee want or need the technology, and how flexible is the licensor willing to be toward prospective licensees?

A word of warning: Experience tends to suggest that where a premium is achieved, subsequent royalty rates are lower unless the technology is a genuine killer application. In other words, the overall amount of money received is often similar whether a premium is paid or not; it is the timing of the receipt of money that changes.

Other matters that will be included in the financial provisions relate to the payment process, including: frequency of financial reports and accounting statements on how much royalty is due; invoicing policies; requirements for financial audits and independent verification of record keeping. In international situations, there may be withholding tax deduction issues where the royalty is paid across jurisdictional boundaries, which may affect the actual, in-hand royalty received. A process for dealing with this should be anticipated in the agreement to enable recovery of paid tax where possible. Various standard forms exist for all of these matters; lawyers can adopt them, and you should discuss the forms with them.

Termination

If the license is to be exclusive or even sole, then, as mentioned, you should have criteria against which that exclusivity is to be reviewed and perhaps reduced or withdrawn. If the licensee fails to exploit the technology appropriately, the loss may be significant, both in terms of pure revenues and the long-term value of the technology.

The basic criteria for termination in a technology transfer arrangement are usually relatively straightforward and standard. Broadly, the most common are breach, failure to comply with performance criteria or to pay money when due, and insolvency/bankruptcy. You should think about any specific criteria that should be included depending on your particular position. For example, a change in the ownership of the license, licensee causing harm to your reputation, or licensee taking a license of a competing technology. Challenging the licensor's IP rights is often grounds for termination in its own right.

Termination for breach may be refined by having different categories of breach: material and nonmaterial as well as remediable and nonremediable. For remediable breaches, you may agree that you will have the right to terminate only if the other side fails to remedy within defined remedy periods. Minor breaches by the licensee that accumulate during a period need to be addressed in the licensing agreement. The usual mechanism is for the licensor to state that in aggregate the minor breaches over a period will constitute a terminable breach. As licensor, you may also want to include compensation provisions for situations where breaches are not remediable but you do not wish to terminate.

The insolvency of a party is a critical point in a license. From a licensee's point of view, the licensor's insolvency causes a number of practical issues. The licensee will need to decide whether to continue or terminate the license depending on a variety of factors. Normally, a licensee will want to continue exploiting the licensed rights as a source of revenue if the license is remunerative (i.e., pays out money). In the situation where a license is not remunerative, a liquidator or receiver of an insolvent business may have legal powers to terminate a license. Even when that is not the case (i.e., the license is remunerative and the liquidator or receiver has no legal powers to terminate the license), of course the issue remains that the licensee may lose the practical support of the licensor, at least temporarily, until the rights are sold to a new licensor. Moreover, the licensee bears the risk that the liquidator or receiver may sell the rights to another party—who may or may not be a good licensor or may even be a competitor of the licensee.

Often termination is not really a relevant remedy for a licensee who suffers breaches by the licensor; the licensee will want to continue with the license and to use the technology. As a licensee, you may try to include alternative compensation mechanisms for breach by the licensor.

As the licensor, dealing with what happens after termination is more complex. Generally, technology transfer agreements set in place mechanisms and marketplace positions that cannot be simply turned on or off. A licensee will have perhaps begun regulatory approval processes (or completed them) or will have established customers who are using or buying the technology in one form or another. You need to take a realistic view of what the market situation may be at termination and build into the license the steps to be undertaken by both parties. As much as you (and the other party) may desire it, you may not be able simply to terminate and walk away. Like any ongoing relationship, a period of businesslike, if not necessarily friendly, post-termination relationship may well be needed to sort out the transfer issues and provide continuity in the market. Of course, you as the licensor may need to put in a lot more effort to effect this; the licensee's financial interest will have largely disappeared so its incentive to cooperate may be low. In order to help with this, it may be worth considering whether to pay the licensee a fee during a post-termination transition phase or allow it to still benefit for a period from the income from the technology.

Know-How Transfer

A crucial element of certain technology transfer arrangements is the effective transfer of know-how. As a licensee, you need to be particularly aware of this issue. It is all very well having the right to use a technology, but if you cannot put it into practice, it is not very useful to you. Even where there is a clear patent at the heart of the technology, likely there is some background information that must be imparted for effective or the most efficient use of the patent.

As discussed earlier in this chapter, in the section "Definitions," a good licensor will have documented as much of this know-how as possible. First and foremost, a licensee needs a complete, accurate, and up-to-date copy of this documentation.

Beyond that document, for some technologies, some of the know-how needs to be demonstrated as "show-how." Training in the technology is part of that process, and you should have specific provisions about training. You need to address what training will be given, where, and who pays what cost. You might include in the license only initial training but have provisions for the licensee to pay for more. If the training is taking place at the licensee's premises, you need to agree who will pay for the trainers' travel and accommodation costs. If it is to be at the licensor's premises, you need to make clear who will pay for the attendee's costs (and how many can be trained).

On top of or instead of training is the idea of mentoring: having a person skilled in the technology working with a licensee for a while to implement, troubleshoot, and show-how. Perhaps, as licensor, you could send a representative to work with a licensor. Of course, this will depend on the technology and the degree of assistance that the licensee needs. It is also worth considering whether you need to provide ongoing technical assistance, perhaps as the technology improves or changes or new applications open up.

The cost and who bears it is important, of course. Perhaps the licensee can buy at consultancy rates. When you are considering how much training or mentoring is needed and who will bear the cost, bear in mind that only after licensees have had effective training and transfer of know-how will they be in a position to exploit the technology effectively and generate the revenue to pay royalties.

Patent Infringements and Licensing

You need to think carefully about issues relating to patent licensing in any technology transfer arrangement. Deciding who should be responsible for taking action for patent infringement by a third party or defending any action brought against your technology is not always straightforward.

If the licensee is the most active exploiter of the IP, then its economic interest in any patent infringement claim may be higher than the licensor's, especially if it is an exclusive licensee. Conversely, if the technology is the capital property of the licensor, then any decisions that may affect its long-term capital value should be controlled by it. As licensor, of course, you profit from the license of the technology and are contractually obliged to give the licensee access to the rights. You must consider very carefully how you are to fulfill your obligations as the licensor of the technology in any case where third parties claim that the technology infringes on their rights.

The law in some territories provides that an exclusive licensee may, of its own initiative, take action to prosecute patent infringement claims against others. However, the technology transfer agreement needs to address the issue specifically to make sure that both parties have the necessary input into any infringement proceedings to be taken and that the responsibilities and liabilities for costs are clearly allocated. It may also be worth reviewing this issue as the technology transfer relationship continues. It should perhaps be the subject of a detailed renegotiation at any renewal of the agreement if there is a shift in the balance of use or exposure of the technology.

In the case of taking action against third-party infringers, generally speaking, no matter how slight the licensor's interest is, it should allow nothing to be done that will destroy the capital value of the technology. Likewise, the licensee must be able to protect its economic value in the income from exploitation of the technology without undue constraint. This means that a license often needs a clearly set out cooperation provision with the sharing of risks and rewards. In other cases, one party or the other will need to be given the lead according to the risk to each party.

Similar provisions will need to be considered in relation to defending infringement proceedings by third parties. Licensees that are actively exploiting the licensed technology often are the target of the first round of such claims. Of course, the licensor has contractually promised to allow the use of a valuable licensed technology to a licensee. In such cases, it may be reasonable to expect the licensor to put the licensee in a good position, whatever the merits of the third-party claims, and to take at its own risk all the steps necessary to do so. This may require you as licensor to procure from the third party a license of its technology. However, if you license in good faith a technology that subsequently becomes the subject of an infringement claim by a third party—for example, in a new territory—a more cooperative approach may well be appropriate. This may be the case where the technology is new and has not been exploited previously. Here the risk allocation should be more evenly spread.

For each and every case, the actual commercial situation and the commercial strengths and weaknesses of each party, plus the foreseeable circumstances of infringement must be considered carefully. Provisions in the agreement relating to infringement are not a time for a pro forma or simple precedent approach but are rather a time to seek to provide for the best possible allocation of risk and reward for the mutual benefit of both parties. If the licensor and licensee are seen to have divided interests or stances on any action it is all the more likely that any subsequent infringement action taken against a third party will fail or a defense against an action brought by a third party will be unsuccessful.

COMPETITION LAW AND ANTITRUST PROVISIONS

Technology transfer arrangements, as noted, may be governed by antitrust and competition law in many jurisdictions. In many cases, technology transfer agreements are considered to be potentially anticompetitive, as they can have the effect of dividing a market, therefore stifling innovation, reducing the access to technology, or reducing the number of players in a market who are able to exploit a particular technology and therefore raising barriers to new competition. However, competition law in the European Union (EU) recognizes that there are benefits to technology licensing too and that a properly constructed technology transfer license can negate all of the points set out above—especially if the parties do not control significant portions of the market.

In the EU, therefore, a specific provision of European law provides for technology transfer (including specifically software licensing) known as the Technology Transfer Block Exemption (TTBE).[3] The TTBE allows for certain provisions that would otherwise be potentially anticompetitive (in the context of EU competition law) to survive on the basis that their overall *economic effect* is to increase competition. Not only does the TTBE provide a number of general exemptions to European competition law for technology licenses, it also sets economic tests and thresholds for these exemptions to apply. Below certain economic thresholds (discussed next), the market power of a business is considered to be such that any licensing arrangements the business undertakes would not have an anticompetitive effect—unless the licensing arrangement includes a listed "Hardcore Restriction" that is considered anti-competitive and prohibited at any economic threshold. (Hardcore restrictions include: restrictions on freedom to set prices, limitations on output, and allocations of customers.) If the market power of the business exceeds the relevant economic threshold, then the "economic effect" test means that a licensing arrangement will automatically fall outside the exemption, in which case, the parties must be able to demonstrate that the "economic effect" of the license is not anticompetitive. Doing this becomes increasingly difficult as the level of market share rises.

The principal thresholds are defined by reference to a share of the market for the particular technology. The market for a new technology can be difficult to define. One of the key tests is substitutability—is there another product or technology that can be used instead? With a genuinely innovative technology, there may be no substitute. The substitute does not need to be exact but needs to allow a user to achieve a similar practical effect. The two relevant threshold levels are 30 percent for "noncompeting" businesses and 20 percent for "competing" businesses, in each case of the combined share of the market. The TTBE defines *competing* and *noncompeting* in economic terms. Unfortunately, in cooperative technology transfer, the licensor and licensee may well be considered competitors. One particular issue for new businesses is that the economic tests in particular are measured throughout the life of any technology transfer licensing arrangements. Especially for rapid growth areas, this can mean that a business may go from being under the economic threshold at the outset of a license to well over the economic threshold for the applicability of the exemption at the end of a license period.

The application of these exemptions and of the economic tests is complex and must be done with proper professional guidance. You need to understand fully the relevant market for the thresholds, and the further complication of the application of the TTBE. Technology transfer licensing arrangements must be constructed carefully.

EXAMPLES: BIOL LIMITED AND BLIZZEN SA

Biol Limited, a British company, has developed a new technology that binds onto the chemical in existing chemotherapy treatments to make them less generally traumatic for the patient. It works by limiting the effect on other cells. On one hand, Biol's market share may be argued as being 100 percent, if you were to define the market scope narrowly as encompassing only Biol's specific unique technology. Other products may not be regarded as substitutable, and Biol's technology could stand alone. Any license of it will fall outside the EU technology transfer block exemption. On the other hand, a number of palliative treatments related to chemotherapy are well established. Consequently, it could be argued that Biol should be regarded as initially having almost no market share. If this interpretation is accepted, then Biol's license agreements, at least at the beginning phases, would fall well within the threshold for the application of the TTBE.

Blizzen SA, a French company, has a technology that automatically compresses and aligns data processed in central processing units (CPUs) and random

(Continued)

EXAMPLES: BIOL LIMITED AND BLIZZEN SA
(*Continued*)

---

access memory (RAM), such that they operate much faster. The technology includes a chip that acts as a gateway for CPUs and RAM. As it is a hardware-based technology, Blizzen has had a hard time getting it adopted by end user equipment manufacturers. Its market share has been only 7 percent up to this year. It has signed a license with a large European chip set and motherboard manufacturer, and its market share is likely to be 28 percent this year and 38 percent next year. Depending on whether Blizzen's license is considered to be with a competitor or not, it is either already out of the scope of the TTBE or will be very soon.

Other jurisdictions have different sensitivities to the anticompetitive or antitrust effects of patent licensing or technology transfer arrangements. Anticompetitive or antitrust issues should always be considered when entering into any sort of exclusive arrangement with a third party. Again, the licensing of technology across jurisdictional boundaries further complicates the structuring of such agreements.

HEADS OF TERMS OR MEMORANDUM OF UNDERSTANDING

Often the best approach to entering into a technology transfer arrangement is first to come up with a memorandum of understanding (MoU) (or heads of terms, as it is known in England). These documents are alternatively referred to as a deal sheet, or a letter of intent (LoI). In general, an MoU is signed by all potential parties, whereas an LoI is a unilateral declaration of intent. In all of these documents, the parties (or party) to them express the intention to enter into serious negotiations and conclude a contract.

As such, the MoU or deal sheet are *informal* documents that record the principal commercial terms of a deal, usually without legally binding either party to it. They can therefore initially be negotiated (though not finalized) directly between the parties before being considered and checked by each party's legal team. Often the heads of terms or MoU incorporates a confidentiality clause and perhaps an exclusive negotiation period that is intended to be legally binding even if the rest is not. (For more on confidentiality agreements, see Chapter 9.)

For the reasons given earlier, the range and diversity of potential technology transfer transactions and the contracts that reflect them means that any sample agreement is likely to be more constraining than useful. There is much more that can and needs to be considered in a technology transfer agreement than what could ever appear in a sample document. If, however, you are able to address the main commercial and technical points at an early stage in negotiations, you are less likely to waste time when the negotiations are more advanced and a more robust and sound deal is likely to be done. It is almost always best to facilitate the discussion of these main points and to create a heads of term or MoU that sets out at an early stage of the negotiations the proposed approach to be taken. It is obvious by the comments just made that you should involve experienced IP lawyers early in the process. Too often lawyers are presented with a heads of terms or MoU signed and agreed between parties. Had the lawyers had the opportunity to comment on these points at an earlier stage, they may have been able to influence, correct, or even bring up other important issues.

Appendix 14.1 (located at the end of this chapter) presents a sample heads of terms or memorandum of understanding that may be usefully used either as the agenda for any first discussion of a technology transfer arrangement or as an internal set of talking points to decide the approach to key issues in advance.

Grant-Backs

A grant-back or license-back is a feature of technology transfer transactions that are used in several scenarios. Where there has been an outright assignment of the technology to a third party or a long exclusive license, a grant-back allows the originating party to continue to use that IP, perhaps for internal purposes, to develop further improvements or associated technology in a different field of use (in other words, a different application) or marketplace (as discussed earlier).

These clauses are also used in research and development (R&D) collaborations where, perhaps, each party grants back to the other a license of the IP that it has developed to ensure that each party comes out of the collaboration with a complete suite of IP rights. Often in these situations the grant-back is limited to a particular field of use, effectively dividing the market for the technology between the R&D partners. Antitrust/competition law issues pertain to the use of grant-backs, particularly within the EU, but also in other jurisdictions where trust or competition law seeks to avoid the structured division of marketplaces. You should seek professional legal guidance as a matter of course when considering these sorts of provisions.

EXAMPLE: MESSA

Messa is a specialist sportswear manufacturer in Denmark. Endo Ltd. is a U.K. defense development business. They collaborated on the manufacture of specialist clothing and footwear. Messa contributed its specialist knowledge of the demands of athletes in training and competing. Endo contributed its specialist knowledge of materials. During the development period, there was a limited grant to each other of the other's existing IP for the purpose of developing the final products only. (This existing IP is often referred to as background IP: any IP a party had *before* the collaboration). Each party retained the IP it developed and jointly developed IP was held jointly. At the end of the development period, each party granted a license-back to the other of all of the developed IP for use by Endo in military-related applications and by Messa in sports-related applications only.

Another common context in which grant-back clauses are found are in more straightforward licenses or technology transfer arrangements where the licensor seeks to get a license back to it of any improvements that the licensee discovers or develops relating to the licensed technology. Again, antitrust and competition law considerations may need to be addressed if you want to do this. In the EU, such grant-backs must comply with the terms of the TTBE that regulates all technology transfer licenses in the EU. The TTBE terms require a high level of mutuality in such clauses.

The use of grant-back clauses can be advantageous to both parties. However, overreliance on grant-back clauses can cause the parties to an arrangement to lose sight of the fundamental reasons for the technology transfer in the first place: the need for dissemination of innovation in order to facilitate the exploitation of a market or of a combined technology that would otherwise either not be available at all to the originator of the technology or that would be difficult for it to exploit. Grant-backs can act to undermine the incentive to innovate if a licensee has to give the licensor access to technology improvements. The limiting effects of antitrust or competition law can make grant-backs less attractive to licensors. They can be very useful but must be drafted carefully.

Cross-Licensing

Cross-licensing is distinguished from grant-backs in that a cross-license is a two-way license between two parties of a technology that may or may not be related. It is a common tool in the electronic and computing fields and notably in pharmaceuticals and biotechnology. Where the technologies are related, the term *patent pool* may be used instead of *cross-licensing*.

The justification between larger companies for cross-licensing or patent pooling is to come to a commercial and practical solution to issues that would otherwise be the subject of infringement proceedings. By cross-licensing, the parties can not only save themselves costs but they can, arguably, bring the technology to the marketplace more quickly (by avoiding the delays of a court action), and therefore benefit consumers. Without cross-licensing, the threat of legal proceedings often means that the technology would not be exploited at all in some territories so as to avoid increasing the potential for damages. (Often damages are calculated by reference to income from the exploitation.) These situations can arise in many ways, but the most common is where there is a parallel development of similar technologies or an improvement to a previously patented technology, a license of which is needed to exploit the successor technology.

Another situation in which cross-licensing is relevant is where each party holds outright a technology that is key to the development or exploitation of the other's technology. This area may be of particular relevance to younger innovation businesses. The advantages of cross-licensing here are not only avoiding the time and effort required to self-develop that part of the technology but the enhancement that the cooperation with another can bring to the product's marketing. For example, patent pooling or cross-licensing often is used where a common format is required in order to disseminate the technology.

For a new innovation business, there are a great many potential hazards in undertaking cross-licensing or joining a patent pool, especially where there is no reasonable parity or bargaining position between the parties. Cross-licensing has been abused when large companies used access to their technology as a lever to require cross-licensing of another party's technology to them. This abuse has enabled the larger business to exploit that other party's technology using its enhanced market position to the ultimate detriment of the smaller party. Many examples of this situation exist, most obviously in personal computing software. If you are going to undertake any cross-licensing, you need to give serious thought to the benefit of licensing-out what may be the key value of your business and what terms you agree to in order to protect your position.

Where there is some parity between the parties or a clear benefit and legal structure to protect each party, patent pooling or cross-licensing can be a powerful enabler of progress, saving many years of frustrating research or diverting energies into working around another party's patent or technology. No small business wants to waste valuable time and resources in unnecessary litigation where a commercial solution can be reached. Cross-licensing and patent pooling recognizes that no single innovator can always come up with all the necessary solutions required to produce a marketable product and that the incorporation of third-party IP can be mutually beneficial where parties are working in a similar environment.

Open Innovation Modes

Some larger enterprises are now actively working with third parties on using cross-licensing to utilize to the fullest their research departments while keeping focused on their core product range or market. This open licensing framework has many guises, but it is essentially a form of cross-licensing. What is more notable is the structural shift that this represents in what are often very large technology businesses. It shows that they recognize that it is no longer possible to have a monopoly over a particular technology. The diversity of solutions and applications is too great. Furthermore, it is obvious to nearly everyone that innovation is not the exclusive preserve of an in-house research department but is possible anywhere in a firm or among its alliance network.

By creating open structures internally and developing strong relationships with innovators externally, these businesses are seeking to ensure that they continue to have access to leading-edge technology. Collaborating with companies that have already adopted open innovation models is potentially advantageous and of lower risk for smaller innovative businesses than the expensive route of entirely self-developed products.

CHAPTER TAKEAWAYS

- Consider the definitions of any technology transfer agreements carefully. Know the answers to these basic queries: What? Who? Where? What for? How long?
- Involve competent legal advisors at an early stage, even when negotiating such nonbinding agreements as deal sheets or preliminary MoUs. Complex legal and business issues are involved. Having an experienced team negotiating such agreements on your behalf will pay off in the long run.
- Consider deal structure provisions at the outset. Put yourself in the place of the other parties. Think through in advance such basic licensing issues as exclusivity and nonexclusivity rights, time, territory, and exploitation rights. Work out

various scenarios and leave yourself room to negotiate a variety of conditions and terms.

- Consider financial provisions to be an integral part of the deal structuring process. Depending on the deal conditions, the financial results will change. The two parts—deal conditions and financial terms—need to be modeled together, not separately.
- Consider issues of nonperformance. If the licensee delays exploitation, the licensor's opportunity cost of lost time and money may be high. Take steps at the outset to try to mitigate this risk through careful selection and screening of licensee candidates. If the licensee is distracted by other issues or runs into difficulties, have adequate provisions for working out ways to resolve differences or, if need be, to terminate the contractual relationship.
- Finally, consider issues of infringement and who bears this risk.

APPENDIX 14.1 SAMPLE HEADS OF TERMS OR MEMORANDUM OF UNDERSTANDING

Technology Transfer

This memorandum of understanding sets out the principal points of agreement between the parties. It is the intention of the parties that they will cooperate and negotiate with each other in good faith to enter into a full form Technology Transfer Agreement incorporating the following agreed terms by no later than [date]. This date may be extended by agreement between the parties. No part of this memorandum of understanding is to be legally binding apart from paragraphs [X and Y] relating to confidentiality and law of jurisdiction.

1. **Parties**
   1.1 Licensor [who should be the actual owner of the intellectual property or an authorized licensee]
   1.2 Licensee [the party who will be exploiting the technology]
2. **Technology**
   [Details of the patents and other intellectual property, including know-how that is the subject of the technology transfer arrangement]
3. **Territory**
   [Be as specific as possible and use legal jurisdictions. If referring to an organization's territory—for example, the European Union—be aware of the issues caused by expansion of that territory during the life of the technology transfer arrangement.]
4. **Term**
   [Initial period and any renewals or extensions]
5. **Purpose/Field of Use**
   [Defined by the technical application, the marketplace, or the point in a process]
6. **Grant**
   [Specify here if the grant will be nonexclusive, exclusive, sole, and what meaning you ascribe to those terms. Also specify if there are likely to be any provisions

or powers to change the grant either by expansion of the territory or fields of use or by reduction of the territory, exclusivity, or field of use.

   Specify any exceptions or limitations

   Define the level of exclusivity.]

7. **Financial Provisions**

   7.1 **Royalty**

   [Specify here royalty and royalty calculation mechanisms and the basis of the calculation. Also specify here any minimum annual payments whether these are advances on royalties or in addition to royalties.]

   7.2 **Advances: premium renewal fee.**

   [Include here an outline of any mechanism for changing the rate of royalty or the payments. This is an important financial provision.

   Also include any other unusual financial provisions, for example, if audit rights are to be particularly onerous, or if there is to be a direct link to the licensee's revenue systems.]

8. **Targets**

   [Here set out any sales or production targets, any targets for royalty rates or minimum returns, whether globally or broken down by territory. Specify the consequences of failing to meet these targets. Options may include payment of the difference between actual returns and agreed minimum returns or a reduction in the territory scope or reduction in the degree of exclusivity.]

9. **Termination and Restrictions**

   [Include here any unusual termination provisions, and identify issues in relation to termination for breach

   9.1 **Time Periods**

   9.2 **Consequences of termination**

   9.3 **Run off sale, period of sale of items made, orders outstanding, transfer of production facilities to a third party.**]

10. **Full Agreement**

    [Set out here the envisaged timetable to negotiation and finalizing a full license. Include a reference to any special terms the license will contain in addition to the commercial terms above.]

11. **Confidentiality**

    Each party shall keep the terms of this arrangement, any negotiations, and any information of the other revealed or disclosed to it or which comes into its possession confidential and secret except as ordered by a court or to the extent that the information is already public knowledge (other than from the receiving party).

12. **Jurisdiction and Law**

    [Here, what is best for the memorandum of understanding may be different from what is best for the formal contract. Also specify the degree to which the provisions of the memorandum of understanding are legally binding—usually only the confidentiality provisions are legally binding.]

Competitive Intelligence and Due Diligence

Competitive Intelligence and Patent Searching

In this chapter, we show you tips on how you can better monitor the external environment and use patent searches effectively so as to be more aware of what your competition is doing and how not to waste money reinventing the wheel when selecting which research and development (R&D) projects to fund. We illustrate the process of patent mining and patent mapping using a straightforward case. In doing so, we demonstrate how you can use both free and commercial sources of information to identify pertinent high-technology sectors, markets, and competition and the most recent research and inventions that have been made in your domain of interest. We also show you how to get started on obtaining basic business and competitive intelligence if there is no large decision-support system in place, and especially if you are working in a fledgling start-up high-tech firm, with limited time and money to spend on these systems. In the end, we recommend that any intelligence-gathering, data-mining, or mapping exercise needs to be accompanied by your own common sense and strategic insight.

Monitoring and identifying opportunities is one of the key activities for innovation companies. For example, Procter and Gamble (P&G) in its "Connect and Develop" program follows open innovation principles to investigate valuable opportunities. In the past, P&G used to source only 10 percent of all innovations externally, but using the open innovation approach, it has set "a target of 50% of innovations found elsewhere [meaning externally]."[1] For managers at P&G at all levels of the company, scanning the horizon and connecting to external innovation is a key part of their strategy to accelerate new product development. P&G wants to grow fast and profitably in order to keep shareholders happy and customers satisfied. Open innovation is an important contribution toward achieving these ambitious targets.

Senior managers of both large and small firms know that they constantly need to evaluate their external environment but do not always have the proper tools or knowledge to do so efficiently and economically. In a recent biotechnology industry survey, Lachman[2] examined the responses from 261 CEOs and licensing executives and concluded that 81 percent of licensing executives were spending too much of their scarce time eliminating out-of-date information. Moreover, when an attractive opportunity was identified, it was overvalued and too expensive for in-licensing due to its high visibility to all subscribers. However, it often appears that managers may be unfamiliar with the latest software tools used by specialists to carry out patent searches to map the patent landscape. In this chapter, we show you how to monitor the external environment and seek new technology trends and valuable opportunities—which we hope will enable you to keep ahead of your competitors.

ASKING THE RIGHT QUESTIONS—DOING VARIOUS PATENT SEARCHES

The challenge in instituting useful competitive intelligence programs is rooted in the abundance of data sources. More practically, how do you cut through the data volume and segregate the relevant and useful details into pertinent information and managerial insights?

You start by posing questions about both your research and development on one hand, and your business and licensing mission on the other hand, before you begin looking for answers. Thus, rather than collecting data, facts, and figures in a random or haphazard manner, the search should become focused, planned, and aimed at efficiently and effectively answering the specific intelligence requirements of the firm or task groups doing the inquiry, whether they are assigned with R&D pipeline development, strategic partnering, or negotiating technology transfer licensing deals. A short list of questions that need to be considered at various phases of the company product development and commercialization processes follows.

When you are still in the early brainstorming phase of research and casting about for creative ideas or innovations to commercialize, you can productively use patent information to get a broad view of key technology areas and identify similar technologies before entering into the research setup process. In this phase you should ask these questions:

- Are you aware of others' R&D efforts in this technology domain?
- Are you effectively using patent documents that are not in force to pick up free technical details (methods) without any extra charge?
- Are there technologies on the market that you could purchase and further develop?

When you are setting up a new research project, you should carefully search and analyze patent information to avoid reinventing the wheel. Ask yourself:

- Are you sure that you are not about to invest R&D resources in something that is already patented or perhaps even launched in the market?

When you intend to file a new patent application, ask yourself:

- Are you aware of all prior art documents?
- Can you get patent protection for your technology, or should you consider other forms of intellectual property (IP) protection (trademark, copyrights, and trade secrets)?

When you are thinking of collaborating with another company and licensing or sharing intellectual property assets, ask yourself:

- Do you know what IP rights your collaborator owns?
- Do you have a proper understanding of the legal status of your own and the collaborator's IP rights?

When you are entering into the market with your product, ask yourself:

- Are you infringing on others' IP rights?
- Are others infringing on your IP rights?
- Can you invalidate those patents that cause a potential threat?

You can get answers to these questions by using databases (explained later in this chapter) or by asking patent information specialists and patent search companies to conduct a search on your behalf.

State-of-the-Art Searches

State-of-the-art searches are carried out to get a broad view of a particular technology area, before a firm invests heavily in a research project. This typically includes analyzing both patent and nonpatent documents on a global basis. R&D managers frequently use such search to redirect the goals of their groups' research projects. They also use this type of search to learn ways to design around technologies already patented or to find free methods for developing a technology (e.g., discovering patents that are not in force because payments have lapsed or because a patent was never granted).

Patentability Searches

Patentability searches, also known as novelty searches, are normally conducted by, or on the behalf of, inventors to familiarize themselves with previous developments in the field of invention. The purpose is to determine if an invention is truly novel or to learn if someone else has already invented it or has published something about it. Patentability searches are critical to allow the inventor to decide whether to spend the time and money to go to the next step and apply for a patent or to develop the creative work further.

Freedom-to-Operate Searches

Managers and their legal advisors will pay for freedom-to-operate searches (also referred to as freedom-to-use searches) when there is a question as to whether a particular invention may or may not infringe on an in-force patent. The term *freedom to design* is preferred when the search involves design patents. A freedom-to-operate search is also conducted when a company plans to enter a new target market; then the search normally is restricted to the market of interest.

Invalidation Searches

Invalidation searches typically are carried out when the company has launched a new product or process and subsequently received a letter from a competitor threatening a lawsuit, injunction, or other type of legal action because of alleged patent infringements. Sometimes such disputes are settled by product withdrawal or by the payment of a licensing fee related to the use of any infringed patents. An invalidation search helps find those patents as well as nonpatent documents that predate the filing date of an accepted or granted patent, to assist with legal opposition or patent invalidation. The purpose of any invalidation search is to discover documents that will show evidence that an issued patent may be invalid.

BUSINESS INTELLIGENCE FOR BENCHMARKING

Business intelligence refers to the process of gathering useful business information critical to making managerial decisions. Its activities include monitoring, analyzing, distributing, and using information on operations. Business intelligence systems help management gain insights and control over how their firm stands on key performance metrics, benchmarked either to a comparison peer group or to other leading firms known for applying best practices for that particular indicator. It relies primarily on internally generated information, which is then compared to external indicators.

Business intelligence describes the process of transforming a company's internally generated data into useful business information and then into insights that enhance management's capabilities to make meaningful decisions. Business intelligence, if executed well, may also help to create a sustainable competitive advantage for your company. For example, each day the firm collects data about customer sales or product needs. Management can analyze these data to pinpoint changes in customer behavior or the customer decision-making processes. This information may then be used by marketing analysts for updating forecasts of the company's sales and financial budget. Business regulatory trends and capacity conditions in the industry may be used to determine who is going to raise or lower their product prices, a critical piece of information for the sales force in the field. In large companies, business trends and industry data are combined with the management information system of the business to generate fact-based support for managerial decisions. These management information systems are essential for managerial control purposes, auditing, and keeping the various functions informed (headquarters, finance, accounting, sales, marketing, purchasing, and production).

COMPETITIVE INTELLIGENCE

Competitive intelligence is broader in scope than business intelligence and focuses on obtaining primarily external insights about rivals, industry trends, and other nonmarket forces (e.g., political, social, regulatory factors) that are needed to make strategic decisions. This is very much a future-oriented, strategic thinking type of process. Competitive intelligence serves to aid and inform senior executives who are responsible for setting the corporate vision and mission of their organizations, and is useful for leading the team of managers who must navigate and steer the company through its global competitive landscape. Competitive intelligence is also vital for business-level managers who need information and insights on how they can create and sustain competitive advantage vis-à-vis their competitors.

Competitive intelligence is primarily concerned with enhancing the firm's capability to listen, monitor, and anticipate competitive forces and trends from outside the firm. It also serves as an early-warning system for management to identify potential threats and new entrants into the industry or market. Management and staff specialists will regularly monitor and update the general political, economic, social, technological, legal, and environmental situation, current and projected, pertinent to the firm. Competitive intelligence uses conceptual frameworks for strategy commonly taught in business schools. Examples are concepts like product or industry life cycles, Porter's Five Forces model, SWOT (strengths, weaknesses, opportunities, and threats), the value chain, and the value net to map out the competitive landscape. For further details on basic strategy, please refer to Chapter 3. Strategists can carry out scenario analyses and industry studies, and use other types of competitive analyses to role-play or simulate the dynamics of industry competition as they try to gauge and assess rivals' potential actions or to identify and co-opt potential collaborators.

CARRYING OUT INFORMATION AND PATENT SEARCHES

It is essential to have a thorough look at granted patents and patent applications before planning a new research project or before a company enters into collaboration with another company or institution. Private companies, especially large ones, publish their inventions in patent literature before, and often instead of, in scientific literature. In fact, approximately 70 percent of patent information is never published anywhere else. The details of an invention must be kept secret before a patent application is submitted. For that reason, patented inventions are disclosed in the patent literature first before they appear in any other literature sources.

High-tech companies should exploit all the possibilities that patent information can provide. Intensive use of patent information allows companies to identify the technical capabilities of an organization and to turn patent information into patent intelligence that assists in structuring collaborative activities.

Free Online Patent Databases

Novices often have a hard time deciding where to begin patent searches from among the myriad of search sites offered on the Internet. While some sites are free, and some are not, it is not always clear what the pay sites offer that the free ones lack. In some cases, seemingly competing information providers share common ownership and even common URLs. What follows is an attempt to sort through this tangle and provide at least a basic guide to the various locales currently on the web for searching patents. We start with examples of free databases and then turn to commercial ones.

A number of free public databases, mostly managed by the world's various patent offices, allow one to:

- Identify the work of known inventors.
- Identify patent applications filed by specific companies or organizations.
- Identify the patent for a particular invention or review patents in a particular technical field.

Since the various patent offices developed the first national patent databases, they are mostly free of charge to the general public but often are not very user friendly. However, a lot of patent data is available if you learn how to use these databases.

If you need some free assistance for patent searching, one possible source is to go to the various patent offices located in each country. Staff will assist you with filing patent documents and conducting searches through free patent databases.

You should, however, keep in mind that free public databases are useful tools, but any search results should be verified in other sources, because it can be difficult to find relevant patent literature through public databases. Still, we recommend free public databases as a starting point for basic patent information and preliminary searches. You may look up relevant information free of charge from the key public databases highlighted next.

Key Free Public Patent Databases

Numerous national databases (e.g., Japan's patent abstracts and South Korea's IP rights information service) can be used for patent searching. However, we recommend using centralized databases, listed next, because most of the key patent documents are available from these databases, and then turning to commercial patent databases for more detailed patent searches.

We recommend that you start your state-of-the-art patent search from the European Patent Office (EPO) databases and then move to full-text databases such as World Intellectual Property Organization's (WIPO's) patent scope and the United States Patent and Trademark Office (USPTO) for more precise searching of patent claims.

European Patent Office Databases: esp@cenet® and epoline®   esp@cenet® is the European Patent Office gateway, created as part of a European initiative.[3] Its "worldwide" format enables searching across a vast amount of patent data (back to 1920 by name, title, or class). You can also search legal status and patent family information through EPO's International Patent Documentation Center (INPADOC) interface. However, keep in mind that the esp@cenet® database allows searching only of original patent titles and abstracts, so you might miss key information that lies in the description and claims sections of patent documents. Moreover, you can search patent applications using only a limited number of search fields. Granted patents are available only for European patents and U.S. patents; you will not be able to see granted claims from other countries' patent offices.

The EPO also provides another important system for monitoring the "legal status" of a patent, which describes all significant steps in the lifetime of an invention, from first publication (in some cases even from the filing) to the end of the patent's term. It includes data such as change of ownership, examination request, grant, revocation, and so forth. The epoline® online services allow researchers to search in the European Patent Register, to monitor registration data, and to use register monitoring tools such as WebRegMT and to use software such as Online Secure File Inspections to check legal status, event history, citations, and patent family data that correspond to a particular patent application.[4] Pertinent information about legal opposition and appeal proceedings, including patent maintenance fees, is stored in the epoline® system, so this is a very useful place to learn about the current status of European patent applications and granted patents, and whether they are still in force.

World Intellectual Property Organization PatentScope Database   The advanced search functions of the PatentScope Database is useful for patent searching, because generally all the key inventions follow the PCT route and the claims and description sections of the patent applications are available for searching.[5] In addition to that, the Patent Cooperation Treaty (PCT) Electronic Gazette contains data relating to PCT international applications. Specifically, you can find these items: Declarations, Written Opinions of the International Search Authority and International Preliminary Reports on Patentability.

Official U.S. Patent and Trademark Office Database   The official U.S. Patent And Trademark Office database provides complete online access to its two patent databases, one for searching issued patents and another for searching patent applications (published since March 15, 2001).[6] Unlike the esp@cenet® database, USPTO allows searching in the claims and descriptions sections of patent documents. The database includes searchable front-page data of U.S. patents (but with revised U.S. classification) plus text of claims and description, all from 1976 onward. Revised versions of patents following litigation and correction slips are not included. Images of patents back to 1790 are available and can be searched for by patent number or current U.S. classification. Applications published on or after March 15, 2001 are available as a separate database in the same way as grants.

A different system provides access to the "legal status" information of U.S. patent applications (where *legal status* means learning if the patents are in force or not). The USPTO Patent Application Information Retrieval (PAIR) system allows you to search and display information regarding the status of a patent application. If a patent application is pending, issued, or published, it will show up on the PAIR display. To access the public PAIR system, you need only to have a patent, application, or publication number to begin the USPTO patent status search.[7]

Other Useful Free Sources   In addition to the preceding databases, some other patent databases cluster information from the sources just listed and offer more advanced search options. The coverage of patent documents in these databases varies, but in general the providers of these databases offer more user-friendly search interfaces for clients. For example, Free Patent Online (www.freepatentsonline .com) and BiOS Initiative Patent Lens (www.patentlens.net) patent search solutions can be used for preliminary patent search purposes to complement the preceding databases. The BiOS Initiative (www.bios.net/daisy/bios/bios/bios-initiative.html) is part of BiOS (Biological Innovation for Open Society www.bios.net).

Also, Google is now offering patent search capabilities to the public through its web site (www.google.com/patents). All of the patents currently available through Google's service come from the USPTO, but Google is likely to expand the coverage to include international patents and patent applications. At the present time, the search interface is fairly simple, the database is not continuously updated, and it is not suited for serious patent information searches. However, the graphical interface and ease-of-use will most likely attract novices to use Google's patent services.

Commercial Patent Databases

The most valuable resource in serious patent research is access to several large commercial patent databases. Commercial patent databases are often more user friendly than noncommercial ones and offer many functions that are unavailable through noncommercial sites.

Commercial patent databases differ from free databases in many ways. The most important distinction is the content of the data. Compared to the original patent data contained in the other services, online databases contain value-added data. The professional database producers often rewrite new informative titles and abstracts where the invention is laid out explicitly and explained in normal technical terms; corresponding parts of the original patent document often attempt to conceal the actual invention. In addition to formal classification systems, such as the International Patent Classification (IPC), the European Classification system (ECLA), United States Patent Classification (USPC) system, and the F-term system used for classifying Japanese patent documents, the commercial database producers often have their own classification and indexing systems. Indexing systems make it possible to conduct precise and effective searching of multiple fields. For example, you can search for "sequences," "polymers," and "companies" at the same time.

In addition to enhanced patent titles and abstracts, commercial databases give researchers an opportunity to view at a glance all of the patents and patent applications resulting from a specific patent application (a patent family). This eliminates the need to go through multiple free patent databases only to discover that, in the end, what were thought to be separate inventions in fact all originate from a single patent application. Pursuing a single invention often leads to many patents throughout the world.

Another common feature in commercial databases is an alerting service. Alerting services automatically run saved searches and e-mail the results to clients, which helps in the monitoring of competitors and industry patent activity. These features enhance the possibility that all relevant records come up in the search and greatly facilitate the assessment of the retrieved patent records.

In addition to these factors that help you find the relevant patent information, commercial companies offer patent information services. Their services enable you to discover relationships and trends in patenting that would be difficult to see when working with patent documents on a one-on-one basis. Patent mapping is often used to identify such trends. We will explain the concept and practice of patent mapping software tools later in a separate section of this chapter.

Patent attorneys and professional patent searchers usually divide commercial patent databases into two categories. Large commercial vendors such as ProQuest Dialog (www.dialog.com), the Scientific and Technical Information Network (STN; www.stn-international.de), and Questel (www.questel.com) offer access to multiple patent databases, which are searchable through professional-level interfaces that require some education and training for proper use. Second-tier commercial databases such as Thomson Innovation (www.thomsoninnovation.com) and Lexis Nexis Total Patent (http://law.lexisnexis.com/total-patent), however, have more user-friendly database interfaces that are sold directly to end users such as researchers, engineers, business developers, and other interested parties. The databases that are made available to end users now offer a better possibility of the effective use of patent literature for all high-tech companies.

We offer brief descriptions of the major commercial database providers on our web site. To access the list, log onto www.innovationtocashflows.com and go to Appendix 15.1, "Selected Commercial Database and Software Tool Vendors." This appendix is part of the book's supplemental online materials.

SEARCHING FOR TECHNICAL AND BUSINESS INFORMATION

In this section we first describe free resources that are available for carrying out technical and business information searches. Then we describe commercial sources of data (news and articles) and various kinds of databases. Finally, we discuss where to go to discover hard-to-find information about strategic alliance transactions and who is doing them.

Free Resources for Technical and Business Information Searching

There are multiple examples of free resources that allow you to search for science- and business-specific information from the Internet. In that sense the challenge of deciding where to begin technical and business information searches is similar to patent searching. As with patent searching, we recommend that you start with the free resources available on the Internet and then move to commercial databases if necessary.

It is important to understand that search engines are all different in the web sites they cover, and in the way they classify these sites. For example, a simple Google search (www.google.com) brings in the results from all web sites; it does not make any distinction between technical articles and other information. To narrow the search, it is important to select those web sites that search articles with technically-oriented information. For instance, we suggest screening these free web sites when searching for technical information:

- Scirus scientific information web site (www.scirus.com)
- Scientific Commons web site (www.scientificcommons.org)
- Google Scholar web site (http://scholar.google.com)
- U.S. National Institutes of Health (NIH) free digital archive of biomedical and life sciences journal literature, the PubMed Central web site (www.pubmedcentral.gov)

Putting yourself on mailing lists and newsgroups, or joining the chat rooms and discussion forums of professional and scientific associations are also useful things to do in order to gain access to fresh insights. In addition, you should use what is called a "feed reader" or a "news reader" to receive web feeds (data formats that are used for serving frequently updated content to users) from interesting blogs or technology news sources. Naturally, you might find a lot of poorly substantiated research material from mailing lists and blogs, but it will not take long to weed out those of poorer quality. The same hold true for discussion forums. Peer-to-peer information, provided by one scientist to another in these forums, can help you pinpoint the research area in which they are both engaged. This in turn can help you to locate potentially interesting licensing opportunities before your competitors.

Commercial Databases for Technical and Business Information Searching

Although a wide variety of news and scientific articles can be accessed through public databases, from the Internet, or from trade associations, it is advisable to use commercial databases to find information in cases where you need to be well aware of others' publications. (Such advice also applies to the experts hired to draft patents.)

From our experience, we know that leading high-tech companies frequently monitor scientific articles and technology news by using alerting services provided by vendors such as ProQuest Dialog, STN, and Wolters Kluwer Ovid Technologies. These information service providers offer an access to technology-specific databases and sophisticated alerts that deliver search results straight to the customer's e-mail inbox. Once an alert arrives in your inbox, it is easy to click and order the complete text of the article highlighted in the headlines.

Even with these science, industry, and business news databases, someone still has to turn that information into business intelligence that is focused and targeted for a specific technology niche. Intelligence aggregators such as MarketResearch (www.marketresearch.com) collect business intelligence reports from independent publishers, consultants, and smaller business intelligence companies and are able to offer a single source for market intelligence to customers worldwide. Using the MarketResearch.com Profound service (www.profound.com/research/), for example, can reduce the expense of business intelligence reports. The service offers individual chapters of business intelligence reports for clients, which are less costly than whole reports. Another approach is to use professional databases provided by companies such as Dialog and STN to search for specific information. For example, the STN Pharmaceutical cluster covers over 50 databases that provide specialized information from the field of pharmaceutical science. Although the cost of using professional services can be high for inexperienced searchers, individuals who are skilled in the art of information searching can find valuable information at a reasonably low cost.

Information Concerning Alliance Formation

After your company has managed to gather patent, technical, news, and business intelligence information about the technology fields of interest, and assuming you now have in place some kind of a knowledge capture system, where the information obtained is constantly being refreshed and updated, the next task is obtaining the hard-to-find information that is essential to have before negotiating a licensing deal or strategic alliance.

One of the more difficult tasks is to get information about recently completed technology deals that have taken place in your *specific* area of interest. This type of information is of crucial importance when it comes to screening deal opportunities and making what are called deal comparisons. To do this type of analysis, you would like to make a pairwise comparison, which means compare two similar deals, with comparable technologies and business models. According to Robert F. Bruner, dean of the University of Virginia Darden School of Business, finance theory suggests that it is better for an investor to take decisions based on opportunity costs, meaning choosing one path over another—"*Either* I invest in this deal *or* I invest in this other deal"—than be faced with a sequence of yes or no decisions, which have to be taken not knowing the opportunity cost.[8] The cost of the lost opportunity can be most easily determined when you can compare two deals side by side and at approximately the same moment in time. Unfortunately, in emerging technologies, you rarely are able to find peer groups and comparable deals, let alone have them happen at the same moment in time, since, by their nature, emerging technologies are often unique.[9]

The Electronic Data Gathering, Analysis, and Retrieval System (EDGAR)[10] can prove helpful for gaining access to those high-tech deal agreements that are filed as material contracts under the public filing requirements of the U.S. Securities and Exchange Commission (SEC), and thus are freely available to the public. Also, some specialty publications such as *Les Nouvelles*, *Genetic Engineering News*, *PharmaDeals Review*, *Bioworld Today*, *Thomson Financial*, and *BioCentury* offer weekly or monthly updates on biotechnology deals and are useful sources for following other types of technology contracts as well. Still, it would be an enormous task for any single person to monitor these sources without the help of companies that are constantly analyzing these kinds of contract agreements in detail.

In the field of biotechnology alliance monitoring, two companies are well worth mentioning: Recombinant Capital and PharmaVentures. Both provide access to valuable, specialized, and proprietary databases that are relied upon extensively for "deal transaction" information by venture capitalists and business development managers in the life sciences.

Recombinant Capital (also known as Recap; www.recap.com) is based in San Francisco, California, and is a consulting firm specializing in biotechnology alliances. It maintains a proprietary database that is searchable and contains vital information on over 13,000 strategic alliances, including earned alliance revenues, product sales, employment agreements, company information, and market capitalization. Furthermore, Recap's database gives key information about biotechnology and pharmaceutical product pipelines of both public and private companies. For example, it shows how many products are in a firm's pipeline and at what stage of clinical trials those products are. Recombinant Capital also shows technology valuations of publicly trading firms (meaning the current value of technology as perceived by public market traders), and the market capitalizations (number of shares times the stock price per share). These data are used in making comparisons of firms for valuation purposes.

PharmaVentures (www.pharmaventures.com) based in Oxford, England, is a consulting firm focused on all aspects of deal making in the pharmaceutical industry, including strategic alliances, licensing, joint ventures, mergers and acquisitions, and equity financing. PharmaVentures' proprietary database, PharmaDeals, is a reliable resource that gives you the latest information and analysis of deal making in the global pharmaceutical industry.

When a start-up venture is contemplating forming high-tech alliances, another important piece of information that the entrepreneurs will need is to identify the key people who are responsible for certain activities in other companies. Many online databases, which can be accessed freely through the Internet, provide some basic information of this type. One of the biggest databases is provided by business.com (www.business.com); its directory contains over 400,000 listings within 65,000 industry, product, and service subcategories and offers contact details of 22 million people. However, there is no substitute for personal networks to identify the real decision makers. One simple but often effective way to reach those people is to use social network services favored by professionals such as LinkedIn (www.linkedin.com) or Plaxo (www.plaxo.com). When using a social networking site, you may also be able to find out the contact details of decision makers, the people to whom they are connected, and other useful facts that are unavailable from traditional printed directories or telephone books. Of course, you also need to be careful about the security of such Internet sites and who is using them and why.

Having done all of these searches, you have completed most of the basic data gathering and information analysis needed for carrying out a competitive intelligence survey. What remains to be done is to complete the technological intelligence portion of your search, a step involving patent data mining.

In the next section we explain what a patent citation search is and how patent information specialists actually conduct patent mining to create patent maps. With these techniques and software tools, patent information specialists are one step closer to turning raw patent data into the technological intelligence you will need for crafting the technology strategy for your firm's future.

GOING FROM PATENT DATA TOWARD TECHNOLOGY INTELLIGENCE

Scientists are eager to learn if their ideas or inventions have already been granted patents or have patents pending so they do not waste time reinventing the wheel. Companies are interested in learning about the risks they face—such as patent infringement or potential litigation—if they were to pursue a particular licensing deal, say as part of a strategic alliance or contractual arrangement. This brings us to a key question: How do leading high-tech firms, R&D laboratories, and university technology transfer offices, turn patent data and scientific information of the kind we have been discussing into useful technological intelligence?

Patent Citation Analyses

The process of securing a patent requires references (citations) to the other patents and published research related to the proposed innovation. After receiving a patent, a subsequent application will, in turn, reference the earlier one. Thus, for any individual patent, there are sets of backward and forward references (or citations) that resemble a family tree, with direct descendants, cousins, and other relations. Patent citation analysis is accomplished by using software and the patent information specialist's training and skills to analyze citation links. Companies can identify external interest in their patents by monitoring the citations they receive from other companies' patents. External citations to a company's patent reveal a close link between the citing patent and the cited patent. The complementary nature of patents can be so great that a company is obliged to resort to either licensing or cross-licensing in order to realize value from its own patents and avoid infringing on others' patents.

Moreover, companies that are citing your patent may be potential licensing candidates for your technology. These leads need to be identified, prioritized, and passed back to the business development and marketing staff for eventual follow-up.

Patent citation analysis is also a valuable tool to identify where to focus R&D efforts. It allows the company to discover what technologies have been developed and to find the open spaces that might be useful for strategically seeking future patents or new breakthroughs.

Patent citation analysis should be carried out through professional patent databases. These databases record patent citations that patent examiners in patent offices have described. In our opinion, the most powerful and useful databases for patent citations searches are Derwent Patents Citation Index and inpadocdb, which cover patent data from all major patent offices (European Patent Office, Germany, United Kingdom, Japan, United States, and PCT database). You can access these databases through STN and Dialog, or by commissioning an analysis directly from patent information specialists. You can also view the forward citations to certain patent documents freely from esp@cenet® for preliminary search purposes.

Patent Mining and Patent Mapping

Patent mapping is the use of published patent documents (or other text) data to create a graphical or physical representation of the relevant documents pertaining to a particular subject area or novel invention. Patent mapping enables companies to identify the patents in a particular technology space, verify the characteristics of these patents, and, most important, identify the relationships among them, to see if there are any zones of infringement.

When management and business developers bring a technology to market, whether it is their own or the technology of someone else, they must critically assess whether they can use the technology's patents without infringing on the rights of another firm or organization (such as a university or government research lab). This means monitoring the patent's scope or uses, also known as the description and claims sections of published patent documents. (Here we are referring to both patent applications and granted patents.) The claims section of a granted patent is shown in Appendix 2.1, "Remmey's Granted Patent" at the end of Chapter 2.

Software and database vendors, such as Clearforest (www.clearforest.com), InXight (www.inxight.com), Search Technology (which markets Vantage Point Software; www.thevantagepoint.com), STN (STN AnaVist; www.stn-international .com/stninterfaces/stnanavist/stn_anavist.html), Thomson Scientific (Thomson Data Analyzer; http://scientific.thomson.com/products/tda/), and Wisdomain (www .wisdomain.com/index.htm), offer software tools for patent data mining that can be used to actively scan and analyze the patents that could be relevant to the company's business or technology development. Multiple decision criteria should be taken into account when purchasing patent mining software. In our experience, the most critical factors are the type of data, the cost and availability of data, and the pricing model.

Arguably, the most important factor in any serious data mining is the type of data that vendors are offering for patent mining. It is difficult to draw serious conclusions from the unstructured raw data that can be accessed through patent office web sites. The initial data should be grouped into database fields with high-quality abstracts produced by indexing specialists with expert knowledge in the relevant area, using data from patent documents.

Other important selection criteria are the cost and availability of data. Some software vendors, for example, Wisdomain, offer data and texts as a part of the subscription offer. Others, such as Thomson data analyzer and STN AnaVist, offer the information separately from the software supplier or, in the case of OmniViz, from a third-party provider.

The companies just mentioned use different pricing models, ranging from pure subscription fees to usage-dependent billing. The subscription model allows you to use the software continuously, but usage-dependent billing might be the better option for small companies because of the modest initial cost. Space does not permit our surveying all the available data mining software tools; instead we recommend reading recent reviews.[11]

A very active and promising application area for data mining is in the pharmaceutical and biopharmaceutical areas, because the quantity of publications is enormous and, furthermore, the cost of pharmaceutical drug development "has risen to over $800 million for a successful product, up more than tenfold from just a decade earlier."[12] In fact, for business development managers and patent lawyers working with pharmaceutical or life science firms, patent mining software tools are critical but often underutilized.

Currently, patent information professionals in developed countries are the most active users of data mining tools. This will change in the coming years. As more business development professionals, technology consultants, and patent advisors become aware of the potential of these tools for transforming patent data into strategic insights and technological knowledge, we expect the customer base to widen. One possibility would be for large multinationals to incorporate patent search specialists into their staff for in-house competitive screening. Another possibility would be for patent specialist advisory firms to move offshore to service centers in Eastern Europe, India, China, Singapore, or South Korea to get access to more specialists.

Whatever the approach will be to carrying out these studies, we need to emphasize the importance of the role of the patent specialist. The person using these patent mining tools must have scientific expertise. Without fundamental training in the sciences and practical experience in high technology, it would be impossible to exercise the judgment needed to carry out these searches in a meaningful manner. It is easy to go astray and draw wrong conclusions from patent searches if they are not done by an expert. Sound patent information analysis depends on having a deep scientific background, a knack for understanding high-tech trends, and the ability to understand and interpret patent documents.

CASE STUDY: PROTEIN CHIPS AND PROTEIN MICROARRAYS

The objective of this case study is to give you real-life insights on how professional patent analysts carry out the patent search and patent mining processes. In this example, we investigate the technology domains of protein chips and protein microarrays in order to find solutions to three questions:

1. What are the key technology sectors within protein chips and protein microarray technology domains according to the patent literature?
2. Which organizations have filed key patents?
3. Who are the most innovative researchers in this particular sector, and what are they working on?

Traditional Approach to Solving This Puzzle

The traditional approach for searching patent information is to log on to one of the free patent offices databases and carry out a tedious search and analysis.

To illustrate the traditional methodology, we conducted a patent search using the esp@cenet® database and the USPTO issued patent database.

A patent search for the keywords "protein biochips or protein microarrays" brings up only 253 individual patent documents from the esp@cenet® database and 240 patent documents from the USPTO issues patent database. (Refer to Figures 15.1 and 15.2.) Clearly, the number of patent publications we found from these two free public databases is very limited. In both cases only a few search terms are allowed per search field. Moreover, no indexing is available using terms from a keyword thesaurus.

Taking a deeper look into the documents that were found with the traditional search becomes problematic as there are no statistical tools available to conduct a more profound analysis. Instead you have to read through many patent documents that disclose the same inventions (as patent family members are not linked together) and draw statistical diagrams in a spreadsheet application such as MS Excel. In addition, the esp@cenet® interface does not allow users to limit the patent search by year, so we had to manually pick out all the relevant documents, a very tedious chore and one prone to errors.

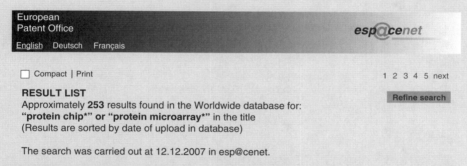

FIGURE 15.1   Traditional Patent Search Results through Esp@cenet

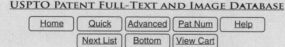

Searching US Patent Collection...

Results of Search in US Patent Collection db for:
"protein chip" OR "protein microarray": 240 patents.
*Hits 1 through **50** out of **240***

The search was carried out at 12.12.2007 in USPTO issued patent database.

FIGURE 15.2   Traditional Patent Search through USPTO-Issued Patent Interface

(Continued)

CASE STUDY: PROTEIN CHIPS AND
PROTEIN MICROARRAYS (*Continued*)

Patent Specialist's Approach to Solving This Puzzle

The patent specialist's search begins by logging into the patent database (in this case using the STN Express 8.2 interface). In the first phase, the professional patent analyst quickly trolls through comprehensive professional databases to reveal key patent publications and other technical documents. A quick keyword search reveals 7,055 documents and, more interestingly, 967 inventions (patent families) from the HCAplus database that is produced by the Chemical Abstracts Service, U.S.A. (See Figure 15.3, "Search String 1.")

In addition to these findings, 642 patent families (inventions) are revealed from the Derwent World Patent Index database that is produced by Thomson Reuters. (See Figure 15.4, "Search String 2.")

```
=> S  PROTEIN ( 2A ) MICROARRAY OR PROTEINCHIP OR PROTEIN CHIP
       2061901  PROTEIN
         50897  MICROARRAY
          6496  PROTEIN ( 2A ) MICROARRAY
           345  PROTEINCHIP
       2061901  PROTEIN
         85381  CHIP
           846  PROTEIN CHIP
                  ( PROTEIN ( W ) CHIP )
L48       7055  PROTEIN ( 2A ) MICROARRAY OR PROTEINCHIP OR PROTEIN CHIP
=> S      L48  AND PATENT / DT
C49        967  PATENT FAMILIES
```

FIGURE 15.3 Search String 1
Source: Adapted from STN Express®. Data provided by FIZ Karlsruhe. STN, STN Express, and the STN Express logo are trademarks or registered trademarks of the American Chemical Society in the United States, or other countries, or both.

```
=> s  protein ( 2A ) microarray or proteinchip or protein chip
      168140  PROTEIN
        3750  MICROARRAY
         162  PROTEIN ( 2A ) MICROARRAY
          19  PROTEINCHIP
      168140  PROTEIN
      198393  CHIP
         470  PROTEIN CHIP
                ( PROTEIN ( W ) CHIP )
L42      642  PROTEIN ( 2A ) MICROARRAY OR PROTEINCHIP OR PROTEIN CHIP
```

FIGURE 15.4 Search String 2
Source: Adapted from STN Express®. Data provided by FIZ Karlsruhe. STN, STN Express, and the STN Express logo are trademarks or registered trademarks of the American Chemical Society in the United States, or other countries, or both.

Although most of the patent documents are found by keyword-based search techniques, a comprehensive patent search always includes "company name" and "inventor's name" inquiries—which is useful, as additional documents may emerge from these detailed searches. Another advantage is that professional patent analysts can employ a company name and inventor name thesaurus to pick up only the relevant documents. For example, a company name search by one of the key patent assignees (Toyobo Corporation) shows that some patent documents are filed by Toyobo Engineering and the Toyobo gene analysis companies. By looking into these documents, subsequent searches show relevant documents with *both* company names. (See Figure 15.5, "Search String 3.")

After doing all the necessary inquiries, the patent search analyst then prioritizes the patent publications by time frame, in this case all patent publications listed during or after the year 2000. Even so, the search results reveal more than 1,000 inventions (patent families) that need to be inspected.

Query 1: Identify the key technology sectors by searching through patent documents published during or after the year 2000.

After the initial data set is created, the searcher checks the patent titles and might quickly read each abstract to make sure that most of the documents indeed are dealing with the protein biochip or protein microarray applications. The only way to do this, given today's technology, is to have a person read

```
=>  e  toyobo co / pa
E1      1      TOYOBASHI GIJUTSU JAPAN / PA
E2   10664     TOYOBASHI GIJUTSU JAPAN / PA
E3      1 -->   TOYOBASHI GIJUTSU JAPAN / PA
E4   10613     TOYOBO CO LTD / PA
E5    9497     TOYOBO CO LTD JAPAN / PA
E6      1      TOYOBO DO BRASIL LTDA / PA
E7      1      TOYOBO DO BRASIL LTDA BRAZIL / PA
E8      1      TOYOBO ENG CO LTD / PA
E9      1      TOYOBO ENG CO LTD JAPAN / PA
E10    14      TOYOBO ENGINEERING CO LTD / PA
E11    12      TOYOBO ENGINEERING CO LTD JAPAN / PA
E12     1      TOYOBO ENGINEERING K K / PA
E13     1      TOYOBO ENGINEERING K K JAPAN / PA
E14     2      TOYOBO GENE ANALYISIS CO LTD / PA
E15     1      TOYOBO GENE ANALYISIS CO LTD JAPAN / PA
```

FIGURE 15.5 Search String 3
Source: Adapted from STN Express®. Data provided by FIZ Karlsruhe. STN, STN Express, and the STN Express logo are trademarks or registered trademarks of the American Chemical Society in the United States, or other countries, or both.

(Continued)

CASE STUDY: PROTEIN CHIPS AND
PROTEIN MICROARRAYS (*Continued*)

through the documents and pick out the most relevant ones. This is where the technological training and experience of the patent searcher is important.

If the patent analyst is comfortable with the data set, then it can be imported to STN AnaVist. The software automatically groups together the consolidated data sets. This means that the concepts of various patent documents are decoded on the basis of a defined, unified language, and patent landscapes are created.

The professional patent analyst can use various approaches to identify specific technology sectors in any technology area. One of the most useful approaches is to take a look at the results of the "Technology Indicators" that the HCAplus database provides (see Figure 15.6). In our case example, using the Technology Indicator analysis reveals that patents which cover diagnosis

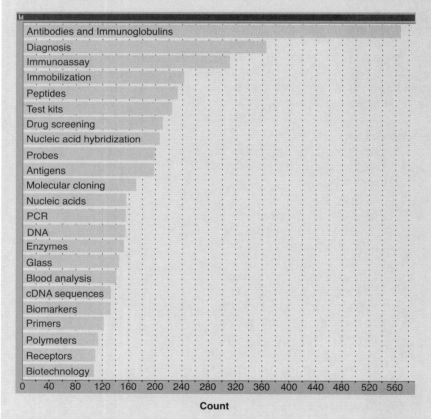

Count

FIGURE 15.6 Priority Patents According to Technology Indicators, Years 2000 to 2006
Source: Adapted from STN AnaVist. Data provided by FIZ Karlsruhe. STN, STN AnaVist, and the STN AnaVist logo are trademarks or registered trademarks of the American Chemical Society in the United States, or other countries, or both.

methods appear to dominate this sector. The real value-added feature is the flexibility of the software interface, which allows the patent specialist to peruse any technology indicators he or she wishes. Merely by touching an area of interest with the mouse pointer reveals the actual documents and the key inventors and patent assignees. This expedites the search techniques and reveals more links with less fatigue than would be possible by traditional methods.

In addition to Technology Indicators, it is possible to analyze technology sectors according to patent classification codes, Derwent World Patents Index® manual codes, Derwent World Patents Index® class, or by looking into the patent maps. Figure 15.7 shows how easy it is to look at the patent map and pick up any technology area of interest for further inspection.

In our example, the patent specialist picked "laser desorption mass spectrometry applications" as a target for further inspection. The results indicate that most of the patents in this domain disclose "computer enabled methods for analyzing liver and heart samples." Furthermore, they appear to apply samples onto protein chips and use laser desorption mass spectrometry to generate mass spectra results (see Figure 15.7).

By linking together various search and analysis techniques, combined with state-of-the-art patent software and comprehensive databases, professional

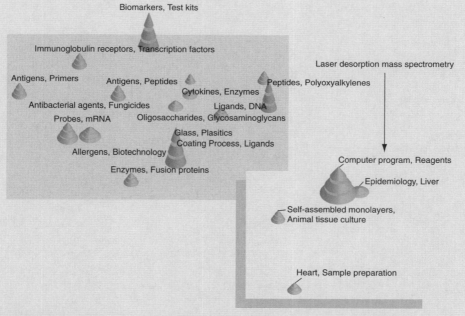

FIGURE 15.7 Priority Patents Clustered in Patent Map, Years 2000 to 2006
Source: Adapted from STN AnaVist. Data provided by FIZ Karlsruhe. STN, STN AnaVist, and the STN AnaVist logo are trademarks or registered trademarks of the American Chemical Society in the United States, or other countries, or both.

(Continued)

CASE STUDY: PROTEIN CHIPS AND
PROTEIN MICROARRAYS (Continued)

patent analysts are able to more quickly and accurately reveal pertinent information of any technology domain.

Query 2: Identify the key organizations and researchers that have filed patents in this particular sector.

Now that our patent analyst has the proper data set identified and defined, he or she can find the patenting activity of key organizations merely by picking the technology areas of interest inside the protein chip or protein microarray technology fields. Figure 15.8 represents the key organizations filing patent in

	2006	2005	2004	2003	2002	2001	2000
Incyte Corp.				6	13	5	2
Diversa Corp.	1	7	1	5	5	4	
Toyobo Co., Ltd.	2	9	9		1		
Ciphergen Biosystems Inc	1	3	8	3	3	1	
Agilent Technologies, Inc.	1			2	7	4	1
Johns Hopkins University		3	3	1	2		
Japan Science and Tech...		4	2	2	1		
Hitachi, Ltd.		2	3		3	1	
Harvard University		1	2	2		3	1
University of California	2	1	2	1	1	1	
Sumitomo Bakelite Co., Ltd.	1	6	1				
Canon Inc.		4		3	1		
Bayer AG		1		4	2		
Avidia Research Institute			1	1		5	
Wyeth		2	2	1		1	
Sirs Lab GmbH	1	2		2		1	
Sense Proteomic Ltd.					2	3	1
Eastman Kodak Co.		3		2		1	

FIGURE 15.8 Key Organizations Filing Patents in Protein Chip and Protein Microarray Technology Area
Source: Adapted from STN AnaVist. Data provided by FIZ Karlsruhe. STN, STN AnaVist, and the STN AnaVist logo are trademarks or registered trademarks of the American Chemical Society in the United States, or other countries, or both.

protein chip or protein microarray technology area in the twenty-first century. It shows that Incyte Corporation initially was an active patent assignee but ceased its patenting activity after the year 2003.

Figure 15.9 shows the results of the search to identify the most innovative researchers in this specialty, information that is useful for identifying and recruiting new employees.

Year	Tang Y Tom	Inamori Kazunori	Elliott Vicki S	Richardson Thomas W	Ramkumat Jayalaxmi	Chawla Narinder K	Swarnakar Anita	Khare Reena	Hafalia April J A	Becha Shanaya D	Katayama Yoshiki	Kable Amy E	Sonofa Tatsuhiko	Marquis Joseph P	Lee Soo Yeun	Baughn Mariah R	Tran Uyen K	Inoue Yusuke	Jin Pei
2006		2																	
2005	7										7		7					5	
2004	1	9									7		7					7	
2003	1	2	4	2	5	3	4	3	4	2		3		3	3	4			4
2002	6	10	10	9	11	9	11	8	9	1		11		10	8	4	6		5
2001	5	4	3	4	1	4	1	3	3	2		1		3	5	3			2
2000	7	2	2				2					2							

FIGURE 15.9   Most Innovative Researchers in Protein Chip and Protein Microarray Technology Area
Source: Adapted from STN AnaVist. Data provided by FIZ Karlsruhe. STN, STN AnaVist, and the STN AnaVist logo are trademarks or registered trademarks of the American Chemical Society in the United States, or other countries, or both.

Making Meaning Out of the Patent Search—Rely on Human Judgment

Patent mining and especially managerial interpretation of patent landscape maps is a powerful new toolkit that should be employed by just about anyone involved in technology transfer, from the university technology transfer office to the business development team at a research intensive start-up. Most firms do not need to have this expertise in-house, but they should rely on competent patent advisory firms to be up to date on this technique.

As with any new technique, however, you should not expect it to make the important strategic decisions for you. You need to be in the driver's seat. You need to frame the right questions for the search to be able to get the right answers. You need to use the results to scan the horizon and properly identify who your competition is: Who are the new potential entrants? What are these firms doing in leading-edge research? Where do they have defendable patents, and where are they most vulnerable? Who are their most prolific researchers? In what technology domains are they being the most innovative? Are your competitors moving to new technology sectors, and should you follow them? What can you patent in the future, or is the entire patent landscape a land mine filled with other companies' patents? What technologies should you in-license (license into your firm) to be able to commercialize your invention?

You can get answers to some of these questions by scrutinizing the patent landscape map. The patent landscape allows you to review in-depth the patent portfolios of competitors and to discover unknown technologies. In fact, the tool allows you to visualize the relationships between a total of nine different fields, including key organizations (most active patent assignees), key inventors, most important technology trends (number of patents per year), and technology indicators (most active area of technology in a peak). (Refer to Figure 15.10.)

Clearly our journey through intelligence-gathering methods has barely scratched the surface. As you can see, many data mining applications can be found in the marketplace. However, these software applications can never take the place of human analysis. Leading high-tech firms and top research centers hire and train patent information specialists, experts with years of industry experience, to decide on the initial search parameters, refine the initial search to confirm that it captures relevant information, and tweak the categories to ensure accuracy and alignment with business objectives. Outstanding patent information specialists are experienced researchers with a basic knowledge of patent law and a formidable expertise in information science and multiple scientific disciplines. They understand how to navigate technology domains and pick out the pertinent competitive trends.

After all is said and done, when the databases have been consulted and cross-checked and the results mapped, human experts still will be needed to review the output of the information search and to transform that information into intelligence. In the past, consulting firms have been the users of data mining and other visualization tools that helped company managers make decisions. In recent years, the situation has changed as corporate information professionals working inside the firm replace outside consultants. Chief information officers are increasingly dealing with business-critical questions and knowledge management systems. They are the ones who have to be able to identify what data should be relied on, what the information means, why it is relevant, who should see the results, and how the key people within the firm will access the intelligence to make timely strategic decisions. Managers increasingly make strategic decisions based on the analysis that information professionals have conducted and present to them, often on a real-time basis through the firm's intranet.

CHAPTER TAKEAWAYS

- *Be expeditious.* Begin your intelligence search by figuring out the questions you want to ask and the types of information you think you might need *before* you begin. Avoid collecting data, facts, and figures in a haphazard manner. Update and revise your search goals as you learn new information. Be willing to backtrack and rethink your plan of attack if you see your chosen strategy is leading to a dead end.

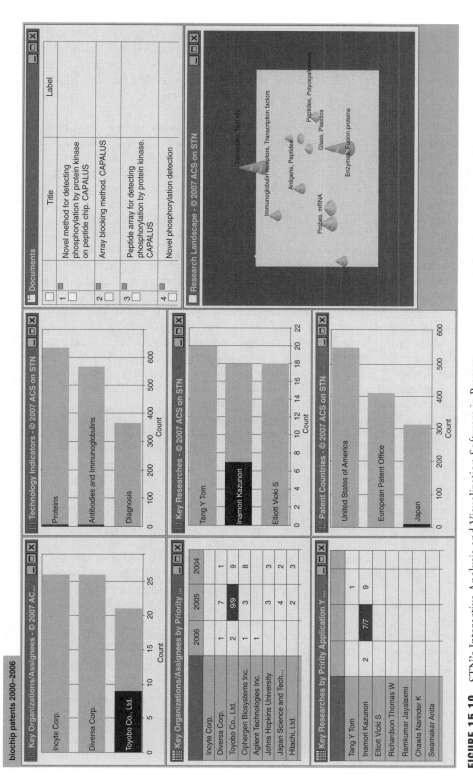

FIGURE 15.10 STN's Interactive Analysis and Visualization Software in Process

Source: Adapted from STN AnaVist. Data provided by FIZ Karlsruhe. STN, STN AnaVist, and the STN AnaVist logo are trademarks or registered trademarks of the American Chemical Society in the United States, or other countries, or both.

- *Know when to seek help.* Preliminary searches using public databases are fine for introducing the novice to the world of patents, but relying solely on free databases will not get you the precision or the results you may need to avoid having to deal with patent infringement lawsuits or wasting time reinventing the wheel. For a truly effective patent search, you may need to turn to specialized service providers.

- *Get to know some patent information specialists.* These professionals are trained and skilled in a variety of proprietary patent databases that contain better-quality (more readable, understandable, and reliable) inputs than those that are contained in the free public databases of the patent offices around the world.

- *Screen, scan, and filter multiple sources of firsthand data.* Primary data from firsthand contact with customers, suppliers, salespeople, experts, and specialists working on the front line are the best way to gain fresh insights about new trends before your competitors. A lot of "information" is actually stale, recycled, and needs to be discarded. Try to keep focused on your goals and objectives.

- *Conferences and networking opportunities abound.* Take advantage of them to find new partners and collaboration leads. Also use them as a chance to keep yourself up to date on industry thinking and competitors' moves.

- *Patent searches, citation analysis, and patent mining tools are indispensable.* But they need to be supplemented and cross-checked with research from other data sources. Do not overlook the hard-to-get information in favor of the easy-to-reach solution. You might be on the wrong path altogether. Search scientific literature sources, web feeds, and other publications. Patent mining is enhanced by new graphical tools used to create patent maps. These tools will continue to get better and more user-friendly as time goes on.

- *There is no substitute for reflecting and figuring out what it all means.* Try to stop now and then to make meaning out of the search results. In other words, connect the dots in the painting. It is easy to get overwhelmed by data, particularly scientific and technology data. To gain competitive intelligence, you need to broaden your search and combine technological insights about the customer, the market, competitors, and new entrants. Remember to look at the big picture now and then.

- *Aim for competitive intelligence and strategic insights.* Focus on decision making, not pure analysis. To be useful to managers, data need to be turned into information; and information needs to be transformed into insights that can be acted on by busy people. These business, market, and technology insights need to go into some type of knowledge management system where they can be disseminated quickly to the decision makers in your organization for further action.

- Log onto our web site at www.innovationtocashflows.com, where you will find these supplemental materials:
  - Appendix 15.1, "Selected Commercial Database and Software Tool Vendors"
  - Glossary
  - Resources (includes recommended books plus online resources, blogs, and many useful web links)

CHAPTER 16

Due Diligence

Richard Lord
Withers LLP

The objective of this chapter is to provide technology entrepreneurs with a better understanding of the process known as due diligence as it affects their business on the journey from innovation to value creation and realization.

Due diligence is relevant to any high-tech or biotech business—whether carrying out the initial analysis of the invention, its patentability and prospects for commercialization; effecting a university spin-off or obtaining seed capital; seeking later-stage venture capital or private equity funding; entering into a strategic alliance or transferring or licensing the intellectual property (IP) to a major corporation; or, ultimately, selling the business or floating shares of the company on a stock exchange.

Any successful business is likely to go through a number of such due diligence exercises during its lifetime, whether as the subject of such an exercise carried out by a third-party inquirer or itself undertaking such an exercise (e.g., if it proposes to acquire another business or enter into a strategic alliance). (In this chapter, we use the generic term *inquirer*, when referring to anyone carrying out due diligence, whether it is a university technology transfer office, a seed capital provider, a private equity or venture capital investor, a strategic alliance partner, a licensee of IP rights, or a purchaser of the business.) It follows that the nature and scope of the due diligence exercise will vary according to the purpose for which it is being carried out and the phase that the business has reached in its life cycle. The inventor or entrepreneur is also likely to need to undertake some form of self due diligence, analyzing the strengths and weaknesses of the invention and, later, his or her business against others in the marketplace prior to, say, seeking outside investment or a purchaser for the business or an initial public offering (IPO).

In this chapter, we examine what exactly people mean when they talk about "doing due diligence," why people do it, and how they go about doing it. We highlight some of the cultural differences in approaches to due diligence. We also look at the options available should due diligence uncover a problem within a business.

However, our overriding aim is to frame the overview of due diligence by reference to the world of high-tech or biotech entrepreneurs as they move from innovation to cash flow, from the laboratory to the marketplace, creating value for his business.

WHAT IS DUE DILIGENCE?

Entrepreneurs no doubt have heard the expression *due diligence* (often shortened simply to *DD*) used many times. They may have a reasonable understanding of what it entails and may even have been through the process at some stage during the life of their business. However, it can often seem a rather vague, ill-defined notion, bandied about knowingly by lawyers, accountants, and other professional advisors. But what exactly does it mean in practice?

Due diligence is a mind-set; it is investigative reporting, detective work if you will. *Diligence* can be defined as care, attention, precision, rigorousness, meticulousness, and thoroughness. It can be defined equally well by its opposites: carelessness, recklessness, negligence, and inaccuracy.

In essence, due diligence is the process of investigating a business before executing the legally binding agreements to give effect to a transaction. The purpose is to gather information, so that the inquirer obtains as full an understanding of the relevant business as possible and determines whether there are any matters that it wishes to have addressed before proceeding to completion of the transaction. It also allows the inquirer to plan its postcompletion strategy.

PRELIMINARY ISSUES BEFORE COMMENCING DUE DILIGENCE

Before we look at the process of due diligence in various contexts, it is important for all concerned to address certain preliminary issues.

Preparation

It should go without saying that any company seeking an investor, strategic partner, or buyer must ensure that it is in the optimum condition to attract them. Consideration should be given well in advance to the information and documentation to which others are likely to want to have access, and also what issues exist within the business that could act as an impediment to the successful conclusion of a transaction. If any such issues are identified, remedial action should, if possible, be taken prior to the start of any third-party due diligence exercise. In other words, the first step is for management itself effectively to carry out a form of internal due diligence.

Management must also identify and, at the appropriate time, instruct the team within the company that will be tasked with ensuring that the transaction proceeds to completion with the minimum disruption to the business, and in accordance with whatever timetable is laid down. It must give careful thought to who should be made aware of the transaction within the company (and also outside the company, say its customers and suppliers). It is normal for only a very limited number of key people to be involved, to minimize both the disruption—since the business must continue to be run—and the risk of information about the transaction getting into the workplace or the wider world, especially to competitors.

As well as establishing the internal team, it will need to appoint external advisors, including some or all of these: legal counsel; accountants and tax advisors; corporate finance advisors; trademark and patent attorneys; scientific advisors and technical experts.

The company may also produce an *information memorandum*. This will provide a summary of the major stages in its history and development; its historic financial performance and financial projections; details of the markets in which it operates and its competitors; details of its key customers and suppliers; and details of key management. Note that, in many jurisdictions, there are strict laws governing the distribution of inducements to enter into investment activities, including business plans, information memoranda, and the like. The company should always seek legal advice before distributing such documents or information. It is also common practice in many jurisdictions for such documents to contain a *legal disclaimer* to protect the company and its corporate finance advisors. As a further layer of protection, the corporate finance advisor may insist on all (or, at least, all material) statements in such document being formally verified before it is released. In addition, many jurisdictions impose criminal or civil penalties or both for making misleading statements with a view to inducing a person to make an investment, so it is essential that any information provided to the inquirer is true and not misleading.

Confidentiality

Clearly, any investigation of a company by a third party and its advisors, and the accompanying release of documentation and information by the company to them, creates issues of confidentiality for the company. The risks only multiply if there is more than one inquirer and if any of them are competitors of the company in some or all of the markets in which it is active. If a deal aborts after the due diligence exercise has commenced, the company is likely to have disclosed significant amounts of its confidential information to third parties but may have little or no adequate protection in law to prevent the use of such information or its further disclosure.

Apart from being concerned to ensure that a third party should not be able to use the information disclosed if the transaction aborts, the company will also want to keep the fact and details of the negotiations and the transaction in general secret from all but the most senior of its employees and, quite possibly, from its customers and suppliers.

The company's concern in this regard may not fit easily with the requirements of the people doing the due diligence, particularly if the inquirer wishes, for example, to carry out interviews with senior employees, key customers, or suppliers, or make site visits to see the business in operation at firsthand.

In certain contexts, it may be more difficult, and ultimately impossible, to ensure that certain third parties do not find out about the transaction prior to completion. For example, with the sale of a business in England (i.e., a sale of some or all of its assets and undertaking, as opposed to its share capital), it may be necessary, prior to completion, to obtain the consent of counterparties to transfer commercial contracts to which the company is party, or the consent of landlords of the company's real estate may be required to transfer any leases to the purchaser. The same may be true of statutory, regulatory, or other licenses, permits, or authorizations that the company holds in connection with the business. On a share sale, some of the company's commercial contracts may contain so-called change of control clauses, giving the counterparty a right to terminate the contract if a third party gains control of the company. In such case, the company may have to obtain the counterparty's agreement not to enforce that clause before the purchaser will proceed.

In any event, the company's concerns about the disclosure of its confidential information will mean that, prior to releasing any information to any third party or its advisors, it should ensure that the third party signs a legally binding confidentiality (or nondisclosure) agreement. Confidentiality agreements and recommended precautions when relying on them are discussed in more detail in Chapters 9 and 11.

Letter of Intent

Another document that is frequently entered into between the parties at the commencement of a transaction is a letter of intent (LoI) (also variously known as heads of terms [heads], heads of agreement, term sheet, or memorandum of understanding [MoU]). Refer to Chapter 10, Appendix 10.1, "Investment Term Sheet," and Chapter 14, Appendix 14.1, "Sample Heads of Terms or Memorandum of Understanding," for examples of two such documents. The purpose of the letter of intent is to record the key terms that have been agreed between the parties, but with the legal detail to be dealt with in the definitive agreements. However, a letter of intent, as the name itself suggests, is only an agreement in principle and, for that reason, should invariably be drafted so as expressly not to constitute a legally binding agreement between the parties (except for certain clauses, to be discussed). This means (at least in common law jurisdictions such as England and the United States) that either party can walk away from the transaction at any time without liability to the other (unless the letter of intent provides for some form of compensation in such event, as will be discussed).

Indeed, in the absence of any agreement to the contrary, parties are generally at liberty in common law jurisdictions to end negotiations at any time prior to the execution of a legally binding agreement; as such jurisdictions do not recognize any implied concept of good faith in relation to contractual negotiations between parties. However, many civil law jurisdictions do recognize the concept of good faith, including France, Germany, Spain, the Netherlands, and Italy. The duty to act in good faith varies from country to country but broadly encompasses obligations to inform the other party of major issues that could influence its decision whether to conclude the transaction, to be diligent in the performance of its obligations, and to observe certain standards of behavior. All of these obligations clearly have implications for the due diligence process if the transaction involves a party in a civil law jurisdiction, and care needs to be taken in such cases.

A letter of intent usually includes a series of conditions to which the completion of the transaction is subject, including the completion of due diligence satisfactory to the inquirer.

As noted earlier, certain clauses of a letter of intent are expressed to be legally binding. In particular, this is the case for any confidentiality provisions in the letter. There may also be provisions as to who is responsible for the costs of the transaction, especially if it aborts. Commonly, the letter includes exclusivity undertakings from the company, pursuant to which it will agree not to negotiate with or solicit interest from third parties during a specified period of time. This allows the other party to the transaction to progress to its due diligence investigations and negotiate the deal, and incur the resulting, potentially significant costs, in the knowledge that it is, during that exclusivity period, the only person with whom the company should be dealing. The letter may then go on to provide that, should the company breach such undertaking and the transaction fails, it will bear the wasted legal and other professional costs and expenses of the other party.

Although the letter of intent is not a legally binding document, except as just indicated, the parties should nonetheless give careful thought to its terms, since it is generally viewed as a morally binding agreement, if not a legally binding one. In addition, it can set the tone for the rest of the transaction and negotiations. If a particular point is of commercial significance to one of the parties, it will want to ensure that that point is agreed in principle at the outset and properly reflected in the letter of intent. It is generally preferable to have any difficult discussions up front, so that any irreconcilable differences (or "deal breakers") in relation to the fundamental terms of the deal are brought to light at that stage, and they can be addressed, or the parties can walk away, before they have spent considerable time and money on an abortive transaction. Of course, while focusing on those key issues, you should be mindful not to allow the letter of intent to assume greater importance than is merited and to delay the transaction before it has even started or set a confrontational tone to the transaction.

HOW LEGAL DUE DILIGENCE WORKS

The inquirer will invariably have carried out some form of initial, commercial due diligence of its own from publicly available information and based on its own knowledge (if any) of the company and the relevant market(s) before it even makes a first approach or indicative offer. However, let us suppose that it has decided to pursue the transaction opportunity and is ready to progress to the next, detailed stage of due diligence.

Due Diligence Questionnaire

Traditionally, the formal legal due diligence process begins with the inquirer's legal counsel sending a detailed due diligence request list or questionnaire to the company and its lawyers. The list usually covers all aspects of the business, although it should always be tailored to the specific business being investigated, with irrelevant questions omitted and more detailed questions included in relation to specific business types (e.g., more detailed IP questions should be put where the company develops, manufactures, licenses, or sells patented pharmaceutical products or is involved in proprietary research and development).

It will then be up to the company and its advisors to provide responses to the questionnaire. Depending on the responses given, further inquiries may be put to the company until the inquirer and its advisors are satisfied that all material issues have been addressed. Even in the absence of such further investigations, the company and its advisors should not assume that, simply by providing responses to the original inquiries, they have done all that they are required to do. If new information comes to light or facts relating to a particular issue change, the company may need to make supplementary disclosure. In fact, the process should be seen as an ongoing process up to completion of the transaction.

Data Room

The company may simply provide written responses to the due diligence questionnaire to the other side and its advisors, together with accompanying documents. Alternatively, it may be that the best way for the company to make information available is to establish a so-called data room. The first of these responses is self-explanatory; it is, however, worth explaining the data room process a little further.

First, a data room may be either physical or virtual. A physical data room is either established at the company's premises or, perhaps more routinely, at the premises of one of its advisors (e.g., its lawyers). Maintaining the data room off-site has the dual advantages of minimizing the on-site interruption to the business and also the risk that employees will become aware of the impending transaction. A virtual data room is accessed online by use of a password. There are specialist providers of virtual data room software and services, for example, Merrill DataSite™ (www.merrilldatasite.com) and TransPerfect Deal Interactive (www.dealinteractive.com). In either case, the company may wish to draw up data room rules for signature by the inquirer and those advisors who are to be granted access. The rules will, among other things, specify at what times the (physical) data room shall be open; how many people may attend at any one time; whether advisors may take or transmit copies out of the room; and so on.

While it may seem like a mundane task, proper preparation of the data room is of great importance and can save time and costs on both sides as the transaction progresses. The company should ensure that the data room contains all relevant documentation. Incomplete, unsigned, or undated documents may waste time, as can the failure to provide documents to which reference is made in the correspondence that is provided. The documents should also be contained in indexed files, preferably with separate files for each company or business area and for each substantial part of the due diligence inquiries (e.g., tax, employment, real estate, commercial contracts, intellectual property, etc.). This organization will enable specialist advisors easy access to the documents on which they need to focus.

Whether a data room is used or the company simply provides written replies to the questionnaire, it is vitally important that the company keeps an accurate and complete record of all documentation and information provided to the other side and its advisors. In particular, it or its legal advisors must retain one copy of the documentation after the transaction has been completed.

In addition, the company must take care not to make any untrue or misleading statements in replying to the due diligence inquiries. If it does, the counterparty may have a claim for a breach of warranty or indemnity (if a warranty or indemnity as to the veracity and accuracy of the information provided is included in the definitive agreement). Untrue statements could also give rise to a common law claim for misrepresentation.

Other Sources of Information

In addition to the documentation and information provided by the company, there are a number of other possible sources of useful information. These may include:

- Searches of the company's corporate records at the relevant public registry
- Searches of the courts in relation to insolvency proceedings
- Searches of public intellectual property registers (see Chapter 15)

- Searches of public real estate registers
- Searches of any other public registers relevant to the business
- The company's own publicly available materials and its web site
- Press articles, industry publications, and proprietary commercial databases
- The Internet generally

Due Diligence Report

The inquirer's solicitors and other advisors, in particular, its financial and tax advisors, will review and assess the mass of information that is provided to them, with a view to preparing their respective due diligence reports.

Depending on the instructions provided, the report(s) may focus only on material issues or may instead constitute a complete analysis of the company. In either case, the report(s) should have an executive summary at the beginning to highlight the main areas of concern that the due diligence review has identified and, importantly, recommendations as to how such issues might be resolved. It is important that advisors are asked to flag any particular issues as the due diligence exercise progresses and not simply wait until the final, or even draft, reports are issued. This will allow management sufficient time to assess the impact of such matters and take whatever course of action they feel is required.

The report(s) should not simply be a dry, legal or financial recital of the company's business, highlighting a series of potential difficulties; instead, they should assist the inquirer to identify key issues and find practical ways to resolve them. After all, it is to be assumed that both parties are spending their valuable management time and hard-earned money in order to complete a deal, and it is the advisors' job, wherever possible, to facilitate and not impede the transaction.

Both the inquirer and its advisors will need to understand how to interpret the mass of information furnished by the company. In particular, the legal advisors must approach due diligence with the right mind-set, understanding what is most important to the inquirer and how to analyze the information provided in the context of the transaction and the inquirer's short- and long-term objectives. As Louis Pasteur remarked, "Where observation is concerned, chance favors only the prepared mind."

NONLEGAL DUE DILIGENCE

While this chapter focuses on legal due diligence, there are a number of other areas of due diligence that may be needed, depending on the nature of the business and various other factors: the time and funds available, the importance of the transaction to the respective parties' businesses, and so on.

Financial Due Diligence

Many, if not most, inquirers will probably view financial due diligence on the company as being equally as important as (if not more important than) legal due diligence. Accordingly, on all but the most basic of transactions, a thorough financial due diligence by tax and financial advisors will be required. This is likely to encompass a review of the company's financial statements and most recent management accounts (or internal cost accounting reports), its tax affairs, financial reporting systems, working capital requirements and the banking facilities or lines of credit available to it, debtors and creditors, and any other financial issues relevant to the transaction and the plans for the business after completion.

The areas to be reviewed by the accountants and lawyers will, inevitably, overlap to an extent, and it is therefore important for a purchaser (and indeed the advisors themselves) that the roles and scope of work are clearly defined from the outset. There should also be ongoing coordination between the lawyers and accountants to ensure that all issues are fully covered and that any problem areas are identified and dealt with as early as possible.

Commercial Due Diligence

Commercial due diligence involves an analysis of the market(s) in which the company is active and its competitive position within those market(s). This may either be done in-house by the inquirer, if it has the resources and expertise, or by specialist commercial due diligence consultants, chartered marketers, or strategic research consultants. (Refer to Chapter 3 for more on strategic analysis and Chapter 15 for more on competitive intelligence searches.) Commercial due diligence is likely to focus on some or all of these elements:

- The company's geographical areas of operation and any associated risks
- Current and anticipated trends in the relevant industry sectors
- The achievability of the company's financial projections
- The company's pricing policy and how it compares to that of its competitors
- The company's key competitors, their strengths and weaknesses
- How the company could improve its market share
- How the company could enhance the strength of its brands and distribution channels
- How clients and suppliers perceive the company's reputation and how it could improve
- Whether any business areas are underperforming and, if so, why
- The company's internal financial reporting and risk management systems and procedures
- A review of the company's key management personnel and their experience, and whether it is appropriately staffed for its future business objectives
- Information may also be freely available from other sources, such as press articles or industry publications, the Internet, and public registers (e.g., company, real estate, and IP registers)
- For more on commercial databases, log onto our web site at www. innovationtocashflows.com and go to Appendix 15.1, "Selected Commercial Database and Software Tool Vendors" for descriptions and URLs of leading database providers.

Management Due Diligence

If some or all of the existing management team will be retained after completion of the transaction, the inquirer will carry out specific due diligence on those personnel. There are various ways that this can be achieved, from interviews (with them and possibly their colleagues, or customers, suppliers, and other third parties with whom they deal) to specific testing and analysis by a specialist human resources firm.

Any such due diligence review will focus on issues such as:

- Management's vision for the company and whether such vision fits with the inquirer's vision
- Management's values, ethical norms, and corporate traditions and whether they are compatible with the inquirer's
- Management's ability to deliver the expected performance
- Whether a viable business plan exists
- Whether the company has the requisite human resources and depth of leadership to take the business forward
- Whether the business has adequate reporting systems and controls
- Whether the company and its employees have compatible ethical standards and practices compared to the inquirer's

Specialist Due Diligence

Depending on the nature of the business being investigated, due diligence on specific aspects may be required. For a business dependent on the ownership and proper protection of its IP rights, or the right to use the IP rights of third parties, an intellectual property audit will be essential. See Chapter 15 for an illustrative case example on how to conduct a patent search.

Other specialist due diligence may include:

- *Technology and operations due diligence* (e.g., where the business is reliant on or manufactures complex technological products or relies heavily on information technology (IT) systems). Issues to be explored would be efficiency, flexibility, and exposure to technological change of the business's manufacturing plant and equipment. In IT-intensive businesses, it is important to verify the compatibility of the business's information systems with the inquirer's and the extent of any additional investment required to upgrade the hardware and software systems to achieve interoperability and compatibility.[1]
- *Regulatory due diligence* (e.g., where the business operates in a sector such as healthcare or pharmaceuticals, defense, telecommunications or broadcasting, or banking and financial services).
- *Environmental and safety audits* to investigate compliance with applicable health, safety, and environmental laws and possible exposures to environmental liabilities (e.g., where the business is involved in heavy industry and manufactures or uses hazardous materials).[2]
- *Real estate appraisals* (e.g., where real estate comprises a major part of the business).
- *Corporate reputation and brand investigation* (e.g., the value of the brand, its perceived strength, and its transferability and suitability for use in other markets, sales channels, or geographic territories).

ISSUES IN CROSS-BORDER DUE DILIGENCE

Due diligence on a cross-border transaction raises various difficulties on a legal, practical, and, sometimes, cultural level.

While the due diligence process described in this chapter is familiar to, and generally accepted by, sellers and purchasers in England, the United States, and other common law jurisdictions, it is not yet standard practice in many countries and so may pose cultural obstacles. Indeed, such investigations may be seen as damaging to the relationship between the parties or as acting in bad faith in some countries. This may be for purely cultural reasons, or because, as opposed to the English position, local laws do provide a reasonable measure of protection to the purchaser, by imposing obligations of good faith on the parties.

Parties in many jurisdictions will also be very reluctant to disclose freely what they consider confidential business information. Some countries' laws restrict what a company may disclose to third parties or require shareholder approval to certain disclosures. Privacy and data protection laws may also impact on the parties' freedom to exchange sensitive information, in particular relating to their employees.

In addition, professional advisors in different countries are likely to have very different understandings of what will be required of them, whether in terms of timing, the scope of their work, the content and style of the due diligence reports, or the procedures to be followed. There should always be one lead firm of lawyers tasked with coordinating the international due diligence; that firm must explain fully to each local firm of advisors what is required and then draw together each local report into a coherent whole for the purchaser. Clear lines of communication are a prerequisite for a successful transaction. Normally, there will be one master due diligence questionnaire, supplemented by individual questionnaires in respect of each jurisdiction.

The lead firm must then ensure that any specific legal, regulatory, or other practical issues in each jurisdiction are brought to the purchaser's attention and that the potential impact is explained and, if necessary, suitable action is taken or provisions are inserted into the sale and purchase agreement.

As well as issues for the advisors to consider, the inquirer should also be undertaking its own "soft" due diligence on the other parties to the transaction, evaluating the cultural differences and deciding how to manage businesses and personnel in two or more jurisdictions once the transaction has been completed. Entering into a transaction with a party in a foreign jurisdiction raises a vast array of issues—language and lines of communication, management style and relations with employees, legal and regulatory differences, political and cultural influences—that will affect the parties. Soft due diligence should identify and address any cultural issues or pending ethical problems before the relationship is consummated.

WHAT IF DUE DILIGENCE UNCOVERS A PROBLEM?

There are a number of options available if the due diligence process reveals a material issue within the company or business. These include:

- Withdrawing from the transaction
- Negotiating appropriate warranty and indemnity protection in the definitive agreements
- Seeking a reduction in the purchase price (on an acquisition) or in the level of funds to be invested or the percentage equity holding in the company that the funds will yield (on an investment)

- On an acquisition, seeking to retain part of the consideration payable to the seller or having part of the consideration placed into an escrow account, subject to satisfaction of certain conditions or milestones by the company
- Insisting that certain issues be resolved as preconditions to completion
- In the case of a proposed share acquisition, restructuring the acquisition as a business purchase and leaving behind the unwanted liabilities or commitments or requiring the seller to transfer the unwanted asset or liability out of the target entity (e.g., to another company in the seller's group)
- Obtaining appropriate insurance cover

A combination of some of these points may be appropriate. Unless the issue is so material as to represent a deal breaker, it is usual for the parties to arrive at some form of agreement as to how the problem should be addressed and how the risk associated with it should be allocated between them.

FROM INNOVATION TO CASH FLOWS AND BEYOND: DUE DILIGENCE DURING THE BUSINESS LIFE CYCLE

Having examined the due diligence process, let us now look at the specific issues that arise in relation to due diligence on a business that owns or uses significant intellectual property rights. While in today's world, nearly all businesses own or license some form of IP rights, for companies in the high-tech or biotech sectors, IP will form a fundamental part of their business. Consequently, an inquirer will be particularly eager to ensure that the company owns what it says that it owns or has the legal right to use whatever IP it does not itself own.

As noted, as a first port of call, public registries will provide details of any registered IP rights. However, searches should not be relied on exclusively, and more detailed and specific inquiries will be required where IP is vital to the business. Obviously, public records show only registered rights; it is probable that a high-tech or biotech business also has material unregistered rights.

The rights in question may include, among others, trademarks and service marks, patents, copyright, design rights, moral rights, rights to inventions, domain names, trade names, confidential information and trade secrets, know-how, database rights, rights in computer software, and rights to goodwill. Some may be registered; many may be unregistered or unregisterable. The rights may also include pending applications, or the right to apply, for registration of such rights.

If there are pending applications for registration of rights, the person carrying out the due diligence will want to verify that the application is likely to succeed and that no objections or oppositions have been received or are likely. Similarly, any applications for rectification or cancellation of registered rights should be investigated, as should any applications that were refused, if important to the business.

The purchaser will also be concerned with ensuring that the business has the right to use any third-party IP rights that are required for the business.

The purchaser may also wish to consider whether rights should be registered in jurisdictions that are or may become important to the business, but where registration has not yet, for some reason, been applied for. If the seller is already aware of this issue, it may consider making appropriate applications prior to seeking a buyer for the business.

By their very nature, unregistered rights can be much more difficult to identify and verify. It will, therefore, be necessary to investigate such rights very thoroughly and to ensure that the business has adequate systems and procedures in place to protect such rights. Employment contracts should be reviewed to ensure that they contain suitable provision, among other things, for any rights created by an employee during the course of employment to belong to the company.

It follows that any company that is considering seeking a purchaser for or an investor into its business should, as far as possible, ensure that its IP portfolio is in good order before the potential purchaser or investor begins its due diligence. A disorganized or neglected portfolio could well spell the end of a potential transaction.

However, whatever the purpose of the due diligence, some fundamental issues need to be investigated when dealing with IP assets. In particular, an inquirer will need to identify and analyze:

- All IP rights owned and used in the business
- Which rights are registered or have applications for registration pending
- What material unregistered rights the business owns
- All licenses of the IP rights of the business out to third parties and all licenses in of IP rights from third parties for use in the business
- Whether any IP rights are shared with third parties
- Any issues concerning the validity, subsistence, or ownership of the rights
- Any actual or potential infringements of the rights owned or used in the business or, conversely, by the business of any third-party IP rights
- How the business manages disclosure of its confidential information to third parties

It is also worth considering what is meant by intellectual property in the context of a transaction. In an investment agreement or acquisition agreement, the definition of the term *intellectual property* normally is very widely drawn and includes, among other things, patents, trademarks and service marks, rights to inventions, copyright, business names, domain names, design rights, rights in software and databases, moral rights, rights in confidential information, and know-how.

Let us now take a look at due diligence in the context of some common but more specific scenarios that may arise during the lifetime of an IP business.

Innovation

The first step on the long road to the commercialization of a new concept is often through a university technology transfer office or through initial contact with the technology transfer team or licensing department inside an established firm. The process usually begins with the submission of an invention disclosure form by the inventor. The typical invention disclosure form usually covers most, if not all, of these areas:

- Basic details of the invention
- A description of the inventive steps, the prerequisites for successful patentability
- The invention's advantages over any similar existing methods or products

- What further development is required and how long it is expected to take
- Any third-party interests in the invention (in other words, those of any person who has funded or otherwise supported the development to date)
- Details of any agreements in force restricting the use of the invention
- Details of any disclosures of the IP that have been made
- Any other information that may help assess the commercial potential of the invention (e.g., details of companies that use similar IP)
- To set up such an invention disclosure system, log onto our web site at www.innovationtocashflows.com and download these files: Appendix 2.2, "Guidelines for Setting Up an Invention Disclosure System for Your Company," and Appendix 2.3, "Sample Invention Disclosure Form."

It is clear that inventors will need to have done their own due diligence prior to approaching the technology transfer team. The disclosure form primarily enables the team to define and establish ownership rights over the relevant invention and to assess its commercial potential and the patentability of the concept. The transfer team also will be eager to identify anyone other than the inventors who may have a claim on the ownership of a patent. (Refer to the section "Access to Innovation through Collaboration with Academic Groups" in Chapter 8 for more discussion on new ventures starting up in a university setting and for more on ownership rights in the context of academic collaborations.)

If the team is satisfied that the concept shows good prospects for commercialization, it will then advance the due diligence to the next level. This will involve market research to verify the commercial value of the IP and its practical applications: How will the university and the inventor be able to create value from the original concept in the real world? The due diligence will also focus on whether to commercialize the concept through a license out or by transferring the IP to a university spin-off company incorporated specifically for that purpose. In the United Kingdom, such entities are often called university "spin-out" companies, whereas in the United States the term is usually "spin-off."[3]

Let us assume that a university spin-off company is formed to carry out further evaluation and testing of a promising new biomedical device. It may receive initial investment from the technology transfer team's own incubator funds; specialist seed capital providers or business angels may have invested; government grants may have been provided; as may funding from other bodies, such as foundations or nongovernmental organizations that invest specifically in new technology companies.

The company progresses well, thanks to the initial funding, and perhaps it has achieved its first proof-of-concept for a new noninvasive gastrointestinal application, but it needs more financing to build a working prototype of its invention and carry out further testing and evaluation. The company turns to venture capital or private equity funds for its next significant infusion of cash.

Outside Investment

The investment process can take anywhere from one month to one year. An average time frame, from consideration of the initial proposal to completing the investment, might be around four to six months. The investor and its team of experts will spend much of this time on the due diligence exercise. Critical to the success of an external investment in a technology business is the quality of information provided or otherwise available to the investor, in particular concerning the IP used in the business.

First, let us make it clear that due diligence in this context, although primarily undertaken by the potential investor, is by no means a one-way street; the company must ensure that it approaches private equity firms whose investment profile fits with its sector, location, and the amount of funding required. After all, the founders of the business are proposing to give up a significant percentage of the company's equity and, with it, invariably, the relative freedom that they have enjoyed up to that point to run the business as they think fit. With such a commitment, and the future of the business at stake, it is imperative that management chooses the right investor with whom to work and take the business forward.

First of all, any external investor will want to see a comprehensive, professional business plan or information memorandum covering all key areas of the business, including its principal products, its place in the market and competitors, brief biographies of its management team, its past and projected future financial performance, and, last but not least, proposed uses of the funds to be invested. However, on the initial approach, it is often better to provide a more concise executive summary to potential investors to grab their attention. Remember that, as noted, legal advice should be sought before distributing such documents to third parties.

A corporate finance advisor will be able to advise the company on how best to present itself and which private equity firms it should approach. Either way, this will be the first due diligence information that the potential investors will receive on the company, and it is crucial that the company gets it right, or it may never even get its foot in the private equity door.

On receipt of a business plan or information memorandum, the potential investor will perform its own initial due diligence, based on the information disclosed in such document. It will probably undertake some form of commercial due diligence. Assuming it decides to proceed, the more formal due diligence process will commence.

In many ways, an investor in a technology business will want to undertake similar due diligence to a purchaser in the context of an acquisition of the same business (to be discussed). Depending on the size of the investment, there may be no discernible difference between the two.

However, there are some key differences. Above all, while you may expect a purchaser of a business to be interested in integrating the business into its preexisting structure as part of its medium- to long-term strategy, an outside investor will invariably be looking toward its ultimate exit from the investment, whether by way of a sale of the business or its stake in it or by way of a stock market flotation. Consequently, it will be very eager to assess the financial forecasts for the business to analyze how long it will take to generate the target return on its investment. It will also do due diligence on how it can exit the investment most efficiently—for example, are there a number of acquisitive groups in the same sector that would be potential purchasers of the business?

Furthermore, given that the management team involved in the business is likely to stay in place after the investment (whereas, on an acquisition, the purchaser very often replaces the existing management team with its own people), an outside investor may pay more attention to due diligence on the key management personnel and is likely to want to interview them separately to gauge their competence and commitment to the business.

Strategic Alliances

Entering into a strategic alliance can be incredibly valuable for any technology business. Such an alliance can take a variety of forms, such as a technology license agreement or collaboration agreement (e.g., for marketing a product or for research and development), an equity or contractual joint venture, a distribution agreement, or a manufacturing or production alliance. (See Chapters 4, 6, 7, and 14.)

It is also one transaction where the entrepreneur and the company should be doing as much due diligence as the counterparty, in order to ensure that the partner with which it enters into a relationship is the right one. For that reason, commercial and management due diligence is likely to be as important as legal due diligence. (Refer to Chapter 7 for more on partner selection in strategic alliances.)

The scope of the due diligence necessary depends on the precise nature of the alliance but, from a commercial perspective, may include some of these points:

- If access to new markets is the driver behind the alliance, can the partner provide access to those markets? What are its distribution channels? How is the partner perceived in those markets?
- Has the partner had any operational problems recently that could adversely affect the alliance and, by extension, the entrepreneur, the business, and their reputation? For example, have there been any significant disputes with customers or suppliers, or other major litigation investigations by governmental or regulatory authorities; problems with other alliances?
- What does the partner want to achieve from the venture? An ongoing commercial relationship? A short- to medium-term relationship in order to break into a market or allow it to attain the next stage of its business life cycle? A trade sale to a third party? The takeover of the other or to be taken over? A listing on a stock exchange?
- What is the partner's business philosophy? Does it fit with that of the entrepreneur?
- Does the partner have the resources, financial and otherwise, to ensure the success of the alliance?
- If manufacture of a product or component is the motive, does the partner have the production capacity necessary to deliver?
- What assets will the partner contribute to the venture? What IP will the partner provide? Is the IP valid? For how long will the IP protection or registration last?
- Who are the partner's key stakeholders and management? Will the entrepreneur and the team be able to work well with them?
- Does the partner have other strategic alliances? What effect might they have on the proposed venture?

These are some examples of commercial due diligence issues that may be relevant in the context of a strategic alliance. Each highlights the need for the entrepreneur to undertake thorough commercial (as well as legal, financial, and other) due diligence on any potential strategic partner. Choosing the wrong partner will almost inevitably have disastrous consequences for the business and could even spell the end of the road.

Sale of the Company

A potential purchaser of a company needs to satisfy itself that it is acquiring what it wishes to acquire and that there are no unwelcome surprises in store. Due diligence allows the purchaser to confirm or, if appropriate, adjust the price that it is prepared to pay.

In transactions governed by common law, a purchaser (or, for that matter, an investor or strategic partner) has a crucial problem to overcome: Common law provides it with almost no built-in, statutory protection, and the overriding principle is that of *caveat emptor*, or buyer beware. A seller is under no legal obligation to disclose any particular information to the purchaser. So, while it is true that the common law can provide a purchaser with a remedy in certain limited circumstances—for example, for a misrepresentation by a seller—a purchaser is potentially exposed unless thorough legal, commercial, and financial investigations are carried out into the target company and its operations, and adequate contractual protections are put in place, before the acquisition is completed. The purchaser's exposure under common law contrasts with the position described earlier in this chapter in relation to the parties' obligations of good faith under many civil law systems.

Because of this exposure, it is standard practice in all but the most straightforward of acquisitions for the purchaser to seek to include extensive warranties and indemnities in the sale and purchase agreement. In this way, the purchaser obtains a measure of protection by contractual means that the common law does not provide and shifts at least part of the risk back on to the seller.

However, even well-drafted warranties and indemnities may not cover every possible area of risk. Even if a particular risk is covered, the sale and purchase agreement will invariably contain limitations on the potential liability of the seller (e.g., as to the time during which the purchaser may make a claim against the seller and the maximum amount that it is permitted to recover). Furthermore, the success of any claim depends on the financial ability of the seller to meet such liability; warranties and indemnities are only as good as the person giving them. In truth, no purchaser will, in any event, want to have to dedicate significant resources, time, and costs to legal proceedings to try and recover damages for a breach of warranty or indemnity after an acquisition has been completed; the purchaser will have its hands full managing its newly acquired business and trying to integrate it into its own structure and operations, which can be a notoriously difficult process.

Purchasers, therefore, should not view warranties as a substitute for a properly conducted due diligence exercise, which can uncover any problem areas, and so give a purchaser the opportunity to take action, before it is legally committed to complete the acquisition. Indeed, warranties are designed to elicit information on the target company—through the disclosure process that the seller will undertake in response to the warranties—as much, if not more, than giving the purchaser a possible remedy.

Yet a purchaser may not be able or may not wish to conduct full (or even any) due diligence. For example, if a transaction has to be completed in a very short time frame, the purchaser may have limited scope to carry out due diligence inquires and may have to limit itself to the key areas of the target's operations. Or, if an acquisition is of relatively minor importance for the purchaser—such as a large concern acquiring a much smaller business—it may perceive the risk to be small and, accordingly, be prepared to forgo a more complete due diligence exercise and rely exclusively (or at least more heavily) on warranties and indemnities in the sale and purchase agreement.

Aside from providing detailed information on the company prior to completion of the acquisition, another important aspect of due diligence is that it allows the purchaser to identify issues that may affect, and plan ahead for, the integration of the target company and its business into the purchaser's operations and structure following completion. Indeed, on the presumption that the purchaser has in effect decided, even prior to making an offer, to proceed with the acquisition absent any deal breakers, due diligence can be seen as the first stage in the future management of the combined businesses.

It is worth mentioning at this point that due diligence in the context of what might be called a "regular" acquisition—one where a single potential purchaser makes an offer for the target business and is generally in greater control of the process, including due diligence—differs from due diligence in connection with a so-called "auction sale" (where the seller invites offers from a number of would-be purchasers in what is, in effect, a bidding war).

The principal difference is that it is the seller who controls the process, the documentation, and the timetable of an auction sale. Generally, the seller issues an information memorandum on the company to prospective bidders. The memorandum contains the key information on the company and allows the prospective bidders to carry out some initial due diligence. After evaluating the initial round of indicative offers, the seller selects the winning bidders for the next round. These second-round bidders will be given access to formal due diligence materials—materials selected by the seller and its advisors, rather than requested by the purchaser by means of a due diligence questionnaire. The second-round bidders will also be provided with a draft sale and purchase agreement, prepared by the seller's lawyers rather than the purchaser's lawyers, as would usually be the case. The remaining bidders then submit further bids, if they wish to pursue the acquisition after completing their initial due diligence, and the seller elects to continue negotiations with one or more of them until definitive agreements are signed with one.

As can be deduced, a purchaser invariably is given less due diligence material on an auction sale and a lower level of protection in the sale and purchase agreement, quite simply because the seller is likely to have a choice of two or more possible buyers and can therefore take up a much stronger negotiating stance. In general, the seller benefits more than the winning bidder does from an auction sale. This is known in M&A as the winner's curse.

However, an auction does come with risks attached for the seller. For example, information is being disclosed to more potential purchasers and their advisors, thus increasing the risk of confidential information leaking into the public domain. One or more of the bidders are likely to be competitors of the seller, so disclosure of sensitive information carries risks if any of those bidders do not proceed. For that reason, a seller conducting an auction sale may be best advised not to disclose its more sensitive commercial and financial data, at least until it has narrowed the field of suitors down to one or two. Also, legal and other professional costs may be increased because negotiations are being held with different potential purchasers.

Stock Market Flotation

The actual process of due diligence on an IPO has many similarities to that carried out on an acquisition. Due diligence on an IPO will cover most, if not all, of the areas of a business that would be covered by due diligence on an acquisition. There is one critical difference, however, that underpins the process on an IPO: The regulations governing admission to trading on the relevant stock exchange prescribe what information the company is required to disclose to investors in its *offering prospectus*—that is, the document through which it seeks to attract investors in the flotation. The listing regulations drive the due diligence process. In essence, therefore, the due diligence agenda is set by the applicable regulations, not by any individual party.

In addition, it is the company and its legal and financial counsel who are primarily responsible for undertaking the due diligence exercise and preparing due diligence reports. Those reports are subject to review and comment by the advisors to the banks that are acting as managers (members of the underwriting syndicate) on the flotation. The lead manager (the bookrunner) serves as the head of the underwriting syndicate. The due diligence reports then form the basis of the disclosures to be made in the prospectus. The prospectus itself may also be subject to approval by the relevant regulatory authority—as is the case in England for a flotation on the main market of the London Stock Exchange—before its release to potential investors.

Another stage in the due diligence exercise on an IPO is the process known as *verification*. In essence, because of the requirements to comply with the rules on disclosure and to ensure that statements made in the prospectus are accurate and not misleading, it is standard practice in many jurisdictions for all statements that will be made in the prospectus to be verified. Verification essentially involves the company's directors, assisted by its legal counsel, confirming the accuracy of each statement in the prospectus, where possible by reference to independent sources. If a statement cannot be verified, it must be modified so that it becomes verifiable or otherwise removed from the prospectus. As a prospectus can easily run to over 100 pages, this verification process can be time-consuming and laborious. However, its ultimate purpose is to protect the company and directors from potential liability to investors, so it is very much a necessary evil.

CLOSING THOUGHTS

It is all very well stressing the importance of proper due diligence and how inadequate due diligence can lead to disastrous consequences. Surely, an entrepreneur might reason, these are just lawyers and other professional advisors trying to generate an even greater fee income for themselves, and the likelihood of anything truly catastrophic coming to pass because of poor due diligence is remote. Numerous web sites and stories highlight the potential pitfalls of inadequate or nonexistent due diligence and how it can cost a party to a transaction dearly.[4] The entrepreneur would do well to heed the moral of their stories.

Nevertheless, despite the many pitfalls for the unwary, due diligence need not be a process to be approached with great trepidation, whether by the entrepreneur or the investor, strategic partner, or purchaser. With good preparation and management, the process should assist the transaction to reach a successful conclusion for all concerned and set the scene for the technology entrepreneur to move on to the next stage in the journey on the road from innovation to value creation and realization.

CHAPTER TAKEAWAYS

- Due diligence is detective work.
- Various types of due diligence exist: legal, financial, commercial, management, and specialist.
- Consider legal, cultural, and practical issues that may arise if different jurisdictions are involved.
- The principle of *caveat emptor* (buyer beware) exists in common law jurisdictions.
- Warranties and indemnities are not a substitute for a properly conducted due diligence exercise.
- Proper preparation is critical to the due diligence exercise.
- Consider the impact of the due diligence process on the company—including the impact on management's time and the risk of the transaction becoming known in the workplace or by the public generally.
- Ensure that the inquirer signs a confidentiality agreement before you disclose any key information on the business.
- Consider signing a nonbinding letter of intent or memorandum of understanding to record the main terms that have been agreed in principle before due diligence commences.
- Consider how the due diligence will be structured: Will a data room be used? If so, will it be a virtual data room?
- Consider strategy and options if due diligence reveals material problems.
- Due diligence is a tool for post-completion planning as much as pre-completion issue spotting.

And, finally, remember:

- Due diligence need not be a nightmare!

Valuing Company Cash Flows

Valuation Using Discounted Cash Flow

In this chapter, we discuss general principles of valuing a business using discounted cash flow (DCF) valuation methods. In Chapter 18, we review accounting basics, discuss equity markets, and then cover other techniques for valuing businesses using multiples and comparable deal transactions. In Chapter 19, we learn how venture capitalists use a shortcut method to value start-up ventures. That chapter also discusses financing rounds and examines how multiple rounds of financing can affect common shareholders through equity share dilution. Chapter 20 discusses how to create financial models of a contractual agreement involving patent licensing rights and the transfer of proprietary technology for a new product under development. Chapter 21 closes Part Six and concludes the book.

Throughout Part Six, we make reference to four capstone cases that allow you to practice the concepts discussed in the text. We have also written our own case studies to illustrate key points. (Our own cases include financial spreadsheet valuation models.) To download any of these files, you will need to register and log onto our web site at www.innovationtocashflows.com. (For further information, refer to pages 605–606 and visit the book's web site.)

WHY VALUATION IS AN IMPORTANT SKILL TO LEARN

If you master the principles of discounted cash flow valuations, you will be able to value technology transfer licensing agreements, strategic alliances, and joint ventures. Furthermore, you can use DCF valuation methods to value your own start-up venture and help you decide how to divide up the pie and allocate the equity shares among the other cofounders, key employees, and outside investors.

Valuation is a basic part of the tool kit for any manager who needs to make investment decisions. As you will soon see, all chief executive officers, chief financial officers (CFOs), and business development managers need to understand valuation as a regular part of their everyday jobs. Line managers need to be able to do valuations in order to pursue value creation strategies and to make wise capital budgeting decisions. Valuation techniques help all managers quantify the risk and return trade-offs of future investment opportunities.

Investment bankers use a combination of methods, including DCF, to value companies for an initial public offering. Professional appraisers are often asked by clients to do asset valuations upon the dissolution of a partnership or a joint venture. Valuations may figure prominently in the probate of the estate of a company owner or key employee upon death. Divorce proceedings may also be about splitting up shared assets, in which case valuations are required.

Venture capitalists, professional fund managers, and financial intermediaries regularly do valuations of the companies held in their equity portfolios. Small business brokers, financial advisors, litigation expert witnesses, and investment bankers use valuation in their advisory roles to companies involved in strategic alliance, mergers and acquisitions (M&A), and corporate restructuring negotiations or in securities markets lawsuits or patent infringement litigation.

In this chapter, we explain how to do DCF valuations and demonstrate their use from building cash flow statements to doing sensitivity analyses. Before going into the numerical details, we define pertinent terminology, explain the basic theory of valuation, and derive the necessary formulas. This is followed by detailed practical examples to illustrate each of the techniques, step-by-step. We have written an illustrative case called PB Electronics Inc. to demonstrate how to value a company from start to finish, using a financial spreadsheet. The spreadsheet contains the formulas to discount the company's cash flows and derive the economic value of the company. The case of PB Electronics Inc. is found in Appendix 17.1, "Using the Enterprise Valuation Method to Value a High-Technology Company," located at the end of the chapter. (The downloadable electronic spreadsheet for PB Electronics Inc. is available on our web site after you log in at www.innovationtocashflows.com.)

COMPOUNDING AND DISCOUNTING MONEY: PRESENT VALUE TECHNIQUES

We begin with the concepts of the time value of money and purchasing power. Money today buys a certain basket of goods or services. More money will be needed a year from now to buy the same basket of goods or services if there is inflation. Purchasing power decreases by the inflation rate. Money put under a mattress also loses value if there is inflation. Money deposited into a bank account will likely be worth more because the bank pays interest on the deposit.

In order to capture the value of money over time, we use the techniques of compounding and discounting. *Compounding* refers to calculating the future value of today's dollar or euro, whereas *discounting* enables us to calculate what a given amount in the future would be worth in the present.

Present value (PV) techniques compute the time value of money. In order to compound money, we multiply its present value by an interest rate factor and calculate a future amount of value. In this example, the interest rate is referred to as the *discount rate*. The term *present worth* has the same meaning as *present value*.

In order to discount money, we divide a future amount of money by an interest rate factor and compute the present value of the money. The basic formula looks like this for discrete discounting (taking a future sum back to the present):

$$PV_0 = \frac{FV_n}{(1+r)^n}$$

where PV_0 = Present Value at time $t = 0$
FV_n = Future Value at time $t = n$
r = Discount Rate of Return
n = Time Period

For example, say you expect to inherit some money in three years time ($n = 3$ years). Using discrete discounting, how much is the future \$15,000 inheritance worth today if the discount rate is 6 percent per year? (Answer: \$12,594.29.)

As another example, this time of compounding money, say that a customer makes a \$10,000 deposit in a bank for $n = 4$ years at an interest rate of 3.5 percent per year, how much money will the person have at the end of three years? Here we know the present value and want to compute the future value. To solve the problem, we use the discrete compounding formula:

$$FV_n = PV_0(1 + r)^n = \$10,000 \times (1.035)^4 = \$11,475.23$$

If you discover that you are a bit rusty on compounding or discounting, you can find a more in-depth discussion and examples in Appendix 17.2, "Time Value of Money", which you can browse or download by logging onto our web site at www.innovationtocashflows.com. In Appendix 17.2, we explain both discrete compounding and continuous compounding, and provide numerical examples.

DEFINITION OF NET PRESENT VALUE

The difference between a present value (PV) calculation and a *net present value* (NPV) is that the cost of the initial investment is included in the latter whereas it is not included in the former. In other words, the *net* present value "nets out" or subtracts the cost of investment from the overall present value calculation.

For example, if the overall PV of the cash inflows for a project are worth \$10,000 and the required investment to build the project is \$1,000 (the cash outflow), then the net present value (NPV) would be \$10,000 − \$1,000 = \$9,000. The NPV of a project or investment is a measure of how much richer the owner will become by undertaking the investment.

Therefore, net present value is the increase (or decrease) in wealth accruing to an investor when he or she makes an investment. Positive NPV projects increase wealth. Negative NPV projects decrease wealth.

$$NPV = -(PV\ of\ cash\ outflows) + (PV\ of\ cash\ inflows)$$

Decision Time at Dynamic Turbine Company

For instance, say the Dynamic Turbine Company is developing an innovative multimillion-dollar jet engine designed to save energy and reduce air and noise pollution for commercial airlines. The required investments for the new turbine are expected to amount to €1.6 billion. The preliminary cash flows are expected to be approximately €900 million per year for five years. Should the company make the investment if its required discount rate (often referred to as the company's "hurdle rate" for projects) is 15 percent per annum? (Note we have shown all results in millions of euros).

$$NPV = -€1,600 + \sum_{t=1}^{5} \frac{€900}{(1.15)^t}$$
$$= €1,416.94$$

Since the NPV result of €1,416.94 million is positive, the company should proceed with the project and make the investment.

Net Present Value and Value Creation

For companies to create value for their shareholders, they need to invest in positive-NPV activities where the higher the NPV, the better. Zero-NPV activities are neutral: They neither create nor destroy wealth over and above the required rate of return. The company should not invest in negative-NPV activities, as they destroy shareholders' wealth. Shareholders would have better alternatives in the capital markets in which to place their funds. Therefore, the acceptance criteria for projects are such that when

$NPV > 0$, accept the investment;

$NPV < 0$, reject the investment;

$NPV = 0$, consider the investment to be marginal.

INTERNAL RATE OF RETURN

The internal rate of return (IRR) is simply the rate of return that causes the net present value of a project to be zero. IRR is commonly used by managers for comparing alternative budget proposals when they are doing capital budgeting. Note that the internal rate of return is an intrinsically derived number—it is not dependent on anything except the cash flows of a particular project or investment. An investment's IRR is defined to be:

IRR = Discount rate at which the investment's NPV equals zero

We return to our earlier example of the Dynamic Turbine Company (with its ecological and energy-saving jet turbine project). To find the IRR, we simply ask: At what rate does the NPV of the project equal zero? By solving the next equation, we compute the internal rate of return for the jet turbine project:

$$NPV = 0 = -€1,600 + \sum_{t=1}^{5} \frac{€900}{(IRR)^t}$$

Solving for the IRR, the answer is 48 percent.

The corresponding acceptance criteria for an investment project is the required cost of capital (specifically it is the *opportunity cost of capital* or the cost of the forgone opportunity). We discuss more about opportunity cost of capital later in the section, "What Is Opportunity Cost?"

If the IRR exceeds the required cost of capital (expressed as a percentage rate of return) then the investment is attractive; if it is less than the required cost of capital, the investment is unattractive. If the IRR equals the required cost of capital, the investment is marginal.

For the Dynamic Turbine Company, its required cost of capital for investment projects, also called the company's *hurdle rate*, is $K = 15$ percent. Since the project's computed IRR of 48 percent vastly exceeds the 15 percent hurdle rate, management should approve the new turbine project.

In general, the acceptance criteria for investment projects are such that for $K =$ the percentage required cost of capital, then if

$$IRR > K, \text{ accept the investment}$$

$$IRR < K, \text{ reject the investment}$$

$$IRR = K, \text{ consider the investment marginal}$$

A word of caution: The IRR technique has a number of problems associated with its use (or misuse). In particular, if there are changes in the signs of the cash flows when you solve for IRR, then you get multiple rates of return. Consult a corporate finance or engineering economy textbook that describes capital budgeting for further discussion about the pitfalls in using IRR. When in doubt, it is best to rely on net present value rather than on internal rate of return for comparing investment proposals.

Investments with a Salvage Value

As another illustration of a net present value investment, consider a project that requires an initial capital expenditure of $40 million at initial time zero, returns $7.5 million in cash at the end of each year for four years, and then has a remaining value (salvage value) of $37.38 million at the end of the fifth year. Determine the net present value or NPV at a cost of capital, $K = 10$ percent, and then determine the IRR.

In this problem we have an initial cash outflow followed by five positive cash inflows. Therefore, to find the NPV we show the capital outlay as a negative number in year 0 (undiscounted), and then sum up the present value of the remaining positive cash flows, shown mathematically below,

$$NPV = -\$40 + \frac{\$7.50}{(1+r)} + \frac{\$7.50}{(1+r)^2} + \frac{\$7.50}{(1+r)^3} + \frac{\$7.50}{(1+r)^4} + \frac{\$37.38}{(1+r)^5}$$

where the discount rate r is equal to the cost of capital, $K = 10$ percent (expressed as a decimal), for this example.

	A	B	C	D	E	F	G	H
1	**ESTIMATED ANNUAL CASH FLOWS ($US)**							
2	Year		**Yr 0**	**Yr 1**	**Yr 2**	**Yr 3**	**Yr 4**	**Yr 5**
3	Cash flow, $ millions		−40.00	7.50	7.50	7.50	7.50	37.38
4	Discount rate	*10%*						
5			**Equations**			**Answer**		
6	Net present value (NPV)		= NPV (B4, D3:H3) + C3			$6.98		
7								
8	Internal Rate of Return (IRR)		= IRR (C3:H3, 0.14)			15%		

FIGURE 17.1   Net Present Value and Internal Rate of Return for an Investment Project with a Salvage Value

We also set up the problem equation in a computer spreadsheet and show you the results in Figure 17.1.

Based on the NPV and IRR calculations, management should clearly accept this investment project proposal. It creates positive NPV of $6.98 million and has an IRR of 15 percent which exceeds the opportunity cost of capital, $K = 10$ percent.

In Figure 17.1, we show you the equations as they would appear in a spreadsheet. To solve for the IRR, we ask: What must the discount rate be to make the NPV of the project equal to zero? To make it work in your spreadsheet's IRR function, you need to make an initial guess. We used 14 percent as the initial value. That is why you see the 0.14 in the spreadsheet equation like this = IRR (C3:H3, 0.14). The spreadsheet then uses trial and error to solve for the IRR. The correct answer is 15 percent. Of course, you may use any financial calculator with an IRR function to solve the problem equally well by trial and error. Having gone through the mechanics of present value, we now turn to the historical roots of valuing a business and explain who invented the method we use today.

MEANING OF INTRINSIC VALUE

John Burr Williams opens his seminal book *The Theory of Investment Value*, with the sage observation, "Separate and distinct things not to be confused, as every thoughtful investor knows, are real worth and market price."[1]

Contrary to what many people believe, the stock market's quoted price for a firm (or its market price) is *not* the same thing as determining the real "true" value or economic worth of a business. So how do professionals value the economic worth of a business? Who invented the discounted cash flow valuation methods commonly used today by financial analysts? Leading scholars of financial investments—such as the legendary Benjamin Graham, whom many consider to be the founder of the profession of security analysis—credit John Burr Williams with inventing the process of valuing a common stock in order to determine its *intrinsic value* or "real economic worth."[2]

In 1938, Williams defined investment value as being the "permanent" value of a business, as opposed to its short-term speculative or market value. We quote his definition in the next passage.

> *Let us define the investment value of a stock as the present worth of all the dividends to be paid upon it. Likewise let us define the investment value of a bond as the present worth of its future coupons and principal. In both cases, dividends, or coupons and principal, must be adjusted for expected changes in the purchasing power of money. The purchase of a stock or bond, like other transactions which give rise to the phenomenon of interest, represents the exchange of present goods for future goods—dividends, or coupons and principal, in this case being the claim on future goods. To appraise the investment value, then, it is necessary to estimate future payments. The annuity of payments, adjusted for changes in the value of money itself, may then be discounted at the pure interest rate demanded by the investor.*[3]

Writing shortly after the Great Depression, Williams was deeply troubled by how many families had lost their fortunes in the U.S. stock market crash of 1929. He wanted to find a better way for individual investors to systematically determine the value of a business. Williams's idea was to discount all future dividends of the firm at the personal interest rate sought by the individual investor. Today, we would call the "pure interest rate sought by the investor" to be the investor's personal "opportunity cost of capital."

What Is Opportunity Cost?

An *opportunity cost* is an expense that is incurred, either directly or indirectly, because of the scarcity of resources. It is the cost of the forgone opportunity.

Consider the potential graduate student who could earn $45,000 a year working full time for a high-technology firm and who chooses instead to pursue doctoral studies at a leading private university, at a cost of $55,000 per year in tuition. The student's total cost of going to school for that year is $100,000: $55,000 cash outlay for tuition and $45,000 in forgone income.[4]

Using the Opportunity Cost of Funds for Economic Analysis

In any economic study, whether for capital budgeting purposes or for investment analysis, the proper discount rate to use is the opportunity cost of funds, that is, the income forgone or the expense incurred because the money was invested in that particular investment project *rather than in other alternative projects of similar risk*. Suppose that a firm always has available certain investment opportunities, such as new projects to expand the business that will earn a minimum of, say, 10 percent. This being the case, the firm's managers would be unwise to invest in other alternative projects earning less than 10 percent. The 10 percent may be thought of as the opportunity cost of not investing in the readily available alternative. The opportunity cost is the economic sacrifice of possible income that might have been obtained by the use of that money elsewhere.[5]

Just to make clear the point about which discount rate to use in valuation, we note that Williams refers to an earlier article, "Investing for True Values," that was written by Robert F. Wiese and published in *Barron's* (1930).[6] While both Williams and Wiese agree on visualizing the firm as a perpetual security (where shareholders would receive an infinite stream of future income payments), they appear to *disagree* on the proper discount rate. Wiese wrote: "The proper price of any security, whether a stock or bond, is the sum of all future income payments discounted at the current rate of interest in order to arrive at the present value."[7] Instead, Williams wisely advises that each individual investor should discount a firm's future dividends, *not* at the current rate of interest (as Wiese says), but at the "pure interest rate demanded by the investor,"[8] (in other words, by each individual investor's *personal opportunity cost of capital*). We agree with Williams.

Personal Rates versus Market Rates of Interest

Williams suggests that each individual investor is likely to have *his or her own perception of the required target rate of interest* for a particular investment. For instance, the opportunity cost of the next best alternative investment for one individual might very well be different than for someone else. The future inflation expectations of one investor might be higher (or lower) than another investor. These differences in inflation expectations may influence the discount rate that individual investors will use to estimate their required inflation adjusted purchasing power returns. Consequently, for financial advisors to private clients, thinking about an individual's opportunity cost of capital is a key insight we can glean from William's theory of investment value. If one person demands say, 12 percent, and the other only 8 percent as the minimum opportunity cost, the same share trading in an equity market or the value of a private company contemplated for purchase will be accorded a lower valuation by the first individual than by the second. The correct conclusion to draw is that there will not be a single point estimate of intrinsic value for a company but a *range of values*. Why? Because various investors and speculators in the markets will have different views about expected inflation, varying opportunity costs, longer or shorter investment time horizons, distinct risk profiles, and personal consumption patterns. Markets, particularly equity markets, are not made up of homogeneous investors but of a heterogeneous population of investors and speculators, each with their own views and beliefs about the future. We have more to say about estimating the cost of equity later in this chapter, and we discuss further the characteristics of equity markets and investor behavior in Chapter 18.

Williams goes on to recommend that a market rate of interest (meaning a discount rate derived from the capital markets)—and *not* a personal opportunity cost of capital—should be applied in valuing an equity security when the individual investor (or financial security analyst) is speaking not for himself personally *but for investors in general*. For instance, if a financial analyst is employed by a large institutional investment firm, say an asset management company that manages highly diversified mutual funds for a broad spectrum of retail investors, then the analyst should use the "pure interest rate as it is expected to be found in the open market in the years to come."[9]

Today, 70 years later, we would interpret William's words to mean that professional analysts valuing publicly traded companies for highly diversified investors (e.g., mutual funds, pension funds, life insurance companies, etc.) ought to use a market-derived and forward-looking long-term and *risk-adjusted* discount rate. By *risk-adjusted discount rate* we mean that a risk premium has been added to the interest rate to adjust for the riskiness of the cash flows of the company that is being valued. Later in this chapter, we explain in detail how to do such risk adjustments using the Capital Asset Pricing Model (CAPM) developed by Nobel laureate Professor William F. Sharpe.[10]

According to modern financial theory, we should incorporate risk adjustments in the discount rate, provided that the cash flow estimates are not similarly adjusted. We do *not* want to double-count the risk by adjusting for risk in the discount rate and the cash flow estimates simultaneously.

Intrinsic Value Is the Fundamental Economic Value of the Firm

Discounting expected dividends at the required risk-adjusted opportunity cost of equity funds is known as determining the intrinsic value of a firm based on *company fundamentals*. Included in fundamentals are such items as the earnings, dividends, assets, capital structure, creditworthiness, management quality, and ability to execute the business plan. Fundamental analysis also includes the strategic outlook of the industry: the intensity of competitive rivalry and factors promoting industry change, possible and probable changes in sales volumes, prices, and costs.

Professor Luis E. Pereiro, an expert on valuing companies in emerging markets, explains the difference between a business's intrinsic value versus its extrinsic value:

> *The term intrinsic means that the value estimate is anchored in the internal business drivers, rather than in the value opinion that a specific potential buyer or seller of the asset may hold. That is, differences in intrinsic values for the same asset derive from differing judgments on the part of analysts, rather than on different investors' opinions. Intrinsic value becomes extrinsic value when investors reach the same value conclusion as professional appraisers. Extrinsic, or fair market value, is that assigned to the asset by the market; that is willing buyers and sellers who are under no coercion to interact and who are all in possession of reasonable knowledge of the relevant facts of the situation"*[11]

For instance, if you were to do such a fundamental appraisal, you would want to assess the breadth and depth of a company's new product pipeline, the quality and quantity of its research and development (R&D), and its ability to raise prices more than inflation. You would look for operating margin improvement due to the installation of new, more cost-efficient technology. Other fundamental factors might include your assessment of the perceived value of the company's intangible assets, such as trademarks, patent portfolios, and customer loyalty. Your views on how these intangibles influence product pricing premiums and market share penetration for a new line of goods would be reflected in your sales forecasts. In fact, your views and opinions on all the economic drivers of the business would show up in the assumptions you use to prepare a complete set of projected income statements, cash flow statements, and balance sheet statements. (For an example, refer to Appendix 17.1

at the end of this chapter with the comprehensive case of PB Electronics Inc., where we illustrate how to do a valuation for a small, privately held, family-run business.)

You also would try to assess the capabilities, integrity, and commitment of management to the extent such things can be determined by outsiders. You would research and be well informed about the political, economic, social, technological, environmental, and legal trends affecting the industry, and where the industry is in terms of its life cycle. You would study the current and future competitive situation confronting the company, as we discussed in Chapter 3. You ought to scrutinize the company's business model, probe the strength and weaknesses of the alliance network surrounding the firm, and question management about the future strategy of the firm and its foreseeable capital expenditure and investment plans. You would need to gather and make sense of a vast array of qualitative and quantitative information in order to carry out an objective economic analysis of a firm's future earnings prospects and risk profile.

Example: Collecting Qualitative Information to Value a Life Science Venture   How might fundamental analysis work in practice? For example, an analyst working for the fund manager of a leading life science investment fund (one with a sizable amount of money under management) would most likely seek the advice and insights of leading medical doctors, biomedical academics, clinical researchers, end users, and patient organizations to get the pulse of new trends and leading research ideas. She would meet frequently with senior managers and business development heads of major pharmaceutical and medical device companies, and talk to leading experts who have specialized knowledge or experience in a particular biotechnology or therapeutic treatment area. If the investment under consideration were significant, the investment fund might spend money to retain experts and have them write up a private report on the market potential of a particular path of treatment or novel medical device. Patent search specialists and other patent agents or patent lawyers might also be hired to give their advice on the freedom to operate of a particular portfolio of patents (either granted or pending). Leading market research firms with proprietary databases would also be contacted and their inputs sought. Professional life science investors would then use this "due diligence" information to make a judgment about whether to invest in a new biopharmaceutical company or medical device spin-off company. (See Chapter 8 for more on business models and alliances in the life sciences; see Chapter 15 on competitive intelligence and patent searching; and refer to Chapter 16 on doing due diligence. In Chapter 19, we show how life science venture capitalists use a measure called the "technology value" to compare unlisted biotechnology companies to quoted comparable companies listed on the stock exchange.)

Discounting Dividends Instead of Earnings or Cash Flows

Some people will look at discounting dividends and object to it by saying that dividends are not relevant. They think we ought to use the present value of future "earnings"; if they have been to business school, they say we should be "discounting future free cash flows" in our formulas. (We introduce free cash flow later in this chapter. For a comprehensive definition, log on to www.innovationtocashflows.com and refer to Appendix 17.3, "Advanced Definition of Free Cash Flows for Use with the Enterprise Valuation Method.")

Actually, *if done correctly*, discounting earnings, free cash flows, or dividends should give the same answer. The logic goes like this. If earnings that are not paid out in dividends are instead retained by the company and successfully reinvested for the benefit of the stockholder, these earnings should eventually produce future dividends, provided management's interests are aligned with shareholders' interests.

Protecting the Rights of Minority Shareholders: The Agency Problem

The crucial difference between actually receiving "dividends" as a minority shareholder and investing in a company that is producing "earnings" was dramatically brought to light in December 2003. At that time, one of the largest corporate scandals in the world showed the misalignment of interests between controlling shareholders and minority equity shareholders. Here is the story. The minority shareholders in an Italian listed company known as Parmalat, based in Parma, Italy, learned about a massive fraud (reportedly over $10 billion, according to Mark Landler and Daniel J. Wakin of the *New York Times*).[12] The scandal eventually led to Parmalat becoming Europe's largest bankruptcy.[13] At the time, Parmalat, which sold dairy milk and processed food products, was the eighth largest publicly listed corporation on the Milan stock exchange and Italy's largest food company, with over 34,000 employees.

Calisto Tanzi was Parmalat's founder, chief executive officer, and controlling shareholder. When news about the scandal broke, Tanzi was jailed in San Vittore (Milan's infamous prison) on suspicion of committing fraud. He and other senior managers were accused of milking the business of cash (no pun intended) over a decade, by creating fictitious assets and diverting funds to hidden offshore accounts. The main lesson of Parmalat is that minority shareholders will receive future dividends only if the controlling shareholders' and senior manager's economic interests are *aligned* with those of the minority shareholders.

So why do we conceptually like the idea of discounting dividends instead of cash flows? Because that is as it should be. After all, a stock is worth only what you as an equity investor can get out of it; long-term equity investors ultimately expect to get dividend income on their equity shares. Be mindful that equity investors have a residual claim on the assets of the company. In the liquidation of a company, equity investors only get their claim paid after everyone else ahead of them has been paid: employees, suppliers, debt holders, and preferred shareholders. Last, but not least, will be the common stockholder, if there is any money left to be distributed.

Permanent Value of the Shares versus Temporary Price Fluctuations   In saying that long-term dividends determine share value, it may appear that we are ignoring the influence that speculative news and earnings announcements can have on a company's share price. Actually we are not. We acknowledge that share prices in the short term constantly respond to new information flowing into the capital markets. Share prices will rise and fall in reaction to pertinent news, and also react to random market noise and market rumors. Benjamin Graham put it this way:

> [T]he market is not a weighing machine, on which the value of each issue is recorded by an exact and impersonal mechanism, in accordance with its specific qualities. Rather should we say that the market is a voting machine, whereon countless individuals register choices which are the product partly of reason and partly of emotion.[14]

We are concentrating on the long-term *permanent* investment value of a company when we discuss intrinsic value; we are not referring to short-term speculative price movements of publicly traded companies. Over the long term, the value of a company is determined by its ability to retain earnings and reinvest them in growth opportunities that earn more than the required cost of capital. If management cannot find such investment opportunities, then the company should return money to its shareholders in the form of dividends. If the management (or majority shareholders) cannot deliver the dividends, sell your shares.

By our insistence on looking ultimately at future dividends and their growth rate, we may be worrying other people, especially entrepreneurs, who need to value their fledgling growth companies. New ventures are not companies that normally pay dividends, nor do their owners expect to receive dividends for many years. After all, these are companies that prefer to retain earnings, if there are any profits at all, to fuel future growth. How can you value companies with no dividends? We examine this dilemma next.

VALUING YOUNG GROWTH COMPANIES WITH NO DIVIDENDS

Some will think that you cannot value a growth company using the dividend discount method because the company does not pay any dividends. Well, in practice, that is not the case. Financial analysts and venture investors do it all the time by looking far forward into the future and envisioning the day when there will be dividends. They imagine the pattern of potential revenues, earnings, free cash flows, and dividends based on their judgment and experience creating financial forecasts for different types of business models. They do this every day, even though looking decades into the future is fraught with risk and high ambiguity. They have to have the courage to "take a view" and put their experience into the forecasts.

Forecasting such things is not easy, especially for young start-ups with no operating history. It is even harder to do forecasts for high-technology ventures that are innovating and producing emerging technology in new untested markets. There is very *high uncertainty* associated with such continuing values. We liken it to peering into a "TV of the future" (TV being the abbreviation not only for television but also for *terminal value* or continuing value of the company). Hard or not, financial analysts and venture capital investors do such estimates every day.

If you want to race ahead and see how to use dividends to value a high-technology growth company, then go directly to the section "Multiple-Period Dividend Growth Model" later in this chapter.

For novices who have never tried it before, we recommend you practice using discounted cash flow techniques and especially try your hand at estimating terminal values. To give you an opportunity to practice using terminal values, we have included a capstone case called Arcadian Microarray Technologies, Inc., available for downloading at www.innovationtocashflows.com. By practicing with this case, you can test your ability to peer into the future and to envision the continuing value of a high-technology venture in perpetuity. Practice also helps you get used to the uncertainty of making forecasts and quantifying your judgment about your company's future earnings. If you do forecasts every day, as part of your job, it will become second nature.

Scenario Analysis Helps to Capture Uncertainty and Fit It into Forecasts

Besides estimating financial statements and determining the size of continuing values in perpetuity, you also will need to do various kinds of *scenario analysis* to try to capture a wide range of possible outlooks for your company. When doing scenarios, it is useful to think of them as answering this question: What could happen to your company's earnings under different states of the world? (Recall that we discussed scenario analysis in Chapter 3 when we described the different external analyses used by strategists and managers.)

Here is how it works in real life. Try to envision different macroscenarios and the political, economic, social, technological, legal, and environmental (PESTLE) forces that impinge on your company (or the particular company you are trying to value). Imagine distinct states of the world as you think about the future for your company and its industry.

We suggest you picture a state of the world where everything goes well, and the new products being launched are wildly successful. This could be called the blockbuster scenario. Picture yet another scenario where the projects produce only good-to-mediocre results; then picture a scenario where poor results and many failures result; finally, envision the disaster scenario, where products are delayed, a factory burns down, and all sorts of calamities occur.

Then forecast the company's income statements, cash flows, and balance sheets under each expected scenario. In order to do these forecasts, you need to pick a time horizon when you think earnings, free cash flows, and dividends will become positive (or visible) for each imagined state. For each set of scenarios, also forecast a long-run continuing value for the company in perpetuity.

The next step is to assign probabilities to the likelihood of each scenario happening (e.g., a 20 percent chance for the blockbuster scenario, a 50 percent chance for the more likely average scenario, followed by a 25 percent poor scenario, followed by a 5 percent chance of the disaster scenario). The probabilities of all the states of the world should always add up to 100 percent.

Then multiply the results of each scenario's cash flow by the expected probability and derive a probability weighted average result (the expected cash flow). Next, discount these expected cash flows back to the present using the appropriate discount rate.

For a fuller explanation of expected cash flows and their role in discounting earnings under uncertainty, refer to Beaver[15] or a leading corporate finance textbook. We also suggest that you read capstone case Proto5 at www.innovation tocashflows.com. The Proto5 case illustrates the *expected* present value technique applied to the valuation of a very-early-stage biopharmaceutical firm.

Cognitive Biases

By constructing scenarios, we are trying to capture the uncertainty of the future and take into account remotely possible events. By doing so, we are systematically attempting to overcome some of the cognitive biases that we all share.

Research on decision making by cognitive psychologists and behavioral finance experts reveals patterns in how human beings cope with ambiguity, complexity, and uncertainty. We tend to use heuristics (rules of thumb) and mental shortcuts to help us think about vague, complex, or uncertain dilemmas. We are all susceptible to many cognitive biases. We examine two of the most important biases (for valuation purposes) in the next paragraphs.

Underestimating Uncertainty   People tend to underestimate the amount of uncertainty and to misjudge the wide variability possible surrounding facts, figures, and future outcomes. Cognitive psychologists and renowned researchers Amos Tversky and Daniel Kahneman[16] describe this tendency as the "illusion of overconfidence." Many experimenters have tested this bias by asking people to guess a value for an unknown quantity, such as the purchase price of a recently acquired company. Subjects are asked a series of questions where they need to make a high estimate and a low estimate so that there is a 90 percent chance that the value will fall within the specified range. If the uncertainty were judged correctly, the true answer should fall within their estimated range for 9 out of 10 questions. For many subjects, however, most of the true answers fall well outside the specified ranges.[17] The cognitive problem is that human beings tend to fail to take into account all of the uncertainty that future events may introduce. This cognitive bias may be a coping mechanism for making a complex world easier to understand.

Overestimating the Near-Term and Dramatic but Highly Improbable Event   People have a tendency to overestimate the influence that immediate and highly visible, but low-probability, events will have on long-term sales and earnings. Such a terrifying event might be a major earthquake or the devastation wreaked by Hurricane Katrina that decimated New Orleans, a once-in-a-century hurricane. Recently acquired information and especially colorfully depicted events are often overemphasized compared to more generally known data—even when the mundane data are more reliable and more relevant. According to University of Virginia Darden Business School professor Elizabeth Olmsted Teisberg, the bias of "vividness" is described in the study by Borgida and Nisbett (1977) and the bias of "availability" and use of heuristics for judging probabilities is discussed in Tversky and Kahneman (1973).[18]

For additional information on how to counteract cognitive biases in negotiating (useful also for equity investors), see the various writings on decision making by James G. March and on rational negotiations by coauthors Max H. Bazerman and Margaret A. Neale.[19] Teisberg discusses the "nine cognitive biases experienced by bright, well-educated, and conscientious people who manage their companies into strategic distress."[20] Teisberg's article is worth reading by anyone interested in improving his or her decision-making skills and mitigating cognitive biases.

OVERVIEW OF DISCOUNTED CASH FLOW METHODS

As we said, discounting cash flows follows the fundamental economic principle that the value of an asset is the present value of the *expected* cash flows from using that asset. The asset may be any type of asset, such as a real property (land, house, or commercial office building), tangible property (equipment inside a factory), or an intangible asset like a patent or a trademark. The two basic approaches to valuing the equity of a company are these:

1. Dividend discount method (or the equity residual cash flow method)
2. Enterprise valuation method (or the free cash flow to the firm method)

We are free to choose whichever of these two approaches makes more sense, given the data available. In theory, either method should give equivalent results. In practice, due to the difficulties of estimating some of the debt and tax-related components, the results may vary. What is extremely important is *not* to combine the approaches: Make a choice and stick with it. If done properly, both methods will give the same answer, provided that the correct cash flows are matched to the proper cost of capital and the appropriate adjustments are made for "leverage" or the borrowings of the company and for tax effects.

In the next section, we explain first the dividend discount method (present value of an infinite stream of dividends, also called the equity residual cash flow) followed by the discounted free cash flow (FCF) or enterprise valuation method. We need to be fluent in both methods in order to master valuation.

PRESENT VALUE OF AN INFINITE STREAM OF DIVIDENDS

In his leading textbook on investments, professor William F. Sharpe acknowledges that John Burr Williams laid the foundation for the theory of investment value when he conceived of the basic dividend discount model, which is the formula for discounting to the present time an infinite stream of dividends.[21] Williams envisioned the value of a business as a stream of dividends stretching into infinity. He reasoned that a company has a perpetual life. Therefore, its value is analogous to a perpetual bond. Instead of looking forward to clipping bond coupons as bondholders do, common equity shareholders expect to receive future dividend payments.

To show the derivation of the dividend discount model, we begin with the formula for valuing perpetual bonds (bonds with an infinite life); instead of yearly bond coupons, however, we substitute yearly dividend payments.

Algebraically the intrinsic value, V_0, of the equity is equal to the present value of an infinite stream of *expected* dividends discounted back at the investor's opportunity cost of equity funds.

$$V_0 = \frac{D_1}{(1+k_e)^1} + \frac{D_2}{(1+k_e)^2} + \frac{D_3}{(1+k_e)^3} + \cdots$$

$$= \sum_{t=1}^{\infty} \frac{D_t}{(1+k_e)^t}$$

where V_0 = intrinsic value of the equity at time $t = 0$
  D_1 = next period dividend at time $t = 1$
   t = time
  k_e = investor's opportunity cost of equity funds

In this equation, the discount rate is assumed to be the same for all periods. Actually because of the infinity symbol ∞ above the summation sign, all expected dividends will be discounted at the same rate, from the moment the investment is made until infinity.

One complication in using this dividend discount model is to forecast *all* future dividends of the business out to infinity. However, by making some simple assumptions about growth rates, the problem can be solved quite nicely using the mathematical properties of infinite series, as we show next.

We shall let g be defined as the growth rate in dividends. That is, the dividend per share at any time t may be seen as equal to the dividend per share at time $t-1$ times a dividend growth rate of g_t, like this:

$$D_1 = D_0(1 + g_1) = D_{t-1}(1 + g_t)$$

Rearranging terms, we may use the same expression to solve for the growth rate of a dividend. For instance,

$$g_t = \frac{(D_1 - D_{t-1})}{D_{t-1}}$$

For example, if a company's expected dividend per share in year 3 is $5.10 per share, and the actual dividend per share expected in year 2 is $5.00 per share, then the computed expected dividend growth, g_3, is 2 percent:

$$g_3 = (\$5.10 - \$5.00)/\$5.00 = 2.0\%$$

ZERO-GROWTH PERPETUITY MODEL

If we assume that the dividend stays the same, year after year, then the dividends have a zero growth rate, or $g = 0$. This is called the *zero-growth perpetuity* model (zero-growth), because we are considering valuing a stream of dividends *in perpetuity*. This simple model is the most conservative way to value a business. To derive the zero-growth perpetuity model expression, we start with the basic equation of intrinsic value:

$$V_0 = \sum_{t=1}^{\infty} \frac{D_t}{(1 + k_e)^t}$$

Because $g = 0$ for this zero-growth model, we can replace D_t by D_0 in the numerator, and then this expression is true:

$$V_0 = \sum_{t=1}^{\infty} \frac{D_0}{(1 + k_e)^t}$$

As D_0 is a constant, it can be moved outside the summation sign, like this:

$$V_0 = D_0 \sum_{t=1}^{\infty} \frac{1}{(1 + k_e)^t}$$

Then, relying on a property of infinite series from mathematics, if $k_e > 0$, then it can be shown that:

$$V_0 = \sum_{t=1}^{\infty} \frac{1}{(1 + k_e)^t} = \frac{1}{k_e}$$

Applying this property to our equation results in the next formula for the zero-growth model:

$$V_0 = \frac{D_0}{k_e}$$

Because $D_0 = D_1$ when the growth rate is zero, this equation may also be written in an equivalent form as:

$$V_0 = \frac{D_1}{k_e}$$

To estimate the approximate value of a stock, we simply place in the numerator the next year's projected dividend and divide by an estimated opportunity cost of equity funds. For instance, if in year 1 we expect a constant dividend of $2.50 per share (forever) and our opportunity cost of equity funds is 10 percent, then the intrinsic worth of the common stock is computed to be $25.00 per share. Remember this estimate is usually conservative, as it makes the assumption that the dividends have zero growth and last forever (in perpetuity).

$$V_0 = \frac{\$2.50 \text{ expected dividend/share}}{0.10} = \$25.00/\text{share}$$

If we multiply this estimate by the total number of common shares outstanding, the final result is the economic value of the equity. Assume that there are 100,000 shares of stock issued and outstanding worth $25 per share, then the company's estimated economic value V_0 would be $2.5 million.

Capitalizing the Income Stream

Whenever you have an income value in the numerator and the cost of funds in the denominator, this is known as capitalizing the income stream. (Real estate brokers often talk about the "cap rate" for pricing rental properties. They simply take the rental income and divide it by their cost of funds—usually the mortgage rate on money borrowed from a bank.)

In the previous zero-growth model equation, we were capitalizing the dividends to estimate the value of a company's equity. Remember that whenever anyone is capitalizing a dividend stream or any other kind of income stream, he or she is making the implicit assumption that the dividend income will have zero growth.

CONSTANT-GROWTH MODEL

If the business is healthy and growing, it is quite reasonable to assume that dividends will increase each and every year. That is to say, the business will produce a steady stream of dividends that grow at some constant rate, g, forever. For this assumption, the intrinsic value of the firm to the equity shareholders is calculated directly by using the next formula:

$$V_0 = \sum_{t=1}^{\infty} \frac{D_0 (1+g)^t}{(1+k_e)^t}$$

Similar to the zero-growth model, we simplify this equation by noting that D_0 is a constant sum, so it can be written outside the summation sign:

$$V_0 = D_0 \left[\sum_{t=1}^{\infty} \frac{(1+g)^t}{(1+k_e)^t} \right]$$

The next step relies on a property of infinite series in mathematics. As before, if $k_e > g$, then it can be shown that the next equation must hold true:

$$\sum_{t=1}^{\infty} \frac{(1+g)^t}{(1+k_e)^t} = \frac{1+g}{k_e - g}$$

Substituting this result into the prior equation yields the valuation formula for the constant-growth model:

$$V_0 = D_0 \left[\sum_{t=1}^{\infty} \frac{(1+g)^t}{(1+k_e)^t} \right] = D_0 \left[\frac{1+g}{k_e - g} \right]$$

Because $D_1 = D_0(1+g)$, we can rewrite the last term as the formula for constant growth expressed as:

$$V_0 = \frac{D_1}{k_e - g}$$

We will be using this constant-growth expression in the next few chapters.

Valuing TechMate Company Using the Constant-Growth Model

As an example of how to use the constant dividend growth model, we assume that the TechMate Company (a hypothetical high-tech company) paid dividends amounting to $D_0 = \$2.80$ per share over the last year. The consensus view of the analysts covering the company is that expected dividends will grow at $g = 5\%$ per year in perpetuity. This means the next year's dividend should be

$$D_1 = D_0(1 + g) = \$2.80 \times 1.05 = \$2.94 \text{ per share}$$

Next we assume that investors require an opportunity cost of equity, k_e, of 12 percent. We enter the three estimates (prospective dividend, required cost of equity, and perpetual growth rate) into the formula. We calculate that the intrinsic value of TechMate Company's common shares, at time $t = 0$, ought to be

$$V_0 = \frac{D_1}{k_e - g} = \frac{\$2.94}{0.12 - 0.05} = \$42.00 \text{ per share}$$

If we compare this intrinsic value with the current market price of the share in the stock market, we can judge if the company's shares are over- or undervalued. Assume that the sellers of this stock are asking $35.00 per share. Since our calculation shows the company is worth $42.00 per share, more than the $35.00 per share asking price, it means the company's stock is trading at a *discount* to its real intrinsic value. We should consider it a bargain and a possible candidate for purchase—if our "margin of safety" and any other investment criteria are satisfied. (Margin of safety is a generic term often found in engineering, which means the margin of error, safety margin, fudge factor, or safety cushion in an estimate.)

To determine the margin of safety, one approach is to compute a ratio of intrinsic value over current market price. For our example, the margin of safety is therefore:

$$\frac{\$42.00 \text{ per share}}{\$35.00 \text{ per share}} = 1.20$$

If we consider a safety margin of 1.20 times to be adequate protection against the risk of errors in estimating the expected cost of equity, the expected dividend, or the expected growth rate, then the company's stock should be purchased. When expressed as a percentage discount, a safety margin of 1.2 is equivalent to a discount of 16.67 percent. (The reciprocal of 1.2 is 83.333 percent, which when subtracted from 100 percent is equal to a discount of 16.667 percent.) Most institutional investors require that a share be undervalued by at least 25 percent to 33 percent (a safety margin of approximately 1.3 to 1.5) before they would start accumulating shares. Hence, for our example, they would most likely wait before accumulating this particular stock, as it is not yet a bargain according to their investment criteria.

If the current *market price* were say $50.00 per share—a price above the estimated intrinsic value range at around $42.00 per share—we would say the share is currently *overvalued* in the marketplace. There is no margin of safety at all, as the shares are too expensive and not a bargain. We would need to continue our search for investment alternatives that are less expensive and that still meet our criteria. No share purchases would be made at current market conditions.

MULTIPLE-PERIOD DIVIDEND GROWTH MODEL

The most general form of the dividend discount model for valuing the common equity of a company is the multiple-period dividend growth model. With this model, we separate the perpetual stream of dividends pertaining to equity shareholders into two parts.

The first part represents a stream of dividends over an explicit forecast period (or the chosen time horizon); the second part represents the continuing value of the dividends in perpetuity, also called the terminal value, or the TV, that is assumed to take place at time $= T$, the moment when the explicit forecast period ends and the continuing value period begins. The terminal value estimate is made when the business has reached its maturity stage.

Keep in mind that we take the *present value* of all the forecast dividends up to and including time T, and then the *present value* of all dividends after time T. We do this by *discounting* the flows of dividends by *dividing* by the opportunity cost of equity for the explicit forecast period (the factor $[1 + k_e]^t$, which will appear in the denominator of the equation). Afterward, we simply sum the two amounts to determine the intrinsic value of the equity.

$$Equity\ Value = \left\{ \begin{array}{c} \textit{Present value} \text{ of dividends} \\ \text{during the explicit forecast period} \end{array} \right\}$$

$$+ \left\{ \begin{array}{c} \textit{Present value} \text{ of dividends} \\ \text{after the explicit forecast period} \end{array} \right\}$$

We abbreviate these words in symbols, where V_{T-} refers to the present value of the dividend flows in years 1 through T and V_{T+} refers to the present value of the infinite stream of dividends extending beyond the forecast horizon, T, like this:

$$V_0 = V_{T-} + V_{T+}$$

$$V_0 = \left\{ \sum_{t=1}^{T} \frac{D_t}{(1 + k_e)^t} \right\} + \left\{ \frac{TV_T}{(1 + k_e)^T} \right\}$$

If the dividends after the explicit forecast period grow at a constant rate in perpetuity, then the terminal value or TV_T at time T may be expressed using either the zero-growth or the constant-growth formulas we derived earlier, depending on our view about the business's growth prospects upon reaching maturity:

■ Zero growth of the dividends in the terminal value:

$$TV_T = Terminal\ Value \text{ (at time } T) = \frac{D_{T+1}}{k_{e\infty}}$$

■ Constant growth of the dividends in the terminal value:

$$TV_T = Terminal\ Value \text{ (at time } T) = \frac{D_{T+1}}{(k_{e\infty} - g_\infty)}$$

In both terminal value expressions, we place the infinity sign next to the cost of equity $k_{e\infty}$ and to the growth symbol g_∞, as reminders that the dividends, estimated opportunity cost of equity, and growth rate are estimated in perpetuity. They should reflect the condition of the business when it is in a steady state of maturity.

All that remains is to substitute the appropriate terminal value expression into the basic equation developed by John Burr Williams for valuing an infinite stream of dividends. When we do so, then we get these equations for the multiple-period growth model, depending on which terminal value condition applies:

- Assuming *zero growth* for the continuing value:

$$V_0 = \left\{ \sum_{t=1}^{T} \frac{D_t}{(1+k_e)^t} \right\} + \left\{ \frac{D_{T+1}}{(k_{e\infty})(1+k_e)^T} \right\}$$

- Assuming *constant growth* for the continuing value (dividends grow at a constant rate in perpetuity):

$$V_0 = \left\{ \sum_{t=1}^{T} \frac{D_t}{(1+k_e)^t} \right\} + \left\{ \frac{D_{T+1}}{(k_{e\infty} - g_\infty)(1+k_e)^T} \right\}$$

where
t = time
V_0 = intrinsic or economic value of the *equity* at time, $t = 0$
D_t = expected dividend at time, t
D_{T+1} = dividend to be received in the *next* period, at time $(T+1)$
k_e = required opportunity cost of equity for the explicit forecast period
$k_{e\infty}$ = required opportunity cost of equity for the continuing value or terminal value period.
g_∞ = expected growth rate of all dividends (in perpetuity)

We have placed the large braces around the two parts of the last equation to emphasize that we are summing up two parts, $V_0 = V_{T-} + V_{T+}$, where the *present value* of the dividends during the explicit forecast period is this expression:

$$V_{T-} = \sum_{t=1}^{T} \frac{D_t}{(1+k_e)^t}$$

and the *present value* of the constant-growth terminal value is this formula:

$$V_{T+} = \frac{D_{T+1}}{(k_{e\infty} - g_\infty)(1+k_e)^T}$$

Normally the equation for the multiple-period dividend growth model is written without braces as:

$$V_0 = \sum_{t=1}^{T} \frac{D_t}{(1 + k_e)^t} + \frac{D_{T+1}}{(k_{e\infty} - g_\infty)(1 + k_e)^T}$$

Caveats on the Use of the Constant Growth Terminal Value Formula

A few words of caution are in order on how to apply the constant-growth terminal value formula. Unless you are very careful with the assumptions used, the constant-growth rate formula is likely to overstate a company's terminal value. There are two pitfalls to avoid. The most common error is to assume a growth rate (in perpetuity) that is too high. The other error is to use an improperly adjusted expected dividend, D_{T+1}, for the terminal value. An error in that expected dividend is magnified for all eternity and can become quite a large mistake. It is critical, therefore, to be sure that the proper operating margins, working capital, and capital expenditures are taken into consideration. (Later we give an example of how to compute the investment in working capital.) Keep in mind when modeling the continuing value period that the dividend flows should be representative of a *mature* business, many years out in the future.

We suggest that the continuing growth g_∞ be modeled assuming a constant rate of growth equal to the long-run growth rate of the economy, say 2 percent to 3 percent a year, plus expected inflation, on the order of say 3 percent for the U.S. economy. This would give an estimate for the long-run growth rate of between 5 percent to 6 percent as an upper limit. The Fisher equation (developed by the economist Irving Fisher in 1896) is often used to convert the real rate of interest into a nominal rate of interest, as shown in the next equation:

$$(1 + \text{nominal interest rate}) = (1 + \text{real interest rate}) \times (1 + \text{expected inflation})$$

When inflation is moderate, the cross product in the Fisher equation may be ignored and the math reduces to this simple approximation:

$$\text{Nominal interest rate} \approx \text{Real interest rate} + \text{Expected inflation rate}$$

For more details, refer to Appendix 17.7, "The Fisher Equation: Taking Inflation Expectations into Account," at www.innovationtocashflows.com.

Valuing Innovatech Inc., a High-Growth Company, Using the Multiple-Period Dividend Discount Model

In this next example, we illustrate numerically how the constant-growth version of the multiple-period dividend discount model may be applied. We shall assume that during the past year an innovative technology company called Innovatech Inc. paid its shareholders a dividend of $0.68 per share. Over the next year, we think

Innovatech will pay a dividend of $1.50 per share. Therefore, our estimate for the dividend growth rate for the first year is:

$$g_1 = (D_1 - D_0)/D_0 = (\$1.50 - \$0.68)/\$0.68 = 121\%$$

For the next year, we expect dividends to increase to $2.25 per share, indicating that $g_2 = (D_2 - D_1)/D_1 = (\$2.25 - \$1.50)/\$1.50 = 50\%$.

After this high spurt of initial dividend growth, we forecast modest growth for the mature phase of the business. We also predict that dividends will grow by 6 percent per year indefinitely.

Even though we now think Innovatech has matured, due to its innovative technology, we expect the company's long-term growth to slightly exceed the average growth rate of the industry for many decades, in other words, that $g_\infty = 6.0\%$. Therefore we estimate that the dividend (in perpetuity) for the terminal value will be $D_{T+1} = D_3 = \$2.25(1 + .06) = \$2.385$.

In another simplification, we also make the assumption that Innovatech, as a growing business, requires the same required equity rate of return as when it reaches maturity, in other words, that $k_{e\infty} = k_e = 15$ percent. We will relax this assumption of equality later in the case of PB Electronics Inc. (Refer to the PB Electronics case in Appendix 17.1 at the end of this chapter.) In PB Electronics Inc., we explain how venture capitalists valuing closely held ventures typically use a *higher* required rate of return, k_e, for the *early stages* of growth, and then a lower required rate of return, $k_{e\infty}$, during the mature state (the terminal value phase) where the risks are expected to be lower than at start-up.

Now, inserting the numbers we explained previously into the dividend discount model formulas, we compute the intrinsic value (per share) of Innovatech:

$$V_0 = \sum_{t=1}^{T} \frac{D_t}{(1 + k_e)^t} + \frac{D_{T+1}}{(k_{e\infty} - g_\infty)(1 + k_e)^T}$$

$$V_0 = \frac{\$1.50}{(1 + .15)^1} + \frac{\$2.25}{(1 + .15)^2} + \frac{\$2.385}{(.15 - .06)(1.15)^3}$$

$$V_0 = \$20.43 \text{ per share}$$

To more clearly make our point about summing up the two parts (the explicit forecast and then the terminal value forecast), we show the estimates for each part separately, using the basic formula:

$$V_0 = V_{T-} + V_{T+}$$

where $V_{T-} = 1.30435 + 1.50132 = \$3.01$ (rounded to two decimals). It is the *present value* of the two dividends paid during the explicit forecast period discounted at the *investor's opportunity cost of equity*, $k_e = 15$ percent.

$V_{T+} = \$17.42$ (rounded to two decimals). It is the *present value* of the terminal value and represents the discounted value of the remaining dividends in perpetuity. (To compute the present value, we discount the terminal value at the investor's opportunity cost of equity, $k_e = 15$ percent).

$V_0 = \$20.43$ per share. The sum of the two parts, is the intrinsic value per share of Innovatech.

Interpreting the Results   At the current stock market price of $P = \$20.00$ per share, then Innovatech appears to be fairly priced. The stock price is approximately equal to the calculated intrinsic value of $20.43 per share. Based on this result, we will *not* purchase the company's shares but seek better investment opportunities elsewhere in the capital markets.

INTRODUCTION TO THE COST OF EQUITY

Up to now, in all the examples in this chapter, we have provided you with the *investor's opportunity cost of equity*, k_e, without explaining where it came from or the challenges involved in estimating it.

The opportunity cost of equity is more difficult to estimate than the cost of debt because it cannot be directly observed in the capital markets. We can observe the cost of debt by looking up the interest rates of government bonds or the current market rates for corporate debt issues. If it is unobservable, how do financial managers and their advisers estimate the cost of equity to use in their calculations?

We answer by saying that the topic of how to estimate the cost of equity is one of the most controversial subjects in corporate finance. It arouses keen debate among practitioners and academics. There is no simple answer as to how to compute this important discount rate.

The Capital Asset Pricing Model (CAPM), which was developed by Sharpe[22], has grown in popularity and is the most widely used technique in the United States for determining a company's expected cost of equity, according to a field survey conducted and published by Robert F. Bruner, Kenneth M. Eades, Robert S. Harris, and Robert C. Higgins. These researchers (all highly respected finance professors) wanted to understand "best practices" for estimating the cost of capital in the United States. They surveyed financial officers from 27 leading corporations and 10 prominent investment banks, and also examined 7 leading finance textbooks.[23] They followed up their questionnaire survey with in-depth personal interviews. The overwhelming favorite approach of the surveyed participants was to use CAPM:

- For the companies, 85 percent used it or a modified version of CAPM.
- For the investment banks, 80 percent used CAPM, and the other 20 percent used either a modified CAPM or a multifactor regression model.
- For the leading textbooks and finance books, 100 percent recommend the use of CAPM.

Pereiro and Galli[24] conducted and published a similar study for Argentine companies and financial advisers. Their study results (in English) were also reported in Pereiro.[25] Researchers in other countries are beginning to investigate best practices for determination of the cost of equity, especially in less efficient financial markets.

The two studies just cited both show that financial professionals make widely different choices about how they select and then modify the inputs for the capital asset pricing model. Consequently, different experts, even when using the same tool—CAPM, can compute significantly different estimates for the cost of capital. For us, the search continues for a better way to determine the expected risk adjusted cost of equity than using CAPM. However, for the time being, CAPM is the most widely used theoretical tool we have. We introduce CAPM in the next section.

CAPITAL ASSET PRICING MODEL

William F. Sharpe published the Capital Asset Pricing Model in 1964 for which he was awarded the Nobel Prize in Economics in 1990.[26] CAPM is a simplified equilibrium model for pricing assets that builds on the earlier work of Harry Markowitz on portfolio diversification. (Markowitz's work is referred to in finance as Modern Portfolio Theory.)

Users of CAPM make important assumptions about how investors and capital markets work. *These assumptions do not always hold true in the real world.* Nevertheless, the elegance and simplicity of CAPM comes from these fundamental assumptions:

- CAPM assumes that all investors are rational, risk averse, and have homogeneous beliefs implying that investors everywhere have the same perceptions in regard to the expected returns, standard deviations (risks), and covariances (or comovements) of securities.
- CAPM assumes that all investors have the same one-period investment horizon. The model does not explain what the length of "one-period" is (in terms of hours, days, or months). It only states that it is for one-period "in the future."
- CAPM assumes that all relevant and public information is available instantaneously to all investors at no cost. The capital markets are assumed to be frictionless, implying no trading costs. Furthermore, investors may either lend (i.e., invest) or borrow money at a risk-free rate that is the same for all investors. For more details on these assumptions, refer to Sharpe, Alexander, and Bailey.[27]

If all these assumptions hold, then CAPM postulates that the opportunity cost of equity is equal to the return on risk-free securities plus the company's so-called *beta* (its systematic risk) multiplied by the equity market risk premium (i.e., the so-called "market price of equity risk"). Each of these terms is defined and discussed in the next section.

The model is popular because it is simple. However, it also poses many challenges when put into practice, especially for finance professionals working in emerging markets or for investors interested in acquiring privately held companies. Because its use (and misuse) is so widespread, we think CAPM needs to be mastered and its applications for valuation practices understood.

Basic Capital Asset Pricing Model Equation

According to CAPM, the expected rate of return for an equity security, k_e, from the point of view of the well-diversified investor who is holding the market portfolio, is postulated to be this equation:

$$k_e = r_f + \beta[E(r_m) - r_f]$$

where k_e = expected rate of return for the security
            β = beta, the systematic risk of the equity security
            r_f = risk-free rate of return
     $E(r_m)$ = expected rate of return on the overall market portfolio

According to CAPM assumptions, all securities are exposed to two kinds of risks: (1) the systematic risk or so-called beta risk, which is defined to be undiversifiable market risk of the market portfolio; and (2) the unsystematic risk, or idiosyncratic risk, which is the diversifiable risk of the individual security. The sum of the systematic risk and the unsystematic risk equals the total risk of the security.

CAPM is a very simple linear model. In essence, it says that there is a linear relationship between the expected cost of equity k_e and the measured systematic risk (the beta risk) of that equity security. By inputting the company's beta, the expected cost of capital for that company can be derived from the CAPM equation. According to CAPM, diversified investors may expect to be rewarded (with higher expected returns) only for bearing market risk (higher betas); they are not rewarded for bearing idiosyncratic or nonmarket risk.

Be mindful that when you are using CAPM and see the term k_e discussed, it refers to the *expected* rate of return or the opportunity cost of capital sought by *highly diversified* investors who are looking into the future. The expected cost of equity is *not* the same thing as the historical cost of equity. The expected estimate is a forward-looking or ex-ante measure; historical costs are backward-looking or ex-post measures based on market conditions in the past.

By definition, the beta of the market portfolio is exactly equal to 1.0. If you were to input a beta of 1.0 into the CAPM equation, you would see that the expected cost of equity k_e is equal to $E(r_m)$, or the expected rate of return on the overall market portfolio. This means that the "average company" has a beta of 1.0, the same as the average beta of the overall market portfolio.

Securities with larger betas have larger amounts of market risk, and therefore investors (according to the theory) demand higher expected returns on equity. Securities with lower betas have less amounts of market risk, and therefore their share prices are less volatile than the market portfolio and investors expect a lower cost of equity.[28]

To use the CAPM for estimating the cost of equity of a particular security, we need only three inputs: the current risk-free rate of government bonds, which is observable from the capital markets; an estimate of the expected market risk premium; and an estimate of the beta for the equity shares of the company. We discuss each input next.

Choosing the Risk-Free Rate

Theoretically, the risk-free rate is the return on a portfolio of securities that has no default risk and has a zero beta. The best real-world alternative to such an ideal risk-free portfolio would be a portfolio made up of government bonds, issued by a country with a government that has a strong credit rating and that is unlikely to default on its debt. For instance, a portfolio made up of U.S. government bonds would qualify. The U.S. bond market has short-term Treasury bills (less than one year in duration) and longer-term Treasury bonds. (For details, see the U.S. Treasury web site at www.treasurydirect.gov).

Some experts would say that the best proxy for a risk-free instrument is a short-term U.S. Treasury bill. For valuing companies, however, we recommend using a longer-term government bond that matches the long duration of the cash flows being valued. (Remember we said the life of a company was infinite.)

Another reason to favor long-term government bond rates is that the rates for short-term Treasury bills are very volatile. In the United States, the longest term government bond is the 30-year Treasury bond. Some countries do not issue such long-term government bonds. If that is the case, then use the longest-term government bond rate available for your market.

Deciding on the Equity Market Risk Premium

The equity market risk premium is the price of equity risk. It is defined as the spread between the expected return on the equity market and the risk-free government bond rate:

$$[E(r_m) - r_f] = \text{expected market risk premium}$$

Like the expected cost of equity, the equity market risk premium is also a forward-looking measure. It is the price premium that investors expect to receive in the future that induces them to hold equity securities rather than government bonds.

We believe that a figure ranging from 5 percent to 7 percent is a good estimate for the U.S. equity market risk premium, defined as the spread between expected rate of return on U.S. equities and the long-term 10-year U.S. government Treasury bonds. For the purposes of this book, we use a figure of 6 percent for the U.S. equity market risk premium. (We discuss academic research that attempts to estimate the equity market risk premium in more detail in Appendix 17.5, "General Principles for Determining the Equity Market Risk Premium," accessible at www.innovationtocashflows.com.

Estimates for the equity market risk premium will vary, depending on whether you are using data series based on an ex-post historical estimate or using ex-ante security analyst forecasts of what investors might be expecting.

For ex-post estimates, the results obtained by doing regressions on historical data depend very much on the time horizon chosen for the calculations and the assumptions used. CAPM is silent on the length of the time horizon; it merely states it is a "one-period" model. Therefore, investors are left on their own to interpret the meaning of time horizon in CAPM.

If you are working and valuing companies in developing economies, consult Bloomberg or the respective web sites of the stock exchanges to download price data needed to estimate the appropriate market risk premiums. Do not just assume your country's market risk premium is the same as the U.S. equity market; it most likely differs.

Selecting the Beta

Finance professionals typically subscribe to commercial financial data providers, such as Bloomberg, Thomson Reuters, Value Line Investment Survey, and Standard & Poor's Compustat database, or are the corporate clients of banks like Goldman Sachs or Morgan Stanley. Each provider calculates and regularly publishes company beta information for their customers. Students typically rely on Yahoo! Finance to find free beta information. Log onto our web site at www.innovationtocashflows.com, download the file called Resources, and go to the entry Yahoo! Finance to find out how to access company betas from the Yahoo! Finance web site.

The betas provided directly from the equity markets are known as levered betas or equity betas because they include the effects of debt in the company's capital structure. Unlevered betas or asset betas in general must be computed using formulas that we introduce and explain in Appendix 17.5 located on our web site at www.innovationtocashflows.com.

To compute the cost of equity from the CAPM equation, the equity beta is needed and should be adjusted to reflect the *target* capital structure of the company being valued. The problem is that the observed equity beta may have a different capital structure from the target debt-to-equity ratio. Hence we need to know how to unlever and relever betas to adjust for differences in indebtedness. In the online Appendix 17.5, we give the equations and more information on how to (1) take an equity beta and (2) unlever it to an asset beta, and then (3) relever it to the new target debt-equity ratio desired. Furthermore we show you how to use these different betas in a comprehensive example. We also briefly explain how to compute betas using stock price data, market indices, and simple regression techniques.

As we said earlier, the "average" company beta is 1.0, by definition. In practice, most securities trading on U.S. stock markets have betas ranging from 0.3 to 3.0. Values beyond these limits are extremely rare.

For instance, telecommunications and electronics companies might have betas ranging from 1.3 to 2.5. (Beta values that are higher than 1.0 mean that these high-technology shares are more volatile that the market average.)

Biotechnology and pharmaceutical companies tend to have lower betas, ranging from 0.3 to 0.85, because these shares normally are not very correlated to the stock market. They therefore tend to be less volatile than the market average. Even if pharmaceutical and biotechnology stocks have low systematic risk (beta risk), they do have high technological risks, but since these kinds of risks are classified under idiosyncratic risk (which are diversifiable), they are not included in the beta measurement.

One of the problems of applying CAPM in the real world, is that the "market portfolio is ill-defined."[29] The CAPM says that the market portfolio is made up of all possible securities (representing all the investible assets in the world). Furthermore, the amount of money invested in each security (or asset class) should correspond to its relative market value. In other words, the index chosen to represent the market portfolio should be a market-capitalization weighted index (like the Wilshire 5000 index) and not an equally weighted index (like the Dow-Jones index). We raise these issues because, depending on how you define the market portfolio and which index you choose for the regressions, you will get significantly different beta results. Be mindful, too, that the beta you compute is highly dependent on the time period selected and the number of years' worth of data used for the regressions.[30]

Now, in theory, we have the three inputs we need to estimate the expected cost of equity for a particular security using CAPM. Once we have computed an estimate for the equity market risk premium, then it should be multiplied by the company's beta, and the result added to the current risk-free rate of long-term government bonds (again, use the longest term government bond available). Be logically consistent in the choice of market when making the calculations. If you are computing betas for the U.S. equity market, then you should use a U.S. risk-free rate and U.S. equity market risk premium. Try not to mix and match inputs from different equity markets.

Simple Numerical Example: Estimating the Expected Cost of Equity for a Publicly Trading Company

We have a publicly trading company, listed on a U.S. stock exchange, whose cost of equity we would like to estimate using CAPM. The current risk-free rate for long-term 10-year U.S. government Treasury bonds is 4.5 percent. The U.S. equity market risk premium is 6 percent. The equity beta (levered beta) of our company is 1.40. What is its expected cost of equity according to CAPM?

$$k_e = r_f + \beta[E(r_m) - r_f]$$

We substitute the values stated into the equation and compute the expected cost of equity (required by well-diversified investors). The answer is 13 percent.

$$k_e = 0.045 + 1.40 \times [0.06] = 0.13 \text{ or } 13\%$$

As you can see, the simplicity of CAPM is seductive. CAPM is popular, widely used, and also widely misused. Be mindful of the theory's simple assumptions and use critical thinking whenever you apply it.

ENTERPRISE VALUATION METHOD

In this section, we introduce the enterprise valuation method and present the basic formulas for businesses experiencing zero-growth, constant-growth, or multiple-period growth conditions. Having already derived the equations for the dividend discount models, we will not repeat the derivations for the enterprise valuation method, as the proofs are similar. We close the section by presenting a new concept, the *weighted average cost of capital* (WACC), pronounced "whack." The weighted average cost of capital is the proper cost of capital to use when discounting free cash flows in the enterprise valuation method.

An Overview of the Enterprise Valuation Method

When we choose to use the enterprise valuation method, our aim is to value *all the assets* of the business. We want to take into account all the claims on the assets held by both the equity and the debt holders. In other words, we want to calculate the present value of expected free cash flows accruing to all common equity shareholders, any preferred shareholders, and all the creditors of the company. To this present value of the entity, we need to add in any surplus or *excess cash*. Excess cash is what the business does not require for usual operations. The sum total represents the total value of the assets of the company, what we will call the company value. From the company value, we then deduce the value of the equity owned by common shareholders indirectly. We take the total value of the assets and subtract off the portions owned by the debt holders, any other creditors, and also the preferred shareholders. What remains is the residual value that belongs to the common shareholders. This is the equity value of the company, or its intrinsic value. It represents the economic value of the equity holdings of the common shareholders.

We graphically depict the enterprise valuation approach in a simple and straightforward company valuation in Figure 17.2. As may be seen from the picture, the intrinsic value of a company is calculated as the present value of the company's free cash flows (to be defined later) over an explicit time horizon. To this sum, we add the present value of the continuing value (the TV). Then we add back any excess cash and marketable securities.

In more complicated cases, we may also have to add back the value of any nonoperating assets. (Usually these are other financial assets to which we would assign their current market value.) Undervalued real estate assets would need to be taken into consideration. We would mark up the historical cost of the real estate assets on the balance sheet to their current fair market prices. A positive difference between historical cost and fair market value is what we would add back to compute the company value. This is known as the excess of real estate value over historical cost. Recall that in general, real estate assets on a company's financial

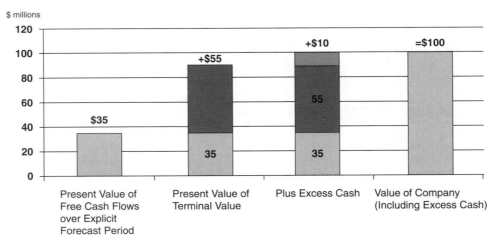

FIGURE 17.2   In the Enterprise Method, Company Value Is Obtained by Summing the Parts

statements are booked at historical cost and are not typically adjusted for any sub-sequent increases (or decreases) in value. (We do note, however, that accounting treatment of real assets depends on local accounting standards; the standards may be very different for those countries that are experiencing high inflation.)

If the company were to have any employee-defined benefit pension plans, then the over- or underfunding of those pension plans would also be included as a "plus," if overfunded, or as a "minus," if underfunded. We talk about pension plans only for completeness sake; defined benefit pensions are not normally a big issue for start-ups. (They usually do not have them.) However, for certain large corporations that have billions of dollars in underfunded pensions, it is a sizable worry. Underfunded pension liabilities reduce overall company valuations and ought to be taken into account when valuing the company.

For our simple example, we do not include any pension liabilities or excess real estate assets. We sum up all the relevant component parts and determine the estimated total value of the company to be $100 million. (Refer to Figure 17.2.)

In the enterprise valuation method, we indirectly estimate the value of the share-holder's equity by subtracting from the total value of the enterprise. Starting with the total enterprise value of the company (found in Figure 17.2), we subtract the market value of short-term debt, long-term debt, any capital leases, operating leases, preferred stock, minority interests, and warrants and stock options from the total value of the enterprise. The equity value is the residual value that remains. In our example, it equals $38 million. (Refer to Figure 17.3.)

Formulas for the Enterprise Valuation Method

Although it appears that the formulas for the enterprise valuation method are similar to those for the dividend discount model, there are two important differences in terms of the inputs to use. First, we substitute free cash flow streams instead of expected dividend streams in the numerator of the equations. Second, we use a different discount rate in the denominator, one that reflects the riskiness of the income streams coming from the total assets of the entire business enterprise rather than the riskiness

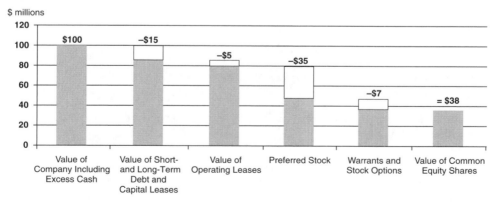

FIGURE 17.3 In the Enterprise Method, the Equity Value Is the Residual that Remains after Prior Claims Are Subtracted

of the dividend stream pertaining solely to the equity shareholders. For discounting free cash flows of the entire enterprise, we need to use the WACC, described later.

We will be using the enterprise valuation method (also referred to as the free cash flow to the firm method) to compute the present value of the free cash flows pertaining to the operations of the enterprise, or its *enterprise value*. The general equation is

$$VE_0 = \frac{FCF_1}{(1 + k_{wacc})^1} + \frac{FCF_2}{(1 + k_{wacc})^2} + \frac{FCF_3}{(1 + k_{wacc})^3} + \cdots$$

$$= \sum_{t=1}^{\infty} \frac{FCF_t}{(1 + k_{wacc})^t}$$

where $VE_0 =$ Present value of the enterprise at time $t = 0$
$FCF_t =$ Free cash flows to the enterprise derived from business operations
$t =$ Time period (usually expressed as annual periods)
$\infty =$ In perpetuity, meaning we will be summing up an *infinite* stream of free cash flows
$k_{wacc} =$ Weighted average cost of capital

Zero-Growth Perpetuity Model for Discounting Free Cash Flows

For the zero-growth case, this is the equivalent FCF formula:

$$VE_0 = \frac{FCF_1}{k_{wacc}}$$

Constant-Growth Model for Discounting Free Cash Flows

For the constant-growth case, this is the equivalent FCF formula:

$$VE_0 = \frac{FCF_1}{k_{wacc} - g}$$

Multiple-Period Growth Model for Discounting Free Cash Flows

For the case where growth of the enterprise extends over multiple periods, this is the equivalent FCF formula:

$$VE_0 = \sum_{t=1}^{T} \frac{FCF_t}{(1 + k_{wacc})^t} + \frac{TV_T}{(1 + k_{wacc})^T}$$

where $TV_T =$ terminal value at time T.

For a company expected to have constant growth at maturity, we may express the terminal value using this constant growth formula:

$$TV_T = \text{Terminal Value} = \frac{FCF_{T+1}}{k_{wacc\infty} - g_\infty}$$

where

TV_T = Terminal value at time T

FCF_{T+1} = Normalized free cash flows for the first year beyond the forecast time horizon

g_∞ = Perpetual growth rate of free cash flows

$k_{wacc\infty}$ = Appropriate weighted average cost of capital for a mature business

If we combine the two last equations, then the general formula for the enterprise value, with a terminal value having perpetual dividends growing at a constant rate may be expressed as:

$$VE_0 = \sum_{t=1}^{T} \frac{FCF_t}{(1 + k_{wacc})^t} + \frac{FCF_{T+1}}{(1 + k_{wacc})^T \times (k_{wacc\infty} - g_\infty)}$$

At this point, we highly recommend that readers turn to Appendix 17.4, "Five Ways to Estimate Terminal Values," at www.innovationtocashflows.com for further examples of how to estimate terminal values. The method and growth estimates for the terminal value should be tailored to fit the circumstances of the business when it reaches maturity.

DEFINING THE WEIGHTED AVERAGE COST OF CAPITAL

According to financial theory, the weighted average cost of capital for a company is calculated by weighting the cost of each source of funds by its proportion of the total market value of the firm. It may be calculated on a before- or after-tax basis. The WACC sounds simple, but questions always arise when applying the formula in practice. Each component in the WACC equation needs to be estimated, and judgment is required. The reason is that these estimates, theoretically, should be forward-looking estimates, not backward-looking ones.

Furthermore, in the real world, many companies have rather complicated capital structures, which may consist of a mixture of straight debt, convertible debt, operating or capitalized leases, preferred equity, stock options, warrants, and common equity shares. Care needs to be exercised when estimating the costs of these different sources of funds.

For simpler capital structures, the general equation for k_{wacc} (on an after-tax basis) is:

$$k_{wacc} = k_d(1 - Tc)\frac{D}{V} + k_{preferred}\frac{P}{V} + k_e\frac{E}{V}$$

where

V = Market value of the total enterprise

D = Market value of debt

P = Market value of preferred shares

E = Market value of the equity shares

k_d = Pretax market expected yield to maturity on noncallable, nonconvertible debt

$k_{preferred}$ = After-tax cost of capital for noncallable, nonconvertible preferred stock (which equals the pretax cost of preferred stock when no deduction is made from corporate taxes for preferred dividends)

k_e = Market-determined opportunity cost of equity capital

Tc = Marginal corporate tax rate

Example of Computing a Weighted Average Cost of Capital

Suppose we have a corporation worth $100 million that has issued a total of $40 million in debt and raised $60 million in equity through its public share offering. The CFO considers that the enterprise is appropriately financed.

Consequently we will assume that the current proportions of 40 percent debt and 60 percent equity will be the "ideal" or "target" capital structure also in the future. Let us assume that the interest rate (we use the yield-to-maturity rate) on the company's corporate debt is 9 percent. We also assume the company's marginal corporate tax rate is 30 percent and the required return to equity shareholders is 20 percent. Then the after-tax weighted average cost of capital is calculated using this next formula:

$$k_{wacc} = \left(k_e \times \frac{E}{D+E} \right) + \left(k_d(1 - T_c) \times \frac{D}{D+E} \right)$$

where k_e = Opportunity cost of equity

k_d = Opportunity cost of debt

T_c = Marginal corporate tax rate

$\frac{E}{D+E}$ = target proportion of equity in the capital structure

$\frac{D}{D+E}$ = target proportion of debt in the capital structure

Substituting the numbers into the formula, we compute that

$$k_{wacc} = \left(0.20 \times \frac{\$60 \text{ million}}{\$100 \text{ million}} \right) + \left\{ 0.09 \times (1 - 0.30) \times \frac{\$40 \text{ million}}{\$100 \text{ million}} \right\}$$

$$= (0.20 \times 0.60) + (0.09 \times 0.70 \times 0.40)$$

$$= 0.145 \text{ or } 14.5\%$$

Therefore, $k_{wacc} = 14.5$ percent is the weighted average return required by diversified investors in the capital markets for this particular company. It represents the *minimum* required opportunity cost of capital for the firm. The k_{wacc} may be used by the firm's managers to evaluate "average risk" investment projects that are available to the company. By "average risk" we mean a typical capital expenditure project for the company that will *not* change the overall risk profile of the firm.

APPLYING THE ENTERPRISE VALUATION APPROACH BY DISCOUNTING FREE CASH FLOWS

In this section, we illustrate how to do the enterprise valuation method step by step. To use this method, we must estimate and decide on four basic inputs and a computation:

1. Forecast the expected free cash flows.
2. Estimate the terminal value (TV), also called the continuing value.
3. Determine the explicit forecast period (or forecast time horizon).
4. Choose the discount rate appropriate to the riskiness of the free cash flows.
5. Compute the equity value from the enterprise value by subtracting any debt and adding back any excess cash.

In steps 1 through 4, we have directly determined the value of the whole enterprise, and in step 5, we have indirectly estimated a value for the equity of the firm. We explain each of these components in the next paragraphs.

Step 1: Free Cash Flows

The first challenge we face is to estimate the relevant cash flows to be discounted. A *simplified* definition of free cash flow (FCF) is that it is equal to (earnings after tax) plus (depreciation and other noncash charges) minus (needed investments in capital expenditures [CAPEX] or incremental working capital). In symbols, the equation may be written like this:

$$FCF = EBIT(1 - T_c) + \text{Depreciation} - \text{CAPEX} - \text{Investments in Working Capital}$$

where
FCF = Free cash flows
$EBIT$ = Earnings before interest and taxes
T_c = Marginal corporate tax rate
Depreciation = Depreciation expenses and other noncash charges
CAPEX = Capital expenditures
Investments in Working Capital (to be defined on page 418)

The reason for starting with the earnings before interest and taxes (EBIT) is that it is the operating income the company earns without regard to how the business enterprise is financed. Consequently, the expression EBIT × (1 − *Tax Rate*) is equivalent to operating income after tax excluding the effects of any debt financing. Adding back in any noncash charges—for instance, depreciation expenses—yields the after-tax cash flow. Of course, the company's management also needs to pay for new capital expenditures and additions to short-term assets; otherwise plant and equipment will wear out and working capital will be inadequate to support sales growth. The annual cash flow that is freely distributable to owners and creditors as dividends—the so-called free cash flow—is thus operating cash flow after tax minus capital expenditures and working capital investments.

Excess Cash   If a company is profitable, it is likely to build up excess cash until such time as it pays out future dividends to shareholders. Excess cash is not the same thing as the required cash needed in daily operations, which is part of working capital (which we discuss next). Excess cash is *surplus* cash. What should you do about the buildup of any excess cash a company accumulates over and above the amount necessary to support operations? We advise you to omit excess cash from the discounted cash flow valuation and to treat it separately as an add-in item at the conclusion of the valuation. We show you how to do this in the PB Electronics illustrative case in Appendix 17.1 at the end of this chapter.

Investments in Working Capital   It is easy to make mistakes when estimating incremental investments in working capital, so we will give a brief refresher of the topic here. *Working capital investment* is defined to be equal to the increase in current assets minus increases in *noninterest-bearing current liabilities*. To do the forecast properly, you need to understand how to estimate investment in working capital. Specifically, working capital investment equals the increase in current assets necessary to support operations, less any accompanying increases in noninterest-bearing *current liabilities*.

What are increases in *current assets*? They are items such as increases in inventory and accounts receivable. What are examples of noninterest-bearing current liabilities? They are items such as accounts payable and accrued wages. The difference will be the net working capital investment that must be financed by creditors and owners. Two examples of interest-bearing current liabilities would be short-term debt and the current part of long-term debt.

To illustrate the calculation, we do a numerical example. Table 17.1 shows how to estimate an investment in working capital that is required to support the launch of a new electronic sensor product. We make two key assumptions:

1. The change in required investment in working capital will be about 20 percent of sales (corresponding to an increase in inventory and accounts receivable net of current assets such as accounts payables, and accrued wages).
2. There is a full recovery of working capital at the end of the product's life (in other words, there is a large salvage value to these working capital investments as the

TABLE 17.1   Determining the Investment in Working Capital

Year	0	1	2	3	4	5
(all figures are in $ thousands)						
New product sales	$0	$60	$82	$150	$170	$125
Working capital at 20% of sales	0	12	16	30	34	25
Annual change in working capital	0	12	4	14	4	(9)
Recovery of working capital						25
Total working capital investment	$0	$(12)	$(4)	$(14)	$(4)	$34

Source: Author's own estimates adapted from an example in Robert C. Higgins, *Analysis for Financial Management*, 8th international ed. (New York: McGraw-Hill, 2007), p. 263.

product line matures in year 5). Be sure to watch correctly the sign convention used for the investment in working capital. An *increase* in working capital will show up as a *use* of funds (indicated by brackets as it will be a negative sum) whereas a *decrease* in working capital will show up as a *return* of funds and therefore be a positive figure. To see the results, refer to Table 17.1.

Advanced Accounting Topics   Log onto our web site at www.innovationtocash flows.com to download Appendix 17.3, "Advanced Definition of Free Cash Flows for Use with Enterprise Valuation Method." In this appendix, we provide advanced readers with a more complete definition of free cash flows, including the treatment of various accounting items, such as operating and capitalized leases, the amortization of goodwill (for countries that still permit it), and foreign currency adjustments. (Up to this point in this chapter, we have ignored off-balance sheet items, goodwill, and other foreign currency translation effects, in order to make the free cash flow explanation simpler and clearer.)

Step 2: Terminal Value

We now face a very important part of the valuation exercise. In many start-up companies, continuing value is a very large percentage of the value. So this topic merits serious discussion. We do not want to be making spreadsheets with 100 years' worth of estimates, nor do we think that that would even be feasible or reasonable. Therefore we think about the value of the enterprise (VE_0) by splitting up the problem of forecasting an infinite stream of free cash flows into two pieces and then summing the parts.

As we said earlier, the enterprise value is equal to the present value of the free cash flows during the forecast period plus the discounted free cash flows after the explicit forecast period is over. The latter is the present value of the free cash flows in perpetuity. The expression (in words) is:

$$VE_0 = (PV \text{ of FCF for years 1 to T}) + (PV \text{ of TV at year T})$$

In symbols, we express it like this:

$$VE_0 = V_{T^-} + V_{T^+}$$

The practical dilemma we face is to know what expression to use for the terminal value. Earlier we offered advice on how to estimate a company's "TV of the future." (See Appendix 17.4 at www.innovationtocashflows.com for five different ways to estimate terminal values using various methods. We also discuss the typical mistakes that arise when making terminal value estimations and describe methods to avoid committing these errors.)

Because we discuss terminal values extensively in Appendix 17.4, our remarks here will be brief. The perpetual constant growth model is the most popular expression for the terminal value. Again, a few strong words of caution when applying it: Any business growing faster than the economy forever must eventually grow to become the size of the economy. There is a limit to how fast a company can grow in perpetuity. Many analysts, even experienced ones, forget this and extrapolate the past high growth rate and use it for the terminal value growth rate. We say the upper limit for the perpetual growth rate g_∞ must be the long-run growth rate of the economy, roughly 2 percent to 3 percent a year for the United States, plus expected inflation. (Refer to Appendix 17.7, located on our web site, for a brief explanation of the Fisher equation that is frequently used to convert from real rates to nominal rates by taking inflation expectations into account.)

If inflation rises, management will need to spend more on both capital expenditures and working capital just to stay even with inflation. This means that free cash flow actually falls even as the perpetual growth rate g_∞ (in nominal terms) rises due to inflation. So unless the person doing the analysis is very careful, especially when working in countries with rising inflation, the perpetual constant growth formula is likely to overstate a company's continuing value, even if the g_∞ is kept to a reasonably low figure.

Step 3: Forecast Time Horizon

We need to determine the time horizon (number of years) over which the free cash flows will be forecast explicitly. Generally, we recommend a forecast on an annual basis looking out over a reasonably long time period of anywhere from five to 15 years, depending on the nature of the business and the turbulence and uncertainty in the industry. For highly volatile wireless businesses, five years might be reasonable. For biopharmaceutical businesses, where the product development periods last a decade or more, 15 years is not unusual.

What tips do we suggest for helping the analyst to decide when to end the explicit forecast period and begin the terminal value period? Our advice is to pick a time frame that is long enough to capture a full business cycle of the company's operation. All industries experience cycles when capacity is constrained, prices are relatively high, and demand is booming, followed by periods when the industry adds too much capacity, pricing power is weak and price wars might ensue, and demand is slack. You want to forecast over the entire cycle.

For practical examples of how different industries have widely varying forecast time horizons, refer to the capstone case Arcadian Microarrays, which you can access by logging onto our web site, www.innovationtocashflows.com. In this case, you can see the forecast time horizons for a movie studio, a soft drink beverage bottling plant, and a toll road.

If you are modeling a start-up company that is launching a series of new products, you will want to incorporate the effect on cash flows of these currently heavy R&D investments and capital expenditures. However, you will also want to include the period of time when these products are in the market and, it is hoped, producing profits, not just causing losses. If you expect heavy competition or a rival to launch a substitute product that will erode your target company's market shares, you need to take that into account in the explicit forecast period. If the company is a mature business, it could very well experience a major turnaround or restructuring effort. You need to make sure your forecast is long enough to capture these effects on the business model. Similarly, the effects of any merger and acquisition activity (actual or planned) need to be modeled—especially the full effect of any synergies as a result of the merger or any additional earnings (or losses) as a result of consolidating the acquisition.

Note: For an illustration of how to financially model a technology licensing agreement and prepare for its negotiation, see our case, Advanced Dermal Delivery, in Chapter 20. To learn how to value an early stage biopharmaceutical research company, refer to the capstone case Proto5 located on our web site. To see how to model the key factors driving the economic value of a joint-venture deal, refer to the capstone case Genzyme-Geltex Pharmaceuticals Joint Venture also located on our web site.

In short, the explicit forecast period should reflect the forecaster's expectations of all known factors at the time of making the spreadsheet models. The flows of cash should reflect any growth rates that are abnormally high or abnormally low compared to industry averages. Our advice is to go out as far into the future as you feel comfortable forecasting—until you believe that the company has reached a steady state of mature growth. By *steady state maturity*, we mean that the company expects to experience, on average, a constant rate of return on new projects during the terminal value period and also expects to invest, on average, a constant percentage of its cash flows into the business each year and to maintain a constant debt-to-equity financing ratio, which is what the enterprise valuation methodology assumes. *The last assumption of a constant debt-to-equity financing ratio is critically important to remember.*

If the debt-to-equity financing ratio is *not* constant, you should not rely on the enterprise valuation method. Instead, you need to use an alternative approach, such as the dividend discount model, and for each year of the forecast carefully change the debt-to-equity ratio.

An even easier approach to valuing companies with changing debt-to-equity financing is a third method, known as the *adjusted present value* (APV) method. It is a valuation technique that is particularly suited for modeling leveraged buyouts. We briefly describe the main differences between APV and the enterprise valuation approach in the next paragraph. (We do *not* cover the APV model in-depth, as it is beyond the scope of this book; even so, we do want our readers to be aware of APV and understand that it may be used to value a highly levered deal or corporate restructuring transaction.)

Adjusted Present Value Method   The adjusted present value method is similar to the enterprise valuation approach. As with the enterprise valuation approach, the APV model discounts free cash flows to estimate the value of operations, and ultimately the value of the total enterprise, after adding back the value of nonoperating assets. From the total enterprise value, the value of debt is deducted to arrive at an equity value. The difference between the two methods is that the APV separates the value of operations into two components: the value of the company as if it were financed by equity 100 percent and the value of the tax benefit that results from debt financing, as interest expenses are tax deductible to the firm. This is the so-called tax shield benefit. The APV method uses an unlevered cost of equity when computing WACC, which we have not yet discussed. For more information on the APV method, we suggest more advanced books on M&A and corporate restructurings or corporate finance. We recommend that APV should be considered whenever debt-to-equity ratios are changing, as in the case of a leveraged buyout or financial restructuring. Since we focus mainly on early-stage ventures, not corporate restructurings, we leave it to others to cover this technique in detail. For instance, see Copeland, Koller, and Murrin (2000) or refer to Bruner (2004) for further discussion and detailed examples.[31]

Step 4: Weighted Average Cost of Capital

For the enterprise valuation method, we need to consider the opportunity cost of funds for both the creditors and the owners of the business. The proper way to think about opportunity costs is to consider what economic returns the debt holders and the equity owners could have earned on alternative, similar-risk investments. Combined, their opportunity costs define the minimum rate of return the company must earn on its assets to meet the expectations of its capital providers. The weighted average cost of capital is simply the weighted average of the cost of equity and the cost of debt. The cost of debt capital should include all interest-bearing debt. It is the interest rate the company is paying for borrowing funds, adjusted for the usual deductibility of interest expense for determining income taxes.

Interested readers should refer to online Appendix 17.5, "General Principles for Determining the Equity Market Risk Premium," to read more about the controversy and debate surrounding the cost of equity and how to estimate it. Refer to online Appendix 17.6, "Estimating the Weighted Average Cost of Capital for the ABC Corporation," for a comprehensive numerical example of how to lever and unlever betas from an industry sample of proxy companies. Both appendixes may be accessed and downloaded after logging onto our web site www.innovationtocashflows.com.

Step 5: Derive the Final Equity Value from the Enterprise Value

Remember that by using free cash flows and the WACC, we have determined an estimate for the value of all the assets of the company that are claimed by both the equity shareholders and the debt holders. Recall the fundamental relationship:

$$\text{Enterprise Value} = \text{Equity} + \text{Debt} - \text{Excess Cash}$$

The basic equation to remember is:

$$EV_0 = E + D - C$$

To calculate the equity value, we must now subtract the debt and add back any excess or surplus cash. By rearranging terms, we solve for the equity value:

$$E = EV_0 - D + C$$

PRACTICAL ADVICE ON SELECTING THE PROPER DISCOUNT RATE

If you are planning on buying a technology company or doing any kind of alliance or joint venture, you must match the discount rate to the level of risk of the expected free cash flows to be received from the target technology company or planned strategic alliance or joint venture. (For an example, log onto our web site to see the capstone case, Genyzme-Geltex Pharmaceutical Joint Venture, for the discount rate used in an actual joint venture negotiation.)

In carrying out analyses for M&As, the same principle holds true. Novices often make mistakes when determining the appropriate discount rate for the target company that is being taken over by the acquiring company. *When you are valuing the target company, you need to choose a discount rate for the stream of economic benefits you expect to receive as an investor in that company.* The discount rate used to value the target should match the riskiness of the target's cash flows.

With the DCF method, the value of an R&D project or capacity expansion project is determined by discounting future expected cash flows at a discount rate that takes into account the expected risk of the project or expansion. Therefore, in principle, all that is needed is to estimate the expected future cash flows of the project and to discount back to the present all these future cash flows, using a discount rate consistent with the level of risk in the project. If the value arrived at through DCF analysis is higher than the current cost of the investment, the DCF calculation would say to go ahead and invest.

When using the dividend discount method of determining the intrinsic value of a company, you should use the investor's opportunity cost of equity as the discount rate. For well-diversified investors, such as the typical mutual fund or index fund investor, the CAPM cost of equity is most often used by U.S. financial analysts as the appropriate market-determined discount rate.

Undiversified investors, such as venture capitalists, will have a much higher opportunity cost of capital than the fully diversified investor who is investing in quoted companies in well-developed capital markets. As we discuss in Chapter 19, venture capitalists invest in early-stage companies, often in the same high-technology sector. Hence venture capitalists are more exposed to unsystematic risk (idiosyncratic risk) than a highly diversified mutual fund manager with a portfolio of shares in listed companies covering a broad spectrum of the economy.

In this chapter, we have focused on exploring how professional financial analysts use DCF methods to value public companies trading in deep, broad equity markets such as the United States. Financial analysts, particularly those valuing mature businesses or publicly trading companies, tend to choose the enterprise valuation method of discounting free cash flows over the dividend discount model for at least two reasons.

1. Free cash flows are easier to use because they are *before* debt-related expense payments. Therefore, you do not have to consider directly the cash flows related to complicated debt securities, which sometimes can be difficult to untangle.

2. Since the free cash flows are before debt-related payments, they are also less likely to be negative numbers. With positive free cash flows, it is easier to compute ratios and multiples. With losses, the ratios are meaningless.

There is a caveat to using the enterprise valuation method. The amount of borrowings and the capital structure of the company *will affect* the overall value of the company, due to the effect that debt (leverage) has on the WACC. These leverage effects need to be carefully included when determining the proper WACC. Sometimes novices unknowingly make an oversimplified assumption by using a single WACC in their valuation formula. In so doing, they neglect to account for a changing debt-to-equity ratio and its effect on the year-by-year WACC calculation. *Remember that the enterprise valuation method as it is commonly applied assumes a constant WACC and a constant debt-to-equity ratio.*

At times, even professional analysts have been misled by companies that rely on off-balance sheet financing or are deceived by a firm's fraudulent behavior. These companies do not always clearly present their true debt levels to shareholders and the investment community. The more borrowings, whether on the balance sheet or off the balance sheet, the more financial risk the company is assuming, and the higher ought to be the cost of debt borrowings. This principle is especially true for a firm that is so highly leveraged that it may be nearing financial distress. In such cases, financial analysts need to be especially wary about some of the assumptions used in determining the weighted average cost of capital, as WACC was not designed to be used for valuing highly leveraged buyouts where debt levels constantly change, nor should it be used for valuing companies in deep financial distress. In particular, the formula for levering and unlevering betas is *not applicable* to situations of high indebtedness.

If you have to make a valuation of a highly leveraged company, you should consult more advanced finance textbooks and professional appraisal articles that address these special issues. We have recommended various chapters in leading finance books that cover these situations in more detail in the endnotes to this chapter. Recommended textbooks that cover more advanced corporate restructuring topics are listed on our web site under "Resources—Finance" (log onto www.innovationtocashflows.com to download the file).

Finally, for advice on ways to approach determining the cost of capital and beta values in emerging country markets, we suggest reading the tips in Pereiro and in Bruner,[32] where they discuss cross-border valuation issues and the current state of the art on this topic, from both practitioner and academic perspectives. Cross-border valuation is beyond the scope of our book.

ESTABLISH AN ESTIMATED RANGE OF VALUATION VALUES

It should be clear that no one approach will suffice for all situations. Multiple valuation methods should be applied. As an illustration, we compute company values using a variety of different company valuation methods. We then plot the results in a bar graph as suggested by Bruner.[33] Refer to Figure 17.4.

Once we do a variety of valuations and have the plot of the range of results, we are faced with the problem of how to combine the results into a composite

Price per share

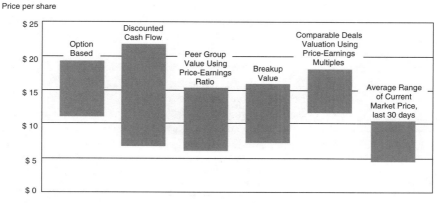

FIGURE 17.4 Results of Various Company Valuation Methods
Source: Author's own estimates adapted from an example in Robert F. Bruner, *Applied Mergers and Acquisitions* (Hoboken, NJ: John Wiley & Sons, 2000), p. 277.

valuation. The process of combining results is called triangulation. The term comes from surveying and navigation. It is a technique of determining the distance between points on the Earth's surface by weighting and combining a series of measurements.[34]

The final weighting of the valuations obtained from various methods should be calibrated based on judgment and experience. It ought to include an honest assessment of the reliability of the data available and used in each method. Those answers that are derived from better-quality and more reliable information should be given more weight than those that are based on poorer-quality data inputs. Judgment needs to be exercised and weightings devised that are clear and replicable. For instance, in the example in Figure 17.4, we might give more weight to the results from the DCF analysis and transaction multiples than the options valuation or peer multiples, breakup, or current market price. Therefore we give higher weight to some answers and lower weights to the others.

Once we decide on the weighting of each input, we simply combine the results as we would a weighted average to produce the "best estimate" range of possible values. Sometimes irregularly high or low values are ignored or thrown out and a weighted average of the remaining values is tabulated. To compute an average or central value the analyst may choose from a variety of measures, including the mean or median. The mean (also called the arithmetic average) is widely used, but suffers from outlier bias. It also weights each variable the same, regardless of the analyst's perception of its importance. The median is the value of the middle item in a group of items arranged in ascending or descending order. The median is better to use in a series with high or low outliers. The final choice of metric depends very much on the situation and the judgment of the analyst.

Figure 17.5 diagrams the overall valuation process, including the final triangulation step. If you refer to the online capstone case, Arcadian Microarray Technologies, located on our web site, you can read a fuller explanation of how to do triangulation to produce a best estimate range of possible values. You will also be able to practice doing it yourself. For additional insights, refer to Pereiro and to Bruner[35]

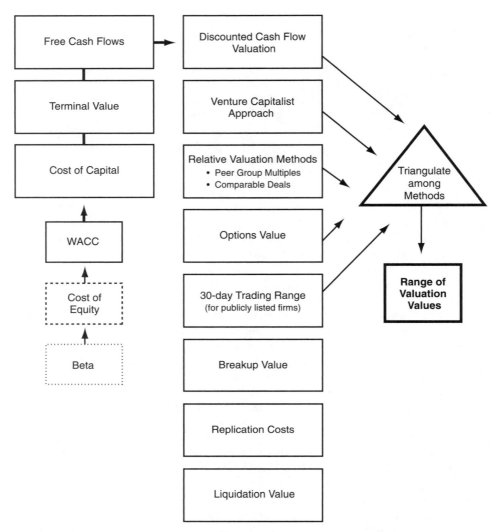

FIGURE 17.5 Developing the Composite Valuation: The Process of "Triangulating" the Final Valuation Results
Source: Adapted from Robert F. Bruner, *Applied Mergers and Acquisitions* (Hoboken, NJ: John Wiley & Sons, 2000), p. 279.

for excellent discussions and practical tips on how to blend estimates derived from different methods to come up with triangulated results.

NEXT STEPS FOR TESTING YOUR KEY ASSUMPTIONS

After plotting and combining the various valuation results as we did in Figure 17.4, we recommend going yet one step further and performing sensitivity analysis on the key data inputs and underlying financial model assumptions.

Sensitivity analysis means varying the inputs (usually one by one) and recalculating the answer. This is best done with a tool such as a spreadsheet, as it is tedious and cumbersome to do by hand or with a financial calculator. Data tables that display the various inputs and the corresponding range of outputs are useful for collecting the results of the sensitivity analyses. Particularly important would be to vary the growth rates of the business's sales forecasts, the operating margins, and the perpetual growth rate in the terminal value. We also advise testing the estimates for the cost of capital.

Scenarios should also be run where two or more variables are changed at the same time and the influence on valuation results recorded. Scenarios can be very useful for making appropriate trade-offs during negotiations of M&A deals or strategic alliance contractual agreements. We illustrate scenarios in Chapter 20 in the Advanced Dermal Delivery, Inc. case, when we do the valuation of a patent licensing and technology transfer agreement.

Simulation techniques are also helpful to understand and model the risks of financial forecasts. A popular software program for doing risk analysis and Monte Carlo simulations is @Risk 5.0, which may be bought separately or as part of a complete Decision Tools Suite developed by Palisade (www.palisade.com). For more information on risk analysis and simulation techniques, see the many tutorials and examples on Palisade's web site. We have used @Risk when teaching executives and MBAs and have found the program to be quite intuitive and user friendly. The user interface resembles a spreadsheet and the graphics are excellent.

Decisioneering (www.decisioneering.com) is another provider of risk assessment software. Decisioneering sells the Crystal Ball add-in package, which also offers a suite of tools useful for simulations and financial modeling and risk assessment. Like Palisade, the company has a helpful web site that will enable you to get started learning about simulations on your own.

NEXT STEPS FOR PRACTICING VALUATIONS

Valuation is a skill and an art. To do it well takes practice and applying the theory and readings to real-life situations. To help you on this part of your journey as an entrepreneur we offer several cases.

The capstone case Proto5 compares and contrasts the discounted free cash flow method with the venture capital method of valuation, which we discuss in Chapter 19. In addition, Proto5 introduces the concept of a decision tree with probability assessments. By using the decision tree technique, you can, for example, take into account the unsystematic risks of a therapeutic drug compound failing clinical trials and incorporate these technological and scientific risks directly into the expected cash flows.

For further practice on doing discounted cash flow valuations and sensitivity analysis, we refer you to the capstone case Genzyme-Geltex Pharmaceuticals Joint Venture that may be downloaded after logging onto our web site www.innovationtocashflows.com. This is an excellent finance and joint venture negotiations case. One of the case exhibits displays a comprehensive spreadsheet model of a discounted cash flow valuation for the proposed 50/50 joint venture between Genzyme and Geltex. The student version of the electronic spreadsheet (with the formulas and data inserted) may be ordered directly from Darden Business Publishing, University of Virginia (https://store.darden.virginia.edu/). The electronic spreadsheet allows you to do sensitivity analysis on all the key value drivers in the deal. Readers familiar with financial modeling will find this particular case ideally suited for doing Monte Carlo simulations.

To illustrate how to do a valuation from start to finish using the enterprise valuation method, we have prepared our own comprehensive case example, called PB Electronics Inc., a company that has obtained the North American distribution rights to a novel high-tech backpack that it plans to sell in the United States, Canada, and Mexico. This case is presented in Appendix 17.1 at the end of this chapter. There you will find detailed income statement forecasts, projected balance sheet figures, and a complete set of free cash flow projections for the company. We also show you the calculations where we compute both the enterprise value and the equity value of PB Electronics Inc. To download the electronic spreadsheet containing the financial valuation model that accompanies the case, log onto our web site, www.innovationtocashflows.

CHAPTER TAKEAWAYS

- *Intrinsic value* reflects the fundamental economic value of the firm. It is what security analysts and professional appraisers mean when they say the "true value" or "real value" of the company. It is based on the economic value of the firm's dividends or free cash flows (in perpetuity) discounted back to the present with an *appropriate* discount rate. Naturally each person will have to exercise her own judgment about the quality, quantity, and extent of dividends or free cash flows the firm will be able to produce over its lifetime when making her valuation appraisal.
- The dividend discount model or equity residual cash flow method was invented by John Burr Williams in 1938. The model derives the equity value of the shares directly. Always use the cost of equity when discounting dividends.
- The enterprise valuation or free cash flow to the firm method values the assets pertaining to the whole firm. This method uses the weighted average cost of equity when discounting free cash flows. It indirectly estimates the value of the common equity as the final residual claim after all the other claim holders have been paid. The procedure is to start with the enterprise value, add back any excess or surplus cash, and subtract the value of any debt or preferred or other claims. What is left over is the residual value to common shareholders.
- The adjusted present value is a third technique for valuing companies. Use the APV method for the appraisal of businesses with changing debt-equity levels, for instance, leveraged buyouts.
- Do *not* mix up the methods. When deciding which technique to use (dividend discount, enterprise value, or APV method), pick the one that makes the most sense given the capital structure, available data, and the goal of the valuation, and then stick with your choice.
- In many start-up companies, continuing value is a very large portion of the value. As we do not want to be making spreadsheets with 100 years' worth

of estimates, we simplify the analysis by estimating a continuing value for the business (or terminal value).

- When deciding on a perpetual growth rate for the terminal value, keep in mind the old saying "Trees don't grow to the sky." Do not implicitly assume high growth rates in perpetuity. Even great companies find their profitability eventually regresses toward the industry average as they grow larger in size.
- The Capital Asset Pricing Model is a financial theory that can be applied to estimate the expected cost of equity. CAPM postulates that in equilibrium, there is a linear relationship between the expected return on any risky asset and its systematic (undiversifiable) risk. The theory is based on a number of simplifying assumptions about rational investor behavior and efficient capital markets.
- Estimating the expected equity market risk premium is controversial. We know that the risk premium fluctuates. New studies by leading-edge investment firms and academic researchers continue to enhance our understanding of financial markets, investor expectations, and the determinants of risk premiums.
- Employ sensitivity analysis and scenario analysis. Systematically doing so will help overcome cognitive biases. These types of risk assessments will yield a range of likely values for the company under different states of the world. They also will help capture and quantify remotely possible outcomes.
- Log onto our web site www.innovationtocashflows where you will find:
  - Electronic spreadsheet to accompany the PB Electronics Inc. case.
  - Appendix 17.2: The Time Value of Money
  - Appendix 17.3: Advanced Definition of Free Cash Flows for Use with Enterprise Valuation Method
  - Appendix 17.4: Five Ways to Estimate Terminal Values
  - Appendix 17.5: General Principles for Determining the Equity Market Risk Premium
  - Appendix 17.6: Estimating the Weighted Average Cost of Capital for the ABC Corporation
  - Appendix 17.7: The Fisher Equation: Taking Inflation Expectations into Account
  - Resources: for recommended finance and valuation books and online finance resources
  - Glossary: for definitions of financial terms used in this chapter

APPENDIX 17.1   USING THE ENTERPRISE VALUATION METHOD TO VALUE A HIGH-TECHNOLOGY COMPANY

To show how to do the enterprise valuation method, we have developed a comprehensive case example—with an integrated set of sales, operating profits, net profit, free cash flow projections, and balance sheet forecasts—for an imaginary company called PB Electronics Inc., with headquarters in Denver, Colorado. It is owned and managed by two brothers, Michael and Carlos Moretti, both experienced entrepreneurs. PB Electronics is a wholesale business that distributes innovative electronic consumer products to specialty retailers in Canada, the United States, and Mexico.

PB Electronics recently acquired exclusive distribution rights to merchandise innovative, rugged, versatile, and extremely lightweight backpacks for North America. The uses of the backpack are many. The most expensive and advanced models would be suitable for mountain climbers involved in high-altitude trekking expeditions. Mid-price backpacks may be used by business travelers who want a combined backpack and computer carrying case. The low-price range is perfect for design-conscious university students who want an all-around backpack they can take to school or on trips.

For all users, the special feature of this backpack is its security. All items placed inside it can be electronically secured and monitored, thereby protecting any personal items or electronic gear stored into the backpack. Embedded throughout the backpack's special woven fabric are a series of powerful nanosensors that allow the backpack to be traced anywhere in the world.

- For instance, during a high-altitude trek, the nanosensors would enable alpine rescue squads to pinpoint the location of the backpack in the event of an avalanche or other natural disaster.
- For business travelers, the backpacks are especially designed to open up easily for hand inspection during airport security controls.
- For college students, the big advantage is their light weight and attractive design. The sensors also would be useful in recovering the backpack if it is stolen or lost.

The patented fabric, tracking sensors, and sleek design were developed by a high-technology alpine trekking equipment firm located near Zurich, Switzerland. The inventors of this high-tech miracle used to work at a Swiss electronics firm noted for its highly automated scientific instruments, laboratory, and industrial weighing systems. SwissExplore AG was founded by Hans Gutmann, Dr. Franz Adler, and Adele St. John, a leading commercial designer with design studios in Basel and Milan. The two electronics whizzes, Hans and Franz, worked for many years developing the nanosenors in their laboratories at SwissExplore, AG, in Greifensee, close to Zurich. Adele was the designer who thought of incorporating the nanosensors into high-tech fabrics and who designed the backpack prototypes. The specially impregnated woven fabric is produced in a factory near Lake Como, in northern Italy, a region noted for its fine silks. The backpacks are made, assembled, inspected, and packaged in a state-of-the-art factory located in Singapore managed by SwissExplore's joint venture partner. The backpacks destined for PB Electronics are packed into a container and shipped on a cargo vessel to the port of Oakland, California. The container is off-loaded onto a truck and driven directly to Denver, to a warehouse rented by PB Electronics.

Financial Projections for PB Electronics

Table 17A1.1 shows Michael and Carlos Moretti's forecast assumptions for projecting PB Electronics financial statements over the next five years (including their best estimate of the sales from the new line of backpacks).

Michael and Carlos expect sales to soar with this new product line, growing from around $1,700,000 in year 1 to about $5,419,000 by year 5. Cost of goods sold is assumed to average about 70 percent of sales, leaving a gross profit margin of 30 percent. The corporate tax rate is projected at a 35 percent effective marginal corporate tax rate (federal plus state taxes). During the high risk start-up phase of the launch, they used 25 percent for their after-tax WACC; and for the terminal value, the cost of capital estimate was lower at 14.7 percent. The before-tax cost of debt was 10 percent and the perpetual growth rate for the terminal value was 4 percent. (Their thinking and justification for each of these values is explained later in the sections, "Forecasting Growth and Inflation" and "Determining the Opportunity Cost of Capital.")

As a general policy, PB Electronics Inc. puts all merchandise deliveries on account with half paid in the current month and half in the following month. The company has no overdue credits and none is anticipated in the future. Sales are typically 40 percent credit (on accounts receivable and collected the next month) and 60 percent cash. Inventory policy is to cover about 80 percent of the sales for the month plus a cash cushion. Next year's rent is expected to be $49,680 per year, and insurance expenses will be about $4,140 per year (prepaid once a year). Depreciation expense is mainly from depreciating the company's rather old delivery truck, office computers, and other equipment. Wages of the sales and administrative staff are paid twice a month. The sale force is paid a combination of a fixed and variable component (bonus) depending on achieving certain sales targets. The two founders are paying themselves only a minimal salary while the other employees are paid a fixed salary. Next year wages and salaries are budgeted at $317,400.

TABLE 17A1.1   PB Electronics Inc.: Financial Forecast Assumptions

Forecast Items	Assumptions for Explicit Forecast Period					
	Year 1 $T = 1$	Year 2 $T = 2$	Year 3 $T = 3$	Year 4 $T = 4$	Year 5 $T = 5$	Year 6 $TV = T + 1$
Sales Forecast (in thousands of $)	$1,700	$2,100	$2,740	$3,800	$5,419	$5,850
Growth Rate in Net Sales (YoY, %)	n/a	23.53%	30.48%	38.69%	42.61%	7.95%
Cost of Goods Sold (as % of Net sales)	70.0%	70.0%	70.0%	70.0%	70.0%	70.0%
Gross Profit Margin (%)	30.0%	30.0%	30.0%	30.0%	30.0%	30.0%
Estimated Corporate Tax Rate (%)	35.0%	35.0%	35.0%	35.0%	35.0%	35.0%
After-Tax WACC	25.0%	25.0%	25.0%	25.0%	25.0%	14.7%
Interest Rate on Borrowed Debt (Before Tax Cost of Debt)	10.0%	10.0%	10.0%	10.0%	10.0%	10.0%
Perpetual Growth Rate for Terminal Value						4.0%

The minimum amount of cash that is required in year 0 for operations is the $23,000 contained in the firm's checking account. By the end of the first year this amount will rise to $24,840. The excess cash (not needed for day-to-day operations) they plan to show as a separate line item called "surplus cash" on the projected balance sheet. The actual surplus or excess cash (in Year 0) was $6,487.

To further finance the growth of the business, the company plans to apply for a $420,000 loan at the end of year 5. Currently the two brothers are providing a line of financing for the business at a rate of 1.5 percent interest *per* month on any credit balances.

After projecting the financial flows for the next five years, the brothers contemplated what to use for the continuing value of the business. They exchanged views about the economy over a cup of coffee.

Forecasting Inflation and Growth

Both men were somewhat worried about future inflation picking up, especially given the large U.S. deficit and unpredictable energy and commodity prices. Years ago, Carlos had read about the famous economist Irving Fisher and remembered Fisher's equation about inflation. In the Fisher equation:

$$(1 + \text{nominal interest rate}) = (1 + \text{real rate of interest}) \times (1 + \text{expected inflation})$$

where the expected inflation rate is the rate expected to prevail over the life of the security and expressed as a per annum figure. When inflation is moderate, the cross product may be ignored and the math simplified to this alternative approximation:

$$\text{Nominal rate of interest} \approx \text{Real Rate} + \text{Expected Inflation Rate}$$

(For more about the Fisher equation, refer to Appendix 17.7 at www.innovationtocashflows.com.)

The two brothers estimated that future U.S. inflation would probably be somewhere between 2 percent to 3 percent per year. They picked 2.5 percent as the average going forward. They thought their own distributor business could grow at a real rate of about 1.5 percent a year in perpetuity, which they believed to be slightly below the long-term U.S. economy growth rate, and hence a conservative estimate. However, they did not think they could get growth much above that rate in real units. They were expecting ever tougher global competition, making it extremely unlikely they could raise prices and still gain market share.

To use the Fisher equation correctly, they knew they should compound the two rates to yield the result of $(1.015 \times 1.025) = 1.04038$ and convert it to a percentage (4.04 percent). They decided to ignore the small difference due to the compounding effect and ended up using 4 percent as their perpetual growth rate estimate for the terminal value.

Determining the Opportunity Cost of Capital

The brothers thought long and hard about what should be the opportunity cost of capital for their business and the riskiness of the free cash flows that were yet to come.

They reasoned that they were both highly dependent on the success or failure of the business, as this was their sole source of income. They were not highly diversified. In fact, they had taken most of their savings out of their personal bank accounts and were using the funds to bootstrap the start-up of the new backpack project. As investors, they felt their risks were more like those of typical venture capitalists, especially compared to the risks being taken by their friends who had placed their savings into broadly diversified and low-cost indexed mutual funds.

The more they read up on the topic of entrepreneurial finance, the more they were convinced that it made sense to use two different estimates for the k_{wacc} (used as the present value discount rate) and the $k_{wacc\infty}$ (used in the terminal value estimate).

After much discussion and more cups of coffee, they finally agreed on a higher venture capital-like rate of $k_{wacc} = 25$ percent for the explicit forecast period (years 0 to 5). They chose to use the CAPM to estimate a $k_{wacc\infty} = 14.7$ percent for the constant growth terminal value expression, after the start-up and ramp-up phases were expected to be completed and the business was in a steady state of growth.

After summarizing and documenting their key forecast assumptions, they next computed the enterprise valuation.

Step-by-Step Determining PB's Enterprise Valuation In this section, Michael and Carlos are going to apply, step-by-step, the process and the equations that were developed earlier in this chapter. They will be using the multiple period enterprise valuation method and assuming constant growth for the continuing value period. That, is they will be using this expression:

$$VE_0 = \sum_{t=1}^{T} \frac{FCF_t}{(1 + k_{wacc})^t} + \frac{FCF_{T+1}}{(1 + k_{wacc})^T \times (k_{wacc\infty} - g_{\infty})}$$

1. Table 17A1.2 summarizes Michael and Carlos's free cash flow estimates for the explicit five-year forecast period.
2. To find the present value of these future free cash flows estimates, the brothers used the venture capital rate of $k_{wacc} = 25$ percent (for the explicit forecast period from years 0 to 5) as the discount rate. The present value of the first five years' free cash flows was $78,378, as shown in the next computation:

$$PV\ FCFs = \frac{\$64,891}{1.25} + \frac{\$21,939}{1.25^2} + \frac{\$17,421}{1.25^3} + \frac{\$7,803}{1.25^4} + \frac{939}{1.25^5}$$

$$PV\ FCFs = \$78,378$$

TABLE 17A1.2   PB Electronics Inc.: Five-Year Projected Free Cash Flows

	Year 0 12/31/Y0	Fcst Yr1 12/31/Y1	Fcst Yr2 12/31/Y2	Fcst Yr3 12/31/Y3	Fcst Yr4 12/31/Y4	Fcst Yr5 12/31/Y5	Fcst (T + 1) TV Period
(All amounts shown are in U.S. dollars)							
Earnings Before Interest and Taxes (EBIT)		$75,024	$93,606	$122,566	$170,615	$243,699	$258,256
Less: (Marginal Corporate Tax Rate) × EBIT		(26,258)	(32,762)	(42,898)	(59,716)	(85,295)	(90,389)
Equals: EBIT (1-Tax Rate)		48,766	60,844	79,668	110,899	158,404	167,866
Plus: Depreciation and Amortization		5,796	6,230	7,696	10,042	13,927	19,860
Less: Capital expenditures		(10,140)	(20,890)	(31,151)	(48,890)	(73,262)	(35,656)
Less: Investment in net working capital		20,470	(24,245)	(38,792)	(64,248)	(98,131)	(26,124)
Equals: Free Cash Flows to the Enterprise		64,892	21,939	17,421	7,803	938	125,947

3. Next they developed their terminal value estimate, using the constant growth formula:

$$TV_T = \text{Terminal Value} = \frac{FCF_{T+1}}{k_{wacc\,\infty} - g_\infty}$$

where TV_T = terminal value at time T

FCF_{T+1} = the normalized free cash flow for the first year beyond the forecast time horizon

g_∞ = perpetual growth rate of free cash flows

$k_{wacc\,\infty}$ = appropriate weighted average cost of capital for the mature business phase

Inputting the data into the formula (using an electronic spreadsheet), they determined this value for the terminal value of their business enterprise (using full decimal points for the computation):

$$TV_T = \text{Terminal Value} = \frac{FCF_{T+1}}{k_{wacc\,\infty} - g_\infty}$$

$$= \frac{\$125,947}{0.147 - 0.04} = \$1,177,071$$

4. The next step was to compute the present value of the terminal value. The question was whether they should use a discount rate of $k_{wacc} = 14.7$ percent or 25 percent to calculate the present value. After verifying the formulas one more time, they realized they needed to discount the terminal value at the $k_{wacc} = 25$ percent rate. They also remembered they needed to put the TV at the end of the explicit forecast period, in other words at time $t = T$, or the *end* of the fifth year and *not* in the sixth year. Consequently, to compute the present value of

the TV, they would need to discount the TV for five years, like this:

$$PV \text{ of the } TV = \frac{\$1,177,071}{(1.25)^5} = \$385,702$$

5. They then summed the present value of the free cash flows from Step 2 with the present value of the terminal value from Step 4 to determine the present value of the enterprise, or VE_0 (which represents the operations of the business).

$$VE_0 = (PV \text{ of } FCF \text{ for years } 1 \text{ to } T) + (PV \text{ of } TV \text{ at year } T)$$

$$VE_0 = \sum_{t=1}^{T} \frac{FCF_t}{(1 + k_{wacc})^t} + \frac{FCF_{T+1}}{(1 + k_{wacc})^T \times (k_{wacc\infty} - g_\infty)}$$

$$= \$78,378 + \$385,702 = \$464,080$$

The amount of $464,080 represents the PV of all cash flows related to the operations of PB Enterprises. It excludes the value of any nonoperating assets, and it also excludes excess cash, which is treated separately (see next step).

6. The final step was to compute the equity value of PB Electronics at time $t = 0$. Michael and Carlos determined this amount indirectly. They started with the enterprise valuation, VE_0, then added in the actual surplus cash from the balance sheet, C, and subtracted the market value of the debt held in year 0. (In fact, there was no debt at time $t = 0$).

$$\text{Equity Value} = VE_0 + \text{Excess Cash} - \text{Debt}$$

$$\text{Equity Value} = \$464,080 + \$6,487 - 0 = \$470,567$$

7. As PB Electronics has 10,000 common shares outstanding, the final intrinsic value per share (equity value per share) is therefore $470,567 divided by 10,000 shares, or $47.06 per share.

Table 17A1.3 provides a summary overview of the enterprise valuation model results for PB Electronics Inc. The complete five-year financial projections for the income statement, balance sheet, and cash flow statements are shown in Table 17A1.4, Table 17A1.5, and Table 17A1.6. The electronic spreadsheets for the PB Electronics Inc. financial forecasts and valuation model may be downloaded from our web site by logging onto www.innovationtocashflows.com and going to the spreadsheet file for the PB Electronics Inc. case.

TABLE 17A1.3 PB Electronics Inc.: Summary of the Valuation Results

	Year 0 12/31/Y0	Fcst Yr 1 12/31/Y1	Fcst Yr 2 12/31/Y2	Fcst Yr 3 12/31/Y3	Fcst Yr 4 12/31/Y4	Fcst Yr 5 12/31/Y5	Fcst (T + 1) TV Period
Enterprise Free Cash Flows		$64,892	$21,939	$17,421	$7,803	$938	$125,947
PV of the FCFs @ 25% for Years 1 to 5, (excluding the TV period)	$78,378						
Estimated Terminal Value (TV) at year 5						$1,177,071	
PV of the Terminal Value @ 25% at year 0	$385,702						
Sum of the PVs of all the FCFs from Operations	$464,080						
Add: Excess Cash and Nonoperating Assets, at time $t = 0$.	$6,487						
Value of the Total Enterprise, at time $t = 0$	$470,567						
Less: Market Value of the Debt, at time $t = 0$	$0						
Value of the Equity	$470,567						
No. of common shares issued and outstanding	10,000						
Intrinsic value per share	$47.06						

TABLE 17A1.4 PB Electronics, Inc.—Projected Income Statement

Projected Income Statement	Fcst Year 1	Fcst Year 2	Fcst Year 3	Fcst Year 4	Fcst T = 5	Fcst T + 1 = 6
All amounts are in U.S. dollars						
Net Sales	$1,700,000	$2,100,000	$2,740,000	$3,800,000	$5,419,000	$5,850,000
Cost of Goods Sold	(1,190,000)	(1,470,000)	(1,918,000)	(2,660,000)	(3,793,300)	(4,095,000)
Gross Profit	510,000	630,000	822,000	1,140,000	1,625,700	1,755,000
Operating Expenses:						
Salaries, Wages, and Employee Benefits	(317,400)	(392,082)	(511,574)	(709,482)	(1,011,759)	(1,092,229)
Rent	(49,680)	(61,369)	(80,072)	(111,049)	(158,362)	(170,958)
Miscellaneous Expenses	(57,960)	(71,598)	(93,418)	(129,558)	(184,756)	(199,451)
Insurance	(4,140)	(5,114)	(6,673)	(9,254)	(13,197)	(14,246)
Depreciation Expense	(5,796)	(6,230)	(7,696)	(10,042)	(13,927)	(19,860)
Total Operating Expenses	(434,976)	(536,394)	(699,434)	(969,385)	(1,382,001)	(1,496,744)
Income from Operations	75,024	93,606	122,566	170,615	243,699	258,256
Interest Expenses	0	0	0	0	0	(42,000)
Earnings before Taxes	75,024	93,606	122,566	170,615	243,699	216,256
Less: Taxes (at 35%)	(26,258)	(32,762)	(42,898)	(59,715)	(85,295)	(75,689)
Net Income	48,766	60,844	79,668	110,899	158,404	140,566
Dividends	0	0	0	0	0	0
Retained Earnings	$48,766	$60,844	$79,668	$110,899	$158,404	$140,566

TABLE 17A1.5 PB Electronics, Inc.—Projected Balance Sheet

All amounts are in U.S. dollars

Projected Balance Sheet	Actual 12/31/Y0	Year 1 12/31/Y1	Year 2 12/31/Y2	Year 3 12/31/Y3	Year 4 12/31/Y4	Year T = 5 12/31/Y5	Year T + 1 12/31/Y6	Assumptions
Cash and Equivalents:								
Required Cash	$23,000	$24,840	$30,685	$40,036	$55,525	$79,181	$85,479	
Surplus or Excess Cash	6,487	71,379	93,318	110,739	118,542	539,480	663,327	"Plug" figures
Total Cash and Equivalents	29,487	96,219	124,003	150,775	174,066	618,661	748,806	
Accounts Receivable	46,000	46,000	56,824	74,141	102,824	146,632	158,294	Grows with sales
Merchandise Inventory	97,520	82,800	102,282	133,454	185,082	263,937	284,929	Grows with sales
Prepaid Insurance	2,300	2,300	2,841	3,707	5,141	7,332	7,915	Grows with sales
Total Current Assets	175,307	227,319	285,950	362,078	467,113	1,036,562	1,199,944	
Property, Plant, and Equipment:								
Equipment, Fixtures, and Other	92,000	102,140	123,030	154,182	203,072	276,335	311,991	Increases by CAPEX
Less (Accumulated Depreciation)	(34,040)	(39,836)	(46,066)	(53,763)	(63,805)	(77,731)	(97,592)	Incr. by depr. exp.
Net Property, Plant, and Equipment	57,960	62,304	76,964	100,419	139,268	198,603	214,399	Grows with sales
Total Assets	$233,267	$289,623	$362,914	$462,497	$606,381	$1,235,165	$1,414,343	
Current Liabilities:								
Accounts Payable	33,810	41,400	51,141	66,727	92,541	131,969	142,465	Grows with sales
Accrued Wages and Commissions	11,500	11,500	14,206	18,535	25,706	36,658	39,574	Grows with sales
Total Current Liabilities	45,310	52,900	65,347	85,262	118,247	168,627	182,038	
Long-Term Debt	0	0	0	0	0	420,000	445,200	
Shareholders' Equity	187,957	236,723	297,567	377,235	488,134	646,538	787,105	
Total Liabilities and Shareholders' Equity	$233,267	$289,623	$362,914	$462,497	$606,381	$1,235,165	$1,414,343	

TABLE 17A1.6 PB Electronics, Inc.—Projected Cash Flow Statement

Projected Cash Flow Statement	Fcst Year 1	Fcst Year 2	Fcst Year 3	Fcst Year 4	Fcst T = 5	Fcst T + 1 = 6
All amounts are in U.S. dollars						
Cash Flows from Activities:						
Net Income	$48,766	$60,844	$79,668	$110,899	$158,404	$140,566
Adjustments to Net Income for Cash Flow:						
Add: Depreciation Expense	5,796	6,230	7,696	10,042	13,927	19,860
Change in Prepaid Insurance	0	(541)	(866)	(1,434)	(2,190)	(583)
Change in Accrued Liabilities	0	2,706	4,329	7,171	10,952	2,916
Change in Inventory	14,720	(19,482)	(31,172)	(51,628)	(78,855)	(20,992)
Change in Accounts Payable	7,590	9,741	15,586	25,814	39,427	10,496
Change in Accounts Receivable	0	(10,824)	(17,318)	(28,682)	(43,808)	(11,662)
Change in Deferred Taxes	0	0	0	0	0	0
Total Adjustments	28,106	(12,170)	(21,744)	(38,718)	(60,547)	34
Net Cash Flow from Operations	*76,872*	*48,674*	*57,925*	*72,181*	*97,857*	*140,600*
Cash Flows from Investing:						
Less: (Capital Expenditures)	(10,140)	(20,890)	(31,152)	(48,890)	(73,262)	(35,656)
Net Cash Flow from Investing	*(10,140)*	*(20,890)*	*(31,152)*	*(48,890)*	*(73,262)*	*(35,656)*
Cash Flows from Financing:						
Less: (Dividends) Add: Equity Issues	0	0	0	0	0	0
Add: Debt Issues	0	0	0	0	420,000	25,200
Net Cash Flows from Financing	*0*	*0*	*0*	*0*	*420,000*	*25,200*
Net Change in Cash and Equivalents	66,731	27,784	26,773	23,291	444,595	130,145
Beginning Cash Balance	29,487	96,219	124,003	150,775	174,066	618,661
Ending Cash Balance	96,219	124,003	150,775	174,066	618,661	748,806

Valuation Using Market Multiples and Comparable Deal Transactions

In this chapter, we introduce the notion of an *economic balance sheet* and we show how it differs from the firm's *accounting balance sheet*. We demonstrate why the *book value* shown in a company's audited accounting statements is different from the company's *market value of the equity*. Then we turn to explore stock markets and their characteristics. We want to know how the market prices of shares are determined. We explain how large-volume traders—by their buying and selling of shares—create that day's market price for a firm's equity shares. This market price may or may not be equal to the firm's fundamental value or intrinsic value that we learned how to derive in Chapter 17. If buyers discover a favorable price discrepancy between the intrinsic value and the market price, it means they have found a potential bargain in the marketplace. Another way to value businesses is by using various market multiples and key financial ratios; we show you how to compute the most important ones. Practitioners use market multiples, financial ratios, and the information from comparable transactions (deals) as a way to capture market sentiment (boom or gloom) and bring it into the pricing picture. Feeling the pulse of the market is important for negotiating the best price for any transaction. Multiples are widely used by financial advisors for valuing merger and acquisition (M&A) targets, private equity sales, and corporate restructurings. They also are used in valuing joint ventures, strategic alliances, or transfers of intellectual property (IP). As with all financial tools and techniques, multiples may be correctly applied or misapplied. We offer guidance on how to avoid the most common pitfalls. We close the chapter by giving a practical example of how to use market information to compute the *technology value* of comparable biotechnology ventures.

ENTERPRISE VALUE OF THE FIRM IS A MARKET VALUE

As in physics, the principle of conservation of mass holds in finance. We learned from Chapter 17 that the enterprise value equals the market value of the total business enterprise. It is defined to be the sum of the parts: the market value of the shareholders' equity holdings, plus the market value of the debtor's holding, less any "excess cash" that could be returned to shareholders in the form of dividends, as shown in the following expression.

$$Enterprise\ Value = \left(\begin{array}{c} Market\ Value \\ of\ Equity \end{array}\right) + \left(\begin{array}{c} Market\ Value \\ of\ Debt \end{array}\right) - \left(\begin{array}{c} Excess \\ Cash \end{array}\right)$$

In symbols, the equation may be written as:

$$EV = E + D - C$$

where EV = enterprise value or the market value of the firm's total assets
  E = market value of firm's shareholders' equity
  D = market value of the debt holdings or liabilities
  C = surplus or excess cash (cash that is not needed for the day-to-day running of the business)

Figure 18.1 presents a graphical depiction of the market value of the enterprise. Observe that the parts are expressed as market values, *not* as accounting values or book values.

The market value of the equity (E) is defined to be the price per share of common shareholder stock, *fully diluted*, issued, and *outstanding*. It is computed simply by multiplying the current share price times the number of fully diluted, issued, and outstanding shares of common stock, where *fully diluted* means all stock options, warrants, convertible debt, and convertible preferred shares are fully converted into equivalent common shares. Treasury shares held by the firm are said to be issued, but they are *not* considered to be outstanding. Consequently, Treasury shares are excluded in calculating the market value of the equity.

Example: A company has 10 million common shares fully diluted, issued, and outstanding—so that all stock options have been converted and are included in the 10 million share count, but no Treasury shares are in the share count. About 40 percent of the common shares are listed and trading on a stock exchange for $25 per share. The market value of the equity (E) equals $25 per share × 10 million fully diluted, issued, and outstanding shares, or $250 million. The market value of equity is equivalent to the term *market capitalization*. Security analysts refer to a listed company's equity market capitalization as its *market cap*.

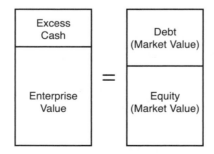

FIGURE 18.1   Enterprise Value of the Firm Is a *Market Value*

The market value of debt (D) is the value of any bonds and long-term debt securities. Listed debt should be *marked to market*, which means that the value for each tradable security has been determined using a current trading price in the financial markets. (It usually is done daily, but the frequency of marking to market depends on the type of financial instrument or derivative product being priced and why it is being done.)

Excess cash has the same meaning as it had in Chapter 17. It refers to monetary assets (cash or marketable securities) that are *not* needed in the day-to-day operations of the business or for capital expenditures. This "surplus cash" may be returned to shareholders in the form of dividends or may be used to repurchase shares. This excess cash should be deducted from our calculations. No investor will pay a premium for cash; neither will owners give away cash for less than it is worth.

Returning to the topic of the market value of debt, we note that not all types of corporate bonds trade readily, so it is sometimes difficult to obtain actual market prices by which to value corporate debt. Therefore, as we pointed out in the last chapter, practitioners doing valuations frequently assume that all long-term debt trades at prices that are about equal to the historical cost when purchased. In other words, the appraiser *assumes* the market value of the debt is equal to its book value. This assumption, most of the time, is tolerable. We do advise caution whenever low-quality bonds or other forms of distressed debt are trading at prices significantly below historical cost or book values—for example, when a firm has a low credit rating and risks defaulting on its debt. When a firm is highly leveraged—meaning the company has borrowed a lot of debt—and especially if has debt with a low-quality credit rating (also known as junk bonds), then the financial community will be concerned that the firm's cash flow may not be sufficient to meet future interest payments. Indeed, the value of such debt can suddenly plunge if market traders think a firm is heading toward default. In these special circumstances, the person doing the valuation needs to keep a watchful eye on actual debt market conditions.

PUTTING THE MONEY TO WORK IN THE BUSINESS

In this section, we explain the *accounting* definitions for a company's three main asset categories.

Net Working Capital in Accounting Terms

The accounting definition of *net working capital* (NWC) is simply current assets (CA) minus current liabilities (CL). The "net" means that the current liabilities are *subtracted* from, or netted against, the current assets. In symbols the formula is:

$$Net\ Working\ Capital\ (NWC) = CA - CL$$

Usually businesses need to have more current assets than current liabilities, so except for rare situations, net working capital is positive. Businesses also need to keep cash on hand to run operations smoothly. This cash is required in the business; therefore, it is not the surplus cash we discussed in the last chapter. Cash may be temporarily invested in short-term liquid investments or easily marketable securities such as Treasury bills, commercial paper, or certificates of deposit. Businesses typically extend credit to their customers (*accounts receivable*). In turn, many businesses are extended credit terms by their suppliers (*accounts payable*). Manufacturing businesses finance inventories (including raw materials, work in progress, and finished goods). We list items relevant to the working capital of businesses next.

Current assets include:

- Cash
- Short-term investments (marketable securities)
- Accounts receivables
- Inventories
- Any prepayments (e.g., office rent, or lease deposits)

Current liabilities include:

- Accounts payable
- Accrued wages and salaries
- The current portion of long-term debt (in other words, any payments due within one year)
- Other short-term debt (less than one year in term)
- Other accrued items, such as income taxes payable

Managers ought to be mindful that the accounting definition of net working capital is slightly different from the *investment in working capital* that we computed for determining free cash flow. Recall that in Chapter 17, for the enterprise valuation method, we defined investment in working capital as operating current assets minus *noninterest-bearing* current liabilities.[1]

Tangible Assets

The tangible assets are the things you can touch. The expression "go out and kick the tires" refers to the independent auditor inspecting the plant and equipment to verify that the physical assets are still in the possession of the company. Tangible assets are found under "plant, property, and equipment" in the balance sheet, often abbreviated as "PP&E." Property assets include land and any physical improvements to that land, such as water and sewer lines, sprinklers and fire protection systems, paving, fencing, and landscaping. Tangible assets may include these categories:

- Land
- Land improvements
- Office buildings, furniture, and office equipment
- Factory structures
- Machinery and machine tools, dies, molds, fixtures
- Laboratory facilities and lab equipment
- Storage units, chillers, coolers,
- Mechanical equipment, heating and ventilation systems
- Trucks, cars, other vehicles
- Construction still in progress

Intangible Assets, Intellectual Property, and Goodwill

Intangible assets include not only the intellectual property of the firm (its patents, copyrights, trademarks, and trade secrets as defined by law) but also the many intangible relationships of the firms and the contractual rights associated with the firm's IP assets. Goodwill, in everyday terms, can mean a person's kindly attitude, benevolence, or cheerful consent. In business, it is often considered to mean the value of a business's reputation over and above its tangible assets. In accounting terms, goodwill represents the difference between the purchase cost and the fair value of net assets acquired in business acquisitions.

Intangible assets lack physical substance (obviously you can't touch them or kick them like tires). Examples of intangible assets would be:

- Customer loyalty to a brand or to a group of practicing professionals, like in a dental, medical, consulting, or legal practice.
- Innovative proprietary processes for carrying out research and development (R&D).
- Employee devotion to the company's vision and mission.
- Firm's social standing in the community dating back for generations.
- Special distributor relationships (e.g., relations with specialized contractor supply houses).
- Company reputation: The firm is known to deal with its investors and stakeholders in an honest, reliable, and dependable way. The firm's management keeps its word and commitments. It delivers on its promises.
- Goodwill acquired through business acquisitions.

Most of a firm's intangible assets (*except* for the last item goodwill acquired through acquisitions) will *not* appear on the firm's accounting balance sheets because such items are not allowed either by U.S. Generally Accepted Accounting Principles (U.S. GAAP) or by International Financing Reporting Standards (IFRS). Hence for most healthy firms, the accounting balance sheet *underestimates* the economic worth of the firm. We explain this fundamental point more in the next section and illustrate it with several drawings to make the message clearer.

WHY ACCOUNTING VALUES ARE *NOT* THE SAME THING AS MARKET VALUES

Accounting values are not equal to market values nor are they the same thing as the economic or fundamental or intrinsic value of a business. The accounting profession is interested in the historical costs of the business. Accountants classify and account for items on the balance sheet quite differently from the way financial investors and managers tend to think about them.

Investors and managers are interested in the forward-looking economic prospects of the business and its ability to sustain earnings. Accountants tend to look backward at the costs. We think it helps to show this discrepancy with words and pictures because we know it is easy to get mixed up between book values and market values when using multiples.

The accounting view is captured in the fundamental definition of accounting, namely that the assets of the firm must always balance with the liabilities owed to creditors of the firm plus the funds provided by the shareholders in the firm. The fundamental accounting equation is

$$\text{Assets} = \text{Liabilities} + \text{Shareholders' Equity}$$

Liabilities represent the *claims* against the assets of the firm: debtors' claims as well as shareholders' claims. Shareholders' equity is on the liabilities side of the balance sheet, not the asset side. Shareholders' equity is a *residual* claim—meaning the investors in the company are the *last to be paid* from the sale of any assets. They may claim only what is left over after all the liabilities have been settled.

With few exceptions, nearly all items shown in the accounting books are recorded at their *historical costs* (in other words, at the prices when purchased). The balance sheet is like a snapshot or picture of the firm's financial position at a single point in time. The balance sheet is determined on a specific day of the year, usually at the end of each quarter or fiscal year.

Shareholders' equity or stockholders' equity as recorded in the balance sheet is equivalent to book value. Sometimes it is called the net worth or the owner's equity or simply the equity of the firm. Yet another label for the book value of the firm is net asset value. The net asset value means the accountant has subtracted the liabilities from the assets and calculated the total, which will always be equivalent to the shareholders' equity by definition. (Recall that subtraction in accounting is the netting of one term against another, hence net assets or net worth.)

Book value is usually *less* than what a viable concern is truly worth, sometimes a lot less, since historical costs do not reflect the future earnings capabilities of the business. As mentioned earlier, book value generally does not include such intangibles as the value of customer loyalty or an end user's affinity to a brand unless they have been acquired by purchasing another company at a premium. Goodwill is the difference between the acquisition price of a firm and the fair market value of its identifiable assets. Goodwill is accounted for as an asset on the balance sheet. A company's *self-created* intangible assets will *not* appear on its balance sheet, because intangibles arising from a firm's own organizational processes and management systems or its own R&D activities are *not allowed* by U.S. GAAP.[2]

For those readers interested in further details on the Financial Accounting Standards Board's *Statement of Financial Accounting Standards* (SFAS) No. 141(R) *Business Combinations* (Revised 2007) and SFAS No. 142 *Goodwill and Other Intangible Assets* (issued June 2001) log onto our web site (www.innovationtocashflows.com) and download the file Appendix 18.1, "Accounting for Goodwill and Intangible Assets."

Do not confuse the term *book value* with the market value of the shareholders' equity. The two are separate and distinct concepts. Figures 18.2 and 18.3 present the fundamental accounting relationship. Figure 18.4 presents the firm's economic balance sheet in the next section.

We can further subdivide the assets and liabilities of the firm into finer categories. On the assets side of the accounting statement, we have the current assets (cash and accounts receivable) plus the property plant and equipment, then any financial assets that the company owns (its investments in affiliated companies or minority

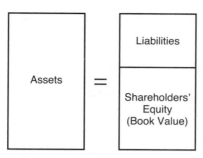

FIGURE 18.2 Fundamental Accounting Relationship

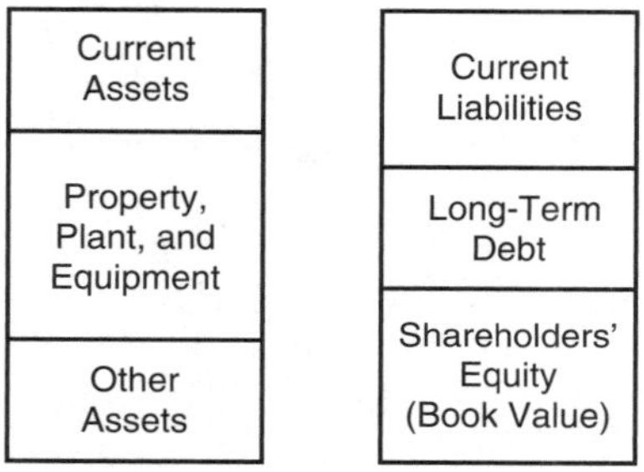

FIGURE 18.3 Accounting Balance Sheet of a Manufacturing Business

participations) or any deferred assets, such as assets under construction or any payments on account. On the liabilities side of the accounting statements, we show the current liabilities (to credit card companies or banks, trade creditors), longer-term debts (loans from banks, longer-term trade credits, finance leases), provisions for pensions or similar legal obligations, provisions for taxes, other reserves, then the subscribed equity capital, legal reserves, and retained profits accounts. The main categories are summarized in Figure 18.3.

ECONOMIC BALANCE SHEET REFLECTS THE CAPITAL MARKET'S VIEW

To a potential investor in a business, the audited balance sheet statements are only a starting point for conducting a proper valuation. They are but one small part of the rich mosaic of information that professionals use to form an appraisal of a business. The market value of a business is captured in its *economic* balance sheet, not the *accounting* balance sheet. An economic balance sheet of a listed company will reflect the views of the traders in the equity markets about the enterprise and its future prospects.

As you saw in prior chapters and as a theme throughout this book, entrepreneurs and investors are keenly interested in understanding the future prospects of a business. They are searching for the answers to these types of forward-looking questions:

- What are the prospects for profitable growth in the industry?
- How robust and scalable is the firm's business model?
- How capable is management at creating value on a sustainable ongoing basis?
- Would they be good alliance partners for our company? Should we make a deal with them?
- What is the competition doing?

We may write an algebraic expression for the economic balance sheet of the firm as being made up of these components:

$$\begin{pmatrix} \text{Value of the} \\ \text{Enterprise} \end{pmatrix} = \begin{pmatrix} \text{Net Working} \\ \text{Capital} \end{pmatrix} + \begin{pmatrix} \text{Tangible} \\ \text{Assets} \end{pmatrix} + (\text{Intangible Assets})$$

Figure 18.4 draws an economic balance sheet. In the depicted economic balance sheet, the total assets are "marked to market" (expressed at market prices, not at historical costs). The items inside the solid lines are what would be recorded on a historical cost basis according to accounting standards. The extended area (in dotted lines) at the bottom indicate: (1) the additional value the market is giving to the intangible assets of the firm that are not recorded in the accounting statements, (2) the additional value that some fixed assets have gained over time from when they were originally purchased (e.g., the value of land or buildings carried at historical cost might be worth more today than when purchased 25 years ago), and (3) any deviations in working capital due to historical accounting versus economic portrayal of the balance sheet.

In Figure 18.4, we are graphically doing what financial analysts call summing up the market value of the assets. The increase in value attributed by the capital markets to this firm's intangible assets is reflected in the right-hand side of the economic balance sheet under the market value of shareholders' equity. This box is

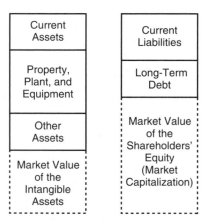

FIGURE 18.4 Economic Balance Sheet of a Manufacturing Firm

much larger than the one on the accounting balance sheet, which is shown as the book value (accounting value) of the equity.

The providers of capital consider the value of the enterprise as being the sum of the market value of the debt and the market value of the equity. These bankers and equity investors, like the entrepreneurs they are backing, look forward in time to envision the prospects for the firm. They think the company is worth far more than the accounting statements show.

FINANCING THE BUSINESS: THE PECKING ORDER OF FINANCE

We pause for a brief aside to discuss for a moment topics relevant to financing the business. In a henhouse, the rooster maintains law and order by pecking at his rivals and at the hens. They line up behind him with the strongest closest to him and the weakest at the tail. Similarly, there is a pecking order of finance, where the various costs of financing may be arrayed not by strength but by their riskiness—with the safest and least risky at the bottom of the pyramid (the risk-free rate or government Treasury bills) and the most expensive and highest risk at the top (equity financing and then venture funds). Refer to Figure 18.5.

In every business, there is a continuum of financing needs which the chief financial officer (CFO) must try to match against the various market providers of capital. The idea is to match the asset to be financed to its appropriate source of financing so as to create a balanced "capital structure" for the firm, where ideally there is not too much debt nor too much equity, but just the right amount of each to optimize risk and return for all the firm's shareholders and debtors. According to Professor

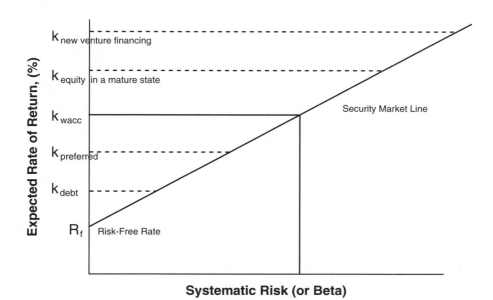

FIGURE 18.5 Pecking Order of Finance

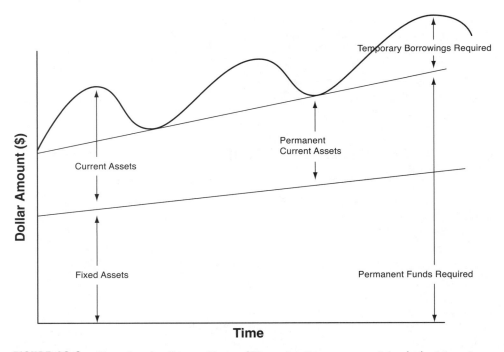

FIGURE 18.6 Choosing the Correct Type of Financing Instrument to Match the Maturity of the Asset
Source: James C. Van Horne, *Financial Management and Policy*, 12th edition, Copyright © 2002 (Upper Saddle River, NJ: Pearson Education, Inc., 2002), 485. Adapted by permission of Pearson Education, Inc.

James C. Van Horne, normally a firm uses "short-term debt to finance seasonal variations in current assets" and uses long-term debt or equity (permanent capital) "to finance the permanent component of current assets."[3] A typical financing policy for a firm is illustrated in Figure 18.6.

A firm that wishes to pursue sound financial policies should strive to match the maturity of the asset with the maturity of the financing instrument. The three basic principles are to:

1. Finance current assets with current liabilities to the greatest extent possible with short-term funding needs (e.g., seasonal changes in working capital) financed by short-term loans and credit facilities.
2. Finance riskier tangible assets that have longer lives, such as plant, property, and equipment, with longer-term debt instruments. Avoid using short-term debt to match long-term capital expenditures; instead, try to match like for like, so fund short-term assets with short-term liabilities and longer-term assets with longer-term debt. Assets such as property, plant, and equipment, are less liquid than current assets; therefore, they are harder to dispose of, if trouble should arise, and thus, they pose higher risks to lenders. These types of longer-lived, less-liquid assets are usually financed by issuing longer-term debt securities, such

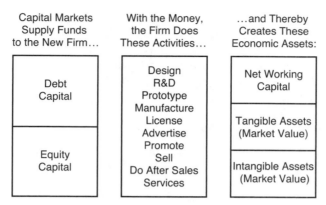

Capital Markets Supply Funds to the New Firm...	With the Money, the Firm Does These Activities...	...and Thereby Creates These Economic Assets:
Debt Capital	Design R&D Prototype Manufacture License Advertise Promote Sell Do After Sales Services	Net Working Capital
Equity Capital		Tangible Assets (Market Value)
		Intangible Assets (Market Value)

FIGURE 18.7   Financing the Economic Value Creation Process of the Firm

as corporate bonds or other types of asset-backed security instruments. As the name suggests, these debt instruments are secured with the collateral of the tangible asset (much like homeowners finance the mortgage of their homes by taking out a home loan backed with the collateral of the home). Long-term capital expenditure building programs and major investment projects should be funded either by long-term debt or by an equity issue, depending on the type of business.

3. Finance the very riskiest intangible assets, such as proprietary R&D, techno-logical know-how, and other intangibles (patents, trademarks, brand loyalty, and company reputation, which can take years to build up and only a single catastrophic event to destroy) with permanent equity capital provided by the shareholders of the firm. The least liquid assets of the firm are its intangible assets (its reputation, brand image), including its IP (patents, trademarks, and copyrights) and the rights associated with the IP. The market for buying and selling IP is thin, narrow, and illiquid. Therefore, assets of this nature are the riskiest and should be financed by the equity shareholders of the firm.

A firm raises money from private investors and from the public capital markets. The money is put to work to financing current operations by supplying funds for working capital and investing in the future through long-term capital expenditures, and funding R&D. The goal of the firm is to create long-term economic value for the company's shareholders and other stakeholders. We depict a firm's sources and uses of funds and the value creation process in Figure 18.7.

IMPORTANT CHARACTERISTICS OF EQUITY MARKETS

Having surveyed key topics in accounting, finance, and capital structure, we now turn to equity markets and discuss some of their important characteristics. We examine stock market mechanics briefly, look at how trading takes place, and make a few pertinent observations about investor behavior.

A stock exchange is a regulated, public marketplace for buying and selling company shares. In a stock exchange, the dealers' bid and ask prices are posted. The *bid-ask spread* is the amount by which the ask price exceeds the bid price. (A seller typically wants more money than the buyer is willing to pay.) What this means is that if you are buying a stock, you must pay the dealer's ask price (the higher price); if you are selling a stock, you receive the dealer's bid price (the lower price).

Who Keeps the Bid-Ask Spread?

The middleman or "market maker" keeps the bid-ask spread. The bid-ask spread is the market maker's reward for taking the risk of providing *liquidity* to the market when others are afraid to trade.

On the NASDAQ, the middleman is called a "broker-dealer" whereas on the NYSE, the dealer is called a "market specialist." On the NYSE, the market specialist is given a special monopoly position to make a market for a particular stock, but in return for that privilege, the NYSE regulations require that the specialist maintain a "fair and orderly market" for trading the shares.

In any market, there are suppliers of liquidity and there are demanders of liquidity. The buyer who wants to immediately purchase a share of stock can place a "market" order. The person who is willing to wait until the price reaches his or her target price can place a "limit" order. Such an order is completed only when the share hits the target price and there are enough shares to fill the order. Such a limit order can take a much longer time to fill than a market order.

A trade is made when a buyer and a seller agree on a price. The trade is "cleared" when the terms of the trade are verified. It is "settled" when the buyer's money is transferred to the seller's account in exchange for the shares.

Most stock exchanges make money by selling real-time data feeds of stock prices to various customers, such as the major brokerages, investment houses, and, of course, service providers such as Bloomberg or Thomson Reuters. These providers then transmit the latest stock prices to interested investors and speculators all around the world.

WHO SETS THE MARKET PRICE OF A STOCK?

As we have said, the *market capitalization* (or market cap or market value) of a listed firm's equity is the value of the firm's equity as determined by the *consensus view* of the traders in the equity market. In truth, the price is set by the marginal trader, that is, the last one who was willing to buy the company's shares.

The largest and most active marginal traders have the most weight in the market consensus. These are major institutional funds managed by professionals. These well-informed and large investors are nicknamed the lead steers; they are the investors who steer the prices in the market.

These large institutional funds buy and sell huge volumes of shares (tens of thousands of shares at a time), as opposed to the small retail customer buying and selling perhaps only hundreds of shares.

Prime examples of lead steers are actively managed mutual funds, momentum funds, and certain types of hedge funds. The trades of the lead steers are often imitated or followed by less sophisticated traders, the so-called noise traders and the uninformed traders. Passive index funds and less active funds (such as pension funds) tend not to be the ones who set the market prices, since they are not actively trading the shares in their portfolios.

The *market value* of a stock is therefore a reflection of the price perceived and acted on by a willing buyer and a willing seller, neither under compulsion to do the trade, and each having full knowledge (disclosure) of the relevant facts. The exchange of shares on the exchange ought to be done on *fair terms* to both sides. (Some of the reasons why stock exchanges are regulated are to prevent fraud and manipulation of stock prices and to enforce full disclosure of relevant information in a timely way.) The point is that the market value is an agreed-on exchange value—which a buyer is *willing* to give and a seller *willing* to take without coercion.

A *deep market* for a stock is characterized by many traders buying and selling large quantities of stock. A thinly traded or illiquid security issue does not have many traders.

Free float refers to the quantity of shares that may be freely bought or sold for a particular stock issue. Free float does not include shares held by insiders, any strategic (long-term) investors, company founders, or large institutional blocks of stocks. Also excluded from free float are restricted stocks (shares that cannot be sold right away).

In many countries, it is not unusual for family businesses to float only a small percentage of their shares on the stock market. The rest remains in the hands of the controlling shareholders. Such stock would have a low percentage of free float.

Finally, the *depth* of a stock market refers to the amount of shares available and the number of interested buyers and sellers. A liquid market is the best for price discovery. (*Price discovery* is the process whereby buyers and sellers trading in a market incorporate new information into stock prices.) A thin market with a low amount of free float tends to be less efficient.

Market Behavior

A dedicated and habitual clothes shopper will claim that he knows when he runs across a good buy. Say, for example, that the object to be purchased is a cashmere sweater. We agree that a habitual shopper—someone who regularly goes to the bazaar or the mall—most likely will know the difference between the offering price in the market and the true worth of that sweater—he will know if he has spotted indeed a bargain or not. Afterward, he may brag to his friends how much he has saved by buying it. In his head, he can calculate the margin of safety on the sweater and tell you (the friend) how much it was underpriced compared to what he considers to be the average price of the same sweater elsewhere. He will make his calculations based on the *relative prices* of similar sweaters in the bazaar and shops he frequents. Note that not all shoppers, either casual or habitual, will share the same opinion.

An experienced, professional cashmere sweater buyer would take a slightly different approach. He would be someone who gets paid to go every day to many different bazaars, in many different locations, around the world. This professional buyer, call him an appraiser, would diligently calculate the cost of raw materials and labor involved in making the sweater. He would have an eye for a particularly striking design or outstanding fit and would know how much extra or premium could be charged for these finishes for various types of clientele. He also would know the margins required for the people involved in selling and distributing the products. The appraiser would have a professional's edge over our habitual shopper who is relying on "relative" prices in merely one bazaar and local stores to make up his view on what is a bargain or not. Our professional appraiser has access to a much richer and deeper set of information than our habitual shopper. The appraiser conducts worldwide searches and therefore has a more global view of the fundamentals affecting cashmere sweater prices.

Of course, over the long term, the performance of the habitual shopper will beat our inexperienced occasional buyer who buys whatever looks like a cashmere sweater at the going market price. The moral of our story is that the professional appraiser is in a far better position than either the habitual shopper or the occasional buyer when it comes to understanding the intrinsic value of cashmere sweaters.

The same situation applies when buying a home, a car, and a company's shares. Sometimes the market price is exaggerated compared to what the item "should" cost.

History books are replete with stories of famous cases where market prices went awry, such as the Tulipomania (seventeenth-century Holland) or the South Sea Bubble (eighteenth-century England).[4] More recently, the dot-com bubble affected many traders around the world, particularly those heavily speculating on TMT (telecom, media, and technology stocks). The Internet frenzy started around 1995–1996 and lasted until about 2001. (Many would say it peaked on March 10, 2000, when the NASDAQ hit 5,132 and then started falling.)

In the global financial crisis of 2007–2009, the value of global stock markets shrank by $30 trillion as of November 22, 2008, or about half their value before the crash.[5] The Dow Jones Industrial Average, which was trading around 13,000 late in 2007, fell to a trading range of 8,000 to 9,000 by the third quarter of 2008. The global real estate bubble of 2001–2007 started bursting with the subprime mortgage crisis in the United States and the cooling down of real estate speculation in England, Spain, and elsewhere. As the subprime mortgage contagion spread, customers began to lose confidence. Customers queued up to take out their deposits at Indy Mac (closed July 11, 2007). The bank run on Northern Rock (September 14, 2007) was the first run on a British bank in over a century. (Northern Rock was eventually nationalized on February 22, 2008.) The U.S. government placed Freddie Mac and Fannie Mae into conservatorship under the Federal Housing Finance Agency on September 11, 2008. Mortgage lender Washington Mutual failed shortly after on September 25, 2008.

During August to November 2008, credit markets all but dried up from the heavy losses of banks and others, not only in mortgage-backed securities but also in credit derivatives, especially collateralized debt obligations (CDOs), and credit default swaps. Banks stopped lending to each other in the interbank market. The Federal Reserve pumped billions of liquidity into the credit markets and rescued Wall Street investment bank Bear Stearns by its sale to JPMorgan Chase. Lehman Brothers, however, the Federal Reserve allowed to collapse. Merrill Lynch preemptively sold itself to Bank of America. Goldman Sachs and Morgan Stanley turned themselves into commercial bank holding companies. The era of the all-powerful "bulge bracket" Wall Street investment bank was over.

As the panic spread, the U.S. government took over insurance giant AIG in exchange for rescue funding from the Fed. Over 300 banks and mortgage-related institutions went into receivership. Others were saved from collapse, such as the merger between troubled U.S. commercial bank Wachovia and Wells Fargo in October, 2008.

Meanwhile, in Europe, Iceland experienced a complete banking sector meltdown while Belgian-Dutch bank Fortis ran aground. Numerous global banking giants were humbled and sought to raise additional shareholder equity, ranging from UBS to Citigroup to Banco Santander. As we go to press, the depth and extent of the global recession is being widely debated in the media.

At Times, Markets Are Driven by Crowd Behavior Why do market bubbles keep occurring? Market behavior has been the subject of intense scrutiny by many authors and noted scholars. A favorite book of ours is by the French author Gustave Le Bon (1841–1931), who wrote *A Study of the Popular Mind*, an investing classic. Because of human nature, markets will tend to overreact either positively (when the crowd is feeling greedy) or negatively (when the crowd is feeling fearful). At times, markets are driven by contagion and crowd psychology. Crowds are susceptible to being influenced and subject to "rapid turning of the sentiments."[6] In any market where prices are driven higher and higher (or lower and lower) by participants trading in them, players may be susceptible to contagion. In general, people making trades based on relative prices are more vulnerable to emotional reactions than people making long-term investment decisions based on fundamental valuations and reason.

Going back to our previous story, if our habitual shopper shops only in downtown Milan or London or Paris and only sees these "luxury" store prices, he may not realize that what appears to him to be a bargain is actually a lot more expensive than what it would cost him in a shop located in a less expensive neighborhood. That is why our "sophisticated" expert shopper, unlike the habitual shopper, scans far and wide for bargains. He calculates values based on his fundamental analysis and global analysis, not just relative prices. By doing so, he strives to discover independently what should be a fair price of a cashmere sweater and does not rely on the opinion of the people at the local bazaar trying to sell him the goods.

Most appraisers are specialists, valuing only what they consider to be within their range of expertise. Being an appraiser and doing appraisals properly requires dedication, training, time, and skill. Relative valuation is usually quicker and costs less to do than fundamental analysis, but always be mindful that relative valuations may be subject to bias and to market bubbles that skew prices too high or too low.

The Market for Buying and Selling Private Companies

We have been talking mainly about traders on stock exchanges buying and selling shares on behalf of institutional investors. Privately held firms are bought and sold off the stock exchange. Small businesses may be bought and sold directly, without the help of a business broker or investment bank, although such direct sales, without intermediaries, are unusual. Larger firms invariably rely on expert advice and assistance, especially regarding complex tax, legal, and accounting matters. Different parts of a business may be sold:

- The firm's entire assets (or pieces of them)
- Only the firm's equity shares
- Only the firm's debts

MEASURES OF VALUE USED IN APPRAISALS UNDER A VARIETY OF CIRCUMSTANCES

In this section, we aim to clarify the meaning of various words, all of which are used to describe a firm's "value" under differing conditions. We want to examine how the value of a company changes when it is being bought and sold in a public market versus a private sale and examine why the value of a liquidated company is so much lower than the value of a company that is up and operating (a "going concern"). Each of these terms is explained in the next paragraphs.

Meaning of *Fair Market Value* in a Private Transaction

If a company is privately held, then no stock market price is available, as the company does not trade on a stock exchange. In such cases, the *fair market value* of the firm's assets would be the price that a willing buyer and seller agree on in an arm's-length transaction (an independent transaction carried out without coercion, and where the parties act fairly and prudently while having full knowledge of all relevant facts and information).[7]

In private market settings, price discovery is slower—it takes more time for buyers and sellers to discover each other and to learn at which price the other party is willing to start the bargaining process. These private equity markets are less efficient than public equity markets because they are less transparent and less regulated, and price discovery is much slower. In these markets, liquidity discounts become much more relevant and important when negotiating a bid-or-ask price for a firm.

The *private placement* market is an important source of financing for certain types of fast-growing smaller companies that need to raise a late round of financing before listing on an exchange. Privately held companies may raise expansion capital by offering for sale new issues of either debt, or equity, or some combination of debt and equity securities to qualified sophisticated investors. (Under U.S. Securities and Exchange Commission [SEC] Rule 501, Regulation D, *sophisticated investors* are high-net-wealth or high-net-income individuals and qualified institutional investors.) In the United States, private placements do not have to be registered with the SEC and require only a private placement memorandum as opposed to an offering prospectus. Disclosure requirements are less stringent than for a full initial public offering (IPO). Private placements can be attractive for companies that qualify for them, because they are quicker to do, cost less than venture capital, and have less onerous reporting burdens than for a full public offering. However, private placements are not for early-stage ventures or start-up companies.

Venture capitalists do invest in very-early-stage companies and therefore experience a large number of investment failures. They also run the risk of having their firm's money tied up for long periods. To compensate them for these risks of not being able to exit an investment, venture capitalists charge more for supplying financing to ventures. In other words, their opportunity cost of funds will need to take into account the lack of timely exit. (We discuss more about the venture capital approach to valuation and the reasons why venture capitalists require such high returns for their funds in Chapter 19.)

Liquidation Value

The *liquidation value* of the firm is the bargain-basement or fire-sale price of a firm that is no longer in business. In a *liquidation sale,* the bankrupt firm is under court order to put up its assets for sale. The sale can be carried out either as an auction (in other words, the assets sold to the highest bidder) or else as a negotiated sale of the entire firm to creditors. With the asset sale proceeds, the firm must pay off all outstanding debts and other liabilities owed to creditors. If there is not enough money to pay off all the liabilities, the shareholders will receive nothing. If any funds are left over, they will be paid out as a final dividend to the equity shareholders. Then the firm will be dissolved.

Going-Concern Value

The *going-concern value* is how much a firm is worth when it is up and running, meaning the firm has a trained workforce, an operating plant, and the necessary permits, licenses, utilities, procedures, and management information systems working. The business is purchasing from its suppliers, satisfying customers, paying its bills, and is operational. Typically the going-concern value will be higher than the book or accounting value, because it includes intangibles such as community and employee relationships.

Replacement Cost

The *replacement cost* is what it would cost (in current dollars or other currencies) to replace comparable plant and equipment today. Replacement cost is usually higher than historical cost because of inflation; however, this may not always be true. Sometimes it is lower, due to economies of scale and other productivity gains from improvements in workforce processes and better procedures (learning effects). For instance, replacing an old computer will be cheaper today than it was five years ago—assuming the same performance and memory features—because of economies of scale and competition, which drive the cost of hardware down. However, customers are also likely to spend the same or even more, as they upgrade their equipment to take advantage of new benefits. The replacement cost should therefore be the cost to replace *comparable* plant and equipment but not upgraded versions. It would exclude the costs related to unsuccessful or inefficient product prototypes.

Replication Costs

Replication costs would be the funds required (in current cost terms) to redevelop and reproduce a process, patent, or other R&D project in exactly the same way as the original and to the same quality standards. Replication costs ought to include all expenses required to duplicate a process in its entirety, including the mistakes, such as the creation and testing of early prototypes that do not work out.

RELATIVE VALUATION BY COMPARING SIMILAR COMPANIES AND TRANSACTIONS

In this section, we explore how you as an entrepreneur may use the information embedded in public equity markets to help you value your high-technology company. We do this valuation two ways. First, we compare your company to other similar companies trading in the public equity markets (using market multiples). Then we compare your firm to other companies recently bought and sold in the mergers and acquisitions (M&A) market for corporate control (using transactions data).

Carrying out relative valuations based on multiples is a methodology that is frequently used by professionals who value companies for a living. Any investment banker working in M&A or corporate finance, and any professional security analyst who works either on the sell side (for security brokerage firms) or on the buy side (for hedge funds, pension funds, mutual funds) will use different sorts of multiples to value different kinds of businesses. Each industry tends to have its own favorite set of multiples that people commonly use to value companies operating in that sector. It is a quick way of communicating relative values among professionals.

Investment bankers and security analysts usually value publicly trading equities or are valuing a business which is mature enough to take public in an IPO. They are experts at valuing public companies.

Venture capitalists and private equity investors value privately held businesses for a living. They are attuned to the problems of valuing high-technology ventures that are still emerging from their nascent states. They are experts at valuing private businesses.

Valuing publicly trading companies in well-developed capital markets using multiples is easier than valuing privately held companies. There is simply more information and data available for public companies than for private companies. The information asymmetries are smaller and the discounts for illiquidity are smaller and more easily quantified. The problems of relative valuations for emerging technology firms are tricky because of a lack of comparable companies. It gets even harder if these emerging technology firms are in less developed capital markets, where lack of data is a huge problem. But let us not get too far ahead of ourselves. First, we solve the easy problems, and then we suggest resources to tackle the harder ones.

Basic Principles of Relative Valuation

The basic idea behind relative valuation is for you (the appraiser) to identify a sample of companies that have similar characteristics to the firm you are attempting to value (the target company). The idea is to compare apples to apples. Once the set of comparable firms is identified, then various financial ratios or multiples are computed for each of the benchmark or proxy companies (e.g., price-to-earnings ratio, market-to-book ratio, etc.) and combined. The results are used to value the target company.

Whenever you construct ratios or multiples, the basic principle is to strive for internal consistency. If the measure you are seeking relates to the total assets of the firm, use an enterprise value and some sort of free cash flow or total sales figure as a ratio or multiple. If the measure relates to the equity shareholders of the firm, use an equity market value and a net income figure (the income pertaining to shareholders after the interest charges have been paid).

Sometimes you will hear brokers talk about trading multiples. A *trading multiple* is nothing more than a ratio derived from stock market data, such as a company's current share price, as opposed to a ratio constructed purely from accounting data or historical information (like a return on equity ratio). If no market data are involved in the derivation of the ratio, then it is an accounting ratio. If stock market pricing data are involved, it is a trading ratio or trading multiple.

Basic Principles of Comparable Transactions

In the *comparable transactions* approach, you are going to compare the target deal to other comparable deals. The first thing to figure out is why the transaction is being contemplated. Always ask: What is the purpose of the deal?

Once you ascertain the purpose, you need to develop a set of search criteria. After doing so, you then determine what sort of databases and other fundamental or economic data you need to access and which ones can you afford to use. Then you set to work and search for as many relevant and comparable deals as you can that fit your criteria, given time and budget constraints.

The principle is always to compare apples to apples and oranges to oranges, so compare venture capital deals to other venture capital deals; M&A deals to M&A deals; leveraged buyouts (LBOs) to LBOs; IPOs to other IPOs. For instance, the purpose of the valuation exercise might be appraise the value of a target company that is being pursued for M&A purposes, but there could also be other motivations, such as conducting a spin-out or spin-off, settling litigation disputes, or determining the costs of bankruptcy. Each appraisal is for a different type of transaction. The prices for one type of deal, say, divestitures, are not comparable to another, such as bankruptcies.

Transactions may also refer to the deal terms for licensing agreements, joint ventures, or other forms of strategic alliances. For instance, IP appraisers search for comparable licensing deals to get a general idea of average royalty rate percentages for a particular industry sector or type of patent. In another search, they might be seeking transactions involving particular consumer brands for valuing a trademark.

As another example, venture capitalists look to see how other venture capitalist funds are pricing deals based on a comparison of recent exit multiples, such as when private companies are sold to trade buyers or are taken public in an IPO. These market multiples are then incorporated into their own exit price valuations. (We explain the venture capital technique in Chapter 19.)

Transactions may be carried out in all sorts of markets: trading stakes in the public stock markets; purchasing majority control of a company in the private market for corporate control; buying and selling minority stakes of companies in the private placement market, where, as we mentioned earlier, companies are bought and sold privately between investors and not traded on a regulated stock exchange. The more transparent and public the market, the more information and details will be revealed about the transaction.

Valuing companies by multiples is considered to be a top-down or macro-view assessment of value. This top-down approach differs from a detailed bottom-up methodology, which we employed in Chapter 17, when we learned about discounted cash flow techniques. In a bottom-up valuation, the appraiser scrutinizes fundamental data and competitor market information, and uses past accounting statements and other financial data to make forecasts and projections of sales, earnings, and cash flow forecasts.

Comparable trading multiples or comparable transactions are *relative valuation* approaches—one company is compared relative to another company or one deal to another (one tulip to another tulip)—of *absolute value* or fundamental value techniques like discounted cash flow. Any relative valuation technique is susceptible to the biases we pointed out earlier, namely of crowd effects and bubbles. We discuss more advantages and disadvantages to this approach next.

Advantages and Disadvantages of Relative Valuation Approaches

We have discussed where relative valuation multiple approaches are widely used by venture capitalists, small-business brokerage firms, M&A specialists, business strategy consultancies, and other types of corporate finance investment bankers to gauge market sentiment. It is vital to bring information about the current state or mood of the capital markets into the valuation process when advising buyers or sellers.

The advantages of multiples are that they are:

- Simple
- Easy to do
- Easy to explain
- Quick
- Good at capturing the sentiment of investors at a snapshot in time

The disadvantages of using relative valuation techniques are also numerous:

- *Biases attributable to market crowd behavior.* Any relative valuation technique is susceptible to the behavioral biases we pointed out earlier, especially those of contagion, loss of perspective, and the influence of periodic market bubbles or crashes on relative price levels.
- *Tendency to compare apples to oranges, not apples to apples.* Finding comparable companies or transactions may require access to proprietary databases, such as those in Bloomberg's or Thomson Reuters. (We describe commercial databases in Chapter 15 and also list others on our web site. Log onto the site www.innovationtocashflows.com and go to "Resources—Proprietary Deal Databases and Company Information.") Sometimes entrepreneurs or financial analysts working for small firms do not have access to these state-of-the-art search tools; or they do not have the money to pay for such services. Another problem is that the databases might not cover emerging new technologies and innovative discoveries.
- *Insufficient sample sizes.* The greatest difficulty with the relative valuation methodology, particularly for biotechnology firms, is that the proprietary technologies being compared are often unique. Hence it is difficult (if not impossible) to find true peer comparables. This is especially a problem in one-of-a-kind biotechnology platform technology companies (called research tool companies

by some analysts) or other specialized medical diagnostic equipment manu-facturers. The firms may be the pioneers in discovering a certain therapeutic compound or in their approach to doing research or the design of a diagnostic device. To be considered a peer, the technology firms being compared should be based on similar technology or therapeutic treatment area. They should have similar business models. They also should have roughly similar R&D focus, be in a similar stage of clinical trials, and have roughly equivalent product pipelines. Of course, in the real world, it is difficult to meet all these criteria simultane-ously. In biotechnology, the sample size may consist of *at most* one to three peer comparables.

- *Problems with cross-border comparisons.* Ideally the comparisons should be carried out on firms trading in the same geographic stock market, in other words, all the peers should be trading in U.S. stock markets, or on the Tokyo stock market or London Stock Exchange. Many times, however, cross-border comparisons are the only alternatives, especially for very specialized technol-ogy companies with sample sizes, perhaps in the ones, twos, or threes. In any cross-border comparisons, the analyst must make careful adjustments for differ-ences in local accounting practices and other factors, to avoid making erroneous comparisons.

- *Survival bias.* Typically larger and more mature biopharmaceutical firms make it through to the IPO stage. When used for early-stage drug development firms, trading multiples need to be adjusted for the size of the firm, the quality of the product pipeline, and stage of clinical trials.

- *Lack of free float.* If you are lucky and find a comparable market "proxy" firm, you still might face the problem that the comparable company shares lack liquidity. This means the shares trade in a thin market and do not have much free float. Under these circumstances, the market prices may be somewhat suspect. This can be a particular problem when the company is still tightly controlled and only a small portion of the shares have been floated. These shares may have "lock-ups," meaning the institutional investors or founder or other insiders owning these shares cannot sell them for a certain number of months after the IPO. When they finally are allowed to sell, blocks of shares may come onto the market, create volatility, exaggerate price movements, and distort price information. Brokers always worry that large blocks of shares may have a noticeable market impact (up or down) on share pricing.

- *Failure to adjust for differences in time.* As we said earlier, markets do experience investor contagion. Market sentiment, or mood, may change swiftly from time to time. It makes no sense to compare multiples belonging to a different time period unless corrections have been made to account for this distortion. Nevertheless, sometimes these adjustments are not done, because of a lack of time or data or inexperience.

TYPICAL RATIOS AND MULTIPLES USED IN RELATIVE VALUATION

Over time, each industry develops its own shortcuts for valuing and comparing firms using multiples and ratios. These shortcut methods evolve through business practice.[8] Here we limit our discussion to the multiples most widely used in valuations.

Basic Per Share Figures

In this section, we show the formulas for calculating six frequently used per share ratios. The calculations are straightforward provided you determine the correct number of shares issued and outstanding. (Getting the number of shares right is not as easy as it looks when there are convertible bonds, warrants, other types of rights, stock options, and complex securities involved.) Listed companies also split their shares, give shares away as dividends, and issue new shares. For these reasons, the formulas ask that the number of shares in the denominator of each ratio be based on a *weighted average* number of common shares issued and outstanding (not just the number of shares at the beginning or at the end of the year).

For instance, if a company has 100,000 shares for 9 months and then issues 1,000,000 new shares bringing the total number of shares to 1,100,000 shares for the last 3 months of the fiscal year, the weighted average total number of shares for the historical 12-month period would be:

$$(100,000 \text{ shares} \times 9/12) + (1,100,000 \text{ shares} \times 3/12) = 350,000 \text{ shares}$$

outstanding on a weighted average basis

Looking ahead, the number of shares to use to calculate the *forecast* earnings per share (or dividends per share, or whatever per share figure is of interest) should be based on the number of shares expected to be outstanding in the year for which the earnings per share estimate is being prepared.

The earnings per share ratio and the dividend per share should be easy to understand. Note that the revenue per share number is called the turnover ratio in the United Kingdom. The reason is that sales revenues refer to "turnover" in the United Kingdom; in the United States, *turnover* means the rotation of inventory (as in inventory turnover), a distinctly different concept.

Book value per share is based on the *accounting book value* per share. We show you two formulas for how to compute this ratio, depending on what you are trying to measure. Cash flow per share also has many different meanings; we show one typical way to estimate it.

- EPS = Earnings per share

$$= \frac{\text{Earnings available for common shareholders}}{\text{Weighted average fully diluted common shares outstanding}}$$

- DPS = Dividend per share

$$= \frac{\text{Total annual dividends paid to common shareholders}}{\text{Weighted average fully diluted common shares outstanding}}$$

- Sales per share (or revenue per share)

$$= \frac{\text{Total Sales}}{\text{Weighted average fully diluted common shares outstanding}}$$

- Cash flow per share

$$= \frac{\text{Cash flow from operations after tax but before interest}}{\text{Weighted average fully diluted common shares outstanding}}$$

- Book value per share

$$= \frac{\text{Book value of common equity}}{\text{Common equity shares outstanding at balance sheet date}}$$

Note that some authors and security analyst handbooks suggest calculating a *tangible book value* ratio. For instance, Cottle, Murray, and Block[9] recommend this next expression:

Tangible book value per share =

$$\frac{\text{Book value of common equity} - \text{goodwill} - \text{other intangible assets}}{\text{Common shares outstanding at balance sheet date}}$$

We add a word of caution on the use of all ratios. Always verify the definitions of ratios (and the adjustments made to them) that are published by financial data providers or found in company annual reports or investment bank or stock brokerage reports. Different analysts and firms use a wide variety of ratio definitions, and the adjustments made to the inputs vary. Be aware that the ratios from one service may not be directly comparable to another; especially watch the numerous ways to define *cash flow*.

Price-Earnings Ratios or Earnings Multiples

Price-earnings ratio (PER) is the most commonly used market ratio on Wall Street and the City of London. It is defined as the price per share of common equity divided by the earnings per share, both figures on a fully diluted basis (meaning all stock options, warrants, and convertible shares should be fully converted into their common equity equivalents). The ratio usually is calculated on the basis of a one-year time period, such as a 12-month fiscal year or calendar year.

For example, if a company announces fully diluted earnings per share of $2.00 for its latest fiscal year, and its current share price is $20.00 per share, then the actual PER is $20.00 divided by $2.00 or 10 times, written as 10×.

Alternatively the price-earnings ratio may be calculated as the total market capitalization of the company divided by 12-months net earnings (before extraordinary items and after any required adjustments).

For instance, a company with a market capitalization of €2 million announces net profits before extraordinary items of €200,000. Then the PER ratio would also be 10× because €2,000,000 ÷ €200,000 = 10.0×.

- Price-earnings ratio $= \dfrac{\text{Price per share}}{\text{Earnings per share}}$

What if the company has no earnings, only losses (a typical situation for many start-up companies)? The PER ratio is meaningless if there are losses. What venture capitalists will do to get around this problem when valuing start-up companies is to apply an industry average multiple to forecasted earnings at some point out in the future, and then discount this future value back to the present at an appropriate discount rate of return. (We illustrate the technique that venture capitalists use to value start-ups in Chapter 19.)

Should the "earnings" in the PER ratio be based on the last trailing 12 months (meaning the most recent 12-month period available), or the latest fiscal year, or on projected earnings? All are acceptable approaches. Because year-to-year changes in earnings, particularly for smaller companies, can be highly volatile, it is very important to clearly indicate the time period used to determine the earnings and explain whether these are based on actual figures or estimated projections.

What about the "price" in the PER ratio? Again, a wide variety of answers are possible depending on the stock brokerage firm or data provider. The price may be the most recent trading price, an average price, an end-of-a-period price, or an anticipated price. Whoever is preparing the valuation needs to document the way each ratio was defined and computed to avoid confusion.

■ Dividend yield $= \dfrac{\text{Dividend per share}}{\text{Price per share}}$

Dividend yield is usually expressed as a percentage.

■ Earnings yield (also called the earnings to price ratio) $= \dfrac{\text{Earnings per share}}{\text{Price per share}}$

The earnings yield is simply the inverse of the price-earnings ratio. If the average price-earnings ratio is 14 times, then the earnings-price ratio (earnings yield) is 7.1 percent.

Diversity of Price-Earnings Ratios   When scrutinizing the vast assortment of price-earnings ratios, it is easy to become bewildered and confused by their inconsistency and diversity. For instance, financial data providers typically update the share price used in calculating the PER of a stock on a daily basis (or even more frequently if they are using a real-time feed of stock prices). However, the earnings per share figure will be for an entirely different time period. A novice might want to go back into the share price history and compute a historical price that matches the time period for the earnings. It is a logically consistent approach and makes perfect sense, but it is not how things normally are done on Wall Street. Stockbrokers and security analysts tend to use current prices and forecasted earnings per share to compute price-earnings ratios; or else they use current prices but in the denominator use the trailing 12-month earnings to compute the price-earnings ratio.

For determining the acquisition premium paid in a hostile takeover, investment bankers often calculate average multiples for the 30 or 60 days prior to the announcement and then compare them to the results on the day of the announcement or for a certain period of time after the takeover (if it is successful). If you wish to do this sort of assessment, simply compare the earnings per share for the latest 12 months and divide it by the average share price (take the mean of the stock price) for 30 or 60 days prior to the announcement and thereby determine an average price-earnings level for a particular stock.

Enterprise Value Ratios or Enterprise Multiples

The enterprise value-to-free cash flow is a popular measure used to compare the relative value of different companies. The enterprise value ratio is a measure of the market value of all the company's assets to the free cash flow that the company generates. It is the total company equivalent to the price-earnings multiple. In this ratio, the value of the whole company (the market value of the debt and equity) is in the numerator of the ratio. Therefore, it makes logical sense and is internally consistent if the denominator of the multiple represents the earnings generated from the whole enterprise. Thus, the proper earnings figure to use is the free cash flow to the firm or the flow of funds available to both debt holders and equity shareholders. (Recall that in Chapter 17 we explained how to derive the free cash flow to the firm.) Refer also to the online Appendix 17.3, "Advanced Definition of Free Cash Flows for Use with Enterprise Valuation Method," accessible by logging onto our web site at www.innovationtocashflows.com.

- Enterprise value to free cash flow $= EV/FCF$

$$= \frac{\text{Market value of the total assets (debt plus equity)}}{\text{Free cash flow to the firm}}$$

- Enterprise Value to Sales ratio $= \dfrac{\text{Enterprise Value}}{\text{Total Sales}}$

The multiple of enterprise value to total sales is a logically consistent ratio because it takes into account the market value of the total company (enterprise value) and divides it into the total sales of the enterprise. Sales are a performance measure of the total assets of the company, so the enterprise value is the correct figure to choose.

Caveat: An inconsistent (but widely used ratio for start-ups) is the price to sales ratio. This is the market value of common stock divided by the total sales of the company. Technically it is not a conceptually correct ratio because sales pertain to total assets, not shareholders' equity. However, if the high-technology start-up has little debt or leases, the difference between the enterprise value to total sales versus an equity market value to total sales ratio ought to be negligible, provided that any excess cash is properly treated. We suggest removing excess cash from the calculation and treating it separately, as a smart buyer will not be willing to pay more for the cash than it is worth.

Balance Sheet Ratios

The market-to-book ratio (M/B ratio) is the *market value* of shareholders' equity divided by the book value of the shareholders' equity of the firm. Book value is sometimes called the net worth of the firm. Net worth or book value is always an accounting measure.

- Market-to-book value ratio $= M/B$

$$= \frac{\text{Market Capitalization of the common equity shares}}{\text{Shareholders' equity (the book value) of the company}}$$

The same result as the market-to-book ratio should be obtained from the per share calculation known as the price-to-book value ratio:

- Price-to-book $= \dfrac{\text{Price per share of common shares}}{\text{Book value per share of common shares outstanding}}$

In healthy, growing, and profitable companies, with intangible assets and good reputations, the market-to-book or price-to book ratio should be much greater than one. However, if market sentiment is extremely negative (as during a major depression), or if for some reason a healthy company is deeply out of favor with the investment community, then a bargain may be discovered in the marketplace if you find a company selling below its book value.

Unfortunately, even these days—as we go to press with the world economy in a major recession—such bargain companies (known as "deep value shares") are still very hard to find. If a company is that cheap, there is something that the market consensus *perceives* as being wrong with the firm's balance sheet, business model, or with the management running it. Or it could be, as is happening now in the banking sector, that the entire sector is facing an unstable macroeconomic environment with higher than normal risks that are difficult to price. *Caveat emptor* on such bargains; it takes strong skills at doing fundamental company analysis plus a lot of courage to go against the consensus view.

Technology Value

Life science venture capitalists commonly refer to technology values, or tech values. Technology value is equivalent to the enterprise value. It is not a ratio but an amount of money. For instance, Biotech Company XYZ has a "tech value" of $15 million.

Technology value is defined to be equal to the market value of the equity plus the market value of the debt, minus any excess cash. The expression is identical to that which we used for enterprise value, only we substitute the words *technology value* in place of *enterprise value*.

- Technology Value = (Equity at Market Value)
                     + (Debt at Market Value) − (Excess Cash)

Technology values are widely used by life science venture capitalists to compare the market valuations of different life science ventures (we do an example in the next section).[10] A biotechnology venture's most valuable assets are its proprietary technology, processes, patents, and other IP rights that have been developed by its talented team of scientists and entrepreneurs. The technology value captures the value of these mostly intangible assets, since such ventures rarely have much debt, few leases, and usually have very little (if any) excess cash. An exception would be if the venture has gone public in a booming equity market and managed to raise more cash than it currently needs. Sometimes after an IPO, a promising drug compound fails a clinical trial and is discontinued. The biotechnology's share price falls, but the cash it raised in the IPO and that it was going to use to fund the clinical trial is still on hand. That is why excess cash can become a significant part of the value of some biotech ventures, depending on circumstances.

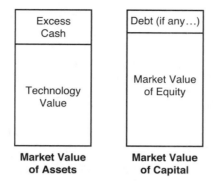

FIGURE 18.8   How Investors Might Perceive a Biotechnology Firm after Its Initial Public Offering

In Figure 18.8, we illustrate how capital market participants would view the assets of a typical later-stage biotechnology firm *shortly after* going public in an IPO. We visualize this company as having two main assets: excess cash and the value of its technology, which we place on the left hand side of the drawing. The market value of debt, if it has any, and the market value of the equity shares are drawn on the right hand side.

With this background information about technology values and how they are used in life science valuations, we now turn our attention to an illustrative case on how to devise a sample of comparable botechnology firms when making a relative valuation.

CASE STUDY: DETERMINING THE TECHNOLOGY VALUE OF A SAMPLE OF COMPARABLE BIOTECHNOLOGY FIRMS

In real life, chief executive officers (CEOs) and CFOs of life science ventures, investors in the life sciences, investment bankers specializing in the sector, heads of business development of large pharmaceutical companies, and all sorts of management consultants and financial advisory firms are interested in tracking relevant data and market sentiment toward life science companies trading in the equity market.

In this case example, we are working as investment bankers. Our firm was given the mandate to be the lead investment bank for a successful biotechnology company. We are helping the senior management team, in particular the CEO and CFO, get the company ready to go public. The listing is planned to take place within the next two months, depending on equity market conditions. Our current task is to do a top-down valuation estimate for the company using the technology values obtained from a representative sample of biotechnology firms.

Like many others who invest and work in the life science and healthcare sector, our investment bank subscribes to a variety of proprietary databases and financial service providers, including PharmaDeals, Recombinant Capital, and of course Bloomberg and Thomson Reuters. The latter are probably the most complete databases on publicly traded companies and emerging market stock markets around the world. (See Chapter 15 for other ideas on data sources.)

Based on experience, we know that the Recombinant Capital's specialized life science database provides us with up-to-date information on product development pipelines and current technology values for firms included in its database. We will use this information in our comparison study.

Finding and Selecting a Proper Sample of Comparable Biotechnology Companies

Our next problem is that there are quite a few biotechnology companies in the Recombinant Capital database. How do we narrow down the choices and devise a proper set of companies to use as our benchmark?

We need to devise a set of comparability criteria. These criteria will help us compare and assess the business models and market forces facing the different companies we are trying to screen:

- Compete in same industry sector
- Target similar customers and clients
- Employ similar technology platform or have a comparable R&D focus
- Have developed comparable product or service offering
- Compete in similar geographic territories and are indeed rivals to each other
- Similar supply chain and logistics functions
- Similar capital structure (use of financial leverage)
- Same stage of growth and company maturity level
- Comparable amount of annual revenues
- Similar growth pattern of cash flows, capital expenditures
- Listed on the same stock exchange or same country where the target company plans to list

We will never find an identical twin to our target company, so we must prioritize our criteria. The first measure, that the proxy company competes in the same industry as the target company, is of overriding importance. Sector effects dominate the other effects. The next four measures explicitly ensure that the comparable company is a competitor or rival to the target company being valued. The final criterion—regarding the stock exchange on which the comparable company is listed—is important for comparability of the data. If the proxy companies are listed on different stock exchanges, trading in different currencies, and subject to different national accounting standards and practices, then the appraiser needs to make cross-border adjustments to the data. To read an explanation on how to do this and to see worked out examples, we recommend Pereiro.[11]

After careful screening and filtering, we narrowed our sample universe down to three publicly traded biotechnology firms that compete in the same therapeutic area as our target company. We call them Firm A, Firm B, and Firm C. They differ widely in terms of their size, market capitalizations, technology values, and excess cash. However, the three proxy firms have similar business models, competitive situations, product development pipelines, and technology platforms. Furthermore, they all are focused on the same therapeutic treatment area as our target firm. (In this case, all three rival firms are leaders in developing novel treatments for oncology, specifically for inhibiting cancerous brain tumors.)

The three firms are disguised, but the data used for the firms are real and come from Recombinant Capital's database. The time period was in the year 2002, when market sentiment toward biotech stocks was quite pessimistic. Given the wide range of factors that affect the valuation of a technology, we hope you realize that the "tech value" is only a preliminary assessment of a firm's value. With this caveat, we will see how to apply the very simple tech value equation using the information in Figure 18.9.

From Figure 18.9, it is clear that Firm A has the highest market value ($308 million) and the highest technology value ($205 million) primarily because stock market investors perceive that is the only firm to actually have had a therapeutic drug make it through clinical trials and then launched into that particular therapeutic drug market. We can further surmise that the investors trading in the stock market perceive Firm A's product pipeline to be better balanced and further along in clinical trials than either Firms A or B. Hence, Firm A's relative market value is much higher than B or C. The amount of excess cash shown for Firm A is over $103 million, which it apparently raised in an IPO and from earlier rounds of financing.

With a market capitalization of over $300 million, Firm A should be classified as a middle-capitalization (mid-cap) biotech firm. It is clearly not a small capitalization (small-cap) start-up company, which typically has a valuation ranging from say $1 million to $5 million. Since a start-up is so much smaller and less mature in its stage of development, it would be unfair to compare the start-up with a publicly traded firm the size of Firm A. However, publicly traded firms might be the only comparable data available. In such a case, we would have to make "size" adjustments (adjust the figure downward) to account for the difference in scale and scope of the two companies.

Firm	Market Capitalization (million, $US)	Excess Cash (million, $US)	Technology Value (million, $US)	Company's Product Portfolio, (Number of Therapeutic Compounds at Each Stage of Drug Development)						
				Preclinical	IND*	Phase I	Phase II	Phase III	NDA[†], Pre-registration	Approved and Launched to Market
A	308	103	205	1	0	2	4	3	0	1
B	67	81	(14)	9	0	2	1	1	0	0
C	13	11	2	3	0	4	4	0	0	0

Notes:
*Investigational New Drug Application
[†]New Drug Application

FIGURE 18.9 Technology Values of Comparable Biotechnology Firms Trading on NASDAQ
Source: Author's own example based on disguised real data from Recombinant Capital.

Turning to Firm B, we see it is much smaller than Firm A in terms of market capitalization, but upon scrutiny of the data, it appears that Firm B has a negative tech value of close to $14 million. What does a negative tech value mean? A negative tech value means that the investors in the stock market think that the technology is worse than worthless; they are saying that management is destroying shareholder value. The market is signaling that this firm might be better off discontinuing operations, handing back the cash to shareholders in the form of dividends, and then disbanding. Remember that these data are from 2002, a time period when market sentiment was very negative; a lot of investors had been burned in the biotechnology bubble that burst after the Internet frenzy a year earlier. If an investor were to have a *different view* of the technology's true worth than the market consensus, then this stock would be a bargain for that investor and should be purchased. However, if the investor were wrong, the firm might go bankrupt, and the investor would lose the money she invested in buying the shares of Firm B.

Firm C is apparently the smallest of the firms (market capitalization is only $13 million). It has plenty of cash on hand, although how long that cash will last depends on its burn rate (the rate at which it consumes cash flow). For example, the burn rate will be very high for a biopharmaceutical company whose drugs are entering into later-stage clinical trials, which is usually why they must do a strategic alliance with a Big Pharma company to get the needed equity infusion to fund these expenditures. According to Figure 18.9, Firm C has 11 products in preclinical through Phase II development but nothing in Phase III, registered, or launched. Consequently, it appears that the investor community is taking a wait-and-see approach to this firm's future and giving it a modest technology valuation at this point in time, pending further clinical trial results. Such a low-tech value might also mean that the investor community perceives high competition for this particular line of therapeutic treatment or that other competitors are likely to reach market launch sooner.[12]

SELECTING THE RIGHT MULTIPLE FOR A GIVEN SITUATION

Deciding which multiple to use when doing a valuation is where the art comes to the foreground of the valuation picture and the science fades to the background. We recommend thinking about the *purpose of the valuation* exercise: IPO, negotiating the sale of a closely held family business? Understanding the *context of the situation* may help you decide the best measure to use. Identify the stage of life cycle, growth rate, type of industry, level of profitability, and level of indebtedness. We offer some suggestions for various situations you may encounter.

Start-Ups and New Ventures

Valuing start-up companies by a multiple of sales is quite common. For start-up companies with no earnings, a PER multiple is meaningless. Therefore, price-to-sales multiples are commonly used to compare fast-growing high-tech companies that might have sales but no profits or earnings.

Example: A target firm's projected next year's sales are projected to be $2 million. At a price-to-sales multiple of 3 to 1, the seller would be asking $6,000,000 for this company. The buyer, however, might be willing to pay only two times sales, a multiple of 2 to 1, or $4,000,000.

Then the negotiations begin....

Caveats: Sales should be normalized over a business cycle and smoothed for seasonal fluctuations. As we mentioned under "Enterprise Multiples," if you are the seller or the buyer, you need to be very clear whether the price in the price-to-sales multiple is referring to an enterprise value (market value of debt plus market value of the equity) or an equity value. For companies with a lot of debt, the ratio chosen can make a big difference in the equity value that is paid. Also, verify if the person doing the valuation is pricing last year's audited sales or next year's projected sales. Sales should *exclude* any extraordinary items that are nonrecurring. No extraneous income or retainer fees should be mixed into revenues, as sometimes happens. The sales should be sales related to normal operations of the company.

Publicly Listed and Well-Established Companies

The most popular ratios are the PER and some multiple of enterprise value. We prefer enterprise value to free cash flow, but some providers and brokerages publish only enterprise value to EBITDA ratios, where *EBITDA* stands for earnings *before* interest taxes, depreciation, and amortization. The problem with EBITDA is that it does not take into account any investments needed in long-term capital expenditures or investments in working capital. The multiples based on EBITDA were very popular with sell-side analysts during the Internet and TMT mania leading to the dot-com crash. Many telecom and cable businesses and their suppliers were valued using enterprise value to EBITDA multiples. The multiples ignored the overinvestment these firms were making in excess optical fiber network capacity, (nicknamed "dark-fiber" investments as the optical fiber was not used [i.e., not lighted] due to overcapacity in the industry).

Besides TMT companies, the other users that compute EBITDA measures are the leveraged buyout specialists. That is because sometimes highly leveraged companies will show only losses after interest expenses and depreciation are deducted, even though they may have positive operating earnings before such charges. Another reason analysts in emerging markets will use EBIT (earnings before interest and taxes) or EBITDA measures is that accelerated depreciation policies or adjustments for high inflation can make cross-border comparisons difficult, especially for capital-intensive industries (e.g., electric utilities or natural gas companies).

Other Special Situations

Book value ratios, especially tangible book value ratios, may be useful as first approximations of value for companies under liquidation. Book values are also useful for valuing commercial banks and certain types of financial groups. (These are often bought and sold as multiples of book value.)

To learn more about ratios and multiples in-depth, we refer you to the fifth edition of *Graham and Dodd's Security Analysis*.[13] In this handbook, the authors carefully explain how to calculate and use at least 39 useful financial ratios and market multiples. This level of knowledge is needed by professional security analysts but is more than the average person needs to know.

In general, financial analysts and investment bankers will calculate for their clients a variety of financial ratios, trading multiples, comparable deal measures and use them to compute company valuations by different methods. It is often left up to the clients' judgment to choose which results are the most meaningful for the types of decisions they need to make.

For more help on multiples and advice on when to use what, we suggest reading the capstone case: Arcadian Microarray Technologies Inc., which is accessible by logging onto our web site (www.innovationtocashflows.com). The case is specifically designed to exercise skills in selecting and using multiples to estimate the terminal value of a high-tech business start-up. (Recall that we introduced terminal values in Chapter 17.)

CHAPTER TAKEAWAYS

- Feeling the pulse of the market is important for negotiating the best price for an acquisition, trade sale, or IPO listing. Investment bankers and venture capitalists use multiples and comparable deal transactions to judge market sentiment (bull market or bear market).
- Multiples are widely used by practitioners. Relative valuations appear in all facets of M&A, private equity, and corporate restructurings, and for valuing joint ventures, strategic alliances, and intellectual property.
- Valuing companies by multiples is a "top-down" or macro-view way of carrying out a valuation assessment. The top-down approach differs from a detailed bottom-up methodology, where we scrutinize fundamental accounting, financial, and market data about the competitors in a particular industry and develop detailed spreadsheet calculations of sales, earnings, and cash flow forecasts.
- Accountants tend to look backward at the costs. With few exceptions, nearly all items shown in the accounting books are recorded at their historical costs (in other words, at the prices when purchased). The balance sheet is like a snapshot of the firm's financial position at a single point in time. As historical costs do not reflect the future earnings capabilities of the business or its intangibles, you should never confuse the term book value with the market value of the shareholders' equity.
- Audited accounting statements are only a starting point for conducting a proper valuation. To a potential investor in a business, the audited accounts are only one small part of the rich mosaic of information that professionals use to form an appraisal of a business. Over the long term, investors and managers are interested in the forward-looking economic prospects of the business and its ability to sustain earnings.
- The equity market's value of a business is reflected in its economic balance sheet, not the accounting balance sheet. The economic balance sheet is being made up of these components:

$$\text{Value of the Enterprise} = \text{Net Working Capital} + \text{Tangible Assets}$$
$$+ \text{Intangible Assets}$$

- You can use the information embedded in public equity markets to help you value your high-technology company. You can either compare your company to other similar companies trading in the public equity markets (using market multiples) or compare your firm to other companies recently bought and sold in the mergers and acquisitions market for corporate control (using transactions data).
- Each industry over time develops its own shortcuts for valuing and comparing firms using multiples and ratios. Deciding which multiple to use when doing a valuation is where the art comes into the foreground of the valuation picture and the science fades into the background. We recommend thinking about the purpose of the valuation exercise for choosing the most appropriate multiple. Thoroughly understanding the context of the situation helps you to decide the best measure to use.
- Log onto our web site at www.innovationtocashflows.com for these files:
  - Appendix 18.1, "Accounting for Goodwill and Intangible Assets"
  - Resources
  - Glossary

CHAPTER 19

Venture Capital Method of Valuation

This chapter gives you an overview of the venture capital and private equity industry. We explain how private equity partnerships (venture capital and buyout
firms) raise funds and put them to work by investing in businesses. We think that
if you, the entrepreneur, understand better how the venture capital industry works,
and especially the competition venture capitalists (VCs) face when raising funds from
their own institutional investors, then you will be better off when it comes time to
sit down at the conference table and negotiate financing for your venture. The more
you know about the people who are financing your venture, the better. The main
purpose of this chapter is to put you in the shoes of the venture capital fund manager. We examine how they think and what are their business models. We discuss
the rationale behind why VCs must charge such high rates for their money. We show
you how to do the venture capital method of valuation through examples. Finally,
we explain how your equity stake as a majority shareholder will be diluted after each
financing round and why you need to be concerned about control and governance
issues whenever you accept venture financing.

ACTIVITIES OF PRIVATE EQUITY INVESTORS: AN OVERVIEW OF THE INDUSTRY

Broadly speaking, investors in privately held companies are referred to as *private
equity investors*. In fact, private equity investors are involved in a wide spectrum of
different activities. Some venture funds invest only in very young companies; other
buyout funds invest only in mature businesses. In Europe, the term *venture capital*
is all-inclusive and means almost all types of investment in unlisted companies,
including what in the United States would be viewed as private equity activities. In
the United States, VCs would be the fund managers of venture capital investment
funds that focus on young and emerging ventures; private equity funds would be
those buyout funds, turnaround funds, and distressed company (or "vulture") funds
that seek undervalued and underperforming *mature* businesses that can be acquired,
restructured, and eventually put on a vigorous path to growth and profitability.

Venture capital and private equity funds normally provide equity capital to their
investee companies, usually in the form of preferred equity (preference shares in
the United Kingdom) and sometimes convertible debt. (Refer to Appendix 10.1 for
a sample investment term sheet or memorandum of understanding.) The VCs and

buyout specialists also put their managerial expertise and operating experience at the disposal of the entrepreneurs.

In exchange for funding, these venture capital and private equity investment funds receive large (often controlling) equity stakes in closely held, illiquid, and normally unquoted businesses. One exception to the general rule about venture capital and private equity funds investing in unlisted companies is a private equity investment vehicle called a PIPE (private investment in public equity). Publicly listed firms, normally smaller companies, sometimes may accept PIPE financing when they need to raise more capital and other alternatives are less attractive. For more about PIPEs and their risks, see Hogoboom 2004, Chaplinski 2003, and Crawford and Chaplinski 2003.[1] Another exception is when a buyout fund acquires a controlling stake in a publicly listed company. Often in such cases, however, as part of the deal, the buyout fund will delist the company from trading on the stock exchange and the company is taken private. (This is called a going-private buyout.)

FINANCIAL INTERMEDIARIES VERSUS PRINCIPAL INVESTORS

Investors who manage money raised from third parties are acting as *financial intermediaries* when they invest these funds on behalf of the others. When investors put their own money to work, or that of their own firms, then they are acting as principal investors.

Most private equity managers—whether VCs or buyout specialists—are acting primarily as financial intermediaries. They raise large sums of money from institutional investors (e.g., pension funds) and wealthy individuals. The private equity fund managers then place these proceeds, over a period of years, into small start-ups or mature businesses, depending on the focus of the investment fund. Even though private equity fund managers are serving as financial intermediaries, they are also doing principal investing because the partners usually contribute a portion of their own money into the funds they manage (this is called coinvesting). By contributing their own money they are not only making the cake but eating it too. Coinvesting helps to align the interests of the fund managers with those of their institutional investors; it is also a way of aligning fund managers' interests with those of the entrepreneurs and other shareholders in whose companies they are buying equity shares, often sizable stakes. Most of the time, VCs and private equity managers aim to gain control of their investee companies, and usually they will have seats on the board of directors. In this way, they are in a position to exercise control over their portfolio companies and replace senior management if strategic targets are not met and performance is weaker than promised.

BUYOUT FUNDS

Buyout specialists tend to focus on mature businesses with the potential to generate abundant cash flow without a lot of capital expenditures. Such businesses are known as cash cows. The investment skills and sector experiences of buyout fund managers are very different from those of the VCs who work with immature, high-technology, emerging growth companies. Buyout teams usually look for family-run businesses, typically manufacturing businesses, with steady cash flows, low levels of indebtedness, and where the chairman or chief executive officer (CEO) of the company is about to retire and may be having trouble finding an appropriate successor. Other suitable targets might be telecom, energy, or infrastructure investments, such as toll roads or electric utilities, which tend to generate steady cash flows. Some buyout funds focus on healthcare businesses (long-term care facilities for the elderly) or health management organizations. Others like to acquire retail businesses with good reputations and loyal followings, or financial firms with similar characteristics. Still others focus on professional service companies with steady customer bases paying regular long-term service fees or subscriptions. For instance, Palamon Capital Partners is a rather unusual European buyout firm in that it is focused purely on acquiring service businesses (no manufacturing) in high-tech, professional services, and finance. In 2007, according to the Private Equity Council, the five largest industries for private equity investment were telecom, finance, energy, retail, and healthcare (www.privateequitycouncil.org).

A *management buyout* (MBO) is when the management team that is taking over comes from within the ranks of the target company. A *management buy-in* (MBI) is when new management comes from outside the target company. If the takeover is financed by borrowings, some form of debt, or debt-like instruments, then the buyout is called a *leveraged buyout* (LBO). Buyout experts expect to restructure the company to make it even more efficient or better able to handle rapid growth, perhaps by merging it with another small company in their portfolio of companies. The new managers intend to use the cash generated to pay back the interest expense on the borrowed debt, and make payments on the principal, thereby reducing the overall debt level. When market conditions are favorable and the company is ready, then they expect to exit, by selling to another trade buyer, by taking the company public, or by selling to another fund of funds. On average, the fund managers hope to exit with high capital gains on their portfolio of companies. An example of a buyout fund firm would be Bain Capital Private Equity, which is well-known for its European activities.

MEGAFUNDS

Megafunds have huge amounts of capital under management (usually over $6 billion per fund). They are financial powerhouses. One example of such a large firm would be General Atlantic, covering the world and offering a full range of private equity investment possibilities—from venture capital, to leveraged buyouts, private investment in public equity, to mezzanine financing (to be defined later). See its web site (www.generalatlantic.com) for more details about the firm and its investments. Other well-known megafunds are APAX Partners; The Blackstone Group; The Carlyle Group; Goldman Sachs (GS) Private Equity; and Kohlberg, Kravis, Roberts & Co.

VENTURE CAPITAL FUNDS

Venture capitalists are a subset of the private equity investor universe. They focus on financing young growth companies. VCs specialize by industry, by technology, by target end customer or market focus, and according to the stage of development of their portfolio companies (investee companies).

Most VCs are classified by the round of financings they tend to do. The first professionals to provide money are known as *seed capital* investors. *Early-stage* investors normally provide the first- or second-round financing. *Late-stage* investors provide for the third or fourth or more rounds of financing. *Mezzanine finance* is the last round of private finance before a company goes public or is sold to a trade sale partner. *Bridge finance* is temporary financing used to fill any funding gaps. For instance, a bridge loan might give the company breathing space to restructure before going public or to wait for the right trade sale opportunity.

Examples of premier West Coast venture capital firms are Kleiner, Perkins, Caufield, and Byers; Institutional Venture Partners; and the Mayfield Fund. In Europe, the 3i Group is one of the oldest established venture capital firms. The original firm started up in 1945 in Britain and 3i was successfully listed on the London Stock Exchange in 1994. Over the last decade, the 3i Group's investments have evolved away from early-stage VC toward later-stage growth capital. Currently 3i's Growth Capital Fund seeks minority stakes worth up to €250 million in established businesses, many of them family-owned and -operated, with high growth potential and enterprise values of €100 million to €1 billion. The 3i Group has also diversified into buyouts, infrastructure, and quoted private equity. Although 3i still maintains a team that manages its established VC portfolio (worth almost €1 billion) of early-stage investments, it is not currently raising fresh VC funds or investing in early-stage ventures. Assets under management for the 3i Group totaled €12.3 billion as of March 2008.

In 2008, Goldman Sachs Mezzanine Partners became the world's largest mezzanine fund family, with its fifth fund raising $20 billion in capital ($13 billion in equity and $7 billion in debt) at its closing on July 8, 2008.[2] GS Mezzanine Partners' Funds I through IV have committed $17 billion to over 100 companies.[3]

Venture Capital Industry in Europe

In general, the venture capital industry in Europe has fewer funds under management and is less developed than that of the United States. U.S. venture capital began shortly after World War II; European venture capital gained momentum only in the early 1980s, first in the United Kingdom, France, and the Netherlands, and then spread to Scandinavia, and southern Germany. Spain and Italy were rather late to the game due to the less developed nature of their equity markets and the reluctance of Spanish and Italian family firms to give up control to outside investors.

For more information on the history of the venture capital industry, see the European Venture Capital Association (EVCA) web site (www.evca.com), the British Venture Capital Association web site (www.bvca.co.uk), and the National Venture Capital Association (NVCA) web site (www.nvca.org). The major venture capital associations also publish regularly updated information and fact sheets on the amount of private equity funds raised, classified according to round of financing, along with useful comparisons to funds raised in earlier years. They also publish timely statistics about exit data, such as the number of initial public offering (IPOs) and size of IPOs by venture-backed firms.

According to the EVCA, there are about 900 specialist venture capital firms located across Europe, of which 170 are located in the United Kingdom. In comparison, venture capital directories, such as Capital Vector, list over 1,830 active venture capital firms for the United States (www.capitalvector.com/faq.html). In 2008, there were over 480 venture capital and private equity firms belonging to the NVCA, according to its web site.

Example of a Seed Capital Fund in Europe   Very early seed capital venture financing is scarce in Europe. Compared to the United States, this segment of the venture capital market is still at a very nascent stage of development. In Europe, most high-tech ventures get their earliest financing from friends and family or as loans and grants from various government bodies. There simply are not that many professionally managed venture funds solely focused on providing seed capital to high-tech ventures. Most VCs in Europe would argue such a focus on "high-technology plus early stage of growth" is too risky. European seed capital funds that do exist are very small; most aim to raise around €10 million to €50 million as a typical fund size. The amount of the initial seed funding provided to portfolio companies is also smaller than in the United States, usually on the order of €100,000 to €1.5 million. Most seed funds are located near major European universities with active research centers for technology or life science.

One example of such a pioneer seed venture capitalist is Lucius Carey, whose fund is based in the Magdalen Centre, Oxford Science Park, near Oxford University, in the United Kingdom. He started out in business as an entrepreneur and then he founded the *Venture Capital Report*, to help other entrepreneurs connect with people who had capital to invest. In 1983, he established his first venture fund, called Seed Capital Ltd., to invest in very-early-stage high-tech ventures. He had realized from his work writing the *Venture Capital Report* that many promising U.K. scientists were having a particularly hard struggle raising seed money for their start-ups. After Seed Capital Ltd., Carey then set up another company, Oxford Technology Management, to serve as the investment manager to a variety of venture funds providing seed capital to enterprises in amounts ranging from £100,000 and occasionally up to £2,000,000. Currently, four of these funds are publicly listed and quoted on the London Stock Exchange: the Oxford Technology Management Venture Capital Funds I through IV. Because these are listed venture capital seed funds, they offer substantially more disclosure about their investment practices and companies than many other unlisted venture capital firms. See Oxford Technology web site (www.oxfordtechnology.com) for further details about the funds, the way they are structured, and information about their respective portfolio companies.

Early-Stage and Later-Stage Funds in Europe   Early-stage venture capitalists usually invest in the first- and second-financing rounds. Like seed capital VCs, they tended to invest close to home. The old rule of thumb was that they should be within one day's travel time to their portfolio companies. Later-stage VCs in general have always had a slightly wider geographical reach. However, the old rule of thumb is changing for all VC stages due to faster transport, better communications, and globalization. Leading European early-stage life science venture capital funds, for instance, will make investments in targeted markets in the United Kingdom, Continental Europe, and the United States.

We mention two European examples to illustrate these trends: Abingworth and Gilde Healthcare Partners, both well-known life science investors. Abingworth started in the United Kingdom. It currently does all stages of life science venture investing and recently opened a fund to invest in undervalued publicly listed life science companies. Over a number of years, Abingworth has added partners and offices on both sides of the Atlantic, in the United Kingdom (London and Cambridge), and in the United States (Menlo Park and Boston) according to their web site (www.abingworth.com).

Gilde Healthcare Partners is based in the Netherlands. It is focused on early- and late-stage investing in therapeutics, diagnostics, and medical devices. The fund has made investments in the United Kingdom, San Diego, Boston, and in target markets of Continental Europe. Gilde Healthcare Partners is one of three separately managed investment funds that make up Gilde Investment Management (Gilde; www.gilde.nl), which was established in 1982 and has offices in the Netherlands, France, and Switzerland. Gilde's funds, as a group, are prominent continental European private equity investors. Besides Gilde Healthcare, Gilde has two midmarket buyout funds, managed by different partners, one focused on the Benelux region and the other on continental western Europe.

As illustrated by these examples, a trend among venture capital firms is to blend early-stage and later-stage investee companies into the same fund portfolio and to diversify their portfolios geographically. The reason is to spread risks and develop more balanced portfolios. We also see venture capital firms branching into PIPEs or adding new partners and diversifying into private equity buyout funds. In addition, we see traditional buyout firms setting up venture capital funds. The boundaries are blurring between these once-distinct segments.

Pan-European Venture Funds and the Rise of Global Venture Capital Firms   Pan-European venture capital firms do exist. We also are seeing the rise of global venture capital firms, although the funds they have under management are orders of magnitude smaller than the megafunds we mentioned earlier. Pan-European and global venture capital firms generally operate with separate offices in each of the important country markets, staffed with local partners who know the local firms and key players in their area of expertise.

An interesting example of a California-based early-stage venture capital firm that has rapidly grown and spread to Europe, Asia, and increasingly around the world Draper, Fisher, Jurvetson (DFJ; www.dfj.com). DFJ is a third-generation VC with family roots firmly planted on Sand Hill Road in Menlo Park, California. Sand Hill Road is the famous road (next to the Stanford University Campus) where many leading high-tech venture capital firms have their main offices. DFJ has been a pioneer in developing a business model that allows it to grow globally while keeping to the old adage of staying within a day's reach. DFJ's globalization strategy has been to set up a federation of independent local partner funds. By doing so, it is diversifying its risks. DFJ has chosen to stay focused on seed capital and early-stage investing but hedges its exposures by spreading investments geographically around the world. Its network gives it access to a much larger and more diverse deal flow than other firms. DFJ has built up a local presence, with affiliated offices in 33 cities and a reach that stretches across the United States to South America, Europe, Israel, Russia, and Asia.

Future Private Equity Industry Challenges As you can see, each venture capital and private equity firm is trying to come up with new ways to attain competitive advantage for itself. The VC and private equity fund managers must simultaneously answer to the needs of their investors and investee companies while at the same time balancing overall risks to their partnerships and the specific risks in their fund portfolios. One of the keys for any private equity or venture capital partnership is to find, hire, and retain top talent. The other is to execute the firm's growth strategy well. The global race is on. As more and private funds are raised, the industry is showing signs of maturing. The challenge going forward for the next generation of leaders is to keep ahead of the increasing number of venture capital and private equity firms located around the world. Still, the basic principles remain the same: VCs and private equity fund managers should work hard to identify excellent leads; qualify these leads through careful and rigorous due diligence; then negotiate good deals for all parties concerned; and finally help their portfolio companies thrive, create value, and grow fast and profitably.

TYPICAL VENTURE'S LIFE CYCLE OF DEVELOPMENT

In this section, we briefly describe the life cycle of a typical high-tech venture that is one of the fortunate few to attain venture capital financing. We give an overview of the entire process of how a venture develops and the type of available financing for each stage of development. We also explain the major sources of funds and the typical uses for the proceeds that are raised. We summarize our observations in Table 19.1, beginning on page 484.

Early Beginnings

When a venture is being conceived, generally the founders finance it, by forgoing salaries and contributing their personal savings into the business. While the entrepreneurs flesh out their business concept, sketch out a business plan, and start talking to potential customers and investors, quite often their friends and family finance these early steps in a new venture's life.

Start-Up Phase

Angel investors are individuals who invest money in early start-ups in exchange for equity stakes. They often are experienced business managers or former entrepreneurs themselves who made a lot of money. They also might be wealthy professionals, doctors, lawyers, or sports figures who may not have a lot of experience in the market or type of business the entrepreneurial team wishes to set up. Each angel investor is unique; the entrepreneurs should investigate his or her background and experiences thoroughly as part of their deal due diligence.

A good way to do angel due diligence is by connecting early to the established angel investor networks in your area. More and more cities across the United States, Europe, and around the world have angel investor networks. Depending on where you live (or went to school), and where your venture is located, you may or may not find local angel investor networks. Web searches, word of mouth, talking to entrepreneurs and alumni from local universities, and connecting with local venture capital associations is the best way to find out if your region has active angel investor networks.

Seed capital, or seed money, generally comes after friends and family and funds contributed by angel investors. Seed capital investors normally are professional venture capitalists who must respond to the needs of their limited partner investors. Most seed capital investors want the venture business to have at least a business plan prepared and a well-developed product idea ready for prototyping, if not already in prototype. If the venture is a web or service business, some sort of demonstration software should be available for the seed capital VC to use and try out. For an idea of what a seed capital VC expects, read the requirements on their web sites and talk to the VC networks or business incubators in your local area.

Early Stages of Development

Early-stage venture capitalists like to get in early, usually on the first or second round of financing. Angel investors and seed money VCs will be helpful in connecting you to early-stage VCs from your local region. If you are going directly from friends and family to first-round financing, then you will need to search local VC directories and use your own personal networks, alumni networks, and professional networks to identify firms interested in your particular business model, market niche, and kind of technology. The first round of financing is usually the hardest to get. At this stage, the enterprise should have a product. It might be searching for more capital to begin scaling up the new process or to finance manufacture of the new product. The venture is unlikely to be profitable at this early stage. Many high-tech firms run out of money before they get to the second round due to unexpected delays or start-up problems. That is why the first round is often referred to as the survival round. By the time of second-round financing, the company should have the management systems, personnel, manufacturing, sales and marketing resources in place and be ready for rapid growth.

Later Stages of Development

Late-stage venture capitalists are investors who usually place substantially larger sums of money into the investee companies than early-stage investors are willing to invest. The main reason for the larger amount is that by the third or fourth round of financing, the company is less vulnerable to setbacks. The perceived business risks, although still high, are lower than in the earlier stages. The number of financing rounds depends on the sector, country (or region), and equity market conditions plus the specific growth needs of the business. Late-stage financing rounds are used to implement the business plan, advance product development, increase manufacturing capacity, extend the marketing and sales efforts, fund working capital increases, and expand internationally. These VCs are experienced at helping to professionalize the company. They can help strengthen the senior team by bringing in new talent and easing out founders who have reached their managerial limits. They advise on getting the company ready for an IPO or trade sale.

Nearing the Exit or Liquidity Event

The exit or liquidity event is when a company's VC investors sell their shares in a trade sale, an IPO, or to another fund. Mezzanine finance and bridge financing are usually the last stages of financing before the exit event. Before an IPO, the controlling shareholders might orchestrate a management succession and replace the founding entrepreneurs with a new executive team, more experienced at growing and operating a public company.

Of course if the venture's products are unsuccessful, or the company runs out of cash, then it is the worst-case exit scenario for the investors. (Refer to Chapter 4 for more on insolvency proceedings, including liquidation and financial reorganizations.)

Table 19.1 summarizes the typical hightechnology venture's life cycle of development.

TYPICAL APPROACH TO CREATING A VENTURE CAPITAL OR PRIVATE EQUITY FUND

Venture capital or private equity funds normally are structured as limited partnerships. In this section, we refer to the creation of a venture capital fund, but the approach is similar for buyout funds and even hedge funds.

The *general partner* (GP) is the entity that is legally responsible and generally liable for the venture capital fund. The general partner decides on the investment focus of the fund, develops the idea, promotes it, and solicits *limited partners* (LPs) to subscribe to the offering by contributing cash. The limited partners have limited liability. Each limited partner is liable only up to the amount of money it has contributed. (Refer to Chapter 9 for more information about limited liability partnerships and limited liability corporations.)

To shield themselves from personal liability, the individuals who are the venture capitalists (or private equity partners, as the case may be) will form a separate investment fund management company, usually some kind of limited liability corporation (LLC)—the specific legal vehicle depends on the local tax rules and corporate law regulations of where the fund is domiciled. The VCs will then designate the investment fund management company as the GP, taking advantage of its LLC structure to gain favorable tax treatment and liability protection. The GP serves as the advisor to the venture capital fund and is also responsible for its day-to-day management. In Figure 19.1 on page 486, we depict the structure of a fictitious venture capital fund that we use as an example to illustrate how a typical venture capital or private equity fund is set up and organized.

In our example, the venture capital fund is called the Venture Capital Investment Fund No. 4 Go-IV-IT Limited Partnership (Go-IV-IT Fund). (See center box in Figure 19.1.) The Go-IV-IT Fund is actually the fourth fund (IV) being raised by this particular group of experienced venture capital GPs. Go-IV-IT is being promoted as a specialized early-stage venture fund (Round 2 financing) that is focused on emerging European information technology (IT) investments. The goal is to raise €200 million from major institutional investors (the LPs). The GP will also coinvest in the fund as indicated by the € (euro) symbol on the diagram.

TABLE 19.1   Venture Life Cycle, Types of Venture Financing, Uses and Sources of Funding

Life Cycle Stage of Development	Type of Venture Financing and Typical Target Rates of Return	Use of Proceeds in a Typical High-Tech Venture	Major Sources of Funding
Early beginnings	Self-financing 50%–70+%	Think up a business concept. Convince others to join in as a team to work on developing the idea. Research, evaluate, and develop an initial idea or concept.	Entrepreneur's savings and loans on personal assets Family and friends
Start-up phase	Seed financing 60%	For product development and initial market research or customer tests. The business is still in the being-created stage and products not yet being sold commercially.	Entrepreneur's own assets Family and friends Business angels Seed venture capitalists Bootstrap financing from a parent company or a corporate venture fund Government grants or loans for new enterprises (small and medium enterprises [SMEs])
Early stage: Survival	1st-round financing 40%	The business has a product and needs capital to begin manufacturing it and selling it; it still has not generated any profits.	Early-stage venture capitalists Government loans for SMEs Suppliers and customers Venture's own business operations
Early stage: 2nd round	2nd-round financing 30%	The business is still losing money but is expected to break even during this stage; it is entering a period of high growth. The infusion of new funds is used to develop the first product, hire personnel, start manufacture, develop sales channel, and fund increased working capital needs.	Early-stage and 2nd-round VCs Government loans for SMEs Suppliers and customers Perhaps some profits reinvested from business operations

TABLE 19.1 (*Continued*)

Life Cycle Stage of Development	Type of Venture Financing and Typical Target Rates of Return	Use of Proceeds in a Typical High-Tech Venture	Major Sources of Funding
Late stage: 3rd, 4th, or more rounds; Ramp-up for rapid growth	3rd-round financing 25%	Same as above plus start work on more new products, finance strategic alliances or small acquisitions. Number of financing rounds depends on the sector and the individual needs of the business. Company should be profitable by this stage while still growing rapidly.	Late-stage venture capitalists Venture's own business operations Suppliers and customers Government-sponsored loans for SMEs Commercial banks for SMEs Investment banks specializing in SMEs
Liquidity event or exit stage	Mezzanine financing Bridge financing 20%	The business should be hitting targets and milestones and being readied for exit of venture investors and takeover by an industrial company, listed in an IPO, or sold to another later-stage mezzanine fund.	Venture's own business operations Suppliers and customers Specialized commercial banks Specialized investment banks
Seasoned company or "mature" financing stage	Securing bank loans Issuing debt securities Issuing new primary equity Selling secondary shares 15%	The company should be profitable and handling growth well. This might be the time to transition to a management team more suited for running a larger corporation than an entrepreneurial start-up.	Business operations Commercial banks Investment banks specializing in IPOs and corporate finance for SMEs

Source: Interviews by the coauthors in 2008 with venture capitalists, private equity investors, and turnaround specialists in Europe and the United States; European Private Equity & Venture Capital Association. "Guide on Private Equity and Venture Capital for Entrepreneurs" (November 2007): 1–39.

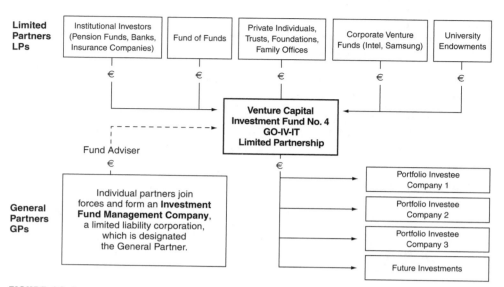

FIGURE 19.1   Structure of a Typical Venture Capital Fund

The GP normally prepares a rather detailed offering memorandum that sets out the fund's strategy, describes how the fund will be managed, lists who within the investment fund management company will be advising the fund, and proposes investment terms and conditions. Some of these investment terms and conditions will be renegotiated with the limited partners in the course of the actual fundraising.

With the GP's offering memorandum prepared, the venture capitalists go out on the road. (They do presentations about their fund in a schedule packed with client visits, what is known as a road show.) Fundraising takes four to six months, after which, if the target amount has been raised, the fund is closed to future investors. The fund managers then start putting the money to work by buying equity stakes in portfolio companies.

Acceptance Rate of Venture Capital

The VCs who manage the investment operations continually search for new companies in which to place funds. They spend their time qualifying prospects, questioning entrepreneurs about their business models, and vetting the founders and their proposed management teams.

An experienced and well-connected venture capitalist team may well receive over 1,000 business plans a year from eager start-up teams. Naturally all the entrepreneurs behind the plans are optimistic and promise high future earnings and growth. Entrepreneurs should be mindful that most business plans will be rejected at the initial screening, which may take as little as five minutes of the VC partner's time. The winnowing-out process is brutal.

For a general venture capital fund, for every 100 business plans that are reviewed, on average only 3.6 percent of the plans will receive funding. For high-tech venture funds, the acceptance rate is even lower, about 2.7 percent, according to researchers from Nottingham University in the United Kingdom.[4] Similar acceptance rates apply in the United States and elsewhere.

The high-tech and life science VCs with whom we work in Europe tell us that for every 100 business plans received, perhaps five venture proposals will make it into the due diligence phase. Only if the venture proposal passes due diligence do the VCs and the entrepreneurs negotiate final financing terms and conditions and conclude a definitive investment agreement contract. In the end, only two to three proposals (out of every 100 business plans received) receive VC funding.

Managing the Fund Day to Day

After the initial investments are made in the portfolio companies, the VCs then need to monitor these investments and make sure the business plans are being executed as scheduled and planned. VCs normally sit on the board of directors of the portfolio companies for which they are responsible. If a crisis arises, VCs keep in close contact with the senior managers of their companies. If things are going smoothly, they will be more hands-off. As members of the board of directors, VCs need to walk a fine line; they should not operate the company directly (e.g., termed "gestion de fait" [*de facto* management] in France) or indirectly (e.g., by setting up a "phantom board" [that lacks independence] as termed in England or the United States). Otherwise the board members could become responsible and liable for the consequences of having managed the company (especially in the case of insolvency proceedings in European countries). This calls for balanced corporate governance between the board and the CEO. The VCs and other board members need to understand clearly each country's local corporate governance code and their duties under the law.

The venture capitalists's fund management performance results depend on how successful they are at disposing the fund's stakes in the various portfolio companies. The VCs work closely with their investee companies to time the exit carefully, according to conditions in the market for corporate control (the merger and acquisitions market [M&A]) or the public stock markets, where an IPO would take place. The exit strategy also depends on the agreements the venture fund has made with each company's entrepreneurs at the time of the initial investment round of financing and subsequent capital infusions. Most VC funds, as a general rule, try to exit from a portfolio company in about three to five years. It may be longer for life science investors, due to the lengthy incubation time of biopharmaceutical and biotechnology ventures. Of course, exit times may also have to be prolonged if the stock markets crash or the economy goes into a major recession and the exit prices are not deemed attractive enough. When a portfolio company is sold, the capital gains are either reinvested in the fund or else distributed to the LPs and GPs according to the investment agreement and how much time still remains for the fund to be operating.

Winding Up the Fund at the End of 10 Years

The normal life span of a private equity or venture capital investment fund is about 10 years, with a possible two-year extension. At the end of 10 to 12 years, the venture or private equity fund is wound up and ceases to operate. The remaining cash is distributed back to the LPs and GPs on a pro rata basis. If any shares of any investee companies still remain in the fund, either because the company has yet to be sold or because it was recently listed and the shares are under lockup and cannot be sold, company shares may be distributed to the LPs in lieu of cash. The choice of how the distribution is done, cash or in-kind shares, often depends on tax considerations and stock market conditions.

Who Are the Limited Partners and What Is Their Role?

The limited partners are typically large institutional investors and wealthy individuals who supply the cash to fund the venture capital fund or private equity buyout fund. These institutional investors may be large company pension funds, important banking groups, large insurance companies (particularly life insurance companies), sovereign wealth funds, funds of funds (funds that invest in other funds), or wealthy individuals or the family offices of high-net-worth individuals. Other important and long-term investors may be major trusts, charitable foundations (e.g., the Gates Foundation or Hewlett-Packard Foundation), and university endowments.

In the United States, certain universities (mostly private) have built up substantial sums of money over the years. For instance, for fiscal year 2007, Harvard's endowment was $34.9 billion (www.hmc.harvard.edu), Yale's endowment topped $22.5 billion (www.yale.edu/investments), and Stanford's endowment was $17.2 billion (www.stanfordmanage.org). Over time, prominent alumni donate money or bequeath family estates to their alma maters' endowment. A certain percentage of the endowment money is spent each year to fund the school's operations, important research projects, or to carry out major capital expenditures (for new campus buildings and the like). Harvard, Yale, and Stanford are known to be longtime and prominent investors in top-tier venture capital and leveraged buyout funds in the United States and increasingly abroad. For further information on how Yale thinks about its venture capital and buyout fund investments, consult the web site of the Yale University Investment Office and read its latest endowment report. Yale has one of the best track records in the world for investing in private equity.

Limited partners are only at risk for the amount of capital they put into the fund; they do not manage the investment fund nor do they have any obligations in advising the fund managers. The LPs expect to be kept informed about the fund's performance and to eventually receive a rate of return on their investment that is higher than they could obtain by investing in public capital markets. They expect this higher return to compensate for the added risk of keeping their funds tied up for long periods of time and of investing in illiquid, privately held new ventures or highly leveraged or distressed firms, depending on the private equity fund's focus.

Remuneration for the General Partners

As the investment manager, the general partner charges a management fee (usually 2 to 2.5 percent) to cover reasonable overhead expenses of operating the fund. Smaller funds tend to charge 2.5 percent, whereas large funds tend to charge slightly less. Normally, the management fee is collected on the *committed capital*. The committed capital is the money promised by the LPs that is to be invested in the fund (the GP's commitments normally are excluded for purposes of calculating the management fee). Following the investment period, then the management fee is charged only on the contributed capital that remains invested in the portfolio companies (including any follow-on investments).

During the early years of the fund, the LPs do not have to provide the committed capital all at once; normally, they will have several years to satisfy the commitment. When the fund managers ask for additional cash, they issue a *drawdown notice*. The management fee usually is paid quarterly for the life of the fund, although sometimes the percentage amount is lowered in the later stages of the fund's life as activities are winding down. The details are negotiated with investors when the fund is formed, and the agreed-on terms and conditions are documented in the final investment agreement.

Carried Interest The incentive portion of the general partner's compensation is called the carried interest. The *carried interest* represents a share of the returns generated on the assets under management (where the returns are the capital gains from the sale of the equity stakes in the investee companies). The incentive compensation normally is given to the GP only if certain conditions are met. Industry practice has the GP receive about 20 percent of the carried interests, and the remaining 80 percent is allocated to the LPs and shared among them in proportion to how much money each has contributed to the investment fund. The details come down to the negotiations between the LPs and the GPs.

Hurdle Rate Before signing the final investment agreement, the LPs typically insist that the carried interest be paid to the GP only after the LPs have received their capital back (their original contribution of funds), plus a return at an agreed-on interest rate on those funds, called the hurdle rate. The LPs do not want the GP to be rewarded for fund performance that is below the cost of interest that the funds could earn elsewhere in the equity markets. Given that the funds are equity funds, the hurdle rate, which represents the LPs' opportunity cost of funds, should be steeper than the cost of Treasury funds. For instance, the terms and conditions might stipulate that no bonus be paid unless the private equity fund performance exceeds that of the expected rate of return for a broad stock market index. Alternatively the benchmark might be a smaller company index, representing the area the investments are expected to be made in.

The carried interest remuneration is meant to motivate GPs and to compensate them for assuming the general liability for the fund. David F. Swensen, the chief investment officer for the Yale Endowment, argues that the incentive compensation should not be a free lunch ticket for the fund managers.[5] If the investment fund does well, the idea is to reward the GP with a share in the upside gains; if the fund does poorly, the carried interest will not be paid out and the GP receives no rewards. In reality, the exact terms and conditions for the carried interest, hurdle rate, and other features vary for each fund. They depend on negotiations between the GPs and the LPs during the fundraising period, with the negotiated outcome documented in the final investment agreement.

What tends to happen in the private equity industry is that the carried interest percentage creeps upward when times are booming. The fund sponsors then have the upper hand, and it is relatively easy to raise private equity funds. In lean times, however, the carried interest percentage eases back down, as the institutional investors gain more bargaining power. Hurdle rates also vary according to economic times and private equity cycles. Fund managers on occasion may also try to increase their management fees above the typical 2 to 2.5 percent range, turning such fees into profit centers rather than just reimbursement for reasonable fund management expenses.

Bear in mind that the LPs normally contribute the lion's share of the funding, on the order of 90 up to 99 percent of the capital to the fund's limited partnership; the remaining 1 to 10 percent is the coinvestment amount contributed by the GPs. Therefore, carried interest may be viewed as a "sweat equity" incentive similar to what is found in real estate development partnerships, where the GP contributes labor, experience, and talents in exchange for a bigger slice of the profits, if any, from the development. As in real estate limited partnerships, the LPs in a private equity limited partnership will contribute proportionately more money but have no say in managing the fund.

Debate is currently under way in the public policy arena to change the U.S. tax treatment of carried interest and private equity limited partnerships. In response to this policy threat, some of the major megafund buyout groups in the industry formed the Private Equity Council. The council's web site publishes these funds' views in white papers and articles (www.privateequitycouncil.org).[6] Since each country's tax laws differ, we advise obtaining specialized tax and legal counsel when forming or structuring any private equity limited partnership.

HOW VENTURE CAPITALISTS IMPROVE THEIR CHANCES FOR SUCCESS

Venture capitalists as an industry make high-risk, high-expected-return investments throughout different stages of a young company's life—from a fledgling start-up to a rapidly growing company that can go public or would make an attractive acquisition. We say high *expected* returns because for every 10 investments that a VC makes, only one will turn out to be a really big success. The gigantic megawins are the ones we excitedly watch in the media (Google, eBay, Amazon); they are extremely rare. The other nine out of 10 investee companies either die an early death, or they limp along. Only occasionally do we read about such failures and also-rans in the newspapers. The winners are the survivors, the losers disappear.

In some ways, VCs are the modern-day version of the gold diggers of the U.S. Wild West or the wildcatters searching for oil in the frontier territories. No one can know ahead of time where the gold nuggets will be found when searching for gold. Nor can anyone know for sure which drilled hole will become the next oil gusher. The secret to finding oil is to go out and drill a lot of holes. The companies that drill the most holes have the best odds of striking oil; their odds are enhanced if they can get access to the best plots of ground with favorable geological formations for finding oil or gas.

Venture capitalists play a similar game of odds. No one can predict with certainty which new venture will be the next Google, so VCs tend to make a large number of small bets on promising companies. To improve their odds, venture capitalists strive to improve their access to deal flow which enhances their search for investment opportunities. They look for great business models. They invest in talented management teams: people who have reliable and honest reputations with relevant sector experience. The VCs learn their particular area of expertise well and focus only on particular high-tech sectors and markets they can understand. If dealing with a new technology, they will seek out the opinions of expert advisors in that scientific and technological domain. If presented with an investment opportunity of substantial size, VCs will spread their risks by investing in combination with other VCs in what is known as an investor syndicate. The lead investor is the one who takes the lead and manages the syndicate on behalf of the other members.

Doing Staged Investing, Setting Milestones, and Planning the Exit

VCs negotiate hard not to pay more cash than they have to up front. They also manage their risks by making staged investments in which the venture's management must meet various business milestones or targets before qualifying for another infusion of capital. They do not put into the venture all the capital it will require up front and in one round. They dole out the funding and give it only when it is needed. The venture has to constantly prove itself by qualifying for the next round.

The other secret to being a good VC is to start planning the exit strategy—even before making the investment. The key point to keep in mind is that VCs must liquidate part or all of their fund's investment in a particular portfolio company in order to reap the capital gains required by their own institutional investors. The success of the exit is critical for their performance, and the key factor in their reward and compensation scheme. The bigger the exit and the sooner it comes, the higher the internal rate of return (IRR) of that particular investment. A delay in the exit and the IRR will be lower; a lower exit price and the IRR will be less. So time to exit and the quality of the exit, in terms of final price terms and conditions, are all crucial factors that a VC will strive to control in order to enhance the fund's return on investment.

The exit time horizon for investment deals varies by sector. For VCs making investments in web-related, consumer electronics, or other fast-moving high-tech communications sectors, the investment time horizon might be on average three to five years. For VCs specializing in the life sciences, the time horizon for their investments will be longer, on average maybe five years and sometimes lasting 10 years or up to the life of the fund.

Choosing the Exit Strategy: Which Market?

The choice of pursuing a trade sale or an IPO is a difficult decision to make a priori. The reason is that at the time of exit (three to more than five years down the road), market conditions may be unpredictably different than they are at the time of investing. The VC must become intimately familiar with at least four markets: the trade sale market (sometimes called the market for corporate control or the M&A market); the public equity markets (where the IPO listing conditions are set); bankruptcy proceedings and reorganization (when things do not work out as they should); and the market for buying and selling portfolio companies to other venture funds. This last market becomes extremely important when the M&A market is flat, the IPO window is closed, and the sale of a portfolio company to another VC firm is the best remaining exit alternative for a venture fund to cash out of an investee company. Ideally, one would have a crystal ball and be able to peer into the future and know where the best exit prices would be obtainable. Alas, such crystal balls have yet to be engineered and produced. The VCs, the boards of directors, and the CEOs with whom they interact do the best they can and exercise judgment on which strategic path to take, depending on the investment context they face at the time they are making their initial decisions. Then they have to live with the consequences of these decisions and the path chosen.

SPECIAL CASE OF LIFE SCIENCE VENTURES: RECENT EXIT TRENDS

For over the last two years, from 2007 to 2008, M&A market conditions have been quite buoyant for sellers of smaller biotechnology and biopharmaceutical companies. In the market for corporate control, the major pharmaceutical companies have been paying record prices to acquire entrepreneurial life science firms. The major players are especially interested in acquiring innovative technology platforms or the patent rights to therapeutic compounds entering the late stages of clinical trials in markets with huge potential, such as cancer, high blood pressure, Alzheimer's, and obesity treatments.

In the summer of 2008, as we are writing this chapter, the dollar is weak and hitting all-time lows, while European and Japanese currencies are strong. Consequently, record-making cross-border deals are in the works. In May 2008, the Japanese company Takeda Pharmaceutical completed its tender offer for Millenium Pharmaceuticals for $8.8 billion in cash (www.mlnm.com); on July 7, 2008, the giant Swiss pharmaceutical Novartis announced it was buying a 25 percent minority stake in eye care company Alcon from Nestlé for $10.4 billion cash, with the right to buy majority control (from Nestlé) in two more stages through the year 2011. Novartis also has announced a string of other smaller acquisitions in biotechnology and biopharmaceuticals (www.novartis.com). On July 21, 2008, Roche announced its intention to acquire the 44.1 percent equity stake in Genentech it does not already own for $43.7 billion, valuing the entire equity of Genentech at around $100 billion (www.roche.com).

Influence of the Exit Decision on Structuring the Alliance Strategy for Early-Stage Biotech Ventures

If the lead VC investor could know ahead of time that a trade sale would be the final exit path, then he or she might conceivably argue at a board of directors' meeting that the CEO of a biotech start-up should enter into *fewer* strategic licensing agreements than if the exit were done via an IPO. The ideal sequence of events leading up to a trade sale would go like this: (1) The CEO engages a major pharmaceutical company in negotiations on licensing the venture's key patents and therapeutic compounds undergoing clinical trials; (2) Wait and see if during the strategic alliance negotiations, the major pharmaceutical company is willing to go one step further and take a minority stake in the venture or even acquire it outright; (3) Because the other VCs who sit on the board typically follow the lead VC investor's advice, the board would vote in favor of the venture being acquired by the bigger company—if such an event were to unfold, and if the timing, terms, and conditions were appropriate; (4) Exit strategy completed.

Alternatively, the lead VC might have a different rationale, arguing the venture should follow a strategic path of negotiating an early licensing agreement on only one key therapeutic treatment (say, cancer), and in only one geographical territory, the U.S. market, for instance. Such an agreement with an important pharmaceutical company would validate the proof of concept while retaining key rights on other therapeutic treatment indications (say, for Alzheimer's or obesity) and keeping other territorial rights, say, in Europe or Japan, to do clinical trials and copromotion. That way, the venture company could learn from the big pharmaceutical alliance while enhancing value by developing the other therapeutic treatment areas on its own and gaining strength and expertise in such higher-value-added downstream activities as later-stage clinical trials or copromotion in key markets. Ideally the key strategic alliance partner would eventually become the trade sale partner, but only at a much later stage in the development cycle, when the company is worth more, if all goes according to plan. The upside is that hving fewer strategic alliances means that the venture's freedom-to-operate is less encumbered (because there are fewer exclusive patent licensing agreements) and hence the venture retains more value for its shareholders. The venture will be worth more to the purchaser, and the exiting investors can reap more profit at the time of the trade sale. The advice to the fledgling biotech or biopharmaceutical start-ups might be summed up as "Don't do more out-licensing deals than are absolutely necessary. Keep focused on a favorable trade sale exit."

Of course, the founding CEO might have an entirely different view from the venture capitalists. On the downside, who is to say such a single focus will bring the best final price? (Doesn't it usually help to be the object of desire of many players to get the highest price, such as the target of a bidding war or auction sale?) The CEO might suggest that it is better to have more than one lead compound validated by a leading biopharmaceutical company to hedge the risk of clinical trial failures. Therefore, the CEO will argue for more out-licensing agreements than might the VCs on the board.

Then again, the wheel of fate takes many a surprising turn. For instance, it might very well be that what appeared to be the ideal strategic alliance partner turned trade sale partner in the eyes of the VC could itself become a takeover target. In the past, the pharmaceutical industry, like many other mature industries, has periodically experienced intense rounds of consolidation. (It appears we may be entering one such period again.) It could be that the favored trade sale partner takes part in an unanticipated merger with another major pharmaceutical company. What at one time, five years earlier, appeared to be the best partner has suddenly become the worst partner due to an unforeseen merger and perhaps problems arising in postmerger integration. What also may happen is that the pharmaceutical company in question decides to change its focus on therapeutic research areas as a result of a merger or restructuring.

Other events might also change the course of decisions, such as clinical trial failures (these definitely eliminate a set of possibilities), unforeseen patent infringement lawsuits, scale-up and manufacturing problems, government health policy changes, medical reimbursement changes, and so forth.

How Exiting by IPO Affects a Biotechnology Venture's Licensing Strategy

For completeness, let us now examine the other option of exiting via an IPO shares listing. Suppose the board of directors, the VCs, and founding CEO of the biotechnology venture all know they want to go the IPO route. What would be the best strategy to pursue in the meantime?

Contrary to the VCs' advice for the trade sale exit, for the IPO route, all the parties involved would most likely recommend that the biopharmaceutical venture make as many out-licensing agreements with as many top-tier biopharmaceutical partners as it possibly could. Then the venture could better its odds of having adequate (and diverse) financing, through up-front payments, milestones, and eventually product royalties, to see it through to the IPO stage. When the conditions for an IPO are right (both from the point of view of the venture's development and the market), the company founders and the VCs would hope that equity market conditions are buoyant. They would hope the equity market "window of opportunity"[7] stays open long enough for them to get all regulatory approvals for the public listing, secure top-tier investment bankers, and have an oversubscribed issue. Then they would hope that the public equity markets stay buoyant during the "lock-up" period (when the founders, VCs, and other insiders are not allowed to sell shares) and that when they finally are able to sell out, that the market is still favorable and the company's pipeline of products hits all the promised milestones. This is the optimistic best-case scenario for an IPO exit.

The True Story of GenPharm International

To bring into focus the implications of these very different exit strategies, trade sale or IPO, we have chosen a capstone case to illustrate the real-life dilemma facing founders and VCs alike. (Refer to the GenPharm International case that is accessible by logging onto our web site at www.innovationtocashflows.com.)

The case deals with the real-life story of what happened to GenPharm International, the biotechnology company cofounded by Dr. Jonathan MacQuitty, and the issues he faced as he pondered an exit offer from Medarex, Inc., a publicly listed, much larger biopharmaceutical concern.

As you are reading this case, try to decide what you would do if you were in MacQuitty's shoes. Think about what we have written on exit strategies. What do you think has been MacQuitty's and his venture capital investors' exit strategy all along? How easy is it to change that exit strategy and adapt it to the company's current situation? The case will give you a chance to practice your skills at peering into your crystal ball, navigating strategic alliance negotiations, and deciding on an exit offer under turbulent, real-world conditions.

VENTURE CAPITAL METHOD OF VALUING YOUNG FLEDGLING FIRMS

In this section, we describe the way venture capitalists value young growth companies. These emerging companies typically have a talented group of scientists and engineers working on proprietary technology and creating innovative products or services. The team may have a few working models or product prototypes in the lab. The company is burning through its cash flow and producing losses rather than profits at this stage of development. The valuation dilemmas facing the first-round VC may be summed up in this quote from a prominent venture capitalist active in biotechnology investing in Silicon Valley who prefers to remain anonymous:

> *You should understand that biotech valuations are seriously unacademic in reality. No one uses option theory; discounted cash flows are rare. You are investing in companies where you cannot do an "earnings per share" calculation until 10 or even 15 years out and where the first revenues are often on a similar time frame. I don't think it's going to be very illuminating to review valuation methodology but maybe that point is itself something worth getting across.*

Contrary to the opinion of this VC, we definitely believe that it is relevant and important for entrepreneurs to know and understand how VCs value companies.

As we explore the VC approach in this section, always remember that the VC method takes the point of view of the *venture capital investor* rather than the company. Consequently, in the VC method, we will be using the *investor's* perceived opportunity cost of capital, *not* the company's required cost of capital. We will call the VC's cost of capital the target rate of return or the required rate of return. It is calculated on a compound annual basis. The time period is from the moment the VC fund buys shares in the venture to the time the VC fund sells its shares in the venture upon exiting the investment.

All the other financial concepts you need to know have been introduced in Chapter 17, namely, cost of the initial investment, terminal value, number of years to exit, opportunity cost of capital, and the by-now-familiar present value formula. The venture capital method of valuation is mathematically simple. It is the lack of precise inputs that makes these sorts of valuations difficult.

Next we discuss the target rates of return required by high-tech VCs in general. Then we give target rates of return required by life science venture capitalists specializing in early-stage biopharmaceutical ventures. Finally we explain how to apply the venture capital method by demonstrating its use with a case example.

Typical Venture Capital Discount Rates of Return

Early-stage venture capital investors typically demand a higher rate of return on investment than later stage venture capitalists. Investors in each successive round, require less expected return because generally speaking, the cash flows become less risky as the high-tech venture matures. Put differently, for most high-tech ventures, the risk of failure tends to decrease with each financing round.

In general, the first five years are particularly fraught with danger for small businesses. Numerous academic and government studies have tried to document the survival rates of small businesses. One such survey conducted by the Swiss Federal Statistics Office showed that more than four-fifths of all Swiss start-ups (from a variety of industries) survive the first year, but only about half survive their first five years of business. Figures are similar for small business start-ups in other countries.[8]

TABLE 19.2   Typical Venture Capital Target Rates of Return by Stage of Development

Stage of Development (Financing Round)	VC Target Rates of Return (Compound Annual Returns)	Typical Range of VC Target Rates of Return
Early beginnings (seed capital)	60%	50%–70% and up
Survival stage (1st round)	40%	30%–50%
Early stage (2nd round)	30%	25%–35%
Late stage (3rd or 4th rounds)	25%	20%–30%
Nearing exit (mezzanine or bridge)	20%	20%–25%
Seasoned small business	15%	12%–18%

Sources: Data updated from Leach and Melicher (2003, 237) based on authors' interviews conducted with venture capitalists in California, Finland, Italy, the Netherlands, and the United Kingdom during August 2008.

In Table 19.2, we depict reasonable target rates of return required by VCs according to the venture's stage of development. These are *target rates of return*; they are what VCs seek or *hope* to earn from investing in a portfolio company. Be aware that the target return is *not* the *actual* rate of return earned on the overall venture fund's portfolio over the 10-year life of the venture capital fund. The actual portfolio returns are *much lower* because most of the portfolio companies fail to earn the target rate of return; others go into bankruptcy or liquidation; and only a handful are big winners. (As the saying goes, "Lemons ripen faster than plums" where "lemons" refer to bad investments and the "plums" are the good investments.)

For instance, a seed-capital venture capitalist who is investigating an investment in a start-up company would target a rate of return of 60 percent compounded annually, with the average range being anywhere from 40 to 70 percent and up. For the next round of financing, the entering investor would ask for a 40 percent compound annual return, according to Table 19.2.

If the time horizon for the seed capital VC were five years, how much money would he make per $1 invested in the venture? Using the present value formula introduced in Chapter 17, we need to compound $1 at a 60 percent rate of return per year for five years.

$$Future\ Value\ (FV) = Present\ Value\ (PV) \times (1 + r)^n$$

Substituting in the numbers, we have:

$$FV = \$1.00 \times (1.60)^5 = \$10.49$$

In VC jargon, this compounded amount of $10.49 would be equivalent to an "exit multiple" of 10.5 times the initial $1 investment. VCs normally do not talk about their target rates of return to the entrepreneurs with whom they are negotiating. What they might do instead is drop a casual hint in conversation, such as "We seek a 10.5 times multiple on our initial investment," or "We like to get out at an exit multiple of between 10 to 11 times."

TABLE 19.3   Biopharmaceutical Required Rates of Return

Biopharmaceutical Company's Development Stage	Life Science VCs' Required Rate of Return	Drug Development Stage
Seed stage	70%–100%	Discovery—generating leads
Start-up stage	50%–70%	Optimizing leads/preclinical
First stage	40%–60%	Phase I clinical trials
Second stage	35%–50%	Phase II clinical trials
Later stage	25%–40%	Phase III clinical trials

Source: Adapted from Patrick Frei and Benoit Leleoux, "Valuation: What You Need to Know," *Nature Biotechnology* (August 2004).

Naturally these target rates of return will vary depending on the industry sector, country of origin, current venture capital market conditions, and general economic conditions—recession or boom, and especially the level of general interest rates.

To learn the VC target rates for your sector, it is best to talk to other entrepreneurs who have recently obtained funding and network with VCs familiar with the market in your local region and for your particular industry. What you do not want to do is go in and pitch your deal to the VC whom you really want to fund your venture and set an initial price that is way too high compared to other deals the VC is seeing. You will not get a second chance to pitch your deal.

In Table 19.3, we provide typical venture capital target rates of return for the biopharmaceutical sector. The early-stage VC fund investing in this sector is exposed to the very high risks of clinical trials failures. Consequently, the target rates of return demanded by life science VCs are generally higher than for other kinds of high-tech investors; you can see this by comparing the higher target rates of return in Table 19.3 with the lower target rates of return in Table 19.2.

CASE STUDY: TSP ENTERPRISES SEEKS VENTURE FINANCING

In this fictional case study, two entrepreneurs decide to go into business together. Carl Strauss, an experienced software programmer, and his colleague Steven Chung, an expert in hardware systems, want to form a company. They met when both were working for United Technologies in Los Angeles and have known each other for a decade. They have come up with an innovative idea for a new virtual gaming platform. Their platform uses a computer storage product that is useful for developing interactive entertainment in the form of digital games and movies, all of which need to process and store massive amounts of data. Carl and Steven, after consulting with their lawyers, decide to incorporate. They have formed a small corporation called TSP Enterprises, Inc. The letters stand for Tourmaline Surf Park, their favorite surfing spot in Pacific Beach (San Diego). Their accountant advised them to issue 2 million shares of common stock (1 million shares each).

Carl and Steven were at home in Los Angeles, working over the weekend to prepare a detailed business plan. They had already begun talking to their network of friends to learn more about the local venture capital community and whom they thought might be interested in funding their company. Their preliminary business plan forecasts that TSP would need $4 million in immediate venture capital investment and that the company would reach a forecasted profit of $7.5 million in year 5. They thought by that time their venture would be ripe for either a trade sale or IPO. Their plan would be to raise all $4 million in one financing round, enough to commence operations and to cover all their cash flow needs until the end of year 5.

On Monday morning, after hearing their business plan pitch, the senior partner at Sapphire Venture Capital and the General Partner of Sapphire Ventures, Ltd., a seed capital fund managed by a team of well-known VCs, said he might be interested in funding TSP Enterprises. He said he would want 1,745,555 in newly issued shares in return for his fund's $4 million investment. As they were leaving the conference room and heading for the elevator, the partner reiterated that Sapphire's offer meant a *premoney* valuation of $4.58 million and a *postmoney* valuation of $8.58 million (defined in the next section). Carl and Steve told him that they would think it over and call him back in the morning with an answer.

Premoney and Postmoney Terminology

Premoney refers to the value of a company's equity *before* it receives a round of external equity financing. *Postmoney* is the value of the company's equity *after* receiving the equity financing. Hence the postmoney valuation of $8.58 million is simply the premoney valuation of $4.58 million plus the $4 million first-round financing provided by Sapphire. In equation form, we can express the relationship this way:

$$\text{Postmoney Valuation} = \text{Premoney Valuation} + \text{Investment}$$

APPLYING THE VENTURE CAPITAL VALUATION METHOD

The venture capital method is based on four simple ideas: money in, money out, time to exit, and discount the venture's future free cash flows at the VCs' target rate of return. The important point to remember is that when deciding on which discount rate to use, the venture capital method takes the point of view of the *investor* rather than of the company. So in the VC method, we want to use the *investor's* opportunity cost of capital, not the company's cost of capital. The concepts you need to know have already been introduced in Chapter 17, namely, initial investment, terminal value, number of years to exit, and opportunity cost of capital, plus the by-now familiar present value formula. We explain the venture capital method step by step next.

1. *Money in.* This is the cash investment today that the venture capital fund plans to make in the new venture. We will use the numbers envisioned for TSP Enterprises, Carl Strauss and Steven Chung's start-up business. Sapphire's investment plans are to put $4,000,000 into the venture at time $t = 0$. Turn to Table 19.4 and refer to the first scenario for TSP Enterprises called "One Financing Round" to follow the explanation of the procedure.

2. *Money out.* This is the amount the business is thought to be worth at the time of exit. The value is computed by the VC based on some market measure, for instance, an earnings multiple of a group of comparable high-tech companies

TABLE 19.4 TSP Enterprises, Inc. and Sapphire Ventures

Scenario A: One Financing Round

Assumptions

Net Income, year 5	$7,500,000
Price-to-earnings Ratio (PER) at Exit, at time t = T	12
Sapphire Venture's Round 1 Investment, at time t = 0	$4,000,000
Sapphire Venture's Target Rate of Return	60%
TSP Common Shares Issued and Outstanding, at t = 0	2,000,000
Exit Assumed at End of Year T =	5 years

Venture Capital Cash Flows and Valuation		t = 0	t = 1	t = 2	t = 3	t = 4	T = 5
Sapphire Investment, at time t = 0	Years	$ (4,000,000)	0	0	0	0	
Terminal Value of TSP at exit, T = 5							$90,000,000
Discount Terminal Value at Sapphire's target rate of return to the present time, t = 0	$8,583,069						
Sapphire's Required Ownership Stake (%) to Earn Their Target Return	46.603378%						
Number of New Shares Issued by TSP for Sapphire Ventures to Purchase	1,745,555						
Price per Share	$2.29153						
Premoney Value of TSP Enterprises	$4,583,069						
Postmoney Value of TSP Enterprises	$8,583,069						
Final Wealth of the Investors	$41,943,040						
Final Wealth of the Cofounders	$48,056,960						
Present Value of Investor's Wealth	$4,000,000						
Present Value of Cofounders' Wealth	$4,583,069						

(relative valuation techniques) or a transaction-based earnings multiple (relying on recent and similar venture capital deals for this type of seed venture being appraised). The VC way of determining the terminal value is simply to multiply the earnings multiple by the terminal year's earnings. In the business plan, Carl and Steven forecast earnings in year 5 to be about $7.5 million. The VC decides a price-to-earnings ratio (PER) of 12 times is appropriate based on a sample of recent deal transactions in the Los Angeles area. So Sapphire estimates the exit value as simply 12 × $7.5 million = $90 million.

The observant reader will wonder why Sapphire used the last year's earnings instead of the earnings forecast for the next period (T + 1)? If you recall, we used the dividends in the period (T + 1) for the dividend discount method and the next period after the terminal year, in other words, free cash flows for (T + 1) in the enterprise valuation method. VCs (and many investment bankers) will argue that given all the uncertainties surrounding the sales forecasts, operating margins, and timing, it does not really matter whether they use earnings for period T or (T + 1). To keep life simple, VCs tend to use the last year's earnings at time T.

3. *Determine the postmoney valuation using the VC's opportunity cost of funds.* We take the VC perspective and use the VC's required rate of return (sometimes called the target rate of return) to discount the exit value (terminal value) back to the present time, $t = 0$. When discounted back to the present by Sapphire's opportunity cost of funds, the exit value is equal to the postmoney valuation. The formula is

$$\text{PV of the Exit Value} = \text{Postmoney Valuation} = \frac{TV}{(1 + r)^t}$$

Sapphire, like most VC's investing in the earliest stages of a start-up, has its own internal target rates of return that it uses for valuation purposes. Sapphire demands a 60 percent compound annual return for seed capital investments (refer to the first row of Table 19.2 for this target rate of return). Substituting in the numbers, we compute the discounted results over the time horizon of 5 years:

$$\text{Postmoney Valuation} = \frac{\$90,000,000}{(1.60)^5} = \$8,583,069$$

4. *Calculate the premoney valuation from the postmoney valuation.* We simply take the postmoney valuation (step 3) and subtract Sapphire's investment amount of $4 million. That is to say,

$$\text{Premoney Valuation} = (\text{Postmoney Valuation}) - (\text{Investment})$$

$$\text{Premoney Valuation} = \$8,583,069 - \$4,000,000 = \$4,583,069$$

We have now verified what Sapphire said at the meeting, namely, that the premoney valuation was $4.58 million and the postmoney valuation is $8.58 million. So far, everything appears to be going smoothly.

5. *Determine the VC's required ownership stake.* Divide the VC's investment at time $t = 0$ (from step 1) by the venture's discounted future terminal value (from step 3.)

$$\text{VC's final ownership stake} = \frac{\text{Initial Investment}}{\text{PV of the Exit Value}}$$

To compute Sapphire's final ownership stake, we insert the initial investment of \$4,000,000 in the numerator and divide it by the result of step 3, which was \$8,583,069. The result is the fraction of ownership = 0.466034 that the VC requires in order to meet the 60 percent target rate of return. Converted to a percentage (by multiplying by 100), the percentage ownership required is 46.60338 percent. (We will keep all the decimals for the moment.) This means the VC wants to own nearly half the company, leaving the founders with the residual, or 53.39662 percent. The two founders, Carl and Steven, will keep majority control of the company.

6. *Determine the number of new shares to be issued and purchased by the VC.* We assume that both Carl and Steven will keep all their shares and will be issuing a new series of shares to be bought by the VC fund, Sapphire Ventures Limited. To get the number of new shares required, we use this reasoning. The \$4 million investment by the VC would be 46.60338 percent of the present value of the exit value (from step 5). Therefore, TSP Enterprises must issue shares to the investor so that the newly issued shares, N, will be equal to the fractional ownership 0.4660338 of the *total* shares outstanding after the new issue, where total shares equals new shares plus current shares outstanding (or the existing shares). In symbols, let

f = VC's fractional ownership

NS = new shares to be issued and purchased by the VC investor

CSO = current shares outstanding

We can express the VC's fractional ownership by this formula:

$$f = \frac{\text{New Shares}}{(\text{New Shares} + \text{Current Shares Outstanding})} = \frac{NS}{NS + CSO}$$

Solving algebraically for the new shares, this expression may be rewritten as the fundamental equation of the venture capital method. This next expression is the one you need to remember:

$$NS = \frac{f \times CSO}{(1 - f)}$$

$$NS = \frac{\left(\dfrac{\$4,000,000}{\$8,583,609}\right) \times 2,000,000 \text{ Current Shares Outstanding}}{1 - \left(\dfrac{\$4,000,000}{\$8,583,609}\right)}$$

$$= 1,745,555 \text{ new shares}$$

7. *Compute the share price of the newly issued shares.* To determine the price of the new shares, we divide Sapphire's $4 million investment by the number of new shares to be purchased (1,745,555) and determine that the price of the new shares equals $2.29/share (rounded to two decimals).

Now we have determined all the key variables to the venture capital method. Any other results may be computed from what we have derived up to this point. For instance, the entrepreneurs may be very interested to learn what their final wealth will be in year 5, if all works out as planned. Their final wealth in year 5 is simply the final exit price (terminal value) multiplied by their ownership stake, which we said in step 5 was $(1 - f)$, or 53.39662 percent, since there is only one financing round. Thus, according to Table 19.4, the entrepreneur's final wealth at the time of the VC exit will be $48,056,960. The wealth of Sapphire Fund in year 5 will be $41,943,040, since they own fewer shares in the company than the entrepreneurs.

ADJUSTING THE VC METHOD FOR MULTIPLE ROUNDS OF FINANCING

Most venture financing is done in stages. Why? Staging lowers the risks of both parties. The VC fund has time to get to know the entrepreneurial team's capabilities better and avoids investing large upfront sums into a venture that could flounder. The entrepreneurs benefit because they will not be charged venture capital rates of return on surplus cash that is deposited in the new venture's bank account and earning only money market rates. We said that the VC method is a simplified approach. It does not distinguish between cash that is put to use right away and cash that sits in the bank. Staged investing reduces the surplus cash penalty.[9]

"Divide to Multiply"

The key to understanding multiple rounds of financing is to get a grip on the notion of "divide to multiply." The basic idea is that entrepreneurs are willing to *divide* up the shares they own in their company to *multiply* their wealth some day in the future. Rather than owning a big slice of a very little pie, their idea is to own a smaller slice in what it is hoped one day will become a much larger pie. When contemplating venture capital financing, the founders must be willing to divide up the shares in their little pie (the venture) and share them with the VCs, in the hope that down the road, everybody will win: The venture becomes a huge success, and founders and VCs are able to multiply their wealth in the end. To see how this works, refer to Table 19.5 and take a look at the scenario called "Two Financing Rounds."

The situation is the same as before. Carl and Steven are the entrepreneurs who cofound the same venture start-up, TSP Enterprises; furthermore, the first-round financing will be done by Sapphire Ventures Ltd., our familiar seed venture capital fund, which is still requiring a 60 percent target rate of return. The only difference is that Carl and Steven are now looking for an early-stage VC fund that is willing to invest a large round of financing at the end of year 2 (we will name this fund R2). We have penciled in a figure of $9 million for round two, and we are now constructing

TABLE 19.5 TSP Enterprises, Inc., Sapphire Ventures, and R2

Panel A: Scenario B: Two Financing Rounds

Assumptions

Net Income at year 5	$7,500,000
Price-to-earnings Ratio (PER) at Exit in year 5	12
Investment Required (at time 0)	$4,000,000
Investment Required (at time, t = 2 years)	$9,000,000
Sapphire Venture's Target Rate of Return	60%
Second Round Investor R2's Target Rate of Return	40%
Initial Shares Issued and Outstanding	2,000,000

	t = 0	t = 1	t = 2	t = 3	t = 4	T = 5
Venture Capital Cash Flows						
Sapphire Ventures Investment at t = 0	$(4,000,000)					
R2's Investment at time t = 2 years		0	$(9,000,000)	0	0	
TSP Enterprises Terminal Value at exit, T = 5 years						$90,000,000

Second-Round Investor (R2)	
Value of TSP at time t = 2, found by discounting the terminal value by R2's target rate of return	$32,798,834
R2 Ownership's Stake Required to Meet Target Rate of Return, at time t = 2	27.44%
Sapphire Ventures	
Value of TSP at Sapphire's Target Rate of Return at t = 0	$8,583,069
Sapphire's Ownership Stake to Earn Required Rate of Return at Time of Exit, T = 5	46.60338%
Retention Ratio (1-R2's stake)	0.7256
Sapphire's ownership stake grossed up by the retention rate for time t = 0	64.22737%
Number of Shares Sapphire Requires to Avoid Dilution	3,590,866
Share Price at Time, t = 0	$1.11394

(Continued)

TABLE 19.5 (*Continued*)

Premoney Value of TSP Enterprises at t = 0 for Initial Number of Shares	$2,227,875	Premoney Value of TSP, t = 2	$23,798,834
Postmoney Value of TSP Enterprises (Premoney + Sapphire's investment)	$6,227,875	Premoney Share Price of TSP, t = 2	$4.2567

Situation of Second-Round Investor R2 (at t = 2 years)

Shares purchased by R2 investor	2,114,297	R2 pays Premoney Share Price
Total Number of TSP Shares Issued and Outstanding after the Two Financing Rounds	7,705,163	
Number of TSP Shares Issued in 2nd Round to R2	2,114,297	
Share Price Paid by R2 (Premoney Price at t = 2 years)	$4.2567	
Premoney Valuation, at t = 2 years	$23,798,834	
Postmoney Valuation, at t = 2 years	$32,798,834	

Panel B: Summary of Scenario B *after* Two Rounds of Financing

Cofounder's Remaining Equity Stake	25.9566222%
Total Shares in Year 5 (initial no. of shares/Cofounder's remaining % stake)	7,705,163
Shares Issued to R2 (second-round venture capitalists)	2,114,297
Shares Issued to Sapphire	3,590,866
Cofounders' Shares (unchanged)	2,000,000
Postmoney Value per Share at T = 5	$ 11.68 per share
Cofounders' Stake Is Worth at T = 5	$ 23,360,960
Sapphire's First-Round Stake Is Worth at T = 5	$ 41,943,040
Second-Round Investor's Stake Is Worth at T = 5	$ 24,696,000

Panel C: Summary of Investor Cash Flows

	Year 0	Year 1	Year 2	Year 3	Year 4	Year 5
Sapphire Ventures, Ltd. Investment Cash Flows	$ (4,000,000)	0	0	0	0	$ 41,943,040
R2 Ventures, Ltd. Investment Cash Flows	0	0	$ (9,000,000)	0	0	$ 24,696,000
Cofounders' Wealth at Exit						$ 23,360,960
TSP Enterprise Exit Value or Terminal Value (ignoring transaction costs)					Total Value	$ 90,000,000

the spreadsheets to see what happens to everyone's stake in TSP and especially what happens to everyone's wealth at the time of exit, still envisioned for the end of year 5.

As shown in Table 19.5, we have kept Sapphire's initial investment of negative $4 million at time $t = 0$ and have inserted a second cash flow of negative $9 million in the column under $t = 2$ to represent R2's investment into the company, representing the money in. The terminal value, or the money out, stays the same as before at $90 million, computed as year 5 earnings of 7.5 million times a PER multiple of 12. Time to exit is still 5 years for Carl and Steven and also for Sapphire. However, for the venture fund, R2, time to exit is only three years, since it puts money into the deal only at the end of year 2. The opportunity cost of funds, target rate of return, for R2 is estimated at 40 percent, per Table 19.2 and the row for "Survival Stage" or first-round financing. Since TSP Enterprises will have survived the first two years, it is reasonable to assume that R2 will require a lower rate of return for an up-and-running company compared to Sapphire, which entered at the seed stage. We insert the inputs into the spreadsheet formulas, and let the computer compute the results.

Not surprisingly, we learn that Sapphire will want to maintain its final ownership stake at slightly over 46.60 percent. However, the pie in terms of shares is now larger after two rounds than it was before with only a single round of financing. The total number of shares issued after two rounds has expanded to 7,705,163. The shares are split up so that R2 receives 2,114,297 shares; Sapphire is issued 3,590,866 shares; and our entrepreneurs keep their founder share stake intact at 2,000,000 shares (1 million shares for each). What is going on? Why is it that Sapphire gets more shares when the founders' number of shares stays the same? The reasons are related to equity dilution. The founders' stake is diluted (watered down or reduced) when R2 enters the picture. However, Sapphire will insist on not being diluted. They want to keep their percentage ownership stake the same; otherwise, they will not meet their 60 percent target rate of return. As more shares are issued, Sapphire needs to acquire proportionately more shares so as to avoid suffering a reduction in its percentage of the holdings. Why would the entrepreneurs be willing to suffer the dilution? The answer lies in the previously described notion of divide to multiply. By allowing their percentage share to be reduced (or diluted), they are allowing more money to come into the venture, thereby enhancing the size of the pie. With the infusion of capital, the entrepreneurs hope to use the financing to avoid running out of cash, to create more value, and, thereby, to make their shareholders and themselves richer in the end. Carl and Steven know that in order to reap any reward at the end, their firm needs to reach the finish line. Better to survive and be diluted than not to survive at all.

If you recall from the first round of financing, the entrepreneurs were worried about losing control of their venture to Sapphire. Carl and Steven were able to hang onto 53.397 percent of their shares, and gave 46.603 percent to Sapphire in exchange for $4 million. After two rounds of financing, Sapphire maintained its equity stake at 46.603 percent; however, Carl and Steven gave up their rights to acquire more shares in the next round of shares that were issued and therefore suffered dilution from 53.397 percent down to 25.957 percent, which is equivalent to their equity stake after R2's financing. In effect, Carl and Steven gave up 27.44 percent and majority control in order to gain $9 million more in second-round financing. The R2 stake is 2,114,297 shares divided by 7,705,163 total shares or 27.44 percent, exactly the same amount by which Carl and Steven were diluted.

The key is for us to understand how Sapphire avoided dilution. It did so by demanding more shares for the scenario of two rounds of financing than it received when there was only one round of financing. With the single round, Sapphire purchased 1,745,555 shares for roughly $2.29 per share (we are rounding to two decimal places on the share price). With the double round, Sapphire purchases 3,590,866 shares at a price of $4 million invested divided by 3,590,866 shares, or $1.11 per share (rounded to two decimals). If you note, Carl and Steven hold onto their 2 million shares; they do not acquire new ones in subsequent financing rounds, and that is why they suffer the dilution. If Sapphire had not been issued all the shares it demanded, it would have suffered dilution, too, and would have had to have lowered its targeted return on investment. Sapphire therefore will try to avoid dilution. Its original investment agreement with Carl and Steven would include conditions for avoiding dilution. (Refer to Chapter 10 where investment agreements are described and the various contract clauses discussed.)

Let us see how we can calculate the ownership percentages and the total number of shares outstanding after two financing rounds of financing. This time we will solve it slightly differently. We will make use of the required rate of return of the venture capital investors, R2 and then Sapphire. This is known as the IRR (internal rate of return) way of expressing the venture capital method. It gives results identical to the present value approach we used earlier, where we discounted the future values to the present. With the IRR method, instead of discounting (dividing) by the compounding factor, we multiply to determine the future values. Both methods make use of the same fundamental relationship. The future value relationship we will be using is:

$$\text{Future Value} = \text{Present Value} \times (1 + R)^n$$

We start with R2's investment and compound it into the future (by multiplying it at R2's required rate of return of 40 percent per year) for the number of years it will be invested into TSP Enterprises (in this case three years, from year 2 to year 5). This is the numerator of our next equation.

Then we calculate the fractional ownership required by R2 at the time of exit, which is at the end of year 5. We do this computation by dividing the future compounded value of R2's investment by the value of the company's terminal value ($90 million). This will be the fractional ownership required by R2 at the time of exit in order to have enough shares on hand to make its target or required rate of return. If R2 buys less than this amount, it will have too few shares to meet its target IRR. If it buys more shares, then it will exceed its target IRR. The result is that to achieve a target IRR of 40 percent compounded for three years, R2 will need to own 27.44 percent of the company at the time of exit. (See the next equation for the computation.)

Second-Round Stake Acquired by R2

$$\text{R2's Fractional Ownership} = \frac{(\text{R2's Investment} = \$9 \text{ million}) \times (1 + .40)^3}{TV = \$90 \text{ million}}$$

$$= 0.27440 \text{ or } 27.44\% \text{ (rounded to two decimals)}$$

The next step is to calculate Sapphire's fractional ownership, recalling that its required opportunity cost is 60 percent and that it makes and then holds its investment for the full five years. We follow the same procedure. We compound (multiply) Sapphire's initial $4 million investment by its target IRR of 60 percent per annum. We do this for five years by raising 1.60 to the 5th power. We now have the numerator of our expression. The denominator will be the terminal value of $90 million, which is the future value of the company at time of exit. Remember when computing fractional ownerships to always match future values of the investment with the future value of the company (future to future). The other possibility (which is what we did for the Round 1 financing) is to match the values of the investments when they were initially made with the value of the company at that same time. There we are matching present values of the investment with the present value of the company (present to present). In order to achieve its target internal rate of return of 60 percent per annum, Sapphire needs to acquire 46.60 percent of the company at the time of exit, at the end of year 5. (See the next equation for the computation.)

First-Round Stake Acquired

Sapphire's Fractional Ownership

$$= \frac{(\text{Sapphire's Investment} = \$4 \text{ million}) \times (1 + .60)^5}{TV = \$90 \text{ million}}$$

$$= 0.46603 = 46.60\% \text{ (rounded to two decimals)}$$

So far, so good, the results are consistent with what we calculated earlier. The last step is to determine the ownership stake held by our two entrepreneurial founders, Carl and Steven. They will hold whatever is left after the others investors have acquired their stakes.

Founders' Remaining Stake after Financing Rounds Completed

Founders' Fractional Ownership $= 1 - (\text{R2's stake}) - (\text{Sapphire's stake})$

$$= 1 - 0.27440000 - 0.46603378$$

$$= 0.25956622$$

Total Shares Issued and Outstanding   The total number of shares after two rounds of financing is then easily found by dividing the founders' stake by their fraction of remaining ownership. To enhance accuracy and avoid rounding errors, we input all the decimals in the data for the denominator of the next equation.

Total Shares after Financing

$$= \frac{\text{Founders' equity stake or } 2,000,000 \text{ shares}}{\text{Founders' Remaining Fractional Ownership or } 0.259566222}$$

$$= 7,705,163 \text{ shares}$$

SUMMARY OF TWO FINANCING ROUNDS
FOR TSP ENTERPRISES

Here we summarize the key data from the two rounds of financing provided to TSP Enterprises, Inc. by our VC funds Sapphire Ventures and R2. These results may also be cross-checked with the data provided in Table 19.5 in the previous section.

First Round of Financing Provided
by Sapphire Ventures Ltd.

$$\text{Share price} = \frac{\$4,000,000}{3,590,866 \text{ shares}} = \$1.113937373 \text{ per share}$$

$$\text{Premoney Valuation of TSP} = \$1.11393737373 \text{ per share} \times 2,000,000$$
$$\text{founders' shares} = \$2,227,875$$

$$\text{Postmoney Valuation of TSP} = \$1.113937373 \text{ per share}$$
$$\times (2,000,000 \text{ shares} + 3,590,866 \text{ shares}) = \$1.113937373 \text{ per share}$$
$$\times 5,590,866 \text{ shares} = \$6,227,875$$

We cross-check the above calculation by quickly taking the premoney valuation and adding to it the first-round financing investments, that is, \$2,227,875 plus the \$4 million investment by Sapphire = Postmoney Valuation = \$6,227,876. The two results match, as they should.

$$\text{Founders' Percentage between 1st and 2nd Rounds}$$
$$= \frac{2,000,000}{5,590,866} \text{ shares} = 35.7726334\%$$

$$\text{Sapphire's Ownership Stake between 1st and 2nd Rounds}$$
$$= \frac{3,590,866}{5,590,866} = 64.2273666\%$$

Retention Ratio   A comment about Sapphire's percentage between the first and second rounds of financing: Another way to calculate this result is to use what is called a retention ratio (refer to Table 19.5). We compute the equity stake Sapphire needs to acquire after two financing rounds by using the retention ratio for the ith financing round, where the retention ratio is defined as:

$$\text{Retention Ratio for Round i} = R_i = (1 - d_{i+1}) \times (1 - d_{i+2}) \ldots (1 - d_{i+n}),$$

where $d_{d_{i+1}}$ = fractional ownership given to the $(i\text{th} + 1)$ subsequent round of investors

n = total number of financing rounds

In our example, for only two rounds of financing, the retention ratio = (1 – second round investor's fractional ownership) = 1 – R2's stake, or (1 – 0.2744) = 0.7256.

If we divide Sapphire's stake (after round 1) by the retention ratio, we are grossing up its ownership stake to take into account the dilution that will come from the later financing rounds. As shown in Table 19.5, right below the line where it says Retention Ratio, you will find we have determined that Sapphire's stake would need to expand from 46.603378 to 64.22737 percent. How did we know? Because we divided Sapphire's stake (after round 1) by the retention ratio of 0.7256 to get 64.22737 percent, which exactly corresponds to Sapphire's ownership stake between the first and second rounds that we computed earlier. It does not matter which way you do it; the results should be identical if you are careful about not truncating decimal points when you do the numbers.

Summary of Second-Round Financing Provided by R2

Shares Issued to R2 = R2's fractional ownership × total number of shares

$$= 0.27440 \times 7,705,163 \text{ shares} = 2,114,297 \text{ shares}$$

Compute the price of R2 shares = \$9,000,000/2,114,297 shares = \$4.2567 per share.

Premoney valuation = \$4.26 per share × 5,590,866 shares outstanding *before* the 2nd round = \$23,798,834.

(Note: For this last calculation, we actually performed it by inputting the share price in our spreadsheet without truncating the decimals to avoid rounding errors.)

Postmoney valuation = premoney valuation + R2's 2nd-round investment, or \$23,798,834 + \$9,000,000 = \$32,798,834.

Cross-check the answer by multiplying the share price (with decimals) times the number of shares outstanding after the 2nd round of financing to see if you get the same result:

\$4.2567 per share × (5,590,866 + 2,114,297 shares issued to R2)

= \$4.256734 per share × 7,705,163 shares or \$32,798,834

(Crosscheck complete.)

Founders' stake between 2nd round and exit

$$= \frac{2,000,000 \text{ shares}}{7,705,163 \text{ shares}} = 25.9566222\%$$

Sapphire's stake between 2nd round and exit

$$= \frac{3,590,866 \text{ shares}}{7,705,163 \text{ shares}} = 46.60337\%$$

R2's stake between 2nd round and exit $= \dfrac{2,114,297}{7,705,163 \text{ shares}} = 27.44\%$

Summary of the Final Wealth of the Investors and Founders at the End of Year 5

Sapphire's final wealth is $41,942,040.

R2's final wealth is $24,969,000.

Carl Strauss and Steven Chung's final combined wealth is $23,360,960.

Sum of all the final wealth figures = exit value = $90,000,000.

MULTIPLE-ROUND VERSUS SINGLE-ROUND FINANCING

Now let us take a look at what would have happened to the valuation of the equity stake of our two entrepreneurs if they had decided to do one large round of financing (a "mega round") with Sapphire alone rather than two rounds with Sapphire and R2. Which is better, one round or two?

To answer this question, we go back to the spreadsheet model we set up for one round of financing (see Table 19.4). Only this time, instead of Sapphire putting up $4 million as the initial investment, we revise the investment to $4 million + the PV of $9 million discounted back for two years at 60 percent (the target rate of return for Sapphire). In other words,

$$\text{Sapphire's Revised Investment} = \$4,000,000 + \frac{9,000,000}{(1.6)^2} = \$7,515,625$$

Having Sapphire invest $7,515,625 up front is equivalent to receiving $4 million from Sapphire at time $t = 0$, and then another $9 million at time $t = 2$. We are realistically assuming that Sapphire will not be willing to lower its target rate of return from 60 percent, because it is still investing the money at time $t = 0$, when TSP Enterprises is still in its infancy. We will call this new model the mega round Scenario. (Refer to Table 19.6.)

As shown in Table 19.6, Carl and Steven will be *far worse off* if they follow the mega round strategy than if they do two rounds of financing. In a mega round scenario, Sapphire Ventures would need to ask for an equity stake of over 87.56 percent, leaving the two cofounders holding the remainder of about 12.44 percent. The lower equity stake for Carl and Steven means the combined wealth of the two founders shrinks to $11,192,960 compared to $23,360,960 with two rounds of financing.

What happened? Carl and Steven are paying a stiff price for their extra cash up front. It is costing them 60 percent per year for all five years if they get it from Sapphire. The entrepreneurs only need the money at the very end of year 2. If they wait, they get the money for a much lower cost from R2 (at 40 percent) than Sapphire is willing to give them.

This last example illustrates the surplus cash penalty we were describing earlier. The venture capital method is actually a very simple valuation technique. It assumes all cash supplied to the venture is being used at the compound rate of return required by the VC, an unrealistic assumption from the company's point of view. It also does not differentiate cash that is put to work in the business and cash that is parked temporarily in a bank account to be used later.

TABLE 19.6 TSP Enterprises, Inc. and Sapphire Ventures

Scenario C: Mega-Round Only with Sapphire Ventures Ltd.

Assumptions

Net Income, year 5	$7,500,000
Price-to-Earnings Ratio (PER) at exit in year 5	12
Sapphire Venture's Mega-Round Investment, t = 0	$7,515,625
Sapphire Venture's Target Rate of Return	60%
TSP Common Shares Issued and Outstanding, t = 0	2,000,000
Exit occurs at time T =	5 years

Venture Capital Cash Flows and Valuation	5 years total	t = 0	t = 1	t = 2	t = 3	t = 4	T = 5
Sapphire's Mega-Round Investment at t = 0		$ (7,515,625)	0	0	0	0	
Terminal Value of TSP at end of T = Year 5							$ 90,000,000
Discount Terminal Value at Sapphire's target rate of return to the present time, t = 0	$8,583,069						
Sapphire's required ownership stake to earn target return	87.56338%						
Number of New Shares issued that Sapphire Ventures would purchase	14,081,537						
Price per share	$0.5337						
Premoney value of TSP Enterprises	$1,067,444						
Postmoney value of TSP Enterprises	$8,583,069						
Final Wealth of Sapphire, at T = 5	$78,807,040						
Final Wealth of the Cofounders, at T = 5	$11,192,960						
PV of Sapphire's Wealth, at t = 0	$7,515,625						
PV of Cofounders' Wealth, at t = 0	$1,067,444						

The main advantage of the VC method its simplicity and ability to handle multiple financing rounds at different rates of return. However, when it comes to valuing surplus cash, the method suffers from many defects compared to a more detailed discounted cash flow calculation.

In the end, it boils down to this: The VC method is equivalent to doing a simple net present value calculation, where NPV = 0, money comes in (the investment) and money goes out (the terminal value) but *only* at the time of exit. Therefore, the internal rate of return (IRR) is equal to the VC's target rate of return. If there are complicated flows of cash coming into and out of the deal, and especially if there is a buildup of surplus cash, it will be better for our entrepreneurs Carl and Steven to develop more detailed cash flow projections and then discount them using either the dividend discount model or the enterprise valuation approach, as we did in Chapter 17. These methods handle the buildup of surplus cash better than the VC method. The cofounders can then compare their results with the VC method and be better prepared for their negotiations with interested venture capitalists.

QUESTIONS WHEN APPLYING THE VENTURE CAPITAL METHOD

The VC method is a simplified valuation approach and poses a number of other quandaries for first-time users. For instance, the next questions might have arisen as you were reading the examples and explanations.

Why Do Venture Capitalists Use Current Multiples to Determine the Terminal Value?

VC industry practice is to use current market multiples for comparable companies (relative valuation or current M&A deal transactions) even though the valuation is projected at some future date when the market conditions are unknowable and most likely will not be comparable to today's market conditions. This industry practice may not seem fair to the entrepreneurs, especially if the VC is using a low multiple due to poor current stock market conditions, such as when the economy is entering a deep recession. However, VCs will be the first to tell entrepreneurs that when markets are buoyant, they also use higher relative multiples to make their calculations. When we ask VCs why they do this, they typically say, "We aren't clairvoyant." VCs think that today's equity markets provide a useful and transparent measure of market sentiment. Their logic is that they have to raise funds from their institutional investors at market prices, so market prices should set the measure for their opportunity cost of funds. Over the course of 10 years, stock market conditions are likely to cycle. Hence over time, and over repeated fund raisings, VCs have come to believe that these effects tend to even out over the long run. The alternative is more complexity without necessarily better results. Bear in mind that the two sides, the entrepreneurs and the VCs, will (if all goes well) enter into due diligence (see Chapter 16) and extended negotiations regarding the final terms and conditions of the financing (see Chapter 10). The quick VC method of valuation is merely one starting point for beginning the shareholder negotiations.

Why Do Venture Capitalists Demand Such High Target Rates of Return?

Most probably, Carl and Steve are thinking they potentially would become a lot richer if the earliest venture capitalists were not so greedy in demanding a 60 percent compound return on investment per year. That estimate seems high to Carl and Steve. What is the rationale for such a high target rate of return? Here are three frequently mentioned reasons.

First, venture investing, especially in emerging companies, is a high-risk business. Higher risks require adequate compensation in the form of higher expected returns. VCs spend a lot of effort gathering good investment leads and qualifying them. As we mentioned in an earlier section (see Venture Capital Acceptance Rate), for every 100 business plans the VCs receive, on average they end up investing in only two or three ventures. And then out of those ventures in which they finally do invest, the VCs will earn outsize returns on only one or two out of every 10 of their investee companies. The odds of success are therefore very low. VCs must ask for high target rates to compensate for the many losers that they know from experience they will have in their portfolios.

Good VCs keep track of their deal flow (the number of leads and business plans they review each year). They also keep track of who among their contacts gives them good leads over time and is consistent at steering them toward good opportunities. They also must keep track of their portfolio's investment histories for their limited partners' information. Consequently over time, the more mature VC firms have an extensive database. They will know their deal flows and their investment hit rate (success rate). Based on these data, they will know what target and realized returns they must have, according to the stage of investing, in order to attract new investment from their limited partners.

A second explanation VCs often give to entrepreneurs who ask about their high target rates of return is that they are providing expertise, advice, their vast networks of connections, and strategic counsel to their investee companies. Instead of billing their services on an hourly rate, as doctors or lawyers do, they bundle their fees into their target rates of return. This approach avoids confrontation between VCs and investee companies over billing charges. Entrepreneurs may argue that VCs are already compensated for their management experience in the management fee that they charge to their limited partners. However, VCs are likely to reply that the management fee covers their costs of obtaining the limited partners' funds and compensates them for the general partners' liability risks associated with managing the fund. They will say that the operating expertise and contacts available to the investee companies should be included in the target rate of return as it is an opportunity cost.

The third rationale for the high target rates of return is that they are the result of the venture capital industry's years of experience of working with entrepreneurs, who tend to be an optimistic group. Talk to VCs and they will tell you that the business plans they read and review always have a happy ending. The business plans are always based on the start-up being a success, usually a huge success, in order to attract the venture capital fund's interest. The forecasts tend to ignore the many ways in which a start-up can fail. Entrepreneurs pitch, or sell, their business plans to the VCs like salespeople in a computer store who pitch the latest electronic product release.

According to finance theory, technically the financial forecasts of the entrepreneurs should present the *expected outcome*s of the venture's profits and free cash flows, not the best-case scenario. But as we said, that is not industry practice. Entrepreneurs are selling their hopes and dreams to VCs in exchange for financing. By experience, VCs have learned that it is easier to discount an entrepreneur's numbers as they are presented in the business plan using a very high target rate of return rather than to try to talk down the forecast numbers to a set of more reasonable expected projections. Everyone feels better; the VCs can use their target rate of return and show they are within the acceptable ranges for the kind of investing they do (e.g., by financing round, by industry, and by geographic focus). The entrepreneurs are motivated to hit the numbers they themselves put down in their own business plans. Psychologically it works better to have the entrepreneurs shoot for their own numbers than for some adjusted forecast developed by the VC that they did not participate in making.

Expected Value Scenario versus Best-Case Scenario

It is important that you understand the difference between a best-case scenario and the expected value of all possible scenarios. To get the expected value, any investor (according to rational economic theory) ought to take into account all the possible states of the world, not just the state of the world when all goes right and the best case results.

To illustrate the principle of expected value, we sketch out three typical scenarios and explain how the method works from the point of view of the VC investor. Everyone knows that when a company fails, it results in a loss of capital for the investors and the entrepreneurs who hold shares. This is the total loss outcome; call it the worst-case scenario. The other possibility we referred to earlier was that the venture just limps along, barely breaking even, with minimal possibilities for a good exit sale and therefore low to zero gains for the VCs and entrepreneurs upon final exit. We will refer to this scenario as the break-even outcome. We assume for purposes of this example that only one out of 10 investments on average turns out to be the really big winner; we refer to this outcome as the home run. This is the best-of-all-possible-worlds scenario that inevitably ends up in the entrepreneur's business plan.

In the real world, what actually happens is that the VC's *realized* rate of return on the portfolio ends up being a blend of all the actual returns from each investment. After the venture capital fund is wound down, the general partner tallies up the winners, the breakeven results, and the losers in the fund's portfolio. The result will be the blended weighted average IRR or final realized rate of return on the portfolio. Of course, to do such IRR calculations properly, the VC carefully needs to take into account the timing of each cash flow, how the funds are reinvested, and what rate of return the funds are actually earning, between the time the VC fund exits a company and when it distributes the final proceeds to the limited partners and the general partner. In real life, it is not easy to do these types of IRR calculations properly, and it is a controversial area, since we are dealing with illiquid portfolio companies that are hard to value. In the notes we suggest two publications that show you the details of how the European Venture Capital Association (EVCA) recommends the determinations be done.[10]

CLOSING THOUGHTS

This chapter explored the world of venture capital and private equity investing. Venture capital is but one segment of a much broader asset class known as private equity. Venture capital is equity financing supplied to early-stage innovative businesses often with proprietary intangible assets and technology. For these ventures, the risks of failure may be high but the hopes for huge rewards are even higher.

Large sums have poured into alternative assets (e.g., venture capital, leveraged buyout, hedge funds, and commodity funds) as pension funds and other institutional investors have rotated out of publicly traded marketable securities such as equity shares and bonds and shifted money into other alternatives. These investors are seeking higher expected returns, but in so doing, they are also taking on greater risks of making investments in less efficient corners of the world's capital markets.

The fund players in these alternative assets compete vigorously for the money of major pension funds, life insurance groups, endowments, trusts, foundations, sovereign wealth funds, and very-high-net-wealth individuals. The general partners in a private equity or venture capital fund are responsible for raising money from their clients, the institutional investors who are the limited partners. (Refer to Chapter 9, where we discuss the formation of limited partnerships and special liability companies.)

The general partners' job is multifaceted. As the chief rainmakers, they must define the focus and strategy of the fund and decide to whom it should be promoted. As principal investors, they coinvest their own money into the fund alongside that of their limited partners. The general partners advise the fund on investment criteria, generate deal flow, and evaluate the proposals. They are the chief negotiators opposite the founders and senior management of the portfolio companies when it comes time to negotiate and settle the final conditions and terms of the financing.

Venture capitalists need to balance their funds' interests with those of the venture's founders, senior management team, and other members of the venture's board of directors. As board members of their portfolio companies, VCs must walk a fine line and not be seen as operating the company and interfering with the entrepreneurs' independence, or else they may end up losing key managers or facing personal liability, especially in the case of the venture being placed into insolvency proceedings. Yet they must sometimes step in when there is a crisis and lead the board of directors, for example, to replace a CEO who is not performing up to expectations.

Accepting venture capital funding for your high-tech venture is a double-edged sword. On one hand, you have capital that comes with an experienced investor interested in seeing your venture not only survive but thrive. On the other hand, you have an experienced and tough investor with high expectations and demands who is now in control of your company. To some extent, the choice of entrepreneurship is a lifestyle choice. The venture capital route is designed to have the company grow fast and gain scale, and have the investors exit at a high multiple. It is not a road all company founders desire. However, for many high-tech ventures, it may be the best choice they have. Our advice and admonition is to seek out and accept funding only from the most highly qualified VC firm you can find. They are not all equal. Pick a general partner you can trust. Do a thorough job of due diligence on the VC before you grab the wrong end of the sword.

CHAPTER TAKEAWAYS

- *Early funding.* Most start-up businesses get their initial capital from the founders' friends and families or angel investors. Each angel investor is unique, and his or her background and experiences should be investigated thoroughly by the entrepreneurs as part of their deal due diligence before accepting any funds.
- *The VC business model.* Venture capitalists finance young, innovative, and very-high-growth businesses. They seek business models with high operating margins that are scalable. They invest in experienced teams of entrepreneurs who have the ability to execute the business model and deliver on milestones. They like ventures that target very large markets with unmet needs. The products and services should offer compelling value for customers.
- *Very few home runs.* The winnowing-out process to receive VC financing is brutal. An experienced and well-connected VC team may well receive over 1,000 business plans a year from eager start-up teams. In general, for every 100 business plans that a VC reviews, on average only 3.6 percent of the plans receive funding. Of those businesses that are funded, only 1 out of every 10 will turn out to be a really big success.
- *VC valuation method is fairly straightforward.* VCs value young start-up companies without previous earnings history or track record. Consequently, venture capitalists use a simplified valuation approach based on these key inputs: Money in, money out, time to exit, and discount at the VCs' target rate of return.
- *Staged investing shares the risks.* The VC valuation method penalizes entrepreneurs who raise too much surplus cash by charging them a high rate for the money. Staged investing is preferable for both the VC and the start-up firm. The VC has time to get to know the entrepreneurial team's capabilities better and avoids investing a large amount into the venture all at once. The entrepreneur gets a better share price by financing in rounds.
- *VC exit influences the alliance strategy in biotech.* The VCs' exit decision often exerts *a strong influence on the alliance* strategy pursued by the portfolio company, particularly in early-stage biopharmaceutical ventures. If the exit strategy calls for an IPO, then the biotech company will tend to form more alliances with multiple partners. If the exit strategy is to be an early trade sale to a strategic partner, then the VC will likely recommend fewer strategic alliances, so as to make the final acquisition process easier, smoother, and more lucrative.
- *A viable VC exit is critical to securing venture financing.* VCs need to be convinced of the viability of the exit strategy before they will invest the venture capital fund's money into the proposed business venture. As the entrepreneur, plan on negotiating a proposed exit strategy with your VCs well in advance of its taking place. Also be prepared to revise and adapt the exit strategy, as capital market conditions change, and subsequent events require changes to the venture's business strategy and modifications to the exit timetable.

CHAPTER 20

Valuing and Structuring High Technology Strategic Alliances

This chapter will help you understand the basics about licensing and determining royalty rates. We are going to show you how to use discounted cash flows to value a simple technology transfer deal. We explore how to structure the valuation of a licensing deal from the point of view of the licensee (the party who wishes to use the rights to the patent) and then briefly cover the point of view of the licensor (the owner of the patent being licensed). Patent licensing deals frequently arise as part of technology transfer agreements and are commonly found in many high-tech industries. If successfully concluded, these in-licensed or out-licensed technologies may become a crucial part of the intellectual assets of a start-up company. The contractual relationships resulting from these agreements eventually form the beginnings of the start-up firm's strategic alliance network.

In our case example, located at the end of this chapter, we aim to show you step-by-step how to value a patent license deal and prepare to negotiate a technology transfer agreement for your own venture. We envision a situation where a small manufacturing company is interested in licensing the patents for a key product component from a larger corporation. The small company hopes to speed up the development and manufacture of a new product line by acquiring the rights to use the technology for a critical component, which it plans to incorporate into a new product that it has under development. Without this critical part and the freedom to use the accompanying patent rights, the smaller company would risk infringing on existing patents if it tried to replicate the component on its own. If it does not launch an innovative new product line quickly, the small company faces margin erosion from stiff competition for its existing products. With the new product line, the venture will be able to meet an important unmet market need for its customers, appealing to them with a much higher value proposition. It will be able to charge a premium product price, improve its margins, and enhance its long-term growth prospects.

The larger corporation appears willing to negotiate a deal. It benefits by receiving additional cash flows from licensing its patents for a new application that it has not developed in-house. It is also able to increase the marginal return on investment of its pool of existing patents.

VALUING LICENSES AS THE PRESENT VALUE OF THE FUTURE BENEFITS OF OWNERSHIP AND DEVELOPMENT

An intellectual property (IP) license for a patent, as explained in earlier chapters, is nothing more than a contractual agreement between two parties, where the licensor owns the patent and all of its property rights, and the licensee agrees to pay a royalty for the use of some of those rights in a specific territory and in a designated way. As you might imagine, there are many ways to allocate these rights between the parties and many different compensation schemes. Think of renting an apartment. Each rental contract between the landlord and the tenant is a negotiation where the two sides bargain over all sorts of terms and conditions: how large a deposit, who is liable for damages, how much notice is required before vacating the premises, are pets allowed and if so, what kind of pets, who is responsible for maintenance of the apartment, replacing broken appliances, painting the walls, cleaning the carpets, and so on.

Negotiating a licensing contract is similar to negotiating a rental contract, only instead of bargaining over an apartment, the two sides are bargaining over rights to use IP. In this chapter, we focus on licensing patent rights. To value a patent licensing agreement, we break the problem into two pieces.

First, we identify all the future economic benefits flowing to the owner of the patent and then subtract from this stream of cash flows any expenses that might be incurred in managing or administering the agreement or protecting against infringers. Imagine the parallel situation of a landlord who owns a multiunit apartment complex. Each month the landlord receives rental income paid by the tenants of the occupied units. From this rental income, the landlord subtracts the monthly fees charged by the property management company that administers the building. If the services of a security guard and a gardener are required, these would also be deductible expenses. After accounting for all income and expenses (including depreciation and taxes), the remainder would be the net income attributable to this apartment building investment.

Second, we determine the economic benefits to the licensee derived from the use of the licensed IP (known as exploiting the property rights). To keep our apartment building analogy going, say one of the tenants in an occupied unit is a self-employed piano teacher who gives piano lessons in the apartment. The teacher recently moved to the complex because she believes she will be able to charge her students more for lessons than before. The reason is that she is located in a much better neighborhood, with good parking. She is also closer to the high school where most of her students are enrolled. After moving to her new apartment, the teacher learns she has been able to recruit more students to take lessons than in her former location. The premium charged per lesson plus the incremental income from the new customers—when added up over time and then discounted back at an appropriate cost of funds—would represent the incremental economic benefit to the piano teacher of moving to the new apartment. From these benefits, we would need to subtract any relevant incremental expenses, such as higher rent, higher gas and electric bills, and so forth, as compared to what she was paying in her former housing situation.

In the two steps just described, both for the licensor and the licensee, we can compute the net present value of the future benefits of ownership and of exploitation by discounting the future streams of expected income offset against expected expenses at a cost of funds appropriately matched to the risk of the cash flows. Therefore, to capture the whole picture of the economic benefits created by the licensing transaction (or in the case of the tenant-landlord analogy), we need to add up all the individual pieces and sum them. We need to take into account not just the net present value of the deal from the landlord's perspective but also the net present value of the economic value created for each of the tenants.

The art of valuing technology transfer agreements comes from the imagination and creativity required to envision these future cash flow streams. We need to imagine the time frame and duration of the various cash flows, their size and frequency of occurrence, and the risks associated with receiving them.

The win-win outcome of a good licensing negotiation is to seek a set of terms and conditions that creates value for both licensor and licensee. We can imagine the two sides bargaining over contract terms much like our landlord and tenant would engage in discussions before the signing of any rental contract. In Table 20.1, we describe the positions of licensor and licensee as each might wish to interpret different contract clauses. Naturally, the two perspectives are quite different. The first column lists contract clauses, the second column shows the licensor's viewpoint, and the third column shows the licensee's viewpoint. The aim of the negotiations is to reach a mutually satisfactory middle ground where each side is able to achieve as many of his or her objectives and priorities as possible while yielding on those points of lesser importance.

Forecasting Future Cash Inflows and Outflows—Licensor

What sort of future income streams might the licensor be receiving? We would expect the contractual arrangement to include up-front payments or fees, periodic milestone payments, and then steady royalties once the product is launched and sold or the patented process is in use. For computing royalties, the basis for the royalty might be net sales to the licensee of products covered by the license. However, it could also be calculated on a per unit basis or any other number of formats.

The cash outflows of the licensor might include such expenses as continuing research and development (R&D) costs, litigation expenses to defend the patent against infringers, charges to indemnify the licensee, plus expenses for administration, audits, and accounting.

Forecasting Future Cash Inflows and Outflows—Licensee

We would imagine the licensee would receive economic benefits in the form of higher premium pricing per unit of product sold due to the novel nature of the patented product being licensed. There might be economic spillovers that would benefit future products under development. For instance, cost savings from learning how to manufacture the new product more efficiently might apply to next-generation products as well. If the economic benefits are cost savings, then we would look for these in improved manufacturing processes, better operating efficiencies, and enhanced operating profit margins due to lower costs. Gains from economies of scale might also be possible as higher production volumes are spread over the same fixed costs. Economies of scope occur when the sales team is able to sell both the old and new products without adding more salespeople. Economies of scope also could

TABLE 20.1 Contract Negotiation Terms as Viewed by the Licensor and Licensee

Contract Terms	Licensor	Licensee
Duration of the contract	Extend the flows of income Seek near-term income Extend the license beyond expiration of the patent by including trade secrets or other proprietary know-how	Delay payments Avoid up-front fees No royalty payments after patent expiration
Amount of the contract	Bargain for as high a royalty rate as possible Front-load the contract Obtain grant-backs and access to any improvements of the technology developed by the licensee Seek nonexclusivity and encourage sublicensing Be paid for extras, technical assistance, and the like	Pay as low a royalty rate as possible Delay up-front payments Avoid giving grant-backs of developments made by the licensee; however, insist on getting the latest version of the licensed technology from the licensor Seek exclusivity Have technical assistance included free of charge
Risk Mitigation	Obtain volume and sales guarantees and minimums Establish performance milestones Include rigorous audit procedures Obtain indemnity from tort or product liability actions brought against the licensee Possibly bargain that further development investments be the responsibility of the licensee	Put licensor at risk for performance Avoid guarantees, if possible; otherwise negotiate performance milestones that can be obtained quickly and that are easily verifiable Seek widest territory and coverage possible Obtain indemnities from licensor, especially against third-party patent infringement lawsuits brought against the licensee Avoid committing to large expenditures, especially in the beginning

arise if the old and new products are able to be distributed through the same logistics and distribution channels.

Cash outflows would be the cost of royalty payments, lump-sum payments, or any other fees paid by the licensee to the licensor or incurred by the licensee in developing the technology on its own. These items typically would include R&D expenses; additional plant, property, and equipment expenditures; engineering costs to get the licensed IP integrated into the product and scaled up for mass production; marketing expenses to change and create the new product packaging and labeling; brand advertising expenses to create customer awareness of the new product; and so forth.

BASIC LICENSING MODEL—SHARING THE ECONOMIC PIE

In Figure 20.1, we show a schematic drawing of the economic benefits accruing to the licensor and licensee (in the form of a pie chart). We assume that the licensor is able to use the patents in various applications and market territories on its own. We also assume that it licenses the use of the patents for certain specific territories and particular applications to a licensee. The licensor receives income streams A and royalty stream R (shown as R in the drawing). The licensee receives income stream B from selling products incorporating the patents and pays to the licensor a royalty stream of cash flows.

Having covered the basic concepts of licensing, we now need to apply the theory to a practical example. For this purpose we have written the next case study. To keep the discussion focused, we have illustrated valuation principles using only DCF techniques. In the real world, financial managers and licensing consultants would likely introduce market multiples and comparable deal transactions into their analysis to capture market sentiment. We demonstrate how to incorporate such multiples into valuations in Appendix 17.4, "Five Ways to Estimate Terminal Values" that is available for download at www.innovationtocashflows.com. We further explain and discuss how to carry out relative valuation for emerging technology companies (using multiples and comparable deals) in Chapter 18.

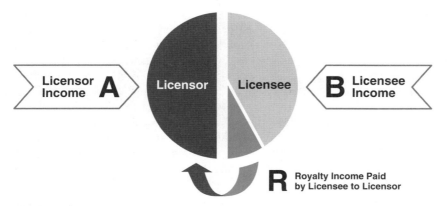

FIGURE 20.1 Economic Benefits Accruing to the Licensor and the Licensee

CASE STUDY: ADVANCED DERMAL DELIVERY, INC. AND THE LAUNCH OF THE NEW TRANSDERMAL PATCH[*]

Advanced Dermal Delivery, Inc. (ADD) is a contract manufacturer specializing in the production of transdermal patches sold to major pharmaceutical and biopharmaceutical companies. ADD, based in San Diego, California, was founded about 10 years ago.[1] The company's entrepreneurial founders, wealthy angel investors, friends, and family have invested $10 million in equity share capital to finance the firm's growth. ADD is privately held; the company founders and insiders own 55 percent of the equity and the rest of the shares are held by outside investors. ADD has a good relationship and a line of credit with a local commercial bank, San Diego Community Bank, which specializes in providing growth financing to small high-technology firms in the area. The founders and senior managers are respected entrepreneurs with strong ties to the local biomedical community of San Diego. The company is a member of the local BIOCOM trade association, a network that helped connect the founders to their local banker.

Current Product Portfolio and Manufacturing Facilities

ADD's annual revenues were approaching $25 million for the year 2008. The company specializes in the manufacture of various adhesive skin patches that are sold to major pharmaceutical companies. The company's main product line is a flexible transdermal patch that is lightweight, hypoallergenic, and comfortable to wear. It is applied simply by peeling off the protective coating and gently attaching it to the patient's skin. In clinical tests, patient tolerance to the patch has been extremely high. The biggest customers for this patch have been well-known pharmaceutical and biotechnology companies with U.S. subsidiaries (e.g., Pfizer, Merck, Novartis, Genentech) and several important consumer health companies (especially Johnson & Johnson, the maker of Band-Aids, a widely recognized and trademarked brand of protective adhesive products).

ADD's most popular patches work in combination with anti-inflammatory drugs to treat pain and inflammation. For instance, consumers buy these transdermal patches in pharmacies and local drugstores as over-the-counter medicines to treat aching backs and strained muscles when they overexert themselves at the gym. Elderly patients buy and apply the patches for temporary relief from arthritis and other localized pain conditions. Patients normally experience fewer side effects with drugs delivered through transdermal patches than from drugs delivered orally.

ADD's products are produced to its customers' (the pharmaceutical companies) specifications and strict quality control procedures. The U.S. Food and Drug Administration (FDA) considers a transdermal patch to be a combination product consisting of a medical device combined with a pharmaceutical drug or biological product that is delivered into the human body. A new transdermal patch and its associated drug (or combination of drugs) must complete intensive clinical trials in order to receive FDA approval. The clinical trials testing and associated expenses are

---

[*]Constance Lütolf-Carroll wrote this case solely as the basis for classroom discussion. The case is not intended to serve as a source of primary data, endorsement, or illustration of effective or ineffective management.

the responsibility of the pharmaceutical companies, not ADD. As a contract manufacturer, ADD produces to specifications and sells its patches at a negotiated price per patch delivered.

ADD has a fully licensed production facility meeting all U.S. FDA Good Manufacturing Practices and Quality System requirements. It has the necessary operating permits, authorizations, and approvals to manufacture state-of-the-art transdermal patches at its Miramar facility, conveniently located close to major hospitals, the University of California, San Diego campus, the Salk Institute, and other biotechnology research centers in the area.

New Product Opportunity

Since the skin acts as a natural defense system for the body's immune system, many medications do not penetrate into the body if applied topically. Consequently, there is a huge unmet medical need for drug delivery systems that work to deliver medicines just under the surface of the skin. Such a delivery system would allow the medicines to reach the bloodstream more quickly. Skin patches would be safer for medical workers than handling hypodermic syringes. A skin patch designed to deliver medicines via a subcutaneous pathway would be well received by the pharmaceutical industry. Especially appealing would be a patch that could be used to administer the latest biological drug compounds for treating chronic illnesses, such as Alzheimer's disease or dementia, and various infectious diseases, such as HIV or hepatitis.

Development of the New Product Technology

ADD has a number of research projects in advanced stages of development. The most promising project involves an enhanced transdermal patch using a new nanodevice. The new transdermal patch safely positions a nanodevice on the patient's skin. Inside the nanodevice is a nanosized pump capable of injecting microquantities of therapeutic medicines upon receipt of the proper electronic signal.[2] The nanosized pump is the result of seven years of development effort by ADD scientists and engineers. The researchers hope to connect their tiny pump to a set of microneedles that can be used to penetrate the skin and deliver drugs to patients. The microneedles that ADD's scientists are testing in the laboratory are the proprietary property of a major ink-jet manufacturer.[3] The patents and technology associated with the microneedles need to be in-licensed by ADD before the prototype could go into full production. (More details about the in-licensing agreement are discussed later.)

Benefits to the Patient

Unlike a normal hypodermic syringe, microneedle penetration is minimally invasive and very quick. The microneedles barely penetrate the skin. The patient feels absolutely no pain, which is a huge advantage over competing systems. Since the device is so small, it can be enclosed and protected within the membrane layers of the transdermal patch. The patient would be unaware that a nanodevice is embedded in the tiny patch.

New System's Benefits to Doctors and Medical Professionals

ADD's new system would allow for closer monitoring of the patient's dosage level. The timing of each dosage could be precisely and automatically controlled. Dosage history would be automatically stored in a small memory chip. The ADD nanodevice would incorporate programmable safety protocols, tailored to each patient's medical history, to prevent adverse drug interactions. Such an integrated system would be vastly preferable to traditional hypodermic syringes or other types of intravenous devices and would be ideal for delivery of expensive biological vaccines, where every drop counts.

Benefits to Pharmaceutical Companies

The key target customers for the new transdermal nanodevice skin patch would be ADD's existing client base of major pharmaceutical companies. By changing the existing drug delivery system from a normal patch to a new nanodevice patch, the pharmaceutical company would be able to extend the time its branded pharmaceutical remained profitably in the market. (A typical branded drug is quickly copied by generics manufacturers after patent expiration of the active ingredient. Once the generic is in the market, customers switch and the branded drug's sales plunge.) However, ADD believed that doctors would likely prescribe for their patients the newer transdermal delivery system (available only to select pharmaceutical manufacturers) instead of the pills or capsules offered by generic drug competitors. Therefore, adopting the new nanodevice patch might represent for one of ADD's pharmaceutical customers a multimillion-dollar market opportunity by helping it fend off competition from generics.

LICENSING DEAL

The key to making all these dreams and visions work is for ADD to obtain the licensing rights to the patented microneedle technology originally developed by the major ink-jet printer manufacturer. If ADD could obtain the license to this patented technology on reasonable terms, and especially if it could secure an exclusive license for the global market, it would be able to speed up the manufacture and launch of its line of new products. Licensing would save years of development time and many millions of dollars in extensive R&D. The license could make ADD a major player in this market niche. (See the next section for a discussion of rival drug delivery systems under development.)

Competition

Numerous drug delivery systems that could be potential competitors to ADD's proposed transdermal microneedle system are in various stages of development. For instance, Pfizer, in 2006, acquired PowderMed Ltd., based in the United Kingdom (www.pfizer.com).[4] PowderMed developed a needleless system using a gold substrate and an inert helium injection system that blasts DNA powders into the subsurface of the skin. (See www.powdermed.com.) One of ADD's main customers, Novartis (www.novartis.com), has been researching and developing transdermal patches, ever since it brought out its first patches to help smokers cut back on nicotine addiction. Other major pharmaceutical companies have developed transdermal patches and successfully introduced them over the years.

An innovative biotechnology company Glide Pharma (www.glide.com), based in Oxford, England, uses an actuator to push solid doses of a pharmaceutical drug into the human skin very rapidly simply through pressure. The Glide actuator is a simple handheld device (about the size of a fountain pen) that patients can easily learn how to use by themselves. When the Glide actuator triggers, the injection is completed almost instantaneously and "the depth to which the drug is injected is consistent and controllable. Injecting the drug in solid dosage form means that the rate of release of the drug can be controlled by incorporating quick dissolving or slow dissolving compounds into the formulations."[5] Glide had four or five pharmaceutical products under development and in various stages of clinical trials. According to information posted on Glide's web site, some of these products were being developed in-house and others were being developed in strategic collaborations with third parties.[6]

UPCOMING LICENSING NEGOTIATIONS

Dr. Joe McCaffrey, the current chief executive officer (CEO) of Advanced Dermal Deliveries, had initially contacted the head of technology licensing at the ink-jet manufacturing company in late May 2008. Initial talks were progressing rapidly and smoothly. The two parties were to meet again, on June 16, 2008, in San Francisco, California, to discuss the terms and conditions to be included in a memorandum of understanding for the strategic partnership. McCaffrey was planning on attending and bringing with him his chief financial officer (CFO) Ms. Victoria Lee, and the head of business development, Dr. Mike Mendoza. The goal was to have a definitive alliance agreement ready to be signed by the end of the fiscal year on December 31, 2008.

Structuring the Basic Licensing Problem

On June 9, Lee was busy preparing for a meeting the next day with Mendoza where they planned to review the preliminary outputs from the financial model that she had built for the upcoming strategic alliance deal. They were both of the opinion that modeling the license deal should be similar to doing a discounted cash flow of an investment project.

To create the basic license model, Lee had developed a simple "base case" scenario for an in-licensing deal where the licensor (the ink-jet manufacturer) would grant patent rights to use its microneedle technology to the licensee (ADD) in exchange for annual royalty payments based on the net sales of new microneedle patches sold. As the licensor appeared willing to do a deal, the main item left to model was the appropriate royalty rate. Therefore, the financial problem Lee was trying to resolve could be stated as: How much can ADD pay in royalties to the ink-jet manufacturer and still meet ADD's target cost of capital?

Lee had built the Base Case Scenario using a 10-year financial forecast without the new microneedle patch (for the years 2009–2018). Scenario A-1 was the Base Case Scenario financial model plus the incremental cash flow effects arising from the new product launch. For Scenario A-1's forecast, Lee estimated the incremental new product sales and additional operating expenses associated with the new product line. Other expenditures, such as increased R&D and new capital equipment purchases, were also included. After comparing the Base Case Scenario to Scenario A-1, Lee expected to see a positive difference in net present value (in other words, the new product is a success, and value is created).

However, the Scenario A-1 financial model did not include a charge for the royalty expenses. Lee added these royalty expenses (as a percentage of new drug product sales) in a separate spreadsheet model called Scenario A-2. She then used trial and error to adjust the royalty rate in Scenario A-2's spreadsheet. She was solving for the *maximum* royalty rate that ADD would be willing to pay and still meet its target rate of return. The correct answer was the royalty rate that makes the net present value of the free cash flows of Scenario A-2 equal to the net present value of the free cash flows of the Base Case Scenario. (This was mathematically equivalent to taking the differential free cash flows of the two scenarios and setting them equal to each other by adjusting the royalty rate.)

The *minimum* royalty that ADD might be charged by the licensor would obviously be zero. Somewhere in between these two high and low values would be the final royalty rate—agreed on during the upcoming negotiations with the ink-jet manufacturer.

CONSTRUCTING THE FINANCIAL FORECASTS AND LICENSING MODEL

The key assumptions used by Lee to build the Base Case Scenario are explained in the next section. These are followed by the assumptions she used for Scenario A-1: new product launch *excluding* royalty payments and Scenario A-2: new product launch *including* royalty payments. Following thereafter is a section with an explanation of the cost of capital assumptions used for all the scenarios.

Although Lee was inputting data estimates for the final financial model calculations on June 9, 2008, she chose to set the valuation date of her net present value calculations as of December 31, 2008, to coincide with the end of the fiscal year. This choice of date greatly simplified her projections. (The end of the fiscal year was also when the strategic alliance was to be finalized, if all went well with the negotiations.)

Base Case Scenario: Status Quo with No New Product Sales

Lee expected that ADD would have sales of approximately $25 million by December 31, 2008. For purposes of the forecast, she projected that base case sales would grow by 2 percent per year in new units, and that prices could be increased in line with estimated inflation, expected to be about 3 percent per year. This meant that sales would rise at the compound growth rate of $(1.02) \times (1.03) = (1.0506)$ or 5.06 percent per year.

When queried by Lee about the sales assumptions, ADD's marketing manager said that he did not anticipate being able to implement major price increases above inflation because of stiff competition faced by the older product lines. Projected future sales volume was conservative, again because of tough competition from other pharmaceutical companies making their own patches in-house and overseas manufacturers' gaining new customers. Consequently, Lee's forecast showed only slight improvement in market share penetration. She also reasoned that the products in the Base Case Scenario would be fairly mature by the end of the time horizon. In fact, during the terminal value period, Lee decided to grow sales only by inflation of 3 percent in her initial set of assumptions. Afterward, she would do further sensitivity tests; she could always raise the growth rate later.

In recent years, ADD's average cost of goods sold (COGS) is about 55 percent of sales, leaving a gross margin of about 45 percent. Lee decided to continue using the historical COGS in her forecasts for the base case. ADD produced transdermal skin patches that were unbranded, so gross margins were lower than for a pharmaceutical company making branded transdermal patches and selling them directly to retail pharmacy stores. Even though its products were unbranded, ADD's innovative technology and stringent quality control manufacturing processes enabled it to charge a higher gross margin compared to commodity industrial products. The Base Case Scenario assumptions that Lee used in her forecast are presented in Table 20.2. What follows are further explanations of operating expenses, capital expenditures, and financing assumptions.

Additional Base Case Assumptions   Research and development (R&D) costs were expensed and not capitalized in the forecast. Marketing and selling expenses were

TABLE 20.2   Advanced Dermal Deliveries, Inc.—Base Case Assumptions

Base Case Assumptions	Actual as of Dec. 31, 2007	Estimated as of Dec. 31, 2008
Net sales for year 0 (in thousands)	$ 23,796	$ 25,000
Compound annual growth rate in sales (% per year)	5.06%	5.06%
Cost of goods sold (% of net sales)	55%	55%
Gross margin (% of net sales)	45%	45%
Research and development expenses (% of net sales)	11%	11%
Marketing and selling expenses (% of net sales)	15%	15%
General and administrative (G&A) expenses (% of net sales, then afterwards G&A grows at the rate of inflation)	10%	10%
Marginal corporate tax rate	38%	38%
Depreciation expense (% of net PP&E, end of prior year)	10%	10%
Days receivables	45 days	45 days
Days payables	45 days	45 days
Days inventory	60 days	60 days
Long-Term debt borrowings	0	0
Shareholders' equity and retained earnings	$10,937	$11,922
Growth rate of TV, g_∞	3.0%	3.0%
Cost of equity, k_e	13.2%	13.2%
Cost of borrowed debt, k_d	8.0%	8.0%

forecast to remain a constant percentage of sales during the forecast time horizon. General and administrative (G&A) expenses were treated as fixed costs. After the initial assumption of G&A equal to 10 percent of net sales, then G&A costs were grown at the rate of inflation for the remaining forecast period. Depreciation was estimated at 10 percent of net property, plant, and equipment (PP&E). The company's marginal corporate tax rate was estimated at 38 percent. Collection time for accounts receivable was 45 days. Accounts payable were paid in 45 days. Inventory turnover was 60 days. Lee made the very conservative financial planning assumption that all accrued salaries, wages, employee benefits, and taxes would be paid immediately in cash. This meant that the only current liabilities shown on the balance sheet would be due to accounts payable, related to the cost of goods sold.

In the Base Case Scenario, the capital expenditures were included in the free cash flow projections but only for the existing business (i.e., not including the envisioned capital expenditures associated with the new microneedle patch product line). See the section "Additional Capital Expenditures" for further discussion of how Lee treated capital expenditures in Scenarios A-1 and A-2.

The company had no need to borrow long-term debt as it was producing generous free cash flows in the Base Case Scenario. Consequently, the weighted average cost of capital (k_{wacc}) was equal to the cost of equity (k_e) because ADD had no debt in its capital structure. Most privately-held high technology companies are conservatively financed, relying heavily on equity financing with very little debt due to high operating risks, so such a target capital structure for ADD was not unusual in the industry.

Because of its good relationship with San Diego Community Bank, ADD had access to a short-term line of credit to finance its short-term borrowing needs. The line of credit was available for a maximum amount of $1 million over 12 months, after which time it must be paid back down to zero. ADD rarely had to draw upon this credit-line. Minimum cash requirements were $150,000. Cash in excess of this amount was shown as excess or surplus cash in the forecasted balance sheets.

To keep the Base Case and Scenarios A-1 and A-2 directly comparable, the surplus cash was treated the same way in each spreadsheet. Also, in all scenarios, all net income was retained and no dividends were paid or surplus cash invested in other projects (except for what was already included in the Base Case). These assumptions were made to isolate the effect that royalties have on the microneedle project—even though ADD would build up a sizeable cash surplus in the years ahead, and conceivably could pay out a hefty dividend or invest the surplus in other projects.

For ease of explanation, the same cost of capital in the terminal value calculation was used as the cost of capital for discounting the operating free cash flows for years 1 to 10. However, these two discount rates do not necessarily have to be the same number. Very often a lower cost of capital is appropriate to use in the terminal value, as the perpetual cash flows might be less risky than the cash flows coming earlier in the life of a start-up company. (Refer to Chapter 19 for more on the Venture Capital Method of Valuation.)

Scenarios A-1 and A-2: New Transdermal Product Launch

The financial forecast assumptions for Scenario A-1 were identical to the Base Case Scenario assumptions *plus* the incremental effects of launching the new microneedle patch *without any* patent license royalty payments. In Scenario A-2, Lee *included* the patent license royalty payments, leaving the rest of the assumptions unchanged from Scenario A-1. The next sections explain the additional forecast assumptions for the new microneedle product line.

Incremental Research and Development (R&D) Expenditures To develop the new microneedle technology and get the prototype ready for scale-up and eventual production, ADD's engineering and new product development team anticipated incremental expenditures of $1,000,000 in year 2009 and $500,000 in year 2010 for Scenarios A-1 and A-2.

The R&D was for further product development, testing, and debugging of manufacturing problems. ADD needed to transfer the microneedle technology (especially the process know-how) from the ink-jet manufacturer to its own new product development team. Then ADD's engineers had to connect ADD's nanopump to the microneedle subassembly and seal the combined final assembly into the transdermal membrane. Increased hardware and software development expenses were also anticipated.

As mentioned earlier, ADD did not intend to do clinical trials, as these are not part of its business model. The pharmaceutical company that wished to purchase the new patches would either carry out clinical trials itself or would outsource the work to a contract research company. Therefore, no clinical trial expenditures were included in ADD's forecasts, since any trials would be coordinated, supervised, and paid for by the pharmaceutical company.

Incremental Capital Expenditures Capital expenditure was a separate item that Lee included in her free cash flow projections. Table 20.3 shows Lee's forecast for capital expenditures for the years 2009 to 2018, followed by projections for the terminal value (continuing value period). The first line of Table 20.3 shows the capital expenditures that Lee included in the Base Case forecast. The second line of Table 20.3 is the incremental capital expenditures required for the new product line. Consequently, these additional capital expenditures appear only in the cash flow projections of Scenarios A-1 and A-2 and not in the Base Case forecast.

For the new microneedle product, Lee's capital spending budget included the purchase of new quality control and test equipment, new production machinery, and money to retool existing equipment. The main challenges to overcome in manufacturing were devising procedures and fine-tuning equipment to properly seal the microneedle device into the transdermal membranes, and then, of course, scaling up production to achieve high volume throughputs. The capital expenditures associated

TABLE 20.3 Forecast Capital Expenditure

Year	2009	2010	2011	2012	2013	2014	2015	2016	2017	2018	TV
Base Case	$ 800	900	1,000	1,100	1,150	1,200	1,300	1,400	1,450	1,550	1,200
Scenarios A1 and A2	$1,000	1,000	1,000	1,000	0	0	0	0	0	0	0

Figures shown are in thousands of U.S. dollars.

with the new microneedle product were planned to be phased in over four years (from 2009 to 2012). Staggering the investments would give management the real option to stop investing in production capacity if the initial sales forecasts turned out to be too optimistic.

Time to Market   The new skin patches were to be ready for the market in two to four years, depending on the testing and approvals process.[7] For the initial sales forecast for Scenarios A-1 and A-2, Lee and Mendoza chose two years as the time of launch. Prior to launch, the company planned to sell small quantities of patches to its pharmaceutical partners for use in their clinical trials testing. That is why some sales are shown even in the first year.

Investment in Working Capital   Investment in working capital must increase as incremental sales from the new products grow. The net effect of (changes in accounts receivable) plus (changes in inventory) less (changes in accounts payable) is reflected as a separate line item in the free cash flow forecast projections.

Uncertainties in the New Product Forecasts   Lee was confident that her estimates were conservative (based on her firsthand discussions with the head of manufacturing, the quality assurance personnel, and head of information technology services) provided that the new patch was able to receive FDA approval in two years. Her other doubts were estimating future sales levels and the timing for the launch of the new product line. Regulatory approval, customer acceptance, and time to penetrate the market were very hard to know ahead of time. She realized she would need to do more sensitivity tests and scenarios with Mendoza in order for both of them to better understand the economic value drivers of the deal. (The results for these analyses are discussed in later sections).

Target Capital Structure and Cost of Equity Applicable to All Scenarios

Like many high-technology companies, ADD had a policy to keep long-term debt to a minimum. The family that controlled the company felt strongly that it should not rely too much on borrowed funds. The company had enough exposure to technological and operating risks that it did not need to add more financial risk by leveraging itself with too much debt.

With no debt, the expected cost of equity, k_e, would be equal to the weighted average cost of capital, k_{wacc}, which is the correct cost of capital to use when discounting free cash flows and estimating the value of the whole enterprise. (Refer to Chapter 17 where discounted cash flow valuation, and methods to estimate the cost of capital are explained.)

Lee planned to use the Capital Asset Pricing Model (CAPM) formula to estimate the expected cost of equity, k_e, and then make an additional adjustment to account for the unsystematic risk of a closely-held and unlisted company like ADD. According to CAPM, the formula for the expected cost of equity is

$$k_e = r_f + \beta(R_m - r_f)$$

Risk-Free Rate r_f On June 9, 2008, the constant maturity rate for the 10-year U.S. Treasury bond was 4.02 percent, and for the 30-year U.S. Treasury bond, the rate was 4.64 percent. Lee found these rates directly from the U.S. Treasury web site that publishes the daily Treasury yield curve rates (www.ustreas.gov/offices/domestic-finance/debt-management/interest-rate/yield.shtml). Lee decided to use the 30-year rate of 4.64 percent for her estimate of the risk-free rate. The longer maturity date better matched the time-horizon of her investment proposal. After all, she was estimating the present value of an infinite stream of cash flows.

Beta Estimation β Lee computed the beta of her company to be about 0.80 using data from Bloomberg and the same techniques as described in online Appendix 17.6, "Estimating the Weighted Average Cost of Capital for ABC Corporation," accessible by logging onto www.innovationtocashflows.com.

Equity Market Risk Premium $(R_m - r_f)$ Lee knew from reading the finance literature that expert opinion varied on what the best way was to forecast the *expected* long-term equity market risk premium. The latest studies she had read indicated that the prospective arithmetic average risk premium for large-capitalization U.S. stocks ranged from 4 percent to 7 percent, depending on which time series of data were used and when the study was conducted. (See online Appendix 17.5 for more details about academic research on estimating the equity market risk premium).

Professors Dimson, Marsh, and Staunton of the London Business School recommended a prospective arithmetic risk premium of 5.4 percent for large capitalization stocks in the U.S. equity market.[8] Furthermore, Ibbotson and Sinquefield suggested adding a 1.5 percent risk premium for small market capitalization stocks (small-caps) to account for the greater bankruptcy risk of smaller firms.[9] Adding these two risk premiums together, Lee determined a prospective equity market risk premium for small-cap stocks to be about 6.9 percent. She substituted into the CAPM formula her estimates for the equity risk premium, risk free rate, and Beta, and computed the expected cost of equity.

$$k_e = r_f + \beta(R_m - r_f)$$
$$= 4.64\% + 0.80(6.9\%) = 10.16\%$$

Later, Lee and Mendoza would do sensitivity analyses and vary the cost of equity to capture the wide range of estimates for the expected market risk premium.

Unsystematic Risk Adjustments

CAPM is a theoretical equilibrium asset pricing model that assumes perfect information and complete capital markets along with various other assumptions. According to many scholars and practitioners, unsystematic risks (also called idiosyncratic risks or company specific risks) are ignored by CAPM, even though they are of vital importance to most entrepreneurs. Such unsystematic risks include

- Liquidity (or its lack thereof) of the equity shares.
- Minority versus majority shareholding.

The equation for CAPM may be modified to account for unsystematic risks—by adding either a risk premium or subtracting a risk discount. The next equation shows the adjusted cost of equity computed using the CAPM with a component included for the unsystematic risk rate premium

$$\text{Adjusted cost of equity} = r_f + \beta(R_m - r_f) + \text{Unsystematic risk rate premium}$$

The opportunity cost of equity for investors in an unquoted, closely-held company like ADD is not comparable to the opportunity cost of equity for investors in a listed company for two basic reasons. First, ADD's family founders are exposed to more unsystematic risk than diversified investors because most of their personal wealth is tied up in the company. (Diversified investors would have their wealth invested in broad market index funds.) Second, ADD's shares, being unlisted, are highly illiquid (could not be easily bought or sold). Lee could see that she had to do an adjustment to her model to account for ADD being an illiquid private company. The question was how to do this adjustment.

According to Luis Pereiro, "Computing unsystematic risk is an intricate task for the appraiser. Academics have not yet developed a full set of models to tackle the issues, simply because the capital asset pricing model (CAPM) mind-set ignores it by design."[10] Pereiro writes that the adjustment for unsystematic (idiosyncratic) risk can be introduced ". . . either into the discount rate, or simply as a straight adjustment . . . to the final stock value computed via the DCF analysis."[11]

If the illiquidity adjustment is made via the discount rate, then the appraiser needs to add a *premium* to the discount rate to account for the higher illiquidity risk. Investors normally will not pay as much for shares that are illiquid as for shares that can be easily bought and sold. A higher discount rate means a lower present value.

If the adjustment is made to the final stock value, then the appraiser needs to give the final valuation amount a "haircut" and shave off an appropriate percentage amount—typically ranging from 20 percent to 40 percent of the total amount—to account for the extra risk of the shares being illiquid. The actual adjustment depends on a variety of factors, including particulars about the company and its industry, as explained next.

For instance, scholars John Koeplin, Atulya Sarin, and Alan C. Shapiro investigated illiquidity discounts on 84 private company acquisitions in the United States and 108 non-U.S. deals during the period 1984 to 1988. For each private transaction, they identified a matching public company that had been acquired about the same time. Then they computed the acquisition price to trailing earnings multiple for each public company and compared it to the same multiple for the matching private company. Based on their methodology, they observed that U.S. private companies were acquired at a discount of 20 percent to 30 percent of the stock's value compared to comparable public companies. Moreover, the discounts for foreign private companies were much higher than in the United States. Foreign discounts averaged 40 percent to 50 percent over the same time period.[12]

More recently, Stanley B. Block used the same methodology as Koeplin et al. for private companies acquired during 1999 to 2006. Block concluded that private companies sold at a discount of approximately 20 to 25 percent below public companies. Furthermore, he discovered that the illiquidity discount was higher for manufacturing firms (30 to 40 percent) and much lower for financial firms (8 to 10 percent).[13]

Based on these previously mentioned sources and empirical studies, Lee chose a 30 percent liquidity discount as a reasonable estimate (expressed as a percentage of ADD's total equity value). Next, she needed to convert this 30 percent liquidity discount into an implied illiquidity risk premium to include in the discount rate of her DCF calculations. To properly handle the compounding of the risk premium over long periods of time, a formula must be used to do the conversion. Pereiro recommends the approach developed by corporate finance and valuation expert Enrique R. Arzac, professor of finance at Columbia Graduate School of Business, who devised the next formula to make the proper conversion.[14]

$$\text{Unsystematic risk rate premium} = d \times (k - g)/(1 - d)$$

where d = discount (as a percentage of the security's equity or enterprise value)
k = DCF discount rate (k_e or WACC)
g = dividend or free cash flow growth rate (in perpetuity)

Lee used Arzac's unsystematic risk rate formula to determine an implied illiquidity risk premium for ADD. She inserted $d = 30\%$, $k_e = 10.16\%$, and $g_\infty = 3\%$ as shown next:

$$= 0.30 \times (0.1016 - 0.03)/(1 - 0.30)$$
$$= 3.07\%$$

Based on this last calculation, ADD's revised expected cost of equity would be $(10.16\% + 3.07\%) = 13.23\%$ or 13.2% after adjusting for the illiquidity risk premium and then rounding to one decimal. She made a mental note that when carrying out later sensitivity tests of the data inputs, she would need to recalculate, using the Arzac formula, the implied risk premium for unsystematic risk whenever she changed the initial estimates of g_∞, or k_e.

Control Premium or Not?   When one company seeks to acquire another, the purchaser typically needs to pay a control premium to acquire a majority stake. For example, if the current control premium is about 25 percent of a target company's market capitalization, then the purchaser of a company with an equity value of $1,000 would need to offer at least $1,250 to buy control from the minority shareholders. Owning a majority shareholding in a business is considered to be less risky than a minority stake, and therefore, the majority position is worth more to the acquirer—the rationale being that a controlling shareholder is able to exercise control and restructure the company in ways that a minority shareholder cannot (e.g., appoint senior management, define compensation and benefit policies, buy or sell assets, deploy resources, and recapitalize or dissolve the business).

Lee needed to decide whether it was appropriate to add a control premium amount to her valuation results for ADD. (Note that the control premium has the opposite effect on total valuation as compared to the illiquidity discount "haircut." The control premium amount is added to the valuation whereas the amount of illiquidity discount is subtracted from the total.)

In their note on valuing private companies, Hatch and Dussin advised, "If the cash flow projections are done assuming the purchaser would exercise control over the existing business, then no control premium should be added to the DCF valuation."[15] Because the family founders already controlled the majority of voting shares in ADD and since their influence was already incorporated into the projections, Lee decided *not* to lower her already adjusted cost of equity to account for the effect of control. Therefore, $k_e = 13.2$ percent remained her best estimate of ADD's adjusted cost of equity (including the illiquidity risk rate premium) for the Base Case Scenario at a terminal value growth rate, g_∞, of 3 percent.

Technological Risk Adjustments for the New Product Launch   Lee contemplated how she was going to handle the technological risks of the microneedle product launch. After all, the new product was still in development and could easily fail in further testing or in scaling up to high-volume production. Lee's spreadsheet model only had a "best case" estimate of sales and profit forecasts, under the unrealistic assumption that the product launch would be 100 percent successful. Instead, proper DCF techniques required the appraiser to use *expected* cash flows, including the risk of failure.[16]

To handle the technological risks and the uncertainties involved in any new high-tech product launch, Lee had three choices. She could either (1) adjust for the technological risk in the incremental cash flows derived from the new product, (2) add a technology risk premium to the discount rate used to discount the incremental cash flows from the new product, or (3) create scenarios of the likely outcomes from the new product launch (including the risk of total failure) and use these to adjust for the risk. Each choice is discussed next.

(1) *Adjust for the technological risk directly in the incremental cash flows.* For this adjustment, she would need probability estimates of the risk of failure. (Refer to the capstone case Proto5 for an illustration of how to use probability estimates to adjust the cash flows for early-stage drug research projects. To download Proto5, go to www.innovationtocashflows.com.) If Lee had probability estimates, she could multiply the incremental cash flows from the new microneedle product launch by the probability estimates and compute the incremental expected cash flows to be received. Unfortunately, Lee did not have any historical data to determine suitable estimates for the microneedle project's expected failure rate. She had tried to get such estimates from her company's production manager, but these statistics were unavailable, as this was the first major project of this kind the company had ever done. She had reached a dead-end.

(2) *Adjust for technological risk through the discount rate.* Lee could simply add a technology risk premium to the cost of equity. (The higher discount rate would take into account the risk of failure, which would *not* be reflected in any cash flow adjustments.) Lee thought about the technological risks over the life of the project. She realized that to model these risks carefully, she ought to take into account the varying pattern of risks year by year. Theoretically, she ought to use much higher discount rates at the earliest stages of the project, when the risks were highest during prototyping. Then she could gradually lower the discount rate for the less risky phases of production and commercialization. She could intuitively imagine the change in risks as the development process progressed. She also knew that there were no hard-and-fast rules on how to estimate such technological risks

for new technologies. She also recognized that ADD expected the prototype to be in production and launched within the next two years, a very short time horizon. The practical problem remained: She had no idea what would be an appropriate technological risk premium to use for the discount rate. She also had no guidelines upon which she could comfortably rely for such a novel product. She searched for another solution.

(3) *Adjust for technological risks through the use of scenarios.* Having discarded choices one and two, Lee contemplated the third possibility: Create plausible scenarios of the likely outcomes from the new product launch (including the risk of total failure) and use these to adjust for the remaining unsystematic risks. Lee did not want to double count any risks that were already incorporated into her modeling of the incremental cash flows from the new product being launched; yet, at the same time, she wanted to be sure that her financial model reflected the chances of the project failing during the scale-up from lab prototype to full-scale production, something which had never been done before.

Looking at the whole situation matter-of-factly, Lee decided that she would pursue choice three and make scenarios and handle the technological risk in this fashion. She would do this together with Mendoza when they met on June 10. (For the results, see the section "Next Step: Developing Scenarios to Quantify the Risks of New Product Failure.")

COMPARING SPREADSHEET RESULTS

After spending the rest of the day and a good part of the evening inputting all the data and constructing the spreadsheets, Lee was ready to double-check her financial model and scrutinize the outputs before sharing them with her colleague, Mendoza, the next day. (To download the electronic spreadsheets of the model, log onto www.innovationtocashflows.com.)

The valuation model for the Base Case Scenario is shown in Table 20.4.

The valuation model for Scenario A-1 (including the introduction of the new microneedle product and associated costs but *without royalty* payments) is presented in Table 20.5.

The valuation model for Scenario A-2 (including all the same financial assumptions as used in Scenario A-1 *plus royalty* payments) is presented in Table 20.6.

Insights from the DCF Analysis before Doing Sensitivity and Scenario Analysis

In the Base Case Scenario (refer to Table 20.4), the computed equity value of ADD is $11,552,000 using a discount rate of 13.2 percent and an infinite growth rate of 3 percent for the terminal value. Because there is no interest-bearing long-term debt in year 0, the firm value equals the equity value.

In Scenario A-1 (see Table 20.5), the equity value is $22,318,000 (nearly double the Base Case Scenario). In Scenario A-1, with no debt in year 0, the firm value equals the equity value. The reason the equity value in Scenario A-1 is so much higher ($22,318,000 − $11,552,000 = $10,766,000) is because no royalty expenses

TABLE 20.4 Advanced Dermal Deliveries—Base Case Scenario

Base Case assumes no new microneedle product and no royalty payments

PANEL A

Pro Forma Income Statement (In thousands of US $)	Historical 2007	Valuation Date Is Dec 31, 2008	Fcst Yr 1 2009	Fcst Yr 2 2010	Fcst Yr 3 2011	Fcst Yr 4 2012	Fcst Yr 5 2013	Fcst Yr 6 2014	Fcst Yr 7 2015	Fcst Yr 8 2016	Fcst Yr 9 2017	Fcst Yr 10 2018	TV Period T+1 = 11
Net Sales—Base Case	23,796	25,000	26,265	27,594	28,990	30,457	31,998	33,617	35,318	37,106	38,983	40,956	42,184
Cost of Goods Sold—Base Case	13,088	13,750	14,446	15,177	15,945	16,751	17,599	18,490	19,425	20,408	21,441	22,526	23,201
Gross Profit	10,708	11,250	11,819	12,417	13,046	13,706	14,399	15,128	15,893	16,698	17,542	18,430	18,983
Less Operating Expenses:													
Research & Development (% of Net Sales)	2,618	2,750	2,889	3,035	3,189	3,350	3,520	3,698	3,885	4,082	4,288	4,505	4,640
Marketing & Selling Expenses (% of Net Sales)	3,569	3,750	3,940	4,139	4,349	4,569	4,800	5,043	5,298	5,566	5,847	6,143	6,328
General & Admin. Expenses (grows with inflation)	2,380	2,500	2,575	2,652	2,732	2,814	2,898	2,985	3,075	3,167	3,262	3,360	3,461
Earnings Before Interest, Taxes, and Depr. (EBITDA)	2,142	2,250	2,415	2,591	2,776	2,973	3,181	3,402	3,636	3,883	4,145	4,422	4,554
Depreciation Expenses (10% of NET PP&E, prior EOY)	630	637	643	659	683	715	753	793	834	880	932	984	1,041
Earnings Before Interest and Taxes (EBIT)	1,512	1,613	1,772	1,932	2,093	2,258	2,428	2,609	2,802	3,003	3,213	3,438	3,514
Net interest expense	0	0	0	0	0	0	0	0	0	0	0	0	0
Earnings Before Tax	1,512	1,613	1,772	1,932	2,093	2,258	2,428	2,609	2,802	3,003	3,213	3,438	3,514
Provision for Taxes	574	613	673	734	795	858	923	992	1,065	1,141	1,221	1,306	1,335
Earnings After Tax	937	1,000	1,099	1,198	1,298	1,400	1,505	1,618	1,737	1,862	1,992	2,131	2,179

PANEL B

Pro Forma Balance Sheet (In thousands of US $)	Historical Dec 31 2007	Valuation Date Is Dec 31, 2008	Fcst Yr 1 FY-2009	Fcst Yr 2 FY-2010	Fcst Yr 3 FY-2011	Fcst Yr 4 FY-2012	Fcst Yr 5 FY-2013	Fcst Yr 6 FY-2014	Fcst Yr 7 FY-2015	Fcst Yr 8 FY-2016	Fcst Yr 9 FY-2017	Fcst Yr 10 FY-2018	TV Period T+1
Assets													
Current Assets:													
Cash and Short-Term Securities	150	150	150	150	150	150	150	150	150	150	150	150	150
Surplus or Excess Cash (PLUG)	768	1,527	2,283	3,044	3,819	4,618	5,500	6,472	7,493	8,571	9,769	11,044	12,882
Accounts Receivable	3,007	3,159	3,319	3,487	3,663	3,849	4,044	4,248	4,463	4,689	4,926	5,176	5,331
Inventories	2,151	2,260	2,375	2,495	2,621	2,754	2,893	3,039	3,193	3,355	3,525	3,703	3,814
Prepaid Expenses	45	45	45	45	45	45	45	45	45	45	45	45	45
Total Current Assets	6,121	7,142	8,172	9,221	10,299	11,416	12,631	13,955	15,344	16,810	18,415	20,117	22,222
Gross Property, Plant, and Equipment	7,000	7,700	8,500	9,400	10,400	11,500	12,650	13,850	15,150	16,550	18,000	19,550	20,750
Less: (Accumulated Depreciation)	(630)	(1,267)	(1,910)	(2,569)	(3,252)	(3,967)	(4,720)	(5,513)	(6,347)	(7,227)	(8,160)	(9,144)	(10,184)
Net Property, Plant, and Equipment	6,370	6,433	6,590	6,831	7,148	7,533	7,930	8,337	8,803	9,323	9,840	10,406	10,566
Purchased Patents, Trademarks, Goodwill	100	100	100	100	100	100	100	100	100	100	100	100	100
Total Assets	12,591	13,675	14,861	16,151	17,546	19,048	20,661	22,391	24,247	26,233	28,355	30,624	32,888
Liabilities and Shareholders' Equity													
Bank Borrowings (short-term)	0	0	0	0	0	0	0	0	0	0	0	0	0
Accounts Payable	1,654	1,738	1,825	1,918	2,015	2,117	2,224	2,336	2,455	2,579	2,709	2,847	2,932
Total Current Liabilities	1,654	1,738	1,825	1,918	2,015	2,117	2,224	2,336	2,455	2,579	2,709	2,847	2,932
Long-Term Debt Borrowings	0	0	0	0	0	0	0	0	0	0	0	0	0
Shareholders' Equity	10,937	11,937	13,036	14,234	15,531	16,932	18,437	20,055	21,792	23,654	25,646	27,777	29,956
Total Liabilities and Shareholders' Equity	12,591	13,675	14,861	16,151	17,546	19,048	20,661	22,391	24,247	26,233	28,355	30,624	32,888

(Continued)

TABLE 20.4 (Continued)

Base Case assumes no new microneedle product and no royalty payments

PANEL C

Projected Free Cash Flows and DCF Valuation (In thousands of US $)	Valuation Date Is Dec 31, 2008	Fcst Yr 1 2009	Fcst Yr 2 2010	Fcst Yr 3 2011	Fcst Yr 4 2012	Fcst Yr 5 2013	Fcst Yr 6 2014	Fcst Yr 7 2015	Fcst Yr 8 2016	Fcst Yr 9 2017	Fcst Yr 10 2018	TV Period T+1 = 11
Base Case Net Sales	25,000	26,265	27,594	28,990	30,457	31,998	33,617	35,318	37,106	38,983	40,956	42,184
Base Case Cost of Goods Sold	13,750	14,446	15,177	15,945	16,751	17,599	18,490	19,425	20,408	21,441	22,526	23,201
Gross Profit	11,250	11,819	12,417	13,046	13,706	14,399	15,128	15,893	16,698	17,542	18,430	18,983
Less Expenses:												
Research & Development Expenses	2,750	2,889	3,035	3,189	3,350	3,520	3,698	3,885	4,082	4,288	4,505	4,640
Marketing and Sales Expenses	3,750	3,940	4,139	4,349	4,569	4,800	5,043	5,298	5,566	5,847	6,143	6,328
General & Admin. Expenses (% of Net Sales)	2,500	2,575	2,652	2,732	2,814	2,898	2,985	3,075	3,167	3,262	3,360	3,461
Depreciation Expenses	637	643	659	683	715	753	793	834	880	932	984	1,041
Earnings Before Interest and Taxes (EBIT)	1,613	1,772	1,932	2,093	2,258	2,428	2,609	2,802	3,003	3,213	3,438	3,514
Less Taxes on EBIT	613	673	734	795	858	923	992	1,065	1,141	1,221	1,306	1,335
plus increase (or minus decr.) in accum. deferred taxes	0	0	0	0	0	0	0	0	0	0	0	0
Net Operating Profits Less Adjusted Taxes (NOPLAT)	1,000	1,099	1,198	1,298	1,400	1,505	1,618	1,737	1,862	1,992	2,131	2,179
Plus Depreciation Expense	637	643	659	683	715	753	793	834	880	932	984	1,041
Less Investments in Working Capital	177	186	196	206	216	227	238	251	263	277	291	181
Less Capital Expenditures	700	800	900	1,000	1,100	1,150	1,200	1,300	1,400	1,450	1,550	1,200
Free Cash Flows	760	756	761	775	799	882	972	1,020	1,079	1,198	1,275	1,838 FCF at (T+1)

Required Rate of Return (discount at WACC) 13.2%
PV @13.2% of Forecasted FCFs Yrs 1 to 10 4,809

Terminal Value (TV) Estimate for Year 10
Perpetual Growth at g = 3% [FCF @Yr11/(Kw – g)]   TV at Yr 10 18,022   g = 3%

Discount the Terminal Value from Yr 10 to Yr 0   0   0   0   0   0   0   0   0   0   0   18,022
PV@13.2% of Terminal Value at time 0   5,216
Present Value of Operations   10,025
Plus Excess Cash (year 0)   1,527
Present Value of the Enterprise   11,552
Less Value of Interest-Bearing Debt   0
Equity Value of Advanced Dermal Delivery, Inc.   11,552

TABLE 20.5 Advanced Dermal Deliveries—Scenario A-1

Scenario A-1 assumes new product line and zero royalty payments

PANEL A

Pro Forma Income Statement (In thousands of US $)	Historical 2007	Valuation Date Is Dec 31, 2008	Fcst Yr 1 2009	Fcst Yr 2 2010	Fcst Yr 3 2011	Fcst Yr 4 2012	Fcst Yr 5 2013	Fcst Yr 6 2014	Fcst Yr 7 2015	Fcst Yr 8 2016	Fcst Yr 9 2017	Fcst Yr 10 2018	TV Period T+1 = 11
Net Sales—Base Case	23,796	25,000	26,265	27,594	28,990	30,457	31,998	33,617	35,318	37,106	38,983	40,956	42,184
New Product Sales (net)		0	100	1,000	4,000	8,000	10,000	11,000	12,100	13,310	14,641	15,080	15,532
(Memo: % YOY Growth in New Product Sales)				900%	300%	100%	25%	10%	10%	10%	10%	3%	3%
Total Net Sales for ADD (Scenario A-1)	23,796	25,000	26,365	28,594	32,990	38,457	41,998	44,617	47,418	50,416	53,624	56,036	57,716
Cost of Goods Sold—Base Case	13,088	13,750	14,446	15,177	15,945	16,751	17,599	18,490	19,425	20,408	21,441	22,526	23,201
New Product COGS at 45% of New Product Sales	0	0	50	500	2,000	4,000	5,000	5,500	6,050	6,655	7,321	7,540	7,766
Total Cost of Goods Sold	13,088	13,750	14,496	15,677	17,945	20,751	22,599	23,990	25,475	27,063	28,761	30,066	30,967
Gross Profit	10,708	11,250	11,869	12,917	15,046	17,706	19,399	20,628	21,943	23,353	24,863	25,970	26,749
Total Gross Profit Margin	45%	45%	45%	45.2%	45.6%	46.0%	46.2%	46.2%	46.3%	46.3%	46.4%	46.3%	46.3%
Less Expenses:													
Royalty Expenses for New Product	0	0	0	0	0	0	0	0	0	0	0	0	0
Research & Development—Base Case	2,618	2,750	2,889	3,035	3,189	3,350	3,520	3,698	3,885	4,082	4,288	4,505	4,640
Incremental R&D for New Product	0	0	1,000	500	0	0	0	0	0	0	0	0	0
Marketing & Selling Expense—Base Case	3,569	3,750	3,940	4,139	4,349	4,569	4,800	5,043	5,298	5,566	5,847	6,143	6,328
Mkt & Selling for New Product (15% of new prod sales)	0	0	15	150	600	1,200	1,500	1,650	1,815	1,997	2,196	2,262	2,330
General & Admin. Expenses (G&A)	2,380	2,500	2,575	2,652	2,732	2,814	2,898	2,985	3,075	3,167	3,262	3,360	3,461
G&A for New Product (5% of new product sales)	0	0	5	50	200	400	500	550	605	666	732	754	777
Earnings Before Interest, Taxes, and Depreciation (EBITDA)	2,142	2,250	1,445	2,391	3,976	5,373	6,181	6,702	7,266	7,876	8,537	8,946	9,214
Depreciation Expense (10% of NET PP&E, prior EOY)	630	637	643	759	873	986	1,097	1,102	1,112	1,131	1,158	1,187	1,223
Earnings Before Interest and Taxes (EBIT)	1,512	1,613	802	1,632	3,103	4,387	5,084	5,600	6,154	6,745	7,379	7,759	7,991
Net interest expense	0	0	0	0	16	0	0	0	0	0	0	0	0
Earnings Before Tax	1,512	1,613	802	1,632	3,087	4,387	5,084	5,600	6,154	6,745	7,379	7,759	7,991
Provision for Taxes	574	613	305	620	1,173	1,667	1,932	2,128	2,338	2,563	2,804	2,948	3,036
Earnings After Tax	937	1,000	497	1,012	1,914	2,720	3,152	3,472	3,815	4,182	4,575	4,810	4,954

(*Continued*)

TABLE 20.5 (*Continued*)

Scenario A-1 assumes new product line and zero royalty payments

PANEL B

Pro Forma Balance Sheet (In thousands of US $)	Historical Dec 31 2007	Valuation Date Is Dec 31, 2008	Fcst Yr 1 FY-2009	Fcst Yr 2 FY-2010	Fcst Yr 3 FY-2011	Fcst Yr 4 FY-2012	Fcst Yr 5 FY-2013	Fcst Yr 6 FY-2014	Fcst Yr 7 FY-2015	Fcst Yr 8 FY-2016	Fcst Yr 9 FY-2017	Fcst Yr 10 FY-2018	TV Period T+1
Assets													
Current Assets:													
Cash and Short-Term Securities	150	150	150	150	150	150	150	150	150	150	150	150	150
Surplus or Excess Cash (PLUG)	768	1,527	667	411	357	1,165	3,747	6,737	9,954	13,428	17,241	21,334	26,065
Accounts Receivable	3,007	3,159	3,332	3,613	4,169	4,860	5,307	5,638	5,992	6,371	6,776	7,081	7,294
Inventories	2,151	2,260	2,383	2,577	2,950	3,411	3,715	3,943	4,188	4,449	4,728	4,942	5,091
Prepaid Expenses	45	45	45	45	45	45	45	45	45	45	45	45	45
Total Current Assets	6,121	7,142	6,577	6,796	7,670	9,631	12,964	16,514	20,329	24,443	28,940	33,553	38,644
Gross Property, Plant, and Equipment	7,000	7,700	9,500	11,400	13,400	15,500	16,650	17,850	19,150	20,550	22,000	23,550	24,750
Less: (Accumulated Depreciation)	(630)	(1,267)	(1,910)	(2,669)	(3,542)	(4,528)	(5,625)	(6,728)	(7,840)	(8,971)	(10,129)	(11,316)	(12,539)
Net Property, Plant, and Equipment	6,370	6,433	7,590	8,731	9,858	10,972	11,025	11,122	11,310	11,579	11,871	12,234	12,211
Purchased Patents, Trademarks, Goodwill	100	100	100	100	100	100	100	100	100	100	100	100	100
Total Assets	12,591	13,675	14,266	15,627	17,628	20,703	24,088	27,736	31,739	36,122	40,911	45,887	50,955
Liabilities and Shareholders' Equity													
Bank Borrowings (short-term)	0	0	0	200	0	0	0	0	0	0	0	0	0
Accounts Payable	1,654	1,738	1,832	1,981	2,268	2,622	2,856	3,032	3,219	3,420	3,635	3,799	3,913
Total Current Liabilities	1,654	1,738	1,832	2,181	2,268	2,622	2,856	3,032	3,219	3,420	3,635	3,799	3,913
Long-Term Debt Borrowings	0	0	0	0	0	0	0	0	0	0	0	0	0
Shareholders' Equity	10,937	11,937	12,435	13,446	15,360	18,080	21,233	24,704	28,520	32,702	37,277	42,087	47,041
Total Liabilities and Shareholders' Equity	12,591	13,675	14,266	15,627	17,628	20,703	24,088	27,736	31,739	36,122	40,911	45,887	50,955

PANEL C

Projected Free Cash Flows and DCF Valuation (In thousands of US $)	Valuation Date Is Dec 31, 2008	Fcst Yr 1 2009	Fcst Yr 2 2010	Fcst Yr 3 2011	Fcst Yr 4 2012	Fcst Yr 5 2013	Fcst Yr 6 2014	Fcst Yr 7 2015	Fcst Yr 8 2016	Fcst Yr 9 2017	Fcst Yr 10 2018	TV Period T+1 = 11
Total Net Sales	25,000	26,365	28,594	32,990	38,457	41,998	44,617	47,418	50,416	53,624	56,036	57,716
Total Cost of Goods Sold	13,750	14,496	15,677	17,945	20,751	22,599	23,990	25,475	27,063	28,761	30,066	30,967
Gross Profit	11,250	11,869	12,917	15,046	17,706	19,399	20,628	21,943	23,353	24,863	25,970	26,749
Less Operating Expenses:												
Royalty Expenses for New Product Sales @ 0 %	0	0	0	0	0	0	0	0	0	0	0	0
Total Research & Development Expenses	2,750	3,889	3,535	3,189	3,350	3,520	3,698	3,885	4,082	4,288	4,505	4,640
Total Marketing and Sales Expenses	3,750	3,955	4,289	4,949	5,769	6,300	6,693	7,113	7,562	8,044	8,405	8,657
Total General & Admin. Expenses	2,500	2,580	2,702	2,932	3,214	3,398	3,535	3,680	3,832	3,994	4,114	4,237
Total Depreciation Expenses	637	643	759	873	986	1,097	1,102	1,112	1,131	1,158	1,187	1,223
Total Operating Expenses	9,637	11,067	11,286	11,942	13,318	14,315	15,028	15,790	16,607	17,484	18,211	18,758
Earnings Before Interest and Taxes (EBIT)	1,613	802	1,632	3,103	4,387	5,084	5,600	6,154	6,745	7,379	7,759	7,991
Less Taxes on EBIT	613	305	620	1,179	1,667	1,932	2,128	2,338	2,563	2,804	2,948	3,036
plus increase (or minus decr.) in accum. deferred taxes	0	0	0	0	0	0	0	0	0	0	0	0
Net Operating Profits Less Adjusted Taxes (NOPLAT)	1,000	497	1,012	1,924	2,720	3,152	3,472	3,815	4,182	4,575	4,810	4,954
Plus Total Depreciation Expense	637	643	759	873	986	1,097	1,102	1,112	1,131	1,158	1,187	1,223
Less Investments in Working Capital	177	201	327	642	798	518	384	410	439	470	354	247
Less Capital Expenditures (Base Case)	700	800	900	1,000	1,100	1,150	1,200	1,300	1,400	1,450	1,550	1,200
Less CAPEX associated with New Product Line	0	1,000	1,000	1,000	1,000							
Free Cash Flows	760	(860)	(456)	155	808	2,582	2,990	3,217	3,474	3,813	4,093	4,731
Required Rate of Return (discount at WACC)	13.20%											
PV @13.2% of Forecasted FCFs Yrs 1 to 10	7,367											
											TV at Yr 10	
Terminal Value (TV) Estimate for Year 10												
Perpetual Growth at g = 3% [FCF @Yr11/(Kw – g)]											46,382	g = 3%
Discount the Terminal Value from Yr 10 to Yr 0		0	0	0	0	0	0	0	0	0	0	46,382
PV@13.2% of Terminal Value at time 0	13,424											
Present Value of Operations	20,791											
Plus Excess Cash (year 0)	1,527											
Present Value of the Enterprise	22,318											
Less Value of Interest-Bearing Debt	0											
Equity Value of Advanced Dermal Delivery, Inc.	22,318	compared to 11,552 in Base Case Scenario										

TABLE 20.6 Advanced Dermal Deliveries—Scenario A-2

Scenario A-2 assumes new product line added with royalty payments

PANEL A

Pro Forma Income Statement (In thousands of US $)	Historical 2007	Valuation Date Is Dec 31, 2008	Fcst Yr 1 2009	Fcst Yr 2 2010	Fcst Yr 3 2011	Fcst Yr 4 2012	Fcst Yr 5 2013	Fcst Yr 6 2014	Fcst Yr 7 2015	Fcst Yr 8 2016	Fcst Yr 9 2017	Fcst Yr 10 2018	TV Period T+1 = 11
Net Sales—Base Case	23,796	25,000	26,265	27,594	28,990	30,457	31,998	33,617	35,318	37,106	38,983	40,956	42,184
New Product Sales (net)	0	0	100	1,000	4,000	8,000	10,000	11,000	12,100	13,310	14,641	15,080	15,532
(Memo: % YOY Growth in New Product Sales)				900%	300%	100%	25%	10%	10%	10%	10%	3%	3%
Total Net Sales for ADD (Scenario A-1)	23,796	25,000	26,365	28,594	32,990	38,457	41,998	44,617	47,418	50,416	53,624	56,036	57,716
Cost of Goods Sold—Base Case	13,088	13,750	14,446	15,177	15,945	16,751	17,599	18,490	19,425	20,408	21,441	22,526	23,201
New Product COGS at 45% of New Product Sales	0	0	50	500	2,000	4,000	5,000	5,500	6,050	6,655	7,321	7,540	7,766
Total Cost of Goods Sold	13,088	13,750	14,496	15,677	17,945	20,751	22,599	23,990	25,475	27,063	28,761	30,066	30,967
Gross Profit	10,708	11,250	11,869	12,917	15,046	17,706	19,399	20,628	21,943	23,353	24,863	25,970	26,749
Total Gross Profit Margin	45%	45%	45%	45.2%	45.6%	46.0%	46.2%	46.2%	46.3%	46.3%	46.4%	46.3%	46.3%
Less Expenses:													
Royalty Expenses for New Product	0	0	21	211	843	1,686	2,108	2,319	2,551	2,806	3,086	3,179	3,274
Research & Development—Base Case	2,618	2,750	2,889	3,035	3,189	3,350	3,520	3,698	3,885	4,082	4,288	4,505	4,640
Incremental R&D for New Product	0	0	1,000	500	0	0	0	0	0	0	0	0	0
Marketing & Selling Expenses—Base Case	3,569	3,750	3,940	4,139	4,349	4,569	4,800	5,043	5,298	5,566	5,847	6,143	6,328
Mkt & Selling for New Product (15% of new prod sales)	0	0	15	150	600	1,200	1,500	1,650	1,815	1,997	2,196	2,262	2,330
General & Admin. Expenses (G&A)	2,380	2,500	2,575	2,652	2,732	2,814	2,898	2,985	3,075	3,167	3,262	3,360	3,461
G&A for New Product (5% of new product sales)	0	0	5	50	200	400	500	550	605	666	732	754	777
Earnings Before Interest, Taxes, and Depreciation (EBITDA)	2,142	2,250	1,424	2,180	3,133	3,687	4,073	4,383	4,715	5,070	5,451	5,767	5,940
Depreciation Expense (10% of NET PP&E, prior EOY)	630	637	643	759	873	986	1,097	1,102	1,112	1,131	1,158	1,187	1,223
Earnings Before Interest and Taxes (EBIT)	1,512	1,613	781	1,421	2,260	2,701	2,976	3,281	3,603	3,939	4,293	4,580	4,716
Net interest expense	0	0	0	0	16	0	0	0	0	0	0	0	0
Earnings Before Tax	1,512	1,613	781	1,421	2,244	2,701	2,976	3,281	3,603	3,939	4,293	4,580	4,716
Provision for Taxes	574	613	297	540	853	1,026	1,131	1,247	1,369	1,497	1,631	1,740	1,792
Earnings After Tax	937	1,000	484	881	1,391	1,675	1,845	2,034	2,234	2,442	2,662	2,839	2,924

PANEL B

Pro Forma Balance Sheet (In thousands of US $) Assets	Historical Dec 31 2007	Valuation Date Is Dec 31, 2008	Fcst Yr 1 FY-2009	Fcst Yr 2 FY-2010	Fcst Yr 3 FY-2011	Fcst Yr 4 FY-2012	Fcst Yr 5 FY-2013	Fcst Yr 6 FY-2014	Fcst Yr 7 FY-2015	Fcst Yr 8 FY-2016	Fcst Yr 9 FY-2017	Fcst Yr 10 FY-2018	TV Period T+1
Current Assets:													
Cash and Short-Term Securities	150	150	150	150	150	150	150	150	150	150	150	150	150
Surplus or Excess Cash (PLUG)	768	1,527	654	267	(310)	(547)	728	2,280	3,916	5,650	7,550	9,672	12,373
Accounts Receivable	3,007	3,159	3,332	3,613	4,169	4,860	5,307	5,638	5,992	6,371	6,776	7,081	7,294
Inventories	2,151	2,260	2,383	2,577	2,950	3,411	3,715	3,943	4,188	4,449	4,728	4,942	5,091
Prepaid Expenses	45	45	45	45	45	45	45	45	45	45	45	45	45
Total Current Assets	6,121	7,142	6,564	6,653	7,004	7,919	9,945	12,057	14,291	16,665	19,249	21,890	24,952
Gross Property, Plant, and Equipment	7,000	7,700	9,500	11,400	13,400	15,500	16,650	17,850	19,150	20,550	22,000	23,550	24,750
Less: (Accumulated Depreciation)	(630)	(1,267)	(1,910)	(2,669)	(3,542)	(4,528)	(5,625)	(6,728)	(7,840)	(8,971)	(10,129)	(11,316)	(12,539)
Net Property, Plant, and Equipment	6,370	6,433	7,590	8,731	9,858	10,972	11,025	11,122	11,310	11,579	11,871	12,234	12,211
Purchased Patents, Trademarks, Goodwill	100	100	100	100	100	100	100	100	100	100	100	100	100
Total Assets	12,591	13,675	14,253	15,483	16,961	18,991	21,069	23,279	25,701	28,344	31,220	34,224	37,263
Liabilities and Shareholders' Equity													
Bank Borrowings (short-term)	0	0	0	200	0	0	0	0	0	0	0	0	0
Accounts Payable	1,654	1,738	1,832	1,981	2,268	2,622	2,856	3,032	3,219	3,420	3,635	3,799	3,913
Total Current Liabilities	1,654	1,738	1,832	2,181	2,268	2,622	2,856	3,032	3,219	3,420	3,635	3,799	3,913
Long-Term Debt Borrowings	0	0	0	0	0	0	0	0	0	0	0	0	0
Shareholders' Equity	10,937	11,937	12,421	13,302	14,694	16,368	18,214	20,248	22,482	24,924	27,586	30,425	33,349
Total Liabilities and Shareholders' Equity	12,591	13,675	14,253	15,483	16,961	18,991	21,069	23,279	25,701	28,344	31,220	34,224	37,263

(*Continued*)

TABLE 20.6 (*Continued*)

Scenario A-2 assumes new product line added with royalty payments

PANEL C

Projected Free Cash Flows and DCF Valuation (In thousands of US $)	Valuation Date Is Dec 31, 2008	Fcst Yr 1 2009	Fcst Yr 2 2010	Fcst Yr 3 2011	Fcst Yr 4 2012	Fcst Yr 5 2013	Fcst Yr 6 2014	Fcst Yr 7 2015	Fcst Yr 8 2016	Fcst Yr 9 2017	Fcst Yr 10 2018	TV Period T+1 = 11
Total Net Sales	25,000	26,365	28,594	32,990	38,457	41,998	44,617	47,418	50,416	53,624	56,036	57,716
Total Cost of Goods Sold	13,750	14,496	15,677	17,945	20,751	22,599	23,990	25,475	27,063	28,761	30,066	30,967
Gross Profit	11,250	11,869	12,917	15,046	17,706	19,399	20,628	21,943	23,353	24,863	25,970	26,749
Less Operating Expenses:												
Royalty Expenses for New Product Sales @ 21.08%	0	21	211	843	1,686	2,108	2,319	2,551	2,806	3,086	3,179	3,274
Total Research & Development Expenses	2,750	3,889	3,535	3,189	3,350	3,520	3,698	3,885	4,082	4,288	4,505	4,640
Total Marketing and Sales Expenses	3,750	3,955	4,289	4,949	5,769	6,300	6,693	7,113	7,562	8,044	8,405	8,657
Total General & Admin. Expenses	2,500	2,580	2,702	2,932	3,214	3,398	3,535	3,680	3,832	3,994	4,114	4,237
Total Depreciation Expenses	637	643	759	873	986	1,097	1,102	1,112	1,131	1,158	1,187	1,223
Total Operating Expenses	9,637	11,088	11,496	12,786	15,005	16,423	17,347	18,340	19,413	20,570	21,390	22,032
Earnings Before Interest and Taxes (EBIT)	1,613	781	1,421	2,260	2,701	2,976	3,281	3,603	3,939	4,293	4,580	4,716
Less Taxes on EBIT	613	297	540	859	1,026	1,131	1,247	1,369	1,497	1,631	1,740	1,792
Plus increase (or minus decr.) in accum. deferred taxes	0	0	0	0	0	0	0	0	0	0	0	0

Net Operating Profits Less Adjusted Taxes (NOPLAT)	1,000	484	881	1,401	1,675	1,845	2,034	2,234	2,442	2,662	2,839	2,924
Plus Total Depreciation Expense	637	643	759	873	986	1,097	1,102	1,112	1,131	1,158	1,187	1,223
Less Investments in Working Capital	177	201	327	642	798	518	384	410	439	470	354	247
Less Capital Expenditures (Base Case)	700	800	900	1,000	1,100	1,150	1,200	1,300	1,400	1,450	1,550	1,200
Less CAPEX associated with New Product Line	0	1,000	1,000	1,000	1,000	0	0	0	0	0	0	0
Free Cash Flows	760	(873)	(587)	(367)	(237)	1,275	1,553	1,636	1,734	1,900	2,122	2,701
Required Rate of Return (discount at WACC)	13.20%											
PV @13.2% of Forecasted FCFs Yrs 1 to 10	2,363											
Terminal Value (TV) Estimate for Year 10											TV at Yr 10 26,480	
Perpetual Growth at g = 3% [FCF @Yr11/(Kw – g)]												g = 3%
Discount the Terminal Value from Yr 10 to Yr 0	0	0	0	0	0	0	0	0	0	0	26,480	0
PV@13.2% of Terminal Value at time 0	7,664											
Present Value of Operations	10,027											
Plus Excess Cash (year 0)	1,527											
Present Value of the Enterprise	11,554											
Less Value of Interest-Bearing Debt	0											
Equity Value of Advanced Dermal Delivery, Inc.	11,554	compared to 11,552 in Base Case Scenario										

for the new product are included and the launch of the new microneedle product is assumed to be successful (with much increased sales and margins).

Scenario A-2 is identical to Scenario A-1 except for one line in the spreadsheet. Go to Table 20.6 Panel C and look under "Operating Expenses" in Scenario A-2 to find the line: "Royalty Expense as a percentage of New Product Sales" in the projected free cash flows forecast.

To solve for the *maximum* royalty rate that ADD should be willing to pay to the ink-jet manufacturer for the microneedle technology, Lee used trial and error. She gradually increased the royalty percentage in Scenario A-2 until the net present value of this scenario matched the net present value of the Base Case Scenario of $11,552,000. The correct answer was a royalty payment equal to 21.08 percent or approximately 21 percent of new product sales. Note that even if ADD were to pay 21 percent, the company would still be able to earn its required cost of capital of 13.2 percent for Scenario A-2 (the same cost of capital as was used in the Base Case Scenario).

If ADD were able to negotiate a lower royalty rate from the ink-jet manufacturer say of 10 percent instead of 21 percent, then it would be able to create a win-win situation for both parties, where each side shares in the economic benefit produced through ADD's new product efforts and the ink-jet manufacturer's microneedle technology.

The positive NPV result indicated that ADD should go ahead with the development project. ADD saves the time and effort of trying to invent the microneedle in-house, something that it is highly unlikely to do, as it does not have the know-how or expertise to develop this type of technology. By successfully concluding a licensing agreement with the ink-jet manufacturer, ADD also gains freedom to operate and avoids infringing on the ink-jet manufacturer's microneedle patents.

NEXT STEP: SENSITIVITY ANALYSIS

It was now the morning of June 10, and time for Lee to meet with Mendoza to jointly review the model's assumptions. Lee explained to him the Base Case and then Scenarios A-1 and A-2. She demonstrated how these two scenarios bracketed the extreme range of royalty rates from 0 percent (unacceptable to licensor) to the high of 21 percent (the maximum tolerable to the licensee). Somewhere in-between would be an acceptable range of shared economic advantage for both sides.

The simplest technique to better understand the uncertainties in a forecast is to apply sensitivity analysis, known as "what if" questions to the financial model. What if ADD's royalty rates varied from 0 percent to 21 percent—what would be the effect on the model's results? Sensitivity testing involves systematically changing one of the variables on which the forecast is based and observing the response.

To begin the testing, Lee and Mendoza together reduced the royalty rate to 10 percent, and observed that the equity value of ADD for Scenario A-2 rose to $17,212,000, a significant gain (nearly 50 percent) over the Base Case equity value of $11,552,000. Table 20.7 shows the complete results of their sensitivity analysis. They tried varying the royalty rate in Scenario A-2 from 0 percent to 21.08 percent (maximum) while keeping everything else the same, (i.e., maintaining the terminal value growth rate, $g_\infty = 3\%$ and keeping the free cash flow discount rate at 13.2 percent).

TABLE 20.7 Royalty Rate Sensitivity Analysis
for Scenario A-2

Scenario A-2 Royalty Rate (%)	Equity Value (in thousands of $)
0—MIN	22,318
2	21,297
4	20,276
6	19,254
8	18,233
10	17,212
12	16,191
14	15,170
16	14,148
18	13,127
20	12,106
21—MAX	11,595

In Table 20.7, Lee and Mendoza could clearly see the economic value created or destroyed by adding the new product line and paying different royalty schemes. To test the limits, Lee and Mendoza inserted the very high royalty rate of 25 percent, and calculated the equity value of $9,553,000 for Scenario A-2 and compared it to the $11,552,000 for the Base Case. They observed a decrease in shareholders' wealth of about $2 million. At such a high royalty rate, ADD would not be earning the 13.2 percent cost of capital expected by its shareholders. The results showed that if ADD were to pay a royalty rate higher than 21 percent, the corresponding financial results would be less than for the Base Case and the new microneedle product would not enhance economic value. Therefore, ADD would have to either negotiate a royalty rate that was lower than 21 percent from the ink-jet manufacturer or not do the deal.

Changing the Cost of Capital

Having done sensitivity analysis on the royalty rate, Lee and Mendoza next were curious to learn what would happen to the results if they raised or lowered the equity market risk premium used in the CAPM formula to estimate the expected cost of equity. Recall that ADD used no debt in its target capital structure. Therefore, the WACC for ADD equaled its cost of equity ($k_{wacc} = k_e$).

When changing the cost of equity, they also took into account the influence of the unsystematic risk adjustment for illiquidity. The next formula repeats the adjusted cost of equity including the unsystematic risk rate premium:

Adjusted cost of equity $= r_f + \beta(R_m - r_f) +$ Unsystematic risk rate premium.

Recall that the unsystematic risk rate premium $= d \times (k - g)/(1 - d)$

where $d =$ discount (as a percentage of the security's equity or enterprise value)
$k =$ DCF discount rate (k_e or WACC)
$g =$ dividend or free cash flow growth rate (in perpetuity)

TABLE 20.8   Base Case Sensitivity Analysis of Different Cost of Equity Assumptions

Equity Market Risk Premium with Small-Cap Adjustment $(R_m - r_f)$ (in %)	CAPM Cost of Equity k_e, (in %)*	Adjusted Cost of Equity Including Illiquidity Risk Premium (in %)**	Base Case Scenario Equity Value (in 1,000s of $)
5.0	8.64	11.1	$14,735
6.0	9.44	12.2	$12,875
6.9	**10.16**	**13.2**	**$11,552**
7.0	10.24	13.3	$11,435
8.0	11.04	14.5	$10,200
9.0	11.84	15.6	$9,290

*K_{wacc} = Ke adjusted because ADD uses no long-term debt in its capital structure.
**Figures rounded to one decimal and used for computing ADD's equity value.

Table 20.8 shows the results of changing the adjusted cost of capital only for the Base Case Scenario (to keep the discussion simpler). However, the same sort of sensitivity analysis could be extended to all the other scenarios and the results compared. The first column shows the equity market risk premium, the second column shows the CAPM cost of equity, the third column shows the adjusted cost of equity including the illiquidity risk premium, and the fourth column shows the equity valuation results of the Base Case Scenario after inputting the revised cost of equity.

Based on their sensitivity analysis of the cost of capital, Lee and Mendoza concluded that a lower cost of capital would make any investment look more favorable, whereas a higher cost of capital would penalize any project. Clearly, if they were to do the same sensitivity analysis on Scenario A-2, it would mean that ADD would need to negotiate a much *lower* royalty rate from the ink-jet manufacturing company when the adjusted cost of capital was higher (say at 15.6 percent) than lower (at 13.2 percent). The difference in these two equity values ($11,552,000 − $9,290,000) amounted to over $2,262,000 in net present value. (Refer to Table 20.8.)

Changing the Perpetual Growth Rate

Lee and Mendoza next did sensitivity analysis on the perpetual growth rate assumed in the terminal value formula. They varied the perpetual growth rate g_∞, of the TV from $g_\infty = 0$ percent up to 6 percent (and at the same time they changed the corresponding adjusted cost of equity). Because g_∞ represents an infinite stream of cash flows, a small increase or reduction in the perpetual growth rate can make a significant difference in the TV calculation and consequently in the equity value of ADD. Table 20.9 shows the results of the sensitivity tests for changing the perpetual growth rate (and its associated adjusted cost of equity), but not changing any other assumptions in the Base Case. The Base Case equity value turned out to be very sensitive to the perpetual growth rate assumption.

TABLE 20.9   Base Case Sensitivity Analysis of Varying the Perpetual Growth Rate

Perpetual Growth Rate (%)	Corresponding Adjusted Cost of Equity (including illiquidity Risk Premium) (%)	Base Case Scenario Equity Value (in 1,000s of $)
0	14.51	9,339
2	13.66	10,622
3	13.2*	11,552 (Original Base Case)
4	12.80	12,685
5	12.37	14,287
6	11.94	16,632

*Inputted 13.2 percent (after rounding) instead of 13.23 percent for consistency with Base Case model assumptions. Other adjusted cost of equity figures inputted with two decimal places for more accuracy.

NEXT STEP: DEVELOPING SCENARIOS TO QUANTIFY THE RISKS OF NEW PRODUCT FAILURE

Sensitivity analysis has both pluses and minuses. Sensitivity analysis usually changes only one variable at a time. However, as seen in the previous section with the perpetual growth rate example, changing the perpetual growth rate implicitly changed the adjusted cost of equity. It would have been incorrect to change one and not the other. Scenario analysis takes a broader view of the modeling problem than sensitivity analysis and allows the appraiser to examine how a number of variables might change simultaneously in response to a particular event or an imagined future state-of-the-world. Scenario analysis also encompasses interrelated risks and uncertainties better than sensitivity tests.

In order to quantify the risks of new product failure due to technological uncertainties, Lee and Mendoza decided to create three distinct technology scenarios: worst, most likely, and best case. The technology scenarios would be incorporated into the spreadsheet assumptions for Scenario A-2: new product launch and royalty expenses included. Each of the technology scenarios would use a 3 percent perpetual growth rate and an adjusted cost of equity (with the illiquidity premium included) of 13.2 percent. The idea is to modify only those variables related to technology risks of the new product launch that are not accounted for in Scenario A-2.

What are typical technological risks? Such risks could be product failure due to mechanical problems with the nanosize pump; design or material specification problems; or delays due to challenges encountered when scaling up the device from a laboratory prototype to a fully-functional transdermal nanodevice that could be manufactured at high volumes. The scenarios needed to envision how these technological risks impacted new product sales and overall profit forecasts.

- *Worst case.* Shutdown of the microneedle project due to unresolved technological problems after two years of development effort. New microneedle net product sales would be zero. Incremental R&D expenses of $1 million in year 2009 and $500,000 in year 2010 would be charged to the income statement, and

$1 million per year in additional capital expenditures for each of the years 2009 and 2010. Therefore total costs to be written off after product failure amounted to $3.5 million. Lee and Mendoza thought the chances of this happening were about 25 percent.

- *Most likely case.* Microneedle product launch delayed by one year due to technological challenges. New product sales, related cost of goods, marketing and sales expenses related to the new product—all these items would shift one year in timing. However, incremental R&D and incremental capital expenditures would not change from the original assumptions; they would be incurred according to the original budget. They gave this scenario a 50 percent probability.
- *Best case.* No delays and everything proceeding smoothly according to plan. They gave this scenario a 25 percent chance of coming true.

In Table 20.10 are the results for the three technology risk scenarios. The second column shows the probability of occurrence of each scenario. The third column is the resulting equity value of Scenario A-2 after making the adjustments appropriate for each scenario. The fourth column shows the Base Case Scenario value computed for perpetual growth of 3 percent and a discount rate of 13.2 percent. The fifth column calculates the net change in equity value under each scenario. Multiplying the probability of occurrence of each scenario (column two) by the resulting equity value of Scenario A-2 (column three), Lee and Mendoza calculated a probability weighted equity value of $10,836,750 for ADD, corresponding to an overall decrease in equity value of $10,836,750 – $11,552,000 or a decrease of $715,250 for all three scenarios combined.

What should Lee and Mendoza do with the technological risk assessment information? The technology risk has the effect of decreasing the maximum royalty amount that ADD should be willing to pay to the ink-jet manufacturer by the amount of the expected change over the Base Case Scenario.

However, looking at the overall size of the expected change (approximately $715,000), they realized that other factors appear to be far more important than the technology risk assessment in this particular instance. The other factors they thought should be analyzed more carefully include: raising or lowering the forecast for Base Case sales; improving (or showing deterioration) in the cost of goods sold; changing the number of days receivables from 45 to 60 days; and so forth.

TABLE 20.10   Scenario A-2: Technological Risk Assessment Using Three Scenarios

Scenario Analysis	Probability of Occurrence	Scenario A-2 Equity Value (in 1,000s)	Base Case Equity Value (in 1,000s)	Decrease in Equity Value (in 1,000s) (column 3 – column 4)	Probability Weighted Equity Value (column 5 x column 2)
Worst Case	25%	$9,421	$11,552	($2,131)	($532.75)
Most Likely	50%	$11,186	$11,552	($366)	($183.00)
Best Case	25%	$11,554	$11,552	$2	$0.50
					Total = ($714.25)

What Lee and Mendoza also learned from doing the technological risk scenarios was the wisdom of ADD *stretching out the new product capital expenditures over four years*. ADD greatly enhanced its flexibility to respond quickly to problems during the launch phase. All in all, they decided it reasonable not to do any further adjustments in their model for technology risks. They thought their time was better spent developing other scenarios and negotiating points.

DEVELOPING OTHER LIKELY SCENARIOS AND NEGOTIATING POINTS

With Monte Carlo simulation,[17] Lee and Mendoza could expand upon their scenario analysis to encompass many more questions about the future states of the world, including such regulatory issues. For instance, a key question for their pharmaceutical company clients would be whether they could obtain timely FDA approval for the new microneedle patch plus therapeutic drug delivery system. If FDA approval were delayed, or denied, how might this impact ADD's new product sales and profits? They also could use simulation techniques to quantify the uncertainties in what appeared to be a gloomy macroeconomic outlook. What if expected inflation rose or fell beyond what they had estimated in their model? What if the business cycle downturn went from a recession into a depression?

Simulation is suitable for observing how operating margins improve (or worsen) in relation to sales increasing (or decreasing); different degrees of customer acceptance and market penetration (or not); and later enhancements of the new microneedle patch, that take place after launch. Monte Carlo simulation is able to quantify the impact of these multiple variables interacting simultaneously on the financial results, something which is difficult (and time consuming) to do in a manual "what if" sensitivity or scenario testing process.

In Lee and Mendoza's experience, no CEO, CFO, or head of business development should walk into an important strategic alliance negotiation with just one scenario prepared. The negotiating team needs to know and understand the economic impact of various contract clauses and how agreement or disagreement on these terms might influence the risks and potential returns of the deal. The negotiators need to be well versed on the deal's economic drivers (in other words, what provisions create positive cash flows and what provisions create negative cash flows for the business)—not only for their side of the deal but also for the other side.

In their opinion, it is good advice to prepare for the upcoming negotiation by taking the point of view of the opposite party and trying to work out the deal terms from the perspective of the other side. In the end, it would be Lee, Mendoza, their boss, Joe McCaffrey, and ADD's intellectual property attorney and legal adviser, who need to come up with a reasonable number of viable alternatives to propose to the other side. They also have to work out what the downside risks might be for ADD if the other side proposes different terms and conditions than they were expecting. They do not want the negotiations to get hung up on haggling merely over the price of royalties; they need to be creative in considering a variety of options. They also know that the better they prepare, the better their chances of remaining calm and flexible during the bargaining sessions.

Next Lee and Mendoza discuss specific contract terms and conditions that they expect will be negotiated with the ink-jet manufacturing company. These terms and conditions will become part of the memorandum of understanding being drafted for the strategic alliance. The final terms and conditions will be incorporated into the definitive strategic alliance contract agreement. Eventually some or all of these items will be incorporated into the financial modeling as Lee and Mendoza see fit.

Technical Assistance from the Licensor

ADD might be interested in incorporating into the license agreement compensation terms for the value of anticipated technical assistance. ADD is not expert in ink-jet printer technology. It might require technical assistance from the ink-jet manufacturer's research team, especially in matters related to cleaning, maintenance, and operations of the microneedle component and its tiny reservoirs where the drug is stored. In some contracts, the technical assistance compensation is included as part of the overall royalty rate with no specific breakdown. In other contracts, it is a clearly specified amount, such as 20 percent of the royalty rate for technical assistance and 80 percent of the royalty for the right to use the underlying intellectual property. The specification of what kind of technical assistance and know-how (or "show-how") should be negotiated. (Refer to Chapters 11 and 14 for information on specifying trade secrets and know-how in technology transfer agreements.)

Up-Front License Fees and Milestone Payments

In ADD's case, the developer of the ink-jet technology is a very large corporation with sizable manufacturing resources and capital. Consequently, up-front payments of license fees (or milestone payments) for this particular licensor might not be critical. In many other instances, however, the reverse holds true. For example, what if a small, high-tech venture with its own proprietary technology seeks to license its patents and software to another major corporation. For the venture, early up-front payments (payments in advance of selling the final product) might be critical to its survival. If it does not receive up-front payments, it might not have the cash flow to be able to wait 6 months, 12 months, 24 months, or more for the product to be launched and royalty payments to be received. Its burn rate is too high to survive for long.

In the negotiations, the licensor will seek to trade-off the receipt of earlier up-front fees and lump-sum payments (linked to milestones) with the receipt of later (and less certain) cash flow streams tied to the royalty payments.

From the Licensee's Viewpoint   If the licensee is supposed to pay up-front payments to the licensor, then normally these payments are treated as operating expenses in the same way that royalty payments are handled. The person building the financial forecasts simply adds a line item called "up-front license payments" or "milestone payments" into the operating expenses of the forecasted income statements at the time they are incurred. These expenses reduce operating income of the license. At the same time, the person doing the model needs to reduce the operating expense of the royalties to offset the new milestone or lump-sum payments. Basically the trade-off is to reduce the present value of a long-term stream of cash payments (the royalties) by an equal amount of discounted up-front lump sum payments, everything else remaining equal in the DCF analysis.

From the Licensor's Viewpoint   On the other side, if the licensor receives milestone payments, these are handled like income. The person building the forecast can add a line "other income" to the revenues of the company. Revenues will be made up of net sales from products and income from licensing fees. The more income the licensor receives from up-front licensing fees, the lower should be the corresponding royalty percentage, all other factors remaining equal in the discounted flows of cash analysis.

But Are They Really Equal?   The old saying "A bird in the hand is worth two in the bush" comes to mind. Up-front payments in cash are less risky than possibly receiving royalties on a new product yet to be proven or launched. Cash in the hand is certain. Royalty payments need to be audited and verified. They are subject to more interpretation as to how they are calculated. The company that should pay the royalties might go bankrupt or face litigation. Any number of intervening factors could prohibit payment from one party to the other. Many licensing deals consist of up-front licensing fees, milestone payments, and royalty payments to try to reduce risk and optimize the deal structure.

How to Set the "Right" Allocation Mix?   Most people facing this situation will turn to industry practice and review current licensing deals for how players in their particular sector allocate the licensing revenues between royalties and up-front licensing fees and milestone payments. It ultimately is a matter of bargaining skill and perceived negotiation power between the parties involved. Senior licensing managers and business development executives whom we asked to share their words of wisdom on this subject answered most frequently: "There are no rules, each case is different."

FINAL TIPS ON NEGOTIATION PREPARATIONS FOR STRUCTURING THE DEAL

By applying their combined forecasting skills, knowledge about discounted cash flow analyses, and experiences from past negotiations, Victoria Lee, Mike Mendoza, and Joe McCaffrey developed a series of likely possibilities, financial alternatives, and associated discounted cash flow figures. They developed an overall sense of the economic drivers of the business. They spent time preparing, doing their homework, and analyzing the effect of various licensing elements and contractual clauses on the economics of their business (from the point of view of ADD) and on the business of the other party (and from the point of view of the ink-jet manufacturer).

   To facilitate the negotiation preparations, we have learned (Chapter 7) that it is useful to make a trade-off table of the key provisions so that in the course of negotiations, the impact of various proposals can be estimated quickly and accurately. Table 20.11 captures the positive (or negative) influences on the results.

   From a trade-off table, the negotiators can quickly realize that the ability to negotiate technical upgrades and the rights to future releases will have more positive

TABLE 20.11   Trade-Off Table of Key Provisions

License Provision #1 (nonexclusivity) Interpretation: This means that if the license is nonexclusive instead of exclusive, the NPV would be *lower* by an estimated $3,000,000.	$(3,000,000)
License Provision #2 (delay in obtaining FDA **approval by one year)** Interpretation: This means that if FDA approval is delayed by one year, it creates an opportunity cost of $1,000,000 in NPV from the delay	$(1,000,000)
License Provision #3 (technical upgrades on **future releases)** Interpretation: The licensee (ADD) would receive rights from the licensor to the next generation of microneedle technology, which is even smaller, better, and faster than the current generation. This would enhance the operating performance of ADD's future products while lowering manufacturing costs. If sales prices could be kept at a premium, this option could be worth even more (hence the range in estimates, as it may not be possible to pinpoint an exact answer).	$1,250,000–$2,400,000
License Provision #4 (reduce royalty **payments by 1%)** Interpretation: ADD pays less royalties to the licensor, thereby realizing these savings.	$500,000

economic input on the overall strategic alliance than haggling over a 1 percent variation in the royalties. The most important negative impact is the choice of exclusive versus nonexclusive rights to the microneedle technology. As pointed out in Chapter 14, where technology transfer licensing contracts were explained in detail, it pays to give careful thought to exclusivity clauses and their ramifications.

Other types of license provisions may be more troublesome to quantify, for instance, provisions that require some form of indemnification (protection against loss). We can imagine where ADD would like to be held harmless in any situation where a third party might sue (or class action suit arise) in the event of the microneedle causing a product liability for the new nanopatch. On the other side, the licensor, especially because it is a large corporation and therefore may be a target for a class action suit, may want some sort of indemnification in the event that ADD's product causes them some kind of harm. The answer to these sorts of questions depends very much on the proposed field of use and the history of infringement or product liability litigation for that particular product (and country or territory). The licensor needs to weigh the consequences of product liability claims and damage awards to the rewards obtained from proceeding with the transaction. This is an area where expert advice and legal counsel is clearly advisable. There are no black-and-white, hard-and-fast rules. Product liability insurance may be a solution, but it is often expensive or unavailable.

For the valuation and quantification of these uncertainties, the general principle is either to raise the discount rate (the more risk, the higher the discount rate) or to introduce probabilities into the calculation of the cash flows using either scenarios or decision trees (these last two are called the expected cash flow approach). In other words, either adjust the cash flows or adjust the discount rate but do *not* do both. That would be double-counting the risk.

For instance, we could make two estimates. In Alternative A, some sort of legal fees need to be paid to settle litigation, but no damage awards. The legal costs of $100,000 would be assumed to take place early in the forecast, for instance, year 3. Alternative B is the scenario of serious litigation where damages and legal fees cost over $1,000,000 and might also occur in year 3. The business development manager might think that neither alternative is very probable and therefore uses a higher discount rate (say, 25 percent) than that used for the other negotiated scenarios (say, 15 percent). This reduces the present value of these less likely scenarios.

Earlier in the section on developing scenarios to quantify the risks of new product failure, we demonstrated how to probability weight the results from three technology risk scenarios. The other technique (decision trees) uses probabilities to adjust the cash flows to reflect the likelihood of future events. Decision trees are well illustrated in the capstone case Proto5 (log onto www.innovationtocashflows.com to download the file) so we will not cover them here.

Merits of a Simple System to Quantify the Trade-Offs during Negotiations

It is easy to get carried away in financial modeling and lose sight of the big picture, which is to come up with a win-win strategic alliance that works and creates value for both parties. Very often in the course of bargaining terms and conditions, negotiators need a quick way to calculate if a proposed licensing provision will yield positive or negative cash flows and if the suggested change is of major or minor consequence for the deal.

We have attempted to demonstrate with this case a systematic way of valuing and structuring a licensing deal step by step and then organizing the final valuation information in a simple trade-off table. Trade-off tables come in handy for the persons doing the negotiations, if they are simple enough and easy to use.

When preparing for a negotiation, it pays to think about presenting the alternatives and permutations of the evolving deal in a modular way. The modules pertain to specific clauses that can then be assembled, discarded, or reassembled easily, depending on how the negotiations evolve. A modular approach keeps options open and creates room for more creative accommodation. By combining modules with a trade-off table, negotiators can bargain without giving away more in economic value than they intended.

CHAPTER TAKEAWAYS

- The win-win outcome of a good licensing negotiation is to seek a set of terms and conditions that creates value for both licensor and licensee. The aim of the negotiations is to reach a mutually satisfactory middle ground where each side is able to achieve as many of its objectives and priorities as possible while yielding on those points of lesser importance.

- The art of valuing technology transfer agreements comes from the imagination and creativity required to envision future cash flow streams. You need to imagine the time frame and duration of the various cash flows, their size and frequency of occurrence, and the risks associated with receiving the cash flows. The risks of a product development project usually are higher in the beginning and decrease as the project goes from the lab and moves into the commercialization phase.

- Small companies rely on diverse teams of people (usually the CEO, CFO, and head of business development) to prepare important deal valuations. The input of other members of the senior management team, scientific advisory board, and board of directors might also be solicited. Finally, it is important to seek the advice of tax, patent, or other IP specialists and legal counsel in order to properly prepare the valuations for deal negotiations.

- Prepare alternative scenarios and think about issues from multiple perspectives. The negotiating team needs to know and understand the economic impact of various contract clauses and how agreement or disagreement on these terms might influence the risks and potential returns of the deal. It is also necessary to make a trade-off table of the key provisions so that in the course of negotiations, the impact of various proposals can be estimated quickly and accurately.

- Refer to Chapter 17 for information on DCF valuation techniques. For more on the use of market multiples and comparable deal transactions in valuations, refer to Chapter 18.

- Interested readers may log onto www.innovationtocashflow.com to download these supplemental resources:
  - Electronic spreadsheets to accompany the case on Advanced Dermal Delivery, Inc. with financial forecasts for ADD's Base Case Scenario, Scenario A-1, and Scenario A-2.
  - Appendix 17.2: The Time Value of Money.
  - Appendix 17.4: Five Ways to Estimate Terminal Values.
  - Appendix 17.5: General Principles for Determining the Equity Market Risk Premium.
  - Appendix 17.6: Estimating the Weighted Average Cost of Capital for the ABC Corporation.

CHAPTER 21

Conclusion

We are reaching the end of our journey. In these closing thoughts, we offer a summary of the key messages in the book, their implications, and our own views about being an entrepreneur and what it takes to be a successful one.

Entrepreneurs start up businesses for all sorts of reasons. For some, their parents and grandparents and great-grandparents were all entrepreneurs, so doing something else never occurs to them. For others, the decision is reached only after their jobs are restructured and they collect a golden handshake. Or perhaps the choice is driven by frustration: hitting the infamous glass ceiling in terms of promotion and not being able to break through. Others may still be in school when they decide that the allure of striking out on their own is too strong to ignore. They hope to become the next Steve Jobs and Steve Wozniak of Apple, Bill Gates and Steve Ballmer of Microsoft, or Larry Page and Sergey Brin of Google.

Sometimes the decision stems from personality: The companies' founders could not work for anyone else. We note that entrepreneurs do tend to be a rather stubborn lot. Does their strong character give them the stamina to persevere against all odds and the naysaying of other people? We have learned from listening to entrepreneurs that many of them cherish the freedom that comes from working independently. They feel uncomfortable being in the bureaucracy of a large corporation. They enjoy more the experience of creating something new from scratch. Stubbornness can also mean that some entrepreneurs are like Don Quixote, they chase windmills forever. They never do get their ideas off the ground and into viable business models. Like Don Quixote, some entrepreneurs find their meaning in life simply from following their dreams. The Don Quixotes of this world are driven by obligation rather than by consequence. I do what I do, because I must do it. Professor James March refers to such behavior as driven by an "obligatory logic." He explains:

> The rules of obligation are different from the rule of consequence. In a consequential logic, a person is "in touch with reality" and asks, What are my alternatives? What are the probable consequences of those alternatives? What are the values to me of those probably consequences? Then the person selects the alternative whose consequences he or she values the most.
>
> In an obligatory logic, a person "in touch with self" and asks, What kind of situation is this? What kind of person am I? What does a person such as I do in a situation such as this?[1]

Professor March makes a point that if deviant ideas were often good ideas, society would have very little problem accepting them. Society could withstand a few mistakes now and then and collectively absorb their cost. The real dilemma, according to March,

> is that although new, deviant ideas are essential to improvement, most of the dramatically imaginative ideas turn out to be bad ones . . . the wild ideas of political crackpots, religious heretics, crazy artists, mad scientists, and organizational dreamers are overwhelmingly foolish, rather than brilliant. Only a tiny fraction of our heretics will ever be canonized, and we cannot identify the saints ahead of time.[2]

In the pages of our book, we shared with you stories and parables about pathfinders. Entrepreneurs are visionary pathfinders; they also are enablers. Entrepreneurial leaders help spot the future pathways for the rest of their team to follow; they also must gather the requisite financial, physical, organizational, and technological resources to sustain the company. They inspire and motivate others to join the venture team they put together. Gaining momentum—going from invention, to innovation, to generating cash flows—is crucial for the venture's survival. Those entrepreneurs whose visions are too far ahead of their times tend to run out of money before investors or customers recognize the genius of their ideas. These ventures never gain momentum. Launching the right products for the market at the right time is an important ingredient for success.

Starting up a high-technology business with a sustainable competitive advantage, a business that is able to rapidly gain market share, generate profits, create jobs, and do something worthwhile for society—that is the challenge. You never really know whether it will work out in the end or not. Silicon Valley is littered with the shipwrecks of ventures that have crashed along the way. Persistence is what it takes to reach the destination, but only time will tell if the business comes ashore whole or in pieces.

Entrepreneurs experience the joys and the heartaches every day that come with being in a start-up. Most entrepreneurs are earning less and working longer hours than they would have been if working at someone else's company. They are facing risks, and making tough decisions, under pressure, and often with little information. The long-term rewards for entrepreneurs, at times, are sizable; at other times, there are no rewards. The stresses are exacerbated if coupled with difficulties in personal relationships (death of a family member or a divorce or a serious illness). These are the days when all entrepreneurs wonder: Do I have the strength to carry on? Most draw on inner determination and stubbornness to get up each morning and put one foot ahead of the other on that long climb up the mountain.

THE BASIC BROTH OF BUSINESS

Many ingredients go into the making of a successful venture regardless of whether it is a high-technology business or not. The basic business ingredients are what we have tried to emphasize in this book; they are like *il brodo*—the broth, the basic potage that is essential for any outstanding soup, stew, or risotto. Preparing the "business broth" is fundamental to any venture's growth; to do otherwise is to handicap its future. Good chefs create an outstanding soup by beginning with a great broth and quality ingredients. The same holds true for entrepreneurs creating a new venture. Our advice is to begin with the finest ingredients you can find, especially these: purpose, values, business principles, and talented people.

It goes without saying that we are believers in these business basics: giving customers value for their money; making and selling safe, quality products; and going beyond the call of duty to serve customer needs. These are not platitudes; these are commonsense business principles that pay off in the end. We may be old-fashioned, but we think entrepreneurs should not be in business simply to make money. The outstanding ones we admire always have a mission as well. For Bill Gates, it was to put a personal computer in every home. For Phil Knight, it was to make the best high-performance shoes and clothing for athletes. We personally believe that business ought to benefit the local community and help society in some way, just as civil society benefits business. Business has a social responsibility not just to be making outsize profits; it also should do its part toward taking care of the environment, saving energy, and responding to social needs.

On a strategic level and in order to obtain external financing, the entrepreneurs need a coherent business model, backed up by a business plan. The business model needs to be focused and realistic, and the business strategy needs to have a clear set of aims, goals, sustainable advantage, and strategic rationale. The entrepreneurs need to be able to visualize the customers or clients who will buy the venture's products or services. The entrepreneurs must identify viable value propositions for these target customers. After all, sales are the lifeblood of any company. Start-ups frequently find that it pays to concentrate on harvesting the low-hanging fruit first, especially at the beginning, to gain sales momentum with some early wins.

The entrepreneurial team needs to make many decisions about which activities to do within the venture's own value chain and which activities to do through strategic partners. The integration of all the pieces must be seamless, the risks controlled, and the performance carefully monitored.

Entrepreneurs must be resourceful. They have to get the business up and running, usually with only a small amount of cash and working capital. Only a lucky few are able to tap into a business angel network or attain seed venture capital financing. More often it is friends and family and the founders themselves who keep the company going with their own funds, and sweat equity, before outside loans or financing starts to flow into the venture.

Always Watch the Cash

Most small businesses are severely undercapitalized. Consequently, cash-hungry small businesses rapidly learn to collect accounts receivable as quickly as possible. They avoid selling to customers who are unable to pay or who have poor credit histories. They stretch payments of accounts payable for as long as possible. They work to make inventories turn over as efficiently as they can. They try to keep inventories in balance—enough to keep things running smoothly, not so little that they have stock-outs. Entrepreneurs soon learn to use the working capital of others to finance supplies. Most also will try to keep costs variable instead of fixed. For instance, they might pay salespeople on commission instead of high fixed salaries. They will share, rent, or lease office space rather than buy it. The smart start-ups usually do not waste money buying fancy office furniture and expensive carpets. They use secondhand furniture. Their employees bargain for discounts wherever and whenever possible. They scrimp and save. They do away with unnecessary frills. The cardinal rule for *any* owner of a small business venture is always to keep focused on the cash flow. Without cash flow, you cannot meet payroll and pay your suppliers.

Picking the Team

A critical task for any entrepreneur leading an organization is to build an excellent team. The young venture should be run by eager people who are willing to go that extra mile (or kilometer) to produce results for the firm. A big problem that the growing company will have is retaining its most talented people. Human resource development needs to be a top priority of any CEO of a new venture. Employees need to be inspired, motivated, and groomed for future leadership positions.

Experienced entrepreneurs tend to hire overqualified people and let the company grow up around them. Experienced people with good track records may appear to be too expensive for a start-up, but experienced supervision is worth its weight in gold. Start-ups have no time to train employees who have no experience. Start-ups need experienced people who not only know what to do but are able to do many different things at once. In a start-up, personnel with multiple skills and multifunctional experience are better than narrow specialists or people with no training at all.

BUILDING THE HIGH-TECHNOLOGY BUSINESS VENTURE

For creating a high-technology venture, the analogy of beginning with an excellent broth, *il brodo*, is equally applicable, but some additional ingredients must be added to fit its special needs, especially if the high-tech start-up is being financed by venture capitalists.

Time is the first spice that livens up the high-tech concoction. In the supercharged time frame required by venture capitalists' exit requirements, the stove's burner is always turned on high. Three to five years is a very short time frame to get started, scale up the business, and hit those milestones.

Given the fast pace inside the company coupled with the turbulent change taking place in high-tech markets, the appropriate business model and application of strategic thinking take on greater importance. The margin of error is smaller than in a conventional business while the technological risks are higher.

Furthermore, high-tech start-ups are different from conventional businesses because of two other factors. One is the importance of managing the intellectual property (IP) rights associated with the scientific and proprietary know-how of the firm. The second is the importance of designing, structuring, and managing strategic alliances to leverage the resources and capabilities of the start-up and create economic value.

Balancing all three elements—managing the high technology, the business aspects, and the IP rights—and getting them to coalesce properly into a well-launched strategic alliance was the bull's-eye target for which our book was aiming.

High-Technology Teams Require More Scientific and Technical Expertise

High-tech start-ups, especially those that are backed with venture capital, need to hire highly qualified employees: people with above-average competencies in specialized fields of science, engineering, mathematics, or computer science that are related to the core competencies of the venture. Technically qualified and scientifically educated people are necessary ingredients in high technology, but technical competencies alone are not enough to turn *il brodo* into a world-class soup, stew, or risotto. To these scientists and engineers, the CEO needs to add other senior managers with skills and experiences in high-tech marketing, sales, production, service, and logistics. Putting together a new team of specialists is no guarantee that they will work together smoothly as an effective and productive team. The team also needs to be seasoned with finance and business development people who know how to value and negotiate strategic alliance deals and who have the necessary knowledge about IP law and contracts to work well with outside legal and financial experts. In general, a high-tech venture demands all these extra ingredients, in addition to the usual business broth.

Diversify the Risks and Use Financial Discipline   We emphasized that most entrepreneurs in high technology take measured risks. They develop viable business models to commercialize the know-how and IP assets of their ventures, and they also take prudent steps to share and diversify the high idiosyncratic risks they face. These risks come from the uncertain and ambiguous technological, market, and operating risks faced by any venture trying to do something completely novel for the first time in an emerging technology. In general, most high-tech ventures do not use debt financing; this lowers their financial risks compared to a leveraged buyout, for instance. We also strongly advise entrepreneurs to avoid remaining a one-product business for long. As soon as possible, diversify both the product and the customer base to lower the venture's exposure to the potential catastrophe of the loss of either the major customer or the failure of the sole product.

Look beyond the Technology and See the Implications

Success in high technology requires both depth of knowledge and breadth of understanding. Depth in scientific or technical understanding alone is not enough; at the same time, the entrepreneurial team needs to see the big picture. True, the team does need to understand the research behind the technology to be able to evaluate it properly, but it also needs to visualize the commercialization possibilities. To do so, the team needs to comprehend broader industry trends. It needs to be cognizant of the threats and opportunities posed by competing technologies, keep abreast of the thinking of market regulators, and assess how customer needs are changing due to sociodemographic changes. Knowing how to scan the horizon and envision possible futures and states of the world under a variety of scenarios should become part of the managerial tool kit of the entrepreneur and the senior team.

In high-tech ventures, a common mistake is for the company's founders to focus on developing and delivering technologically perfect products for their clients. They miss the importance of putting in adequate time and effort to connecting with customers, listening to their needs, making sales calls, and closing sales. They spend too much of their time and effort testing, refining the product, and fixing bugs.

Managing Intellectual Property Rights in High Technology

High-tech entrepreneurs know that the innovative use of IP rights is important for increasing investor returns in their venture. However, the field of IP rights is somewhat esoteric. Albert Einstein worked in a patent office and Abraham Lincoln was a patent attorney; though giants in their own right, neither was an entrepreneur. Entrepreneurs in turn may know a lot about business or be experts in the science and technology, but often they know very little about managing IP rights. In fact, they may not even be paying attention to them at the outset of a start-up, when so many other pots on the front burners need stirring. Quite often the entrepreneurial team learns about its ignorance of IP laws by making mistakes. The start-up infringes on someone else's patent or trademark and gets sued; or it winds up having to negotiate a cross-licensing agreement under duress; or it has to admit that it wasted precious time and money reinventing something that was already on the market, but no one in the start-up knew about it until it was too late; or it gives away exclusive licensing rights to too many territories for too many fields of use, without realizing the consequences.

Although a handful of patents is a start for the aspiring inventor, it certainly is not enough to create a viable and sustainable business. Robert H. Remmey III had what he thought was a terrific idea and even was granted a patent for his invention of a new system of reusable book tabs (recall the story in Chapter 2). Remmey learned the hard way how exasperating it can be for inventors to get big companies interested in investing resources to commercialize their inventions.

The Remmey patent story brings us to the other message we hope we conveyed, and which we owe to Henry Chesbrough from his book *Open Innovation: New Imperative for Creating and Profiting from Technology*:

> *There is no inherent value in technology* per se. *The value is determined instead by the business model used to bring it to market. The same technology taken to market through two different business models will yield different amounts of value...a mediocre technology pursued within a great business model may be more valuable than a great technology in a mediocre business model.*[3]

In other words, in order to value a technology transfer agreement (say, for licensing both patent and trademark rights), we need to understand the proposed business model and the complementary assets needed for exploiting the patent and the trademark. Only when we begin to understand how these rights are going to be commercialized, and the investments required, can we proceed to forecast the future cash flows, work out the various permutations of the deal, and compute their net present values. We showed you how to do such financial valuations, including sensitivity checks and scenarios, using the Advanced Dermal Delivery Inc. case in Chapter 20.

In addition to the discounted cash flow analysis, we also emphasized the importance of using contingent claims thinking when structuring both investor agreements and alliances involving technology transfer agreements. We mentioned that entrepreneurs and their chief financial officers can also use other simulation techniques (e.g., Monte Carlo simulation) to assess the risks in a proposed alliance or joint venture deal. We included the Genzyme-Geltex Pharmaceuticals Joint Venture capstone case (log onto www.innovationtocashflow.com) to let you see how to use quantitative analysis to help you prepare for negotiating an equity joint venture.

A real option is when a manager buys the right, but is under no obligation, to invest or disinvest in a real asset at some future time. Real options can be quite valuable, especially under conditions of high uncertainty. Real options capture the value of managerial flexibility: to accelerate investment spending when growth conditions are favorable; to avoid losses by deferring spending if the economic outlook deteriorates; to abandon a project before a deadline if the project turns out not to be meeting expectations; or to switch from one operating mode to another (building an electric power plant that runs on both coal and natural gas). Given the importance of making decisions about IP rights for a high-tech business, success in crafting and implementing a coherent patenting strategy can be crucial to creating real options for the venture. For instance, enhancing the ability of management to change direction on technological investments through cross-licensing agreements and patent pools is important for some high-tech industries, since managers cannot predict ahead of time with absolute certainty which patents will become valuable and which ones will not. The chosen patenting strategy, whether offensive or defensive, needs to be thought out early in the life of the high-tech venture and then woven into the underlying competitive strategy of the firm. The implication of real options for managers is that flexibility is valuable. Strive to conserve or build flexibility into your IP strategies.

We suggested that ventures keep appraised of the patent landscape and explored the latest state-of-the-art methods for conducting patent searches and doing competitive intelligence. Scanning specialized patent databases around the world is critical for gaining insights on what rivals are doing, what technological research they are conducting, and who the lead investigators are. The last thing a venture can afford to do is reinvent the wheel.

We also emphasized the importance of keeping abreast of any new patent applications or granted patents that could erode the venture's freedom to use (freedom to operate). Small high-tech firms must be vigilant so as to avoid infringing on others' patents. Finding out after a product is launched that patents have been infringed is way too late. It can lead to costly litigation and even the failure of the business as precious time to market is lost. Check for patent infringement issues early in the research and development phases.

Patents are not a permit to do something; instead, they give their owners the right to prohibit others from doing something that falls within the scope of the patent. Enforcing that right costs money. Patents are expensive up front (patent filing fees, translation fees, patent agent and patent attorney fees, renewal fees, litigation fees, etc.) and only yield an indirect value over the longer term. The costs of patents need to be carefully budgeted. The benefits from patents accrue by converting competitors into customers, receiving patent licensing revenues, increasing the firm's market reach, and preventing the venture's rivals from selling infringing products.

Seek expert advice early in the process of setting an IP strategy. Advisors will help you assess better what IP rights to pursue and in which territories to pursue them, and what IP not to pursue. Oftentimes it is best to use a combination of IP rights (patents, trademarks, design rights, trade secrets, or copyright) and competitive strategies (e.g., secrecy, faster learning, quicker new product introductions, and more nimble strategy execution) to keep ahead of rivals.

Dealing with Strategic Uncertainty and Ambiguity through Alliances

In the turbulent environment that surrounds a high-tech venture, the engine of internal growth may not be sufficiently powerful to keep up with the demands of a rapidly changing market. Or the new venture might not be able to meet the growth and return constraints placed on it by outside investors. Strategic alliances and joint ventures can give a high-tech start-up the crucial boost it needs by making it possible to leverage its strengths with outside help.

To be worthwhile doing, alliances need to make commercial sense, if not right away, then at least over the long term. Successful alliances create economic value. Over time, they enhance the long-term intrinsic value of the venture's business. In general, if alliances or joint ventures do not accomplish this basic economic goal, the parties will lose interest in participating and the alliance may flounder unless there are some overriding strategic reasons for continuing the collaboration that are not reflected in the numbers.

Structuring deals requires finding mutually satisfactory solutions so that the interests of multiple parties are served. The design of a strategic alliance depends on many related factors. We stressed the importance of knowing the strategic intent for the collaboration and being aware of the goals and aims of both sides to the negotiation. Other important factors to consider are the criteria and selection process for picking the alliance partner and the composition of the alliance team and choice of external advisors. Many deal design and structuring issues are interlinked, such as the context, contents, risks, size of the investment, importance of the alliance to each party, and overall complexity of the processes to reach an agreement. Changes in one part of the system will cascade and impact other interconnected parts. Research shows that careful planning and implementation of the joint venture or alliance launch will enhance the odds of success. It is normal for the goals of any collaborative alliance to evolve and change over the lifetime of the relationship. Be aware of the dynamics of the relationship and have contingency measures in place to terminate the alliance if the need arises.

Due Diligence   Conducting due diligence is a fundamental part of the investment process. We explored how to do due diligence in detail, as many executives might not be aware of all that it entails. We pointed out that due diligence is conducted at various times during the evolution of a business, not only at the time when the venture capitalist is thinking of investing at the earliest stages of the business. Due diligence is also done later on, for instance, at the time of investor exit via a trade sale to an industrial strategic investor. Due diligence must be done by the investment bankers who are preparing the shareholder prospectus for an initial public offering. Due diligence is also required upon sale of the business to, say, another venture capital fund or mezzanine investor. Due diligence is also done and is extremely important when searching for a suitable strategic alliance collaborator (or joint venture partner or both). Due diligence requires an inquisitive mind-set and attentive attitude toward both risks and opportunities. Search for ways to mitigate the risks and capitalize on the opportunities. We emphasized that cultural expectations and reactions to due diligence differ, especially in Europe, where some countries have a legal system based on *bona fide* (good faith) whereas others are based on *caveat emptor* (let the buyer beware). Be alert to local context and cultural sensitivities.

Valuation   Valuation is a fundamental skill required of any business manager. A solid grasp of finance is important not just to price negotiation trade-offs but also to estimate the profit or loss impact of various legal vehicles and deal structures, ranging from strategic alliances, contractual joint ventures, equity joint ventures, to mergers and alliances. Is it better to in-source or out-source this technology? Should we share the risks through a joint venture? Can we make more incremental profits by commercializing this licensing strategy on our own or by engaging in a cross-licensing deal with another partner?

We examined both discounted dividends and discounted free cash flow techniques of valuing businesses and illustrated the methods with several examples. We also explored the use of market multiples and comparable deals transactions. Venture capitalists and investment bankers use these methods to bring market sentiment into their pricing decisions. Rather than take the usual perspective of the entrepreneur, we switched sides and took the role of the general partner in a venture capital fund. We explained how a venture capital fund is set up as a limited partnership and how the general partner raises money from institutional investors. We explored what a venture capitalist needs to do to survive and thrive in his or her highly competitive industry. Entrepreneurs have a tendency to look for financing only from their own point of view. We tried to show the perspective of venture capitalists and private equity investors and reveal what motivates them, how they hedge their risks, and how early-stage venture capital investments fit into the overall picture of the private equity industry.

We also illustrated the way venture capitalists value ventures using their shortcut techniques. We discussed the penalty entrepreneurs pay if they raise too much cash up front. Venture capitalists charge high rates for the use of their funds' capital. For the entrepreneurs negotiating with venture capitalists, the art of the deal is to estimate how much money the start-up needs for a particular financing round, including some extra to provide for unexpected calamities, but without having so much money that surplus cash is left lying idle at a very high cost. At the same time, the entrepreneur needs to obtain enough cash to make it to the next round of financing without running out of money.

Limits of Financial Theory to Capture Real Options Values in Early-Stage Research and Development Projects   We have also pointed out some of the limits of traditional corporate finance methods in modeling early-stage research investments. Traditional finance focuses on estimating cash flows under uncertainty using expected values. It generally assumes a passive investment with unvarying risk. If risk varies, which often happens in research and development (R&D) projects, multistage growth models or decision trees can be employed. We briefly mentioned that Monte Carlo simulations and the like are other techniques managers may use for modeling and quantifying investment risks.

In the very earliest phases of research and discovery, a potential barrier to fully exploiting IP rights is the lack of quantitative tools to value them. The tools we have today do provide estimates of the value of real options but under rather simple constraints. When the phases of the investment project are no longer independent but linked, and perhaps are contingent on management decisions taken by competitors, the real options valuation problems become complex, and we lack elegant ways to solve them.

Especially in the earliest discovery phases of research, uncertainty often reigns: The final applications are unclear, the customer is undefined, and the nature and timing of future earnings streams is cloudy. In fact, at these very early stages of invention, it is hard to visualize the most appropriate business model when a plethora of different models may be applicable and the commercialization possibilities are still so far away. At the end of the day, senior venture capitalists and those responsible for making technology licensing and patenting decisions for early-stage R&D must rely on their years of experience and judgment or "street smarts" to shift and weigh qualitative management factors that financial theory has yet to figure out how to capture in quantitative real options models.

Joe Wilson, CEO of Xerox, also talks about this struggle to "envision the future" when he describes the early days of Haloid's true position as

> *a little company just breaking even after the war—a company with meager financial resources, without much research and engineering competence, with a small thinly spread sales force and obviously without specialized plants because xerographic products had not been made before by any man anywhere. I must confess that if we had fully foreseen the magnitude of the job, the millions needed for research and new capital, the marketing complexities, the manufacturing problems involved in making new things work right and reliably all over the world in all temperatures and humidities, we probably would not have had the fortitude to go ahead. But we did.*

We agree sometimes it is better not to know what you are getting into. To know too much at the beginning is too intimidating. Better to let serendipity run its course and trust in hope and hard work. You prepare as best you can and then strive to keep your options open.

Joe Wilson's inspiring entrepreneurship is what our book, *From Innovation to Cash Flows*, is all about. We are describing the often-arduous journey to get from the lab into the marketplace with products and services that are capable of satisfying and delighting customers, year after year.

What makes a successful company is a mixture of many components, but we believe that the most important ingredients are:

- *Mutual trust.* To be able to believe in the word of the other founders and senior management team. The founders of the venture must have absolute trust in each other's integrity; otherwise, there will be a conflict of values at the top.
- *Vision.* To be able to recognize the commercial possibilities of an innovation and the potential of others' talents and build a team.

- *Will and determination.* To be ready to go through painful days and long nights of hard work. If it were easy, someone else would have already done it. You need to stay the course.
- *Lifestyle.* To be willing to forgo a steady monthly paycheck, in the hope and dream of creating a viable business. If safety and security is what you crave, then entrepreneurship is probably not for you. But if you want more freedom and want to test your personal limits, then entrepreneurship certainly is a choice to be considered.

We have tried to include in the previous chapters the key elements you need to conceive, start up, and build a new venture. We have seasoned the book with stories and anecdotes from our own personal experiences as high-tech entrepreneurs. We have also shared with you the practical experiences and wisdom of our contributors. We hope that all these ingredients combined will help you turn your ideas into innovations and eventually into profitable businesses. We also hope that our advice will enable you to find your own pathway from innovation to cash flows.

Notes

Foreword

1. For pursuing disruptive technologies, see Christensen 1997 for an introduction to managing disruptive technologies. For opening up your innovation process to external sources of ideas and technologies, see Chesbrough 2003 for an introduction to open innovation. For constructing more open business models to create and capture value from your ideas, see Chesbrough 2006 for a discussion of creating and advancing open business models. And for co-creating value with your customers, see Prahalad and Krishnan 2008 for a discussion of co-creation of value with customers.

CHAPTER 1 Creativity and the Entrepreneurial Process

1. According to Anne M. Mulcahy, current chair and CEO of Xerox Corporation, this verse by Robert Browning was a favorite of Joe Wilson, the visionary CEO and entrepreneur who transformed his family's tiny Haloid Corporation into the mighty Xerox Corporation.
2. Mind maps are mental pictures clustering key ideas and then drawing connections among them. First originated by Tony Buzan, the actual inspiration for mind maps comes from Leonardo da Vinci's notes and drawings found in his famous notebooks (according to Gelb 1998, 169).Today, 40 years after the invention of mind maps, many software programs are available to help you sketch out your ideas and link concepts together creatively. Enter into Google the words "mind maps" for the latest lists, links, and sample drawings. To learn how to create your own mind maps, see Gelb 1998. You can teach yourself how to draw mind maps from the chapter on Arte and Scienza and the associated exercises on pp. 176–191.
3. For an interpretation of "essence" in creativity, refer to Ray and Myers 1986, 3–10. Michael L. Ray is the John G. McCoy–Banc One Corporation Professor of Creativity and Innovation and of Marketing, Emeritus, at the Stanford Graduate School of Business. Rochelle Myers is the founder of the Art and Growth Studio and the Myers Institute for Creative Studies in San Francisco. Ray, a prolific author and scholar, pioneered the famed Stanford course on personal creativity in business that helped legitimize the study of creativity in business schools.
4. Bolles 2004.
5. Gelb 1998.
6. Dr. Harold J. Leavitt was the Walter Kenneth Kilpatrick Professor of Organizational Behavior and Psychology, Emeritus, at Stanford Graduate School of Business until he passed away, at age 85, as we were writing this book. Leavitt firmly believed that "organizational success should be judged in human terms." His academic peers at Stanford consider him one of the creators of the field of organizational behavior. Leavitt is the author of the best-selling *Managerial Psychology* textbook (1986), now in its fifth edition, and translated into 18 languages. He was a professor of one of the coauthors, and he will be missed, as he was a visionary educator.
7. Quotes are from Leavitt 1986, 10–11.

8. Ibid., 6.
9. See Leavitt 1988, 1–21.
10. Ibid., 1.
11. The Yale School of Management, in March 2006, announced a major overhaul of its MBA curriculum for the academic year 2006–2007. For details of the changes, see also 2006, B5, downloaded from www.yale.edu/opa/download/newsYale/MBA_Programs_Blend_Disciplines_701106.pdf (accessed May 23, 2008). The Stanford Graduate School of Business announced on June 6, 2006, that it would radically change its curriculum. The news was reported by Gloeckler 2005, www.businessweek.com/bschools/content/jun2006/bs2006065_4760_bs001.htm (accessed May 23, 2008).
12. For emotional intelligence, see Goleman 1995, which made the *New York Times* Best Seller list for 18 months. *Soft skills* include leadership competencies, such as being able to negotiate, communicate, and influence others, as well as interpersonal relations skills and traits, such as listening and being empathetic.
13. See Goleman, Boyatzis, and McKee 2002, especially 253–256.
14. See Strebel and Keys 2002, 1–23. This book describes and explains what makes an effective learning experience for executives. It illustrates how IMD's world-renowned professors are incorporating relevant content, implementation skills, and emotional intelligence into their executive education teaching. IMD, based in Lausanne, Switzerland, is Europe's leading business school for executive education.
15. See the documentary film *Building the Gherkin* (2005) directed by Mirjam von Arx for live footage and commentary on the Gherkin while it was under construction. As the filming started four months before construction, by which time design was more or less finalized and planning permission had been granted, von Arx re-created some of the early planning and design events in retrospective interviews with Carla Picardi (Project Director, Preconstruction Phase), Robin Partington (Director of Foster & Partners and lead project architect), and Peter Wynne Rees (City Planning Officer, The Corporation of London). In one segment of the documentary, Partington illustrates the evolution of the building's design using three-dimensional working models. For more details, consult the film's web site: www.buildingthegherkin.com (accessed on April 16, 2008).
16. We recommend the book by Ellis (2006), which is the source of these inspiring stories. We also thank Bill Falloon, senior editor John Wiley & Sons, for giving us the Ellis book as a gift, when we were in the midst of writing our own.
17. Carlson's perseverance might have been strongly influenced by his difficult childhood. He grew up in poverty and suffered greatly. We think there is truth to the old saying "Necessity is the mother of invention."
18. Ibid., 41.
19. Ibid.
20. Ibid.
21. Ibid., 41–42.
22. Ibid., 42
23. Ibid.
24. Ibid.
25. Ibid.
26. Ibid., 43.
27. Ibid., 42.
28. Ibid., 44.
29. Ibid., 49.
30. Ibid., 71–72.
31. Ibid., 46.
32. Ibid., 49.

33. Ellis poignantly paints the picture of Haloid as being "in an increasingly untenable strategic position. Little Haloid could never win over the long haul, in direct competition against such formidable giants as DuPont, Agfa, and Kodak. Haloid was the classic polar bear on an iceberg heading toward the equator." Ibid., 20.
34. Ibid., 64–65. In the words of Joe Wilson himself, "We believe first in innovation—throughout the company. We want to create new services that have not been rendered before and secure a profit from them. Our best rewards have come from things of this sort, like the 914 [the first Xerox copy machine]—unheard of at the time it was introduced, but now one of the most successful products in America. This is the first principle." Ibid., 372.
35. Ibid., 64–65.
36. Chesbrough 2006, 116.
37. Chesbrough (2006, 35–37) describes a small software company named GO Corporation, which was funded by Kleiner, Perkins, Caufield & Byers, a premier venture capital firm, based in Palo Alto, CA. The GO Corporation developed an operating system for pen-based personal computer products called PenPoint. Nevertheless, the managers and backers of GO made a fatal strategic mistake in its business model. GO floundered because it was too open and disclosed critical information to the wrong people which killed the company. For more about the problems experienced by single product companies, read Chesbrough (2006, 41–42, and 116–117).
38. Worldwide sales numbers of video game consoles by platforms and expressed in units are from Grant 2008a, 186.

CHAPTER 2   Protecting Your Invention

1. Grant 2008b, 291.
2. Ibid., 150–155 for a discussion on how to appraise the profit-earning potential of a firm's resources and capabilities.
3. Ibid., 292.
4. The academic literature provides a wealth of information about the pros and cons of being a first mover or second mover in high-tech industries. See Lieberman and Montgomery 1988; see also Oster 1999, 51–82, for a more general discussion of entry strategies and incumbent advantages.
5. For the history of the world famous Pininfarina family business, started in 1930 and based in Turin, Italy, go to their web site www.pininfarina.it. The business has more than 3,000 employees (2,000 in Italy, 400 in France, 600 in Sweden, and about 100 in Germany).
6. *Irvine & Ors v TalkSport Limited.* 2003.
7. This is the German advertising slogan for Audi, a luxury automobile maker wholly owned by Volkswagen AG of Germany. When translated, *Vorsprung durch technik* means "advancement through technology" or "a head start through technology."

CHAPTER 3   Understanding Strategy Basics

1. Grant 2008b, 19.
2. Key success factors are referred to in some strategy textbooks as "critical success factors" (CSFs). See Johnson and Scholes 2002, 151–152.
3. For a simple, easy-to-understand guide on how to write a business plan for a technology company, download this business plan guide, which explains what to do step by step and includes helpful templates. It is designed for a California start-up, so company incorporation rules and taxation laws in your home country will need to be

addressed: www.connect.org/resources/docs/Springboard_Business_Plan_Guide.pdf (accessed May 15, 2008). Most business parks that feature venture incubators offer help and advice to entrepreneurs on how to develop business plans. Also consult your local chamber of commerce or regional development agencies for further resources. See also the U.S. Small Business Administration Site for an extensive guide to further resources for entrepreneurs: www.sba.gov/smallbusinessplanner/index.html.

4. Porter 1996, 64.
5. Adapted from Hill and Jones 1988, 3–4.
6. Adapted from Saloner, Shephard, and Podolny 2001, 19–23.
7. Ibid., 23.
8. Prahalad and Hamel 1990, 79–91.
9. Kay 1994.
10. To say a person is "competent" is to mean a person has an above-average skill at doing something. For instance, a competent composer would be a musician skilled at composing original scores of music or one who has a competency in music composition. We think the terms *core competence* and *critical capabilities* may be used interchangeably.
11. Prahalad and Hamel 1990, 81.
12. Ibid., 84.
13. Barney 1991, 99–120.
14. See Pascale 1984, 47–72.
15. The International Institute for Management Development (IMD) was created in 1990 in a merger between IMI, founded by Alcan Aluminum, Ltd. and IMEDE, founded by Nestlé Corporation SA; both business schools were formerly independent. Currently, IMD is based in Lausanne, Switzerland. It is recognized as one of the world's leading business schools and is particularly noted for its executive education programs.
16. Malnight and Keys 2007. Article is downloadable from the IMD web site: www.imd.ch/research/publications/pfm.cfm (accessed on May 31, 2008).
17. *The McKinsey Quarterly* conducted its latest global survey in March 2008 and received 1,306 responses from a worldwide representative sample of business executives, 41 percent of whom are CEOs, other senior-level executives, or board directors. All data are weighted by gross domestic product of constituent countries to adjust for differences in response rates. For complete survey results and more details, see "How Companies Act on Global Trends: A McKinsey Global Survey" 2008. Contributors to the development and analysis of the survey include Elizabeth Stephenson, an associate principal in McKinsey's Chicago office, and Adarsh Pandit, a consultant in the New York office.
18. World Commission on Environment and Development 1987, 43.
19. Porter 1980, 12.
20. Carter Bales, P.C. Chatterjee, Donald Gogel, and Anupam Puri published a McKinsey staff paper (1980) outlining a rigorous approach for determining how companies achieve and sustain a cost advantage. Their paper first introduced the concept of the business system. Shortly thereafter, Fred Gluck (1980) wrote an article that describes how the business system concept could be used in strategy formulation. Porter (1985) referred to Gluck's article and introduces his version of the value chain. For more on the history of McKinsey classic strategy tools, see McKinsey & Company 2008a.
21. Porter 1985.
22. Adam Brandenburger of Harvard Business School and Barry Nalebuff of Yale University are experts in game theory and the study of strategic interactions. They coauthored the book *Co-opetition* and thereby popularized a strategy framework they called the "Value Net." Brandenburger and Nalebuff 1997, 16.
23. Ibid., 108–114.
24. Ibid., 109.
25. Teece 1986.

26. Gallagher and Park 2002, 67.
27. Porter 1990, 14. Professor Michael Porter and other Harvard Business School professors cofounded the Monitor Group in 1983. The firm grew to become a global strategy consultancy, headquartered in Cambridge, Massachusetts. Monitor specializes in growth strategies for corporations, governments, and nonprofit organizations. It works closely with national and regional governments, advising them on economic development policy and strategies. For details of actual case studies, see www.monitor.com (accessed on May 15, 2008).
28. Penrose 1959.
29. Wernerfelt 1984, 171–180; Barney 1991, 99–120; and Grant 2008b, 123–168.
30. Adapted and modified from Grant 2008b, 143–149.
31. See www.dilbert.com by Scott Adams. This remark appeared in a Dilbert cartoon printed in the European edition of the *International Herald Tribune* on January 20, 2007.
32. For more about the history and development of the 7-S Framework, refer to McKinsey & Company 2008b.
33. Grant 2008b, 176–177.
34. Saloner, Shepard, and Podolny 2001, 74.
35. Ibid., 2001, 75–89.
36. Roberts 2004, 17.
37. Saloner, Shepard, and Podolny 2001, 65–92; Roberts 2004, 17–18 and 164–176; and Grant 2008b, 137–138.
38. Roberts 2004, 19.
39. Ibid., 32–33.
40. Ibid., 34.
41. See Teece, Pisano, and Shuen 1997, 509–533. Refer also to Eisenhardt and Martin 2000, 1105–1121.
42. Tushman and O'Reilly 1997, 14. For over 30 years, Tushman and O'Reilly have collaborated on research studies and also on teaching and mentoring executives.
43. Tushman and O'Reilly coined the expression *ambidextrous organizations*. They use the term to refer to firms (or business units within larger firms) that support different competencies, structures, cultures, and processes. They think that diversity in organizational design elements is part of the key to creating innovation streams. *Innovation streams* are two or more fundamentally different kinds of innovation that help enable an organization to take advantage of emerging technology cycles so as to actively develop products and services to extend or replace existing ones. For more on the "tyranny of success" and how organizations attempt to cope with it, see Tushman and O'Reilly 1997. For their latest research on "ambidexterity" in organizations and its influence on corporate strategy and organizational design, see their research paper: O'Reilly and Tushman 2007. This paper contains an excellent survey and accessible summary of the dynamic capabilities strategy literature.
44. Lütolf-Carroll worked for McPherson in 1983 when he was dean at the Stanford Graduate School of Business. This quote is based on the author's personal recollections and notes at the time.

CHAPTER 4   Strategies to Grow, Restructure, or Harvest Your Business

1. Managers and key employees may be offered attractive early retirement packages (known as golden handshakes) to voluntarily leave a company during a reorganization, merger, or acquisition. The generosity of these remuneration packages differs widely from one country to the next, depending on local labor laws, country regulations, the strength

and importance of unions, and individual company policies. The cost of such layoff packages needs to be carefully determined and included in any restructuring plan financial projection. For some executives, these golden handshakes may provide the seed capital they need to start up their own companies and fund them for the first few months or years of operation.

2. For example, customers give informal feedback through frequent interactions with field service technicians and customer support teams. More formally, customers may interact with the company through sophisticated, online customer relationship management software and other processes that feed back into new product design, development, and manufacturing enhancements. Strategic alliance partners may be hard-wired into the real-time online databases of their network partners. Shared communities of practice where researchers and other professionals can exchange views and share best practices are common in many professions and industry groups. All these interactions create conditions for learning for those firms willing and able to listen to what markets have to say to them and capable of processing the information and learning from what their outside antennae are telling them.

3. See Nestlé's web site for these press releases: Nestlé Press Release of June 17, 2002, and Nestlé Press Release of January 19, 2006, www.Nestle.com (accessed June 20, 2008).

4. Anslinger, Klepper, and Subramaniam, 1999, 16–27. The example is from p. 18.

5. For an excellent description of the Clariant and Ciba Specialty Chemicals (now Ciba) spin-offs, see these two web sites: www.clariant.com/corporate/internet.nsf/vwWebPp. ByID/B4E9CB47E92E455BC125712C0052516C (accessed June 20, 2008) and www.ciba.com/index/cmp-index/cmp-about/cmp-abo-history.htm (accessed June 20, 2008).

6. McDonald's Annual Report 2006, 48; Chipotle's SEC 10-K Report 2006, p. 40.

7. See the AT&T web site link www.att.com/Common/files/pdf/t_awe_exchange.pdf to download the Exchange Offer details.

8. See United States District Court of the Southern District of New York, Final Approval Order and Settlement, signed by Judge Miriam Cedarbaum, October 20, 2006, AT&T Corporation: AT&T Wireless Group Tracking Stock. For details on this class action lawsuit, consult the Stanford Law School Class Action Clearinghouse in Cooperation with Cornerstone Research. The specific AT&T Wireless Class Action Suit link is: http://securities.stanford.edu/1016/AWE00/index.html.

9. For more details, see the company's web site at www.syncobio.com.

10. See the Investopedia general web site (www.investopedia.com) for in-depth information about finance. Specifically for information on leveraged buyouts, consult this link: www.investopedia.com/terms/l/leveragedbuyout.asp (accessed June 20, 2008).

11. Read more about disruptive technologies in Christensen 1997. Also see Burgleman, Christensen, and Wheelwright 2003; Hayes, Pisano, Upton, and Wheelwright 2004.

12. Leonard-Barton 1992, 11.

13. Tushman and O'Reilly 1997, 37.

14. Ibid., 36–37. See O'Reilly and Tushman 2007. The paper is downloadable from http://ssrn.com/abstract=978493 (accessed June 9, 2008).

CHAPTER 5   Key Elements of a Business Model

1. We thank our friend and former professor George Foster, the Paul L. and Phyllis Wattis Professor of Management and Director of the Stanford Executive Program for Growing Companies, for sharing with us over the years his insights, research, and course notes on entrepreneurship, early-stage companies, the role of financial analysts and venture

capitalists, and currently, his research on sports management "best practices." It was from one of Foster's PowerPoint slides on eBay's early days that we picked up the idea for this introductory set of questions, which we modified only slightly from his list.
2. Chesbrough 2006, 35.
3. For more on value networks in the academic literature, see Christensen and Rosenbloom 1995, 233–257.
4. See Saloner, Shepard, and Podolny 2001 for a lucid description of these components of business strategy, which are the building blocks for developing and implementing a strategy.

CHAPTER 6 Introduction to Strategic Alliances

1. Visit the home page of the open source initiative for more about the open source movement, www.opensource.org/ (accessed June 24, 2008). For definitions of open source licenses, refer to www.opensource.org/license (accessed June 24, 2008).
2. For more on informal alliances and consortia, see Johnson and Scholes 1999, 452–455. For entrepreneurial alliances, see Dollinger 2008, 357–364. For networks and deal origination, see Bruner 2004, 183–204.
3. Lawrence Berkeley National Laboratories is a member of the national laboratory system supported by the U.S. Department of Energy through its Office of Science. It is managed by the University of California (UC) and is charged with conducting unclassified research across a wide range of scientific disciplines (www.lbl.gov).
4. This commentary is based on the EBI web site and various press releases of UC Berkeley, BP, and a report filed by the Associated Press at the time of the bid award. See Berkeley press release of February 2, 2007: http://berkeley.edu/news/media/releases/2007/02/01_ebi.shtml. See BP press release of February 1, 2007: http://www.bp.com/genericarticle.do?categoryId=2012968&content-Id=7028142. Refer to the article "Universities, BP Create 'Energy Biosciences' Unit. Oil Giant Puts Up $500 million in Quest for Cleaner Power" dated February 2, 2007, from MSNBC Online news, www.msnbc.msn.com/id/16946015/.
5. To govern and manage the research consortium, BP and UC Berkeley have created a governance board to share leadership responsibility. The board is composed of an equal number of BP positions and partner institutions. Each of the partner institutions has representation on both the EBI's executive committee and governance board, but none of the individual partners constitutes a majority of either body or has veto power over either body. An appointed director has overall day-to-day responsibility for ensuring research program development and implementation, including budget, personnel, and staffing. The director reports directly to the governance board. The executive committee is the steward of the EBI's mission and its implementation; it reviews and recommends the yearly research program and develops operating policies and practices. The research program requires the approval of the EBI's governance board.
6. The BP and Regents of the University of California Master Agreement of November, 7, 2007, may be downloaded from the Energy Biosciences Institute web site at http://67.199.70.53/images/stories/pressroom/FINAL_EXECUTED_11-14.
7. See the web site of Invest Northern Ireland at www.investni.com for an excellent online guide titled "Joint Ventures" prepared by L'Estragne and Brett Solicitors for Invest Northern Ireland's Business Information Services publications. The guide gives an overview of the principles to consider when contemplating the formation of either nonequity or equity joint ventures. It is written in language understandable to entrepreneurs who are not lawyers.

8. Beamish 2003, 120–139.
9. Dollinger 2008, 119.
10. Source of data is from the homepage of the International Franchise Association. See its web site at www.franchise.org (accessed on June 25, 2008).
11. See link for the MySQL acquisition announcement, www.mysql.com/news-and-events/sun-to-acquire-mysql.html (accessed June 23, 2007).
12. See the profile section of the Sony Ericsson web site for more information about the joint venture at www.sonyericsson.com/cws/corporate/company/aboutus/ profile (accessed on June 23, 2008).
13. See Nokia's web site under investor relations for the Symbian announcement, dated June 24, 2008, at www.nokia.com.
14. The Symbian operating system market share data are from the Reuters report filed by O'Brien 2008.
15. See follow-up commentary on Nokia's Symbian announcement by McDougall and Hoover 2008: www.informationweek.com/story/showArticle.jhtml?articleID= 208801196 (accessed June 28, 2008).
16. These market share data are from the online Reuters report filed by O'Brien 2008.
17. See Nokia Annual Report, 2004, for details of the Psion, Ltd. buyout, which Nokia announced on February 16, 2004. For commentary about the Psion announcement, see Dano 2004, http://rcrnews.com/apps/pbcs.dll/article?AID=/ 20040216/SUB/402160737 (accessed June 28, 2008).
18. Grove, 1996; Saloner, Shepard, and Podony 2001, 287–290.
19. Rigby 2008.
20. Dossani and Kenney 2003, 7–35. Download working paper at http://aparc.stanford.edu/ publications/went_for_cost_stayed_for_quality_moving_the_back_office_to_india./ (accessed June 28, 2008).
21. Diana Farrell, Director of the McKinsey Global Institute, 2006 points out that the most popular offshore sites for IT and banking service functions are overheating and no longer the "bargains" they once were. She recommends that businesses take a longer and broader view of these strategic decisions, and look at a variety of strategic factors besides lowering labor costs.
22. Rigby 2008.
23. Joseph W. Rottman and Mary C. Lacity interviewed 159 participants from 40 different companies, including 21 offshore client organizations. Among the participants were 45 from biotechnology and 18 from financial services firms. Interviews took place in the United States and in Bangalore, Hyderabad, and Mumbai, India, or at offshore outsourcing events. (Refer to Rottman and Lacity 2006, 56–53).
24. MacCormack et al. 2007a; MacCormack et al. 2007b. The MacCormack studies are worthwhile reading if you are involved in or contemplating an offshore outsourcing project at your firm. See also the extensive bibliographies in the publications of Dossani and Kenney (2003).
25. Hundertmark, Olinto do Valle, and Shulman 2008, 2.
26. Bassar 2008.
27. The first production sharing agreement (PSA) to our knowledge was introduced in Indonesia in 1966; now they are common in the petroleum industry. Two rather controversial production sharing agreements involve major oil discoveries on the Sakhalin Island, on the eastern shoreline of Russia. The Sakhalin I project was being led by Exxon Neftegaz, in conjunction with consortium members SODECO, ONGC Videsh, and two Rosneft subsidiaries (Sakhalinmorneftegaz and RN Astra). Total capital expenditure for the project, approved in 2003, was set at $12.8 billion, according to U.S. Energy Information Administration statistics. See the U.S. government's Energy Information Administration web site (www.eia.doe.gov) for more information on PSAs. The link to the Sakhalin project

is www.eia.doe.gov/emeu/cabs/Sakhalin/Background.html (accessed on March 20, 2008).

28. Continental AG press release 2007.

CHAPTER 7 Managing Alliances

1. Bamford, Ernst, and Fubini 2001, 90.
2. Bruner 2005, 13–54 and 352–362. On pages 13–54, Bruner surveys the academic research literature to explore the fundamental reasons behind M&A failure. On pages 352–362, he compares twenty cases of merger failure. The analytical metrics he uses are (1) *Complexity* (makes it difficult to understand what's going on); (2) *Tight Coupling* (absence of flexibility causes the crisis to radiate through the organization); (3) *"Business Not as Usual"* (trouble in one or more parts of the firm); (5) *Cognitive Biases* (mental "filtering" causes decision makers to discount risks and the crisis); (6) *Management Choices* (decisions that increase the risk of the firm or deal); and (7) *Team Implementation* (flaws in team processes or composition hamper response to the crisis).
3. Ibid., 10.
4. Bamford, Ernst, and Fubini 2004, 90–100.
5. Bleeke and Ernst 1991, 127–135.
6. Ibid., 127.
7. We first read this line (from an anonymous source) in an article by Jacobs (1995, 308).
8. For instance, entrepreneur and venture capitalist Lucius Cary, in the United Kingdom, successfully raised capital for his start-up using the open approach. See Cary 1998, pp. 49–53, for the dilemmas facing the first-time entrepreneur seeking to raise capital and wondering about how to go about doing it.
9. Pereiro 2002, 222.
10. Trigerorgis 1997, 15.
11. In the 1960s, decision scientists proposed using simulation and decision-tree analysis (Hertz 1964; Magee 1964) to capture operating flexibility associated with production decisions. Stuart C. Myers (1977) recognized the idea of thinking about "growth options." Interest in the field of real options has been steadily growing, as more knowledge accumulated about valuing financial options and applying the techniques to real options. Practitioners also were more interested in understanding more fully why discounted cash flow methods undervalued certain types of strategic investments decisions where managerial flexibility was involved. See Trigeorgis 1997, 1–21, for a summary of the real options literature.
12. See also Bruner 2004, 435–437 for more ways to classify real options and 531–546 for deal design in M&A.
13. Ibid., 531, 544–545.
14. We thank Dr. Margaret Mullally for suggesting this saying.
15. Bamford, Ernst, and Fubini 2004, pp. 90–100.
16. MacCormack, Forbath, Brooks, and Kalaher 2007b.
17. See Gomes-Casseres 1993, 3.
18. Kaplan and Norton 1996, 1–322.
19. This quote is from Grant 2008b, 150, who is paraphrasing Hamel and Prahalad 1999, no page cited by Grant.
20. Excerpted from March with Levinthal, "The Myopia of Learning," reprinted in March 1999, 217. The article originally appeared in *Strategic Management Journal* 14 (1993): 95–112.
21. The idea behind this type of an alliance progress review came from the Darden Strategic Alliances Project led by Professor Robert E. Spekman. Refer to web site http://faculty.darden.virginia.edu/alliance_drs/index.htm (accessed on May 15, 2009). We

have modified his checklist of questions and tailored them for the situation of a new venture's team defusing a conflict in its first strategic alliance or joint venture.
22. Watkins 2002, 1–8.

CHAPTER 8   How Alliances Complete the Value Chain in Biotechnology and Pharmaceutical Business Models

1. Biotechnology has an extremely broad scope and encompasses a plethora of disciplines. *Biotechnology* may be defined as the integration of diverse disciplines from the biological sciences with other science disciplines (e.g., physics, chemistry, engineering, medical sciences, and information science) to develop specialist techniques and products for medical and therapeutic purposes (therapeutics, vaccines, diagnostics) or for industrial and agricultural purposes. The terms *biotechnology* and *(bio)pharmaceutical* are used interchangeably in this chapter. For convenience, we use the short-hand expression (bio)pharmaceutical to refer to a company which carries out either biotechnology and pharmaceutical or else biotechnology and biopharmacueutical development activities within the same firm. See pharmaceutical definition in Note 2 and biopharmaceutical (without parenthesis around the "bio") in Note 3.
2. Pharmaceutical companies research, develop, and/or produce chemical-based drugs at early, intermediate, or late stages of development. In general, these companies have multibillion-dollar drug revenues and are usually fully integrated. Nowadays the product pipeline of these companies consists of a mixture of chemical-based drugs and biopharmaceuticals. Leading global pharmaceutical companies are GlaxoSmithKline and Astra Zeneca International based in the United Kingdom, Merck & Co. and Pfizer Inc. in the United States, Roche and Novartis in Switzerland, NovoNordisk in Denmark, and Takeda Pharmaceutical Company Ltd. in Japan.
3. Biopharmaceutical companies research, develop, or produce drugs at early, intermediate, or late stages of development. *Biopharmaceuticals* can be defined as therapeutic compounds that are derived from biological sources. Biopharmaceuticals can include a wide variety of (recombinant) therapeutic proteins (such as antibodies), vaccines, blood plasma–derived products, and nucleic acids. The vast majority of companies in this domain are usually not fully integrated. Pioneering biopharmaceutical companies include Genentech, Amgen, Hybritech (since absorbed into Eli Lilly & Co.) and Chiron (now part of Novartis). Other successful biopharmaceutical companies are Biogen Idec, Gilead Sciences, Genyzme Corporation, all based in the United States, and Élan Corporation, based in Ireland.
4. In a recent article by Bonabeau et al. (2008) these stages were recognized as having fundamentally different goals, strengths, and approaches; furthermore, these stages are the basis of the "Chorus" model of product development recently adopted by Eli Lilly.
5. Latin for "in glass" but as used in the context of pre-clinical and clinical trials, it refers to animal cell cultures in the laboratory environment, usually in plastic containers.
6. The equivalent in Europe is a clinical trial application for an investigational medicinal product (IMP).
7. We define *proof of principle* (POP) as a broader related term, and distinct from proof of concept. POP is an indication that a discovery will function as it was expected to function, but also with respect to the potential to generate revenues. Proof of principle is particularly important for financiers of a drug or medical device development project and is often a requirement for venture capital investment.
8. The drug product may be produced via an alliance with a contract manufacturing organization (CMO). It is preferable, however, to use the same partner for all clinical phases

and for large-scale manufacture, in order to minimize costs associated with technology transfer and proof of equivalence. Normally it is advisable to choose a partner that has two or more separate and validated manufacturing sites so that market supply is more secure in case one facility is temporarily not operating.

9. These calculations were carried out on investigational drugs. The data are from a survey based on the research and development costs of 68 randomly selected new drugs from 10 foreign-owned and U.S.-owned pharmaceutical firms. Details can be found in DiMasi, Hansen, and Grabowski 2003, 163.

10. DiMasi and Grabowski 2007, 1.

11. Small and medium-size enterprises (SMEs) may be categorized using a definition adopted by the European Commission: Medium-size companies are those with fewer than 250 employees, with yearly revenue of less than €50 million or a balance sheet total less than €43 million. Small-size companies are those with fewer than 50 employees, with yearly revenue of less than €10 million or a balance sheet total less than €10 million. Microcompanies are those with fewer than 10 employees, with yearly revenue of less than €2 million or a balance sheet total less than €2 million. The criteria must be applied to the company as a whole (including subsidiaries located in other member states and outside the European Union).

12. Chesbrough 2006, 1.

13. Chesbrough 2003, 53.

14. Chesbrough 2006, 1.

15. Deeds et al. 1999.

16. Given et al. 2005, 1.

17. The U.S. Congress enacted the Bayh-Dole Act (PL 96–517, Patent and Trademark Act Amendments of 1980) on December 12, 1980.

18. Jean-Pierre Garnier was the former CEO of GlaxoSmithKline, based in London and in Philadelphia. Garnier 2008, 71.

19. Garcia, 2006.

20. EMEA 2007.

21. Genzyme Corporation annual report 2007.

22. *Genomics* is the study of gene function and the mapping of large sets of genes within or between genomes.

23. One or more genes have been knocked out or switched off. The knock-out mouse is then compared with the normal mouse on behavioral and biochemical levels. Researchers can thus more easily determine the function of a gene or a number of related genes.

24. These are the costs incurred when a customer changes from one product to another product or from one supplier to another supplier. For technology platforms or for medical devices, these costs include not only technology transfer costs but also retraining costs of specialized personnel to operate the new systems, in addition to validation costs. Often the organization must absorb the expenses of changing over legacy software and database systems to the new standards as well.

25. Papadopoulos 2000, IT3–1T4.

26. van Arnum 2007.

27. *Business Insights* 2007.

28. *Bioinformatics* is the application of computer technology to the management of biological information. Specifically, it is the science of developing computer databases and algorithms to facilitate and expedite biological research, particularly in genomics. Bioinformatics evolved rapidly once automated sequencing became available. Currently there is an enormous task of making sense of the genomic data that comprise our DNA.

29. WHO 2007.

30. Alzheimer's Association 2008.

31. WHO 2006.

32. Burrill 2008.
33. Chesbrough 2003, 2006.
34. Khilji et al. 2006.
35. *Nature Biotechnology*'s Bioentrepreneur web site at: www.nature.com/bioent/ index.html. BCG conducted an extensive and detailed survey in 2005 and 2006, "collating the views and experiences of executives at over 90 vendors in China and India and of officers at several government research institutes in the two countries, and of senior executives at over ten biopharmaceutical multinational corporations (MNCs) operating there." Goodall et al. 2006, 1.
36. Frew et al. 2008.
37. For more on Biocon Ltd. see Konrad, Nichols-Nixon, and Chandrasekkar 2006 for the IVEY Business School case "Biocon Ltd.: Building a Biotech Powerhouse(A)."
38. Howe 2006.
39. The founder of Innocentive, Dr. A. Bingham, had over 25 years of experience with Eli Lilly and Company in pharmaceutical research and development, research acquisitions and collaborations, portfolio management, and R&D strategic planning. Innocentive is seen as a source of innovation for companies such as Eli Lilly, Boeing, Dow Chemical, and others. Dr. Bingham retired from his position as VP Lilly Research Laboratories in 2005 and now serves as a member of the board of Innocentive.
40. FDA 2005.

CHAPTER 9 Contract Law, Key Legal Agreements for Business, and Incorporation Issues

1. In the United States, lawyers are called attorneys. In the United Kingdom, there are two types of lawyers, solicitors and barristers. You would retain a solicitor to advise you on the terms of any contracts. If specialist advice is required, your solicitor might instruct a barrister specialized in that area. In the case of a dispute in a higher court, a barrister (upon the instructions of your solicitor) would normally represent you. Only a solicitor can instruct a barrister. You would not be able to approach a barrister directly.
2. U.S. contract law is not uniform: Each of the 50 states has developed its own principles in this area, and therefore not all states require the four elements exactly as set forth here. However, the concepts discussed in this chapter are generally applicable, to one degree or another, throughout the United States.
3. For example, most corporate entities in civil law European countries require minimum capital to be injected at the time of incorporation as prescribed by law. See Germany's joint stock company (AG) or limited liability company (GmBH) or Italy's joint stock company (S.p.A.) or limited liability company (S.r.l.).
4. Other forms of partnership are available in the United States, such as LLPs (limited liability partnerships) and LLLPs (limited liability limited partnerships), although they are not common choices for entrepreneurs seeking to establish a start-up business.

CHAPTER 11 The Intellectual Property Landscape

1. For example, see Gowers 2006. Andrew Gowers was commissioned by the U.K. Treasury to carry out an independent review of the U.K. Intellectual Property Framework. His report *Gowers Review of Intellectual Property* is available for downloading at www.hm-treasury.gov.uk/d/pbr06_gowers_report_755.pdf (accessed December 19, 2008).
2. European Patent Convention, Article 52(2)(c), October 5, 1973.
3. The World Intellectual Property Organization has a number of links to articles and research on the patentability of software on its web site at www.wipo.int.

4. Under the copyright regimes in most countries, in order for a work to qualify for copyright protection in that country, either the author of the work must be a national of or domiciled in that country, or the work must have first been published in that country.
5. The U.S. Copyright Office web site can be accessed at www.copyright.gov.
6. The three main copyright conventions are the Berne Convention, the Universal Copyright Convention, and the Rome Convention. More recently, the World Intellectual Property Organization (WIPO) Copyright Treaty has come into force in a number of territories, including the United States and the United Kingdom.
7. United States Code, Duration of Copyright: Works Created on or after January 1, 1978, Section 302 of Title 17.
8. Copyright Designs and Patents Act 1988, Section 91(1).
9. Article 1(1)(i) of Regulation 772/2004 on the application of Article 81(3) of the Treaty to categories of technology transfer agreements (OJ 2004 L123/11).
10. The Uniform Trade Secrets Act, Section 1.
11. Restatement of Torts, paragraph 757, comment b (1939).
12. *Saltman Engineering Co. Limited v. Campbell Engineering Co. Limited*, 1948, 65 Reports of Patent Cases 203, at 215. (England)
13. *Coco v. AN Clark (Engineers) Limited*, 1969, Reports of Patent Cases 41, at 47. (England)
14. See also Chapter 16 for advice on setting up a data room, which is where a target company places and stores pertinent documents of a proprietary and confidential nature. The information may be accessed only by authorized personnel on a strict need-to-know basis, for instance, when carrying out due diligence for a pending merger or acquisition transaction.
15. Trademark Act of 1946, 60 Stat. 427, as amended, codified in 15 U.S.C. 1051, paragraph 1117.

CHAPTER 12   The Basics about Patents

1. *Chiron Corporation v. Organon Teknika Ltd.*, 10 FSR 325 (1995), p. 6, column 2, paragraph 2, lines 7–9.
2. Baker and Bissell 2008, www.designcouncil.org.uk/en/About-Design/Business-Essentials/Invention/Invention9 (accessed April 30, 2008).
3. U.K. Intellectual Property Office 2006, www.ipo.gov.uk/about/about-ourorg/about-history/about-history-patent.htm (accessed April 30, 2008).
4. Patentgesetz von Venedig, n.d., www.wolfgang-pfaller.de/venedig.htm (accessed April 30, 2008).
5. Stobbs 2000.
6. Sweet and Maxwell 1998.
7. *The King v. Arkwright* 1785, p. 57, lines 22–30.
8. European Patent Convention, Art. 52(1), October 5, 1973.
9. European Patent Convention, Art. 52(2), October 5, 1973.
10. United States Code, 2008. Title 35, Chapter 10, paragraph 101. Inventions patentable.
11. World Intellectual Property Organization, n.d. *Paris Convention for the Protection of Industrial Property*, www.wipo.int/treaties/en/ip/paris/trtdocs_wo020.html (accessed April 30, 2008).
12. Ius Mentis 2007, www.iusmentis.com (accessed April 30, 2008).
13. World Trade Organization, n.d., www.wto.org (accessed April 30, 2008).
14. World Intellectual Property Organization, n.d., www.wipo.int (accessed April 30, 2008).
15. European Patent Office, 2007, www.epo.org/topics/news/2007/070522.html (accessed April 30, 2008).

CHAPTER 13   General Patenting Strategies in High-Technology Industries

1. Download the brochure "Why Researchers Should Care about Patents" from the European Commission web site, http://ec.europa.eu/invest-in-research/pdf/download_en/patents_for_researchers.pdf (accessed June 15, 2008).
2. *Prima facie* (Latin, on the first appearance) is a fact presumed to be true unless it is disproved. "In common parlance the term prima facie is used to describe the apparent nature of something upon initial observation. In legal practice the term generally is used to describe two things: the presentation of sufficient evidence by a civil claimant to support the legal claim (a *prima facie* case), or a piece of evidence itself (*prima facie* evidence)." Quoted from the Free Dictionary, http://legal-dictionary.thefreedictionary.com/Prima+facia (accessed June 2, 2008).
3. *Collins Concise English Dictionary.*
4. Deloitte 2007, www.deloitte.com/dtt/cda/doc/content/ce_tmt_Managing-IP_160807(4).pdf (accessed June 2, 2008).
5. Sandburg 2001, www.law.com (accessed June 15, 2008).
6. Fishman 2005.

CHAPTER 14   Navigating Technology License Agreements

1. Note there are differences between the U.S., U.K., and E.U. approaches to the protection of trade secrets or know-how, but this is beyond the scope of this chapter. We use the term *know-how* in this chapter to refer to secret and substantial technical information. For more in-depth information on this point, see Chapter 11.
2. *Jurisdiction* means a legal territory. This is not always the same as a country (although it can be). It can be a state (in the U.S. context), or a part of a unitary country. For instance, Scotland is part of the United Kingdom as is England, but Scotland is a separate legal jurisdiction, with its own rules of contract and litigation.
3. Commission Regulation on the Application of Article 81(3) of the Treaty to categories of Technology Transfer Agreements (772/2004/EC), April 27, 2004.

CHAPTER 15   Competitive Intelligence and Patent Searching

1. Meller 2008. See also www.etp.ciaa.be (accessed on May 8, 2008).
2. Lachman 2004, 11–15.
3. European Patent Office, n.d., esp@cenet, http://ep.espacenet.com (accessed on May 8, 2008).
4. European Patent Office, n.d., epoline, "Online Services—the Way to Do IP," www.epoline.org/portal/public (accessed on May 8, 2008).
5. World Intellectual Property Organization, n.d., PatentScope database, www.wipo.int/pctdb/en/ (accessed on May 8, 2008).
6. United States Patent and Trademark Office 2008, "Patent Full-Text and Full-Page Image Databases," www.uspto.gov/patft/index.html (accessed on May 8, 2008).
7. United States Patent and Trademark Office 2008, Patent Electronic Business Center, www.uspto.gov/ebc/index.html (accessed on May 8, 2008).
8. The idea of deciding on a deal based on "either this or that" versus "yes" or "no" comes from Bruner 2004, 187. Refer to Bruner 2004, 183–204, for useful tips on popular screening criteria for deal searches.

9. Professor Luis E. Pereiro has written extensively about valuation of companies in emerging markets. See Pereiro 2002, 247–318 for an explanation of how to do multiples-based comparisons as professional appraisers would do them.

10. U.S. Securities and Exchange Commission 2008, SEC Filings and Forms (EDGAR), www.sec.gov/edgar.shtml (accessed on May 8, 2008).

11. Trippe 2003. See also Eldridge 2006.

12. Chesbrough 2006.

CHAPTER 16 Due Diligence

1. For more on technology due diligence, see Hamscher 1997. Available for free download from the web site: www.hamscher.com/Docs/Tdd_US.pdf (accessed: April 30, 2008). See also Hildebrand and Klosek 2003, library.findlaw.com/ 2003/Dec/1/133278.html.

2. See Bruner 2004, Chapter 8, "Due Diligence," for more issues to consider when carrying out due diligence pertaining to mergers or acquisitions.

3. Shane 2004, 4 defines a university spin-off as "a new company founded to exploit a piece of intellectual property created in an academic institution." In the United States, the term university spin-off is commonly used, whereas in the United Kingdom, such newly-formed companies may be referred to as university "spin-out" companies.

4. For example, see "Due Diligence Horror Stories," www.astutediligence.com/ Diligence_Horror.htm#ip (accessed on April 6, 2008).

CHAPTER 17 Valuation Using Discounted Cash Flow

1. Williams, originally printed 1938, reprinted 1964. Readers may be able to find old copies of the original edition (now out of print) in university libraries or specialized book shops.

2. See Graham, Dodd, and Cottle 1962, 450, for John Burr Williams's contribution: "There is also a well-established financial principle which states that the investment value of a common stock equals the 'present worth' of all its future dividends." This sentence is followed by a footnote citing Williams's book. Afterward Graham et al. write: "To apply this principle in practice would require dividend projections for, say, between 40 and 50 years. We do not believe that estimate for so remote a future can be made with enough dependability to be really useful. The investor may, however, assume a permanent or 'built-in' growth rate for common stocks in general, derived basically from the reinvestment of undistributed earnings and buttressed by the country's long-term financial history. Where significantly higher rates of growth are assumed for some favored enterprise, we think that the specific projections should be limited to, say, four years and that the attractive longer-range prospects should be allowed for, less definitively, in a higher-than average multiplier."

3. Williams 1938, 55.

4. Note that this simple example neglects income taxes; it also assumes the student has no earnings while in school and that the student's room and board expenses are the same while at school as on the job.

5. Entrepreneurs who seek venture capital financing often think the discount rates used by VCs are very high. The entrepreneurs think their business model and business plan to be attractive, but they have no way of comparing it to other investment deal proposals received by the VCs. We talk more about the perspective of the venture capital investor in Chapter 19. To negotiate financing for your venture, you need to understand the thinking and requirements of VCs.

6. Wiese 1930, 5.

7. Wiese, quoted in Williams 1938, 55.
8. Williams, 1938, 55.
9. Ibid., 59.
10. Sharpe 1964, 425–442.
11. Pereiro 2002, 38.
12. Landler and Wakin 2004.
13. "Parmalat is the largest bankruptcy in European history, representing about 1.5 percent of Italian GNP—proportionally larger than the combined ratio of the Enron and WorldCom bankruptcies to the US GNP." Celani 2004.
14. Benjamin Graham in Graham and Dodd 1934, 23.
15. Beaver 1989, 79–103.
16. Tversky and Kahneman 1974, 1124–1131.
17. Teisberg 1991a, 1.
18. See Ibid., 2 where Teisberg cites Borgida and Nisbett 1977, 258–271 and Tversky and Kahneman 1973, 207–232.
19. March 1999 and 1994; Bazerman and Neale 1992.
20. Teisberg 1991b. We frequently suggest that our MBA students read this article by Teisberg "Why Do Good Managers Choose Poor Strategies" in our ESADE Business School strategy courses. For other recommended strategy books and articles, log onto our book's web site at www.innovationtocashflows.com and go to "Resources – Strategy and Management."
21. Sharpe, Alexander, and Bailey 1995, 523.
22. Sharpe 1964.
23. Bruner, Eades, Harris, and Higgins 1998, 13–22.
24. Pereiro and Galli 2000.
25. See Pereiro 2002, 83-91.
26. Sharpe 1964, 425–442.
27. Sharpe, Alexander, and Bailey 1999, 228.
28. Technically, the *beta* of a security is defined as the standardized covariance between the return on the security and the return on the market. The intuition behind beta is that it measures the sensitivity of a change in the return of an individual security to the change in return of the market portfolio. Said another way, beta is the responsiveness of the security's return to market movements. For example, a stock with a beta of 2.0 means that if the overall stock market goes up, this particular stock will do far better (twice as well). Unfortunately, if the market goes down, this same stock will also do worse (twice as poorly) than the market that day. The returns on the stock are magnified two times those of the stock market. Adding a high-beta stock to a diversified portfolio contributes more beta risk to the portfolio than an "average" security contributes with its beta of 1.0.
29. See Sharpe, Alexander, and Bailey 1999, 232.
30. See the article by Reilly and Akhtar 1995, 33–52 for a demonstration of the benchmark problem. These researchers computed an average beta for the 30 stocks in the Dow Jones Industrial Average during three alternative time periods using three different proxies for the market portfolio: (1) S&P 500 Index, (2) Morgan Stanley world Stock Index, and (3) Brinson Partners Global Security Market Index (GSMI). The average beta ranged from a low of 0.820 to a high of 1.264 in their study. The same study results are summarized in a leading investments textbook (refer to Reilly and Brown 2003, 267–270).
31. See Copeland, Koller, and Murrin 2000, 146–150, or Bruner 2004, 393–423.
32. Pereiro 2002 and Bruner 2004.
33. Bruner 2004, 277.
34. Ibid.
35. Pereiro 2002, 81 and 316–317; and Bruner 2004, 277.

CHAPTER 18   Valuation Using Market Multiples and Comparable Deal Transactions

1. In Chapter 17, we defined *investment in working capital* as "operating current assets minus noninterest bearing current liabilities." Operating current assets are the increase in trade accounts receivables and inventory needed by the business but excludes surplus cash. Noninterest-bearing current liabilities are changes in accounts payable, accrued wages and salaries, and other accrued expenses but exclude the current portion of long-term debt and any other interest-bearing short-term debt. For a more advanced explanation of how to reorganize the accounting statements to economic financial statements, see Chapter 9, "Analyzing Historical Performance" in Copeland, Koller, Murrin, and McKinsey 2000, 157–200, especially the discussion on noninterest-bearing current liabilities on pp. 160–162. For the nonfinancial executive, we suggest Ward and Price 2006, which simply and expertly walks you through the accounting jungle and shows you how to construct economic representations of balance sheets from historical accounting statements. See also Higgins 2007, 342 to learn more about determining investment in working capital as used in free cash flow calculations.

2. The Financial Accounting Standards Board (FASB) has been working jointly with the International Accounting Standards Board (IASB) to improve reporting transparency by eliminating some of the more significant and pervasive differences between IFRS and U.S. GAAP. As these rules and standards are being revised continuously, readers are advised to consult the FASB's web site for the latest updates (www.fasb.org).

3. Van Horne 1995, 443.

4. A classic work on the subject of manias is Charles Mackay's *Extraordinary Popular Delusions and the Madness of Crowds*, originally published in 1841 and 1852, reprinted 1980.

5. *The Economist* 2008, 11.

6. Le Bon 1982, 10, 20–21.

7. See Smith and Parr 2005, 304 for the International Assets Valuation Standards Committee discussion of fair market value, which the British define somewhat differently from the Americans. The British refer to "open market value" and intend it to mean "the best price at which an interest in a property might reasonably be expected to be sold by private treaty at the date of valuation assuming: (a) a willing seller; (b) a reasonable period within which to negotiate the sale taking into account the nature of the property and the state of the market; (c) values will remain static throughout the period; (d) the property will be freely exposed to the market; and (e) no account is to be taken of an additional bid by a special purchaser." The definition of open market value comes from Rees 1998, 481.

8. For instance, financial analysts covering the retail industry will often compare same-store sales growth of different retail companies in order to see how much the growth in sales is due to existing stores and separate that information from growth in sales due to building new stores. Mixing up both sets of numbers would provide a confusing picture for investors.

9. Cottle, Murray, and Block 1988, 335.

10. James E. Hatch and Paul Asmundson 2001 of Richard IVEY School of Business have written an excellent case based on a real biotechnology company called Chromos Molecular Systems whose management was trying to decide where and how to go public. One of the co-authors used this case to teach leading South Korean biotech executives about valuation issues of biotechnology firms. The case asks students to decide how to value the firm and where to list this high-tech company—in which country (Canada or the United States?) and on what stock exchange (Toronto Stock Exchange or NASDAQ?). The case exercises students' skills in deciding on their own criteria for picking proxy companies among a large sample of possible biotech competitors. It also contains data to illustrate

how life science security analysts incorporate a number of elements into their thinking processes when pricing an IPO, including technology values.

11. The best explanation we have read on doing international comparisons using comparable company and transaction methods is in Pereiro 2002. In particular, we highly recommend his Chapter 6, "Relative Valuation in Emerging Markets: Comparable Companies and Transactions," pp. 247–318. Also of interest is Chapter 7, "Valuing Technology Startups in Emerging Markets," pp. 319–385. In Chapter 7, Pereiro values a closely held Web start-up venture called Patagonia.com. In July 1999, Patagonia.com was positioned as "one of the most promising personal finance web sites" in Latin America. The valuation done by Pereiro takes place in early 2000, when the investor consortium that controlled Patagonia.com was considering whether to sell the company to a strategic investor or list the company on a U.S. stock market and take it public. Pereiro does an excellent job explaining how he chose the sample of comparable companies and how to systematically take into account the effect of the benchmark companies being at different stages of maturity to the target company. He also adjusts the equity value computed for the unsystematic risk of being a small, privately held company and for the technology bubble. Actually, his book has numerous practical examples in every chapter that clearly show readers what to do and how to approach the nitty-gritty details of valuations in messy emerging markets. We might add that one of the co-authors has had executive MBA students use Pereiro's book to help them value private businesses ranging from wireless ventures in emerging markets in the Middle East and Russia, to pricing a potential acquisition by a major forest products company seeking to expand in Russia.

12. For more on valuing privately held firms, see Hatch and Dussin 2001. For issues concerning the valuation of biotechnology firms, see Hatch 2008.

13. Cottle, Murray, and Block 1988.

CHAPTER 19 Venture Capital Method of Valuation

1. Hogoboom 2004, may be downloaded from the web site: www.sec.gov/info/ small-bus/gbfor25_2006/hogoboom_invest.pdf (accessed August 8, 2008). See also the Darden technical note by Chaplinsky 2003 and the Darden case by Chaplinski and Crawford 2003.

2. Dow Jones Equity Analyst, July 8, 2008. Downloadable from www.reuters.com/article/ pressRelease/idUS110280+08-Jul-2008+PRN20080708 (accessed December 28, 2008).

3. Data is from Goldman Sachs' web site (www2.goldmansachs.com/services/investing/ private-equity/mezzanine/index.html) under "Private Equity— Mezzanine Funds" (accessed December 28, 2008).

4. Lockett, Murray, and Wright 2002, 1009–1030.

5. David F. Swensen is the successful and highly regarded chief investment officer and manager of Yale's endowment. He has written two best-selling books on institutional investing (Swenson 2000) and on personal portfolio investing (Swensen 2005). For more on the pros and cons of various compensation arrangements found in nontraditional asset classes (e.g., private equity, venture capital, and hedge funds) read his first book, especially Swensen 2000, 278–289.

6. In particular, see the policy paper "Private Equity Funds Tax Treatment of Carried Interests," www.privateequitycouncil.org/public-policy/legislative/ private-equity-funds-tax-treatment-of-carried-interests (accessed on August 8, 2008).

7. The latest biotechnology IPO windows were in 1997, 2000, and 2004 according to Edwards, Murray, and Yu 2006, 509–515.

8. These figures are from a report by Allen 2008. Allen reports that according to Professor Heiko Bergmann of the Small and Medium-sized Business Institute at St. Gallen University, "the [Swiss start-up] failure rate, while high, is comparable with the international average." The article explains that the Swiss Federal Statistics Office

"measured the success rate of all firms that started up in Switzerland between 2000 and 2004 by counting how many were still in business in 2005. More than four-fifths survived the first year, but only half of Swiss start-up firms survived their first five years of business, with many failures attributed to lack of market knowledge or unrealistic expectations. The statistics also showed that start-ups in the construction and industrial sectors were more likely to succeed in the long term (60 per cent were still running in the fifth year) than in the service industries such as computer sciences and insurance (which had a 47 per cent five-year survival rate)." There were "36,427 firms founded in Switzerland in 2007, up 6.3 per cent on 2006, and the third annual increase in a row." The full report may be found at www.swissinfo.org/eng/front.html?siteSect=109&ty=st&sid=8621979 (accessed on February 17, 2008).

9. See Leach and Melicher 2003, 285–330 for detailed spreadsheet examples of valuing a venture using three different methods, what they refer to as the maximum dividend method, the pseudo dividend method, and the delayed dividend approximation method. By working through these three methods, the reader will see how the venture capital approach is a shortcut that is similar in its treatment of surplus cash to the delayed dividend approximation method. We refer to the VC method in our book as the money in, money out, time to exit, discount by the VC's target rate of return method. We do so as a reminder that the VC method makes the simple assumption that all the money provided by a VC financing round is held inside the venture until the time of the VC exit. The funds that are put to use and those that are still in cash and waiting to be deployed are charged the *same* discount rate. This is a simplification that should not be overlooked. Entrepreneurs seeking venture capital or private equity financing will soon realize that financing the entire venture's present and future cash needs in a single early round will result in huge loss of value for them. The entrepreneurs will be better off (suffer less dilution in their holdings) by financing in stages. Actually, financing in stages is the usual approach.

10. For more information on how to calculate the IRR or discounted cash flows of a private equity fund, refer to the European Venture Capital Association (EVCA) web site for two free publications: "The EVCA Reporting Guidelines" (June 2006), pp. 27–32 for the IRR calculations; and the "International Private Equity and Venture Capital Valuation Guidelines" (October 2006), pp. 22–23, for a discussion on how to compute the discounted cash flows from an investment portfolio. Both publications may be downloaded from the EVCA web site (www.evca.eu) under these links: www.evca.eu/uploadedFiles/Home/Toolbox/Industry_Standards/evca_reporting_guidelines_2006.pdf and www.evca.eu/uploadedFiles/Home/Toolbox/Industry_Standards/evca_international_valuation_guidelines.pdf.

CHAPTER 20   Valuing and Structuring High Technology Strategic Alliances

1. Advanced Dermal Delivery, Inc. (ADD) is a fictitious company and its products are imaginary.

2. In the case, "nanosize pump" means a very small pump that is produced using nanotechnology. In real life, the Swiss firm Debiotech SA, based in Lausanne, Switzerland, has a registered trademark on the name nanopump. For more information on the nanopump®(™) of Debiotech SA, consult their web site at Debiotech SA, www.debiotech.com/ products/msys/chronojet.html.

3. Because this is a fictitious case, no ink-jet manufacturer is named. For an example of a real microneedle skin patch that is under development, see the HP Labs web site, www.hpl.hp.com/news/2008/jan-mar/skin_patch.html?jumpid=reg_ R1002_USEN (accessed August 21, 2008). HP Labs licensed its microneedle technology to a small company named Crospon of Galway, Ireland.

4. Pfizer's financial statements for 2006 show a $322 million in-process research and development charge related to the PowderMed, Ltd. acquisition, recorded during the

fourth quarter 2006. See Pfizer's web site under Investor Relations, www.pfizer.com/
files/news/2006q4_earnfin1.pdf.

5. The Glide Pharmaceuticals Technology Limited (Glide Pharma) actuator mechanism
is described in the Oxford Technology 3 Venture Capital Trust Newsletter. 2007,
(September 11), pp. 1–2. Available from www.oxfordtechnology.com/downloads/new-
letters/OT3_newsletter.pdf (accessed December 30, 2008).

6. Detailed information about Glide Pharma—its history, business model, partnering strategy, and product pipeline—may be found on the company's web site,
www.glidepharma.com (accessed August 20, 2008).

7. This time-to-market estimate is consistent with what is stated in the HP Labs press
release for the Crospon licensing agreement. For details, see note 3 and the HP Lab we-
blink, www.hpl.hp.com/news/2008/jan-mar/skin_patch.html?jumpid= reg_R1002_USEN
(accessed August 21, 2008). The faster time-to-market estimate was used to keep the
spreadsheet shorter. However, sensitivity analysis should be conducted for delays in product launch and the corresponding impact on the forecast results. Alternatively, Monte
Carlo simulation could be used to quantify the uncertainties, especially if multiple risk
factors are modeled at the same time.

8. Dimson, Marsh, and Staunton 2002, 193.

9. Francis and Ibbotson 2002, 30; Ibbotson Associates 1999, 10, 18, 23, and 256.

10. Pereiro 2002, 176. (See also the field survey by Bruner, Eades, Harris, and Higgins
1998,13–28). The Bruner survey indicated that 86 percent of the leading finance textbooks
and trade books advise adjusting beta for the idiosyncratic risk of an investment (but do
not specify how to do so), whereas 14 percent do not even address the problem. (See
Bruner survey Exhibit 2, in *ibid.*, 18–19). Furthermore, when companies were asked
whether they adjusted discount rates for project risk, the survey questionnaires provided
a wide range of written responses: "Rarely, but at least on one occasion we have for
a whole new line of business." "We do sensitivity analysis on every project." (Bruner
survey Exhibit 10 in *ibid.*, 25).

11. Pereiro 2002, 176. Pereiro also explains and illustrates various methods and approaches
to adjust for unsystematic risk in unlisted, tightly controlled, small businesses in emerging
markets. See Pereiro 2002, 175–221.

12. Koeplin, Sarin, and Shapiro 2000, 94–101. Downloadable from http://ssrn.com/abstract=
251776 (accessed February 14, 2009).

13. Block 2007, 33–40.

14. Pereiro 2002, 185; Arzac 1996.

15. Hatch and Dussin 2008, 15. This note by Hatch and Dussin (2008, 1–18) is highly
recommended. It contains an easy to follow discussion about DCF and comparable
valuation techniques that are appropriate for small, privately-held firms, including the
use of discounts for illiquidity and small size based on various empirical studies. The note
explains idiosyncratic risk adjustments clearly and gives a simple example using an ad
hoc method developed by Aswan Damodaran, professor of finance at the Stern School of
Business, New York University (www.damodaranonline.com).

16. Readers will find an interesting discussion on the pitfalls to avoid when using risk-adjusted
cash flows in the *2007 Cumulative Supplement* to Smith and Parr 2007, 23–39. See also
the Financial Accounting Standards Board's FASB *Statement of Financial Accounting
Concepts* No. 7: Using cash flow information and present value in accounting measurements, issued in February 2002.

17. See the *2007 Cumulative Supplement* to Smith and Parr 2007, 51–54 for a succinct
explanation of Monte Carlo techniques. Monte Carlo simulation software is often sold
as an add-in for Excel spreadsheets. For more information, consult the web site of Palisade Corporation (www.palisade.com). See Palisade's Decision Tools Suite and the software product called @Risk that does Monte Carlo simulation. Refer also to Crystal
Ball by Decisioneering, now part of Oracle. See Oracle's web site for product details
(www.oracle.com/crystalball/index.html).

References

3M Corporation. 2007. 3M innovation—How it flourished. In *A Century of innovation: The 3M story*, 29–48. St. Paul, MN: 3M Company (electronic book). http://multimedia. mmm.com/mws/mediawebserver.dyn?6666660Zjcf6lVs6EVs666IMhCOrrrrQ- (accessed June 5, 2007).

Agreement on Trade Related Aspects of Intellectual Property Rights (TRIPS). World Trade Organization (WTO). www.wto.org/english/tratop_e/trips_e/t_agm0_e.htm.

Allen, Matthew. 2008. Half of start-ups fail after five years, *Swissinfo*, Zurich, Switzerland. www.swissinfo.org/eng/front.html?siteSect=109&ty=st&sid=8621979 (accessed February 17, 2008).

Alsop, Ronald. 2006. MBA Programs blend disciplines to yield big picture. *Wall Street Journal*. July 11, p. B5. www.yale.edu/opa/download/newsYale/MBA_Programs_Blend_Disciplines_701106.pdf (accessed May 23, 2008).

Alzheimer's Association. 2008. Alzheimer's disease facts and figures. www.alz.org/news_and_events_13106.asp.

Anslinger, Patricia L., Steven J. Klepper, and Somu Subramaniam. 1999. Breaking up is good to do. *McKinsey Quarterly* (1): 16–27 (February).

Article 1(1)(i) of European Commission Regulation 772/2004 on the application of Article 81(3) of the Treaty Establishing the European Union to categories of technology transfer agreements (OJ 2004 L123/11).

Arzac, Enrique R. 1996. The cost of capital: A synthesis. Working paper. Columbia University Graduate School of Business.

AstraZeneca. 2006. AstraZeneca and Pozen Inc. sign deal to develop and commercialise naproxen and esomeprazole fixed dose combinations utilising Pozen's proprietary technology for the treatment of chronic pain. August 6. www.astrazeneca.com/press-release/5265.aspx.

AT&T. 2001. *An information guide for AT&T share owners*. www.att.com/Common/files/pdf/t_awe_exchange.pdf (accessed May 16, 2008).

Athanassakos, George. 1995. *Equity valuation: A guide to discounted cash flow and relative valuation nethods*. Monograph. Clarica Financial Services Research Centre. Wilfrid Laurier University, Waterloo, Ontario, Canada.

Athanassakos, George. 2005. Note on the discounted cash flow-based valuation methodology as tested by a public market transaction. 9B05N021. Richard Ivey School of Business, University of Western Ontario, Ontario, Canada.

Baker, Graham, and Peter Bissell. 2008. Ten lessons from successful inventions. In *Invention*. London: Design Council. www.designcouncil.org.uk/en/About-Design/Business-Essentials/Invention/Invention9 (accessed April 30, 2008).

Bales, Carter, P.C. Chatterjee, Donald Gogel, and Anupam Puri. 1980. Competitive cost analysis. McKinsey Staff Paper, McKinsey & Company, Inc. www.mckinseyquarterly.com/strategy.miin00.asp (accessed May 31, 2008).

Bamford, James, David Ernst, and David G. Fubini. 2004. Launching a world-class joint venture, *Harvard Business Review* 82, no. 2 (February): 90–100.

Barney, Jay. 1991. Firm resources and sustained competitive advantage. *Journal of Management* 17: 99–120.

Bassar, Shanny. 2008. Analysts raise infrastructure spending forecasts. *Dow Jones Financial On-line News*, June 23. www.efinancialnews.com/assetmanagement/index/content/2451016799 (accessed June 23, 2008).

Bazerman, Max H., and Margaret A. Neale. *Negotiating rationally.* 1993. New York: Free Press.

Beamish, Paul W. 2003. The design and management of international joint ventures. In *International management: Text and cases,* 5th ed., 120–139. New York: McGraw-Hill.

Beaver, William H. 1989. *Financial reporting: An accounting revolution.* Englewood Cliffs, NJ: Prentice-Hall.

Bleeke, Joel and David Ernst. 1991. The way to win in cross-border alliances. *Harvard Business Review* 69, no. 6 (November-December): 127–135.

Block, Stanley B. 2007. The liquidity discount in valuing privately owned companies. *Journal of Applied Finance.* vol 17, no. 2 (Fall–Winter): 33–40.

Bodily, Samuel E. and Robert F. Bruner, and Pierre Jacquet. 1999. Genzyme/Geltex pharmaceuticals joint venture. Case. UVA-F-1254, version 2.2. Darden Business Publishing, University of Virginia. (April 20).

Bolles, Richard N. 2004. *What color is your parachute: A practical manual for job-hunters and career-changers.* Berkeley, CA: Ten Speed Press.

Bonabeau, Eric, Neil Bodick, and Robert W. Armstrong. 2008. A more rational approach to new-product development. *Harvard Business Review* 86, no. 3 (March): 96–99.

Borgida, E., and R.E. Nisbett. 1977. The differential impact of abstract versus concrete information on decisions. *Journal of Applied Social Psychology* 7, 258–271.

Bruner, Robert F. 2004. *Applied Mergers & Acquisitions.* Hoboken, NJ: John Wiley & Sons.

Bruner, Robert F. 2004. Due diligence. In *Applied Mergers & Acquisitions,* 183–204. Hoboken, NJ: John Wiley & Sons.

Bruner, Robert F. 2004. An introduction to deal design in M&A. In *Applied Mergers & Acquisitions,* 531–546. Hoboken, NJ: John Wiley & Sons.

Bruner, Robert F. 2005. *Deals from hell—M & A lessons that rise above the ashes.* Hoboken: John Wiley & Sons.

Bruner, Robert F., and Sean Carr. 2005. *Arcadian Microarray Technologies, Inc.* Case. UVA-F-1496 (December 9).

Bruner, Robert F., Kenneth M. Eades, Robert S. Harris, and Robert C. Higgins. 1998. Best practices in estimating the cost of capital: Survey and synthesis. *Journal of Financial Practice and Education* (Spring-Summer): 13–28.

Burgleman, Robert A., Clayton M. Christensen, and Steven C. Wheelwright. 2003. *Strategic Management of Technology and Innovation,* 4th ed. New York: McGraw-Hill/Irwin.

Burrill, G. Steven. 2008. Biotech 2008: A global transformation. A presentation for the conference titled Wisconsin Life Sciences Transformation: World Perspectives & Wisconsin's Advantage. February 21. Madison, WI. www.burrillandco.com.

Business Insights. 2007. Optimizing partnerships with contract organizations: Effective management, key issues, and the development of virtual pharmacos 167 (November). www.researchandmarkets.com/reports/c78869.

Cary, Lucius. 1998. *Lucius Cary's guide to raising capital for the smaller business.* Oxford, UK: Seed Capital Ltd. and Venture Capital Report Ltd.

Celani, Claudio. 2004. The story behind Parmalat's bankruptcy. *Executive Intelligence Review*, January 16. www.larouchepub.com/other/2004/3102parmalat_invest.html (accessed September 4, 2008).

Chaplinsky, Susan. 2003. Note on PIPES: Private equity investment in distressed firms. UVA F-1412. University of Virginia, Darden School Foundation.

Chaplinski, Susan, and Richard Crawford. 2003. MicroStrategy Incorporated: PIPE. Case. UVA F-1368. University of Virginia, Darden School Foundation.

Chesbrough, Henry. 2003. *Open innovation—The new imperative for creating and profiting from technology.* Boston: Harvard Business School Press.

Chesbrough, Henry. 2006. *Open business models: How to thrive in the new innovation landscape.* Boston: Harvard Business School.

Chesbrough, Henry, Wim VanHaverbeke, and Joel West, eds. 2006. *Open innovation: Researching a new paradigm.* Oxford: Oxford University Press.

Chiron Corporation v. Organon Teknika Ltd. 10 FSR 325, 1995, p. 6, column 2, paragraph 2, line 7–9.

Christensen, Clayton M. 1997. *The innovator's dilemma: When new technologies cause great firms to fail.* Boston: Harvard Business Press.

Christensen, Clayton M., and Richard S. Rosenbloom. 1995. Explaining the attacker's advantage: Technological paradigms, organizational dynamics, and the value network. *Research Policy* 24 (2): 233–57.

Clariant corporate web site: www.clariant.com/corporate/internet.nsf/vwWeb Pages-ByID/B4E9CB47E92E455BC125712C0052516C (accessed May 14, 2008).

Coco v. AN Clark (Engineers) Limited. 1969. Reports of Patent Cases 41, at 47 (England).

Continental AG press release. 2007. Energy storage systems for the GM Chevrolet "E-Flex" electric vehicle propulsion system. June 21. www.conti-online.com/generator/www/com/en/continental/portal/themes/press_services/press_releases/products/automotive_systems/gt_pr_2007_06_21_gm_en.html (accessed March 20, 2008).

Contract Pharma. Contract services, including contract manufacturing, for the pharmaceutical industry. www.contractpharma.com (accessed December 7, 2008).

Copeland, Tom, Tim Koller, Jack Murrin, and McKinsey & Company. 2000. *Valuation: Measuring and managing the value of companies,* 3rd ed. Indianapolis, IN: John Wiley & Sons.

Copyright Designs and Patents Act 1988, United Kingdom, Section 213.

Copyright Designs and Patents Act 1988, United Kingdom, Section 91(1).

Cordis Europa. See under the EU Cooperation programme, the European technology platforms (ETPs), and Research for the benefit of SME programmes. http://cordis.europa.eu/fp7/sme_en.html (accessed December 7, 2008).

Cottle, Sidney, Roger F. Murray, Frank E. Block, with the collaboration of Martin L. Leibowitz. 1988. *Graham and Dodd's Security Analysis,* 5th ed. New York: McGraw-Hill.

Cowen & Co. Investment bank for high technology and life sciences. www.cowen.com (accessed December 7, 2008).

Decision of the Fourth Board of Appeal of the Office for Harmonization in the Internal Market of the European Union of 27 September 2007–R 708/2006–4–Tarzan Yell (Sound Mark).

Deeds, D.L., D. DeCarolis, and J. Coombs. 1999. Dynamic capabilities and new product development in high technology ventures: An empirical analysis of new biotechnology firms. *Journal of Business Venturing* 15: 211–229.

DeGarmo, E. Paul, John R. Canada, and William G. Sullivan. 1979. *Engineering economy.* New York: Macmillan.

DiMasi, J.A., and H.G. Grabowski. 2007. The cost of biopharmaceutical R&D: Is biotech different? *Managerial and Decision Economics* 28: 469–479.

DiMasi, J.A., R.W. Hansen, and H.G. Grabowski. 2003. The price of innovation: New estimates of drug development costs. *Journal of Health Economics* 22, 151–185.

Dimson, Elroy, Paul R. Marsh, and Mike Staunton. 2005. *Global investment returns yearbook for 2005.* London: ABN-AMRO and London Business School, 180.

Dollinger, Marc J. 2008. Networking and alliances. In *Entrepreneurship: Strategies and resources,* 4th ed., 357–364. Lombard, IL: Marsh Publications.

Dossani, Rafiq, and Martin Kenney. 2003. Went for cost, Stayed for quality?: Moving the back office to India. Working Paper, Walter H. Shorenstein Asia-Pacific Research Center (APARC) Stanford University, November. http://aparc.stanford.edu/publications/went_for_cost_stayed_for_ quality_moving_the_back_office_to_india.

Dow Jones Private Equity Analyst. 2008. U.S. private equity firms raise $132.7 billion in 1st half of 2008, 3% behind last year's record pace. (July 8). www.reuters.com/article/pressRelease/idUS110280+08-Jul-2008+PRN20080708 (accessed December 28, 2008).

Due diligence horror stories. www.astute diligence.com/Diligence_Horror.htm#ip (accessed April 6, 2008).

The Economist 2008. *Where have all your savings gone?* vol 389, no. 8609 (December 6), p. 11.

Edwards, M., F. Murray, and R. Yu. 2006. Gold in the ivory tower: Equity rewards of outlicensing. *Nature Biotechnology* 24 (5): 509–515.

Eisenhardt, Kathleen M., and Jeffrey A. Martin. 2000. Dynamic capabilities: What are they? *Strategic Management Journal* 21: 1105–21.

Eldridge, Jeanette. 2006. Data visualisation tools—A perspective from the pharmaceutical industry. *World Patent Inform* 28 (1) (March): 43–49.

Ellis, Charles D. 2006. *Joe Wilson and the creation of Xerox.* Hoboken, NJ: John Wiley & Sons.

Energy Biosciences Institute. EBI Fact Sheet. http://67.199.70.53/index.php?option=com_content&task=view&id=51&Itemid=90.

European Medicines Agency. The European Union and the FDA working together to create common application for orphan designation for medicines. Doc. Ref. EMEA/557391/2007). Orphan drug status definition. www.emea.europa.eu/pdfs/ general/direct/pr/55739107en.pdf (accessed July 6, 2008).

European Patent Convention, Article 52(1), October 5, 1973.

European Patent Convention, Article 52(2), October 5, 1973.

European Patent Convention, Article 52(2)(c), October 5, 1973.

European Patent Office. 2007. The "big five offices" move towards closer cooperation. www.epo.org/topics/news/2007/070522.html (accessed April 30, 2008).

European Patent Office. epoline database. Online services—the way to do IP. www.epoline.org/portal/public (accessed on May 8, 2008).

Farrell, Diana, and the McKinsey Global Institute. 2006. Smarter offshoring. *Harvard Business Review* 84, no. 6 (June): 84–92.

Financial Accounting Standards Board. 2002. Statement of Financial Accounting Concepts No. 7: Using cash flow information and present value in accounting measurements. (February): 1–53. Downloadable from: www.fasb.org/pdf/con7.pdf (accessed on February 14, 2009).

Fisher, Irving. 1896. Appreciation and interest. *Publications of the American Economic Association* 11, 1–100.

Foster, George, and Andrea Higuera. 2002. GenPharm International. Case. IB38. Stanford Graduate School of Business. (September 5).

Frew, Sarah E., Stephen M. Sammut, Alysha F. Shore, Joshua K. Ramjist, Sara Al-Bader, Rahim Rezaie, Abdallah S. Daar, and Peter A. Singer. 2008. Chinese health biotech and the billion-patient market. *Nature Biotechnology* 26, 37–53. DOI: 10.1038/nbt0108–37. www.nature.com/nbt/journal/v26/n1/abs/nbt0108–37.html.

Frost & Sullivan. 2008. Widening innovation—Productivity gap in the pharmaceutical industry—New challenges and future directions. www.frost.com/prod/servlet/market-insight-top.pag?Src=RSS&docid=128394740 (accessed June 12, 2008).

Frueh, Feliz W. 2005. Personalised medicine, what is it? How will it affect healthcare? 11th Annual FDA Science Forum. April 26. www.fda.gov/cder/genomics/scienceForum 2005.pdf.

Garcia, S. 2006. Trends in life science partnering, collaborations and strategic alliances. Fenwick and West LLP publication. www.fenwick.com.

Garnier, Jean-Pierre. 2008. Rebuilding the R+D engine in Big Pharma. *Harvard Business Review* 86, no. 5 (May): 69–76.

Gelb, Michael J. 1998. *How to think like Leonardo da Vinci: Seven steps to genius every day.* New York: Bantam.

Genentech, Inc. Herceptin (Trastuzumab) HER2—metastastic breast cancer treatment. www.herceptin.com/hcp/index.jsp (accessed December 7, 2008).

Genzyme Corporation. 2007. Annual report, p. 10. www.genzyme.com.

Given, Ruth, Glenn H. Snyder, and Dong Wei. 2005. Critical factors for alliance formation: Insights from the Deloitte research biotech alliance survey. A Deloitte Research Life Sciences Study. June: 1–24. Deloitte Research, part of Deloitte Services LLP. www.deloitte.com/dtt/cda/doc/content/DTT_DR_BIOTECH_June05Final%282%29.pdf (accessed July 6, 2008).

Gloeckler, Geoff. 2005. Stanford's new-look MBA: A top B-school moves to tailor its program to fit the needs of individual students and challenge them at their separate skill levels. *BusinessWeek.com*, June 5. www.businessweek.com/bschools/content/jun2006/bs2006065_4760_bs001.htm (accessed May 23, 2008).

Gluck, Fred. 1980. Strategic choice and resource allocation. *McKinsey Quarterly* 1 (Winter): 22–33.

Goldman Sachs. Private equity—Mezzanine funds. www2.goldmansachs.com/services/investing/private-equity/mezzanine/index.html (accessed September 8, 2008).

Goleman, Daniel. 1995. *Emotional intelligence.* New York: Bantam.

Goleman, Daniel, Richard Boyatzis, and Annie McKee. 2002. *Primal leadership: Realizing the power of emotional intelligence,* Boston: Harvard Business School Press, especially Appendix B, Emotional Intelligence: Leadership Competencies.

Goodall, Simon, Bart Janssens, Kim Wagner, John Wong, Wendy Woods, and Michael Yeh. 2006. The promise of the East: India and China as R&D options. *Nature Biotechnology*, July 25. DOI: 10.1038/bioent910. www.nature.com/bioent/2006/060701/full/bioent910.html.

Google Patents. 2008. www.google.com/patents (accessed May 8, 2008).

Google Scholar. 2008. http://scholar.google.com (accessed May 8, 2008).

Gowers, Andrew. 2006. *Gowers Review of Intellectual Property.* (December). This document is found on the U.K. Treasury's web site, go to www.hm-treasury.gov.uk/d/pbr06_gowers_report_755.pdf (accessed December 19, 2008).

Graham, Benjamin, and David L. Dodd. 1934. *Security analysis.* (Reprint of the classic 1934 ed.) New York: McGraw-Hill.

Grant, Robert M. 2008a. *Cases to accompany contemporary strategy analysis,* 6th ed. Malden, MA: Blackwell Publishers.

Grant, Robert M. 2008b. *Contemporary strategy analysis,* 6th ed. Malden, MA: Blackwell Publishers.

Grove, Andrew S. 1996. *Only the paranoid survive.* New York: Doubleday.

Hamel, Gary, and C.K. Prahalad. 1994. *Competing for the future.* Boston: Harvard Business Press.

Hamscher, Walter. 1997. Technology due diligence. *PriceWaterhouse Review* (December). www.hamscher.com/Docs/Tdd_US.pdf (accessed April 30, 2008).

Hatch, James E. 2008. *Note on valuing a biotech company.* 9B08N005. Richard Ivey School of Business, The University of Western Ontario. (March 11).

Hatch, James E., and Paul Asmundson. 2001. Chromos Molecular Systems, Inc. Case. 9B01N001. Richard Ivey School of Business, The University of Western Ontario. (June 20).

Hatch, James E., and Dennis Dussin. 2001 and 2008. Note on private company valuation. 9B01N009. Richard Ivey School of Business, The University of Western Ontario. Originally issued July 11, 2001, revised and updated on June 30, 2008.

Hatch, James E., and Aseema Singh. 2002. Proto5. Case. 9B02N019. Richard Ivey School of Business, The University of Western Ontario. (Nov. 29).

Hayes, Robert H., Gary P. Pisano, David M. Upton, and Steven C. Wheelwright. 2004. *Operations, strategy, and technology: Pursuing the competitive edge.* Indianapolis, IN: John Wiley & Sons.

Higgins, Robert C. 2007. *Analysis for financial management,* 8th ed. New York: McGraw-Hill/Irwin.

Hill, Charles W.L., and Gareth R. Jones. 1988. *Strategic management: An integrated approach.* Boston: Houghton Mifflin.

Hogoboom, John D. 2004. Private investment in public equity: An overview. *New Jersey Law Journal,* August 16. www.sec.gov/info/smallbus/gbfor25_2006/hogoboom_invest.pdf (accessed September 8, 2008).

Howe, Jeff. 2006. The rise of crowdsourcing. *Wired Magazine.* www.wired.com/wired/archive/14.06/crowds.html.

Hundertmark, Thomas, André Olinto do Valle, and Jeff A. Shulman. 2008. Managing capital projects for competitive advantage. *McKinsey Quarterly* online ed. (June): 1–10. www.mckinseyquarterly.com/Managing_capital_projects_for_competitive_advantage_2163.

Investopedia. 2008. Leveraged buyout (LBO). www.investopedia.com/terms/l/leveragedbuyout.asp (accessed April 30, 2008).

Irvine & Ors v TalkSport Limited. 2003. EWCA Civ 423, (England and Wales Court of Appeal): April 1, 2003.

Ius Mentis. 2007. Internet law, IP law and technology explained, for lawyers and engineers. www.iusmentis.com (accessed April 30, 2008).

Jacobs, Nancy L. 1995. Evaluating investment performance. In *Portable MBA in investment,* ed. Peter L. Bernstein. New York: John Wiley & Sons, p. 308.

Johnson, Gerry, and Kevan Scholes. 1999. Networks. In *Exploring corporate strategy, text and cases,* 6th ed., pp. 452–455. Harlow, Essex, UK: Pearson Education, Financial Times Prentice-Hall imprint.

Kaplan, Robert S., and David P. Norton. 1996. *The balanced scorecard: Translating strategy into action.* Boston: Harvard Business Press.

Kay, John. 1994. *Foundations of corporate success: How business strategies add value.* New York: Oxford University Press.

Kellogg, David, and John M. Charnes. 2000. Real-options valuation for a biotechnology company. *Financial Analysts Journal* (May-June): 76–87.

Koeplin, John, Atulya Sarin, and Alan C. Shapiro. 2000. The private company discount. *Journal of Applied Corporate Finance.* Vol. 12, No. 4, (Winter): 94–101. http://ssrn.com/abstract=251776 (accessed February 14, 2009).

Khilji, S.E., T. Mroczkowski, and B. Bernstein, 2006. From invention to innovation: Toward developing an integrated innovation model for biotech firms. *Journal of Product Innovation Management* 23 (6): 528–540.

The King v. Arkwright, 1785, 1. *Law Reports of Patent Cases: 1602–1842* by William Carpmael, p. 57, lines 22–30. London: Printed and Published by A. Macintosh, 1851.

Lachman, Ranan. 2004. The biotech licensing challenge. *Drug Discovery and Development* (October): 11–15.

Landler, Mark, and Daniel J. Wakin. 2004. The rise and fall of Parma's first family. *New York Times,* January 11. http://query.nytimes.com/gst/fullpage.html? res=9A03E1DA1630F932A25752C0A9629C8B63 (accessed August 25, 2008).

Lax, David A., and James K. Sebenius. 1986. *The manager as negotiator: Bargaining for cooperation and competitive gain.* New York: Free Press.

Leach, Chris J., and Ronald W. Melicher. 2003. *Entrepreneurial finance.* Mason, OH: South-Western, a division of Thomson Learning.

Leavitt, Harold J. 1986. *Corporate pathfinders: How visionary managers use imaginative strategies to shape the future of their companies.* New York: Dow Jones Irwin.

Leavitt, Harold J. 1988. On teaching what we haven't taught. Research Paper Series No. 1005, Stanford University Graduate School of Business (August). https://gsbapps. stanford.edu/researchpapers/library/RP1005.pdf (accessed March 9, 2008).

Leonard-Barton, Dorothy. 1992. Core capabilities and core rigidities: A paradox in managing new product development. *Strategic Management Journal* 13: 111–125, in the Special Issue: Strategy Process: Managing Corporate Self-Renewal (Summer).

Lieberman, Marvin B., and David B. Montgomery. 1988. First-mover advantages. *Strategic Management Journal* 9: 41–58.

Lint, Onno, and Enrico Pennings. 2001. An option approach to the new product development process: A case study at Philips Electronics. *R & D Management* 31 (2): 163–172. DOI 10.1111/1467–9310.00206.

MacCormack, Alan, Theodore Forbath, Peter Brooks, and Patrick Kalaher 2007a. From outsourcing to global collaboration: New ways to build competitiveness. Working paper 07–080, Harvard Business School.

MacCormack, Alan, Theodore Forbath, Peter Brooks, and Patrick Kalaher. 2007b. Innovation through global collaboration: A new source of competitive advantage. Working paper 07–079, Harvard Business School.

Malnight, Thomas, and Tracey Keys. 2007. Surf the storm: Global trends survey results. *Perspectives for Managers* 152 (November). www.imd.ch/research/publications/ pfm.cfm (accessed May 31, 2008).

March, James G. 1994. *A primer on decision making: How decisions happen.* New York: Free Press.

March, James G. 1999. *The pursuit of organizational intelligence.* Malden, MA: Blackwell Publishers.

March, James G., and Daniel A. Levinthal. 1993. The myopia of learning. *Strategic Management Journal* 14: 95–112.

McDougall, Paul, and J. Nicolas Hoover. 2008. Nokia's Symbian deal rewrites the smartphone rules. *InformationWeek*, June 28. www.informationweek.com/story/showArticle. jhtml?articleID=208801196 (accessed June 28, 2008).

McKinsey & Company, 2008a. "Classic McKinsey frameworks that continue to inform management thinking," dated July 2008, downloadable at www.mckinseyquarterly. com/Strategy/Strategic_Thinking/Enduring_ideas_2170 (accessed December 12, 2008).

McKinsey & Company, 2008b. "Enduring Ideas: The 7-S Framework", March 2008, downloadable at www.mckinseyquarterly.com/Enduring_ideas_The_7-S_Framework_2123 (accessed December 12, 2008).

Meller, Steve. 2008. *Open innovation: Food and pharma opportunities.* Paper presented at the European Technology Platform (EPT), Food for Life, Food-Pharma Industry workshop, January 31–February 1, Cork, Ireland. See also www.etp.ciaa.be.

Nature Biotechnology's Portal. Bioentrepreneur—from bench to boardroom. www.nature. com/bioent/index.html (accessed June 30, 2008).

O'Brien, Kevin J. 2008. Nokia in deal to make mobile software free. *International Herald Tribune*, June 25, Technology & Media Section, European ed., 15.

O'Reilly, Charles, and Michael L. Tushman. 2007. Ambidexterity as a dynamic capability: Resolving the innovator's dilemma. Research Paper Series No. 1963, Stanford University Graduate School of Business (March). http://ssrn.com/abstract=978493 (accessed May 15, 2008).

Orphan drug status definition. www.emea.europa.eu/pdfs/general/direct/pr/ 55739107en. pdf.

Oster, Sharon M. 1999. *Modern competitive analysis,* 3rd ed. New York: Oxford University Press.

Oxford Technology. 2007. *Oxford Technology 3–VCT Newsletter.* About companies: Glide Pharma. (September 11): 1-2. www.oxfordtechnology.com/downloads/newletters/OT3_newsletter.pdf. (accessed December 30, 2008).

P&G: Connect + Develop, Procter & Gamble's Innovation Portal. https://secure3. verticali. net/pg-connection-portal/ctx/noauth/PortalHome.do.

Papadopoulos, Stelios. 2000. Business models in biotech. *Nature Biotechnology,* 18 Industry Trends: A snapshot of biotechnology. Supplement: IT3-IT4. www.nature.com/nbt/journal/v18/n10s/abs/nbt1000_IT3.html.

Pascale, Richard T. 1984. Perspectives on strategy: The real story behind Honda's success. *California Management Review* 26 (3) (Spring): 47–72.

Penrose, Edith. 1959. *The theory of the growth of the firm.* New York: John Wiley & Sons.

Pereiro, Luis E. 2002. *Valuation of companies in emerging markets: A practical approach.* New York: John Wiley & Sons.

Pereiro, Luis E., and M. Galli. 2000. La determinación del costo del capital en la valuación de empresas de capital cerrado: una guía práctica. (The determination of the cost of capital in the valuation of corporations: A practical guide) Buenos Aires: Instituto Argentino de Ejecutivos de Finanzas y Universidad Torcuato Di Tella.

Porter, Michael E. 1979. How competitive forces shape strategy. *Harvard Business Review* 57, no. 2 (March-April): 137–145.

Porter, Michael E. 1980. *Competitive strategy: Techniques for analyzing industries and competitors.* New York: The Free Press.

Porter, Michael E. 1985. *Competitive advantage: Creating and sustaining superior performance.* New York: The Free Press.

Porter, Michael E. 1996. What is strategy? *Harvard Business Review* 74, no. 6 (November-December): 61–68.

Porter, Michael E. 1990a. The competitive advantage of nations. *Harvard Business Review,* 68, no. 2 (March-April): 73–93.

Porter, Michael E. 1990b. *The competitive advantage of nations.* New York: The Free Press.

Porter, Michael E., and Rebecca E. Wayland. 1995. Global competition and the localization of competitive advantage. Proceedings of the Integral Strategy Collegium, Graduate School of Business, Indiana University. *Advances in Strategic Management,* vol 11, part A. Greenwich, CT: JAI Press.

Prahalad, C.K. and Gary Hamel. 1990. The core competence of the corporation. *Harvard Business Review* 68, no. 3 (May–June): 79–91.

Prahalad, C.K., and M.S. Krishnan. 2008. *The new age of innovation.* New York: Doubleday.

Pratt, Shannon P. 2001. *Business valuation discounts and premiums.* New York: John Wiley and Sons.

Private Equity Council. 2008. Private equity funds tax treatment of carried interests. www.privateequitycouncil.org/public-policy/legislative/private-equity-funds-tax-treatment-of-carried-interests (accessed August 8, 2008).

Ray, Michael L., and Rochelle Myers. 1986. *Creativity in business.* New York: Doubleday.

Reilly, Frank K., and Rashid A. Akhtar. 1995. The Benchmark error problem with global capital markets. *Journal of Portfolio Management* 22, no. 1 (Fall): 33–52.

Reilly, Frank K., and Keith C. Brown. 2003. *Investment analysis and portfolio management.* 7th ed. Mason, Ohio: South-Western, Thomson Learning.

Restatement of Torts. 1939. *American Law Institute,* paragraph 757, comment b.

Rigby, Darrell. 2008. Bain & Company's management tools: Offshoring. www.bain.com/management_tools/tools_offshoring.asp?groupCode=2.

Roberts, John. 2004. *The modern firm: organizational design for performance and growth.* New York: Oxford University Press.

Roche.com. Background information: The AmpliChip CYP450 DNA chip. www.roche.com/med_backgr-ampli.htm (accessed July 6, 2008).

Rottman, Joseph W., and Mary C. Lacity. 2006. Proven practices for effectively offshoring IT Work, *MIT Sloan Management Review* 47 (Spring): 56–63.

Saloner, Garth, Andrea Shepard, and Joel M. Podolny. 2004. *Strategic management.* Hoboken, NJ: John Wiley & Sons.

Saltman Engineering Co. Limited v. Campbell Engineering Co. Limited. 1948. 65 Reports of Patent Cases 203, at 215 (England).

Sampath, Prabakar. 2008. Widening innovation—Productivity gap in the pharmaceutical industry—New challenges and future directions. Frost & Sullivan. April 22. www.frost.com/prod/servlet/market-insight-top.pag?Src= RSS&docid=12839470.

Sebenius, James. 1996. Introduction to negotiation analysis: Structure, people, and context. Note. Harvard Business School no. 9–896–034.

Shane, Scott Andrew. 2004. *Academic entrepreneurship: University spinoffs and wealth creation.* Northhampton, Ma: Edward Elgar Publishing.

Sharpe, William F. 1964. Capital asset prices: A theory of market equilibrium under conditions of risk. *Journal of Finance* 19 (3): 425–442.

Sharpe, William F., Gordon J. Alexander, and Jeffery V. Bailey. 1995. *Investments.* Upper Saddle River, NJ: Prentice-Hall.

Shockley, Richard L. Jr., Staci Curtis, Jonathan Jafari, and Kristopher Tibbs. 2002. The option value of an early stage biotechnology investment. *Journal of Applied Corporate Finance* 15 (2) (Fall).

Smith, Gordon V., and Russell L. Parr. 2005. *Intellectual property: Valuation, exploitation, and infringement damages.* Hoboken, NJ: John Wiley & Sons.

Smith, Gordon V., and Russell L. Parr. 2007. Risk-adjusted cash flows, pp. 23–39. In *Cumulative supplement to Intellectual property: Valuation, exploitation, and infringement damages.* Hoboken, NJ: John Wiley & Sons.

Springboard Business Plan Guide. www.connect.org/resources/docs/Springboard_Business_Plan_Guide.pdf (accessed May 15, 2008).

Statement of Financial Accounting Concepts No. 7. Using cash flow information and present value in accounting measurements. 2000. Norwalk, CT: Financial Accounting Standards Board of the Financial Accounting Foundation.

Stephenson, Elizabeth, and Adarsh Pandit. 2008. How companies act on global trends: A McKinsey global survey, conducted in March 2008. *McKinsey Quarterly* (April): 1–9. www.mckinseyquarterly.com/How_companies_act_on_global_trends_A_Mc-Kinsey_Global_Survey_2130_abstract (accessed July 6, 2008).

STNAnaVist. STN Interfaces, FIZ Karlsruhe. www.stn-international.com/stninterfaces/stnanavist/stn_anavist.html(accessed May 8, 2008).

Stobbs, G.A. 2000. *Software patents.* New York: Aspen Publishers.

Strebel, Paul, and Tracey Keys, eds. 2005. *Mastering executive education: How to combine content with context and emotion—The IMD guide.* Edinburgh Gate, Harlow, UK: Pearson Education Ltd.

Sweet & Maxwell. 1998. *A practical guide to patent law.* 3rd ed. London: Sweet & Maxwell.

Tadelis, Steven. 2007. The innovative organization: Creating value through outsourcing. *California Management Review,* 50, no. 1 (Fall): 260–277.

Teece, David J., Gary Pisano, and Amy Shuen. 1997. Dynamic capabilities and strategic management. *Strategic Management Journal* 18: 509–533.

Teisberg, Elizabeth Olmsted. 1991a. Strategic response to uncertainty. Note. Harvard Business School no. 9–391–192, published April 11, 1-12. DOI: 10.1225/391192.

Teisberg, Elizabeth Olmsted. 1991b. Why do good managers choose poor strategies? Note. Harvard Business School no. 9–391–172, published March 5, 1–9. DOI: 10.1225/391172.

Trademark Act of 1946. 60 Stat. 427, as amended, codified in United States Code, Title 15, paragraph 1127.

Trigeorgis, Leon. 1996, reprinted 1997. *Real options: Managerial flexibility and strategy in resource allocation.* Cambridge, MA: MIT Press.

Trippe, Anthony J. 2003. Patinformatics: Tasks to tools. *World Patent Information* 25 (3) (September): 211–221. DOI: 10.1016/S0172-2190(03)0079-6 (accessed July 6, 2008).

Tushman, Michael L., and Charles A. O'Reilly III. 1997. *Winning through innovation: A practical guide to leading organizational change and renewal.* Boston: Harvard Business Press.

Tversky, Amos, and Daniel Kahneman. 1973. Availability: A heuristic for judging frequency and probability. *Cognitive Psychology* 5: 207–232.

Tversky, Amos, and Daniel Kahneman. 1974. Judgement under uncertainty: Heuristics and biases. *Science* 185, 1124–1131.

UK Intellectual Property Office. 2006. *History of patents.* www.ipo.gov.uk/about/about-ourorg/about-history/about-history-patent.htm(accessed April 30, 2008).

United States Code. 2008. Title 17. Paragraph 302. Duration of copyright: Works created on or after January 1, 1978.

United States Code. 2008. Title 35. Chapter 10, paragraph 101. Inventions patentable.

United States District Court of the Southern District of New York. Final Approval Order and Settlement signed by Judge Miriam Cedarbaum. October 20, 2006, *AT&T Corporation: AT&T wireless group tracking stock.* http://securities.stanford.edu/1016/AWE00/index.html Stanford Law School Securities Class Action Clearinghouse in association with Cornerstone Research (accessed February 10, 2008).

United States Patent and Trademark Office. Patent Electronic Business Center. 2008. www.uspto.gov/ebc/index.html(accessed May 8, 2008).

United States Patent and Trademark Office. Patent Full-Text and Full-Page Image Databases. 2008. www.uspto.gov/patft/index.html (accessed May 8, 2008).

U.S. Securities and Exchange Commission. SEC Filings and Forms (EDGAR). 2008. www.sec.gov/edgar.shtml (accessed May 8, 2008).

Van Arnum. 2007. CMOs expand biologic manufacturing. http://pharmtech.findpharma.com/pharmtech/article.

Van Horne, James C. 1994. *Financial markets rates and flows*, 4th ed. Upper Saddle River, NJ: Prentice-Hall, p. 77.

von Arx, Mirjam, 2005. *Building the Gherkin: A documentary film.* www.buildingthegherkin.com (accessed April 16, 2008).

Watkins, Michael D. 2002. Negotiating strategic alliances. Note. Harvard Business School no. 9–902–166, June 20, 1–8. DOI: 10.1225/902166.

Watkins, Michael D. 2003. Analyzing complex negotiations. Note. Harvard Business School no. 9–903–088, December 1, 1–22. DOI: 10.1225/903088.

Webster's new world dictionary of the American language, 2nd college ed. 1970. New York: World Publishing Company.

Weeds, Helen. 2002. Real options and game theory: When should real options valuation be applied?" Working paper, Cambridge University.

WHO aging data. www.who.int/features/factfiles/ageing/en/index.html (accessed December 7, 2008).

WHO obesity data. www.who.int/mediacentre/factsheets/fs311/en/index.html (accessed December 7, 2008)

Williams, John Burr. 1938. *The theory of investment value.* Cambridge, MA: Harvard University Press. Reprinted 1964 by North-Holland Publishing Company, Amsterdam.

World Intellectual Property Organization. See under Paris Convention for the Protection of Industrial Property. www.wipo.int/treaties/en/ip/paris/trtdocs_wo020.html (accessed April 30, 2008).

About the Authors

Constance Lütolf-Carroll is an entrepreneur and educator. She earned a BS (honors) in civil engineering from UC Berkeley where she was a Regents Scholar. She holds an MBA from Stanford Graduate School of Business. In 1986, she joined the faculty of ESADE Business School, Ramon Llull University, in Spain. From 2000–2009, Constance was responsible for teaching the core strategy course in ESADE's full-time MBA program. Currently, she is Lecturer at ESADE and a member of the Business Policy department. For the Executive MBA (EMBA), she teaches international business strategy. For the MBA and MSc programs, she teaches the finance elective on international portfolio management.

She is also a visiting professor at other prominent business schools. In Finland, Constance was honored as the Saastamoinen Foundation Visiting Professor 2002 by the Helsinki School of Economics, where she has been teaching regularly in the MBA and EMBA programs for the last twelve years. In 2001, she began teaching international investment management for the MBA and EMBA programs at Rotterdam School of Management, Erasmus University, in the Netherlands. Each summer since 2004, she has been invited to teach in the Korean Executive MBA program at the Seoul School for Integrated Science and Technology (aSSIST) in Seoul, South Korea. As of 2005, she is co-teaching on mergers and acquisitions, merchant banking and corporate restructuring for the Master in Corporate Finance program at SDA Bocconi, in Milan, Italy.

Constance started her career working as a refinery engineer for Exxon Company USA and eventually became a registered civil engineer in California. After her MBA, she joined Ibercorp SA, a leading securities brokerage in Spain, and served on the board of directors of Iberiancorp Gestion BV in the Netherlands. At Baring Securities (now ING) in Mexico, she was deputy director of equity research. More recently she has consulted for leading British asset management firms and has been involved in a variety of start-up ventures.

Constance serves as board member and principal of a family business Netspan AG that she cofounded with her husband in 1997. Netspan AG, based in Switzerland, is an Internet applications service provider for small and midsize companies. Her professional memberships include Tau Beta Pi (the engineering honor society), Prytanean Women's Honor Society (the oldest collegiate women's honorary society in the United States), and the Stanford Alumni Association in Italy, where she has been both an officer and board member. Constance enjoys swimming, walking, and advising her students on their start-up ventures and business projects.

Antti Pirnes is Chairman and a Founding Partner of patent and business intelligence company Patiq Ltd., with head office in Espoo, Finland. He earned an MSc degree in Biotechnology from the University of Helsinki and completed the Biotechnology Management Program at the Helsinki School of Economics and the

Intellectual Property Rights management program in the Lifelong Learning Institute at Espoo, Finland. Antti has worked as a research team leader for the biomedicine company UniCorp, as specialist advisor for a corporate finance company, and as a patent analyst at VTT Technical Research Centre of Finland, the largest contract research organization in northern Europe.

At Patiq Ltd., Antti works closely with many high-technology entrepreneurs, innovators, venture capitalists, research managers, and company executives who wish to identify new technology opportunities and to benefit from inventions. He focuses on showing his clients which inventions of other parties already have patent protection and where other firms and researchers are concentrating their research efforts. He also estimates how likely it is that other patents will interfere with his clients' proposed or current business activities.

About the Contributors

Tom Brand is a Chartered Patent Attorney, European Patent Attorney, European Trade Mark Attorney, and Registered Trade Mark Agent, and is a partner of W.P. Thompson & Co., a European prosecution firm specializing in the protection of intellectual property. Expertise within the firm includes patents, trademarks, designs, and copyrights and covers an extensive range of technologies from electronic engineering and mechanical sciences to chemistry and biotechnology. W.P. Thompson & Co. was established in 1873 and has grown to four offices, three in England and one in Germany, to better serve its substantial client base, both in the United Kingdom and around the world. Tom earned his B.Sc. (Honors) and PhD degrees in Chemistry from the University of Manchester. He is a Chartered Chemist and has a legal master's degree in intellectual property litigation from the Nottingham Law School. After finishing his PhD, Tom entered the patents profession, joining W.P. Thompson & Co.'s London office. After completing his training with the firm, Tom gained further experience working for another private practice in the trademarks field and as corporate patent counsel for Unilever plc, experience that gave him valuable insight into the strategic considerations of large corporations in connection with intellectual property and further experience with the European Patent Office and other patent offices worldwide. Tom's practice now encompasses a wide range of clients from around the world and from many different technology areas. He also maintains a strong interest in trademarks and a substantial trademark practice, and is a contributor to *The Trade Mark Handbook* (Sweet & Maxwell) and is a tutor for the Institute of Trade Mark Attorneys in the United Kingdom.

Anthony R. Indaimo is the Chairman and Head of the International Commercial Practice Group at Withers LLP, an international law firm dedicated to the business, personal, and philanthropic interests of entrepreneurs. Withers LLP is a full service firm and regularly acts for financial institutions, entrepreneurs, public and privately owned businesses, and senior business executives. Established in London, in 1896, Withers LLP has steadily grown to include offices in Italy, Switzerland, Hong Kong, and the United States with associated offices in key commercial centers throughout the world. Anthony has extensive experience in corporate, commercial, and corporate finance transactions. His work involves the acquisition and disposal of businesses and shares for private and public companies, joint ventures, and capital raising. Anthony, who is fluent in Italian, has particular emphasis in his work on cross-border transactions, especially the United Kingdom, United States, and Italy. He earned his Bachelor of Jurisprudence and Bachelor of Law from the University of Western Australia. His professional memberships include the British Italian Law Association, the Business Club Italia, and the British Chamber of Commerce for Italy. He has cowritten various articles about AIM (formerly the Alternative Investment

Market), London's successful secondary stock market, and on the merger of the London and Italian stock exchanges. He lectures extensively on raising capital for growth companies and listing on AIM, and these have included lectures with the London Stock Exchange in Athens, Geneva, London, Madrid, Milan, and Zurich. He has also spoken at various seminars on in-bound investment into the United Kingdom with *Think London* and was a cosponsor with the LSE on a series of seminars on listing investment funds in New York and Greenwich.

Conan Chitham is a Partner at Withers LLP and an experienced commercial intellectual property lawyer. He earned his MA in Law from Trinity Hall, Cambridge University. He advises on noncontentious intellectual property (IP) matters and on issues relating to acquisition, creation, and exploitation of IP, and has worked on the whole range of value-realizing deals involving IP. He also has extensive experience of advising in IP issues in relation to the development of technologies, both by established businesses and new operations. Conan has written numerous articles in journals such as *Communications Law, Copyright World,* and *Trademark World.* He is a Council Member of The Licensing Executive Society and a member of the Institute of Trade Mark Attorneys, the City of London Solicitors Company, and City of London.

Nicole Hirst is a Solicitor in the Intellectual Property Group at Withers LLP, based in London, where she advises on intellectual property and commercial litigation with particular emphasis on trademark, copyright, and patent infringement cases. She is an Associate Member of the Institute of Trade Mark Attorneys, the Law Society of England & Wales, and the British Italian Law Association. She attended Reading University where she obtained an LLB. She also obtained a Diploma in Commercial Intellectual Property from Nottingham Trent University. She contributed to the U.K. chapter on *World Intellectual Property Rights and Remedies* published by the Center for International Legal Studies.

Caroline Hughes was until recently a Solicitor in the IP Group at Withers LLP based in London. She advised on intellectual property and information technology matters, with particular emphasis on brands, licensing, and the commercial exploitation of intellectual property rights. She graduated from the University of Manchester with an LLB (English Law and French Law) before qualifying as a solicitor. She has contributed various legal articles including the Intellectual Property chapter in *Tolley's Charities Manual* and the U.K. chapter in *World Intellectual Property Rights and Remedies* published by the Center for International Legal Studies. She is now working as an in-house solicitor for a media company in a wide ranging legal and commercial role.

Nadia Ignatius is a Senior Associate at Withers LLP. Her practice consists primarily of advising domestic U.K. and international clients on general company and commercial matters. She assists her clients in setting up corporate legal structures and commercial contracts such as agency, distribution, franchising, outsourcing, and sponsorship agreements. She earned her Bachelor of Commerce (Legal) degree at the University of the Witwatersrand in Johannesburg, South Africa, was admitted as a solicitor in England and Wales in 1993, and joined Withers LLP in 1995. She is a fluent Italian speaker and gives talks regularly at seminars and other events organized by Withers LLP in Italy. She is a member of the Law Society of England & Wales and the British Italian Law Association.

Richard Lord was until recently a Senior Associate in the International Commercial Practice Group at Withers LLP. He has extensive experience in corporate, commercial, and corporate finance transactions. His work involved the acquisition and disposal of businesses and shares for private and public companies, raising capital, and doing a wide range of commercial and contractual transactions. Richard, who is fluent in Italian and was based in the firm's Milan office for over four years, had an emphasis in his work on cross-border transactions, particularly involving Italy. He graduated from the University of Lancaster with a BA (Modern Languages) before qualifying as a solicitor. He has lectured extensively on raising capital for growth companies and listing on the AIM market of the London Stock Exchange, including lectures in Italy and Switzerland. Richard has recently become an in-house lawyer at a FTSE 100 company.

John d'A. Maycock was a Partner at Withers LLP and head of the firm's Intellectual Property Group, from which he retired in June 2008 and is now a consultant. He has 30 years of specialist experience in intellectual property (IP), both contentious and noncontentious. He joined Withers LLP from his niche practice, Maycock's. He earned his MA and LLM degrees from Gonville & Caius College, Cambridge, and is a solicitor and Registered Trade Mark Agent. John has considerable experience in advising on the creation, exploitation, management, defense, and enforcement of IP rights. He is well versed in the management and conduct of proceedings in an international context and regularly advises on competition law issues at European and national levels in the context of the exploitation of IP. John has written various legal articles and is a contributor to the IP chapter in *Tolley's Charities Manual* and to the U.K. chapter in the *World Intellectual Property Rights and Remedies* published by the Center for International Legal Studies. He holds various professional memberships including the Law Society of England and Wales, the Institute of Trade Mark Attorneys, the International Association of Practitioners in Industrial Property, the European Community Trade Mark Association, the Union of European Practitioners in Intellectual Property, the Licensing Executives Society, and the Pharmaceutical Trade Marks Group and is an associate member of the Chartered Institute of Patent Agents.

Gabriel Monzon-Cortarelli is a Senior Associate in the International Commercial Practice Group at Withers LLP. He has extensive experience in advising on cross-border mergers and acquisitions, focusing on Italian, U.S., and Latin American transactions and on international capital markets, representing both issuers and underwriters in debt and equity offerings. He also assists Italian and other European, U.S., and Asian issuers who wish to list on AIM of the London Stock Exchange. Gabriel regularly participates as a speaker and lecturer at corporate finance events, such as the AIM listing conferences in Spain. He is a frequent contributor in the Italian corporate press on capital market matters. Gabriel is fluent in Italian and Spanish. He graduated with an LLB (Honors) in Law from University College London, London, and an LLM in Banking and Finance Law from Fordham University School of Law, New York. He is admitted to practice as an attorney in the State of New York and as a solicitor in England and Wales.

Margaret M. Mullally has extensive experience as a Research Scientist and Manager of multidisciplinary and international research programs within the biopharmaceutical and medical domains. Margaret is Senior Business Development Manager at PHARMO Institute for Drug Outcomes Research, based in the Netherlands, an independent scientific research services organization providing integrated patient database and professional analysis services across a range of pharmacotherapeutic areas. Margaret received her PhD in Protein Biochemistry from the School of Biotechnology, Dublin City University, Ireland, in 1996. She subsequently held postdoctoral positions at the Molecular Genetics and Pharmaceutical Biology departments at the University of Groningen, the Netherlands. Her 10 years of research made her an expert in therapeutic protein and peptide drug engineering, design, and preclinical evaluation and coordination of Phase I studies. She is author of several scientific peer-reviewed publications and holds an international patent covering cytokine design. Margaret has been successful in the promotion of academic-industrial partnerships and the establishment of international scientific collaborations at the Nijmegen Centre for Molecular Life Science, the Netherlands. She earned her MBA degree from the Rotterdam School of Management, Erasmus University, the Netherlands, in 2008. She provides strategic advice on research and development pipeline and market strategies for the biopharmaceutical industry.

About The Web Site

The web site for *From Innovation to Cash Flows* is meant to enhance the learning experience of our book's readers. By registering and logging onto your personal account at our web site, you will gain access to many useful and practical materials. To receive these free benefits, you will need to follow these two simple steps:

1. Visit the book's web site at http://www.innovationtocashflows.com
2. Follow the instructions on the web site to register as a new user.

What You will Find on the Web Site

By logging onto your account at www.innovationtocashflows you will be able to browse and download valuable capstone cases, useful sample legal contracts, and complimentary financial valuation models that accompany the cases we wrote. Our book's experts contributed a large and comprehensive glossary of key terms (business, legal, and scientific). In the resources section, you will find lists of recommended textbooks, and useful articles, URL's, and blogs, arranged by topic.

These are the chapter appendices and files that will be accessible to registered site users:

Appendix 2.2: Guidelines for Setting Up an Invention Disclosure System for Your Company

Appendix 2.3: Sample Invention Disclosure Form

Appendix 3.1: Porter's Cluster Theory Applied to San Diego's Biotechnology Cluster

Appendix 3.2: Fictional Case Study of WineOnline.com

Appendix 7.1: Real Options versus Financial Options

Appendix 7.2: Overview of the Negotiation Process

Appendix 9.1: Sample Confidentiality Agreement

Appendix 11.1: International Intellectual Property Treaties and Conventions

Appendix 11.2: Comparison of Design Right and Registered Design

Appendix 15.1: Selected Commercial Database and Software Tool Vendors.

Appendix 17.2: Time Value of Money

Appendix 17.3: Advanced Definition of Free Cash Flows for Use with Enterprise Valuation Method

Appendix 17.4: Five Ways to Estimate Terminal Values

Index

Page numbers followed by "n" refer to material found in the Notes.